Lecture Notes in Artificial Intelligence   7507

Subseries of Lecture Notes in Computer Science

T0217403

Lecture Notes in Artificial Intelligence   7507

Subseries of Lecture Notes in Computer Science

LNAI Series Editors

Randy Goebel
University of Alberta, Edmonton, Canada
Yuzuru Tanaka
Hokkaido University, Sapporo, Japan
Wolfgang Wahlster
DFKI and Saarland University, Saarbrücken, Germany

LNAI Founding Series Editor

Joerg Siekmann
DFKI and Saarland University, Saarbrücken, Germany

Chun-Yi Su   Subhash Rakheja
Honghai Liu (Eds.)

Intelligent Robotics and Applications

5th International Conference, ICIRA 2012
Montreal, QC, Canada, October 3-5, 2012
Proceedings, Part II

 Springer

Series Editors

Randy Goebel, University of Alberta, Edmonton, Canada
Jörg Siekmann, University of Saarland, Saarbrücken, Germany
Wolfgang Wahlster, DFKI and University of Saarland, Saarbrücken, Germany

Volume Editors

Chun-Yi Su
Concordia University
Department of Mechanical and Industrial Engineering
Montreal, QC H3G 1M8, Canada
E-mail: cysu@alcor.concordia.ca

Subhash Rakheja
Concordia University
Department of Mechanical and Industrial Engineering
Montreal, QC H3G 1M8, Canada
E-mail: rakheja@alcor.concordia.ca

Honghai Liu
The University of Portsmouth
School of Creative Technologies
Portsmouth, PO1 2DJ, UK
E-mail: honghai.liu@port.ac.uk

ISSN 0302-9743　　　　　　　　　　e-ISSN 1611-3349
ISBN 978-3-642-33514-3　　　　　　e-ISBN 978-3-642-33515-0
DOI 10.1007/978-3-642-33515-0
Springer Heidelberg Dordrecht London New York

Library of Congress Control Number: 2012946931

CR Subject Classification (1998): I.2.8-11, I.5.3-4, I.4.8-9, K.4.2, J.2, J.3, C.3, C.2, G.1.10

LNCS Sublibrary: SL 7 – Artificial Intelligence

Typesetting: Camera-ready by author, data conversion by Scientific Publishing Services, Chennai, India

Printed on acid-free paper

Springer is part of Springer Science+Business Media (www.springer.com)

Preface

The Organizing Committee of the 5th International Conference on Intelligent Robotics and Applications aimed to facilitate interaction among participants in the field of intelligent robotics, automation, and mechatronics. Through this conference, the committee intended to enhance the sharing of individual experiences and expertise in intelligent robotics with particular emphasis on technical challenges associated with varied applications such as biomedical applications, industrial automations, surveillance, and sustainable mobility.

The 5th International Conference on Intelligent Robotics and Applications was most successful in attracting 271 submissions addressing state-of-the-art developments in robotics, automation, and mechatronics. Owing to the large number of submissions, the committee was faced with the difficult challenge of selecting the most deserving papers for inclusion in these lecture notes and for presentation at the conference, held in Montreal, Canada, October 3–5, 2012. For this purpose, the committee undertook a rigorous review process. Despite the high quality of most of the submissions, a total of 197 papers were selected for publication in 3 volumes of Springer's Lecture Notes in Artificial Intelligence, a subseries of Lecture Notes in Computer Science.

The selected articles were submitted by scientists from 25 different countries. The contribution of the Technical Program Committee and the referees is deeply appreciated. Most of all, we would like to express our sincere thanks to the authors for submitting their most recent work and the Organizing Committee for their enormous efforts to turn this event into a smoothly running meeting. Special thanks go to Concordia University for their generosity and direct support. Our particular thanks are due to Mr. Alfred Hofmann and the editorial staff of Springer-Verlag for enthusiastically supporting the project.

We sincerely hope that these volumes will prove to be an important resource for the scientific community.

July 2012

Chun-Yi Su
Subhash Rakheja
Honghai Liu

Conference Organization

International Advisory Committee

Jorge Angeles	McGill University, Canada
Suguru Arimoto	Ritsumeikan University, Japan
Hegao Cai	Harbin Institute of Technology, China
Tianyou Chai	Northeastern University, China
Clarence De Silva	University of British Columbia, Canada
Han Ding	Huazhong University of Science and Technology, China
Sabina Jeschke	RWTH Aachen University, Germany
Ming Li	National Natural Science Foundation of China, China
Zhongqin Lin	Shanghai Jiao Tong University, China
Ding Liu	Xi'an University of Technology, China
Jinping Qu	South China University of Technology, China
Bruno Siciliano	University of Naples, Italy
Mohammad Siddique	Fayetteville State University, USA
Mark W. Spong	University of Texas at Dallas, USA
Kevin Warwick	University of Reading, UK
Ming Xie	Nanyang Technological University, Singapore
Youlun Xiong	Huazhong University of Science and Technology, China

General Chairs

Chun-Yi Su	Concordia University, Canada
Rama B. Bhat	Concordia University, Canada
Xiangyang Zhu	Shanghai Jiao Tong University, China

Program Chairs

Subhash Rakheja	Concordia University, Canada
Jangmyung Lee	Pusan National University, South Korea
Camille Alain Rabbath	DRDC, Canada

Publicity Chairs

Tongwen Chen	University of Alberta, Canada
Li-Chen Fu	National Taiwan University, Taiwan
Shuzhi Sam Ge	National University of Singapore, Singapore

Naoyuki Kubota	Tokyo Metropolitan University, Japan
Kok-Meng Lee	Georgia Institute of Technology, USA
Ning Xi	City University of Hong Kong, Hong Kong
Xiaohua Xia	University of Pretoria, South Africa
Peter Xu	University of Auckland, New Zealand
Huayong Yang	Zhejiang University, China
Bin Yao	Purdue University, USA
Xinghuo Yu	Royal Melbourne Institute of Technology, Australia
Chaohai Zhang	Harbin Institute of Technology, China

Organized Session Chairs

Mirco Alpen	Helmut Schmidt University, Germany
Shengyong Chen	Zhejiang University of Technology, China
Weidong Chen	Shanghai Jiao Tong University, China
Xiang Chen	University of Windsor, Canada
Xinkai Chen	Shibaura Institute of Technology, Japan
Mingcong Deng	Tokyo University of Agriculture and Technology, Japan
Jun Fu	Massachusetts Institute of Technology, USA
Xin Fu	Zhejiang University, China
Haibo Gao	Harbin Institute of Technology, China
Yueming Hu	South China University of Technology, China
Yangmin Li	University of Macau, Macau, SAR China
Zhijun Li	South China University of Technology, China
Guangjun Liu	Ryerson University, Canada
Xinjun Liu	Tsinghua University, China
Daniel Schilberg	RWTH Aachen University, Germany
Yandong Tang	Shengyang Institute of Automation, CAS, China
Danwei Wang	Nanyang Technological University, Singapore
Enrong Wang	Nanjing Normal University, China
Caihua Xiong	Huazhong University of Science and Technology, China
Simon Yang	University of Guelph, Canada
Hongnian Yu	Staffordshire University, UK
Jianhua Zhang	Shanghai University, China
Youmin Zhang	Concordia University, Canada
Limin Zhu	Shanghai Jiao Tong University, China

Publication Chairs

Honghai Liu	University of Portsmouth, UK
Xinjun Sheng	Shanghai Jiao Tong University, China

Award Chair

Farhad Aghili   Canadian Space Agency, Canada

Registration Chairs

Zhi Li   Concordia University, Canada
Sining Liu   Concordia University, Canada

Finance Chair

Ying Feng   South China University of Technology, China

Local Arrangement Chairs

Wen-Fang Xie   Concordia University, Canada
Chevy Chen   Concordia University, Canada

International Program Committee

Amir Aghdam   Concordia University, Canada
DongPu Cao   Lancaster University, UK
Qixin Cao   Shanghai Jiao Tong University, China
Jie Chen   Beijing Institute of Technology, China
Mingyuan Chen   Concordia University, Canada
Zuomin Dong   University of Victoria, Canada
Guangren Duan   Harbin Institute of Technology, China
Shumin Fei   Southeast University, China
Gang Feng   City University of Hong Kong, China
Huijun Gao   Harbin Institute of Technology, China
Luis E. Garza C.   Tecnológico de Monterrey, México
Andrew A. Goldenberg   University of Toronto, Canada
Guoying Gu   Shanghai Jiao Tong University, China
Jason J. Gu   Dalhousie University, Canada
Peihua Gu   University of Calgary, Canada
Zhi-Hong Guan   Huazhong University of Science & Technology,
                              China
Shuxiang Guo   Kagawa University, Japan
Lina Hao   Northeastern University, China
Henry Hong   Concordia University, Canada
Liu Hsu   Federal University of Rio de Janeiro, Brazil

Huosheng Hu	University of Essex, UK
Qinglei Hu	Harbin Institute of Technology, China
Chunqing Huang	Xiamen University, China
Wei Lin	Case Western Reserve University, USA
Derong Liu	University of Illinois at Chicago, USA
Min Liu	Tsinghua University, China
Peter X. Liu	Carleton University, Canada
Jun Luo	Shanghai University, China
Tao Mao	Dartmouth College, USA
Daniel Miller	University of Waterloo, Canada
Yuichiro Oya	University of Miyazak, Japan
Hailong Pei	South China University of Technology, China
Juntong Qi	Chinese Academy of Sciences, China
Joe Qin	University of Southern California, USA
Yaohong Qu	Northwestern Polytechnical University, China
Lbrir Salim	The University of Trinidad and Tobago, Trinidad and Tobago
Inna Sharf	McGill University, Canada
Yang Shi	Victoria University, Canada
Gangbing Song	University of Houston, USA
Jing Sun	University of Michigan, USA
XiaoBo Tan	Michigan State University, USA
Yonghong Tan	Shanghai Normal University, China
Yong Tang	South China University of Technology, China
Gang Tao	University of Virginia, USA
Didier Theilliol	University of Lorraine, France
Hong Wang	University of Manchester, UK
Xingsong Wang	Southeast University, China
Pak Kin Wong	University of Macau, Macau, SAR China
Shaorong Xie	Shanghai University, China
Xin Xin	Okayama Prefectural University, Japan
Zhenhua Xiong	Shanghai Jiao Tong University, China
Bugong Xu	South China University of Technology, China
Jianxin Xu	National University of Singapore, Singapore
Deyi Xue	University of Calgary, Canada
Zijiang Yang	Ibaraki University, Japan
Dingguo Zhang	Shanghai Jiao Tong University, China
Guangming Zhang	Nanjing University of Technology, China
Yanzheng Zhao	Shanghai Jiao Tong University, China
Wenhong Zhu	Canadian Space Agency, Canada

List of Reviewers

We would like to acknowledge the support of the following people, who peer reviewed articles from ICIRA 2012.

Achint Aggarwal
Farhad Aghili
Jose Alarcon Herrera
Mirco Alpen
Nicolas Alt
Philippe Archambault
Ramprasad Balasubramanian
Mark Becke
Andrey Belkin
Francisco Beltran-Carbajal
Stanley Birchfield
Swetha Sampath Bobba
Hans-Joachim Böhme
Itziar Cabanes
Yifan Cai
Yang Cao
Zhiqiang Cao
Alberto Cavallo
Abbas Chamseddine
Mingyuan Chen
Xiang Chen
Wei Chen
Diansheng Chen
Xinkai Chen
Shengyong Chen
Yixiong Chen
Xiang Chen
Weidong Chen
Chaobin Chen
Shengyong Chen
Chevy Chen
Zhao Cheng
Yushing Cheung
Dong-Il Cho
Yunfei Dai
David D'Ambrosio
Krispin Davies
Hua Deng
Mingcong Deng
Wenhua Ding
Xuejun Ding
John Dolan

Mitchell Donald
Xiao-Gang Duan
Su-Hong Eom
Ole Falkenberg
Yuanjie Fan
Yongchun Fang
Wei Feng
Simon Fojtu
Gustavo Freitas
Klaus Frick
Zhuang Fu
Jun Fu
Xin Fu
Luis Garza
Shuzhi Sam Ge
Jason Geder
Hernan Gonzalez Acuña
Guo-Ying Gu
Tianyu Gu
Yongxin Guo
Zhao Guo
Roger Halkyard
Jianda Han
Lina Hao
Mohamed Hasan
Syed Hassan
Michal Havlena
Jiayuan He
Sven Hellbach
Abdelfetah Hentout
Katharina Hertkorn
Trent Hilliard
Johannes Höcherl
Joachim Horn
Mir Amin Hosseini
Qinglei Hu
Yonghui Hu
Jin Hu
Chunqing Huang
Jidong Huang
Aitore Ibarguren
Satoshi Iwaki

Markus Janssen
Qiuling Jia
Ying Jin
Balajee Kannan
Jun Kanno
Bijan Karimi
Mohammad Keshmiri
Sungshin Kim
Alexandr Klimchik
Yukinori Kobayashi
Tim Köhler
Naoyuki Kubota
Xu-Zhi Lai
Lin Lan
Marco Langerwisch
Jangmyung Lee
Sang-Hoon Lee
Min Lei
Yan Li
Shunchong Li
Jing Li
Zhijun Li
Hengyu Li
Nanjun Li
Yinxiao Li
Qingguo Li
Yangming Li
Zhi Li
Binbin Lian
Junli Liang
Guanhao Liang
Miguel Lima
Xinjun Liu
Han Liu
Chengliang Liu
Peter Liu
Chao Liu
Jia Liu
Sining Liu
Jun Luo
Xiaomin Ma
Yumin Ma
António Machado
Werner Maier
Jörn Malzahn

Mohamed Mamdouh
Ida Bagus Manuaba
Tao Mao
Farhat Mariem
Luis Mateos
Iñaki Maurtua
Aaron Mavrinac
Deqing Mei
Yi Min
Lei Mo
Abolfazl Mohebbi
Vidya Murali
Mahmoud Mustafa
Keitaro Naruse
Ashutosh Natraj
Myagmarbayar Nergui
Bin Niu
Scott Nokleby
Farzad Norouzi fard
Farzan Nowruzi
Ernesto Olguín-Díaz
Godfrey Onwubolu
Tomas Pajdla
Chang-Zhong Pan
Lizheng Pan
Ricardo Pérez-Alcocer
Andreas Pichler
Charles Pinto
Erion Plaku
Peter Poschmann
Radius Prasetiyo
Marius Pruessner
Juntong Qi
Xiaoming Qian
Guo Qiwei
Yaohong Qu
Mohammad Rahman
Ahmed Ramadan
Christian Rauch
Laura Ray
Hamd ul Moqeet Riaz
Martijn Rooker
Miti Ruchanurucks
Kunjin Ryu
Iman Sadeghzadeh

Thomas Schlegl
Christian Schlette
Sven Severin
Inna Sharf
Karam Shaya
Huiping Shen
Huimin Shen
Xinjun Sheng
Thierry Simon
Olivier Simonin
Dalei Song
Zhenguo Sun
Tadeusz Szkodny
XiaoBo Tan
Wenbin Tang
Yandong Tang
Alberto Tellaeche
Didier Theilliol
Christopher Tomaszewski
Abhinav Valada
Prasanna Velagapudi
Tianmiao Wang
Xiaoyan Wang
Xinmin Wang
Jingchuan Wang
Yancheng Wang
Xin Wang
Enrong Wang
Ralf Waspe
Zhixuan Wei
Graeme Wilson
Jonas Witt
Christian Wögerer
Pak Kin Wong
Olarn Wongwirat
Chong Wu
Yier Wu
Jianhua Wu
Min Wu
Xiaojun Wu
Baihua Xiao
Fugui Xie
Rong Xie
Shaorong Xie
Pu Xie
Wen-Fang Xie

Le Xie
Xin Xin
Jing Xin
Zhenhua Xiong
Rong Xiong
Caihua xiong
Bugong Xu
Bin Xu
Xiong Xu
You-Nan Xu
Deyi Xue
Zijiang Yang
Jie Yang
Chenguang Yang
Wenyu Yang
Jing Yang
Chang-En Yang
Lin Yao
Gen'ichi Yasuda
Michael Yeh
Zhouping Yin
Yong-Ho Yoo
Haoyong Yu
Xinghuo Yu
Mimoun Zelmat
Shasha Zeng
Jie Zhang
Zhengchen Zhang
Gang Zhang
Xiaoping Zhang
Jianjun Zhang
He Zhang
Dingguo Zhang
Yifeng Zhang
Xuebo Zhang
Yequn Zhang
Jinsong Zhang
Wenzeng Zhang
Chaohai Zhang
Yanzheng Zhao
Pengbing Zhao
Zhaowei Zhong
Hangfei Zhou
Li-Min Zhu
Asier Zubizarreta

Table of Contents – Part II

Robotics for Rehabilitation and Assistance

Mechatronics and Integration Technology in Electronics and Information Devices Fabrication

Man-Machine Interactions

Manufacturing

Micro and Nano Systems

Mobile Robots and Intelligent Autonomous Systems

Motion Control

Multi-agent Systems and Distributed Control

Multi-sensor Data Fusion Algorithms

Wireless Master-Slave FES Rehabilitation System Using sEMG Control

Zuozheng Lou, Peng Yao, and Dingguo Zhang*

State Key Laboratory of Mechanical System and Vibration
Shanghai Jiao Tong University
Shanghai, China, 200240
dgzhang@sjtu.edu.cn

Abstract. A new kind of functional electrical stimulation (FES) rehabilitation system is presented in this paper, which can assist the paralyzed patients caused by stroke to perform specific exercise following the therapist's intention. The master-slave rehabilitation concept is firstly introduced into the FES system. This system consists of a master unit and a slave unit, and the two units are connected through wireless communication. Surface electromyography (sEMG) of the master side (therapist) is used as the control command for slave side (patients). Experiments are conducted on the upper limb of healthy subjects and the performance is satisfactory. The system exhibits four useful features: noninvasive technique, master-slave control, wireless communication, and "one to N" training mode.

Keywords: FES, EMG, Rehabilitation, Master-slave, Wireless control.

1   Introduction

According to the World Health Organization (WHO) and other leading reports, the number of stroke patients is about 5.8 million each year and altogether there are about 300 million stroke patients all over the world [1]. Physical or exercise therapy is a very important and effective method in early rehabilitation stage for paralyzed patients. In traditional rehabilitation, the movement of stroke patients is accomplished under the therapist's help. Generally it relies on some simple mechanical instruments. In this way, the patient is passive to generate the movement, which requires physical therapists to contribute a very heavy physical labor. As an alternative choice, functional electrical stimulation (FES) technique is becoming more and more important in rehabilitation field, and it has been widely recognized by the medical rehabilitation professions for its good performance in the limb rehabilitation [2].

FES uses electrical pulses of low level for restoration of motor function by activating skeletal muscle to generate the desired movements for paralyzed patients. FES was usually controlled by manual of either a therapist or a patient, which heavily depends on the continuous attention of the therapist or patient manipulation. In recent years, some new technologies such as bio-sensor technology made FES more

---

* Corresponding author.

C.-Y. Su, S. Rakheja, H. Liu (Eds.): ICIRA 2012, Part II, LNAI 7507, pp. 1–10, 2012.

advanced and popular. For example, electromyography (EMG) plays an important role as a source to control FES. EMG is a technique for evaluating and recording the electrical activity produced by skeletal muscles and it detects the electrical potential generated by muscle cells if muscle cells are activated [3]. Surface EMG (sEMG) is mainly applied in artificial limb (prosthesis) control and has achieved a big success in previous research. Differently, for FES control, EMG may bring some new challenges [4]. As a pioneer work, Graupe and Kohn firstly introduced EMG into FES control [5]. In their research, EMG signal of the upper torso was obtained and then mapped to FES electrical pulses to make paralyzed patients walk.

With the development of FES, more muscle groups involved with the desired motions should be stimulated, which needs more control signals. More signals mean that more wires are needed, which may lead to inconvenience and make big troubles for free movements. A better way to solve this problem is to use wireless systems. In the past, only a few works adopted telemetry technique for FES application. In 1989, Jennings developed a wireless system which used infrared transmission of pushbutton signals and provided on/off switching of electrical stimulation [6]. In 1996, Matjačić and his group developed a functional electrical stimulation system using the telemetry system based on wireless control (radiofrequency medium). This system has successfully made use of a new technique of radiofrequency that had superiority in wireless communication [7]. Christa et al. developed a wireless, wearable joint angle transducer to enable proportional control of an upper-limb neuroprosthesis by wrist position in 2009 [8]. In this wearable controller, wrist position measured by gigantic magneto resistive sensing technique was used as the control source.

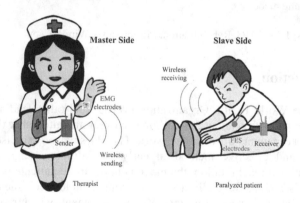

Fig. 1. Principle of the wireless master-salve FES rehabilitation system

To our knowledge, previous FES in rehabilitation engineering application was basically designed for the independent system of individual patients so that patients could achieve a particular motor function. However, they didn't relate to any concept of "master-slave" rehabilitation training at all, and there is no precedent for the application of FES system that includes the mode of "teaching" (from therapist) and "learning" (from patients). Our work will explore this idea and make it into practice. The principle of the idea is shown in Fig.1. We can see that EMG, wireless communication, and FES are the major three important techniques needed for the system.

2   Methodology

2.1   System Structure

The architecture of the system is shown in Fig.2, which consists of a master unit and a slave unit. The number of slave units can be extended from one to N (N>1) if more patients participate. Master unit contains EMG acquisition, EMG processing (feature extraction and classification algorithms), motion recognition, and wireless transmitter. EMG sensors measure the sEMG information from the concerned muscle groups in the forearm of the therapist; the EMG information is processed to predict the motion; the motion will be encoded and be sent to the slave unit as the control signal. Slave unit contains wireless receiver, controller, and FES stimulator. Slave unit receives the motion information and stimulate the targeted muscle groups of the patients in order to make the patients get the same motions as that of the therapist.

When the therapist is doing certain rehabilitation movements, sEMG information related to the movements is collected through sEMG electrodes. Raw EMG is amplified and transmitted to computer for analysis through blue tooth. After the feature extraction and classification processing in PC software, the motion information is acquired. The encoder encodes the motion information and then wireless transmitter transports it to slave unit. The slave unit gets the motion information and decodes it; the stimulation pattern is produced by the controller according to the specific motion. FES instrument generates the desired electrical stimulation pulses to the paralyzed muscles accordingly via electrodes, so that patients perform the same motions as that of the therapist.

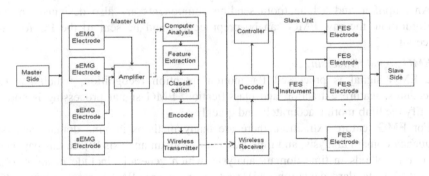

Fig. 2. Block diagram of components in wireless master-salve FES system proposed

2.2   Master Unit Design

1). EMG Signal Acquisition
Fig. 3 shows the wearable sEMG acquisition system used in master side. This system is self-designed and it is the most important part of master unit.

In such system, eight EMG channels are designed on a soft wearable belt. There is a velcro tape (hooks & loops fastener) on the back of the soft belt such that it can be bound to the forearm of the therapist easily. Each channel is an integrated component consisting of three dry electrodes (metal bars): two for EMG potential acquisition and the other one for reference. This double differential detection way can reduce the EMG crosstalk. The self-designed system has some merits. Firstly, different from the traditional EMG electrodes that should be attached over the specific muscles, there is no need to locate the desirable muscles using our EMG sensors, and it is convenient for the users especially the beginners who are not familiar with the muscle location. Secondly, the common wet EMG electrodes with gel are mostly disposable (one-time used), but our EMG electrodes can be used for many times in a long time duration, so it is an environment-friendly device. Thirdly, it looks like a sport belt, which is cosmetically acceptable, and it can be designed into a sleeve in future.

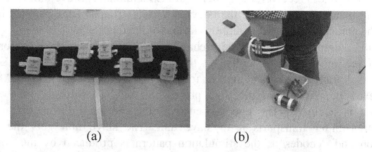

(a)   (b)

Fig. 3. (a) The self-designed sEMG sensors for the master side (the therapist). It has eight channels attached on a wearable belt. (b) The sEMG acquisition system is bound to the forearm of a subject.

An amplifier and a blue tooth sending components are also designed. In such configuration, the raw EMG can be preprocessed and be sent to the PC for later processing.

2) EMG Signal Processing
The EMG signal is processed for motion intention recognition, which has two procedures: feature extraction and classification. EMG signal processing is core to identify the limb motion accurately and quickly.

For EMG feature extraction, there are many methods in time domain analysis, frequency domain analysis, and time-frequency domain analysis [9]. In this paper, we focus on methods in time domain analysis, which generally include mean absolute value (AV), standard deviation (std), root mean square (RMS), zero crossing (ZC), and variance (VAR). These feature extraction algorithms are given as follows:

(1) Mean absolute value (AV):

$$AV = \frac{1}{N}\sum_{i=1}^{N} x_i \qquad (1)$$

where N is the sample length of the signal segment, x_i is the *i*-th sample of the signal segment.

(2) Standard deviation (std):

$$std = \sqrt{\frac{\sum_{i=1}^{N}(x_i - \overline{x})}{N-1}}$$

(2)

where $\overline{x}$ is the average of x_i

(3) Root mean square (RMS):

$$RMS = \sqrt{\frac{1}{N-1}\sum_{i=1}^{N}x_i^2}$$

(3)

(4) Zero crossing (ZC):

$$ZC = \sum_{i=1}^{N}\text{sgn}(-x_i x_{i-1}), \text{sgn}(x) = \begin{cases} 1 & if \quad x > 0 \\ 0 & otherwise \end{cases}$$

(4)

(5) Variance (VAR):

$$VAR = \frac{1}{N-1}\sum_{i=1}^{N}x_i^2$$

(5)

In our experiment, AV, RMS, and ZC are extracted as features for classification. The algorithm is simple and can be calculated quickly.

For classification, artificial neural networks (ANN), linear discriminant analysis (LDA), support vector machine (SVM) and fuzzy logic system are widely used. According to the experience from previous researchers, simple statistical procedures and ensemble methods proved very competitive, mostly producing good results "out of the box" without the inconvenience of delicate and computationally expensive hyperparameter tuning [10]. SVM has such characteristics and match the requirement, so it is selected as the classifier in this work.

SVM is a popular machine learning tool for regression and classification. It uses a kernel function to implicitly map the input vector into a high-dimensional space, and maximize the margin between classes based on computational statistical theory. The main idea of SVM is to create a space of optimal decision hyperplane, and the sample at both sides of hyperplane can get its maximum distance, in order to ensure that the SVM model has good generalization performance. The basic framework for the SVM is binary-class linear classification model: $y(x) = w^T \cdot \varphi(x) + b$, where w is a weight vector, b is a bias and $\varphi(x)$ is a non-linear kernel map and the kernel function is $k(x, x') = \varphi(x)^T \varphi(x')$. The radial basis function is used for SVM classifier because of its superior performance in pattern recognition [9]. We adopt the LIBSVM (Library for Support Vector Machines) package for SVM classifier design here, which is developed by Chang and Lin [11]. It is easy and convenient to use, and the open source codes are provided freely online.

The protocol of above EMG processing algorithms in our paradigm will be implemented in two separate stages: training and testing. The algorithm should be trained well first, and then it is applied in testing stage.

2.3   Slave Unit Design

Wireless communication component should send the motion code from master side to the slave side. The MSP430f149 (TI Inc. Texas U.S.) microcontroller is selected to be the core chip of the communication system. Two pieces of nRF24L01 chip (Nordic Semiconductor Inc. Norway), the single chip 2.4GHz transceiver, are chosen as transceiver and receiver of the radio signals respectively (see Fig. 4(a)).

MSP430F149 is used to get motion mode information after EMG processing in PC, and then encodes it for wireless transition. One nRF24L01 chip is for sending and the other is for receiving data. MSP430F2011 decodes the information and sends signal to control FES instrument (Compex motion II). The controller has "one to N" mapping mode, which can allow one master unit to control several certain muscles in one or more slave units.

In slave unit, a commercial FES device (Compex motion II, Switzerland) is used. It has two analog input channels and four output (stimulation) channels (that can stimulate four muscles one time). The analog input channel of the FES device is interfaced with wireless receiver. Fig. 4(b) shows the slave unit components and location of FES electrodes on the subject. In this case, the surface electrodes are attached to the forearm, and through the electrodes, electrical pulses can stimulate the muscles to generate wrist flexion-extension and radial-ulnar flexion.

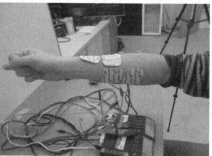

Fig. 4. (a) Wireless communication component. (b) FES system: Arrangement of surface stimulation electrodes on the forearm of a subject can be observed.

2.4   Experimental Design

1) Subjects

The experimental study has been conducted on 3 healthy subjects. All experimental procedures were approved by the local ethics committee and the subjects gave written informed consent, in accordance with the Declaration of Helsinki. All the subjects are male and their age is in twenties. Each subject plays two roles (therapist and patients) one time respectively. When the subject acts as the therapist, he should perform four types of movements regarding wrist joint: wrist flexion, wrist extension, wrist radial flexion, and wrist ulnar flexion. We will verify that the patient can follow the corresponding motions.

2) Experimental Procedure
The experimental protocols are designed for master side and slave side separately. For master side, the EMG data are collected. For salve side, the FES is applied.

Master side: Before the data collection, the instruction photographs of wrist motions are shown to the participants. They can practice the desirable movements for a moment in order to be familiar with the experimental procedure. During the experiment, the subject lays his upper arm on the table, and lifts up his forearm. Then the wrist motions are performed with natural force as usual. In each trial, the participants are instructed to sequentially perform four classes of motion 20 times. Each contraction is performed for 5 s and separated by 5 s rest interval. The experiment is conducted for 4 trials on every participant. The participant can relax after each trial. In EMG processing, the first two trials are assigned as a training stage and the rest two trials as testing stage.

Slave side: Surface FES is used to stimulate muscles corresponding to the four motions performed in master side: wrist flexion, wrist extension, wrist radial flexion, and wrist ulnar flexion. The targeted muscles are: forearm radial flexor, forearm ulnar flexor, forearm extensors and forearm flexors. Different from the master side, the muscle location should be identified accurately for each subject in order to actuate the concerned muscle and generate the desired motion. So the experimenter should try several times in order to find the exact muscle location in a trial-and-error way.

Several points should be noted here. First, surface electrodes are usually attached on the skin above the desired peripheral nerves or muscle's moving point (moving point refers to the point on the epidermis where electrode is placed on to stimulate muscle contractions with the minimum current). Secondly, the size of the electrode should vary with the size of the muscle to be stimulated. Big muscles should adopt large electrodes, and a small muscle is with small electrodes. Thirdly, stimulation current intensity can't be too large to exceed the tolerance of patients, which will cause painful or uncomfortable feeling.

3   Results and Discussion

We tested the stability and accuracy of the system in a variety of environments (including electromagnetism shield room, open room with no radiofrequency interference, room with microwave therapy instruments). The result showed that the system functioned well in all the environments, except that the interference has the same frequency as that of our wireless equipment. In most environments, the distance between master unit and slave unit can be as long as 20 m.

Fig. 5 shows an example of how the subject performed the same action according to the therapist. Since the participants are healthy persons, a large plate is paced between the master side and the slave side such that the slave side cannot see the motion of the master, and he will not intend to control the motion using his force voluntarily. Therefore, the motion of slave side is purely driven by FES. This way can avoid cheating in the present paradigm.

Fig. 5. Experiment shows the slave side (the left subject) can successfully perform the same action as that of the master side (the right subject)

The performance of the designed system was tested on three subjects. Each subject participated in master side and salve side one time separately. Table 1 shows the accuracy that three subjects follow the therapist motion, i.e. the recognition accuracy from EMG signals. The general performance is very good (over 90%). The sEMG signals of the therapist could be detected to control the FES instruments successfully.

Table 1. The accuracy rate that the slave side follows the master side (subjects A, B, C act in master side)

Wrist motions	subject A (%)	subject B (%)	subject C (%)	Mean (%)
flexion	97.25	95	97.25	96.5
extension	96.25	90	95	93.75
radial flexion	95	87.25	95	92.42
radial flexion	92.5	90	92.25	91.58
Mean	95.25	90.56	94.88	93.56

Table 2. Electrical stimulation intensity (current amplitude) for muscles of three subjects in slave side

subject	flexor (mA)	extensor (mA)	radial flexor (mA)	radial flexor (mA)
A	18	17	19	21
B	13	14	15	17
C	15	16	19	18

In the salve side, the four classes of wrist motions are generated by contraction of four muscles respectively. The artificial electrical pulses should be controlled in order to make the muscle generate the appropriate force. The exact value of stimulation intensity is determined in a trial-and-error way for each subject individually, because the muscle force-generating levels are different in different persons. The intensity of the applied electrical pulse is low at beginning and gradually increased to the expected level that can activate the muscle to generate the desired motions.

Table 2 shows the stimulation intensity for the muscles in three subjects. Actually, there are three parameters determining the intensity of electrical pulses: current amplitude, pulse width and pulse frequency. The pulse width and frequency are set as constants for all muscles in three subjects (pulse width is 300 us and frequency is 30 Hz). It means the current amplitude is the only controlled variable that represents the stimulation intensity.

It is well known that the traditional FES technique can maintain muscle activity, prevent muscle atrophy, reduce spasm, and increase the functional skills of paralyzed patients. It is very helpful for the patients' rehabilitation and may significantly improve the quality of their lives. Besides the above well-recognized merits, our proposed prototype of wireless FES rehabilitation system using sEMG control has three more advantages.

First of all, the system offers the distinctive advantage of wireless communication. The experimental result shows that distance between the therapist and patients can be as long as 20m. It saves space in the treatment and overcomes the traditional FES limitation in a very limited range of operation.

Secondly, the system changes the traditional way of exercise rehabilitation. Therapists do not need physical contact to assist paralyzed patients to do the training, and this system can achieve the goal of several patients following a therapist to do rehabilitation training at the same time, which is a "1 to N" concept, greatly reducing the workload of therapists. Due to the smart design of EMG electrodes, the system facilitates the therapists since it can relieve the tedious preparation on placement of EMG sensors. In a word, it is more practical.

Lastly, when paralyzed patients watch the therapist's motion, they tend to do the same motions in mind, but their paralyzed limbs cannot move. FES can help them accomplish the task. During this process, patients can get a strong inductive effect from vision, which will enhance the rehabilitation performance and neural plasticity.

However, there are a few flaws during the experiment. One obvious flaw is the time delay between the therapist and the patients, which is 400 ms on average. It is mainly caused by the time of muscle responds to FES, which is a problem that exists in most FES systems.

4　Conclusion and Future Work

The prototype of wireless master-slave FES rehabilitation system was developed in this work, which has functions of EMG sensing, EMG processing, wireless communicating, and FES actuating. Experiments were conducted on three subjects to test the performance. Results showed that the slave side can follow the master side successfully. The effectiveness of such system was validated.

At present, only motion of wrist joint is considered, and complex motions of whole arm with multiple degrees of freedoms will be tried in future. We will also develop an integrated FES instrument, which will cover 2-4 input channels and 4-8 output channels. In this way, more series of muscle can be stimulated and makes the system more portable.

The internet-based communication will be introduced in future. The remote master-slave control will be realized, so the master side and the slave side can be located in two faraway places even two countries. In such way, the distance can be extended more than that in the present wireless communication way.

This concept can also be used for normal persons in some teaching-learning cases. For example, if a person wants to learn playing a musical instrument such as guitar, our proposed system can be used. In such case, the salve side is the learner, and the master side is a musician (teacher). The EMG from the musician's arm can be acquired to control the finger motions of the learner via FES so that the learner can play the guitar well even he is a layman [12].

Acknowledgments. This work was supported by National Natural Science Foundation of China (No. 51075265), the State Key Laboratory of Mechanical System and Vibration (Grant No. MSVMS201112), and SJTU Student Innovation Project (No. S020IPP001008).

References

1. Truelsen, T., Heuschmann, P.U., Bonita, R., et al.: Standard method for developing stroke registers in low-income and middle income countries: experiences from a feasibility study of a stepwise approach to stroke surveillance (STEPS Stroke). The Lancet Neurology 6, 134–139 (2007)
2. Cauraugh, J., Light, K., Kim, S., et al.: Chronic motor dysfunction after stroke: recovering wrist and finger extension by electromyography triggered neuromuscular stimulation. Stroke 31, 1360–1364 (2000)
3. Kamen, G.: Electromyographic Kinesiology. In: Robertson, D.G.E., et al. (eds.) Research Methods in Biomechanics. Human Kinetics Publ., Champaign (2004)
4. Zhang, D.G., Guan, T.H., Widjaja, F., Ang, W.T.: Functional electrical stimulation in rehabilitation engineering: a survey. In: Proceedings of the 1st International Convention on Rehabilitation Engineering and Assistive Technology (i-CREATe), pp. 221–226 (2007)
5. Graupe, D., Kohn, K.H.: A critical review on EMG- controlled electrical stimulation in paraplegics. CRC Critical Review in Biomedical Engineering 15(3), 187–210 (1987)
6. Jenings, S.J.: Wire-free switch system for electrostimulation in paraplegic locomotion. In: Proceedings of the 3rd International Workshop on Electrostimulation, Baden, Vienna, pp. 327–330 (1989)
7. Matjačić, Z., Munih, M., Bajd, T., et al.: Wireless control of functional electrical stimulation systems. Artificial Organs 21(3), 197–200 (1997)
8. Christa, A., Wheeler, P., Peckham, H.: Wireless wearable controller for upper-limb neuroprosthesis. Journal of Rehabilitation Research & Development 46, 243–256 (2009)
9. Chen, X.P., Zhu, X.Y., Zhang, D.G.: A discriminant bispectrum feature for surface EMG signal classification. Medical Engineering and Physics 32(2), 126–135 (2010)
10. Meyer, D., Leisch, F., Hornik, K.: The support vector machine under test. Neurocomputing 55, 169–186 (2003)
11. Chang, C.C., Lin, C.J.: Libsvm: a library for support vector machines (2001), http://www.csie.ntu.edu.tw/~cjlin/libsvm
12. Tamaki, E., Miyaki, T., Rekimoto, J.: PossessedHand: Techniques for controlling human hands using electrical muscles stimuli. In: Proceedings of the 29th CHI Conference on Human Factors in Computing Systems, pp. 543–552 (2011)

Intelligent Prescription-Diagnosis Function for Rehabilitation Training Robot System

Lizheng Pan[1], Aiguo Song[1,*], Guozheng Xu[2], Huijun Li[1], and Baoguo Xu[1]

[1] School of Instrument Science and Engineering, Southeast University,
Nanjing 210096, China
a.g.song@seu.edu.cn, plz517@sina.com.cn
[2] College of Automation, Nanjing University of Posts and Telecommunications,
Nanjing 210003, China

Abstract. A prescription-diagnosis function based on integrating support vector machine and generalized dynamic fuzzy neural networks (SVM-GDFNN) is developed to automatically recommend a suitable training mode to the impaired limb. Considering the outstanding generalization ability and misclassified samples mainly distributed nearby the support vector for SVM method, SVM is adopted to recommend a preliminary prescription diagnosis for the sample and GDFNN is employed to rediagnose the sample nearby the support vector. Finally, the training mode of impaired limb is prescribed according to the designed principles. In addition, wavelet packet decomposition is applied to extract the features representing the impaired-limb movement performance. Clinical experiment results indicate that the suggested method can effectively reduce the misdiagnosis and serve with a high diagnostic accuracy. Meanwhile, the designed rehabilitation system well manages the promising prescription-diagnosis function, improving the intelligent level.

Keywords: Rehabilitation robot, Support vector machine (SVM), Generalized dynamic fuzzy neural networks (GDFNN), Feature extraction, Prescription diagnosis.

1   Introduction

Neurologic injuries such as stroke and spinal cord injury (SCI) cause dysfunction to neural system, which generally results in upper-limb impairment and motion disabilities. Nowadays, in many countries, more and more people experience a new stroke each year, and approximately 80% of first-time acute stroke survivors suffer from upper-limb impairment [1, 2]. Fortunately, clinical outcomes have shown that intensive and repetitive robot-assisted movement exercises present a positive effectiveness in improved performance of impaired-limb movements [3].

In the last few years, there was increasing interest in using robotic devices to provide rehabilitation therapy for neurologic injuries [4]. To gain the maximal

---

* Corresponding author.

C.-Y. Su, S. Rakheja, H. Liu (Eds.): ICIRA 2012, Part II, LNAI 7507, pp. 11–20, 2012.

effectiveness and promote the intelligent level, many investigators have done a lot of work on control strategies. Ref [5] presented an adaptive and automatic task-presentation strategy to enhance the recovery of upper extremity functions in patients with stroke, which engaged the patient intensively, actively, and adaptively in a variety of realistic functional tasks. A standard model-based, adaptive control approach was adopted to learn the patient's abilities and assist in completing movements, which achieved assistance-as-needed by adding a novel force reducing term [6]. Podobnik explored a haptic robot and virtual environment to motivate the patient's participation largely, and investigated the coordination between load force and grasp force for a special reaching-grasping exercise in robot-aided upper extremity rehabilitation [7]. Ref [8] has examined the usefulness of psychophysiological measurements (heart rate, skin conductance, respiration, and skin temperature) in a biocooperative feedback loop that adjusted the difficulty of an upper extremity rehabilitation task. In addition, surface EMG signals were applied to control the exoskeleton robot and assist the motion of physically weak individuals [9]. In the literature, many contributions have focused on control strategies and control performance and clinical effectiveness of different training modes. However, during the robot-assisted rehabilitation exercises, the training modes are generally predetermined by physiotherapist according to the condition of the impaired limb, it means that the exiting rehabilitation robots lack the function to automatically recommend a suitable training mode to the impaired limb.

In this paper, a novel prescription-diagnosis method which well combines the characteristics of support vector machine (SVM) with generalized dynamic fuzzy neural networks (GDFNN) is proposed to realize automatically recommending suitable training mode to the impaired limb. Firstly, the features of impaired-limb movement performance are extracted. Secondly, due to its good generalization ability, SVM is used to recommend a preliminary training-mode prescription according to the patient's movement ability features. Then, GDFNN is employed to rediagnose the samples nearby the support vector for the SVM is prone to make misdiagnosis in the area. Finally, based on the designed decision-making mechanism, the suitable training mode is recommended to the impaired limb. Clinical experiment results indicate that the suggested method serves with a high diagnostic accuracy, and the designed upper-limb rehabilitation system well manages the promising function.

2   SVM-GDFNN Prescription-Diagnosis Algorithm

2.1   SVM and GDFNN

SVM is a self-supervision neural learning method and its essential approach is to deal with a non-linear classification or regression problem in mapped higher dimensional space by nuclear functions [10, 11]. SVM has become a new focused issue following the neural network, and is widely used in fault diagnosis and classification [10, 12].

Given training vectors (x_i, y_i), $x_i \in \mathbb{R}^n$, indicator vector $y_i \in \{+1, -1\}$, $i=1,2,...,N$, in two classes, and SVM for classification solves the following primal optimization problem:

$$\min(\frac{1}{2}w^T w + C\sum_{i=1}^{n}\xi_i) \qquad \text{s.t.} \quad \begin{cases} y_i(w^T\phi(x_i)+b) \geq 1-\xi_i \\ \xi_i \geq 0 \\ i=1,2,...,n \end{cases} \qquad (1)$$

where ξ_i is the slack variable, C is called soft margin parameter, w and b are the weight vector and threshold, respectively, in function $f(x)=(w\bullet x)+b$.

After applying Lagrange function and using the primal-dual relationship, the optimal w and decision function are expressed as following [11]:

$$\begin{cases} w = \sum_{i=1}^{n} y_i\alpha_i\phi(x_i) \\ f(x) = \text{sgn}(\sum_{i=1}^{n} y_i\alpha_i K(x_i,x)+b) \end{cases} \qquad (2)$$

where $\phi(x_i)$ maps x_i into a higher-dimensional space and $K(x_i,x)$ is the kernel function.

The Eq.(2) is similar to neural networks, and the output is linear organization with each support vector, which is shown as in Fig. 1.

The methods to deal with multi-classification with SVM include all at once, one against one, one against all, and error-correcting output code, etc. One against one SVM combines each two of k-class samples, and constructs $k(k-1)/2$ two-class problems, which performances with a high speed, and is widely applied in practice. Usually, vote method is adopted to make decision, and the sample belongs to the category which obtains the most votes. However, the SVM is prone to misclassify the sample nearby the support vector, when it is adopted to deal with multi classifications.

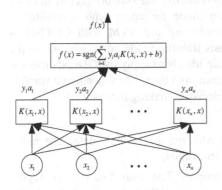

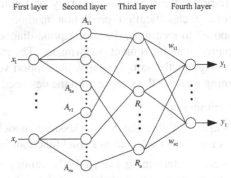

Fig. 1. Schematic diagram for SVM   **Fig. 2.** The GDFNN with MIMO

GDFNN based on elliptical basis functions is functionally equivalent to the TSK fuzzy system with neural network, adjusting and identifying the parameters at the same time, which is suitable for real-time modeling and control of MIMO systems

[13]. According to the characteristic of GDFNN, it is also suitable for dealing with classification problem [14]. The network structure of GDFNN with MIMO is shown in Fig. 2. There are four layers in this network structure, as following:

First layer: input layer, each node represents an input linguistic variable.

Second layer: membership function layer, each input variable includes u Gaussian membership functions A_{ij} ($j = 1, 2, ..., u$).

Third layer: T-Norm layer, each node represents the *IF* section of fuzzy rule.

Fourth layer: output layer, each node represents the sum of weighted input variables:

$$y_p(x_1, x_2, ..., x_r) = \sum_{j=1}^{u} w_{jp} \cdot \phi_j \tag{3}$$

where y_p is the value of *pth* output variable, ϕ_j is the output of *jth* rule, w_{jp} is the weight factor of *jth* rule and y_p (i.e., the *THEN* section of fuzzy rule). The w_{jp} is expressed as:

$$w_{jp} = \alpha_{j0}^p + \alpha_{j1}^p x_1 + ... + \alpha_{jr}^p x_r \qquad j = 1, 2, ..., u \tag{4}$$

where α_{ji}^p ($j = 1, 2, ..., u; i = 0, 1, ..., r; p = 1, 2, ..., z$) is real parameter.

In the fuzzy system, this layer performs defuzzification function, taking into account the impact of all membership functions.

2.2   SVM-GDFNN Classification Algorithm

The analysis result of misclassified data with SVM method shows that the misclassified data-samples are mainly distributed nearby the support vector. In order to improve the diagnosis accuracy of training mode for upper-limb rehabilitation robots, a classification prediction method combining the SVM with GDFNN is proposed to recommend a prescription-diagnosis training mode corresponding to the impaired-limb movement performance. The main idea is to apply the GDFNN method to rediagnose the sample nearby the support vector, and then recommending a suitable training mode to the sample with the designed decision-making mechanism.

Algorithm steps:

Step1: Building the SVM classifier model with training sample data. The radial basis function is selected as kernel function, in this paper.

Step2: Determining the GDFNN training samples. The score line (i.e. the region nearby support vector) is determined according to the SVM training model and self-classification accuracy, where all data-samples are selected as the GDFNN training sample.

Firstly, the value of each training sample is calculated by the following function which is similar to the decision function in Eq.(2).

$$v_m = \sum_{i=1}^{n} y_i \alpha_i K(x_i, x_m) + b \qquad (5)$$

Then, distinguish the samples with the following function, and ordering the training samples according to the calculated values.

$$f_m = \frac{v_m}{v_{mean}} \qquad (6)$$

where v_{mean} is the mean of the class which v_m belongs to, with Eq.(5).

Finally, the $S_k(1 - acc_k + 5\%)$ samples are selected as the training samples for GDFNN from the smallest f_m. S_k is the total number of the training samples in the kth classifier, and acc_k is self-classification accuracy of the kth classifier.

Step3: Training the GDFNN with the total samples selected by step2.

Step4: Designing decision-making mechanism. The prescription-diagnosis training mode of the sample is finally determined by the designed decision-making mechanism, using the proposed SVM-GDFNN algorithm.

The prescription-diagnosis algorithm based on SVM-GDFNN is shown as in Fig. 3.

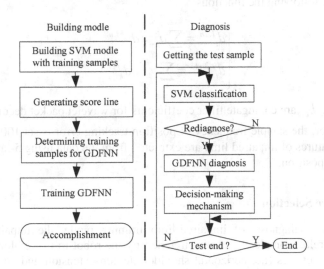

Fig. 3. The flow chart of SVM-GDFNN algorithm

3   Feature Extraction of Impaired-Limb Movement Performance

In clinic, according to the active grade to complete the exercise action, the training mode is divided into three types, namely, passive exercise, assistive-active exercise, and active-and-resistive exercise. Obtaining the effective features of impaired-limb movement performance is a key factor to realize smart prescription diagnosis for training mode. Due to the differences in muscle activity performance and condition of central nervous system, the impaired limb presents different influence on the robot control performance when the patient is asked to relax completely and is stretched by the robot to move along the predefined trajectory [15]. In this paper, the movement features is extracted from the position tracking errors of two passive actions.

3.1   Wavelet Packet Decomposition

Wavelet transform is widely applied in signal denoising and feature extraction [16]. In the orthogonal wavelet transform, the process can be expressed as the space subdivision, i.e. $C_0 = A_1 \oplus D_1 = A_2 \oplus D_2 \oplus D_1 = \cdots$, which applies the multi-scale decomposition only in A space. Wavelet packet transform provides a more flexible way of decomposition, band with multi-level division and high frequency band with further decomposition, and adapts to select the appropriate frequency band to match with the spectrum of the signal according to signal characteristics, which effectively improves the time-frequency resolution.

Wavelet packet decomposition algorithm [17]: $\{d_l^{j,2n}\}$ and $\{d_l^{j,2n+1}\}$ are calculated with $\{d_l^{j+1,n}\}$ following the functions:

$$\begin{cases} d_l^{j,2n} = \sum_k a_{k-2l} d_k^{j+1,n} \\ d_l^{j,2n+1} = \sum_k b_{k-2l} d_k^{j+1,n} \end{cases} \tag{7}$$

where a_k and b_k are conjugate filter coefficients for wavelet packet decomposition.

In this paper, the sample frequency of position tracking error is set 100Hz, and the movement features of impaired limb are extracted from the data using 5-layer wavelet packet decomposition.

3.2   Feature Selection

For prescription diagnosis of impaired-limb training mode, the impaired-limb is conducted to relax completely and is stretched by the robot to move along two-type predefined trajectories (i.e. horizontal shoulder flexion-extension and vertical elbow flexion-extension exercise movements). The position tracking errors of two-type movements are recorded, and then corresponding features are extracted to represent the characteristics of impaired-limb movement performance.

There are 32 decomposed coefficients with 5-layer wavelet packet decomposition, namely, d(5,0)~d(5,31). In order to reduce the dimension of feature vector and represent the impaired-limb condition effectively, five indices are considered to represent the impaired-limb movement performance, namely, energy sum of wavelet packet coefficients, absolute sum of high-frequency coefficients, absolute sum of low-frequency coefficients, absolute sum of d(5,0) and d(5,1), energy sum of position tracking errors. Thus, 10-dimention feature vector is generated to represent the impaired-limb condition with 2-type movements, which as the input feature vector of prescription-diagnosis classifier.

4   Prescription-Diagnosis Function for Rehabilitation Robot

4.1   Upper-Limb Rehabilitation Robot System

Whole Arm Manipulator (WAM) of American Barrett Technology Inc. is a high-performance dexterous mechanical arm with four degree-of-freedom (4-DOF) and naturally back-drivability [18]. The robot system supplies high open software based on Ubuntu Linux, and the researcher can develop advanced control algorithm and experiment on the platform. It was commendably applied in Chicago rehabilitation center in America. In this paper, the constructed upper-limb rehabilitation robot system based on WAM is shown in Fig. 4. The hardware system mainly consists of WAM and self-developed 3-D force sensor [19] and arm support device. The 3-D force sensor installed on the end-effector works for detecting the interaction force between the endeffector and the impaired limb online, and support device is supplied to brace impaired limb.

The software of rehabilitation system was developed on Ubuntu Linux system with a real-time module Xenomai. According to clinical training exercises, three control modules have been developed to conduct the patient with helpful rehabilitation movements, namely, passive control strategy, assistive-active control strategy, and active-and-resistive control strategy. The main control-loop thread shown in Fig. 5 is the key section for the whole control system. This research aims to investigate the intelligent diagnosis function of training mode for upper-limb rehabilitation robot, so the developed control strategies of different training modes are not introduced in this paper. The designed control system with prescription-diagnosis function for rehabilitation robot is shown as in Fig. 6.

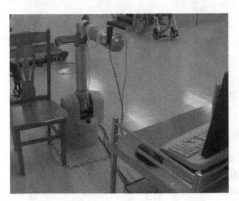

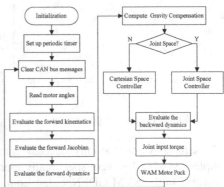

Fig. 4. WAM rehabilitation robot system   **Fig. 5.** WAM control loop flowchart

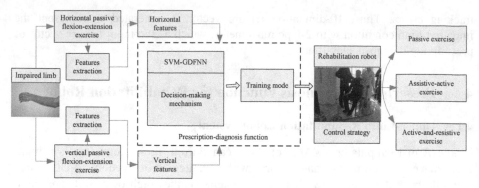

Fig. 6. Rehabilitation system with prescription-diagnosis function

4.2   Clinical Experiment Results

In order to verify the effectiveness of the proposed algorithm, clinical trials were conducted in Nanjing Tongren Hospital Motor Rehabilitation Center. 26 subjects who suffered from upper-limb motor dysfunctions caused by stroke or traumatic brain injury were selected and all the subjects' impaired-limb movement data-samples were recorded on WAM rehabilitation robot system. In addition, the movement data-samples of 5 subjects without dysfunctions were also recorded in order to investigate the issue completely. Four data-samples were selected from each subject at different time, and 124 data-samples were obtained.

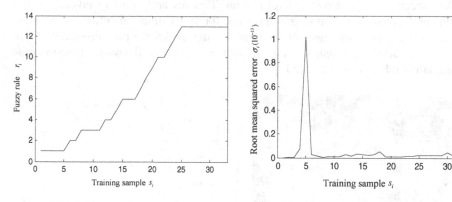

Fig. 7. Fuzzy rule generation   **Fig. 8.** Root mean squared error

74 samples were randomly selected as training samples, another 50 samples as test samples. 33 samples were specifically identified as the training samples of GDFNN according to the SVM-GDFNN algorithm, and then the GDFNN model was build as the rediagnosis model by the identified 33 samples. During the establishment of GDFNN, the process of generating fuzzy rules and the training root mean squared error are shown in Fig. 7 and 8, respectively. Thirteen generated fuzzy rules indicate

that the GDFNN method online amends fuzzy rules according to the importance of the fuzzy rules during the model building, which effectively avoid generates redundant fuzzy rules. From the profile in Fig. 8, it is evident that the training error quickly converges to the target error, which indicates that the GDFNN is outstanding in learning ability.

Using the proposed SVM-GDFNN algorithm, the 50 test samples were carried out to present prescription-diagnosis function. In the process of diagnosis, there were 17 samples undergoing GDFNN rediagnosis; 5 wrong diagnoses were rectified and 1 original correct diagnosis was wronged with the designed decision-making mechanism. In addition, in order to demonstrate the performance of the algorithm completely, the single SVM and GDFNN methods were applied to work for the prescription diagnosis, respectively, and the specific results are shown in Table 1.

Table 1. Diagnosis performance comparison %

Method	SVM-GDFNN	SVM	GDFNN
Self-diagnosis accuracy	94.59	86.49	97.3
Accuracy	92	84	78

The results in Table 1 obviously indicate that GDFNN has the best self-diagnosis accuracy, presenting remarkable learning ability; however, its generalization ability is not so much satisfactory. SVM well manages the balance between generalization ability and model structure with principle to minimize structural risk. The proposed SVM-GDFNN effectively integrates the characteristics of SVM and GDFNN methods, which greatly improves the prescription-diagnosis accuracy.

5   Conclusions

Intelligent level plays an important role for rehabilitation robot in clinic application. In this research, according to the characteristics of SVM and GDFNN methods, the SVM-GDFNN method is proposed to develop prescription-diagnosis function, which effectively manages the virtues of two methods and improves the diagnosis accuracy. Experimental results show that the designed rehabilitation system can automatically recommend a suitable training mode to the impaired limb with high accuracy, applying the suggested method to develop prescription-diagnosis function. The rehabilitation system with prescription-diagnosis function for training mode can effectively avoid the limitation of traditional rehabilitation robot and improve the intelligent level in clinical application. In future work, we need explore more effective feature extraction or classification method to serve this promising prescription-diagnosis function with higher accuracy. Meanwhile, through a large number of clinical experiments, a more intelligent and humanistic expert system would be developed, which benefits the patient with a high quality rehabilitation exercise.

Acknowledgements. The authors would like to thank the volunteers in the clinical experiments. This work was supported by the National Natural Science Foundation of China (No. 61104206), the Natural Science Foundation of JiangSu Province (BK2010063), the Industrial Technology Project Foundation of ChangZhou Government (CE20100022).

References

1. Culmer, P.R., Jackson, A.E., Makower, S.: A control strategy for upper limb robotic rehabilitation with a dual robot system. IEEE/ASME Transactions on Mechatronics 15, 575–585 (2010)
2. Xu, B.G., Peng, S., Song, A.G.: Robot-aided upper-limb rehabilitation based on motor imagery EEG. Int. J. Adv. Robotic Sy. 8, 88–97 (2011)
3. Bovolenta, F., Sale, P.: Robot-aided therapy for upper limbs in patients with stroke-related lesions: Brief report of a clinical experience. Journal of Neuro Engineering and Rehabilitation 8 (2011)
4. Laura, M.C., David, J.R.: Review of control strategies for robotic movement training after neurologic injury. Journal of NeuroEngineering and Rehabilitation 6 (2009)
5. Choi, Y., Gordon, J., Kim, D.: An adaptive automated robotic task-practice system for rehabilitation of arm functions after stroke. IEEE Transactions on Robotics 25, 556–568 (2009)
6. Wolbrecht, E.T., Chan, V., Reinkensmeyer, D.J., Bobrow, J.E.: Optimizing compliant, model-based robotic assistance to promote neurorehabilitation. IEEE Transactions on Neural Systems and Rehabilitation Engineering 16, 286–297 (2008)
7. Podobnik, J., Novak, D., Munih, M.: Grasp coordination in virtual environments for robot-aided upper extremity rehabilitation. Biomedical Engineering-Applications Basis Communications 23, 457–466 (2011)
8. Novak, D., Mihelj, M., Ziherk, J.: Psychophysiological measurements in a biocooperative feedback loop for upper extremity rehabilitation. IEEE Transactions on Neural Systems and Rehabilitation Engineering 19, 400–410 (2011)
9. Gopura, R.A.R.C., Kiguchi, K.: An exoskeleton robot for human forearm and wrist motion assist-hardware design and EMG-based controller. Journal of Advanced Mechanical Design Systems and Manufacturing 2, 1067–1083 (2008)
10. Nuryani, N., Ling, S.S.H., Nguyen, H.T.: Electrocardiographic signals and swarm-based support vector machine for hypoglycemia detection. Annals of Biomedical Engineering 40, 934–945 (2012)
11. Chang, C.C., Lin, C.J.: LIBSVM: A library for support vector machines. ACM Transactions on Intelligent Systems and Technology 2, 27:1–27:27 (2011)
12. Kim, K.J., Ahn, H.: A corporate credit rating model using multi-class support vector machines with an ordinal pairwise partitioning approach. Computers & Operations Research 39, 1800–1811 (2012)
13. Wu, S.Q., Er, M.J., Gao, Y.: A fast approach for automatic generation of fuzzy rulers by generalized dynamic fuzzy neural networks. IEEE Trans. Fuzzy Systems 9, 578–594 (2001)
14. Lim, W.K., Er, M.J.: Classification of mammographic masses using generalized dynamic fuzzy neural networks. Medical Physics 31, 1288–1295 (2004)
15. Ju, M.S., Lin, C.C.K., Lin, D.H., Hwang, I.S.: A rehabilitation robot with force-position hybrid fuzzy controller: Hybrid fuzzy control of rehabilitation robot. IEEE Transactions on Neural Systems and Rehabilitation Engineering 13, 349–358 (2005)
16. Sina, Z.M., Alireza, A., Javad, A.: A fast expert system for electrocardiogram arrhythmia detection. Expert Systems 27, 180–200 (2010)
17. Rosso, O.A., Martin, M.T., et al.: EEG analysis using wavelet-based information tools. Journal of Neuroscience Methods 153, 163–182 (2006)
18. Xu, G.Z., Song, A.G., Li, H.J.: Control system design for an upper-limb rehabilitation robot. Advanced Robotics 25, 229–251 (2011)
19. Song, A.G., Wu, J., Qin, G., et al.: A novel self-decoupled four degree-of-freedom wrist force/torque sensor. Measurement 40, 883–891 (2007)

Human Behavior Recognition
by a Bio-monitoring Mobile Robot

Myagmarbayar Nergui, Yuki Yoshida, Nevrez Imamoglu,
Jose Gonzalez, and Wenwei Yu

Medical System Engineering Department, Graduate School of Engineering, Chiba University,
1-33 Yayoi-cho, Inage-ku, Chiba 263-8522 Japan
myagaa@graduate.chiba-u.jp

Abstract. Our ultimate goal is to develop autonomous mobile home healthcare robots which closely monitor and evaluate the patients' motor function, and their at-home training therapy process, providing automatically calling for medical personnel in emergency situations. The robots to be developed will bring about cost-effective, safe and easier at-home rehabilitation to most motor-function impaired patients (MIPs), and meanwhile, relieve therapists from great burden in canonical rehabilitation.

In order to achieve our ultimate goal, we have developed following programs/algorithms for monitoring subject activities and recognizing human behaviors. 1) Control programs for a mobile robot to track and follow human by three different viewpoints 2) Algorithms for measuring and analyzing of lower limb joints angle from RGB-D images from a Kinect sensor located at the mobile robot, and 3) Algorithms for recognizing gait gesture. In 2), compensation with colored marks was implemented to deal with the joint trajectory error caused by mixing-up and frame flying during tracking and following human movement by the mobile robot. In 3), We have proposed a Hidden Markov Model (HMM) based human behavior recognition using lower limb joint angles and body angle.

Experiment results showed that, joint trajectory could be analyzed with high accuracy compared to a motion tracking system, and human behavior could be recognized from the joint trajectory.

Keywords: Mobile robot, home healthcare, human behavior recognition.

1   Introduction

Home healthcare system has attracted more and more attention than before, because of increasing elderly population, and the improvement of medical treatment and prevention of lifestyle diseases. Main objective of research and development of home healthcare system is to enable monitoring and caring for people at their homes, thus reduce hospital admissions and long term in-hospital stays. In this study, we focused on bio-monitoring of motor-function impaired patients (MIPs) at home. Two important technical steps are 1) observing their motions and behaviors, 2) recognizing

C.-Y. Su, S. Rakheja, H. Liu (Eds.): ICIRA 2012, Part II, LNAI 7507, pp. 21–30, 2012.
© Springer-Verlag Berlin Heidelberg 2012

their behaviors from observed motions. There are many ways of observing human motions, for example, a smart home system which is equipped with full motion capture sensors, cameras, and some other wearable sensors, such as, accelerometers, EMG sensors and so on. However, smart home monitoring systems and motion capture systems are costly and only effective in limited areas, thus not suitable for at-home monitoring.

The mobility of autonomous robots might be a solution. If a robot could move to follow MIPs, keeping observing MIPs from a good viewpoint, in order to measure the joint trajectory with sufficiently high accuracy, and the behavior of MIPs could be recognized from the joint trajectory, then bio-monitoring with a mobile robot in an indoor environment would be quite practical.

Using mobile robots to track and follow human subjects is not a new research topic. There have been research works using mobile robots equipped with various sensors such as vision sensors, laser range finders, audio sensors and integration of them [2-5]. The targets of most of these systems are to track and follow persons. In addition, these systems use expensive sensors, such as LiDAR, and so on.

Our research ultimate goal is to develop autonomous mobile home healthcare and rehabilitation robots which are required not only tracking and following, but also accurately measuring and recognizing the motion of MIPs in an indoor environment.

Three main steps to realize the bio-monitoring robot in this study are: 1) to develop control programs for a mobile robot to track and follow human by three different viewpoints, such as, lateral view, front/back view and from a middle angle between lateral view and front view; 2) to develop algorithms for measuring and analyzing of lower limb joints angle from RGB-D images from a Kinect sensor located at the mobile robot, and 3) to develop algorithms for recognizing gait gesture, and evaluating the patients' motor functions.

In 2), the Kinect sensor, a product of Microsoft Research, contains a RGB camera, a Depth sensor (captures distance data of object), and a multi-array microphone. Due to its reasonable price, it is quite popular nowadays in robotics research. However, during tracking and following human movement by the mobile robot, the skeleton points extracted by Kinect SDK are quite inaccurate due to mixing-up and frame flying, which affects accuracy of the joint trajectory. We implemented compensation [1] with colored marks was implemented to deal with the problem.

Regarding human behavior recognition, research efforts have been done to use image processing methods, pattern recognition and classification algorithms for image sequential features [7-10]. In 3), we have proposed a Hidden Markov Model (HMM) [6] based human behavior recognition using lower limb joint angles and body angle. This is because that statistical nature of the HMM could render overall robustness to gait representation and recognition.

The paper is organized as follows: In section 2, we explain about the mobile robot used and its components. Section 3 presents our human motion tracking and measurement system by a mobile robot. Section 4 presents human behavior recognition procedure. Section 5 gives the experiments and the results of our system. In section 6, we draw conclusion.

2   The Mobile Robot Used and Its Components

2.1   Mobile Robot and Kinect Sensor

In this study, our mobile robot, a pioneer-3dx robot of Adept Technology Inc, is equipped with 8 ultrasound sensors, a Kinect sensor, a controller (rotating table) of the Kinect sensor movement, and a notebook computer. Fig.1 shows our mobile robot and its components.

A pioneer-3DX robot, is the world's most popular research robot. The Pioneer's versatility, reliability and durability have made it the reference platform for robotics research. The base Pioneer 3-DX platform arrives fully assembled with motors with 500-tick encoders, 19cm wheels, tough aluminum body, 8 forwardfacing ultrasonic (sonar) sensors, 3 hot-swappable batteries.

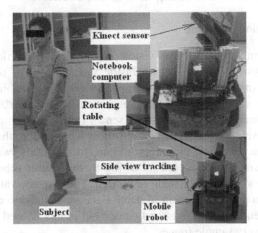

Fig. 1. Our mobile robot with its components and side view tracking

We used the Kinect for Windows SDK and OpenCV2.2 library on Windows 7 operating system for a robot vision. The RGB camera in the Kinect captures a color image, whereas the depth sensor or infrared camera captures depth image data or distance data of the object.

2.2   Kinect Camera Movement Controller

We used a rotating table to control the movement of the Kinect camera in a horizontal plane. We installed the rotating table between the base of The Kinect sensor and stand-up tool of The Kinect. The Kinect sensor itself has a vertical tilt. Thus, the Kinect sensor is able to rotate in vertical and horizontal plane. Now, we have two dimension movement of the Kinect camera. Why we needed 2D movement is to manage different kinds of human tracking and following by a mobile robot while keeping the tracking human inside the vision area in case that the robot avoiding obstacles and can not come near by tracked human.

2.3   Software Platform

The Mobile Robotics Programming Toolkit (MRPT) was used as the software platform. The MRPT is an open source and it is released under the GPL. The MRPT is basically writing on C++ programming language. We have written our full program in Microsoft Visual C++ 2010 Express. There are many kinds of libraries and SDK available for the Kinect sensor. For example, OpenKinect, OpenNI, NITE, FAAST, Official windows SDK of Microsoft and so on in different platforms. The natural user interface (NUI) API in the Kinect for Windows® Software Developer Kit (SDK) enables applications to access and manipulate these data. Notebook computer is a Macbook Pro (2.2GHz quad-core Intel Core i7).

3   Human Motion Tracking and Measurement

3.1   Human Motion Tracking

The most challenging thing for the vision based target detection of the human following robot is to keep target person inside image frame of the Kinect camera while robot is moving. In order to track and follow a human, in our system, we controlled our robot motion by using the skeleton tracking point data of human from the captured depth image data of the Kinect sensor (with 1.2- 3.5m skeleton tracking range). Then, we developed our tracking and following algorithm that is kept a certain distance between the robot and the target human. In this study, we developed three different types of human tracking and following by the mobile robot, such as, lateral view, front/back view and middle angle of human. The distance values of lower limb points from skeleton points of human in depth data are utilized to control the robot's velocity, and difference of left/ right and center hip points is used to control robot's rotational angle at every sample frame.

3.2   Measurement

In measurement of lower limb joints' motion, we used lower limb skeleton points of human tracking in the depth image data of the Kinect sensor in three dimension coordinates. Then, we have developed several algorithms for angle calculation of lower limb joints based on measurement data. Mentioned above, Kinect for Windows SDK Beta from Microsoft Research has 20 points of skeleton tracking data. Following sections explain about our developed algorithms for joint angle calculation.

3.2.1 Algorithm for the Measurement of the Lower Limb Joint Angle
First, we developed the joints angle calculation algorithm (called algorithm A) for using original skeleton points, but results were not good, and the Kinect original skeleton points are not at correct position of human joints, and also flying out during human movement.

3.2.2 Algorithm for Correcting the Skeleton Points Using Color Markers in RGB Image

Then, we developed a new algorithm to improve drawbacks of original skeleton points of the Kinect sensor. The new compensation algorithm (called algorithm B shown in Fig 2) of correcting the original skeleton points shows the method of the calculation of the joint angle of correcting the skeleton points using color markers in RGB image. Comparison results of algorithm A and algorithm B shows in Fig 3 and Fig 4.

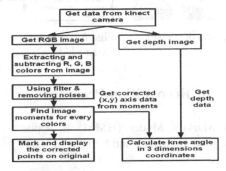

Fig. 2. Algorithm for correcting the skeleton points using color markers in RGB image

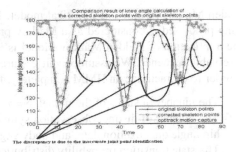

Fig. 3. RGB image with skeleton points (yellow ones are original skeleton points, others are the corrected points)

Fig. 4. Comparison result of knee angle calculation of the corrected skeleton points with original skeleton points

3.2.3 Algorithm for Making Assumption of Missing/Hidden Points

We got another problem for applying color markers to human while tracking and following by lateral views, that some joint points are missing or hidden (Fig 5). Then we developed a new algorithm (called algorithm C) in Fig 6 for making assumption of missing/hidden points in Table 1.

Table 1. Assumption of Missing Points and Calculation of Its Positions

Missing points	Assumption position of x, y axis
Knee and ankle both points of one side	Same as another side
Knee point of one side	Same as another side
Ankle point of one side	Calculate missing point based on geometric method

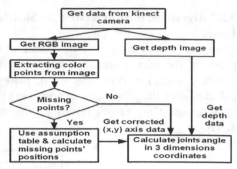

Fig. 5. Missing/hidden points of one side

Fig. 6. Algorithm of making assumption of missing/hidden points

4 Human Behavior Recognition Procedure

In this study, Hidden Markov Model (HMM) is applied for human behavior recognition based on the joint angle data and body angle data.

4.1 Hidden Markov Models

Hidden Markov Model is a statistical model. In a Hidden Markov Model, the system being processed is considered as a Markov process, which has unknown parameters. The application of Hidden Markov Model is to discover the sequence of states using observable sequence. We assumed gait gesture states by 6 different states in Fig .7. In order to characterize an HMM completely, following elements are needed.

> The number of states of the model, N=6
> The number of distinct observation symbols per state, M=19, both side knee and hip angle quantization data, and body angle quantization data
> The state transition probability distribution A={a_{ij}} $a_{ij} = P(q_t = S_j \mid q_{t-1} = S_i)$
> The observation symbol probability distribution ins state j: $b_j(k) = P(V_k \ at \ t \mid q_t = S_j)$
> The initial state distribution: $\pi_i = P(q_1 = S_i)$
> The model parameters notation: $\lambda = (A, B, \pi)$

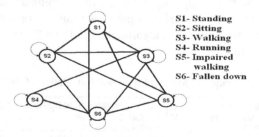

S1- Standing
S2- Sitting
S3- Walking
S4- Running
S5- Impaired walking
S6- Fallen down

Fig. 7. Coded gait gesture states

4.2   Calculation of Gait Joint Angles, Data Recording and Preprocessing Data

Calculation of gait joint angles and data recording were done based on algorithm C (Fig.6). Here is a brief explanation about calculation of the joint angle (hip and knee), we used x, y, and z axis data of shoulder center, hip, knee, ankle joint points in the skeleton data of the Kinect camera. Calculating the distance data between two certain points in 3D:

$$\text{Equations:} \quad ax = x_{hip} - x_{knee}; \quad ay = y_{hip} - y_{knee}; \quad az = z_{hip} - z_{knee}; \tag{1}$$

$$bx = x_{knee} - x_{ankle}; \quad by = y_{knee} - y_{ankle}; \quad bz = z_{knee} - z_{ankle};$$

To get the knee (hip) angle from three skeleton points (hip, knee, and ankle) or 2 lines data above calculated distance data in 3D dimension, we used a cross product and a dot product functions.

$$i = (ax * bx) + (ay * by) + (az * bz) \tag{2}$$

$$j = ((ax * ax) + (ay * ay) + (az * az)) * \\ * ((bx * bx) + (by * by) + (bz * bz)) \tag{3}$$

Finding knee angle from equations (2) and (3):

$$Knee\_angle = a\cos(i / \sqrt{j}) \tag{4}$$

Hip angle is calculated based on shoulder center, hip and knee joints data. In order to recognize fallen down and impaired walking case, body angle was calculated based on shoulder center, hip center point and virtual ground points. Before applying for HMM, the joint angle data were quantized by several levels shown in Table 2.

Table 2. Quantization of Angle Data

Threshold Value		Quanti-zation Level	Threshold Value		Quanti-zation Level
Knee angle	> 170	1	*Hip angle*	> 160	7
	150-	2		< 160	8
	130-	3	*Body angle*	> 150	9
	120-	4		120-150	10
	90-120	5		< 120	11
	< 90	6			

5   Experiments and Results

We developed an algorithm to control mobile robot motion to track and follow human subject based on depth data of the Kinect camera. Three different types (front view, lateral view, and from a middle angle between lateral view and front view) of human motion tracking and measurement system by the mobile robot were also developed. We developed several algorithms for the measurement and calculation of lower limb joint angle (shown in Fig. 2 and Fig.6) based on RGB-D images of tracked human subjects from a Kinect sensor located at the mobile robot. Our first algorithm, called algorithm A, is the measurement and calculation of lower limb joints angle based on original skeleton points of depth data of the Kinect sensor. We made measurement experiment on it, but its result was not good, due to not accurate skeleton points of human and frame flying-out during mobile robot motion. In order to enhance skeleton points' accuracy of lower limb, we developed a new compensation algorithm (called algorithm B shown in Fig 2) of correcting the original skeleton points using color marks attached at human lower limb joints. This algorithm B uses RGB-D image data getting from the Kinect sensor of tracked human for measurement and calculation of lower limb joints.

We compared the algorithm A and B of our motion tracking and measurement with the Optitrack motion capture (10 V100:R2 cameras). Comparison results of algorithm A, and algorithm B with Optitrack motion capture shows in Fig 3 and Fig 4. Our algorithm B result shows similar to reference motion capture system.

From lateral view tracking, we got another problem for applying color markers to human joints, that some joint points are missing or hidden (Fig 5). Then, we developed a new algorithm (called algorithm C) in Fig 6 for making assumption of missing/hidden points. This algorithm C became our final system of motion measurement and angle calculation of human lower limb joints.

After developing several algorithms of motion measurement system, we developed human behavior recognition process by using Hidden Markov Models based on preprocessed calculated lower limb joint and body angle data measured and recorded from lateral view tracking.

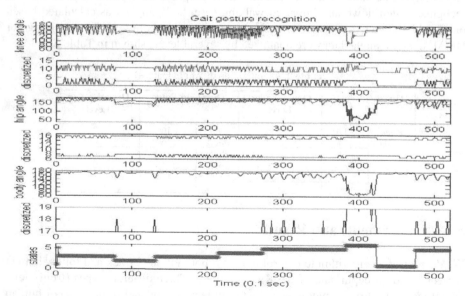

Fig. 8. Human Gait behavior recognition results. y axis is: a) knee angle b) quantized data of knee angle c) hip angle d) quantized data of hip angle e) body angle f) quantized data of body angle g) recognized states/most likely decoded states (Viterbi paths), x axis is time.

HMM were built from one series data. Different series of joint and body angle data were performed to recognize the gait gesture using HMM and to find the most likely decoded paths (Viterbi paths).

In our human behavior recognition experiment, 6 subjects (1 female (30s) and 5 males (20s-30s)) were conducted, and asked to do to following activities: walk and run with different types of speed (1.5km/h-6km/h), stand up, sit down, and fallen down towards front and back. In the impaired walking case, every subject was asked to wear ankle constrained simulated gait and walk with 1-1.5km/h speed. Experiment series data of human behavior recognition process (Walking-sitting-walking -running-impaired walking-fallen down-standing-impaired walking) is shown in Fig 8.

In Fig.8, y axis is: a) knee angle of both legs b) quantized data of knee angle c) hip angle of both legs d) quantized data of hip angle e) body angle (calculated based on shoulder center, hip center and virtual ground points) f) quantized data of body angle g) recognized states/most likely decoded states (Viterbi paths), x axis is time. From Fig.8, we can see that recognized states are 3-2-3-4-5-6-1-5, this means walking (S3)-sitting (S2) - walking (S3) –running (S4) - impaired walking (S5)-fallen down (S6)-standing (S1)-impaired walking (S6) states from coded gait gesture states in Fig.7. Table 3 shows the summarized results of correct rate of gait gesture states of all subjects' data.

Table 3. Corrected rate of all subjects

Subject	Corrected rate						
	S1	S2	S3	S4	S5	S6	Overall
1	100	100	99.1	98.0	91.0	98.1	97.7
2	100	100	99.2	97.9	90.5	98.1	97.61
3	100	100	99.1	97.2	90.1	98.0	97.4
4	100	100	99.3	98.1	91.2	98.2	97.8
5	100	100	99.0	97.6	90.1	98.1	97.5
6	100	100	98.9	97.0	90.0	98.0	97.3
AVG	100	100	99.1	97.6	90.5	98.1	97.5
STDEV	0	0	0.14	0.45	0.51	0.07	0.18

We can see that states S1 and S2 (standing and sitting) are recognized by 100%, because these states are stable. Impaired walking state S5 is recognized by 90-91%, and the lowest rate in all states. 9-10% of incorrect rate is mix-up of other states. This means impaired walking does not have symmetric features same as normal walking. Our human behavior recognition process (almost 97-98%) from Table 3 is the most accurate than any other gait gesture recognition method, because we applied HMM for two hip angle, two knee angle and body angle data. Human gait gesture is basically depends on gait cycle and gait joint motions. When HMM's observation symbols are more, then system's recognition is more accurate. In our case, 19 observation symbols were used.

6   Conclusion

We have developed control programs for a mobile robot to track and follow human by three different viewpoints; lateral view, front view and from a middle angle between lateral view and front view. We also have developed algorithms for measurements of lower limb joints motions and angle calculation of joints motions based on RGB-D image of tracked human. We also investigated the accuracy of joint measurement. Because the original skeleton points of the Kinect sensor is mixing-up and frame flying during procedure of tracking and following human movement by a mobile robot, the error of joint trajectory measurement was very big. However, after applying a colored mark compensation algorithm and missing point correction algorithm, the error could be corrected to a certain extent. This shows the feasibility of joint trajectory measurement through the mobile robots in real time. Finally, we proposed a method of human walking behavior recognition from lateral view tracking by applying HMM based on preprocessed lower limb joint angles and body angle without any attached sensors to human body. Method of applying HMM for gait joint angle motion data is more accuracy than any other gait gesture recognition methods, due to joint motions basically express gait gesture. Our proposed method brings the high rate of recognition of human walking behavior and is effective in indoor environment.

References

[1] Nergui, M., Yoshida, Y., Gonzalez, J., Koike, Y., Sekine, M., Yu, W.: Human Motion Tracking and Measurement by a Mobile Robot. In: ICIUS, Chiba, Japan (2011)
[2] Kwon, H., Yoon, Y., Park, J.B., et al.: Person tracking with a mobile robot using two uncalibrated independently moving cameras. In: IEEE International Conference on Robotics and Automation, Barcelona, Spain, pp. 2877–2883 (2005)
[3] Gupta, M., Behera, L., et al.: A Novel Approach of Human Motion Tracking with the Mobile Robotic Platform. In: 13th International Conference on Modelling and Simulation, UKSim (2011)
[4] Cunha, J., Pedrosa, E., et al.: Using a Depth Camera for Indoor Robot Localization and Navigation. In: Robotics Science and Systems (RSS) Conference 2011, on Campus at the University of Southern California, Poster Presentation P5 (2011)
[5] Biswas, J., Veloso, M.: Depth Camera based Localization and Navigation for Indoor Mobile Robots (2011), http://www.cs.cmu.edu/~mmv/papers/11rssw-KinectLocalization.pdf
[6] Rabiner, L.R.: A Tutorial on Hidden Markov Models and Selected Applications in Speech Recognition. Proceedings of the IEEE 77(2) (February1989)
[7] Wang, L., Tan, T., et al.: Silhouette Analysis-Based Gait Recognition for Human Identification. IEEE Transactions on Pattern Analysis and Machine Intelligence 25(12) (December 2003)
[8] Uddin, M.Z., Kim, T.S., et al.: Video-based Human Gait Recognition Using Depth Imaging and Hidden Markov Model: A Smart System for Smart Home. In: SHB 2010 - 3rd International Symposium on Sustainable Healthy Buildings, Seoul, Korea, May 27 (2010)
[9] Rohila, N., et al.: Abnormal Gait Recognition. International Journal on Computer Science and Engineering 02(05), 1544–1551 (2010)
[10] Pushpa Rani, M., et al.: An efficient gait recognition system for human identification using modified ICA. International Journal of Computer Science & Information Technology 2(1) (February 2010)

Differentiated Time-Frequency Characteristics Based Real-Time Motion Decoding for Lower Extremity Rehabilitation Exoskeleton Robot

Yuanjie Fan and Yuehong Yin

The State Key Laboratory of Mechanical System and Vibration, The Robotics
Institute, Shanghai Jiao Tong University, Dongchuan Rd. 800, 200240 Shanghai, China
{fantian,yhyin}@sjtu.edu.cn

Abstract. Decode the human motion intension precisely in real time is the key
problem in coordinated control of the lower extremity exoskeleton. In this
research, the relationship between frequency characteristics of sEMG (surface
electromyographic) and muscle contraction is established in real time according
to the biomechanism of skeletal muscle; DPSE (Differentiated Power Spectrum
Estimation) method is applied to extract frequency characteristics from sEMG
precisely and quickly; offset compensation is added to prevent noise
disturbance during feature extracting of the sEMG with lower SNR (signal-to-
noise ratio). Corresponding experiments on knee joint are conducted by
prototype exoskeleton robot. EMGBFT (EMG Biofeedback therapy) based on
force and haptic is applied as information feedback. Results show the human-
machine interface can decode human motion intension and assist or resist
movement of the wearer in real-time.

Keywords: Differentiated power spectrum estimation, skeletal muscle
contraction, rehabilitation exoskeleton, Human-machine interface.

1 Introduction

The lower extremity exoskeleton robot, a special artificial limb which enwraps the
lower limbs of the human body, is an integrated application of the exoskeleton robots
in lower artificial limbs. Many scholars have conducted research and are still
conducting research in this area since late 1960s, when the first active exoskeleton
was developed. BLEEX of UC Berkeley [1], Lokomat system of Hocoma [2], hybrid
assistive limbs (HAL) of Tsukuba University [3], Orthosis exoskeleton of Technical
University of Berlin [4], ALEX of University of Delaware [5], the LOPES
exoskeleton robot [6], and ORTHOSIS exoskeleton system [7], rehabilitation
prototype of NTU [8], etc., are some of the representative exoskeleton robots. Some
of them have already been successfully applied to clinical gait correction and aid of
walking, thereby it is recognized that robot-assisted rehabilitation is becoming
increasingly common in patients after stroke. However, the requirement of real-time
control for lower extremity exoskeleton is strict, decode the human motion intension

C.-Y. Su, S. Rakheja, H. Liu (Eds.): ICIRA 2012, Part II, LNAI 7507, pp. 31–40, 2012.

precisely in real time becomes the key point in the coordinated control of the human-machine system.

Angle and force information are conventional and precise signals widely used in control systems, while they can only provide information of the quasi-static and hysteresis motion intention of the human body. EMG (Electromyographic) signals are 30~100ms prior to body movements, 0.01–10 mV, 10–500 Hz. Comparing with angle and force information, biological EMG signals are better for the reason that they can reflect human motion intention in advance and indirectly imply muscle activity information including contraction force and speed of the muscle. It has already been used in motion identification and EMGBFT during clinical rehabilitation. We have also conducted a series of research to establish the relationship between frequency characteristics of sEMG and muscle contraction; discover the frequency of AP (action potential) corresponds to the active level of muscle fiber and determine the contraction force [9-11]. Unfortunately, sEMG signals are formed by the potentials generated by electrically activated muscle cells, signal samples overlapped with each other among the many APs, which are non-stationary signals. It makes it difficult to predict and feedback human motion intention precisely in real time by sEMG signals.

Neural network [12-14], fuzzy clustering, wavelet packet, linear discriminant analysis, and ICA (independent component analysis), etc. are some of the representative methods to cluster the sEMG signals of different human motion intention [15-18]. While these methods is complicated and needs a huge amount of signal samples, and cannot meet the strict requirement of real-time process control. Fortunately, the frequency characteristics of APs can be extracted from frequency domain of sEMG signals, which imply the muscle contraction, by effective spectrum analysis. Normal spectrum analysis methods include classic PSE (power spectrum estimation) based on Fourier transform and the model based power spectrum estimation. These methods are asymptotically unbiased estimation to the actual spectrum, and are widely used in spectrum analysis. However, sEMG is 10-400Hz, PSE with signal samples less than 200ms will result in lower frequency resolution and cannot identify the signals with lower frequency. Meanwhile, PSE with longer signal samples will result in average effect, and reduce the characteristic frequency. Gabor transform, Wigner-Ville transform and wavelet transform are time-frequency analysis. These methods can avoid average effect, while they still need a large amount of signal samples and have poor real-time performance. DPSE can help extracting the characteristic frequency accurately in real time, and then realize real-time motion decoding, motion control and information feedback by sEMG signals.

The motivation of this paper is to develop an effective and real-time human-machine interface. The joint torque of human knee is predicted by establishing the relationship between frequency characteristics of sEMG and muscle contraction, which is based on the biomechanism of skeletal muscle. By means of differentiated AR PSE, the time-frequency characteristics of the sEMG can be extracted precisely in real time. It is applied to real time motion control of the exoskeleton robot and information feedback during EMGBFT. Experimental results show the real-time human-machine interface can decode human motion intension and assist or resist movement of the wearer in real-time.

2   Real-Time Relationship between Frequency Characteristics of sEMG and Muscle Contraction

According to our previous research, the active contraction force of the skeletal muscle can be expressed as (1):

$$F_a = \eta \frac{A_z \alpha \beta n_0 c}{s} \int_0^L x\rho(x,t)dx \approx \eta \cdot \beta \cdot F_{max} \quad (1)$$

Where F_{max} is the maximum contraction force; β is the active level of the muscle that shown as (2), which is fitted by sigmoid function to simplified the calculation; η is the active ratio of muscle fiber, calculated by normalized RMS (root mean square) value of sEMG, calculated as (3):

$$\beta = \frac{[Ca^{2+}]_{sp}^2}{[Ca^{2+}]_{sp}^2 + [Ca^{2+}]_{sp} k_{-1}/k_1 + k_{-0}k_{-1}/k_0 k_1} = \frac{a}{1+e^{-b \cdot f}} + c \quad (2)$$

$$RMS = \sqrt{\frac{1}{N}\sum_{i=1}^N v_i^2} \quad (3)$$

in which N is the number of sample points, v_i is the voltage value of the ith sample point. In this paper, N is 400, and sampling interval is 500μsec.

The parameters of the sigmoid function, shown in Fig. 1, can be obtained by least square method: a=2.014, b=0.02107 and c=-1.06. f is the characteristic frequency of sEMG signal.

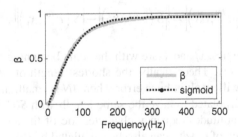

Fig. 1. Frequency of AP versus active level of muscle fiber

3   Differentiated Power Spectrum Estimation (DPSE)

The frequency of APs can be extracted from frequency domain of sEMG signals, which imply the muscle contraction, by effective spectrum analysis. Normal power spectrum estimation methods include: Fourier transform based classic spectrum estimation and mode based spectrum estimation. Autoregressive power spectrum estimation (AR PSE) regards signal samples as an AR process with p order. It is not based on the common assumption of a data window on the signal samples, which makes the estimation has better frequency resolution and variation. AR PSE based on Burg algorithm is used in the paper to estimate the spectrum density of sEMG, as (4):

$$S_{AR}\left(e^{j\omega}\right)=\frac{\sigma^2}{\left|A\left(e^{j\omega}\right)\right|^2}=\frac{\sigma^2}{\left|1+\sum_{k=1}^{p}a_k e^{-j\omega k}\right|^2} \tag{4}$$

in which $\omega=2\pi k/N$, k=0,1,..., N-1. The system input is a white-noise sequence with 0 average and σ^2 variance. According to the power spectrum derive from AR PSE, the characteristic frequency can be expressed as (5):

$$f = \sum_{i=0}^{N-1}\left(\left|S\left(x_k\right)\right|\cdot\omega_i\right)\Big/\sum_{i=0}^{N-1}\left|S\left(x_k\right)\right| \tag{5}$$

in which $S(x)$ is the PSE of signal samples x, ω_i is frequency, and N is the length of PSE. It can calculate the characteristic frequency of t_0+dt, t_0 is the start point of x and dt is the length of x.

However, sEMG is 10-400Hz, PSE with signal samples less than 200ms will result in lower frequency resolution and cannot estimate the signals with lower frequency. Meanwhile, PSE with longer signal samples will result in average effect, and reduce the characteristic frequency. Differentiated method is applied to solve the problem. It can be proved that the increment of the PSE is asymptotically unbiased to the PSE of additional signal samples. The PSE of additional signal samples dx can be obtained by calculating the difference of PSEs of signal sequences with different length, x_1 and x_2, as (6). The method can reduce the amount of signal samples considerably and improve the real-time performance.

$$\left|S\left(e^{j\omega},dx\right)\right|=\left\|S\left(e^{j\omega},x_2\right)\right|-\left|S\left(e^{j\omega},x_1\right)\right\| \tag{6}$$

Where x_k is signal samples, x_1 and x_2 are with the same beginning, and the length are N and $(N+\Delta N)$ respectively. Theoretically, the shortest length of ΔN can be 1. But the variation of AR PSE will result in huge error when ΔN is small. ΔN is 20 in this paper. $S(e^{j\omega}, x_1)$ is linear interpolated to have the same length with $S(e^{j\omega}, x_2)$. The amplitude of $S(e^{j\omega}, dx)$ is the amplitude-frequency characteristic of the signal samples dx. The characteristic frequency of $t_{dx}+dt_{dx}$ can also be calculated by (6).

4   Motion Decoding in Real Time

4.1   Signal Acquisition and Preprocess

The sEMG signals of the muscles are acquired in real time by self-made sEMG signal acquisition processor with 10 times pre-amplification,10~500Hz band pass filter, 50Hz notch filter , 500 times main gain and A/D conversion.

4.2   Power Spectrum Estimation

Differentiated AR PSE based on Burg algorithm is applied in this paper to analyze spectrum of sEMG signals, as described in section 3. SNR is low when the contraction force is small, so offset compensation is added to prevent noise disturbance during feature extracting of the sEMG with lower SNR, as (7). Since the offset is much smaller than the true signal, the extracted features can show the real characteristic frequency with small disturbance when the contraction force is high.

$$x = x_{EMG} + x_{offset} \tag{7}$$

In which x is the signal samples; x_{EMG} is sEMG signals; x_{offset} is the added offset.

4.3   Motion Decoding

The muscle contraction force can be calculated by (1), and the joint torque is the resultant force of corresponding muscles, as (8):

$$\tau = \sum_i F_i \cdot l_i (\theta) \tag{8}$$

In which F_i is the muscle contraction force, is the moment arm of corresponding muscle, which is related with joint angle θ.

However the moment arm is changeable with different people. It is difficult to measure the exact value by normal ways. Fuzzy neural networks (FNN) based on Takagi-Sugeno-Kang model [19] are established to determine the moment arm. The topological structure is shown in Fig. 2(a). The output of the network is the the predicted moment arm, computed as (9):

$$O_l^5 = y_l = \frac{\sum_{i=1}^r \mu_{A^i}(\xi) \cdot g_i}{\sum_{i=1}^r \mu_{A^i}(\xi)} \tag{9}$$

In which r is the number of rules, $\mu_A(\xi)$ denotes the membership degree of the ith rule when the input is ξ, g_i is the output membership functions.

Hybrid learning algorithm [20] is the combination of back propagation algorithm and least square method and it is used to learn and obtain the parameters of the membership function and consequent parameters.

5   Experimental Results and Discussion

5.1   Experiment Setup

The experimental setup, as shown in Fig. 2(b), consists of the exoskeleton robot, a PC, a self-made DAQ card, a self-made motion control card, and a self-made EMG signal processor. Fig. 2 (c) is the mechanics diagram of one leg of the lower extremity exoskeleton. Considering the statistical data of the human body, the key parameters of the exoskeleton are as follows: l_1= 0.422m, d_1= 0.26687m, d_2= 0.055785m, m_1= 4.3kg, m_2= 0.51kg, α= 8.403°, β=14.534°.

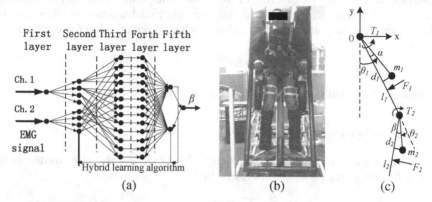

Fig. 2. (a) Fuzzy-neural network, (b) Experiment setup, (c) mechanics diagram

5.2   Experiment Process

The experiment has been carried out with a healthy male subject of age 29 and a healthy male subject of age 26. One leg of them was bound with a leg of the exoskeleton. Biceps muscle and quadriceps muscle of thigh are two main muscles that related to knee joint movements. Considering the measurability and intensity of the sEMG signals, and in order to trace the knee muscle locations that determine the kinetic characteristics of the human knee, two channels of EMG signals are applied to control the knee flexion and extension: ch1, biceps muscle of thigh; ch2, quadriceps muscle of thigh.

The experiment was divided into two stages: the offline test stage and online movement-assist control stage. In the first stage, sEMG signals and interaction force were sampled under different joint angle. Recorded data were used as the training sample to modify the parameters in the neuro-fuzzy network to predict the moment arms of the subject's knee joint muscles. Then the muscle force and joint torque can be calculated by sEMG signal samples as (1) and (9), and were compared with the recorded force data. Meanwhile, human active joint torque was feed back by pressure of the gasbag that mounted at the arm. Each experiment included 30 tests and lasted about 5 minutes. In the second stage, the exoskeleton was controlled to assist the movement of the wearer. DPSE was used to evaluate the joint torque of human knee. The desired torque is twice of the human active joint torque. The control torque was the difference between the desired torque and active human joint torque. The exoskeleton is blocked and the output joint torque is measured by force sensor. The experiment included 10 tests and lasted about 2 minutes.

5.3   Experimental Results

The experimental results of offline testing are shown in Fig. 3. PSEs with and without offset compensation were compared. Normal and differentiated AR PSE are also compared and used to predict joint torque. Methods with STFT and Welch modified periodogram are also compared. The RMS values of the errors are shown in Table 1. DPSE is 6.4% smaller than normal PSE and AR model based PSE has the best performance. Pressure feedback corresponds to human active joint torque applied as information feedback during EMGBFT, and the result is shown in Fig 3(f). The raw sEMG signals, output torque and assist torque of the exoskeleton during coordinated control are shown in Fig 4.

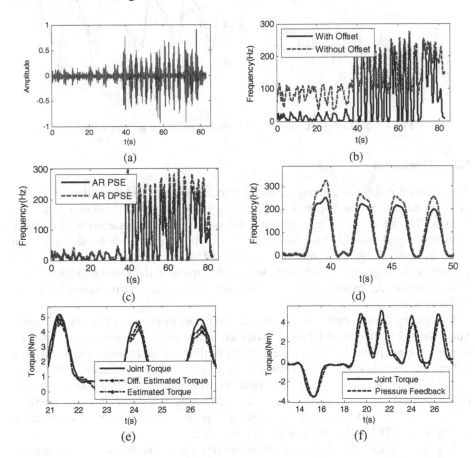

(a)

(b)

(c)

(d)

(e)

(f)

Fig. 3. (a) is the original sEMG signal; (b) is the characteristic frequency curves that with and without offset compensation; (c) is the characteristic frequency curves that with normal and differentiated AR PSE; (d) is the part view of Fig. (c); (e) is the real joint torque and estimated joint toque with different methods; (f) is the human active joint torque and pressure feedback.

Table 1. RMS values of the eatimated torque errors with different methods

	Differentiated PSE	Normal PSE
AR Model	0.4780	0.5257
Welch	0.5039	0.5894
STFT	0.7623	0.7502

Unit: N

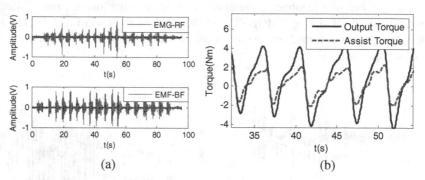

(a)   (b)

Fig. 4. (a) is raw sEMG signals, (b) is the output torque and assist torque

5.4 Discussion

The contraction force is determined by the frequency of AP and the collected amount of motor neuron. So the amplitude and frequency is higher when the contraction force is high. The added offset compensation did not affect the characteristic frequency when the signal samples have higher SNR. On the contrary, when the contraction force is low, SNR is lower. The added offset compensation will lower the characteristic frequency significantly, which correspond to the actual condition of the human muscle. As shown in Fig. 3(b), the curve with offset compensation has better performance.

Comparing the two curves in Fig. 3(c) and (d), both of them have the similar trend. Since the AR model based DPSE take full advantage of the previous signal samples, less new signal is needed. It can improve the real-time performance, and meanwhile reduce the average effect. As shown in Fig. 3(c) and (d), differentiated AR PSE is about 50ms in advance and its peak value is 10% bigger. Table 1 also shows the DPSE method has better performance. But RMS values with STFT based DPSE is bigger, which is different from the other two. It may caused by the poor variance properties of STFT and result in worse performance.

Fig. 3(e) shows both of the controllers can decode the human motion intention in real time. While the DPSE based estimated joint torque is 50ms prior to that obtained by normal estimation method, and its peak value is 10% bigger. It corresponds to the estimation of characteristic frequency, which further proves the estimation by DPSE has better performance. The peak value is slightly smaller than the actual torque, which may caused by the added offset compensation.

Fig. 4 shows the output torque is about twice of the assist torque and equal to the desired torque, which means the controller can decode human motion intension and assist movement of the wearer in real time. However, there still exist some errors. DPSE may inadequate to extract all the information of muscle activity precisely in real time. The information transmitted by sEMG signal concern the quantum effect of Na+ and K+. Ambiguous understanding of the mechanism of EMG generation may lead to inaccurate information extraction during the exoskeleton control.

6   Conclusion

An effective and real-time human-machine interface is built in this paper. The joint torque of human knee is predicted by the established relationship between frequency characteristics of sEMG and muscle contraction. By means of differentiated AR PSE, the time-frequency characteristics of the sEMG can be extracted precisely in real time. EMGBFT (EMG Biofeedback therapy) based on force and haptic is applied as information feedback. Experimental results show the human-machine interface can decode human motion intension and assist movement of the wearer in real-time.

In order to make feature extraction more precise and the controller more stable, the time-frequency domain characteristics of sEMG signals and new methods including wavelet, fractal, etc. need to be introduced. Besides, the closed-loop control system with multi-sensor integration and information fusion will be applied to the control of multi-joint exoskeletons in future work, e.g., two legs of human body. Last but not the least, the performance of the system in clinical treatments will also be evaluated in the next stage.

Acknowledgment. This work was supported by the National Natural Science Foundation of China (61075101,60643002), the National Basic Research Program of China (2011CB013203),the Science and Technology Intercrossing and the Medical and Technology Intercrossing Research Foundation of Shanghai Jiao Tong University (LG2011ZD106,YG2010ZD101).

References

1. Adam, B.Z., Kazerooni, H., Chu, A.: Biomechanical design of the Berkeley Lower Extremity Exoskeleton (BLEEX). IEEE/ASME Trans. Mechatron. 11(2), 128–138 (2006)
2. Riener, R., Lunenburger, L., Jezernik, S., Anderschitz, M., Colombo, G., Dietz, V.: Patient-Cooperative Strategies for Robot-Aided Treadmill Training: First Experimental Results. IEEE Trans. Neural Syst. Rehabil. Eng. 13(3), 380–394 (2005)
3. Lee, S., Sankai, Y.: Power assist control for leg with HAL-3 based on virtual torque and impedance adjustment. In: IEEE Int. Conf. Systems, Man and Cybernetics, pp. 256–267 (2002)
4. Singla, E., Dasgupta, B., Kondak, K., Hommel, G.: Optimal design of an exoskeleton hip using three-degrees-of-freedom spherical mechanism. In: ISR/Robotik 2006-Joint Conference on Robotics, Munich, pp. 10–19 (2006)

5. Banala, S., Kim, S., Agrawal, S., Scholz, J.: Robot assisted gait training with active leg exoskeleton (ALEX). IEEE Trans. Neural Syst. Rehabil. Eng. 17(1), 2–8 (2009)
6. Veneman, J., Kruidhof, R., Hekman, E., Ekkelenkamp, R., van Asseldonk, E., van der Kooij, H.: Design and evaluation of the LOPES exoskeleton robot for interactive gait rehabilitation. IEEE Trans. Neural Syst. Rehabil. Eng. 15(3), 379–386 (2007)
7. Gordon, K., Ferris, D.: Learning to walk with a robotic ankle exoskeleton. J. Biomech. 40, 2636–2644 (2007)
8. Low, K., Yin, Y.H.: An integrated lower exoskeleton system towards design of a portable active orthotic device. Int. J. Robot. Autom. 22(1), 32–42 (2007)
9. Yin, Y.H., Guo, Z., Chen, X., Fan, Y.J.: Study on biomechanics of skeletal muscle based on working mechanism of myosin motors: An overview. Chin. Sci. Bull. (in press, 2012)
10. Yin, Y.H., Guo, Z.: Collective mechanism of molecular motors and a dynamic mechanical model for sarcomere. Sci. China-Technol. Sci. 54(8), 2130–2137 (2011)
11. Yin, Y.H., Chen, X.: Bioelectrochemical control mechanism with variable-frequency regulation for skeletal muscle contraction-Biomechanics of skeletal muscle based on the working mechanism of myosin motors (II). Sci. China -Technol. Sci. 55(8), 2115–2125 (2012)
12. Yin, Y.H., Fan, Y.J., Xu, L.D.: EMG & EPP-Integrated Human-machine Interface between the Paralyzed and Rehabilitation Exoskeleton. IEEE T. Inf. Technol. B. 16(4), 542–549 (2012)
13. Fan, Y.J., Yin, Y.H.: Mechanism Design and Motion Control of a Parallel Ankle Joint for Rehabilitation Robotic Exoskeleton. In: Proceedings of the 2009 IEEE International Conference on Robotics and Biomimetics, Guilin, China, pp. 2527–2532 (2009)
14. Kaveh, M., Sridhar, K., Tom, C.: Real-Time Classification of Forearm Electromyographic Signals Corresponding to User-Selected Intentional Movements for Multifunction Prosthesis Control. IEEE Trans. Neural Syst. Rehabil. Eng. 15(4), 535–542 (2007)
15. Levi, J.H., Erik, J.S., Kevin, B.E., Bernard, S.H.: Multiple Binary Classifications via Linear discriminant Analysis for Improved controllability of a Powered Prosthesis. IEEE Trans. Neural Syst. Rehabil. Eng. 18(1), 49–57 (2010)
16. Bogey, R.A., Perry, J., Gitter, A.J.: An EMG-to-Force Processing Approach for Determining Ankle Muscle Forces During Normal Human Gait. IEEE Trans. Neural Syst. Rehabil. Eng. 13(3), 302–310 (2005)
17. Catherine, R.K., Daniel, P.F.: Medial Gastrocnemius Myoelectric Control of a Robotic Ankle Exoskeleton. IEEE Trans. Neural Syst. Rehabil. Eng. 17(1), 31–37 (2009)
18. Kukolj, D., Levi, E.: Identification of complex systems based on neural and Takagi–Sugeno fuzzy model. IEEE Trans. Syst., Man, Cybern. B 34(1), 272–282 (2003)
19. Lee, W.J., Ouyang, C.S., Lee, S.J.: Constructing neuro-fuzzy systems with TSK fuzzy rules and hybrid SVD-based learning. In: Proc. IEEE Int. Conf. Fuzzy Systems, pp. 1174–1179 (2002)

3D Semantic Map-Based Shared Control
for Smart Wheelchair

Zhixuan Wei[1,2], Weidong Chen[1,2], and Jingchuan Wang[1,2]

[1] Department of Automation, Shanghai Jiao Tong University, and Key Laboratory of System Control and Information Processing, Ministry of Education of China, Shanghai 200240, China
[2] State Key Laboratory of Robotics and System (HIT), Harbin 150001, China
{zhixuan.wei,wdchen,jchwang}@sjtu.edu.cn

Abstract. The previous perception and control system of smart wheelchairs normally doesn't distinguish different objects and treats all objects as obstacles. Consequently it is hard to realize the object related navigation tasks such as furniture docking or door passage with interference from the obstacle avoidance behavior. In this article, a local 3D semantic map is built online using a low-cost RGB-D camera, which provides the semantic and geometrical data of the recognized objects to the shared control modules for user intention estimation, target selection, motion control, as well as parameters adjusting of weight optimization for addressing different target. With the object information provided by 3D semantic map, our control system can choose different behaviors according to user intention to implement object related navigation. A smart wheelchair prototype equipped with a Kinect is developed and tested in real environment. The experiments showed that the 3D semantic map-based shared control can effectively enhance the smart wheelchair's mobility, and improve the collaboration between the user and the smart wheelchair.

Keywords: Smart Wheelchair, 3D Semantic Map, Shared Control.

1   Introduction

To improve the mobility of the smart wheelchair and the collaboration between the user and the smart wheelchair is a currently important research topic worldwide, especially facing unknown indoor environment and accurate tasks. Smart wheelchair is required to cognize the environment, to estimate the intention of user, and to timely adjust the control strategies, so as to achieve accurate and complex operations such as door passage and furniture docking. Previous shared control cannot solve these problems, because it has weak environment perception, which means that it cannot distinguish different objects so that treats all objects as obstacles. Taking door passage as an example, in order to ensure safety, the best method is to pass through it along the perpendicular bisector of the door, but the previous control algorithm does not guarantee this. Another example is the docking into the table, which need to detect the table and determine the docking position and orientation. Previous shared control is almost impossible to solve such problem. In this article, we used shared control and 3D

C.-Y. Su, S. Rakheja, H. Liu (Eds.): ICIRA 2012, Part II, LNAI 7507, pp. 41–51, 2012.

semantic map on smart wheelchair to improve its environment perception and hence mobility and collaboration.

Various shared control has been proposed since 1990s [1]. They can be divided into two categories according to the control level a user takes part in: behavior level sharing and planning level sharing.

Behavior level sharing is a commonly used method in the early stage. There are usually two ways for a wheelchair to cooperate with a human. The first way is that a wheelchair goes towards a direction that a user points out and the assistive system provides some obstacle avoidance algorithm to ensure safety [2]. In the second way, the user's commands are treated as a behavior which is executed with other autonomous behaviors (e.g. obstacle avoidance behavior, wall follow behavior).

Planning level sharing takes the user's intention into account while doing planning. The wheelchair follows orders coming from a planner, and user expresses his or her intention by moving the joystick. When the user's intention conflicts with the planner's order, the control system will modify the user's command [3] or re-plan the task [4], [5]. The user's intention of doing a certain task (e.g. door passage) is measured by defining intention prediction functions [4].

A new kind of shared control method was recently proposed in [6] and [7]. They defined an efficiency function to evaluate the user's control ability and adjusted the user's control weight according to the function value. Inspired by above works, in our previous work [8], we proposed a minimax algorithm for optimizing the weights of both commands of user and machine. All methods mentioned above, however, don't distinguish objects in environment but consider them all as obstacles.

Many 3D technologies have been applied to smart wheelchair since 2005. Stereo vision-based SLAM is used for the smart wheelchair navigation in [9]. But the maps only contained geometry information without object information. The 3D model is segmented into distinct potentially traversable ground regions and fitted planes to the regions in [10]. The planes and segments were analyzed to identify safe and unsafe regions and the information was captured in an annotated 2D grid map called a local safety map. But they still cannot distinguish different objects either.

Rusu et al. [11] proposed a novel framework for semantic 3D object model acquired from point cloud data. The functionality of this framework included robust alignment and integration mechanisms for partial data views, fast segmentation into regions based on local surface characteristics, and reliable object detection, categorization, and re-construction. The computed models were semantic, i.e. they inferred structures in the data, which are meaningful with respect to the robot task. Such objects include doors, handles, supporting planes, cupboards, walls, and movable smaller objects. The point clouds are resulting from a 3D laser scanner. For smart wheelchair application, the mapping approach is still facing the issues on real-time computation, low-cost sensor and human-wheelchair cooperation.

In this article, system architecture of shared control for smart wheelchair is presented. A local 3D semantic map is online built with use of a low-cost RGB-D camera, which provides the semantic and geometrical data of the recognized objects to the shared control modules for user intention estimation, target selection, motion control, as well as parameters resetting of weight optimization for addressing different target, A smart wheelchair equipped with a Kinect is developed as experimental platform for studying the effectiveness of the proposed method.

2 System Architecture

As shown in Fig. 1, our approach is based on the previous shared control (below the dash). 3D semantic map contain the target information from 3D object detection and object feature extraction. At the same time, user intention is estimated to determine whether the user would like to reach the target. If not, the shared control will work as usual; if yes, the 3D semantic map will plan the motion to drive the wheelchair to the target, and the output of motion control (linear and angular velocity commands) will replace the output of joystick, meanwhile the 3D semantic map will adjust the internal parameters of the shared control to adapt to the different situations.

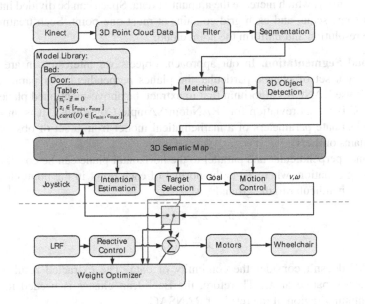

Fig. 1. System architecture

3 3D Semantic Map Building

In this article, we use shape-based method to build 3D semantic map. The point cloud data obtained from the RGB-D camera is firstly filtered and down-sampled to reduce the amount of data. Secondly, RANSAC algorithm is used to segment the data in accordance with the horizontal plane and vertical plane, then European clustering is used to make segmentation region finer. Finally, each region is matched using a priori model library in order to identify object, and to extract object feature for navigation.

Pass Through Filter. Pass through filter is used to reduce the amount of date by removing the useless points, such as the points which are too far or the points higher than the wheelchair and the user. O_i is the point cloud and p (x, y, z) is a point:

$$O_i = \{p(x, y, z) | x \in (x_1, x_2), y \in (y_1, y_2), z \in (z_1, z_2)\} . \tag{1}$$

Sparse Outlier Removal. Using RGB-D camera, measurement errors lead to sparse outliers which corrupt the results even more. They complicate the estimation of local point cloud characteristics such as surface normals or curvature changes, leading to erroneous values. The sparse outlier removal module corrects these irregularities by computing the mean μ and standard deviation σ of the nearest neighbor distances, and trimming the points which fall outside the $\mu \pm \alpha \cdot \sigma$ [11]. The value of α depends on the size of the analyzed neighborhood.

Down Sample. The point cloud data obtained from RGB-D camera has high resolution and uneven density, which increase the amount of data. Space can be divided into voxel grids with some scale, and each grid contains at most one point. Such treatment can reduce the resolution and uniform the point cloud.

Point Cloud Segmentation. In our approach, objects we interested in are usually structured by a set of planes, particular the planes perpendicular or parallel to the ground. We use RANCAS algorithm first to extract the above-mentioned planes [12].

RANSAC is an abbreviation for "RANdom SAmple Consensus". It is an iterative method to estimate parameters of a mathematical model from a set of observed data which contains outliers.

The planes perpendicular and parallel to the horizontal plane can be constrained by the following equation, where $\vec{n_i}$ is the normal of each point in the point cloud data, and z-axis perpendicular to the ground:

$$\vec{n_i} \times \vec{z} = 0 . \tag{2}$$

$$\vec{n_i} \cdot \vec{z} = 0 . \tag{3}$$

RANSAC doesn't consider the continuity of data. The extracted results usually contain many separate areas. Therefore, the Euclidean cluster is needed to get the biggest continuity region of the result of RANSAC.

Model Matching. Common objects of the indoor environment can usually be described with some common-sense constraints, which include the plane normal, the range of area and height, etc. For example, a table can be described as follow:

$$\begin{cases} \vec{n_i} \cdot \vec{z} = 0 \\ z_i \in [z_{min}, z_{max}] \\ card(O) \in [c_{min}, c_{max}] \end{cases} . \tag{4}$$

where $card(O)$ is the number of points in the plane. Because each voxel grid contains at most one point after down sample, the number of points can be estimated to a plane area. So $card(O) \in [c_{min}, c_{max}]$ is the constraint of the desktop area.

In last step, RANSAC extracts the plane $ax + by + cz = d$. Hence $x = 0$ and $y = 0$ will get $z_i = d/c$. And $\overrightarrow{n_i} \cdot \vec{z} = 0$ is the constraint using RANSAC to extract planes parallel to the horizontal plane.

As result the algorithm have detected the object and marked the points in the point cloud which belong to the object to build 3D semantic map. These objects are candidates for the target selection module.

Object Feature Extraction for Navigation. Since our aim is to improve the wheelchair mobility, the details should be extracted according to different objects. One of the important details is to obtain the current goal for motion control in navigation, such as the orientation and the midpoint of the door, the position and orientation for docking, and the size of free space of the table.

4   Shared Control

The share control has two key parts: the reactive control and the weight optimization. The reactive control provides basic obstacle avoidance using MVFH&VFF methods [3], [4]. The weight optimal algorithm optimizes three indicators which will be discussed in the following section to obtain weight of reactive control and user.

Weight Optimization. In our previous work [8], indicators of wheelchair's performance were proposed: *safety, comfort* and *obedience*. *safety* measures the probability of collision. *comfort* measures the variation of angular velocity. *obedience* measures the degree of obedience to the user's control intention. These indicators are defined as:

$$safety = 1 - \exp(-\alpha \cdot dis) . \tag{5}$$

$$comfort = \exp(-\beta|\omega - \omega_0|) . \tag{6}$$

$$obedience = \exp(-\gamma|\xi - \xi^*|) . \tag{7}$$

where, dis measured the distance between the wheelchair and the nearest obstacle in its path; ω and ω_0 are the desired and current angular velocity; ξ^* is the orientation of user command calculated from the user's input v_{mach} and ω_{mach}; ξ is the orientation of final command determined by v and ω; α, β and γ are constants.

The aim of weight optimization is to maximize all three indicators. However, these indicators are usually contradictory to each other. Therefore, there is no absolute optimum solution for maximize the three indicators at the same time. So we proposed of solving this problem is: always improve the smallest indicator among the three. In accordance with this principle we choose the minimax method to simplify this multi-objective optimization problem to a single objective one (Eq. 8).

$$\begin{cases} \max_\kappa(\min(safety, comfort, obedience)) \\ s.t. \\ v(t) = v_{user}(t) \\ \omega(t) = \kappa\omega_{user}(t) + (1 - \kappa)\omega_{mach}(t) \\ 1 \geq \kappa \geq 0 \end{cases} \tag{8}$$

where, κ and $(1 - \kappa)$ is the user weight and the reactive control weight; $v(t)$ and $\omega(t)$ is the linear and angular velocity to be sent to the wheelchair. This equation means that finding the user weight is equivalent to finding the proper κ to maximize the objective function $\min(safety, comfort, obedience)$ under the restrictions stated after s.t.. As the linear velocity in MVFH is equal to $v_{user}(t)$ as long as there is no possible collision, we restrict $v(t)$ to be equal to $v_{user}(t)$.

Eq. 8 as a linearly constrained nonlinear programming problem, there is generally no analytical solution, since we use one-dimensional search algorithm to solve the optimization: First, use rough search algorithm to determine the interval that contain the maximum of the objective function $\min(safety, comfort, obedience)$; Second, implement Golden section search algorithm in the interval mentioned above to find the κ at maximum of the objective function.

Intention Estimation and Target Selection. Human should always be dominant in shared control. The command of machine plays a role of optimizing or revising user's order, which is why it is necessary to estimate user's intention.

Our proposal uses interactive method for user intention estimation. A local map is shown in system interface. A red arrow in the interface represents the orientation of the joystick on wheelchair. Once an object is detected as the destination, the object will be marked by green frame. At this moment, if the user holds the joystick pointing toward the object, the system will understand that the user intends to approach and the green frame will turn red to feedback to the user. This process is called target selection. Otherwise, pointing away from the object or releasing the joystick mean rejecting target and treating the object as obstacle, just as the previous shared control.

Motion Control. Target selection results in two effects. One is replacing the user commands by motion control commands to control the wheelchair automatically. The user's order through joystick is considered as user's intention on destination rather than direct control for velocity of the wheelchair. The velocity is calculated by motion control according to the position and orientation of the wheelchair and the goal. The other is the modification on parameters of shared control. For example, the threshold of obstacle avoidance is decreased to succeed passing through the narrow door or to perform fine manipulation; increase the obedience indicator to improve the accuracy of the tracking trajectory of the wheelchair.

We use a real-state feedback controller [13] to calculates the linear and angular velocity according to the relative position of the wheelchair and the target (Eq. 9).

$$\begin{cases} v = k_r r \\ \omega = k_a a + k_b b \\ r = \sqrt{\Delta x^2 + \Delta y^2} \\ a = -\theta + \mathrm{atan2}(\Delta x, \Delta y) \\ b = -\theta - a \end{cases} \quad (9)$$

where Δx and Δy are position difference between the wheelchair and the target, θ is the orientation of wheelchair. The three variables above are with reference to the world coordinate system. k_r, k_a and k_b are constants.

5   Experiment and Results

Wheelchair Prototype. The wheelchair prototype [8] as shown in Fig. 2, is based on an ordinary electric wheelchair. The wheelchair is equipped with mobile robot sensors including LMS200 laser range finder (LRF), Kinect, odometry etc. A computer running Linux is used to implement the proposed shared control and 3D semantic mapping algorithm. A Smart Motion Controller (SMC) based on a DSP processor is adopted to execute motion control commands for wheelchair. Kinect is connected to the computer for obtaining 3D point cloud. The system software is developed based on ROS [14] and PCL [15].

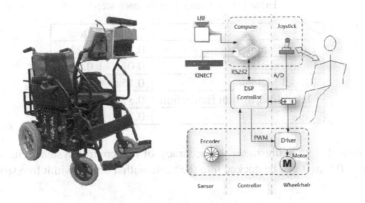

Fig. 2. Wheelchair prototype

Experimental Environment and Task. The experiment is implemented in the laboratory environment as shown in Fig. 5(a). The tasks of the experiments are driving the wheelchair starting from the passageway, then passing through a doorway to get into the laboratory, and finally docking into the table.

The blue line in Fig. 5(a) is the trajectory recorded by the odometry of wheelchair. Dashed part means that the wheelchair was controlled by motion control when the 3D semantic map detected the target and user intention selected the target. And the solid part means that the wheelchair is in the manual mode.

3D Semantic Map Building. Fig. 3 illustrates how 3D semantic map work with a table as example. The first column is the raw data obtain by Kinect. The next column is the 3D semantic map with parts of intermediate results, such as marking the surface of table and the wall, projecting the obstacle on the ground. The third column is the user interface shown on the PC which marks the target with green frame before select it. The last column shows the user interface after user select the target.

Table 1 shows the processing time for each step of map building in Fig. 3. It can satisfy the requirement of real-time of navigation system basically.

Fig. 3. D semantic map building and target selection

Table 1. Processing time for each step

	Table	Door
Down Sample	0.23s	0.23s
Segmentation	0.01s	0.05s
Model Matching	0.15s	0.96s
Detail Information Extraction	0.39s	0.02s
Total	0.78s	1.26s

Shared Control. Fig. 4 illustrates the accuracy of our control system. The width of wheelchair is 0.5m. It can be docked into the table with a 0.67m width free space.

Fig. 4. Docking into the table

Fig. 5(b) shows the comparison of trajectories with and without the 3D semantic map. As shown, when passing through the doorway, the wheelchair controlled with 3D semantic map took an arc to align the center of the door and passed through the doorway vertically. The wheelchair controlled without 3D semantic map, however, passed very close to one side, which is very dangerous. When docking into the table, the wheelchair controlled with 3D semantic map docked autonomously and precisely. On the opposite, the wheelchair couldn't approach to the table and failed to dock.

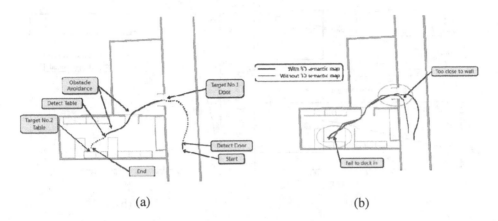

(a)   (b)

Fig. 5. (a) Experimental environment and task; (b) Comparative experiment

Fig. 6 illustrates the three indicators and user weight for every moment in the trajectory with and without 3D semantic map. In order to show more clearly, the data in the figure is $(1 - value)$. The comparison declares that all indicators have been improved. The wheelchair will switch to automatic mode after target selection. The parameter of *safety* is reduced and the linear and angular velocity is calculated by machine, so the *safety* and *smooth* indicators are improved. Therefore, the *obedience* indicator also has been improve.

Fig. 7(a) shows the relationship between the user weight and three indicators and the objective function $min(safety, comfort, obedience)$ when the wheelchair was in the location of the first point marked as "obstacle avoidance" in Fig. 5(a). Fig. 7(b) shows the Golden section search algorithm search process. Algorithm was converged after 18 steps, and error was less than 0.0001. It illustrates that the search interval gradually converge to the maximum value of the objective function fast and precisely.

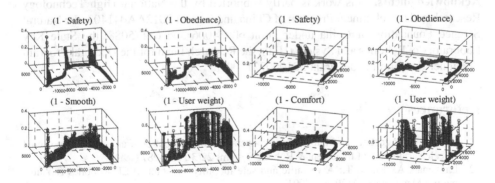

Fig. 6. Comparison of indicators of shared control with (right) and without (left) 3D semantic map

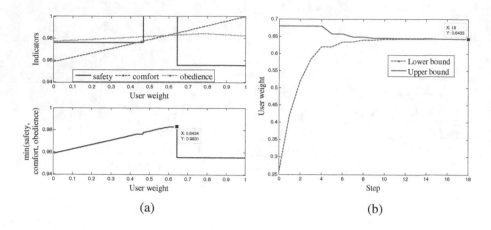

(a)   (b)

Fig. 7. (a) Diagram of the indicators changes with user weight; (b) Convergence process of search algorithm

6   Conclusion and Future Works

This paper presents a 3D semantic map based-shared control for smart wheelchair. 3D semantic map is used to enhance the environment perception of wheelchair. The wheelchair is able to recognize different objects in unknown indoor environments, and with this information the wheelchair can assist the use to implement object related navigation tasks such as door passage or furniture docking. Further, the cooperation between human and wheelchair is improved based on the map. The experiments with real wheelchair and in real world illustrate the validity of the proposed method. In the future, the robustness and stability of the system for more complex environments will be further investigated.

Acknowledgments. This work is partly supported by the National High Technology Research and Development Program of China under grant 2012AA041403, the Natural Science Foundation of China under grant 60934006 and 61175088, the State Key Laboratory of Robotics and System (HIT), the Research Fund for the Doctoral Program of Higher Education under grant 20100073110018.

References

1. Bourhis, G., Agostini, Y.: Man-machine cooperation for the control of an intelligent powered wheelchair. Journal of Intelligent & Robotic Systems 22(3), 269–287 (1998)
2. Lankenau, A., Rofer, T.: A versatile and safe mobility assistant. IEEE Robotics & Automation Magazine 8(1), 29–37 (2001)
3. Parikh, S.P., Grassi Jr., V., Kumar, V., et al.: Integrating human inputs with autonomous behaviors on an intelligent wheelchair platform. IEEE Intelligent Systems 22(2), 33–41 (2007)

4. Carlson, T., Demiris, Y.: Human-wheelchair collaboration through prediction of intention and adaptive assistance. In: IEEE International Conference on Robotics and Automation, Pasadena, CA (2008)
5. Demeester, E., Hüntemann, A., Vanhooydonck, D., et al.: User-adapted plan recognition and user-adapted shared control: A Bayesian approach to semi-autonomous wheelchair driving. Autonomous Robots 24(2), 193–211 (2008)
6. Poncela, A., Urdiales, C., Pérez, E.J., et al.: A new efficiency-weighted strategy for continuous human/robot cooperation in navigation. IEEE Transactions on Systems, Man and Cybernetics, Part A: Systems and Humans 39(3), 486–500 (2009)
7. Urdiales, C., Peula, J., Barrue, C., et al.: An adaptive scheme for wheelchair navigation collaborative control. In: Association for the Advancement of Artificial Intelligence. Fall Symposium, Washington (2008)
8. Li, Q., Chen, W., Wang, J.: Dynamic shared control for human-wheelchair cooperation. In: IEEE International Conference on Robotics and Automation, Shanghai, China (2011)
9. Bailey, M., Chanler, A., Maxwell, B., et al.: Development of Vision-Based Navigation for a Robotic Wheelchair. In: IEEE 10th International Conference on Rehabilitation Robotics, Noordwijk, Netherlands (2007)
10. Murarka, A., Kuipers, B.: A stereo vision based mapping algorithm for detecting inclines, drop-offs, and obstacles for safe local navigation. In: IEEE/RSJ International Conference on Intelligent Robots and Systems, St. Louis, MO (2009)
11. Rusu, R.B., Marton, Z.C., Blodow, N., et al.: Towards 3D Point cloud based object maps for household environments. Robotics and Autonomous Systems 56(11), 927–941 (2008)
12. Schnabel, R., Wahl, R., Klein, R.: Efficient RANSAC for Point-Cloud Shape Detection. Computer Graphics Forum 26(2), 214–226 (2007)
13. Siegwart, R., Nourbakhsh, I.R.: Introduction to autonomous mobile robots. The MIT Press (2004)
14. Robot Operating System (ROS), http://www.ros.org/
15. Rusu, R.B., Cousins, S.: 3D is here: Point Cloud Library (PCL). In: IEEE International Conference on Robotics and Automation, Shanghai, China (2011)

Nonlinear Sliding Mode Control Implementation of an Upper Limb Exoskeleton Robot to Provide Passive Rehabilitation Therapy

Mohammad Habibur Rahman[1], Maarouf Saad[1],
Jean Pierre Kenné[1], and P.S. Archambault[2]

[1] École de Technologie Superieure, 1100 Notre-dame Ouest, Montreal, Canada
[2] School of Physical & Occupational Therapy, McGill University, Montreal, Canada
mhrahman@ieee.org, {maarouf.saad,jean-pierre.kenne}@etsmtl.ca,
philippe.archambault@mcgill.ca

Abstract. Treatment for upper extremity impairment following a stroke or other conditions relies on rehabilitation programs, especially on passive arm movement therapy at the early stages of impairment. An exoskeleton robot (*ETS-MARSE*) was developed to be worn on the lateral side of upper-limb to rehabilitate and assist daily upper-limb motion. We have implemented a nonlinear sliding mode control technique to maneuver the *ETS-MARSE* in providing different passive rehabilitation exercises that include single and multi joint movement exercises. To evaluate the robustness and tracking performance of the controller, exercise involving healthy human subject were performed, where spasticity (a resistance) on arm movement which often found to subjects following a stroke was added artificially. Experimental results show the efficient performance of the controller to maneuver the exoskeleton to provide passive rehabilitation therapy.

Keywords: ETS-MARSE, Exoskeleton Robot, Passive Rehabilitation Therapy, Arm Spasticity, Sliding Mode Control.

1 Introduction

Full or partial upper extremity impairments are common consequences of conditions such as geriatric disorders and/or following a stroke or other conditions such as sports, falls, and traumatic injuries [1-4]. According to the World Health Organization, stroke affects more than 15 million people worldwide each year [5]. Among these, 85% of stroke survivors will incur acute arm impairment [6]. This results in an increased burden on their families, communities and society as well. Treatment of arm impairments mostly relies on rehabilitation therapy.

Recent studies revealed that patients receiving robot-aided rehabilitation gained significant improvement in their arm mobility [3, 7]. In our previous research, we therefore have developed upper extremity exoskeleton robots [8-10] to rehabilitate individuals with upper limb dysfunction. It has already been shown in several studies that robotic devices are able to provide consistent training [1] with high reliability and

C.-Y. Su, S. Rakheja, H. Liu (Eds.): ICIRA 2012, Part II, LNAI 7507, pp. 52–62, 2012.
© Springer-Verlag Berlin Heidelberg 2012

accuracy [10, 11]. In this paper, we have presented a 7DoFs exoskeleton robot, *ETS-MARSE* which was designed to be worn on the lateral side of the upper limb and is able to provide every variety of movement to the shoulder, elbow, forearm and wrist.

Several hypotheses exist as to how upper extremity rehabilitation may be improved. It was found from several studies that intensive and repetitive therapy significantly improve motor function [2]. Therefore the key factors of the therapy (i.e., the intensive and repetitive movements of the affected extremity) need to be integrated in rehabilitation paradigms and this can be done through rehabilitation robotics.

As a key requirement to provide passive rehabilitation and/or passive arm movement assistance, a consistent high dynamic tracking performance of a controller is required to maneuver the robot in an efficient, smooth and continuous manner. Beside, robustness of the controller is necessary to cope with uncertainties, for instance the mass of the human upper-limb which varies from person to person.

The robustness of the sliding mode control (SMC) can theoretically ensure perfect tracking performance despite parameters or model uncertainties [12]. Moreover, the SMC is simple in structure, has good transient performance and is fast in response. We therefore consider the SMC as a good solution to deliver a consistently high dynamic tracking performance. Note that to eliminate/reduce chattering of the control signal that originates from the discontinuous *sign* function of SMC, in this paper we have replaced the discontinuous term with a *sat* function [12].

In experiments, we have implemented trajectory tracking (both joint space and Cartesian trajectory tracking) that corresponds to the recommended rehabilitation exercises [13] with the *ETS-MARSE*. Experiments involved healthy human subjects. It is expected that the controller (SMC with *sat* function) will be able to maneuver the *ETS-MARSE* effectively to provide passive rehabilitation therapy. In the next section a brief description on passive arm therapy is presented. An overview of the *ETS-MARSE* is presented in section 3. Section 4 describes the control strategy of the *ETS-MARSE*. In section 5, experimental results are presented and finally the paper ends with the conclusion and future works in section 6.

2   Upper Limb Passive Rehabilitation Therapy

Passive arm movement therapy is the very first type of physiotherapy treatment given to patients, mainly to improve their passive range of movement (RoM). In this therapeutic approach, patients remain relaxed (i.e., the therapy does not require subject's participation) while therapy in the form of different joint based movements [13] are employed by physiotherapists, skilled caregivers, and/or trained family members [4, 14]. To be noted, this therapy is the key treatment for the patients who are unable to actively move their arm throughout their complete range of motion following a surgery [13] at the shoulder joint, elbow joint or wrist joint due to the dislocation of the joints; or as the result of a stroke mostly due to spasticity and increased muscle tone [14]. A quantitative measurement of spasticity (in terms of force required in achieving the maximal pain free range of movement and corresponding velocity of movement during elbow joint motion) can be found in [15].

3   Upper Extremity Exoskeleton Robot, *ETS-MARSE*

We have developed a 7DoFs wearable upper-limb exoskeleton robot named *ETS-MARSE* (Fig. 1), which is comprised of a shoulder motion support part, an elbow motion support part, a forearm motion support part and a wrist motion support part. Its shoulder motion support part having 3DoFs is responsible for assisting horizontal flexion/extension (RoM: -50^0 to 90^0) and vertical flexion/extension motion (RoM: 0^0 to 140^0), and internal/external rotation of shoulder joint (RoM: -85^0 to 70^0).

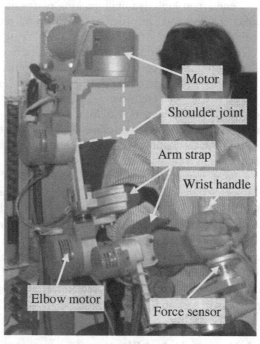

Fig. 1. ETS-MARSE with human subject. A7DoFs exoskeleton robot was designed and developed to rehabilitate and ease daily upper-limb motion.

The elbow motion support (1DoF) is responsible for flexion/extension motion (RoM: 0^0 to 120^0), forearm motion support part (1DoF) is responsible for pronation/supination movement (RoM: -85^0 to 85^0), and wrist motion support part (2DoFs) is responsible for assisting radial/ulnar deviation (RoM: -25^0 to 20^0), and flexion/extension (RoM: -50^0 to 60^0) of wrist joint. As seen in Fig. 1, a six-axis force/torque sensor (Nano-17, ATI) is instrumented underneath the wrist handle to measure instantaneous reaction forces between the subject's wrist and the robot end-effector. For safety reasons, mechanical stoppers were added to limit the joint movements within the anatomical range of upper limb. Detailed of human upper limb range of movement can be found in [8].

4   Sliding Mode Control (SMC)

In this research we have implemented SMC approach in trajectory tracking (both joint space trajectory and Cartesian trajectory) of the *ETS-MARSE*. The dynamic behaviour of the *ETS-MARSE* can be expressed by the rigid body dynamic equation as:

$$M(\theta)\ddot{\theta} + V(\theta,\dot{\theta}) + G(\theta) + F(\theta,\dot{\theta}) = \tau \tag{1}$$

where, $\theta \in \mathbb{R}^7$ is the joint angles vector, τ is the generalized torque vector, $M(\theta) \in \mathbb{R}^{7\times7}$ is the inertia matrix, $V(\theta,\dot{\theta}) \in \mathbb{R}^7$ is the coriolis/centrifugal vector, $G(\theta) \in \mathbb{R}^7$ is the gravity vector, and $F(\theta,\dot{\theta}) \in \mathbb{R}^7$ is the nonlinear coulomb friction vector which can be expressed as:

$$\tau_{friction} = F(\theta,\dot{\theta}) = c.sgn(\dot{\theta}) \tag{2}$$

where, c is the coulomb-friction constant. Equation (1) can be written as:

$$\ddot{\theta} = -M^{-1}(\theta)[V(\theta,\dot{\theta}) + G(\theta) + F(\theta,\dot{\theta})] + M^{-1}(\theta)\tau \tag{3}$$

$M^{-1}(\theta)$ always exists since $M(\theta)$ is symmetrical and positive definite. The general layout of the sliding mode control technique is depicted in Fig. 2.

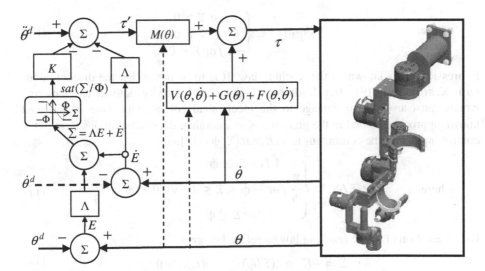

Fig. 2. Schematic diagram of SMC with boundary layer neighboring to the sliding surface

The first step in the sliding mode control is to choose the sliding surface S in terms of the tracking error. Let the tracking error for each joint be defined as:

$$e_i = \theta_i - \theta_i^d \qquad \cdots \qquad (i = 1,\cdots,7) \tag{4}$$

and the sliding surface as:

$$S_i = \lambda_i e_i + \dot{e}_i \qquad \cdots \qquad (i = 1, \cdots, 7) \qquad (5)$$

where, θ_i^d is the desired trajectory for joint i, and S_i is the sliding surface of each DoF. Let, $\Sigma = [S_1 \quad S_2 \quad \cdots \quad S_7]^T$ be the sliding surface for the *ETS-MARSE*. Therefore, we have

$$\Sigma = \begin{bmatrix} \lambda_1 e_1 + \dot{e}_1 \\ \vdots \\ \lambda_7 e_7 + \dot{e}_7 \end{bmatrix} \qquad (6)$$

Equation (5) is a first order differential equation, which implies that if the sliding surface is reached, the tracking error will converge to zero as long as the error vector stays on the surface. Considering the following Lyapunov function candidate:

$$V = \frac{1}{2} \Sigma^T \Sigma \qquad (7)$$

which is continuous and nonnegative. The derivative of V yields:

$$\dot{V} = \Sigma^T \dot{\Sigma} \qquad (8)$$

By choosing $\dot{\Sigma}$ as given in equation (9) relation (8) is ensured to be decreasing.

$$\dot{\Sigma} = -K \, sign(\Sigma), \ \forall t, K > 0 \ \Rightarrow \ \dot{V} < 0 \qquad (9)$$

where, $$sign(\Sigma) = \begin{cases} 1 \ for \ \Sigma > 0 \\ 0 \ for \ \Sigma = 0 \\ -1 \ for \ \Sigma < 0 \end{cases} \qquad (10)$$

Expression (9) is known as the reaching law. It is to be noted that the discontinuous term $K.sign(\Sigma)$ in (9) often leads to a high control activity, known as chattering which can cause severe damage to the mechanical components. One of the well known approaches found in the literature is to smoothen the discontinuous term in the control input with the continuous term $K.sat(\Sigma/\phi)$ [12].

where, $$sat(\Sigma/\phi) = \begin{cases} 1 \ for \ \Sigma \geq \phi \\ \dfrac{\Sigma}{\phi} \ for - \phi \leq \Sigma \leq \phi \quad \forall t, 0 < \phi \ll 1 \\ -1 \ for \ \Sigma \leq \phi \end{cases} \qquad (11)$$

Using equation (11), the reaching law therefore becomes:

$$\dot{\Sigma} = -K . sat(\Sigma/\phi), \qquad \forall t, K > 0 \qquad (12)$$

Therefore and considering:

$$\ddot{\theta}^d = [\ddot{\theta}_1^d \quad \ddot{\theta}_2^d \quad \cdots \quad \ddot{\theta}_7^d]^T, \ \dot{E} = [\dot{e}_1 \quad \dot{e}_2 \quad \cdots \quad \dot{e}_7]^T, \text{ and } \Lambda = \begin{bmatrix} \lambda_1 & 0 & 0 \\ 0 & \ddots & 0 \\ 0 & 0 & \lambda_7 \end{bmatrix}.$$

$$\Sigma = \Lambda E + \dot{E} \quad \Rightarrow \quad \dot{\Sigma} = \Lambda \dot{E} + \ddot{E} \qquad (13)$$

where, $\ddot{E} = \ddot{\theta} - \ddot{\theta}^d$. Thus, equation (13) can be written as:

$$\dot{\Sigma} = \Lambda\dot{E} + \ddot{\theta} - \ddot{\theta}^d \tag{14}$$

Substituting the value of $\ddot{\theta}$ from equation (3) in equation (14) we obtain,

$$\dot{\Sigma} = \Lambda\dot{E} - \ddot{\theta}^d - M^{-1}(\theta)\left[V(\theta,\dot{\theta}) + G(\theta) + F(\theta,\dot{\theta})\right] + M^{-1}(\theta)\tau \tag{15}$$

Replacing $\dot{\Sigma}$ by its value given in equation (12)

$$-K.sat(\Sigma/\phi) = \Lambda\dot{E} - \ddot{\theta}^d - M^{-1}(\theta)\left[V(\theta,\dot{\theta}) + G(\theta) + F(\theta,\dot{\theta}) - \tau\right] \tag{16}$$

The torque τ can be isolated and thus yields:

$$\tau = -M(\theta)\left(\Lambda\dot{E} - \ddot{\theta}^d + K.sat(\Sigma/\phi)\right) + \left[V(\theta,\dot{\theta}) + G(\theta) + F(\theta,\dot{\theta})\right] \tag{17}$$

where, K and Λ are diagonal positive definite matrices. Therefore the control law given in equation (17) ensures that the control system is stable.

Note that the same SMC approach can be used to track both Cartesian and joint space trajectories. It can be seen from the Fig. 2, that the controller inputs are the joint space variables $(\theta^d, \dot{\theta}^d, \ddot{\theta}^d)$, therefore an inverse kinematic solution is required to convert Cartesian variables $(X_d, \dot{X}_d, \ddot{X}_d)$ to joint space variables. The inverse kinematic solution of a redundant manipulator (DoFs >7) can be obtained by using the pseudo inverse of Jacobian matrix $J(\theta)$ [16] as:

$$\dot{\theta} = J^{\dagger}\dot{X} \tag{18}$$

where, $J^{\dagger} = J^T(JJ^T)^{-1}$ is the pseudo inverse generalized.

5   Experiments and Results

Experimental set up of the *ETS-MARSE* system is depicted in Fig. 3. The control algorithm is executed in NI-PXI-8108 [17]. The outputs of the controller are the joints torque commands. However, the torque commands are converted to motor currents, and finally, to reference voltage as the voltage value is the drive command for the motor drivers. The motor driver cards which carry the motor drivers were custom-designed to fit in the slots of the main board.

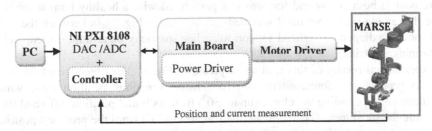

Fig. 3. Experimental setup of *ETS-MARSE* system. It consists of a CPU processor (NI PXI-8108) with a reconfigurable FPGA (field-programmable gate array), a main board, seven motor driver cards, and a PC.

In experiments, the trajectory tracking performance of the *ETS-MARSE* was evaluated with the SMC. Figure 4 shows the experimental results of shoulder joint vertical flexion/extension motion (0^0-90^0). The exercise also known as pointing movement exercise. The topmost plot of Fig. 4 compares the reference trajectories (desired joint angles, dotted line) to measured trajectories (or measured joint angles, solid line). The 2nd row of the plots shows the error as a function of time i.e., deviation between desired and measured trajectories. It is obvious from the figure that the tracking performance of the controller was excellent as it is found that the measured trajectories overlapped with the desired trajectories with tracking error less than 0.7^0. The generated joint torques corresponding to the trajectory is plotted in the bottom row.

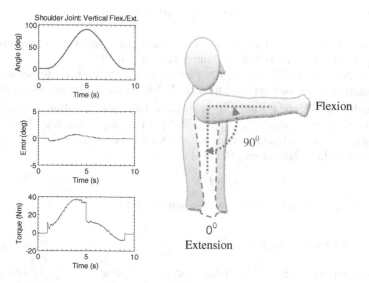

Fig. 4. Pointing movement exercise (performed with healthy human subject having body weight 65kg and height 165 cm)

Further, to evaluate the robustness as well as the tracking performance of the controller, another experiment demonstrating a co-operative and simultaneous movement of both elbow and forearm was performed with a healthy human subject. Note that an elastic rubber band was tied-up (as seen in Fig. 5) in between the end-effector and a diagonal overhead support to realize spasticity on arm movement while performing this trial.

Experimental results of this trial are depicted in Fig. 6. The objective of this task was to pronate the forearm (up to -75^0) from a neutral position (0^0), while simultaneously extending the elbow (up to 30^0) from its initial position (90^0) and then reversing the movement (i.e., supinate the forearm ($+75^0$) from the pronated position while simultaneously flexing the elbow (up to 118^0) from its extension position. It can be seen from the force plots (Fig. 6a) that the maximum resistive forces/perturbations exerted by the elastic rubber band were F_x=5.86N, F_y=11.6N, and F_z=45.2N. As in previous exercises, the tracking error was found to be very small which was below 2^0.

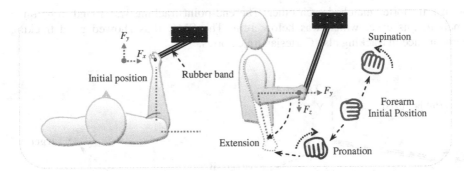

Fig. 5. Schematic diagram of a spastic arm movement exercise that involves simultaneous movement of elbow and forearm

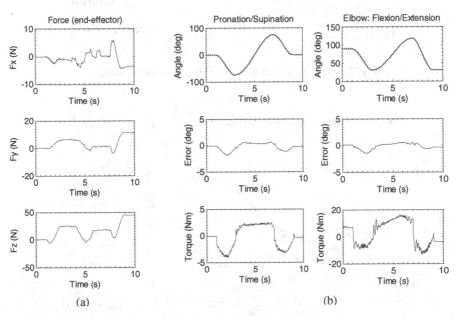

Fig. 6. A co-operative and simultaneous movement of elbow and forearm

The schematic diagram of the Cartesian trajectory tracking (reaching) exercises is shown in Fig. 7. This exercise began at point-X with the elbow joint at 90^0 and then followed path XY to reach Target-A. The objective of this exercise is to reach different targets (in 3D plane) one after another, which involves movement of the entire upper limb's joints. As shown in this figure, to reach two targets in 3D plane, the exercise follows the path XY-YX-XZ-ZX.

Figure 8 shows the experimental results of reaching movement exercises which were performed with a healthy human subject in seated position where initial position of shoulder joint vertical flexion was at 5^0, and that for elbow joint was at 90^0. It can be seen from the plots that the measured (solid line) and desired (dotted line) end point trajectories matched each other. The end-point tracking was found to be quite small in this case, which was below 1cm. The SMC thus showed good tracking performance in tracking also Cartesian trajectories.

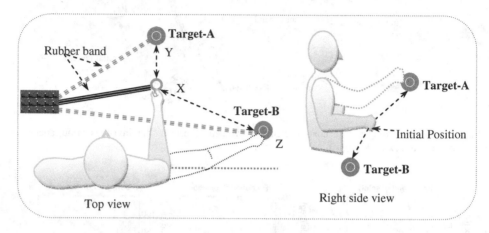

Fig. 7. Schematic diagram of a reaching movement exercise

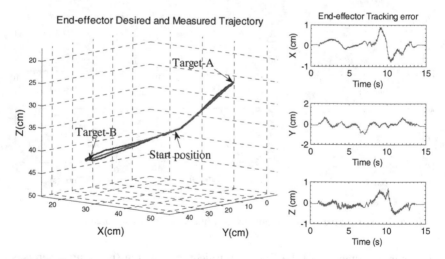

Fig. 8. Cartesian trajectory tracking of *ETS-MARSE* representing reaching movement

Finally, to realize the spasticity on multi-joints arm movements, the same (Cartesian trajectory tracking) reaching exercise was performed again but by adding artificial resistance to arm movements using an elastic rubber band as depicted in Fig. 7. The trial was carried out with the same subject (weight: 65kg, height: 165cm) of previous trial. The maximum resistive forces/perturbations exerted by the elastic rubber band in this case were F_x=22.9N, F_y=9.8N, and F_z=34.67N. Also in this case, the end-point tracking error was found to be small (below 2.5cm).

From these experimental results, it can be concluded that the SMC is quite robust and can effectively maneuver the *ETS-MARSE* to perform passive rehabilitation therapy.

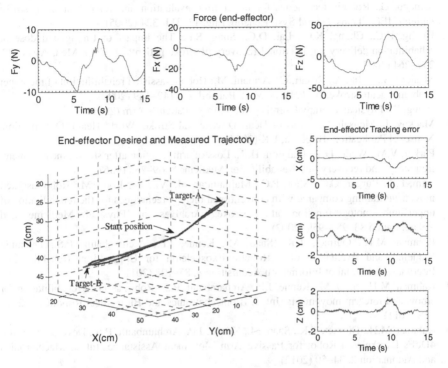

Fig. 5. Reaching movement exercise realizing spasticity on multi-joint arm movements

6   Conclusion

A nonlinear sliding mode control technique was employed in maneuvering the *ETS-MARSE* (a 7doFs exoskeleton robot) in trajectories tracking representing passive rehabilitation exercises. The SMC was found to be quite robust to deal with different types and conditions of exercises; e.g., single and multi-joint movement exercises; joint based and Cartesian based exercises that also include specific case of arm impairment where subjects show spasticity on arm movements. A brief discussion on passive rehabilitation therapy is given. The technical requirements of robot-assisted therapy are presented. A brief description of the *ETS-MARSE* is also presented. Experimental results demonstrate the efficient performance of the SMC in driving the *ETS-MARSE* to provide passive arm movement therapy.

It is to be noted that once resistance to passive arm movements in individuals has diminished it is essential that they practice active movements Future works therefore include in developing a control strategy to provide active arm movement therapy.

References

1. Colombo, R., Pisano, F., Micera, S., Mazzone, A., Delconte, C., Carrozza, M.C., Dario, P., Minuco, G.: Robotic techniques for upper limb evaluation and rehabilitation of stroke patients. IEEE Trans. Neural Syst. Rehabil. Eng. 13, 311–324 (2005)
2. Huang, H.C., Chung, K.C., Lai, D.C., Sung, S.F.: The impact of timing and dose of rehabilitation delivery on functional recovery of stroke patients. J. Chin. Med. Assoc. 72, 257–264 (2009)
3. Masiero, S., Celia, A., Rosati, G., Armani, M.: Robotic-assisted rehabilitation of the upper limb after acute stroke. Arch. Phys. Med. Rehabil. 88, 142–149 (2007)
4. Wang, D.: Physical Therapy Exercises for a Stroke Patient's Arm (2011)
5. Mackay, J., Mensah, G.: Atlas of Heart Disease and Stroke. World Health Organization, Nonserial Publication, Brighton, UK (2004)
6. Parker, V.M., Wade, D.T., Langton, H.R.: Loss of arm function after stroke: measurement, frequency, and recovery. Int. Rehabilitation Medicine 8, 69–73 (1986)
7. Lum, P.S., Burgar, C.G., Shor, P.C., Majmundar, M., Van der Loos, M.: Robot-assisted movement training compared with conventional therapy techniques for the rehabilitation of upper-limb motor function after stroke. Archives of Physical Medicine and Rehabilitation 83, 952–959 (2002)
8. Rahman, M.H., Ouimet, T.K., Saad, M., Kenne, J.P., Archambault, P.S.: Dynamic Modeling and Evaluation of a Robotic Exoskeleton for Upper-Limb Rehabilitation. International Journal of Information Acquisition 8, 83–102 (2011)
9. Rahman, M.H., Saad, M., Kenne, J.P., Archambault, P.S.: Robot assisted rehabilitation for elbow and forearm movements. Int. J. Biomechatronics and Biomedical Robotics 1, 206–218 (2011)
10. Rahman, M.H., Ouimet, T.K., Saad, M., Kenne, J.P., Archambault, P.S.: Development of a 4DoFs Exoskeleton Robot for Passive Arm Movement Assistance. Int. J. Mechatronics and Automation 2, 34–50 (2012)
11. Dobkin, B.H.: Strategies for stroke rehabilitation. Lancet Neurol. 3, 528–536 (2004)
12. Slotine, J.J.E., Li, W.: Applied nonlinear control. Prentice-Hall, Englewood Cliffs (1991)
13. Department of Rehabilitation Services, Brigham and Women's Hospital, http://www.brighamandwomens.org/Patients_Visitors/pcs/rehabilitationservices/StandardsofCare.aspx
14. Post-Stroke Rehabilitation Fact Sheet. In: Health, N.I.o. (ed.) National Institute of Neurological Disorders and Stroke. National Institutes of Health, Bethesda, MD 20892, USA (2011)
15. Kumar, R.T., Pandyan, A.D., Sharma, A.K.: Biomechanical measurement of post-stroke spasticity. Age Ageing 35, 371–375 (2006)
16. Siciliano, B., Sciavicco, L., Villani, L.: Robotics: Modelling, Planning and Control. Springer, London (2009)
17. National Instruments, N.: NI PXI-8108-2.53 GHz Dual-Core PXI Embedded Controller. National Instruments (2012), http://sine.ni.com/nips/cds/view/p/lang/en/nid/206087

sEMG-Based Control
of an Exoskeleton Robot Arm

Baocheng Wang[1], Chenguang Yang[2], Zhijun Li[1,3,*], and Alex Smith[2]

[1] Department of Automation, Shanghai Jiao Tong University, Shanghai, China
[2] School of Computing and Mathematics, Plymouth University, UK
[3] College of Automation Science and Engineering, South China University
of Technology, Guangzhou, China
zjli@ieee.org

Abstract. This paper investigates the processing of surface electromyographic (sEMG) signals collected from the forearm of a human subject and, based on which, a control strategy is developed for an exoskeleton arm. In this study, we map the motion of elbow and wrist to the corresponding joints of an exoskeleton arm. Linear Discriminant Analysis (LDA) based classifiers are introduced as the indicator of the motion type of the joints, and then with the force of corresponding agonist muscles the control signal is produced. In the strategy, which is different from the conventional method, we assign one classifier for each joint, decomposing the motion of the two joints into independent parts, making the recognition of the forearm motion a combination of the results of different joints. In addition, training time is reduced and recognition of motion is simplified.

Keywords: sEMG, LDA, exoskeleton, force estimation.

1 Introduction

Myoelectric signals (MES) can be used to detect a human user's motion intention. The information extracted from MES, recognized as patterns, can be used in a control system, known as a myoelectric control system (MCS), to control rehabilitation devices or assistive robots. The most important advantage of myoelectric control is hands free control compared with other types of control system, such as body-powered mechanical systems (e.g. joysticks and keyboards), which are based on the user's motion.

The research community has focused on the use of some signal-processing techniques to achieve accurate decoding of the MES. Using off-line approaches,

* Corresponding author. This work is supported by the Marie Curie International Incoming Fellowship H2R Project (FP7-PEOPLE-2010-IIF-275078), the Natural Science Foundation of China under Grants (60804003, 61174045, 61111130208), the International Science and Technology Cooperation Program of China (0102011DFA10950), and the Fundamental Research Funds for the Central Universities (2011ZZ0104).

C.-Y. Su, S. Rakheja, H. Liu (Eds.): ICIRA 2012, Part II, LNAI 7507, pp. 63–73, 2012.

the accuracy of MES pattern recognition can be greater than 90%, through the use of various classifiers, such as linear discriminant analysis [1], time-delayed artificial neural networks [2], Gaussian mixture models [3], and Support Vector Machines (SVM) [4]. The above mentioned studies show a promising future in estimating motion intention utilizing complicated but powerful classifiers; however, the ease of use of such strategies have been left open because, in most cases, the output of the classifier is categorical and discrete. For example, in [5], P. Shenoy et al. implemented SVM to recognize eight patterns of human forearm movement for online control of a manipulator, where the only function of MES is to indicate the motion direction of corresponding joints; however, the velocity and torque of the motors are predefined. To overcome the shortcomings mentioned above, more sophisticated approaches have been proposed in the literature. P. K. Artemiadis et al. [6] exploited force and position tracking sensors to establish a state space model to produce a continuous output (including position and force) after training. In [7], J. Kuan et al. employed linear regression to fit EMG signals, with the torque measured by force sensors during the training stage. Many researchers [6][7] utilized force and position tracking sensors to establish the relationship between sEMG and force or position during the training phase, and employ only sEMG in online control. Since the force and position tracking sensors are necessary in these works, control with only sEMG during training and testing phases is not investigated.

Without using expensive force and position tracking sensors, we propose a control strategy based on sEMG and validate it in real-time online control. Two LDA based classifiers are assigned for the two joints and, combined with the estimated force from the EMG signals collected on the dominating muscles of relevant joints, are utilized to produce the control signal. Only sEMG signals are utilized in the whole process. The output of the classifier is the direction of the joint motion, and the estimated force is the force that the robot will exert in that direction. Since the recognition of joint motion is independent, the training can proceed one joint after another instead of the whole forearm and as a result of this the motion of the forearm can be more flexible.

The rest of this paper is organized as follows: in the next section a general view of the structure of the robot arm is presented. In section 3 the strategy mentioned above will be discussed in detail. Section 4 presents methodologies used for data acquisition and the experiments. Section 5 provides the experimental study and analysis of the results. Finally, in section 6 conclusions are presented.

2   Structure of The Robot Arm

The developed upper limb rehabilitation exoskeleton robot is a 5 degree-of-freedom wearable robot with an open-control architecture, developed by our laboratory for human movement and manipulation exercises. The developed robot is shown in Fig. 1(a). The wrist actuator can apply a maximum of $2.4Nm$ and the elbow $3.4Nm$. Every joint is equipped with a Harmonic Drive Transmission (HDT), the inherent zero backlash of which is essential for the exoskeleton.

The robot joints are actuated by Maxon DC brushless servo motors and harmonic gear transmissions. The harmonic drive built into the exoskeleton robot are manufactured by Harmonic Drive Systems Inc. (model SHD-17-100-2SH for joints 1 and 2, model SHD-14-100-2SH for joints 3 and 4, and CSF-32- 50-2A-GR for joints 5). Joint positions are measured through resolvers at the joint output axis, with a resolution of 1000 pulse/cycle output revolutions.

All the motors are controlled in torque mode. The calculated joint torque is directly sent to the servo driver. The calculated torque can be transferred as the current of motors by the servo driver, which can be described by $T_m = K_T \cdot T_c$ where T_m is the motor torque, K_T is the motor torque constant, and T_c is the desired current sent to the servo driver in the form of a two-byte floating-point number.

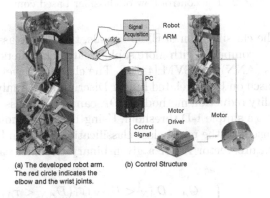

(a) The developed robot arm. The red circle indicates the elbow and the wrist joints.　　(b) Control Structure

Fig. 1. Configuration of the system

3　sEMG-Based Control Method

3.1　Classifier Based Control

Suppose that the relation of motion between the elbow and wrist is small. The potential motion state of each joint is $y_i \in Y^4$ with

$$Y = \{0\ (Rest), 1\ (Flexion), 2\ (Extension), -1\ (Non - Determined)\} \quad (1)$$

If all the kinds of motion (i.e. Rest, Flexion, and Extension) are required to be classified by only one classifier, the total number of classes (9) would be the square of a single joint's motion classes(3), which will increase according to the class numbers of each joint exponentially. It would be time consuming for training so many classes, and the performance of the classifier may be degenerated without enough samples in each class. As a result we can assign each joint with a classifier. For example, the input of the classifier assigned to the elbow is a feature vector x_i extracted only from the sEMG signals controlling the elbow, and the output is y_i. The total number of classes (6) is reduced to the sum of the joints' motion classes (3). The control diagram is shown in Fig. 2. It is well

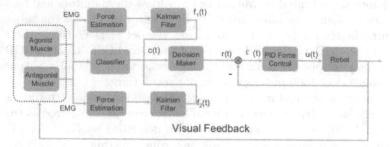

r(t): Reference Force ε (t): Error of Force u(t): Output Force

f$_i$(t): Force of i-th Channel c(t): Class ID t is the time instance

Fig. 2. The control flow of classifier based control

known that in the classification of EMG signals, the LDA classifier has a pretty good performance compared with more sophisticated classifiers such as Artificial Neural Networks (ANN) and SVM [4] [14]. The classifier developed in this work is constructed based on Uncorrelated Linear Discriminant Analysis (ULDA) [13]. As a dimensionality reduction method, ULDA can reduce class-pair specific decision boundaries to a simple 1-D threshold. Using 1-vs-1 technology and majority votes, it can be used for the multi-class classification problem [15]. The class association of a feature vector N for a given binary classifier can be assigned as follows:

$$C_{AB} = \begin{cases} C_A, (D_{AN} < D_{BN}) \cap (D_{AN} < \tau_A) \\ C_B, (D_{BN} < D_{AN}) \cap (D_{BN} < \tau_B) \\ C_{NM}, else \end{cases} \qquad (2)$$

where C_{AB} is the class output for the binary classifier; C_A, C_B,, and C_{NM} denote membership to class A, B, or neither; τ_A and τ_B are adjustable thresholds; and D_{AN} and D_{BN} are the normalized distance between N and class A and B. The decision maker in Fig. 2 is applied to make the decision of the current motion intention estimation more robust. We assume that the user holds his/her motion for a period of time T_M. If the following condition is met, the decision will change. $c(t)$ is the class label at time t (see Fig. 2); $c(t-1)$ is the previous label; T_S is the sampling time.

$$c(t) \neq c(t-1), \quad c(t-1) = \cdots = c(t - T_M/T_S) \qquad (3)$$

The decision maker can select the produced reference force based on the rules illustrated in Table 1. When the output of the decision maker is 0 (relaxed state), the output force of the controller would be a predefined value, which denotes the force that the robot needs to produce when the user is relaxing (to counteract the weight of the exoskeleton). On the other hand, the corresponding surface EMG is inevitably less constrained in online control than in the training phase, and can be representative of contractions that are unknown to the controlling classifier.

In this case there is no unanimous selection among the binary classifiers, and the output is defaulted to the -1 (Non-Determined) class. In order to maintain the continuity of the motion, the control signal does not change.

Table 1. The reference force's source

y_i	Source of Reference Force
1	Agonist Muscle
2	Antagonist Muscle
0	Hold Force
-1	Last Source

3.2 Force Estimation

In general, the approach of estimating force from EMG signals can be sorted into two categories; muscle-model based and model-free. In the former, a Hill-type muscle model with a calibration process can be used to calculate muscle forces using activation and muscle tendon lengths as the input [8] [9]. A model-free approach avoids the modelling process and adopts regression techniques [10] [11]. In order to obtain the accurate torque of relevant muscles, force sensors need to be attached to the human limb.

Since the interaction between human and robot is in real time, a human is involved in the control loop naturally. Since the actuator is subjected to physical constraints we transfer the percentage of maximum torque limit of human joints to the torques of the corresponding robot joints. In order to obtain the true estimation force from the sEMG signals, a high pass filter, the cut-off frequency of which is much larger than conventional 20Hz, is used to remove approximately 99% of the sEMG signal power, which is mainly due to fatigue, tissue filtering properties and the differential amplification process [12]. The non-linearity between the sEMG and force is also considered.

The Kalman filter is utilized as a post-process technique to reduce the estimation noise. Following the approach proposed in [10], we see that:

$$\hat{x}_k^- = \hat{x}_{k-1}, \quad P_k^- = P_{k-1} + Q, \quad K_k = P_k^- (P_k^- + R)^{-1},$$
$$\hat{x}_k = \hat{x}_k^- + K_k(z_k - \hat{x}_k^-), \quad P_k = (1 - K_k)P_k^{-1} \tag{4}$$

where x is the true value of the force; $\hat{x}_k^-$ is estimated prior state; $\hat{x}_k$ the estimated posteriori state; P_k^- the priori estimate error covariance; P_{k-1} the posteriori estimate error covariance; Q the process noise covariance; K_k Kalman filter gain; R the measurement noise covariance; and z_k the calculated force value.

The reference force ($r_i(t)$, see Fig. 2) is produced by the estimation of force as shown in Eq. (5).

$$r_i(t) = m_i + (sgn(F_i) \cdot L_i - m_i) \cdot |F_i|/100 \cdot p$$
$$|r_i(t)| < L_i, \quad i = \{0 \ (elbow), 1 \ (wrist)\} \tag{5}$$

where m_i is the hold force when the input force is zero; F_i the force of agonist or antagonist muscle; p the proportional coefficient; and L_i is the limit of the input force. In the sense of proportional control, the user can obtain a much larger force range compared with his/her own.

4   Process of sEMG Signals

4.1   Data Collection

A four-channel EMG signal was collected from four locations on the upper limb (i.e. biceps-short head, triceps-long head, flexor carpi radialis, extensor carpi radialis), using bipolar electrodes. For the elbow joint, we define the biceps as the agonist muscle, and the triceps as the antagonist muscle. For the wrist, flexor carpi radialis is defined as the agonist muscle, and extensor carpi radialis as the antagonist. The raw signals were digitally sampled at 1024 Hz, band-pass filtered from 10 to 500 Hz using a digital fourth-order Butterworth filter, and a notch filter was used to remove unwanted line-frequency (50 Hz). In the training stage, the user performed six joint motions (i.e. classes). The motions isometric and consist of: elbow rest, elbow flexion, elbow extension, wrist rest, wrist flexion, and wrist extension. Each contraction was held for 8s, with 3-5s rest between adjacent contractions. The suite of six states was repeated 5 times in total. A two-fold cross-validation was employed to evaluate the performance of the classifier. Maximum force information has been included in the data, collected in the above training process.

4.2   Data Analysis

The force signal is estimated from the filtered EMG signals. The whole procedure of estimation is illustrated in Fig. 3. First, the EMG signal is high-pass (cut-off frequency F_{cut}) filtered to remove most of the power energy in the low frequency range. In larger muscles where motor unit recruitment continues into the upper end of the force range and the firing rate has a lower dynamic range, the relationship between force and the amplitude of EMG signal is relatively non-linear. The non-linear relationship is described by Eq. 6 [16].

$$EMG_N = 100 \frac{e^{(-EMG_L \xi)} - 1}{e^{(-100\xi)} - 1} \tag{6}$$

Fig. 3. The flow of force estimation

where $EMG_L = EMG$ linearly normalized to 100% of maximum; $EMG_N = EMG$ non-linearly normalized to 100% of maximum; and $\xi =$ constant to define exponential curvature. In the second strategy, the input of the classifier has to be a feature vector extracted from the raw filtered EMG signals. First, the original data needs to be segmented. A segment is a sequence of data limited in a time slot, which is used to estimate signal features. Real-time constraints enforce a delay time of less than 300 ms between the onset of muscle contraction made by a user, and a corresponding motion in the device [17]. In order to achieve real-time control, the segment we set is 100ms, which produces a 10Hz control command flow. After segmentation the next important step is the feature extraction, which reveals the underlying information between different patterns, having a strong effect on the performance of the classifier. D. Tkach et al. [18] conducted a study of many time-domain features, including the Autoregression Coefficient (AR) feature, although this is generally regarded as frequency feature. They concluded that Mean Absolute Value (MAV), Waveform Length (WL), and AR are the most insensitive features to three disturbances, including EMG electrode location shift, variation in muscle contraction effort, and muscle fatigue. Meanwhile, Farina and Merletti [19] have pointed out that a segment length shorter than 125 ms are to be avoided for the extraction of AR feature, because they lead to high variance and bias. For the above considerations, the features we finally selected were MAV and WL, which produce 4-dimensional feature vectors for the two classifiers respectively. The mathematical definition of these features is described in Table 2.

Table 2. Mathematical Definition of Features, Given s_i as the i-th signal, and N the number of samples in a segment

$MAV = \frac{1}{N} \sum_{i=1}^{N} \lvert s_i \rvert$
$WL = \sum_{i=1}^{N} \lvert \Delta s_i \rvert; \ \Delta s_i = s_i - s_{i-1}$

5 Experiment and Analysis

The chosen values for the parameters mentioned above are: $T_M = 800ms$, $T_{resh} = 1$, $\xi = 0.2$, $F_{cut} = 410Hz$, $Q = 5e - 3$, $R = 1e - 6$. We conducted the force estimation experiment, the result of which is shown in Fig. 4. Because the Root Mean Square (RMS) of the original EMG signals has to be extracted in a sampling time of 100ms both of the original EMG signals and force estimation are down-sampled to show a comparison. The blue curve denotes the original EMG signals, the green one denotes the force estimation, and the red one is the RMS value. In the middle zone between of 10ms and 70ms, the RMS and the estimated force is nearly identical, except that the RMS is a little larger than the force. This is because of the filtered low frequency energy, which is mainly the indicator of the fatigue of the muscle instead of its force. However, in the beginning, because the computation of the RMS has included the subsequent information, it cannot initialize from zero. Similarly, the RMS cannot reflect the change of EMG signals in the last sector.

An experiment using the selected feature set was carried out. The Principal Components Analysis (PCA) technique was applied to reduce the 4-dimensional original feature vector to a 2-dimensional one, which is easy to plot in a plane. The processed feature vectors of EMG signals collected in the elbow and wrist are shown in Fig. 5, which shows the distribution of 50 feature vectors, and the red, green, and blue color denotes that $y_i = 0$, 1, 2 respectively. From the figure, the feature set we selected is suitable for the discrimination between patterns, and in addition, the time-domain has little need for a long data segmentation; it is well suited for the real-time control problem.

The recognition accuracy of the two classifiers was investigated using two-fold cross-validation. The results of this test indicated that the classifiers perform well on the sample data, with 90% for the elbow and 95% accuracy for the wrist. Four kinds of rough trajectory of the elbow and wrist were predefined: flexion and extension of elbow with resting wrist, flexion and extension of wrist with resting elbow, flexion and extension of wrist with flexed elbow and flexion and extension of both of wrist and elbow. The PID force controller must be properly tuned before the online control process can be successfully carried out. In the view of motors, force is realised with current. By using the driver's self-contained software, the motor winding is energized with a high-frequency current in order

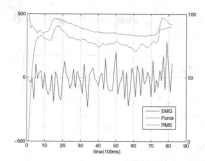

Fig. 4. The estimation of force

(a) Features depicting elbow motion   (b) Features depicting wrist motion

Fig. 5. Feature vectors of reduced dimensions

to identify the dynamic response for resistance and inductance. The result of the test is a set of well-tuned current controller parameters, and the tuning process is automatic without human intervention. This results in a root mean square (RMS) error of 2.8.

The results of the control strategy are shown in Fig. 6. In the figures, the red line denotes the force estimated from the agonist muscle, and the green line denotes the force estimated from the antagonist muscle. From the difference of the two kinds of force, we can distinguish which kind of motion the user is performing. When the force of the agonist muscle is much larger than that from the antagonist muscle, the motion is flexion; otherwise it is extension. If the two kinds of force are almost the same and have small values, the user is resting the relevant joint. The position of the joints is depicted in the blue curve, which is not the aim of our control scheme. In the second strategy, the decision maker outputs the decision as the extension motion, which is illustrated in black circles in Fig. 6. In addition the right axis expresses the position of the relevant joints in degrees.

In Fig. 6, the intention of the first two trajectories is followed closely. However, in Fig. 6(c), almost all of the intention of rest of corresponding joints are recognized as flexion, which indicates that the classifier has a poor online performance. The poor performance of recognition is because of the transient signals of on-line experiments, compared with the isometric contraction signals collected for training. Even in this case the position of relevant joints still follows the user's intention due to the small amplitude of the flexion force, which makes the strategy robust to the error of the recognition when performing online. The results shown in other trajectory imply that the classifier performs especially well in the flexion and extension movement. Fig .6(e) show that although the force is fluctuating, the position of the joint remains stable.

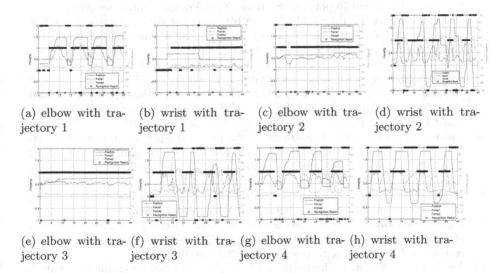

(a) elbow with trajectory 1   (b) wrist with trajectory 1   (c) elbow with trajectory 2   (d) wrist with trajectory 2

(e) elbow with trajectory 3   (f) wrist with trajectory 3   (g) elbow with trajectory 4   (h) wrist with trajectory 4

Fig. 6. Records using the classifier based strategy

6   Conclusion

This paper has presented a control strategy based on upper limb sEMG signals. The strategy is based on the ULDA classifier. Each joint's motion is recognized by one classifier. Using this approach –which may more meaningfully reflect usability– the user can train each classifier by each joint's motion, and in the recognition phase the combined motion of many joints will be natural. In addition to the indicator of the user's motion, the force which the user exerted is also estimated to control the robot, making the motion of the robot an amplifier of the user's force.

References

1. Englehart, K., Hudgins, B.: A robust, real-time control scheme for multifunction myoelectric control. IEEE Trans. Biomed. Eng. 50(7), 848–854 (2003)
2. Au, A.T.C., Kirsch, R.F.: EMG-based prediction of shoulder and elbow kinematics in able-bodied and spinal cord injured individuals. IEEE Trans. Rehabil. Eng. 8(4), 471–480 (2000)
3. Huang, Y., Englehart, K., Hudgins, B., Chan, A.D.C.: A Gaussian mixture model based classification scheme for myoelectric control of powered upper limb prostheses. IEEE Trans. Biomed. Eng. 52(11), 1801–1811 (2005)
4. Oskoei, M.A., Hu, H.: Support Vector Machine-based Classification Scheme for Myoelectric Control Applied to Upper Limb. IEEE Trans. Biomed. Eng. 55(8), 1956–1965 (2008)
5. Shenoy, P., Miller, K.J., Crawford, B., Rao, R.P.N.: Online Electromyographic Control of a Robotic Prosthesis. IEEE Trans. Biomed. Eng. 55(3), 1128–1135 (2008)
6. Artemiadis, P.K., Kyriakopoulos, K.J.: Estimating Arm Motion and Force using EMG signals: On the Control of Exoskeletons. In: IEEE/RSJ International Conference on Intelligent Robots and Systems, Nice, France (September 2008)
7. Kuan, J., Huang, T., Huang, H.: Human Intention Estimation Method for a New Compliant Rehabilitation and Assistive Robot. In: SICE Annual Conference, The Grand Hotel, Taipei, Taiwan, August 18-21 (2010)
8. Lloyd, D.G., Besier, T.F.: An EMG-driven musculoskeletal model to estimate muscle forces and knee joint moments in vivo. J. Biomech., 765–776 (2003)
9. Hayashibe, M., Guiraud, D., Poignet, P.: EMG-to-force estimation with full-scale physiology based muscle model. In: IEEE/RSJ International Conference on Intelligent Robots and Systems, St. Louis, USA, October 11-15 (2009)
10. Nakano, T., Nagata, K., Yamada, M., Magatani, K.: Application of least square method for muscular strength estimation in hand motion recognition using surface EMG. In: International Conference of the IEEE EMBS, Minneapolis, Minnesota, USA, September 2-6 (2009)
11. Hoozemans, M.J.M., van Dieen, J.H.: Prediction of handgrip forces using surface EMG of forearm muscles. J. Electromyogr. Kinesiol., 358–366 (2005)
12. Potvin, J.R., Brown, S.H.M.: Less is more: high pass filtering, to remove up to 99% of the surface EMG signal power, improves EMG-based biceps brachii muscle force estimates. J. Electromyogr. Kinesiol., 389–399 (2004)
13. Ye, J., Li, T., Xiong, T., Janardan, R.: Using Uncorrelated Discriminant Analysis for Tissue Classification with Gene Expression Data. IEEE Trans. Comput. Biol. Bioinf. 1(4) (2004)

14. Lorrain, T., Jiang, N., Farina, D.: Influence of the training set on the accuracy of surface EMG classification in dynamic contractions for the control of multifunction prostheses. Journal of Neuro Engineering and Rehabilitation (2011)
15. Scheme, E.J., Englehart, K.B., Hudgins, B.S.: Selective Classification for Improved Robustness of Myoelectric Control Under Nonideal Conditions. IEEE Trans. Biomed. Eng. 58(6), 1698–1705 (2011)
16. Potvin, J.R., Norman, R.W., McGill, S.M.: Mechanically corrected EMG for the continuous estimation of erector spine muscle loading during repetitive lifting. Eur. J. Appl. Physiol. 74, 119–132 (1996)
17. Hudgins, B., Parker, P., Scott, R.: A new strategy for multifunction myoelectric control. IEEE Trans. Biomed. Eng. 40(1), 82–94 (1993)
18. Tkach, D., Huang, H., Kuiken, T.A.: Study of stability of time-domain features for electromyographic pattern recognition. Journal of NeuroEngineering and Rehabilitation (2010)
19. Farina, D., Merletti, R.: Comparison of algorithms for estimation of EMG variables during voluntary isometric contractions. J. Electromyogr. Kinesiol. 10, 337–349 (2000)

Approaches of Applying Human-Robot-Interaction-Technologies to Assist Workers with Musculoskeletal Disorders in Production

Gunther Reinhart, Ruediger Spillner, and Yi Shen

Institute for Machine Tools and Industrial Management,
Technische Universität München
Boltzmannstraße 15,
85748 Garching/Munich, Germany
{Gunther.Reinhart,Ruediger.Spillner,Yi.Shen}@iwb.tum.de

Abstract. In the course of the demographic change companies will have to tackle the challenges of an ageing workforce. Since older employees, especially blue-collar workers are more likely to show an attrition of their working ability, manufacturers need to take preventive and compensative measures: first to maintain health and well being of their employees, second to integrate those with already reduced working ability and third to further increase productivity. On workplace level the concept of a production assistance robot offers a promising approach, combining support and relief for the worker with the benefits of automation directly in the value added chain. This paper summarizes several approaches, where adding simple low level intelligence to industrial robots results in economically and ergonomically effective assistance functions.

Keywords: assembly, human-robot-interaction system, robot assistance.

1 Introduction

1.1 Demographic Change and Challenge

Europe is undergoing a drastic demographic transformation: Driven by rising life expectancy, low fertility rate and limited immigration its populace is ageing (2004: 39 yrs., 2050: 49 yrs.; median of EU 25). In consequence the workforce available will become older, but also will decline roughly 20 % in the next 40 years, shortening potential GDP-growth. While the aged society demands sustainable social protection, resulting in an increase of social expenditures, the effective rate of retirees to employees will double from 37 % to 70 % in 2050. Thus, fewer will have to support more, whilst still competing in a global and volatile market (Fig. 1). Facing this challenge the EU economy is vitally dependant on fostering the workforce of older people. It is necessary to increase that group's participation on the labour market as well as to raise the effective retirement age, possibly beyond 65, being both productive and a relief to public finances [1]. Hence, accompanying social and

C.-Y. Su, S. Rakheja, H. Liu (Eds.): ICIRA 2012, Part II, LNAI 7507, pp. 74–84, 2012.

political incentives, innovative production technologies are needed to enable employees to prolong their working life and to strongly increase the effective per capita productivity.

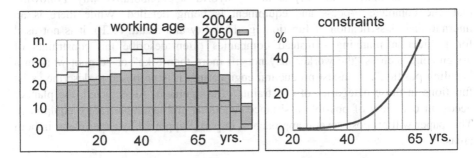

Fig. 1. Left: Projected age cohorts, showing gain and loss of the EU 25 populace from 2004 to 2050 [1]. Right: Incidence of constraints relevant to the assignment of production workers in % (regression) [2].

1.2 Effects of Age and Health on Working Capability

Ageing is a strongly individual and partially reversible process. As a general trend certain attributes like dexterity, perception or strength decline progressively from the mid twenties on, contrariwise experience and related competences grow. Decay and development of the abilities are subjected to genetic disposition, environmental effects, health, training and disuse. Thus, age cannot be linked to a limited working capability, however, the acquisition of constraints is the more likely, the older the employee. According to [2] 5 % of blue collar workers show constraints relevant to their assignment at the age of 40, deteriorating to 47 % at 60. A major factor cutting the working capability is ill health, resulting in absenteeism and early retirement. Among the work related health problems and occupational diseases, musculoskeletal diseases are the most prevalent. Concerning manufacture, the main risk factors are handling of heavy loads, repetitive work or working at high speed and painful, tiring postures [3], [4].

1.3 Production Assistance Robots

Production assistance robots feature both that is needed to tackle this challenge. Automation to increase productivity efficiently, supplemented by the flexibility of human cooperation combined with the most versatile ability to relief production employees from wearing, overstraining work. As a complement to the definition of service robots that exclude manufacturing applications [5], we define a production assistance robot as "a robot, that semi or fully autonomously supports humans in the process of creating added value, e.g. in manufacturing operations". The state of the art of human-machine-cooperation is given in [6]. Further details on production assistance robots are provided by [7].

The integration of robot assistance starts with planning of the workplace (re-) design, see Fig. 2. Considering the requirements of the assembly process and the (dis-) abilities of the worker assigned, each single process step is assessed if it best carried out automated, manually or in any hybrid or collaborative way. Following that, the complete process and equipment is being detailed. While there is an international classification of functioning, disability and health (ICF), it is not used for production planning - instead companies often describe the constraints of assignment, such as "the worker may not lift more than 8 kg" or "cannot work in a kneeling position". To assist production engineering, it is proposed to describe assist functions in those categories of constraints of assignment. As depicted, the planner needs an overview of possible assistance functions and available safety equipment. This paper will propose several approaches, in parts supported by experiment, in both areas.

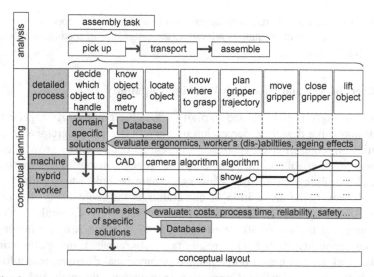

Fig. 2. Planning steps to design and integrate robot assistance on workplace level

2   Alleviating Short Cycled, Repetitive Work

With abating quickness ageing employees find it harder to perform in production lines with short working cycles and quick, repetitive handling processes. Due to the simplicity of the task, experience can hardly be used to compensate. The standard interventions are to either slow the production line, reduce the number of tasks by moving a part to another working place up- or downstream or lastly to assign the worker to a less demanding working place. In contrast, the applied robot assistance aims to keep the worker at the current assignment without need of further personnel. The basic approach is to relief the worker of a part of his tasks, which a robot can safely and timely execute in parallel, providing the worker with more time to finish the remaining task. Based on the estimated loss of productivity; it was assumed, that an improvement of 10 % would be adequate. Fig. 3 depicts the selected pick and place operation of a module from a container to an assembly rack. To ensure safe interaction a robot with intrinsic safety features (light-weight, elastic joints, collision detection) was chosen [8]. To keep a low-cost profile, it was aimed to omit additional sensors to precisely track and pick parts or to detect previously emptied slots in the container. Fig. 3 illustrates the targeted process. To cope with already opened batches with an unknown number of missing parts, the robot moves the end-effector through a slit in the container until a collision is detected (a), which stops the robot. Analyzing the direction of the impact, e.g. using the residual, allows differentiating between expected and unexpected collision along the path of (a). In the former case the robot would stop and then start the gripping process, in the latter case it would stop, drive back and restart process (a). This differentiation, which was tested separately with a force-sensor, is not failsafe. However it is assumed to only occur rarely, resulting in a false pick, which the human at the workplace easily can rectify. Closing the gripper (b), the robot centers and holds the module compliantly. It then lifts (c) and transports the part to an assembly rack. Using the chamfered surface of the rack, the robot pulls the part in the right position (e), allowing a pick of low precision in step (b). The desired contact forces were programmed exploiting the robot's position control. Using an offset, the compliance can be used like a spring, as done in (e). Reducing the offset after insertion of the module averts the lashing movement of the robot when releasing the grasp under tension. The experimental setup demonstrated that a low-cost, retrofit robot assistance to alleviate demanding short cycled work is an applicable concept. The preparation including administration, engineering and programming took 53 h. The installation at the working place was done in 3 h. Given, system and a template of the desired function were available to the respective company a retrofit integration within a day seems feasible. Moreover, a temporary application in cases of reversible disabilities to accelerate resumption of work, e.g. after accidents, could be conceived.

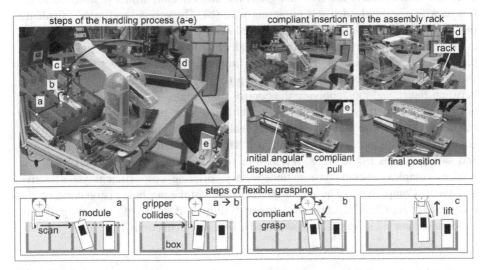

Fig. 3. Top: Robot integrated in a workplace scenario handling a module from a container to an assembly rack. Letters a-e show the steps of the process. Bottom: Details on the pick operation, which tolerates displacement and rotation of modules and container in the range of several cm.

3   Lighten Handling and Assembly of Heavy Parts Effectively

The assembly of a counterweight in a dishwasher base part represents an archetype application suited for robot assistance. The worker has to lift a 7 kg counterweight out of a lattice box. After turning and stepping to the assembly line he moves the weight over the base part and sets it down in a cavity. Based on Methods Time Measurement (MTM) data, this process takes 6.15 s in a 37 s working cycle. To illustrate the strain: in a two hour shift the worker moves 1.4 tons. As aggravating factor, the distal location of the mounting area and of the parts in the lattice box require the worker to bend and lean over, stressing his back, while holding the weight stresses fingers, arms and shoulders.

In the following for each of the three phases (pick up, transport, insertion) a specific problem and a solution will be discussed.

3.1   Efficient Cooperative Pick Up

To pick parts from the loose stack in the lattice box the robot needs precise data for localisation. This could be provided by machine vision or by a worker positioning the robot manually. Both alternatives can be comparatively costly, the first for its hard- and software, the second for its slow process speed, which safety restrictions would dictate. As a new approach, the worker is to manually fasten a gripping tool to the respective part and the robot then autonomously grabs the tool. Fig. 4 illustrates the concept proposed. In step (a) the robot automatically moves to a waiting position, while the worker is separated from the robot's work space by a safety light curtain. Then the worker enters the area and grabs the end-effector, which is fastened to the flange with a spring loaded self retracting wire (b). The spring is adjusted to balance the weight of the end-effector. When pulled onto a stacked counterweight, the end-effector centres the part using circumferential, chamfered metal sheets, and fixates the part with a standard vacuum gripper. When finished, the worker leaves the area which signals the robot to continue with next step (c). By detecting the angle of the wire between flange and tool, applying the control rule (angle $\rightarrow$ 0), the robot moves first horizontally until it is directly over the tool and then moves down, until a latch catches and fixates the tool to the flange. Finally, the robot lifts the counterweight and continues with the assembly operation (d). This design allows the worker to swiftly and safely use his haptic skills, reliefs him from handling the heavy part itself and renders complex machine vision unnecessary, offering cost-efficient yet effective assistance. Comparing to a quote for the realisation of the machine vision concept, the cooperative approach is estimated to cost only half to third, assuming 4 s of cooperation in a 37 s cycle, single shift and a five year deduction.

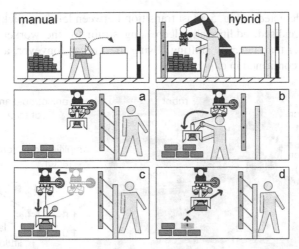

Fig. 4. Top left: Scheme of manual scenario assembling heavy parts. Top right: Scenario for hybrid pick up; a-d: Scheme of the hybrid pick up process.

3.2   Speeding Up Cooperative Handling

To allow manual guidance of a RV60 robot it was equipped with a safe control (ISO 13849 Part I) and an input device featuring a force sensor, emergency switch and an enabling device (ISO 10218 Parts I-II). When not enabled, the robot carries out a stop category 2, permitting the resumption of guided operation within half a second - paramount for acceptance. As a comprehensible and common concept of interaction, a non linear control was implemented transforming the force applied by the worker into the tool's velocity, see Fig. 5. To compensate for less strength in lateral directions, an anisotropic amplification of the force input has been found useful. The robots behaviour can be switched between fine motion for positioning and gross motion for transport just by exerting more or less force [9], [10]. The intermediate hysteresis stabilises the transition between the different amplification factors. The distance to obstacles limits the speed as shown in Fig. 5. Virtual walls are applied to avoid collisions or to guide the tool along a defined path by reducing only the orthogonal velocity to zero at the wall's coordinates. If the tool penetrates the virtual barrier, it is being pushed back smoothly, using a spring-damper-transfer function [11]. In this setup, the stability of control is limited by delay, amplification and stiffness of the kinematic chain of user and robot. In consequence this impairs the potential cooperative working speed and thus the robot assistance's economical value. Depending on the user, handling speeds between 200-500 mm/s were realised. The approach found to further increase handling speed was to decouple the resulting velocity from several sources of instability. This was put into practise using a "virtual conveyor", which basically is adding a preset override of a tangential velocity output to a virtual wall. To speed up lateral movement, the worker drives the tool into the conveyor wall, where it is automatically being pulled sideways, until it either reaches the end of the conveyor or the worker pulls the tool away from the wall. Using two conveyors, as depicted in Fig. 5 a fast transition between left (e.g. pick) and right (e.g. place) can be realised, additionally decreasing strain for the worker, since forward pushing is easier than laterally shifting. Using the virtual conveyor, a stable speed of 1 m/s could be confirmed in experiments.

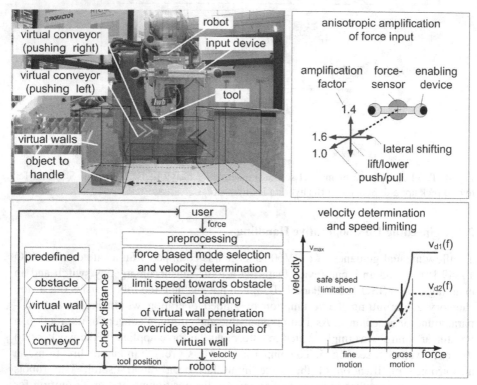

Fig. 5. Top left: Robot with virtual conveyors to ease and speed up transporting a weight between two virtually confined volumes; Top right: anisotropic amplification of input forces; Bottom left: Principle design of the applied control architecture. Bottom right: Non linear transformation of input force to output velocity.

3.3   Assisting Positioning for Assembly

Let it be assumed that the robot assistant has stopped at a waiting position holding the assembly part before this process starts. The insertion of the counterweight in the base part requires a positioning precision of ± 0.7 mm. If the base part is properly aligned and fixated, the robot could be used like a press. Activating the enabling device the part automatically is set down and the robot returns into waiting position. Given a starting distance of 250 mm between the assembly partners, adding the time to grasp the input device, this takes about 3 s. If the base part is only inaccurately positioned and the manual guidance described in 3.2 is being used, the process takes about 8-11 s. The reason reckoned for this long duration is, that the user has no adequate reference point to control the movement due to the assembly part occluding the relevant characteristics of the base part. Considering that the latter situation of the base part is a common case in manual assembly, a method that assists and thus quickens the positioning seems worthwhile. To tackle this, an approach baptized "feature fetching" is envisioned, that consists of three major steps. Before operation, a reference feature on the assembly part and a distinct structure element of the base part are chosen, both of which coincide when assembled. In this case, these are a rib of the base part fitting to a cavity of the assembly part, see Fig. 6. In the next step, the worker guides the robot over the base part while a sensor attached to the flange scans for features derived from said structure element. The rib is being detected e.g. searching for vertical edges with minimum length. When found, these features are mapped in base coordinates using the synchronised tool position. In a third step, areas of attraction are established on top of all localised features. When the worker guides the reference feature into the cone shaped attractor area, a virtual force is added to the user input and lightly pulls the tool to the centre. Below the tip of the cone, the lateral movement is inhibited, so the part can be moved precisely vertically, already aligned for assembly. The currently fetched feature can be highlighted in a display. This way the user can chose between several, even falsely identified features. A proof of concept is in development.

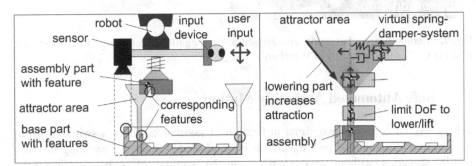

Fig. 6. Targeted setup for feature fetching and details on the attractor area

4   Assisting Complex Assembly Motion

Inserting a driver seat in the auto-body demands a complex motion path. Passive handling devices can only deliver limited support, e.g. in terms of assisted degrees of freedom. The basic idea for a cooperative assembly was to let the worker control the assembly movement manually. This was dropped later on due to quality and ability reasons which an experiment revealed. A proband had to insert a lightweight cardboard double of the seat, collisions were listed and located. Even with training and optimal inserting method the incidence of collisions did not go below 3 % (N=90). The assessed reasons are seen in the limited space, occlusions as well as unrestraint degrees of freedom. It was concluded to assist the worker by providing a predefined insertion path. At a point of choice, the robot synchronizes with the assembly line motion. The worker then detaches the input device allowing him to control the insertion process by tilting the input device, as depicted in Fig. 7. The path can be run for- and backwards and offsets can be added permitting corrections online. The mobile input device facilitates and securing the process. In case the worker releases the enabling device, it is supposed to stop the robot's ideomotion, yet not the synchronized locomotion, as that would stop the whole assembly line. With this design, separating fences can be left aside increasing operational and planning flexibility. Process reliability will improve. The worker is unburdened of the wearing handling task and can continue with further assembly at the car body right after the robot assistant is finished, potentially saving throughput time.

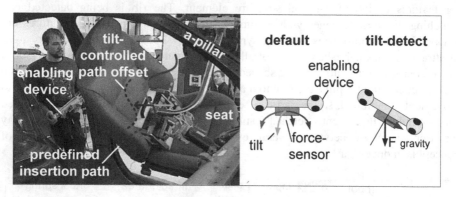

Fig. 7. Inserting a driver seat along a predefined path, using tilt control (realized in cooperation with the LRT of the University of Würzburg)

5   Safe Automated Assembly Motion

To achieve an economical optimal utilization of assistance robots a switching from cooperative to automated task execution is demanded. Whilst the handling of parts within scenarios without task sharing can be secured by existing contactless approaches [6], [7], [10], the automated assembly step itself cannot yet be executed safely in the presence of a human worker without enabling devices or tactile sensors. As a new approach a model-based safety concept is introduced and targets the design of an optoelectronic shield around the aimed assembly position detecting intrusions and thus preventing collisions. The core consists of three linked modules. First, a system model is designed using the real-time robot data providing its tool position and orientation. In combination with a mathematical pinhole model of a selected laser scanner [12] and a CAD-based virtual representation of the assembly base part, sensor distance measurement data can be simulated.

The virtual data is being compared with the real measurement data of the assembly scenario where the laser scanner is attached to the robot tool. The real data is prone to four types of errors (noise, signal quality, e.g. diffuse reflectance, object displacements and sampling issues). The error handling is covered in an online matching module and aims at filtering false negatives with direct effect on the system's robustness. This can be tackled by implementing a matching score, ray aggregation, a Kalman filter, or error modeling [13], [14]. A negative result triggers the robot's trajectory modification, e.g. a stop. It is assumed, that the likelihood of the virtual data creating false positives for a multitude of measurement points at the same time is close to zero and thus will have no safety impact. Ongoing work strives to prove the concept by experiment and calculation.

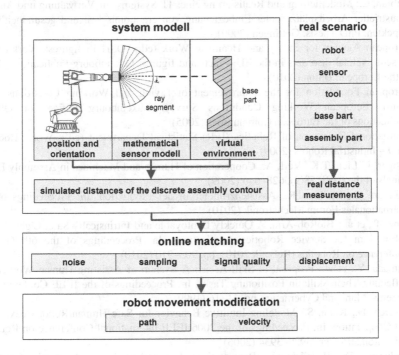

Fig. 8. System architecture of the safety concept

6 Summary

Due to the demographic shift, the value of manual workforces will increase continuously in the near future, The integration of human-robot-interaction technologies as simple and yet intelligent assistance systems within industrial assembly represents an effective method to tackle this challenge and enable the efficient task sharing with respect to both humans' and robots' abilities. Along the assembly steps gripping, handling, positioning and assembly, generic assistance approaches taking into account safety issues for cooperative task execution are presented and discussed.

Acknowledgement. This work was part of the project "FitForAge" funded by the Bayerische Forschungsstiftung.

References

1. EU Commission (ed.): Europe's demographic future: Facts and figures on challenges and opportunities. Luxembourg Office for Official Publications of the European Communities (2007)
2. Dubian, C.: Modellierung und Realisierung eines IT-Systems zur Verwaltung und Analyse industrieller Arbeitsplätze unter Einbeziehung von ergonomischen und gesundheitlichen Aspekten. PhD Thesis, Göttingen (2009)
3. European Agency for Safety and Health at Work (ed.): OSH in figures: Work-related musculoskeletal disorders in the EU – facts and figures. Luxembourg Publications Office of the European Union (2010)
4. European Foundation for the Improvement of Living and Working Conditions (ed.): Fourth European Working Conditions Survey. Luxembourg Office for Official Publications of the European Communities (2005)
5. International Federation of Robotics (IFR) Statistical Department (ed.): World Robotics 2009 – Industrial Robots (2009)
6. Krüger, J., Lien, T.K., Verl, A.: Cooperation of Human and Machines in Assembly Lines. Annals of the CIRP 58(2), 628–646 (2009)
7. Reinhart, G., Spillner, R.: Assistenzroboter in der Produktion. In: Proceedings of the Internationales Forum Mechatronik (2010)
8. Lenz, T., et al.: BioRob-Arm: A Quickly Deployable and Intrinsically Safe, Light-Weight Robot Arm for Service Robotics Applications. In: Proceedings of the 6th German Conference on Robotics (Robotik 2010), pp. 905–910 (2010)
9. Yamada, Y., et al.: Proposal of Skill-Assist: A System of Assisting Human Workers by Reflecting Their Skills in Positioning Tasks. In: Proceedings of the IEEE Conference on Systems, Man, and Cybernetics, pp. 11–16 (1999)
10. Henrich, D., Kuhn, S.: Modeling Intuitive Behavior for Safe Human/Robot Coexistence and Cooperation. In: Proceedings of the 2006 IEEE International Conference on Robotics and Automation, pp. 3929–3934 (2006)
11. Surdilovic, D., Radojicic, J.: Robust Control of Interaction with Haptic Interfaces. In: Proceedings of the IEEE International Conference on Robotics and Automation 2007, pp. 3237–3244 (2007)
12. Friedmann, M., Petersen, K., von Stryk, O.: Simulation of Multi-Robot Teams with Flexible Level of Detail. In: Carpin, S., Noda, I., Pagello, E., Reggiani, M., von Stryk, O. (eds.) SIMPAR 2008. LNCS (LNAI), vol. 5325, pp. 29–40. Springer, Heidelberg (2008)
13. Nandy, S., Chakraborty, G., Kumar, C.S., Ray, R., Shome, S.N.: Error Modeling of Laser Range Finder for Robotic Application using Time Domain Technique. In: Proceedings of the International Conference on Signal Processing, Communications and Computing 2011, pp. 1–5 (2011)
14. Teusch, C.: Model-based Analysis and Evaluation of Point Sets from Optical 3D Laser Scanners. Shaker, Aachen (2007)

Simulation Study of an FES-Involved Control Strategy for Lower Limb Rehabilitation Robot

Yixiong Chen, Jin Hu, Feng Zhang, and Zengguang Hou

State Key Laboratory of Management and Control for Complex Systems Institute of Automation, Chinese Academy of Sciences, Beijing 100190, China

Abstract. This paper proposes a functional electrical stimulation (FES)-involved control strategy for self-made exoskeleton lower limb rehabilitation robot for the training purpose of paraplegic patients caused by spinal cord injury (SCI) or stroke. Two muscles (Vastus Medialis and Riceps Femoris) are stimulated to produce active torque around knee joint which can be considered as a redundant actuator besides electrical motor. During the predefined trajectory tracking task, electrical motors compensate for the gravitational torque of the entire human-robot system, while the muscles provide torque calculated by a PD position/velocity controller based on the tracking error. The FES-induced torque control is accomplished with combination of feedforward and feedback controller, former of which is obtained by applying off-line trained neural networks to map the relationship between desired active torque and FES parameters. Simulation results obtained by using Simulink toolboxes in Matlab verify the feasibility of this control strategy.

Keywords: Rehabilitation robot, FES, torque control, muscle model.

1 Introduction

Patients who have spinal cord injury (SCI) or stroke always suffer from motor disorder, poor blood circulation on the affected limbs as well as psychological problems. Rehabilitation exercises are required to restore the lost movement function of paralyzed limbs which will help the patients out of the predicament physiologically and psychologically. Traditional rehabilitation method is executed by moving the paralyzed limbs repeatedly with the help of physical therapist, and is time-consuming and laborious [1], [2]. Due to the rapid development of robotics, this manual treatment is gradually replaced by rehabilitation robot designed for active training and repetitive movement exercise for paraplegic or hemiplegic patients [3]. This advanced rehabilitation technique enhances the effect of rehabilitation and also decreases the economical cost.

Functional electrical stimulation (FES) involves artificially inducing a current in specific motor neurons to generate muscle contractions [4]. Many FES based studies, both open loop and closed loop control have shown satisfactory results in movement restoration [3], [5]. Since the significant meaning of the FES in rehabilitation, it has been combined with robot for better rehabilitation effect in recent years. A critical factor to be considered during FES-involved training is the timing and intensify of FES which determine the participation of the stimulated muscle, and another factor is what role

C.-Y. Su, S. Rakheja, H. Liu (Eds.): ICIRA 2012, Part II, LNAI 7507, pp. 85–95, 2012.

the rehabilitation robot plays during the training. There are basically two types of solution to these problems. The first one is by setting a desired interaction force/torque between human and rehabilitation robot during certain training task such as leg pressing and cycling motion. Timing and intensity of FES are controlled based on the measured force/torqe, and the rehabilitation robot is used to support the gravity of the limb as well as to provide assistant or active resistent during the training [1]. Another solution is by detecting the patients' intention of motion, either by means of force/torque sensor or electromyography (EMG). Then the FES, whose intensity depends on the measured voluntary force/torque or EMG, "gives a hand" to the relative muscle to help the limb completing certain motion [6].

In this paper, we propose an FES-involved control strategy for self-made exoskeleton lower limb rehabilitation robot for the training purpose of completely paraplegic patients. These patients have no voluntary control of there lower muscles which can only be activated by FES. This control strategy is based on the concept of "soft robot", in which the FES-stimulated muscles are considered as another type of motor. Our control strategy is inspired by an assumption that the limb motion caused by stimulating relative muscles in a controllable manner is likely to enhance the rehabilitation effect compared with purely passive limb motion. In this control strategy, the rehabilitation robot and human lower limb are assigned with a predefined trajectory tracking task, and electrical motors of the rehabilitation robot compensate for the gravitational torque of the entire human-robot system, while the stimulated muscles provide the torque calculated by a PD position/velocity controller according to the tracking error. This paper is organized as follows. In Section II, the simplified system model and its dynamic analysis will be introduce; the FES-stimulated muscle model as well as the approach to its inverse model will be given; also, the control strategy will be depicted in detail. Section III represents the Matlab simulation results which can demonstrate the feasibility and effectiveness of this control strategy. The last section comes up with conclusion and future work.

2   Methods

2.1   Simplified Model of Human Leg and Robot

The plant to be simulated is based on a self-made exoskeleton lower limb rehabilitation robot which have 3-DOF corresponding to hip, knee and ankle joint, respectively. All three joints are driven by electrical motors, and equipped with encoders and torque sensors to get angle position, angular velocity and torque of each joint. Link length of the robot can be adjusted to ensure perfect alignment of the robot joints and human joints. During training, the patient's leg is attached to the robot links by straps, with feet fastened to the pedal. For simplification, it is assumed that the mass of the system is evenly distributed and the ankle joint is maintained at a fixed angle so that the human leg together with robot can be considered as an evenly distributed two-link system. Picture of the real robot and its simplified model are shown in Fig.1.

To get the dynamic of the system, Lagrange-Euler method is employed, and is defined as

$$\frac{d}{dt}\frac{\partial L}{\partial \dot{q}_i} - \frac{\partial L}{\partial q_i} = \tau_i \tag{1}$$

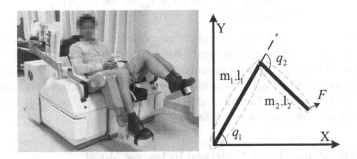

Fig. 1. Picture of the rehabilitation robot and its simplified model. q_i, m_i, and l_i represent joint angle, mass of link and length of link for joint i, respectively. F is the interaction force between the robot and human leg at end-effector.

where L is the Lagrange function which is the difference between kinetic energy K and potential energy P of the entire system. q_i $\dot{q}_i$ and τ_i are joint angles, angular velocities and joint torques of the i-th joint, respectively.

By computing formula (1), dynamic of the system can be written in the following form

$$M(q)\ddot{q} + C(q,\dot{q})\dot{q} + G(q) = \tau \tag{2}$$

where $M(q)$ is the 2×2 inertia matrix; $C(q,\dot{q})$ is the 2×2 Coriolis/centripetal matrix; $G(q)$ is the 2×1 gravity vector. They are given as

$$M = \begin{bmatrix} (\frac{1}{3}m_1 + m_2)l_1^2 + \frac{1}{3}m_2l_2^2 + m_2l_1l_2\cos q_2 & \frac{1}{3}m_2l_2^2 + \frac{1}{2}m_2l_1l_2\cos q_2 \\ \frac{1}{3}m_2l_2^2 + \frac{1}{2}m_2l_1l_2\cos q_2 & \frac{1}{3}m_2l_2^2 \end{bmatrix}$$

$$C = \begin{bmatrix} -\frac{1}{2}m_2l_1l_2\dot{q}_2\sin q_2 & -\frac{1}{2}m_2l_1l_2(\dot{q}_1 + \dot{q}_2)\sin q_2 \\ \frac{1}{2}m_2l_1l_2\dot{q}_1\sin q_2 & 0 \end{bmatrix} \tag{3}$$

$$G = \begin{bmatrix} (\frac{1}{2}m_1 + m_2)gl_1\cos q_1 + \frac{1}{2}m_2gl_2\cos(q_1 + q_2) \\ \frac{1}{2}m_2gl_2\cos(q_1 + q_2) \end{bmatrix}$$

where m_i, l_i represent the mass and the length of link i, respectively.

Since the system has redundant driven actuators (motors and muscles), the joint torque τ in equation (2) can be divided into two parts, namely τ_r which is generated by electrical motor and τ_m which is generated by the FES-induced contraction of relative muscles. There are several methods to detect muscle-produced torque, one of which is by using the force sensor attached on the end-effector where the foot is fastened to the pedal. Similar to the entire system's dynamic, human leg dynamic can be described as [7]

$$M_h(q)\ddot{q} + C_h(q,\dot{q})\dot{q} + G_h(q) = J(q)^T F \tag{4}$$

where $M_h(q)$, $C_h(q,\dot{q})$ and $G_h(q)$ are the inertia matrix, the Coriolis/centripetal matrix and the gravity vector of human leg, respectively. $J(q)$ is the 2×2 Jacobian matrix represented as

$$J = \begin{bmatrix} -l_1 \sin q_1 - l_2 \sin(q_1 + q_2) & -l_2 \sin(q_1 + q_2) \\ l_1 \cos q_1 + l_2 \cos(q_1 + q_2) & l_2 \cos(q_1 + q_2) \end{bmatrix} \qquad (5)$$

F is the force imposed to the leg at end-effector detected by the force sensor. Define $F_s(q)$ to be the measured interaction force when human muscles are kept relaxed at position q, which is collected in the pre-trainning stage as the robot running in predefined trajectory. In the training stage, if the muscle is active by FES, there will be a difference between the measured force F and $F_s(q)$. That is $\Delta F = F - F_s(q)$, from which muscle-produced torque can be calculated: $\tau_m = J(q)^T \Delta F$.

2.2 FES-Stimulated Muscle Model and Its Inverse Model

During the training stage, two human muscles (Vastus Medialis and Riceps Femoris) will be stimulated to produce partial torque around knee joint. A biological model developed by Riener is employed to simulate the muscle response to FES. The active moment of FES-induced muscle contraction is described as two parts, namely activation dynamics and contraction dynamics, while the passive torque of the muscle is described as passive elastic and passive viscous properties [8]. The original model has two inputs for activation dynamics which are stimulation pulse width and frequency, however, in this simulation study, stimulation frequency for each muscle is fixed constantly at 50Hz, resulting in a simplified model shown in Fig.2.

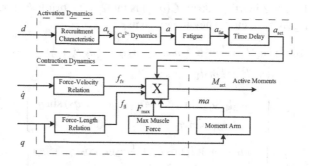

Fig. 2. Activation dynamics and contraction dynamics of the muslce

In the activation dynamics, four components are used to calculate the activation of muscle. They are the recruitment characteristic, calcium dynamics, muscle fatigue and a time delay. The recruitment characteristic shows the relationship between the FES pulse width and the percentage of motor unit activated by FES. The recruitment characteristic a_r is given as

$$a_r = a_f\{c_1\{(d - d_{thr}) \arctan[k_{thr}(d - d_{thr})] - (d - d_{sat}) \arctan[k_{sat}(d - d_{sat})]\} + c_2 \qquad (6)$$

where d is the pulse width of FES, d_{thr} and d_{sat} denote pulse width values corresponding to threshold and saturation. The shape of the recruitment curve is describe using c_1, c_2, k_{thr} and k_{sat}. a_f is introduced to represent the frequency characteristic and is a function of the stimulation frequency in [8]. Since the stimulation frequency is fixed at 50Hz, here

a_f is a constant. Calcium dynamics presents the mechanism that calcium ion released from sarcoplasmic reticulum, and is expressed using the following two-order linear relation

$$T_{ca}^2 \ddot{a} + 2T_{ca}\dot{a} + a = a_r \qquad (7)$$

where T_{ca} is the time constant, and a denotes non-fatigue muscle activation. Fitness function is introduced to depict the effect of muscle fatigue and recovery phenomenon using the following first-order relation

$$\frac{dfit}{dt} = \frac{0.55a(fit_{min} - fit)}{T_{fat}} + \frac{(1 - fit)(1 - 0.55a)}{T_{rec}} \qquad (8)$$

where fit is the fitness of the muscle, while fit_{min} is the minimum fitness. Time constants for fatigue and recovery are given as T_{fat} and T_{rec}. Final activation a_{act} is the product of fitness fit and non-fatigue activation a with a constant time delay T_{del}.

In the contraction dynamics, three parts are involved, i.e., maximum isometric force F_{max}, force-length relation f_{fl} and force-velocity relation f_{fv}. Product of these three parts denotes the maximum force F_m which can be produced by the stimulated muscle at certain joint angle and angular velocity. After F_m being scaled by the activation a_{act} calculated in the activation dynamics, the active force of the stimulated muscle can be obtained. The final active moment is the product of active force and moment arm of the muscle. The force-length relation is given as

$$f_{fl} = \exp\{-[(\bar{l} - 1)/\varepsilon]^2\} \qquad (9)$$

where $\bar{l}$ is the muscle length normalized with respect to the optimal muscle length l_{opt}, and ε is a shape factor. The force-velocity relation is given as

$$f_{fv} = 0.54 \arctan(5.69\bar{v} + 0.51) + 0.745 \qquad (10)$$

where $\bar{v}$ is the muscle velocity normalized with respect to the maximum contraction velocity v_m of the muscle. The muscle length and velocity can be calculated using joint angle, angular velocity and moment arm of the muscle described in detail in [8].

Unlike active moments which are calculated separately for each muscle, the passive joint moments of all the muscles are assigned to the joints. Passive joint moments are considered as the sum of two components: passive viscous moment m_{vis} and passive elasitic moment m_{ela}. The former has a linear relation with angular velocity, while the latter is a function of the joint angle described in detail in [9].

For the FES-induced torque control, a inverse model of the stimulated muscle is usually implemented as a feedforward controller [10]. To get the inverse model, there are basically two methods, first of which is by calculating the inversion of the direct model, and second of which is by considering the muscle as a black box and identifying the input-output relation using experiment data. In this paper, the second method is utilized to obtain the inverse model of the stimulated muscle.

Since neural network has been the most commonly used in modeling and control [11], a three layer neural network is constructed and trained to be the inverse model of muscle using sampling data collected in the pre-training stage. As mentioned above, the direct muscle model contains dynamic items such as calcium dynamics and fatigue dynamics which requires the past input and output to be feedback into the network otherwise the dynamics characteristic of the system can not be represented. However, the delay due to calcium dynamics is tiny compared to the change rate of the input, so the error caused by ignoring this item is in acceptable range. As for the fatigue dynamics, error resulting from ignoring this item can be eliminated by the feedback controller (described in the following part). Therefore, for the sake of simplicity, a static neural network is constructed whose structure is shown in Fig.3.

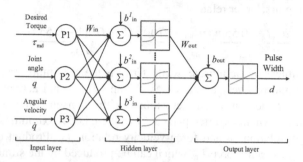

Fig. 3. Neural network structure of the inverse model for the stimulated muscle

The Input layer of the network has three nodes for three inputs: the desired torque to be induced by FES, the joint angle and the angular velocity. The hidden layer has 50 neurons based on former experience whose transfer function is tan-sigmoid function. The output layer has only one neuron from which the pulse width of the FES is calculated. The transfer function of the neuron in output layer is linear function. Note that there are two independent neural networks for two muscles (Vastus Medialis and Riceps Femoris).

2.3 Control Strategy

The general idea of FES-involved control strategy can be easily understood by comparing purely passive control strategy, in which the end-effector of the human-robot system is required to track predefined trajectory. The position/velocity control loop is accomplished by PD feedback controller with gravitational and elastic torque compensated using a feedforward controller. Taking passive joint moments into account, the system dynamics expressed in (2) can be rewritten as

$$M(q)\ddot{q}+C(q,\dot{q})\dot{q}+\tau_{vis}(\dot{q})+G(q)+\tau_{ela}(q)=\hat{\tau}_{g+ela}(q)+\tau \tag{11}$$

where τ_{vis} and τ_{ela} are passive viscous and elastic moments, while $\hat{\tau}_{g+ela}$ is the sum of estimated gravitational torque of the entire system and the passive elastic moment of muscles, both of which has a nonlinear relationship with joint angle q. Considering the passive elastic moment as another kind of gravitational torque, gravity compensation method described in [12] is employed to estimate $\hat{\tau}_{g+ela}$. τ in equation (11) is calculated using the following PD control law

$$\tau = K_p e + K_v \dot{e} \tag{12}$$

where e is the error between desired and actual joint angle; $\dot{e}$ is the error between desired and actual angular velocity. The derivative gain matrix K_v and the proportional gain matrix K_p are selected positive definite. Note that in the case of purely passive control strategy both τ and $\hat{\tau}_{g+ela}$ are produced by electrical motors of the rehabilitation robot.

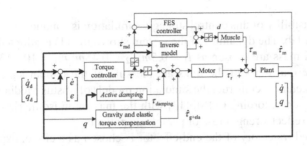

Fig. 4. Control architecture for FES-involved training strategy

As shown in Fig.4, in the FES-involved control strategy, τ is partially produced by FES-induced muscle contraction which is denoted as τ_{md}. Since the gravity and the passive elastic of the entire system is compensated by motors, τ is relatively small, and is mostly within the range that muscle can produced by means of FES. What's more, a limiter is employed to ensure that the desired muscle torque τ_{md} won't extend the ability of muscle. And the exceeded torque will still be produced by motors. Since only Vastus Medialis and Riceps Femoris are stimulated, redundancy just exist in knee joint (these two muscles response for knee extension and flexion, respectively). The limiter for hip joint is set at zero, which means all the computed torque for hip joint is still generated by motor.

The rehabilitation robot should have a damping behavior to the human leg, which is embodied using active damping $\tau_{damping}$ produced by motors. To counterweight the damping torque, desired muscle torque τ_{md} is increased through the feedback mechanism. The active damping torque is expressed as

$$\tau_{damping} = -J^T(q)K_D J(q)\dot{q} \qquad (13)$$

where K_D is the damping matrix through which the strength of damping behavior of the robot can be adjusted, while J is the Jacobian matrix given in (5).

To control the active muscle torque induced by FES, combination of feedforward and feedback controller is employed. The neural network trained to obtain the inverse muscle model serves as the feedforward controller, while a PD controller serves as the feedback controller. The total pulse width d of the FES delivered to the muscle is the sum of the pulse width predicted by the inverse model and the pulse width resulting from the PD controller [10]. Since the actual active torque of the FES-induced muscle τ_m can not be obtain directly, method to detect active muscle torque through force sensor described in the former section is used to calculate the muscle torque $\hat{\tau}_m$. In real situation, error is inevitable between τ_m and $\hat{\tau}_m$, however, for simplicity in simulation, assumption has been made to consider them equal. Note that τ_{md} is generated by two muscles (Vastus Medialis and Riceps Femoris), and which one to be stimulated is determined by the sign of τ_{md}. For a positive τ_{md}, Vastus Medialis will be stimulated; on the contrast, for a negative τ_{md}, Riceps Femoris will be stimulated.

3   Simulation

To verify the feasibility of this control strategy, simulation is conducted using Simulink toolboxes in Matlab. The dynamics of the system shown in (11) is adopted as the plant. Link length and mass are chosen as $l_1 = 0.5m$, $l_2 = 0.45m$, $m_1 = 10+13kg$ and $m_2 = 3.5+12kg$. Note that mass of the links are the sum of the human leg and the robot links. The parameters to construct the simulation models of Vastus Medialis and Riceps Femoris are chosen according to [8], [13] with the maximum isometric force reduced to 45 percent to reflect strength loss of paraplegic patients.

The predefined trajectory of the end-effector is chosen as a circle, expressed in the Cartesian space coordinates as $x=0.73-0.1\cos(0.5\pi t)$, $y=0.1\sin(0.5\pi t)$. Desired joint angle q_d and desired angular velocity $\dot{q}_d$ can be derived from the inverse kinematics and Jacobian matrix.

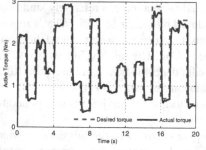
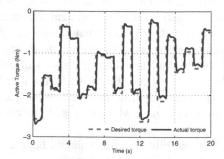

(a) Result of Vastus Medialis inverse model   (b) Result of Riceps Femoris inverse model

Fig. 5. Validation result of neural network-based inverse muscle model

To train the networks used as inverse muscle models for Vastus Medialis and Riceps Femoris, sampling points are collected separately at pre-training stage which last 60 seconds in total for each muscle. During the robot running in the predefined trajectory, FES with random pulse width d uniformly distributed on the interval [0 400] μs is delivered to the muscle, and each random pulse width last 2 seconds. The active torque produced by FES, the knee angle and angular velocity construct a three dimension input vector for the neural network, while the pulse width forms the output. The whole procedure is divided into six fractions, inserted with rest time of 30 seconds, aiming to ensure that the fatigue effect of stimulated muscle can be ignored. There are 6227 sampling points collected during the whole procedure, and Levenberg-Marquardt algorithm is utilized to train the neural network. Both neural networks for Vastus Medialis and Riceps Femoris are trained for 300 iterations. The final mean square error of the network for Vastus Medialis is $1.54\mu s$ and $2.88\mu s$ for the Riceps Femoris network. To validate the networks, they are input with random desired active torque (0 to 3Nm for Vastus Medialis and -3 to 0Nm for Riceps Femoris) during the robot running in the predefined trajectory, and the outputs of the networks (estimated FES pulse width corresponding to the desired active torque) are delivered to the direct muscle models. If the trained networks are precise inversion of the direct muscle models, there should be slight errors between the desired active torque and actual active torque. Fig.5 shows the validation results, from which the effectiveness of the networks can be clearly verified.

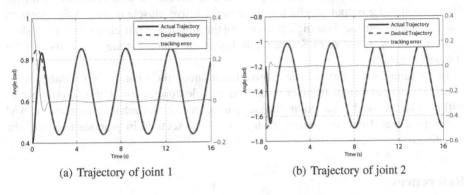

(a) Trajectory of joint 1   (b) Trajectory of joint 2

Fig. 6. Tracking performance of the human-robot system

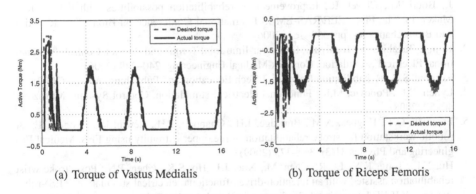

(a) Torque of Vastus Medialis   (b) Torque of Riceps Femoris

Fig. 7. Results of the FES-induced active torque

During the training stage, the initial joint angles are chosen as $q_0 = [0.4\ -1.2]^T$, and the initial joint angular velocities are chosen as $\dot{q}_0 = [0\ 0]^T$. The damping matrix K_D is set as $K_D = \mathrm{diag}(20, 20)$. Torque limiter for the desired active muscle torque in knee joint is set at ± 3Nm. Fig.6 shows the tracking performance of the human-robot system. The tracking errors are almost less than 0.01 rad (0.574 deg) after 2 seconds for both joints. Fig.7 shows the computed torque τ_{md} and the actual active torque produced of the relative muscle, which proves the effectiveness of the FES feedforward and feedback controller. All these simulation results demonstrate the feasibility of this FES-involved control strategy which require the relative muscle to be stimulated in a controllable manner, and the controller developed in section II is capable to achieve this goal.

4 Conclusion

In this paper, a FES-involved control strategy for a lower limb rehabilitation robot is presented and the controller used to accomplished this task is developed. The human-robot model is simplified as a two-link system. A mathematical model of muscle response to FES developed by Riener is employed for simulation. To get the inverse model of the stimulated muscle for the control purpose, neural networks are constructed and trained. Predefined trajectory tracking of the end-effector is well achieved by torque PD controller, the output of which is the desired active muscle torque. A feedforward and feedback controller is sufficient to control the stimulated muscle to produce desired active torque by means of FES. The feasibility of this control strategy is proven by the simulation results.

In the future, voluntary muscle contraction in incomplete paralyzed patients will be taken into account apart from FES-induced muscle contraction. Hip-related muscles will also be involved in the control strategy to achieve better rehabilitation effect. And experiment based on this control strategy will be executed in practice to verify the effectiveness.

References

1. Metrailler, P., Blanchard, V., Perrin, I., Brodard, R., Frischknecht, R., Schmitt, C., Fournier, J., Bouri, M., Clavel, R.: Improvement of rehabilitation possibilities with the Motion-Maker. In: The First IEEE/RAS-EMBS International Conference on Biomedical Robotics and Biomechatronics, pp. 359–364 (2006)
2. Koji, I., Takahiro, S., Toshiyuki, K.: Lower-limb Joint Torque and Position Controls by Functional Electrical Stimulation. Complex Medical Engineering, 240–249 (2006)
3. Kommu, S.S.: Rehabilitation Robotics. I-Tech Education and Publishing, Austria (2007)
4. Lynch, C.L., Popovic, M.R.: Functional electrical stimulation. Control Systems Magazine, 40–50 (2008)
5. Freeman, C.T., Hughes, A.M., Burridge, J.H., Chappell, P.H., Lewin, P.L., Rogers, E.: A robotic workstation for stroke rehabilitation of the upper extremity using FES. Medical Engineering and Physics 31(3), 364–373 (2009)
6. Hu, X.L., Tong, K.Y., Li, R., Chen, M., Xue, J.J., Ho, S.K., Chen, P.N.: Post-stroke wrist rehabilitation assisted with an intention-driven functional electrical stimulation (FES)-robot system. In: IEEE International Conference on Rehabilitation Robotics, pp. 1–6 (2011)
7. Khatib, O.: A unified approach for motion and force control of robot manipulators The operational space formulation. IEEE Journal of Robotics and Automation 3(1), 43–53 (1987)
8. Riener, R., Fuhr, T.: Patient-driven control of FES-supported standing up a simulation study. IEEE Transactions on Rehabilitation Engineering 6(2), 113–124 (1998)
9. Riener, R., Edrich, T.: Identification of passive elastic joint moments in the lower extremities. Journal of Biomechanics 32(5), 539–544 (1999)
10. Ferrarin, M., Palazzo, F., Riener, R., Quintern, J.: Model-based control of FES-induced single joint movements. IEEE Transactions on Neural Systems and Rehabilitation Engineering 9(3), 245–257 (2001)

11. Chang, G.C., Lub, J.J., Liao, G.D., Lai, J.S., Cheng, C.K., Kuo, B.L., Kuo, T.S.: A neuro-control system for the knee joint position control with quadriceps stimulation. IEEE Transactions on Rehabilitation Engineering 5(1), 2–11 (2007)
12. Heredia, J.A., Yu, W.: A Modified PD Control of Robot Manipulator Using Neural Network Compensator. In: International Joint Conference on Neural Networks, vol. 3, pp. 1999–2004 (1999)
13. Delp, S.L.: Surgery simulation: A computer graphics system to analyze and design musculoskeletal reconstructions of the lower limb. Ph.D. dissertation, Stanford University, Stanford (1990)

Development of a Rehabilitation Robot
for Upper-Limb Movements

Chao Lv[1], Le Xie[1,*], Wei Shao[1], Hai-long Yu[1], Yuan Wang[1],
Jin-wu Wang[2], and Ning Nan[2]

[1] National Digital Manufacturing Technology Center, Shanghai Jiao Tong Univ., Shanghai,
China
[2] Med-X Research Institute, Shanghai Jiao Tong Univ., Shanghai, China
lexie@sjtu.edu.cn

Abstract. This paper analyzes the kinematics of human upper-arm and
develops a 6DOF exoskeleton upper-limb hemiplegic rehabilitation training
robot. It describes the mechanical structure and implementation function of
each module of the robot system, and it also describes a design for the
movement data collection. The robot can assist the patient's upper-limb to do
active movement training which simultaneously involves multiple joints and a
total of 7DOF of human upper-limb, that is, shoulder flexion/extension,
shoulder abduction/adduction, shoulder internal rotation/external rotation,
elbow flexion/extension, forearm supination/pronation, wrist extension/flexion
and wrist ulnar deviation/radial deviation

Keywords: Robot, Rehabilitation, Upper-limb.

1 Introduction

Rehabilitation process can help hemiplegic patients get rid of learned non-use atrophy
of muscle, and, more important, have a positive effect on neurological restoration of
the limb function [1].

Traditional human-assisted therapy for mobility impairments is labor-intensive and
inefficient. Robotics technology can transform the rehabilitation clinics from
primitive manual operations to more technology-rich operations. They may be used to
assist the movements of the disabled limbs, improve training quality, quantify healing
effect, optimize training scheme, increase productivity and reduce cost [2].

According to different supporting and guiding ways of the robots on the limb, the
existing rehabilitation robots can be divided into two types: end-effector-based robots
and exoskeleton robots.

When training on an end-effector-based robot system, only a few parts of the
upper-limb, usually hand or wrist, are attached to the robot; movements are guided by
the end-effector. There's no direct relationship between the robot's joints and the
human body joints.

---

* Corresponding author.

C.-Y. Su, S. Rakheja, H. Liu (Eds.): ICIRA 2012, Part II, LNAI 7507, pp. 96–102, 2012.
© Springer-Verlag Berlin Heidelberg 2012

However, when using an exoskeleton robot, which is a wearable bionic device originally used for military to enhance strength and endurance of soldiers, every active parts of the upper-limb, such as hand, forearm and upper-arm, can be attached to the robot. The exoskeleton robot can guide movements of all these parts thus providing determined and comfortable assistance to every segment of the upper-limb[3][4].

In this paper, an exoskeleton robot for upper-limb rehabilitation is developed.

2   Design of the Mechanical Structure of an Exoskeleton Rehabilitation Robot

The human upper limb has numbers of different joints, and its physical movement is very flexible. All these bring considerable difficulties for the design of the exoskeleton robot.

Hocoma, a Swiss company, has developed an exoskeleton robot named ArmeoSpring, which can assist human upper-limb for 5 degrees of freedom of movement: shoulder flexion/extension, shoulder abduction/adduction, shoulder internal rotation/external rotation, elbow flexion/extension and forearm supination/pronation. The system also has gravity compensation, could be used by patients with incomplete paralysis or paresis for active motion training [5].

This paper has developed an exoskeleton rehabilitation robot to assist human upper-limb for 7 degrees of freedom of movement: shoulder flexion/extension, shoulder abduction/adduction, shoulder internal rotation/external rotation, elbow flexion/extension, forearm supination/pronation, wrist extension/flexion and wrist ulnar deviation/radial deviation. And all these anatomical axes are aligned with robot axes.

During the design of the exoskeleton, firstly, a certain degree of simplification is made to the model of every joint.

The shoulder joint is modeled as a center fixed ball-and-socket joint which has 3DOF. The elbow is modeled as a compound joint which allows 1DOF of the elbow and 1DOF of the forearm. The wrist joint is modeled as an elliptic joint which possesses 2DOF; the slight offset of the rotational axes of the flexion/extension and the radial/ulnar deviation is ignored.

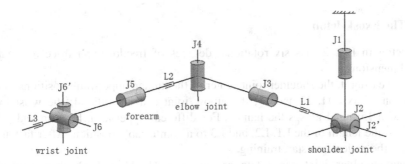

Fig. 1. Human upper-limb joints model

We followed the idea that the robot axes coaxial with the anatomical axes to design the robot. So as long as we modeled the human upper-limb joints, we can determine the robot's joints model. Take the right arm as an example, we can see the model we built in Fig. 1. The correspondences between model DOF and human upper-limb DOF are showed in TABLE I.

Table 1. The correspondences between model DOF and human upper-limb DOF

Joints	Human upper-limb DOF	Model DOF
Shoulder	flexion/extension	J2
	abduction/adduction	J2'
	internal rotation/external rotation	J3
Elbow	flexion/extension	J4
Forearm	supination/pronation	J5
Wrist	extension/flexion	J6
	ulnar deviation/radial deviation	J6'

In the model, J2 and J2' are two forms of one same axis. That is to say, axis J2 and J2' can convert to each other when axis J1 rotates to different angles,. The shoulder joint can perform flexion/extension around axis J2, and abduction/adduction around axis J2'. Similarly, J6 and J6' are two forms of one axis when axis J5 rotates to different angles.

In addition, there are three length adjustable to meet specific parts of different limb sizes: upper-arm length adjustment (L1), forearm length adjustment (L2) and palm length adjustment (L3).

3   Development of Exoskeleton Rehabilitation Robot

Following the design idea in Section 2, we developed a rehabilitation robot which includes exoskeleton, chassis and seat, gravity compensation and data acquisition. The following will be the design and implementation of these parts described in detail.

3.1   The Exoskeleton

Exoskeleton in Fig. 2, has six rotational degrees of freedom and three adjustable length dimensions.

When wearing it, the shoulder joint center of the human upper-limb positions to the intersection of axis J1, J2 and J3; the elbow joint coaxial with J4; the wrist joint coaxial with J5; hand grasps the handle. For different upper-arm, forearm and palm size, adjust the length of the L1, L2, and L3 to a comfortable position. After fastening the straps, the patient can start training.

Human shoulder joint can rotate around axis J1, J2 and J3, three mutually perpendicular axes. In this way, the shoulder would perform flexion/extension around axis J2, and, after rotating appropriate degrees around axis J1, would also perform abduction/adduction around axis J2. Moreover, it can rotate around axis J3 to perform internal rotation/external rotation. Human elbow joint can rotate around axis J4 to perform flexion/extension. Human forearm can rotate around axis J6 to perform supination/pronation. When forearm rotate around axis J6 to appropriate positions, the wrist joint would rotate around axis J5 to perform flexion/extension or ulnar deviation/radial deviation separately. The structure axis J6 can finish the extension and flexion movement in the wrist, so the data acquisition card can gain the data from the wrist and it also can train the wrist of the patients.

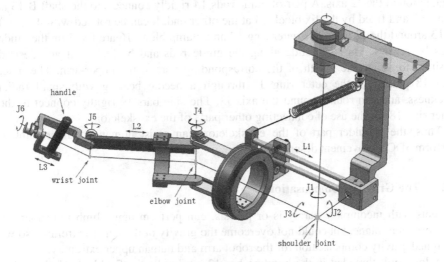

Fig. 2. Schematic diagram of exoskeleton

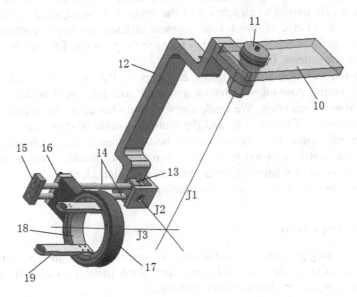

Fig. 3. Shoulder part of the exoskeleton. 10 base board, 11 shaft A, 12 bending bar, 13 shaft B, 14 guide rods, 15 fix block, 16 clamp block, 17 outer ring, 18 inner ring, 19 side bars.

The shoulder part (Fig. 3) of the exoskeleton will be given a detailed description now.

The shaft A 11 links with the base board 10 through a thrust bearing and a deep groove ball bearings, and can rotate around the axis J1. The two bearings withstand the axial load and radial load respectively. The bending bar 12 rigidly connects to the bottom of shaft A 11 and can be rotated with the shaft A 11 around the J1 axis. The shaft B 13 links with bending bar 12 by a pair of deep groove ball bearings and can rotate around the J2 axis. A pair of guide rods 14 rigidly connects to the shaft B 13 at one end, and fixed by the fix block 15 at the other end. It can be rotated with the shaft B 13 around the J2 axis. The outer ring 17 and clamp block 16 are fixed on the guide rods by screws. They can slide along the guide rods and be locked at any desired position to adjust the length of the corresponding part of the upper-arm. The inner ring 18 placed in the outer ring 17 through a needle bearing with small radial thickness, and can rotate around the axis J3. The side bars 19 rigidly connect to the inner ring 18 for the use of connecting other parts of the exoskeleton.

Thus, the shoulder part of the exoskeleton can assist human shoulder joint to perform 3DOF movement described above.

3.2   The Gravity Compensation

Patients with incomplete paralysis or paresis, can perform upper-limb movement in the horizontal plane, but could not overcome the gravity of the upper extremity, so we designed gravity compensation for the robot arm and human upper extremity.

A long bolt threaded in the bending bar 12, and pulls the fix block 15 through a tension spring, by stretching the spring to compensate gravity of the robot arm and human upper extremity. The elongation of the spring can be adjusted by the bolt, in order to provide a range of stretch force to meet different training requirements. The proposed design is an actual useful design because the position of the spring is always offside from the patients. Chassis and seat

Exoskeleton requires a solid frame as support. Patients accept rehabilitation training by sitting position, so chassis and rack locations need to have a stable relationship with each other. We made the seat and chassis structure as a whole to ensure the stability of the chassis, and the mutual position of chassis and seat. Base board 10 rigidly connects to the chassis by bolts to support the whole exoskeleton. Just sit on the seat in appropriate location to make the shoulder joint center of the human position to the intersection of axis J1, J2 and J3, and then wearing the exoskeleton robot, a patient can perform training.

3.3   Data Acquisition

During the training process, we need to obtain the robot posture information of each joint in order to know the state of human upper-limb motion, so each rotation axis equipped with an angular displacement transducer.

A special structure is designed to install the angular displacement transducer for Axis J3, shown in Figure 4. The gear shaft 20 links with the outer ring 17 through a pair of deep groove ball bearings, one end of it rigidly connects to the shaft of the transducer 21 and the other end of it rigidly connects to the small gear 23 which meshes with the large gear 24. The large gear 24 rigidly connects to the inner ring 18 by screws. The shell of the transducer 22 is rigidly connected to the transducer installation base 21 which rigidly connects to the outer ring 17 by screws. Thus, the rotational angle of inner ring 18 will be passed to the gear shaft 20, in order to measure the rotational angle information of inner ring 18 relative to outer ring 17.

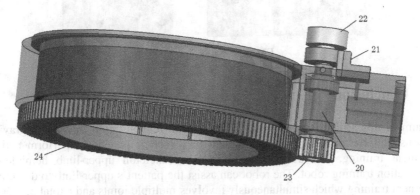

Fig. 4. Transducer installation for axis J3. 20 gear shaft, 21 transducer installation base, 22 transducer, 23 small gear, 24 large gear.

Fig. 5 shows the schematic diagram of the robot and Fig. 6 shows the robot prototype.

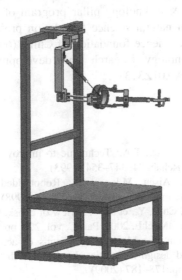

Fig. 5. A shematic diagram of the robot

Fig. 6. Robot prototype

4   Conclusion

The aim of this article is to provide an upper-limb rehabilitation robot with gravity compensation for patients with incomplete paralysis or paresis to perform active movement training. We developed a 6DOF exoskeleton upper-limb hemiplegic rehabilitation training robot. The robot can assist the patient's upper-limb to do active movement training which simultaneously involves multiple joints and a total of 7DOF of human upper-limb. The robot can enrich rehabilitation means and improve the efficiency of training.

Furthermore, software with the virtual reality training system can be combined to enhance paralysis rehabilitation.

Acknowledgment. The work described in this paper was supported by Key projects from the national science & technology pillar program of China (2009BAI71B06), Major program of national natural science foundation project of China (61190124, 61190120), National nature science foundation of China (60873131) and The project from national high technology research and development program of China （2006AA01Z310, 2009AA01Z313）.

References

1. Taub, E., Miller, N.E., Novack, T.A.: Technique to improve chronic motor deficit after stroke. Arch. Phys. Med. Rehab. 74, 347–354 (1993)
2. Krebs, H.I., Hogan, N., Aisen, M.L., et al.: Robot-aided neurorehabilitation. IEEE Transactions on Rehabilitation Engineering 6(1), 75–87 (1998)
3. Yang, C.-J., Zhang, J.-F., Chen, Y., et al.: A review of exoskeleton-type systems and their key technologies. In: Proc. IMechE. 2008, Part C, vol. 222, pp. 1599–1612 (2008)
4. Gopura, R.A.R.C., Kiguchi, K.: Mechanical designs of active upper-limb exoskeleton robots state-of-the-art and design difficulties. In: IEEE 11th International Conference on Rehabilitation Robotics, pp. 178–187 (2009)
5. http://www.hocoma.com/

Dynamic Optimization with a New Performance Index for a 2-DoF Translational Parallel Manipulator

Gang Zhang, PinKuan Liu, and Han Ding

State Key Laboratory of Mechanical System and Vibration, School of Mechanical Engineering,
Shanghai Jiaotong University, Shanghai 200240, China
{zgrobot,pkliu,hding}@sjtu.edu.cn

Abstract. The dynamic analysis and optimization problem of a 2-DoF Translational Parallel Manipulator (TPM) is addressed in this paper. Based on the principle of virtual work and the concept of link Jacobian matrix, the explicit expressions of the dynamic model of the 2-DoF TPM in the global task space are derived. Using the dynamic model, a global and comprehensive dynamic performance index (GCDPI) is proposed to evaluate the manipulator capabilities in terms of dynamic manipulability and dexterity in the prescribed task space. The dynamic optimization problem, which aims at providing the largest, the most isotropic and the most uniform dynamic manipulability of the 2-DoF TPM in the task space, is formulated as the minimization of GCDPI subjected to a set of appropriate constraints. Optimization results showed that the dynamic manipulability of the 2-DoF TPM with optimized kinematic and inertial parameters improves greatly in the prescribed task space. The dynamic equations are also incorporated in the hardware in the loop simulation of the 2-DoF TPM and experimental results show the tracking errors of the linear motor can be improved greatly when a nonlinear computed torque feedforward controller is implemented in addition to the cascade position controller.

Keywords: translational parallel manipulator, operational space formulation, global and comprehensive dynamic performance index (GCDPI), hardware in the loop simulation (HILS).

1 Introduction

Dynamic analysis plays an important role in the control and simulation of parallel manipulators. In the literature, there are mainly three formulations used in the dynamic analysis of parallel manipulators: Newton-Euler (N-E) formulation, Lagrangian formulation and the principle of virtual work. The N-E formulation [1], requiring the equations of motion to be written once for each body of a manipulator, leads to a relatively large system of equations expressed in terms of the constraint forces, resulting poor computational efficiency. Lagrangian formulation [2-3] provides a well analytical and orderly structure, which is better for the derivation of closed-loop dynamic equations used for control purpose. However, due to the presence of passive and non-actuated joints in parallel manipulators, explicit relations between these coordinates have to be calculated, leading to complex dynamic

C.-Y. Su, S. Rakheja, H. Liu (Eds.): ICIRA 2012, Part II, LNAI 7507, pp. 103–115, 2012.

equations. Unlike the traditional N-E and Lagrangian formulation, the principle of virtual work [4-5], which does not require considering the constraint forces, have been used to systematically derive a minimum set of equations of motion for parallel manipulators.

Dynamic performance is one of the most significant factors in the development of fast and accurate robotic manipulators. Several dynamic performance indices have been presented for dynamic optimization of robotic manipulators. Asada [6] proposed the concept of "generalized inertia ellipsoid" (GIE) to represent the capability of velocity change of the end-effector. However, the GIE did not relate actual actuator force input to end-effector accelerations. Yoshikawa [7] extended the concept of kinematic manipulability and defined "dynamic manipulability ellipsoid" (DME) on the basis of the relationship between joint driving force and acceleration of the end-effector to quantify the arbitrariness of changing the acceleration under the constraint of the joint driving force. Khatib and Burdick [8] defined the "isotropic acceleration", which is the largest, most isotropic and most uniform bounds on the magnitude of end-effector acceleration at both low and high velocities. Ding et al. [9] proposed "comprehensive dynamic performance index" (CDPI) for evaluating dynamic merit and developed a procedure for the optimization of dynamic performance for redundant manipulators in the worse case. Ma and Angeles [10] defined the "dynamic isotropy" and proposed the "dynamic condition index" to measure the dynamic coupling and numerical stability of the generalized inertia matrix of manipulators. Doty et al. [11] proposed the wretch ellipsoid, the twist ellipsoid and the dynamics frame-acceleration ellipsoid to deal with the non-homogeneity issues between properties governing linear and angular motions. All these tools developed in previous works are based on the choice of kinematic and inertial parameters of manipulators to meet the proposed dynamic performance indices.

In this paper, the dynamic analysis and optimization problem of a 2-DoF translational parallel manipulator[12] is investigated. Firstly, the geometric description of the 2-DoF TPM is given in Section 2. Then, the dynamic analysis of the 2-DoF TPM is performed and explicit expressions of the dynamic model in the global task workspace are derived in section 3. Moreover, based on the dynamic model in the operational space, a global and comprehensive dynamic performance index (GCDPI) is proposed in section 4 to evaluate the manipulator capabilities in terms of dynamic manipulability, dexterity and isotropy in the prescribed task workspace. The dynamic optimization problem is then formulated as the minimization of the GCDPI subjected to a set of appropriate constraints. Afterwards, optimization results are presented and hardware in the loop simulation results are given to validate the derived dynamic model in Section 5. Conclusions are drawn in section 6.

2   System Description of the 2-DoF TPM

The 2-DoF translational parallel manipulator investigated in this paper is shown in Figs.1. It is composed of a moving platform, a fixed base, two sliders and two kinematic chains. The two sliders are parallel configured and horizontally mounted on the fixed base. The moving platform is connected to the sliders by two identical kinematic chains, each containing a parallelogram linkage ($P_1 P_2 S_2 S_1$ and $P_3 P_4 S_4 S_3$).

Since the parallelogram linkage can keep the moving platform parallel to the slider, the output motion of the TPM is a 2-DoF rigid translation of the moving platform with respect to the fixed base. As a result, the 2-DoF TPM can be denoted as 2- P(Pa), where P is the actuated prismatic joint and Pa stands for the planar parallelogram linkage. From Fig.1, it can be seen that the 2-DoF TPM is over-constrained since only one parallelogram is sufficient to keep the moving platform parallel to the fixed base. The adoption of over-constrained mechanism is to enable the static and dynamic symmetry and improve the stiffness in the direction normal to the plane of motion. In order to improve the dynamic performance and positioning precision of the 2-DoF TPM, each slider is directly driven by a permanent magnet synchronous linear motor (PMSLM), in which the coil windings are mounted on the slider and the permanent magnets are fixed horizontally on the fixed base as a stator. Each PMSLM is equipped with an optical linear scale of sub-micrometer resolution for displacement measurement. By integrating the advantages of parallel mechanisms and direct drive technology, the over-constrained 2-DoF TPM can provide high-speed and high-precision 2-DoF translational motions in a plane.

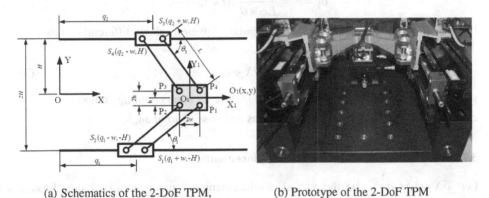

(a) Schematics of the 2-DoF TPM,   (b) Prototype of the 2-DoF TPM

Fig. 1. Schematic model and prototype of the 2-DoF translational parallel manipulator

3 Dynamic Analysis

In this section, the principle of virtual work is applied to derive the governing equation in the task workspace for the 2-DoF TPM. First, the kinematic equations of the 2-DoF TPM are derived. Based on the principle of virtual work and the concept of link Jacobian matrix, the dynamic equations of the 2-DoF TPM in the global task workspace are derived.

3.1 Kinematic Equations of the 2-DoF TPM

As shown in Figs.1, a reference coordinate system O-XY is fixed on the fixed base and a body coordinate system $O_1 - X_1 Y_1$ is rigidly attached to the geometric center of the moving platform. The distance between the two parallel configured sliders is $2H$, the dimension of the moving platform is $2w \times 2h$ and the length of links of the parallelogram is L. $q = [q_1, q_2]^T$ is the vector of joint space coordinates, where q_1 and q_2 are the displacements of linear motors. $X = [x, y]^T$ is chosen as the generalized coordinates of the 2-DoF TPM, where (x, y) is the coordinates of the origin O_1 with respect to the reference coordinate system O-XY. $\theta = [\theta_1, \theta_2, \theta_3, \theta_4]^T$ is the vector of passive joint angles of the link with $\theta_1 = \theta_2$ and $\theta_3 = \theta_4$.

If $x \neq q_1$ and $x \neq q_2$, the inverse kinematics can be written as

$$\begin{bmatrix} \dot{q}_1 \\ \dot{q}_2 \end{bmatrix} = \begin{bmatrix} 1 & \tan\theta_1 \\ 1 & \tan\theta_3 \end{bmatrix} \begin{bmatrix} \dot{x} \\ \dot{y} \end{bmatrix} \tag{1}$$

where $J = \begin{bmatrix} 1 & \tan\theta_1 \\ 1 & \tan\theta_3 \end{bmatrix}$ is the Jacobian matrix of the 2-DoF TPM.

From Equations(1), the angular velocities of the passive joint can be written as

$$\omega_i = \dot{\theta}_i = \frac{\dot{y}}{L\cos\theta_i}, (i = 1, \cdots, 4). \tag{2}$$

If the inverse Jacobian matrix J is non-singular, Equation can be differentiated to obtain the joint space acceleration, i.e.,

$$\ddot{q} = J\ddot{X} + C_0 \tag{3}$$

where $C_0 = [\dot{y}^2 / L\cos^3\theta, \dot{y}^2 / L\cos^3\theta_3]^T$ is the acceleration coupling component expressed in terms of generalized velocities and passive joint angles.

3.2   Computation of the Virtual Displacements

Let $\delta X = (\delta x, \delta y)^T$ be the virtual displacements of the generalized coordinates. From Equation(1), the virtual displacements of the actuated joints and the links of the parallelogram can be computed, i.e.,

$$\delta q = J\delta X, \delta\theta_i = \frac{E}{L\cos\theta_i}\delta X, (i = 1, \cdots, 4). \tag{4}$$

where $\delta q = (\delta q_1, \delta q_2)^T$, $E = |0 \quad 1|$ and $\delta\theta = (\delta\theta_1, \delta\theta_2, \delta\theta_3, \delta\theta_4)^T$.

Assuming that the links of the parallelogram are straight beams with the same cross section and the mass center of the link is at the midpoint of the link, from Fig. 1 (a), the coordinates of the mass center of link S_iP_i can be easily calculated,

$$\begin{bmatrix} x_i \\ y_i \end{bmatrix} = \begin{bmatrix} x - (-1)^i w - \dfrac{L}{2}\cos\theta_i \\ y - h - \dfrac{L}{2}\sin\theta_i \end{bmatrix}, i = 1, 2; \begin{bmatrix} x_i \\ y_i \end{bmatrix} = \begin{bmatrix} x - (-1)^i w - \dfrac{L}{2}\cos\theta_i \\ y + h - \dfrac{L}{2}\sin\theta_i \end{bmatrix}, i = 3, 4. \tag{5}$$

The virtual displacement of the center of mass of link S_iP_i is related to the virtual displacements of the generalized coordinates by the link Jacobian matrix J_i, i.e.,

$$\delta X_i = J_i \delta X, J_i = \begin{bmatrix} 1 & 0.5\tan\theta_i \\ 0 & 0.5 \\ 0 & 1/L\cos\theta_i \end{bmatrix}, (i=1,\cdots,4,). \tag{6}$$

where $\delta X_i = [\delta x_i, \delta y_i, \delta\theta_i]^T$, J_i is the link Jacobian matrix of i-th link.

3.3   Applied and Inertial Wrenches

From Equation(6), the acceleration of the mass center of link $S_iP_i(i=1,\cdots,4)$ can be easily computed,

$$\ddot{X}_i = J_i\ddot{X} + C_i, i = 1,\cdots,4 \tag{7}$$

where $\quad \ddot{X}_i = \begin{bmatrix} \ddot{x}_1 \\ \ddot{y}_i \\ \ddot{\theta}_i \end{bmatrix}, C_i = \begin{bmatrix} \dot{y}^2/2L\cos^3\theta_i \\ 0 \\ \dot{y}^2\sin\theta_i/L^2\cos^3\theta_i \end{bmatrix}.$

Thus, the resultant of applied and inertial forces exerted at the center of mass of the link can be obtained as

$$F_i = \begin{bmatrix} \hat{f}_i \\ \hat{n}_i \end{bmatrix} = \begin{bmatrix} -m_i\ddot{x}_i \\ -m_i\ddot{y}_i \\ -I_{oi}\ddot{\theta}_i - \omega_i \times (I_{oi}\omega_i) \end{bmatrix}, i=1,\cdots,4. \tag{8}$$

where $\hat{f}_i$ and $\hat{n}_i$ are the inertial forces and torques acting at the center of mass of link S_iP_i, m_i is the mass of the i-th link and $I_{oi} = R_iI_iR_i^T$, I_i is the inertia tensor of i-th link with the axis normal to the plane of motion about its center of mass, R_i is the rotation matrix of the i-th $(i=1,\cdots,4)$ link.

Since the gravitational force is applied normally to the plane of motions and the moving platform has no rotational movement, the resultant applied and inertial forces exerted at the center of mass of the moving platform can be obtained as

$$F_p = \begin{bmatrix} \hat{f}_p \\ \hat{n}_p \end{bmatrix} = \begin{bmatrix} f_p - m_p\ddot{X} \\ n_p \end{bmatrix} \tag{9}$$

where m_p is the mass of the moving platform, f_p, n_p are the external forces and moments exerted at the center of mass of the moving platform.

3.4   Dynamic Equations of Motion in the Global Task Space

Let $\tau_i(i=1,2)$ be the actuating forces of the linear motors, the principle of virtual work can be stated as

$$\delta q^T\tau + \delta X^T f_p = \delta X^T m_p\ddot{X} + \sum_{i=1}^{2}\delta q_i^T m_S\ddot{q}_i + \sum_{i=1}^{4}\delta X_i^T F_i \tag{10}$$

where m_s is the mass of the slider, which includes the mass of the coil winding on the linear motors. Note that the input forces and inertial forces have been isolated applied at the center of the moving platform for the convenience of dynamic analysis.

Substituting Equations(6) and (7) into Equation(10), one can yield

$$J^T \tau + f_P = M\ddot{X} + C, \tag{11}$$

where

$$M = J^T M_s J + M_P + \sum_{i=1}^{4} J_i^T M_i J_i, M_s = \begin{bmatrix} m_s & 0 \\ 0 & m_s \end{bmatrix}, M_P = \begin{bmatrix} m_P & 0 \\ 0 & m_P \end{bmatrix},$$

$$M_i = \begin{bmatrix} m_i & 0 & 0 \\ 0 & m_i & 0 \\ 0 & 0 & I_i \end{bmatrix}, C = J^T M_s C_0 + \sum_{i=1}^{4} J_i^T M_i C_i.$$

If the Jacobian matrix J is nonsingular, the dynamic equations of motion in the operational space can be determined by the inverse transpose of the Jacobian matrix

$$\tau = J^{-T}(M\ddot{X} + C - f_P). \tag{12}$$

4   Dynamic Optimization

The objective of dynamic optimization is to determine a set of geometric and inertial parameters of the 2-DoF TPM with respect to desired dynamic performance indices. In this section, a global and comprehensive dynamic performance index (GCDPI) is proposed and the dynamic optimization problem is formulated as the minimization of the GCDPI subjected to a set of appropriate constraints.

4.1   Dynamic Performance Analysis

The dynamic performance of a parallel manipulator is strongly dependent on the inertial and acceleration characteristics of the mechanism. Since both GIE [6] and DME [7] are based on the relationship between the accelerations of the end-effector in the task workspace and the generalized input forces/torques in the joint space, the input force of the linear motors in Equations (12) can be simplified by neglecting the nonlinear inertial and Coriolis forces,

$$\tau \approx J^{-T} M \ddot{X} \tag{13}$$

where $J^{-T}M$ is the generalized inertia matrix of the 2-DoF TPM.

The dynamic manipulability measure, which is the product of the singular values of the generalized mass matrix, is proportional to the volume of the dynamic manipulability ellipsoid in the task workspace. It is an effective tool to measure the maximum and minimum accelerations of the 2-DoF TPM, which is defined as [7]

$$\eta_1 = \left| \frac{\det J}{\det M} \right| \tag{14}$$

where det() is the determinant of matrix. The smaller the dynamic manipulability measure, the higher the end-effector's acceleration in the task workspace. The distribution of dynamic manipulability measure of the 2-DoF TPM is symmetrical with the X-Axis and the end-effector has higher acceleration and better dynamic performance if the moving platform is close to the X-Axis in the task workspace.

When the dynamic manipulability performance in different directions of the task workspace is considered, the condition number of the generalized mass matrix should be considered. The dynamic dexterity index (κ_D), which is configuration dependent, is defined on the basis of the condition number of the generalized inertia matrix [11],

$$1 \leq \kappa_D = \frac{\sigma_{max}}{\sigma_{min}} \leq \infty, \tag{15}$$

where σ_{max} and σ_{min} are the maximum and minimum singular values of the generalized inertia matrix and $1,\infty$ correspond to the isotropic and singular configuration, respectively. In order to obtain global dynamic performance measure of the parallel manipulator, global conditioning index (GCI) [13] should be used to assess the distribution of dynamic dexterity index over the whole workspace. Similar to the global dexterity measure proposed in [14], a global dynamic conditioning index (GDDI) is defined to describe the isotropy of the dynamic manipulability in the prescribed task workspace , which is defined as

$$1 \leq \eta_2 = \frac{\int_{W_t} \kappa_D dw_t}{\int_{W_t} dw_t} \leq \infty \tag{16}$$

where W_t is the prescribed task workspace of the 2-DoF TPM in which the dynamic performance is evaluated. Since GDCI is incapable of describing the deviation of the maximum and minimum conditioning number of the generalized mass matrix, another dynamic conditioning index, denoted by η_3 , is defined to describe the uniformity of the dynamic manipulability in the prescribed task workspace of the 2-DoF TPM,

$$1 \leq \eta_3 = \frac{\max(\kappa_D)}{\min(\kappa_D)} \leq \infty \tag{17}$$

where $\max(\kappa_D)$ and $\min(\kappa_D)$ represent the maximum and minimum value of κ_D in the task workspace. Thus, the global and comprehensive dynamic performance index (GCDPI) can be defined as

$$\eta_D = \sqrt{(w_1\eta_1)^2 + (w_2\eta_2)^2 + (w_3\eta_3)^2} \tag{18}$$

where $w_i \neq 0, (i = 1, \cdots, 3)$ are the weights being placed upon different performance indices. This dynamic performance index aims at providing the largest, most isotropic and most uniform dynamic manipulability capacity of the 2-DoF TPM in the prescribed task workspace.

4.2   Constraints

To avoid singularity and get better force transmission behaviors, the workspace index (*WI*) used in the kinematic optimization [12] is adopted as the constraint in the dynamic optimization, which is stated as

$$1 \leq WI = \frac{y_{\max}}{y_w} \leq \infty \tag{19}$$

As illustrated in Fig.2, $y_{\max}$ and y_w represent the reachable workspace and the prescribed task workspace along the Y-axis.

In order to keep high stiffness and acceptable positioning accuracy, the static deflection δ_z of the link due to the weight of the links in the parallelogram and moving platform should be smaller than $\delta_{\max}$. Using the method of superposition, the deflection of the link at the point of P_i can be calculated as

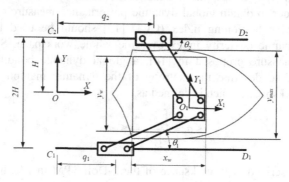

Fig. 2. Reachable workspace and prescribed task workspace of the 2-DoF TPM

$$\delta_z = \frac{m_p g L^3}{12 EI} + \frac{m_i g L^3}{8 EI} \tag{20}$$

where g is the Gravitational acceleration, E and I are the Young's Modulus and Moment of Inertia of the link $S_i P_i$.

From the above discussion, the dynamic optimization problem of the 2-DoF TPM can be generalized as the minimization of an objective function under nonlinear equality and inequality constraints. It can be formulated as follows:

To find a set of design variables $[x_1, x_2, x_3, x_4, x_5]^T \in \mathbb{R}^5$ such that

$$\min \ \eta_D$$

Subject to

$$15° \leq |\theta_i(X,q)| \leq 75° \quad i = 1, \cdots, 4$$

$$1 \leq WI \leq 1.5$$

$$\delta_z \leq \delta_{\max}$$

$$x_i \in [x_{i,\min}, x_{i,\max}] \quad i = 1, \cdots, 5$$

$$\forall (x, y) \in (x_w, y_w)$$

5   Simulation and Experimental Results

5.1   Optimization Results

Based on the dynamic model derived in the above sections, a computer program is developed in MATLAB/Simulink®. The nonlinear dynamic optimization is solved by the Sequential Quadratic Programming (SQP) algorithm available in the MATLAB® Optimization toolbox with η_i calculated by

$$\eta_1 = \frac{\max(w_{D,ij})}{\min(w_{D,ij})}, \quad \eta_2 = \frac{1}{M \times N} \sum_{i=1}^{M} \sum_{j=1}^{N} \kappa_{D,ij}, \quad \eta_3 = \frac{\max(\kappa_{D,ij})}{\min(\kappa_{D,ij})}, \tag{21}$$

where $w_{D,ij}$ and $K_{D,ij}$ are the values of dynamic manipulability measure and condition number of the generalized mass matrix calculated at node (i,j) of $(M-1) \times (N-1)$ equally meshed task workspace. Note that in Equation (21), the dynamic manipulability measure has been normalized and the ratio between the maximum and minimum value of the dynamic manipulability measure has been used in the process of dynamic optimization.

Since all the dynamic performance indices have the same optimum value of 1, which corresponds to isotropic and uniform dynamic manipulability of the 2-DoF TPM, the weights placed upon different performance indices in Eq.(21) are all set to unity in the process of dynamic optimization.

The investigated 2-DoF TPM is designed to have a prescribed task workspace $x_w \times y_w = 70mm \times 70mm$ with submicron accuracy. The design variables of the dynamic optimization problem and the optimization results are listed in Table.2. In order to avoid local optimization values, a set of original values has been used in the optimization process and the maximum number of the iterations taken is set to 1000, the termination tolerance on the design variables x are all set to 1exp(-12).

Table 1. Original values and optimized results of parameter variables of the 2-DoF TPM

Design variables	Content	Unit	Original values	Optimized results
x_1	H-h	m	0.100	0.0785
x_2	L	m	0.141	0.1679
x_3	m_S	kg	1.5	1.3175
x_4	m_P	kg	1.2	1.3175
x_5	m_i	kg	0.5	0.3646

Fig.3(a) shows the dynamic manipulability ellipsoids (DME) of the 2-DoF TPM with original geometric and inertial values. It can be seen that the DME is symmetric about the X-Axis and the shape of the DME changes rapidly from a perfect circle to a long and narrow ellipsoid when the platform moves away from the X-Axis.

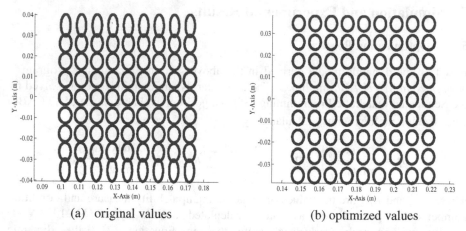

(a) original values   (b) optimized values

Fig. 3. Distribution of DME with original and optimized geometric and inertial values

Fig.3(b) shows the dynamic manipulability ellipsoid of the 2-DoF TPM with optimized geometric and inertial values. It can be seen that the area of the DME is larger than the one with original values. The DME is uniform even at the boundary of the prescribed task workspace, that is, the dynamic manipulability of the optimized mechanism is more isotropic and more uniform than the one with original geometric and inertial values.

The optimized geometric and inertial results have been applied to the development of a 2-DoF TPM (Fig.1 b) in the laboratory of Shanghai Jiaotong University for the industrial applications requiring high-speed and high-precision motions.

5.2   Hardware in the Loop Simulation

Base on the kinematic and dynamic equations of the 2-DoF TPM, a cascade PI/PI controller with velocity/acceleration feedforward compensation and its combination with computed torque feedforward compensation has been developed. The block diagram of the controller is shown in Figure.4, in which K_{VF} is the velocity feedforward gain, τ_{ffc} is the feedforward computed torques and K_E is the force constant of linear motors.

The primary structure of the PI/PI cascade position controller is simple tuning. The PI/PI cascade controller is augmented by velocity (VFC) feedforward compensation, which is used to improve the command response of the velocity without producing stability problems. The gains of velocity feedforward controller are typically values of 0.8-0.95, which can be tuned experimentally.

Because of the direct drive nature of the 2-DoF TPM, the robot nonlinear dynamic cannot be neglected for controller design purpose. This is particularly true in the case where high speed and high precision motions are requested. Based on the estimated dynamic model in the global task workspace, a feedforward of computed torques controller (CTC) can be used to compensate for the nonlinear dynamic forces

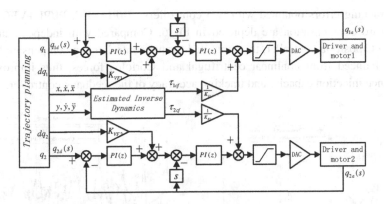

Fig. 4. PI/PI+VFC/AFC controller with computed feedforward compensation

(including Coriolos and centrifugal) along the prescribed trajectory in the task space, the computed forces of the linear motors can be stated as

$$\tau_{ffc} = \hat{J}^{-T}(\hat{M}\ddot{X} + \hat{C} - \hat{f}_P). \tag{22}$$

where the caret ($\wedge$) refers to the estimated values for the inverse dynamic equations.

The controller is implemented on the dSPACE real-time control platform, a suitable platform for the hardware in the loop simulation (HILS) [15]. All the parameters in the proposed controllers can be tuned experimentally. The prescribed trajectory in the simulation is that the moving platform translates along a circle of radius 30mm in the task space with predefined speed. The trajectory in the hardware in the loop simulation can be expressed as

$$x = \sqrt{L^2 - (H - h)^2} + 0.03\cos\omega t, \, y = 0.03\sin\omega t, (0 < \omega t < 2\pi). \tag{23}$$

The trajectory is chosen to be simple and relatively slow but capable of providing insight into the effect of dynamic compensation. The generalized input forces of the linear motors are plotted in Fig.5, where τ_i represent the driving forces of linear motor respectively.

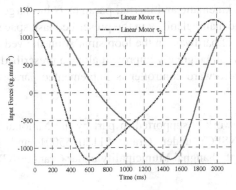

Fig. 5. The generalized input forces of linear motors versus time in HILS

The tracking errors obtained with two controllers: PI/PI+VFC, PI/PI +VFC+CTC feedforward compensation are depicted in Fig.6. Compared with independent joint PI/PI+VFC position controller, the computed torque controller can compensate for the impacts induced from nonlinear centrifugal and Coriolos forces, thus improve the disturbance injection capacity and tracking accuracy of the feedback controller.

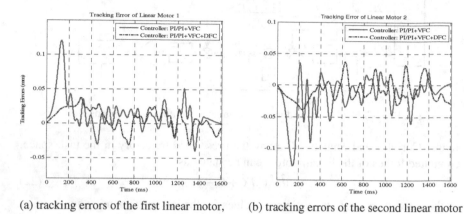

(a) tracking errors of the first linear motor,   (b) tracking errors of the second linear motor

Fig. 6. Tracking errors of the linear motors with different controllers

6 Conclusions

In this paper, the dynamic analysis and optimization problem of a 2-DoF TPM is investigated. The following conclusions can be drawn:

(1)Based on kinematic analysis and the principle of virtual work, explicit expressions of the dynamics for the 2-DoF TPM in the global task space were derived.

(2)A global and comprehensive dynamic performance index was proposed and a dynamic optimization problem was formulated, simulation results show that the 2-DoF TPM with optimized kinematic and inertial parameters has larger, more isotropic and more uniform dynamic manipulability in the prescribed task space.

(3)Experimental results of hardware in the loop simulation showed that the tracking errors of the linear motors can be greatly improved along a prescribed trajectory when a nonlinear computed feedforward controller is implemented parallel to the cascade position controller.

Acknowledgement. This work is supported in part by the National Natural Science Foundation of China (NSFC) under Grant 51120155001 and the Science & Technology Commission of Shanghai Municipality under Grant 09JC1408300.

References

1. Dasgupta, B., Mruthyunjaya, T.S.: A Newton-Euler formulation for the inverse dynamics of the Stewart platform manipulator. Mechanism and Machine Theory 33(8), 1135–1152 (1998)
2. Lee, K.-M., Shah, D.K.: Dynamic Analysis of a Three-Degrees-of-Freedom in-Parallel Actuated Manipulator. IEEE Journal of Robotics and Automation 4(3), 361–367 (1988)
3. Yiu, Y.K., et al.: On the dynamics of parallel manipulators (2001)
4. Wang, J., Gosselin, C.M.: A new approach for the dynamic analysis of parallel manipulators. Multibody System Dynamics 2(3), 317–334 (1998)
5. Tsai, L.W.: Solving the inverse dynamics of a Stewart-Gough manipulator by the principle of virtual work. Journal of Mechanical Design, Transactions of the ASME 122(1), 3–9 (2000)
6. Asada, H.: Geometrical Representation of Manipulator Dynamics and Its Application to Arm Design. Journal of Dynamic Systems, Measurement and Control, Transactions of the ASME 105(3), 131–135 (1983)
7. Yoshikawa, T.: Dynamic Manipulability of Robot Manipulators. Journal of Robotic Systems 2(1), 113–124 (1985)
8. Khatib, O., Burdick, J.: Dynamic Optimization in Manipulator Design: The Operational Space Formulation (1985)
9. Ding, H., Li, Y.F., Tso, S.K.: Dynamic optimization of redundant manipulators in worst case using recurrent neural networks. Mechanism and Machine Theory 35(1), 55–70 (2000)
10. Ma, O., Angeles, J.: The concept of dynamic isotropy and its applications to inverse kinematics and trajectory planning, pp. 481–486 (1990)
11. Doty, K.L., et al.: Robot manipulability. IEEE Transactions on Robotics and Automation 11(3), 462–468 (1995)
12. Zhang, G., Liu, P., Ding, H.: Optimal Kinematic Design of a 2-DoF Translational Parallel Manipulator with High Speed and High Precision. In: Jeschke, S., Liu, H., Schilberg, D. (eds.) ICIRA 2011, Part I. LNCS, vol. 7101, pp. 445–454. Springer, Heidelberg (2011)
13. Gosselin, C., Angeles, J.: Global performance index for the kinematic optimization of robotic manipulators. Journal of Mechanisms, Transmissions, and Automation in Design 113(3), 220–226 (1991)
14. Wu, J., et al.: Dynamic dexterity of a planar 2-DOF parallel manipulator in a hybrid machine tool. Robotica 26(1), 93–98 (2008)
15. Quijano, N., Passino, K., Jogi, S.: A Tutorial Introduction to Control Systems Development and Implementation with dSPACE. Tutorial, The Ohio State University, Columbus, OH (2002)

Research of Piezoelectric Printing Actuator for High-Power White LED Phosphor Coating

Qiwei Guo, Yueming Hu, Zhifu Li, and Ge Ma

Engineering Research Center for Precision Electronic Manufacturing Equipments of Ministry of Education, College of Automation, Science and Engineering, South China University of Technology, Guangzhou 510640, P.R. China

Abstract. Phosphor coating is one of the key steps in high-power LED packaging processes, among which the design of phosphor droplet jetting actuator is the pivotal technology. In this paper, the forming process of the phosphor droplets will be described, and a piezoelectric droplet printing actuator model about the phosphor fluid movement in the nozzle and the pressure cabin is used to define two criterions for producing phosphor droplets. These criterions can be used to design the piezoelectric actuator, the cabin structure and to select the piezoelectric actuator material. And all these developed models will help to understand the phosphor drop formation process and can be applied in phosphor jetting actuator designs.

Keywords: High-power LED, phosphor coating, piezoelectric printing actuator, phosphor droplet.

1 Introduction

It has been widely accepted that high-power light-emitting diodes (LEDs) will substitute the traditional light sources due to its capability of energy saving and high luminous efficiency. The phosphor powder which makes the blue LED generate white light is general used with the silica gel, in the reason of the density of phosphor powder far more outweigh than the silica gel. If it cannot be coating on the surface of the LED chip symmetrically, the mixed phosphor glue will have slow precipitation problems, which will lead to some precipitation or concentration appear in phosphor layer, and the quality of the LED will be degraded.

Therefore, in high-power white LED the packaging process, the phosphor coating technology is considered to be the key process which can highly affect the quality of white LED luminous efficiency.

So far, there are several methods to coat phosphor power on the surface of the LED chip. They all have their own advantages and disadvantages. However, none of them can coat the phosphor symmetrically on LED chip surface and get a flat phosphor layer. Recently, a new coating technology has been brought into LED phosphor coating process. It can coat the phosphor symmetrically and rapidly around the LED chip by using a piezoelectric inkjet printing head. Compared with the conventional methods,

C.-Y. Su, S. Rakheja, H. Liu (Eds.): ICIRA 2012, Part II, LNAI 7507, pp. 116–126, 2012.

this new technology has the benefits of low cost, simpler processing, and a high rate of material utilization. However, there are still many obstacles in front of this new technology, such as the absence of the reliable piezoelectric inkjet head for phosphor solution prevents the application on the manufacturing electronic products due to the difficulty of the precise control of droplet size and elimination of the satellite droplet.

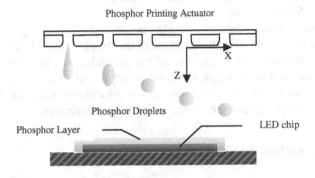

Fig. 1. Schematic of Phosphor Droplet ejection

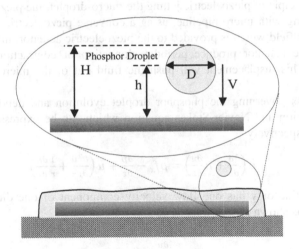

Fig. 2. Schematic of Phosphor Droplet Deposition on LED Chip

Dispensing droplets from a piezoelectric inkjet print head, which contains an array of 64 to 256 nozzles (Fig. 1), is the state-of-the-art of phosphor coating technology. Each nozzle responds very quickly and jets out the phosphor droplets with a volume of several picoliters, generally ranging from 80 down to 14 pl. The droplets with micrometer sizes of 30 to 220 µm are subsequently directed onto LED chip surface. Some manufacturing and fluidic issues have been encountered. The first one is the alignment and eccentricity of nozzles. The accuracy of the phosphor droplet deposition location could suffer from very small angular deviation. Second, the jetting speed is another decisive issue. Large jetting speed could lead to the splash phenomena causing nonuniformity of the phosphor layer on the LED chip surface. Third, improper fluid viscosity is liable to generate an undesired phosphor layer formation. Among the three issues, the first one has been documented in detail by previous researchers. For instance, the precision of the droplet deposition location needs to be well under ±20 μm for a 1500-μm gap between the nozzle and the LED chip surface. Thus, the present investigation focuses on the last two issues.

In this paper, the models of a single phosphor droplet jetting from piezoelectric actuator and the equilibrium characteristic of the droplet on the LED chip surface will be given. Furthermore, two criterions of the piezoelectric phosphor actuator will be defined to use to design the piezoelectric actuator and pressure cabin structure, including the selection of the piezoelectric actuator form and materials. The influence of the phosphor supply parameters on the jetting is also described.

2   Theoretical Formulation

The modeling is based on a finite volume discretization to solve the transient phosphor jet flow and a finite element method to compute the piezoelectric jetting process. Base on the basic principle of piezoelectric jetting the micro-droplet, the piezoelectric actuator is connecting with micro-pipeline, using a converse piezoelectric effect and the periodic electric field which is provided to the piezoelectric actuator, in order to force the piezoelectric actuator produce periodic elongation or contraction deformation displacement. This displacement will push the fluid out of the micro-pipeline into micro-droplet.

The equations governing the phosphor droplet evolution and deposition are the continuity equation and Navier-Stokes equation which can be expressed in the following from, respectively:

$$\rho\left(\frac{\partial u}{\partial t} + u\frac{\partial u}{\partial z}\right) = \rho f_x - \frac{\partial p}{\partial z} + \mu\left(\frac{\partial^2 u}{\partial r^2} + \frac{1}{r}\frac{\partial u}{\partial r}\right) \tag{1}$$

The micro-pipeline only has one flow velocity component of one direction, continuous equation is shown as follows:

$$\frac{\partial u}{\partial z} = 0 \tag{2}$$

If not considering external pressure difference and volume force, equations (1) can be simplified as:

$$\rho\frac{\partial u}{\partial t} = \mu\left(\frac{\partial^2 u}{\partial r^2} + \frac{1}{r}\frac{\partial u}{\partial r}\right) \tag{3}$$

Where u is the fluid axial velocity, μ is the fluid viscosity, ρ is the fluid density, and r is the micro-pipeline diameter coordinate.

According to a smooth micro-pipeline with its radius R and the diameter D, the boundary conditions is shown as follows:

$$u|_{t=0} = 0, \ u|_{r=R} = U_w(t), \ \frac{\partial u}{\partial r}|_{r=0} = 0 \tag{4}$$

Where $U_w(t)$ is piezoelectric actuator movement speed, because of the periodic motion of the actuator, according to Fourier's law, the pulse can be considered the sum of the component which changes base on the sine regular, the plural from of the periodic speed is formulated as:

$$U_w(t) = U_0 e^{i\omega t} \tag{5}$$

Where U_0 is the amplitude, ω is the pulse circular frequencies, $\omega = 2\pi f = \frac{2\pi}{T}$, f is the pulse frequencies, T is the pulse cycle.

If we make these physical quantities dimensionless as follows:

$$\bar{u} = \frac{u}{U_0}, \ \bar{t} = \frac{\mu}{\rho R^2}t, \ \bar{r} = \frac{r}{R} \tag{6}$$

Then the equation (3) can be computed as:

$$\frac{\partial \bar{u}}{\partial \bar{t}} = \left(\frac{\partial^2 \bar{u}}{\partial \bar{R}^2} + \frac{1}{\bar{r}}\frac{\partial \bar{u}}{\partial \bar{r}}\right) \tag{7}$$

The boundary conditions of (7) are shown as follows:

$$\bar{t} = 0, \bar{u} = 0; \ \bar{r} = 0, \frac{\partial \bar{u}}{\partial \bar{r}} = 0; \ \bar{r} = 1, \bar{u} = e^{i\beta^2 t} \tag{8}$$

Where β is the dimensionless radian frequency, $\beta = R\sqrt{\frac{\omega}{\gamma}}$, γ is fluid motion viscosity.

By using separation variable method to solve the equations (7), and satisfy the boundary conditions, we can get:

$$\bar{u}(\bar{r}, \bar{t}) = Re\left(\frac{I_0(\sqrt{i}\beta\bar{r})}{I_0(\sqrt{i}\beta)} e^{i\beta^2 \bar{t}}\right) \tag{9}$$

Where I_0 is the zero order deformation Bessel function.

After integrating equation (9) along the pipeline radius, the dimensionless the average speed can be calculated as follow:

$$\bar{u}_m(\bar{t}) = 2\int_{\bar{r}=0}^{1} \bar{r}\bar{u}(\bar{r}, \bar{t})d\bar{r} \tag{10}$$

from equation (5), (6), (9) and the definition of β, under the periodic piezoelectric actuator, according to the certain types of micro pipeline, the fluid velocity amplitudes depends on the driving voltage, the higher the driving voltage, the greater the velocity amplitude, and the distribution of the fluid velocity is determined by the driving frequency.

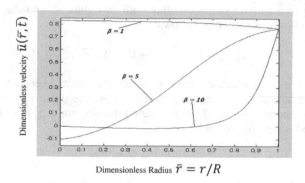

Dimensionless Radius $\bar{r} = r/R$

Fig. 3. Section distribution of different pulse frequency velocity along with the micro pipeline

Fig. 3 is the section distribution of the velocity $\bar{u}(\bar{r}, \bar{t})$ in different pulse frequency ($\beta = 1,5,10$) with the micro pipeline, while the corresponding moment $\omega t = \pi/4$, of which the abscissa denotes is the pipeline's radius, value between 0~1. In the lower frequency, the pipeline internal velocity is even, its profile similar with the piston type; While the increase of the frequency, the pipeline internal velocity will decrease, its profile similar with wavy; The higher the frequency, the slower of the fluid motion response, and leave the increasing distance of the solid wall, the velocity attenuation will become more serious, in the center micro channel has the minimum velocity, which is almost zero.

3   Two Criterions of the Production of Phosphor Droplet in Piezoelectric Printing Actuator

Fig. 4 shows a typical structure of piezoelectric printing head, which including the piezoelectric actuators (built by a thin metal film and piezoelectric ceramic together), pressure cabin, fluid channel and nozzle. (The following discussions all assume in a vacuum device, and not consider the impact of the atmospheric pressure.)

According to the observation of the experiment phenomenon, we can divide the injection of phosphor droplet process into four stages:

1)   The internal fluid in the pressure cabin state kinetic equilibrium, the fluid surface near the nozzle concave into shape of crescent, as shown in fig. 5 fluid surface at time $t = t_0$;
2)   Piezoelectric actuators will have deformation in the influence of voltage pulse, extruding the internal fluid of the pressure cabin, which will cause the internal fluid pressure $p(t)$ rise, the velocity of the fluid at the nozzle will be accelerated to $U_0(t)$;
3)   When the pressure arrive maximum in the nozzle, as shown in fig 5, $t = t^*$, the surface convex of fluid become a largest spherical, and a grain of phosphor droplet jets from the nozzle, as shown in fig. 5, $t > t^*$;

4) The piezoelectric actuator recovery to the original shape, the internal cabin will produce negative pressure, and the fluid surface near the nozzle place will concave into a crescent shape again.

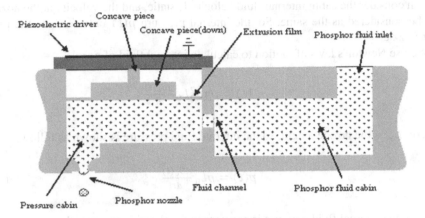

Fig. 4. The structure of the piezoelectric printing head

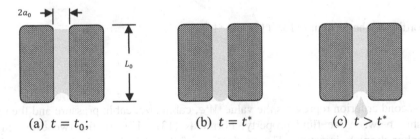

(a) $t = t_0$; (b) $t = t^*$; (c) $t > t^*$

Fig. 5. The diagram of the fluid surface near the nozzle at different jetting moments

From formula (11) we can get,

$$We = \frac{\rho U_0^2(t^*)a_0}{\sigma} > 4 \qquad (12)$$

Where We is the Webber value, which stands for the specific value of the phosphor fluid inertia and its surface tension. The formula (12) is the first criterion of the phosphor droplet production.

From the second condition we can get

$$V_{eject} = \int_0^{t^*} U_0(t)\pi a_0^2 dt \geq \frac{4}{3}\pi a_0^3 \qquad (13)$$

According to the cabin internal fluid motion situation and the finite element analysis results, it can be seen that when cabin internal pressure rises, the internal fluid movement velocity is very small, and the fluid movement velocity is much higher at the nozzle, so the velocity changes drastically from cabin to nozzle joints. Approximately, we can consider the cabin internal fluid velocity is static, and the velocity at the nozzle can be considered as the same. So, the internal pressure $p(t)$ only force to the fluid near nozzle.

We use Newton's laws of motion to calculate internal fluid of nozzle,

$$F(t) = \rho \pi a_0^2 L_0 \frac{dU_0(t)}{dt} \tag{14}$$

Where L_0 is the nozzle length, so the internal fluid pressure is shown as follow.

$$p(t) = \rho L_0 \frac{dU_0(t)}{dt} \tag{15}$$

Assume the internal fluid pressure is constant in accelerating process, then

$$U_0(t) = \frac{p}{\rho L_0} t \tag{16}$$

According to the formulas (13), (14) and (16)

$$We \geq \frac{8}{3} \frac{p a_0^2}{\sigma L_0} \tag{17}$$

The second criterion represents the value We, cabin size, cabin pressure and the relationship between the fluid property. Formulas (13), (17) are the two criterion of phosphor droplets injection. The production of the phosphor droplets must satisfy these two conditions.

4 The Design of Piezoelectric Printing Actuator

The design process of the piezoelectric printing actuator is basically according to the application requirements, determining the diameter of the phosphor droplet size, initial velocity, and working frequency, then referring the criterions of droplets producing process to design the piezoelectric actuator, pressure cabin structure. Hence the working state of the piezoelectric actuator is closely related to its structure, so the design process of the piezoelectric printing actuator should also include the design of the pressure cabin structure.

4.1   The Design of Piezoelectric Material

The selection of piezoelectric ceramic material requires a big reaction displacement. Because so far the modified PZT (zirconium lead titanate) has the most number of applications in micro displacement field, among which PZT-5 has a very low Q_m, a large K_p, a medium D_{33}, a large reaction displacement which under in 90 kV/cm can produce 0.6% reaction displacement. When under low voltage, it basically has a linear relationship between reaction displacement and electric field, and it has a stable performance and widely used in the production of converse piezoelectric effect of electronic components. So the piezoelectric ceramic material should choose PZT-5.

The metal film material should choose brass, because brass has a good corrosion resistance, and the second is that the elastic modulus is small in commonly metal, which is easy to bend.

4.2   The Design of the Piezoelectric Actuator Size

The design of the piezoelectric actuator size includes the diameter and thickness. The piezoelectric actuator requires two conditions, one is the resonant frequency, and the other is the vibration amplitude.

The resonance frequency of the piezoelectric actuator general is selected according to the request of application, and then uses this resonance frequency to calculate the size of the actuator. The relationship between the resonance frequency and the piezoelectric will be given in following pages.

Because the thickness of the piezoelectric actuator is far less than its diameter, the piezoelectric actuators can be simplified to the round thin with uniform thickness; the circular plate thickness t is equal to the piezoelectric actuator total thickness. Equivalent of circular plate density , the elastic modulus E , Poisson's ratio v and diameter D can use the average values of brass and the piezoelectric ceramics.

According to the thin circular plate vibration theory, in the vacuum, the difference equation of the vibration displacement is presented below:

$$\frac{\rho}{W}\frac{\partial^2 \xi}{\partial t^2} = 0 \tag{18}$$

Where ρ is the density of circular plate, and the variable $= \frac{Et^2}{12(1-v^2)}$, we can get the resonant frequency:

$$f_a = \frac{\pi t}{4\sqrt{3}D^2}\sqrt{\frac{E}{\rho(1-v^2)}}\beta_{mn}^2 \tag{19}$$

When piezoelectric actuators vibrating under first order frequency, $\beta_{mn} = \beta_{01} = 1.015$.

Formula (19) indicates that the resonance frequency of the piezoelectric actuator is proportional to the circular plate thickness t, inverse ratio to the diameter square of the piezoelectric actuator; After the selection of piezoelectric actuator materials, Formula (19) can be simplified as:

$$f_a = K \frac{t}{D^2} \tag{20}$$

Where K is constant. In actual application, while internal cabin filled with fluid, the frequency of piezoelectric actuator can make the following fixed:

$$f_w = \frac{f_a}{\sqrt{1+\xi\Gamma}} \tag{21}$$

Where $\xi = \rho_w D / \rho_m t$, ρ_m is the circular plate density, ρ_w is the liquid density; Γ is the dimensional 1 correction factors, for phosphor fluid in a resonant frequency vibration.

According to the general engineering design, formulas (19)-(21) can satisfy the design accuracy requirement, we can use formulas (19)-(21) to design the piezoelectric actuator size. In order to design more precise for piezoelectric actuator frequency, first, we can use Rayleigh-Ritz method to calculate the free vibration frequency of piezoelectric actuator, and then use formula (21).

The vibration amplitude of piezoelectric actuator is the premise of phosphor droplets creation. Based on the discussion of the droplet criterions, according to the application requirements, the fluid pressure to jetting phosphor droplets can be roughly defined, and the piezoelectric actuator deformation value can also be calculated.

Fig. 4 shows structure: when piezoelectric actuators vibrating, ignore the loss at the entrance, the internal pressure can be shown as:

$$p = K_v \frac{\Delta h}{K_s h_c} \tag{22}$$

Where Δh is the piezoelectric actuator vibration amplitude, K_s is the fluid volume compression coefficient, h_c is the pressure cabin depth; $K_v = \Delta V / \frac{\pi}{4} D^2 \Delta h$ is the volume coefficient, D is the pressure cabin diameter. When piezoelectric actuator is in the small amplitude vibration, K_v can be approximately considered as a constant. According to phosphor fluid criterion 2 is stricter; we can substitute formula (22) into (17) and gain the criterion:

$$\Delta h = \frac{3}{8} \frac{We}{K_v} \left| \frac{L_0}{a_0} \right| \left| \frac{h_c \sigma}{a_0} K_s \right| \tag{23}$$

In the actual design we usually consider the entrance loss [7], the piezoelectric actuator Δh often takes 2 ~ 5 times to the calculated value. In the calculation above, we do not consider the influence of the internal bubble, but if the internal pressure cabin mixes with bubbles, which will lead to the practical value of Δh dozens of times larger than the calculation value. So in the actual design, we should avoid to have bubbles in the pressure cabin.

The vibration amplitude and actuator size have the following relation:

$$\Delta h = K_p U_v \frac{D}{t} \tag{24}$$

Where K_p is the structure coefficient, U_v is the power supply voltage. When the voltage is invariant, we can use formulas (21), (23), (24) to design actuator size.

4.3   The Design of Pressure Cabin Structure Parameter

Because the cabin diameter is approximately equal to the diameter of the piezoelectric actuators, the selection of nozzle diameter must according to the application request, so the pressure cabin structure parameters design indicates the cabin depth design, the cabin entrance diameter size design and the nozzle diameter design.When piezoelectric actuator vibrating, the fluid inside cabin will flow from the entrance to the nozzle at the same time. Consider the viscosity of phosphor fluid, the boundary layer thickness can be calculated according to the formula:

$$\delta = \sqrt{\psi t_w} \tag{25}$$

where ψ is the phosphor fluid viscosity. When nozzle diameter above 50 μm, we can consider the boundary layer thickness is far less than the entrance and nozzle radius, then can consider the fluid velocity at the entrance and nozzle are the same, so the fluid loss at the entrance can be calculated as:

$$Q_{loss} = \frac{r_{in}^2}{r_{in}^2 + a_0^2} \tag{26}$$

Where r_{in} is the entrance radius. In order to reduce the entrance flow loss, the value of r_{in} is generally small, r_{in}/a_0 can be about 0.5.According to the formula (23), it is known that the cabin depth h_c is proportional with the piezoelectric actuator amplitude Δh, so we should try to reduce the value of the cabin depth h_c in the piezoelectric actuator design .

5   Conclusion

For the discussions above, we can have the following conclusions. First, the Navier-Stokes models based on the analysis of phosphor droplets jetting process are proposed, which proves that the increase of the actuator frequency will cause the decrease of the fluid velocity in the internal pipeline, and the higher the frequency, the slower of the fluid motion response. Second, The two performance criterions of producing phosphor droplets are proposed, which is believed to provide a useful improving for designing the piezoelectric printing actuator. Third, in this paper, we also propose many formulas to design the piezoelectric printing actuator according to the application requirements, including determining the diameter of the phosphor droplet size, initial velocity, working frequency and most importantly the pressure cabin structure of piezoelectric printing actuator.

Acknowledgments. The project was supported by the momentous special program of Guangdong provincial department of science and technology.

References

1. Bogy, D.B., Talke, F.E.: Experimental and theoretical study of wave propagation phenomena in drop-on-demand ink jet devices. IBM J. of Research and Development 28(3), 314–321 (1984)
2. Daualer, G.: Design of a Drop-On-Demand Delivery System for Molten Solder Microdrops. MIT, Massachusettes (1995)
3. Kohnen, A.S.: Drop-On-Demand Ink Jet Printing for Three Dimensional Printer Application. MIT, Massachusettes (1995)
4. Gohda, T., Kobayashi, Y., Okanao, K., Inoue, S., Okamoto, K., Hashimoto, S., Yamamoto, E., Morita, H., Mitsui, S., Koden, M.: A 3.6-in 202-ppi full-color AMPLED display fabricated by ink-jet method. In: Proceedings of the SID 2006 Digest (2006)
5. Wijshoff, H.M.A.: Structure- and fluid-dynamics in piezo inkjet print-heads, PhD thesis (2008)
6. Beasley, J.D.: Model for fluid ejection and refill in a impulse drive jet. Photographic Science and Engineering 21(2), 77–82 (1977)
7. Antohe, B.V., Wallace, D.B.: Acoustic phenomena in a demand mode piezoelectric inkjet printer. Journal of Image Science and Technology 46, 409–414 (2002)
8. Kwon, G., Kim, W.: A waveform design method for high speed piezo inkjet printing based on self-sensing measurement. Sens. Actuator A, Phys. 140, 75–83 (2007)
9. Shatalov, M., Chitnis, A., Yadav, P., Hasan, M.F., Khan, J., Adivarahan, V., Maruska, H.P.: Thermal analysis offlip-chip packaged 280 nm nitride-based deep ultraviolet light-emitting diodes. Appl. Phys. Lett. 86, 201109 (2005)
10. Hou, B., Rao, H., Li, J.: Phosphor coating technique with slurry method in application of white LED. In: Proc. SPIE, vol. 6841, p. 684106 (2008)

Development of OLED Panel Defect Detection System through Improved Otsu Algorithm

Jian Gao, Zhiliang Wang*, Yanyun Liu, Chuanxia Jian, and Xin Chen

Key Laboratory of Mechanical Equipment Manufacturing & Control Technology,
Ministry of Education, School of Electromechanical Engineering,
Guangdong University of Technology, Guangzhou, 510006, China
Jian_gao2004@163.com

Abstract. OLED (Organic light-emitting) displays have been called the next generation of display devices for their unique properties: colorful images, large viewing angle, light weight and power efficiency. Complex manufacture processing makes the screen have some defects. Detecting the defects will help to improve the quality. In this paper we concentrate on detecting these defects and proposed a corner-points based method, where the corner-points are extracted from the skeleton image and used as the control points for the subtract operation. We proposed an improved Otsu method to determine the image segmentation threshold by recursive process. Based on the algorithm proposed, a system for OLED screen defect detection was developed. The test result shows that the developed system can detect most of the defects on the panel.

Keywords: OLED Panel; Defect Detection, Image Segmentation, Otsu Method, Subtraction Operation.

1 Introduction

OLED (Organic Light-Emitting Diode) screen has gradually become a new generation of display device. They have the advantage of wide view angle, uniform display, quickly reaction, can be made into a flexible panel and are energy efficient. They are widely used in MP3, MP4, mobile phone, digital camera and mobile terminal field. Complex manufacturing processes inevitable introduce a variety of panel defects, for example, blemish defect, line defect and Mura defect [1-3]. These defects influence the OLED's luminescence uniformity, image clarity and operation life. So that develops a high speed and high precision testing system for OLED display defect detection becomes important to guarantee the OLED display screen quality.

In recent years, optical detection technology based on machine vision has received a lot of attention in the field of electronics equipment. Image segmentation and band-pass filtering technology has been used in surface defect detection, such as printed circuit board surface detection, thin film transistor liquid crystal display (TFT-LCD) defect detection [4-5]. TFT-LCD defect detection algorithms are mainly

---

* Corresponding author.

C.-Y. Su, S. Rakheja, H. Liu (Eds.): ICIRA 2012, Part II, LNAI 7507, pp. 127–134, 2012.

implemented in spatial domain or frequency domain. Seong Hoon Kim showed the OLED screens that contain defect (include blemish defects and Mura defects) compose of defects and periodic texture background. In frequency domain, defects correspond to high frequency components and periodic texture backgrounds correspond to low frequency component. A high frequency filter can filter periodic texture background and leaving only defects information [6]. The novelty of this method is it uses a window function to smooth the image instead of filtering it in the frequency domain. The smoothed image is subtracted from the original image, and image of the defect is obtained. But the problem is that: due to the periodic texture background boundary is also corresponded to the high frequency component, after filtering and subtraction operation they will still remain. They are treated as defects, which make the results not accurate.

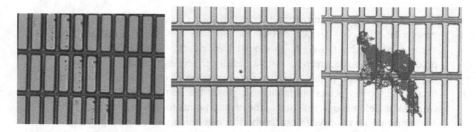

Fig. 1. Typcal OLED screen defect

S.Fan use a regression diagnostic method to detect the defects of a TFT-LCD. They assumed that a panel without defects is light consistent and uniform brightness, while a panel with defects exhibits local brightness, contrast and background inconsistencies [7]. This method first breaks the image into sub-blocks and calculated the average gray for each block. This average value substitutes the gray of the entire region. A defect-free image is used to reconstruct the background, and then the background is subtracted from the original image. Judge the existence of defects according to a pre-set evaluation function to see whether the gray level residuals fall within a range. This method can achieve the purpose of automatic detection, but the processing is complicacy and the parameters of the function should be calibrated manually. TSAI developed an image reconstruction algorithm which is based on a one-dimensional Fourier transform; this method has a good effect for obvious texture picture [8]. Lu proposed a detection algorithm based on independent component analysis [9]. Zhang et al. developed an algorithm based on polynomial surface fitting, which can detect blemish defects from complex backgrounds [10-11]. In the feature extraction field, the methods considers the contrast, area, size, location, contour, shape and brightness uniformity of the target and then establish the blemish defects model. However, this method has a certain ambiguity, the weight of each factor is difficult to determine, and the test results demonstrated a degree of uncertainty. Therefore, in the field of TFT-LCD screen defect detection there are exist some useful algorithms, but exist a general method that can solve the identification for all types of defects[12]. These algorithms are not suitable for rapid industrial production, due to the long processing time.

OLED displays have some differences from TFT-LCD screens at the micro level, mainly in: OLED pixel consists of three separate sub-pixels; the three sub-pixels are the same in appearance except for the luminescent materials. Sub-pixel and wires are neatly arranged on the panel. OLED displays are not the same with TFT-LCD on the microstructure, so it has some special features on the image display. Complex manufacturing processes make the panel contain defects which result in pixel light-emitting abnormal. These defects are come from environment or operating process including dust and foreign matter. Aiming at a variety of defects on OLED panel, this paper presents a block scan detection system.

2   Detection System Descriptions

The system structure used for OLED display defect detection is shown in Fig.2. The detection system includes a CCD camera, motion control card, frame grabbers, XY motion platform, light and other peripheral equipment. The motion control card drivers the XY platform so that the lens scans the OLED capturing different images. The images collected by CCD camera are transformed by the image acquisition card to the PC where the image processing and defect recognition is completed. A representative sample of the captured OLED display pixel image is shown in Fig.3.

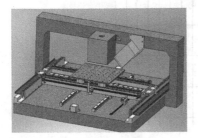

Fig. 2. Display detection platform structure   **Fig. 3.** A captured OLED display pixel image

The basic methodology of the detection system is: extract the OLED display skeleton from captured image based on thinning technology, and create an ideal template which is then subtracted from the original image; determine the image segmentation threshold by a improved Otsu algorithm; and identify defects by image binarization.

3   OLED Display Defect Detection Algorithm

3.1   Extracted Skeleton Template by Thinning Technology

In this paper, the skeleton information of the OLED display image is extracted by image thinning technology, the initial corner information can be extracted based on the "+" mask. A complete control point map needs to be generated through the procedure of projecting the skeleton images to determine the distribution of the initial corner, finding the right distance and adding missing points. This map is used for standard templates creation and subtraction computation. The skeleton is a topological description of the graphical geometry. It is a linear geometry and is placed at the center of symmetry of the graphics, with the same topology as the original graphics, and retains the original shape. The method has been widely used in computer vision, biological shape description, and pattern recognition, industrial inspection, and image compression fields.

Generally, image objects maintain the 8-neighborhood connectivity, the background maintain 4-neighborhood connectivity, it is often used a 3 × 3 template. The relationship between pixel and its eight neighborhoods used as criterion for join or not. Image thinning method is applicable for skeleton extraction in the discrete space. It should be set standards based on the pixel neighborhood information to maintain the original shape of the topology, connectivity, and single-pixel width, while retain some of the abnormal area (the defects area). The thinning algorithm used in this paper does a statistical discrimination on every region of the image, if the statistical results meet the criterion, its center pixel of this region is simply deleted. Repeat the procedure and delete the pixels conform the conditions until the results no longer change. The skeleton of the original OLED panel image can be obtained as shown in Fig.4 (corresponding to the image of Fig.3).

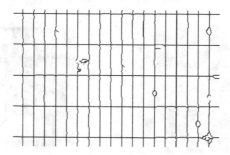

Fig. 4. Skeleton extracted by image thinning algorithm

3.2   Skeleton-Based Corner-Points Extraction

In computer vision, contour feature points (for example, the corner points, the cut point and inflection point) are the basic characterization of the target shape primitives, which plays a decisive role on the target shape. This paper presents an effective characteristics corner extraction method: using a standard "+"mask to loop through the OLED skeleton images, the points matching skeleton mask and in the intersection is the corner, the flowchart of the algorithm is shown in Fig.5. The corner detection result for the image skeleton in Fig.4 is shown in Fig.7(a). Due to defects, the distribution of corner points is not uniform and some corner points are not accurately determined. Therefore, a completion procedure for corner picture is needed.

Through computing the distance and difference between the two control points, the missing control points can be added. Gray value of pixels in a straight line were accumulated and projected along X and Y-direction were shown in Fig.6. Projection along X-direction creates peaks which correspond to vertical segment line; similarly,

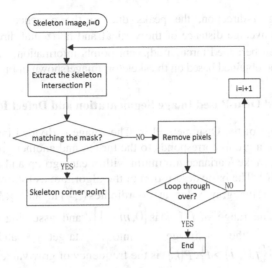

Fig. 5. Flowchart of control points extraction

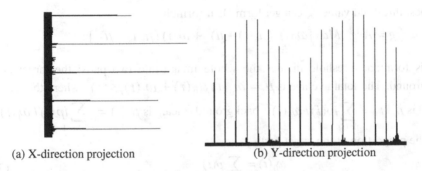

(a) X-direction projection   (b) Y-direction projection

Fig. 6. Skeleton projection image along the X and Y-directions

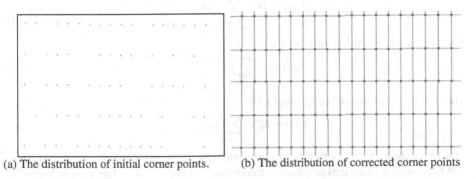

(a) The distribution of initial corner points.   (b) The distribution of corrected corner points

Fig. 7. Distribution maps of corner points for the OLED display images

projection along Y-direction, the peaks due to the presence of horizontal lines. Calculateing the average distance of the vertical and horizontal direction, the missing control points can be added through adjacent points information, and the ideal corner points can then be obtained based on the skeleton image(shown in Fig.7(b)).

3.3   Improved Otsu-Based Image Segmentation and Defect Identification

The basic concept of the Otsu method is: The image is divided into two groups by a setting threshold, a group corresponds to the target, and another group corresponds to the background. Make Variance minimum within each group and maximum between the groups [14-16]. The basic description of the algorithm as follows:

Denoted $f(i, j)$ the gray value at coordinates (i, j) in an $N \times M$ image, the total average is μ. The range of $f(i, j)$ is $[0, m-1]$, and assuming that the threshold t segment the image into target and background: $\{f(i, j) \leq t\}$ and $\{f(i, j) > t\}$. $P(k)$ is the frequency of gray value k, so:

$$p(k) = \frac{1}{MN} \sum_{f(i,j)=k} 1 . \tag{1}$$

The best threshold value g can get form Otsu formula:

$$g = Arg \max_{0 \leq t \leq m-1} [\omega_0(t) \ (\mu_0(t) - \mu)^2 + \omega_1(t) \ (\mu_1(t) - \mu)^2] \tag{2}$$

In this formula, threshold divides the whole image into two parts: the target and background. The total average is $\mu = \omega_0(t)\mu_0(t) + \omega_1(t)\mu_1(t)$, where the target mean is $\mu_0(t) = \sum_{0 \leq i \leq t} ip(i) / \omega_0(t)$, background mean is $\mu_1(t) = \sum_{t \leq i \leq m-1} ip(i) / \omega_1(t)$.

And the proportion of the target part:

$$\omega_0(t) = \sum_{0 \leq i \leq t} p(i) \tag{3}$$

The number of points in target part:

$$N_0(t) = MN \sum_{0 \leq i \leq t} p(i) \tag{4}$$

The proportion of the background part:

$$\omega_1(t) = \sum_{t < i \leq m-1} p(i) \tag{5}$$

The number of points in background part:

$$N_1(t) = MN \sum_{t < i \leq m-1} P(i) \tag{6}$$

The processing of Otsu's threshold determination is looped through 256 gray levels, and finds which value makes variance maximum between classes; this gray value is the optimal threshold (T). However, it is necessary to recalculate the mean and the number of pixels on both sides when looping through every gray level and the computation is very large. So, this paper presents an improved Otsu method, which loops through the entire image in a recursive way, and greatly reduces the computational load. The methodology of the recursive algorithm described as follows:

Assume the total number of pixels in an image is n, the total average is μ, gray histogram is h. s_1 s_2, s_3 is the sum gray value for total image, target part and background part. Set the initial conditions:

$$n_1^{(0)} = 0,\ n_2^{(0)} = 0,\ \mu_1^{(0)} = 0,\ \mu_2^{(0)} = 0, s_1^{(0)} = 0,\ s_2^{(0)} = 0,$$

and $t = 0$ (the range of t is [0,254]), the recursive expression for the variance between their classes is:

$$\sigma^2 = n_1^{(t+1)}\left(\mu_1^{(t+1)} - \mu\right)^2 + n_2^{(t+1)}\left(\mu_2^{(t+1)} - \mu\right)^2 \tag{7}$$

In this formula, $n_1^{(t+1)} = n_1^{(t)} + h^{(t)}$, $n_2^{(t+1)} = n - n_1^{(t+1)}$, $s_1^{(t+1)} = s_1^{(t)} + t * h^{(t)}$,

$s_2^{(t+1)} = s - s_1^{(t+1)}$, $\mu_1^{(t+1)} = s_1^{(t+1)} / n_1^{(t+1)}$, $\mu_2^{(t+1)} = s_2^{(t+1)} / n_2^{(t+1)}$, when σ^2 is the

maximum, threshold $T = t + 1$.

In recursive call processing, $t = t + 1$ until the recursion end, $t = 254$ .The improved algorithm can improve the computational efficiency by 80%.

Integrating the various algorithms proposed above, such as: thinning method to extract the skeleton, completion of control points and the improved Otsu image segmentation algorithm. This paper develops an OLED-oriented defect detection system through Visual Studio 2008 and VC++ 6.0 programming language. The system is validated through several OLED image examples, and the testing results show that the developed system can detect most of the defects on the panel. The original image in Fig.3 was analyzed by this system developed and the results were shown in Fig.8. It is found that the system can efficiently identify the defects from OLED image.

Fig. 8. OLED display defect detection result

4   Conclusions

Various types of defects accurse during the manufacture of OLED display screen. This paper focuses on an automatic defect detection system. It proposed a subtraction method based on the skeleton template to detect defects. It described an improved Otsu method in image segmentation, and determines the threshold by a recursive algorithm. To show the effectiveness of the OLED defect detection system, the system is tested by some image samples. The results show the developed system can detect the defects accurately. Further research work will focus on improving the accuracy for completing skeleton control point, and enhance the robustness of the system. This paper improves the automatic detection and quantification of defect on the OLED screen and will be of great use to OLED screen manufactory an similar industries.

Acknowledgments. This work is supported by National Basic Research Program of China (973 Program, Grant No.2011CB013104), by Key Joint Project of National Natural Science Foundation of China(Grant No. U1134004) and by Guangdong Provincial Science and Technology R&D Project (Grant No. 2009B091300057).

References

1. Hyvarinen, A.: Independent component analysis algorithms and applications. Neural Networks (13), 411–430 (2000)
2. Lin, H.D.: Automated Detection of Color Non-Uniformity Defects in TFT-LCD. Neural Networks (1), 2384–2391 (2006)
3. Kim, J.H.: A High—speed high—Resolution Vision System for the Inspection of TFT-LCD. In: IEEE International Symposium on Industrial Electronics, vol. (1), pp. 101–105 (2001)
4. Tachibana, K.: Study on Moire between screen and panel structure in a LCD rear projection for HDTV. In: Display Research Conference, pp. 143–146 (1991)
5. Lee, K.B.: Defect Detection Method For TFD-LCD Panel Based on Saliency Map Module. In: IEEE Region 10 Conference, vol. A, pp. 223–226 (2004)
6. Kim, S.H., Kang, T.G., Jeong, D.H.: Region Mura Detection using Efficient High Pass Filtering based on Fast Average Operation. In: The International Federation of Automatic Control, vol. (6), pp. 8190–8195 (2008)
7. Pratt, W.K., Sawkar, S.S.: Automatic blemish detection in liquid crystal flat panel displays. In: Proc. SPIE, vol. (1), pp. 25–30 (1998)
8. Tsai, D.M.: Automatic Defect Inspection of Patterned TFT—LCD Panels Using 1—D Fourier Reconstruction and Wavelet Decomposition. International Journal of Production Research (3), 4589–4607 (2005)
9. Lu, C.J.: Defect Defection of Patterned TFT-LCD Surfaces Using Independent Component Analysis. In: Chinese Industrial Engineering Seminar, pp. 1–10 (2004)
10. Zhang, Y., Zhang, J.: Automatic Blemish Inspection for TFT-LCD Based on Polynomial Surface Fitting. Opto-Electronic Engineering 33(10), 108–114 (2006) (in Chinese)
11. Zhang, Y.: Application of Fuzzy Expert System in Defect Inspection of TFT-LCD. Journal of Optoelectronics. Laser 17(6), 719–723 (2006)
12. Lee, J.Y.: Automatic Detection of Region-Mura Defect in TFT-LCD. IEICE Transactions on Information and Systems E87-D(10), 2371–2378 (2004)
13. Serra, J.: Image Analysis and Mathematical Morphology, vol. (1). Academic Press, San Diego (1982)
14. Otsu, N.: A threshold selection method from gray-level histogram. IEEE Transactions on System, Man, and Cybernetics SMC-9(1), 62–66 (1979)
15. Jing, X.J., Cai, A.N., Sun, J.: Image segmentation based on 2D maximum between-cluster variance. Journal of China Institute of Communication 22(4), 71–76 (2001)
16. Li, L.L., Deng, S.X.: Binarization Algorithm Based on Image Partition Derived from Da-Jing Method. Control & Automation 21(8-3), 76–77 (2005) (in Chinese)
17. Liu, Y.Y., Gao, J., Zhao, W.M.: Defect Inspection for OLED Display Based on Skeleton Template. Microcomputer & its Applications (2011) (accepted)

The Linkage Control Strategy for the Two-Phase Flow Dispensing System

Jinsong Zhang[1,2] and Jianhua Zhang[1,2,*]

[1] School of Mechatronics Engineering and Automation, Shanghai University, China
[2] Key Laboratory of Advanced Display and System Applications of Ministry of Education,
Shanghai University, China
jhzhang@staff.shu.edu.cn

Abstract. The fluid dispensing technology has been widely used to deliver all kinds of fluids in electronic industry. This paper first put forward an initial approach based on the direct driving principle to dispense the liquid with a high consistency and precision. According to the direct driving principle, the gas-liquid slug flow should be formed as a stable pattern in the micro-channel while the flow rate ratio between the gas and liquid is in an appropriate range. The linkage control strategy had been done to realize the two-phase flow during the dispensing process. The two-phase flow dispensing system had seven sub-systems for integration to achieve the multi-functions. The control sub-system is the most important unit applying the industry personal computer to connect and control other sub-systems. It undertakes three main tasks, communication, data processing and feed-back control. As a result, the stream of compressed air injected into the continuous liquid stream controlled by the peristaltic pump, the bubbles and droplets appeared in the micro-channel separately and uniformly.

Keywords: linkage control, dispensing system, direct driving principle, two-phase flow.

1   Introduction

The fluid dispensing becomes one of the key technologies in electronic industry due to all kinds of fluids widely application, e.g. chip placement, thermal silica filling, chip and substrate interconnection, *et al*. The fluid dispensing technology implements an accurate process for fluid distribution instead of a controllable way [1].

With the dispensing technology experienced several stages of development, the non-contact jetting dispensing technology has been proved to be predominate [1]. Compared with the contact dispensing technology, the non-contact dispensing technology has a higher working efficiency without the Z axis movement. Taking great progress, a lot of dispensing technologies have been developed and promoted to the market. The typical applications of the non-contact fluid dispensing technology

---

* Corresponding author.

C.-Y. Su, S. Rakheja, H. Liu (Eds.): ICIRA 2012, Part II, LNAI 7507, pp. 135–144, 2012.

can be divided into the two sorts according to the driving methods of the mechanical needle and the compressed air.

For the mechanical dispensing system, it often has a mechanical needle and a metal body, and the mechanical needle can realize a reciprocating motion in the chamber of body to siphon in and spray out the liquid [2]. When the mechanical needle reaches the bottom of the chamber, it stops on the in-wall of the body and separates the liquid stream into two parts. This is a process to cut off the continuous liquid and transfers the kinetic energy from the needle to the liquid, so that the impact exists in the region between the outlet of the nozzle and the front of the needle [3, 4]. The front part of the liquid can spray out of the nozzle to the substrate. During the process of the liquid dispensing, the moving needle impacts on the in-wall of the body periodically to induce wear. It will degrade the lifetime of the mechanical dispensing system.

Another typical technology is time-pressure dispensing system driven by the compressed air [5, 6]. The driving medium is the gas acting on the back of liquid to squeeze it out of the syringe from the nozzle. The complex control of the compressed air by time and pressure regulates the dispensing volume preciously, as the electromagnetic valve works in a high frequency. The time-pressure dispensing is widely used due to its flexible operation and simple structure. While the liquid surface falls down of after dispensing, the compressed air in the syringe takes a larger space. This increases the control difficulty of compressed air and also generates a potential problem of the liquid volume consistency [7].

As mentioned above, the two dominant dispensing technologies have advantages and disadvantages based on the different driving mediums. In the view of engineering fluid dynamics, all the common dispensing technologies are the fluid motion of single-phase flow referring to the indirect driving principle. Under this driving principle, the driving force comes from the mechanical or gas medium to act on the back of the liquid and transfer the kinetic energy from the moving medium to the static liquid. As a result, the liquid are crushed and separated into some droplets spraying out of the nozzle onto the substrate (Fig.1).

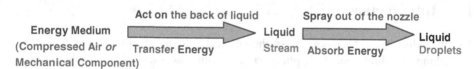

Fig. 1. The diagram of the indirect driving principle for the fluid dispensing technology

2   Direct Driving Principle

This paper first put forward an initial approach, the direct driving principle, to apply the linkage control strategy achieving the liquid dispensing based on the gas-liquid two-phase flow theory.

2.1   Two-Phase Flow Theory

In view of engineering fluid dynamics, the direct driving principle used for the liquid dispensing can be considered to obey the gas-liquid two-phase flow dynamics. Hereby, the gas and liquid are the two kinds of fluids, which present a hydro-flow pattern in the mixing micro-channel simultaneously.

The gas-liquid two-phase flow theory indicates that when the gas and liquid streams have been induced from the two tubes with different flow rates, there is a special flow pattern of the hydro-flow existing in the mixing micro-channel. The common flow patterns, such as bubble, slug, churn, slug-annular, annular et al. had been found in the micro-channel with a diameter for 1.45mm [8]. The transformation of the different flow patterns from each other is depended on the flow rate ratio between the gas flow rate and the liquid flow rate. Figure 2 shows the flow pattern has a high relevance with the gas and liquid superficial velocities. It is interesting that the slug flow pattern takes a large area in the flow pattern map with a widely range of the flow rate ratio. This means that the gas-liquid slug flow is a stable pattern and easy to be obtained with the appropriate flow rate ratio.

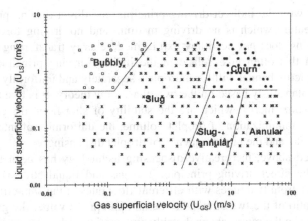

Fig. 2. Flow pattern map as observed for a 1.45mm diameter circular test section [8]

The different morphologies of flow patterns are shown in figure 3. Referring to the slug flow, the gas and liquid streams are totally separated to be bubbles and droplets with uniform volume and interval in micro-channel. This stable flow pattern can be adopted to dispense liquid droplet due to no bubble and droplet mixing each other.

The basic theory to form the gas-liquid slug flow in micro-channel is the instability mechanism of the gas stream flowing with the liquid stream. These phenomena appear not only in the horizontal micro-channels with the cross-section of circle, triangle, rectangle and square [9-14], but also in the vertical micro-channels with the cross-section of circle and square [15-18]. The boundary conditions also have the significant effects on the pattern shift, e.g. the micro-channel shape, micro-channel length, micro-channel diameter, convergence angle, wetting angle [19] et al.

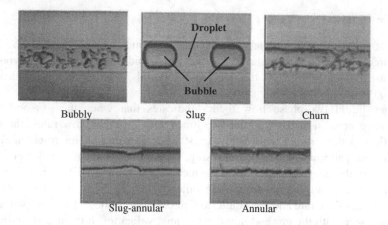

Fig. 3. The morphologies of different flow patterns in the micro-channel [8]

2.2   Advantages of Direct Driving Principle

In comparison with the indirect driving principle, the direct driving principle has a predominant feature which is no driving medium and no driving force. The liquid stream dispensing does not need any extra kinetic energy transferring from the gas stream, though this often takes place in the indirect driving principle. The liquid stream in the micro-channel will form droplets separately and uniformly driven by the gas stream spontaneously based on the two-phase flow theory. It is true the gas-liquid slug flow has some merits, which are the stability of slug flow, the consistency of droplet size, the minimization of droplet volume, the uniformity of interval between bubble and droplet and the high frequency of droplet dispensing.

As mentioned above, the creative dispensing technology has been first proposed according to the direct driving principle. The gas and liquid streams inject into a mixing chamber from two tubes with different flow rates at the same time. Changing the flow rate ratio of the two streams to be an appropriate value, the gas-liquid slug flow will appear in the micro-channel stably and continuously. During the dispensing procedure, bubbles will disappear in the air alternatively and droplets will spray on the substrate and periodically (Fig. 4).

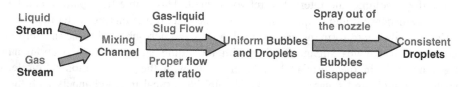

Fig. 4. The diagram of the direct driving principle for the fluid dispensing technology

The direct driving principle has the unique property is that the gas-liquid slug flow in the micro-channel generates the "switch effect". This means if one phase enters the micro-channel, another phase should be blocked not to enter it. Thus, it can meet the requirements of the dispensing technology on the micro volume, good consistency, high controllability, accuracy and frequency and without any back haul.

Table 1. The advantages of the direct driving principle for the fluid dispensing technology

Flow Property	Driving Medium	Gas Control	Liquid Control	Dispenser	Droplet Volume	Accuracy & Frequency	Back Haul
Slug Flow	No	Simple	Simple	Simple	≤ Nano Liter	High	No

3   Linkage Control Strategy

The direct driving principle has some advantages for its application on the fluid dispensing technology. However, how to establish a liable and reliable system is still a great challenge since there is no existing apparatus for reference.

3.1   Design Scheme

For the design tasks from the customer requirements, the design scheme of the two-phase flow dispensing system was presented including seven sub-systems. After sub-system integration, the two-phase flow dispensing system should achieve the multi-functions (Fig. 5).

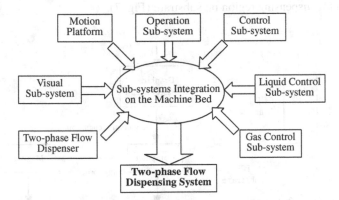

Fig. 5. The schematic of design scheme for the two-phase flow dispensing system

The relationship among different sub-systems is shown in figure 6. In it, the control sub-system is the most important unit to connect and control other sub-systems. It undertakes three main tasks, communication, data processing and feed-back control, to perform the two-phase flow dispensing.

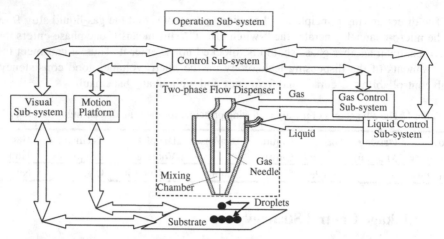

Fig. 6. The relationship among different sub-systems for the two-phase flow dispensing system

3.2   Implementation Scheme

Industry personal computer (IPC) was the core unit for communication, analysis, calculation and display during the linkage control strategy for the integrated system.

After the system starting and initialization, CCD camera captured the trace images of the dispensing region on substrate, and it recognized and transformed the trajectory coordinates to IPC real-time. IPC calculated the motion compensation data and then sent the commands to the motion controller. The platform was driven to move following the coordinates, while the two-phase flow dispenser was automatically positioned to the dispensing region on substrate (Fig. 7).

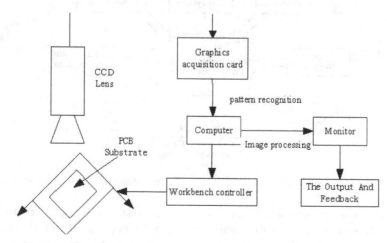

Fig. 7. The schematic of the linkage control strategy for the motion platform

Figure 8 plots the linkage control strategy for the gas and liquid sub-systems.

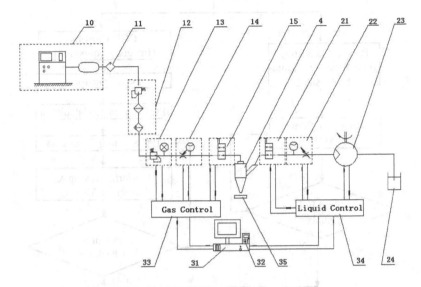

Fig. 8. The schematic of the linkage control strategy for the gas and liquid sub-systems
Compressed Air Source (10), Air Dryer (11), Universal triple Collector (12), Air-pressure Control Unit (13), Air-flow Control Unit (14), Gas Electromagnetic Valve (15), Liquid Electromagnetic Valve (21), Micro-flow Control Unit (22), Peristaltic Pump (23), Liquid Container (24), Operation sub-system (31), Control & Communication Unit (32), Gas Control Unit (33), Liquid Control Unit (34), Substrate (35), Two-phase Flow Dispenser (4).

Both of the gas and liquid control sub-system have to connect the two-phase flow dispenser by hard and soft tubes with the quick connectors, respectively. In detail, the gas inlet was located on the top of the dispenser and the liquid inlet was installed at the side of the dispenser, however they were above the mixing chamber with a convergence angle (<35°). This structure design benefited for the slug flow formation when the two streams entered and mixed in the micro-chamber.

According to the direct driving principle, the gas stream was introduced into the liquid stream at the micro-chamber. After that, a gas-liquid two-phase flow was formed in the micro-channel of the nozzle and the liquid stream was cut by gas bubbles to be uniform and micro-volume droplets spraying out of the nozzle (Fig. 9).

In the implementation scheme, to ensure the system achieving the two-phase flow dispensing, the gas and liquid control sub-systems had been automatically controlled by PID circuits. The gas pressure was maintained as a constant by the high precision

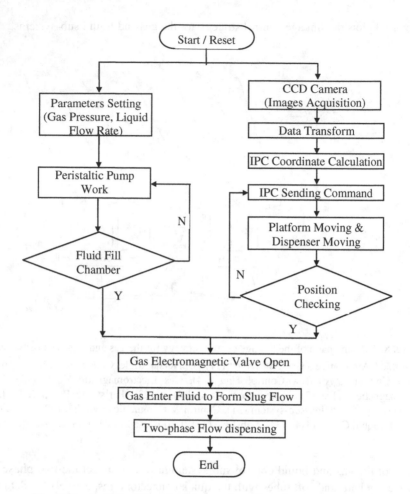

Fig. 9. The work flow chart for the two-phase flow dispensing system

pressure controller and the liquid flow rate was adjusted by the high precision and double-head peristaltic pump. This minimized the pulse effects of the gas and liquid during the dispensing process. The input of the gas and liquid were governed by the electromagnetic valve with a high frequency. After the peristaltic pump input a continuous liquid stream into the chamber of dispenser, the compressed air stream was also introduced into it with an appropriate flow rate ratio. Due to the instability mechanism, the gas stream was crushed to be lots of bubbles, which cut and separated the liquid stream to be uniform droplets periodically.

It took 15 months to fabricate the prototype machine of the two-phase flow dispensing system (Fig. 10).

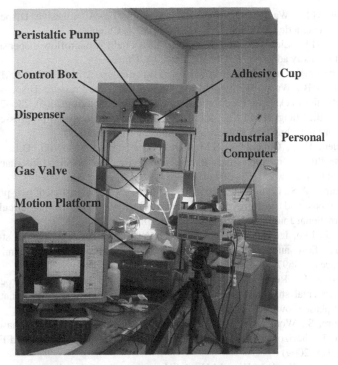

Fig. 10. The picture of the two-phase flow dispensing system

4   Conclusions

This paper first put forward an initial approach based on the direct driving principle to dispense the liquid consistently and preciously. The gas-liquid slug flow in the micro-channel was a stable pattern to form uniform bubbles and droplets periodically, when the gas and liquid streams had an appropriate flow rate ratio. Based on the design scheme, the linkage control strategy had been done in the two main aspects to realize the slug flow during the dispensing process. After manufacturing and integration, the prototype machine of the two-phase flow dispensing system had been established. This is the first dispensing system adopted the direct driving principle in the world.

Acknowledgments. The authors acknowledged the financial supports granted by the National Natural Science Foundation of China (NO. 11172163) and the National Basic Research Program of China (973 Program) (NO. 2011CB013103).

References

1. Zhao, Y.X., Chen, X.D., Chen, X.: A review of fluid dispensing in microelectronic packaging. Hydraulic and Pneumatic 2, 52–54 (2006)
2. http://www.nordson.com

3. Deng, G.L., Wang, J.Q., Xie, J.H., Peng, Z.Y.: A Adhesive Dispenser Driven by Electromagnetic Attraction. P: CN 201220197Y, China
4. Zhang, H.H., Liu, H.Y., Shu, X.Y., Xu, Y.L., et al.: A microflow dispensing apparatus for high viscosity adhesive. P: CN 101190429A, China
5. http://www.musashi-engineering.co.jp/index_sc.html
6. Chen, X.B., Wang, W.J.: Off-Line Control of Time-Pressure Dispensing Process for Electronics Packaging. Electronics Packaging Manufacturing 26(4), 286–293 (2003)
7. Hong, B., Wang, H.M., Cao, J.J., Li, X.Q., Li, Z.W.: Research progresses of quantitative dispensing technology. Review and Comment 16, 1–2 (2009)
8. Triplett, K.A., Ghiaasiaan, S.M., Abdel-Khalik, S.I., Sadowski, D.L.: Gas-liquid two-phase flow in microchannels Part I: two-phase flow patterns. International Journal of Multiphase Flow 25, 377–394 (1999)
9. Pamitran, A.S., Choi, K.-I., Oh, J.-T., Hrnjak, P.: Characteristics of two-phase flow pattern transitions and pressure drop of five refrigerants in horizontal circular small tubes. International Journal of Refrigeration 33, 578–588 (2010)
10. Yue, J., Luo, L., Gonthier, Y., Chen, G., Yuan, Q.: An experimental study of air-water Taylor flow and mass transfer inside square microchannels. Chemical Engineering Science 64, 3697–3708 (2009)
11. Agostini, B., Revellin, R., Thome, J.R.: Elongated bubbles in microchannels. Part I: Experimental study and modeling of elongated bubble velocity. International Journal of Multiphase Flow 34, 590–601 (2008)
12. Saisorn, S., Wongwises, S.: An experimental investigation of two-phase air-water flow through a horizontal circular micro-channel. Experimental Thermal and Fluid Science 33, 306–315 (2009)
13. Choi, C.W., Yu, D.I., Kim, M.H.: Adiabatic two-phase flow in rectangular microchannels with different aspect ratios: Part II - bubble behaviors and pressure drop in single bubble. International Journal of Heat and Mass Transfer 53, 5242–5249 (2010)
14. Elcock, D., Honkanen, M., Kuo, C., Amitay, M., Peles, Y.: Bubble dynamics and interactions with a pair of micro pillars in tandem. International Journal of Multiphase Flow 37(5), 440–452 (2011)
15. Zhao, T.S., Bi, Q.C.: Co-current air-water two-phase flow patterns in vertical triangular microchannels. International Journal of Multiphase Flow 27, 765–782 (2001)
16. Sun, B., Wang, R., Zhao, X., Yan, D.: The mechanism for the formation of slug flow in vertical gas-liquid two-phase flow. Solid-State Electronics 46, 2323–2329 (2002)
17. Kim, N.-H., Sin, T.-R.: Two-phase flow distribution of air-water annular flow in a parallel flow heat exchanger. International Journal of Multiphase Flow 32, 1340–1353 (2006)
18. Li, F.-C., Kunugi, T., Serizawa, A.: MHD effect on flow structures and heat transfer characteristics of liquid metal–gas annular flow in a vertical pipe. International Journal of Heat and Mass Transfer 48, 2571–2581 (2005)
19. Peng, P., Zhang, J., Zhang, J.: Numerical study on gas and liquid two-phase flow in microchannel used in fluid distribution process. In: 2011 International Conference on Electronic Packaging Technology & High Density Packaging, pp. 756–760. IEEE Press, Shanghai (2011)

The Transient Temperature Field Measurement System for Laser Bonding Process

Junfeng Ge[*], Yuneng Lai[*], Yuanhao Huang, and Jianhua Zhang[**]

Key Laboratory of Advanced Display and System Applications (Shanghai University),
Ministry of Education, School of Mechatronics Engineering and Automation,
Shanghai University, Shanghai, 200072, China
jhzhang@staff.shu.edu.cn

Abstract. Laser bonding technology is widely used in encapsulation field. However, the uneven temperature field in the laser bonding influences the bonding quality. This paper is to study the effect of temperature on the laser bonding quality. The designed system has a human-machine interface and its measurement accuracy reach$\pm1°C$. The multiple temperature measurement system is developed for laser bonding process based on K-type thermocouple. This system is composed of a host computer by PC software Visual Basic 6.0 and a lower controller whose core is MSP430F149. The host computer is used for human-machine interface interaction, controlling the lower controller through serial communication protocol. According to the instructions from the host computer, the lower controller executes the corresponding temperature measurement action, and then survey data from multi-channel thermocouples is transferred to the host computer through a serial port. The temperature can be displayed curves and saved. This system has wider measuring temperature range, higher temperature measurement precision and high sensitivity and can meet the transient temperature field measurement need of laser bonding. The temperature measurement range of the system is 0 to 1000 °C and the measurement accuracy of the system reaches$\pm1°C$ using the single chip MSP430F149 with 12-bit ADC module.

Keywords: Transient temperature measurement system, K type thermocouples, SCM, Visual Basic 6.0.

1   Introduction

Recently, laser bonding technology as one of localized heating methods becomes the hotspot of encapsulation researches and has been widely used in the encapsulation of different substrates such as OLED, LED and MEMS encapsulation. However, the laser bonding quality, including air tightness and connection strength is influenced greatly by the transient temperature field in the laser bonding process. The laser

---

[*] These authors have contributed equally to this work.
[**] Corresponding author.

C.-Y. Su, S. Rakheja, H. Liu (Eds.): ICIRA 2012, Part II, LNAI 7507, pp. 145–152, 2012.
© Springer-Verlag Berlin Heidelberg 2012

bonding temperature distribution in the process is highly heterogeneous, therefore, the temperature control in the laser bonding process is very important [1-4]. A temperature measurement system is firstly developed according to the future application in the laser bonding temperature control to reduce its nonuniformity. The transient temperature field measurement system not only can be used for laser bonding process but also other related occasions which are sensitive to temperature. The contact temperature measurement system for laser bonding process is proposed based on K-type thermocouple. A friendly human-machine interface by visual basic 6.0 is designed for the application on laser bonding. The laser bonding temperature field measurement system has a good measurement accuracy and real-time display function. The system keeps a high measurement accuracy $\pm 1\,^\circ$C in a wide range of 0 to 1000 $^\circ$C using the single chip MSP430F149 with 12-bit ADC module.

2   System Design

A multiple temperature measurement system is developed for laser bonding process based on K-type thermocouple. The K-type thermocouple is widely used in industry due to its fast response time, high measurement temperature, simple structure and low cost. The temperature collection system using K-type thermocouple is suitable on a wider range than the system using other thermocouple [5, 6]. 8-channel K-type thermocouples are installed in the fixture below bonding area, shown in Fig.2. Temperature conversion chip AD595 is a complete instrumentation amplifier and thermocouple cold junction compensator used with K-type thermocouple. This system is composed of a host computer by PC software Visual Basic 6.0 and a lower controller whose core is MSP430F149.

2.1   The Thermometry Principle of K-Type Thermocouple

A thermocouple is a device consisting of two different conductors (usually metal alloys) that produce a voltage proportional to a temperature difference, between either ends of the two conductors. The contact of two different conductors produces contact electromotive force and a kind of conductor with different temperature applying for its two ends produces thermoelectromotive force. Their addition is the total electromotive force of thermocouple loop, $E_{AB}(T,T_0)$, which is shown in formula (1).

$$E_{AB}(T,T_0) = \int_{T_0}^{T} S_{AB} dT \tag{1}$$

$$V_{out} = (41\mu\text{V}/^\circ\text{C}) \times (T - T_0) \tag{2}$$

In above formula, T and T_0 represent the temperature of hot junction and cold junction respectively; S_{AB} represents seebeck coefficient, and its value depends on the relative property of electrode material.

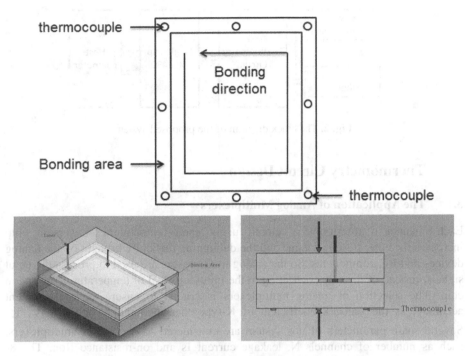

Fig. 1. The position distribution of 8-channel thermocouples

The voltage change of K-type thermocouple is 41 μV with the temperature change of 1 °C. Therefore, a corresponding relationship of voltage to temperature for K-type thermocouple is shown as formula (2). T is obtained by the computation of formula (2) when T_0 is definite value. In general, working end of the thermalcouple is placed in the temperature field and free end is connected to measuring circuit. The temperature conversion chip AD595 is integrated with the function of measurement of T_0, simplifying the measurement circuit.

2.2   System Composing

A single chip MSP430F149 is applied in this temperature field measurement system due to its high performance and low power consumption. The MSP430F149 incorporates a 16-bit RISC CPU, a flexible clock system and peripherals such as 12-bit ADC and serial port. The thermometry circuit has one 8-channel analog multiplexers CD4051 with three binary control inputs and temperature conversion chip AD595. The visual interface built in host computer Dell has the function to send collection command and display the temperature figure. The block diagram of the whole system structure is shown in Fig.2.

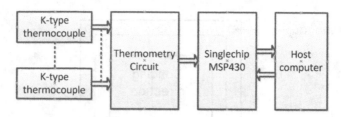

Fig. 2. The block diagram of the proposed system

3 Thermometry Circuit Design

3.1 The Application of Analog Multiplexers

Each channel of thermometry circuit using each temperature conversion chip increases the cost, system volume and the debugging difficulty brought by the analog devices and RC components. So the analog multiplexers are used to process the input signals, instead of directly connecting to the input terminal of temperature conversion chip. The selection of analog multiplexers is crucial to ensure the measurement accuracy, as the seebeck coefficient of K-type thermocouple is only 41 μV /$^\circ$ C.

Several main parameters of this system are considered to choose the multiplexers, such as number of channels N, leakage current Is and on-resistance Ron. The 8-channel analog multiplexers CD4051 is selected due to its low channel leakage of 10pA and low on-resistance of 80 Ω.

3.2 The Application of Temperature Conversion Chip

Temperature conversion chip AD595 is widely used in temperature measurement field. It simplifies thermometry circuit due to the functions of instrumentation amplifier and thermocouple cold junction compensator. Low power design is employed in AD595 to minimize measurement error caused by self-heating. An unload AD595 operates with a total supply current 160 μA, but it is also capable of delivering in excess of 5mA to a load. The AD595 can be powered from a single ended supply and temperature below 0 $^\circ$C can be measured by including a negative supply. The AD595 is calibrated by laser wafer trimming to match the characteristic of type-K thermocouple inputs. It combines an ice reference with a calibrated amplifier to produce a high level (10mV/ $^\circ$C) output directly from thermocouple signal. The AD595 is gain trimmed to match the transfer characteristic of K-type thermocouples at 25 $^\circ$C, to achieve a temperature proportional output of 10mV/$^\circ$C and accurately compensate for the reference junction over the rated operating range of the circuit. The seebeck coefficient of K-type thermocouple is 41 μV /$^\circ$ C, and the gain for AD595 is 247.3 (10mV/ $^\circ$C divided by 41 μV /$^\circ$ C). An adjusted value 11 μV for AD595 is considered to calculate the output voltages in order to ensure 250mV output at 25 $^\circ$C. The actual output voltage is determined by the transfer functions (3).

$$V_{out} = (V_K + 11\mu V) \times 247.3 \tag{3}$$

According to the characteristics of AD595, the output voltage of AD595 is not completely proportional to temperature difference between the hot end and cold end of thermocouples. Output values for intermediate temperatures are interpolated to achieve accurate temperature values. The temperature from 0°C to 1000 °C is divided into 51 parts by 20°C every interval. Linear interpolation is carried out in host computer to obtain the temperature of measurement terminal based on output voltage of AD595. The schematic diagram of temperature measurement circuit is shown as Fig.3. Eight thermocouples are placed in the laser bonding field sequentially. All the grounding terminals of the thermocouples are connected to the IN+ terminal of AD595AD. The terminals T_0 to T_7 of the thermocouples are respectively connected to the terminals X_0 to X_7 of CD4051BCM. One of the thermocouple signals is selected to be to the terminal IN- of AD595AD from the terminal X of CD4051BCM, following the control signals of CA, CB and CC from the single chip MSP430F149.

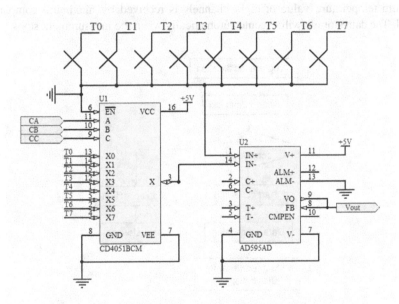

Fig. 3. The position distribution of 8-channel thermocouples

Eight output terminals of K-type thermocouples are respectively connected to the input terminal of analog multiplexers CD4051 and the input terminal 1 of AD595. The output terminal of CD4051 is connected to the input terminal 14 of AD595. The output voltage of AD595 is enlarged twice by operational amplifier, and then input to the terminal P60 of single chip MSP430F149. The analog value is converted to the digital signals by the 12-bit ADC function of MSP430F149, and then the digital signals are transferred to the PC by serial port.

4   Software Design

In this temperature measurement system, a standard serial communication interface RS232 is used to transfer signals. The development environment of PC software is Visual Basic. The software realizes the functions of sending the collection command, converting temperature data, displaying the temperature figure, achieving eight channels' maximum temperature value and storing all the temperature data. Thermocouples have nonlinear outputs related to temperature and linearization techniques are necessary. To solve the problem of linearizing the sensor, the reference table of the AD595 is established in the Visual Basic. The Celsius can be searched through the table correlating with the sampled data, and the problem of linearization will be solved easily. The final measurement accuracy of the system reaches±1 °C. The program flow of the PC software is shown in Figure 4. The collection starts after sending collection command to the single chip MSP430F149. The data frames received by PC are separated and converted to eight channels of temperature values in Visual Basic 6.0. The instant temperature curves are displayed in different colors. Each maximum temperature value of eight channels is received by maximum comparison method. The data storage will execute automatically when the measurement stops.

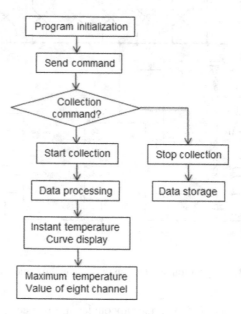

Fig. 4. The program flow of the PC software

The main function of MSP430F149 is switching eight thermocouple inputs to execute ADC and sending the digital signals to PC based on the command of host computer. The programming is simplified due to the application of the ADC module. The flow charts of main program and subprogram are respectively shown in Figure 5(a) and Figure 5(b).

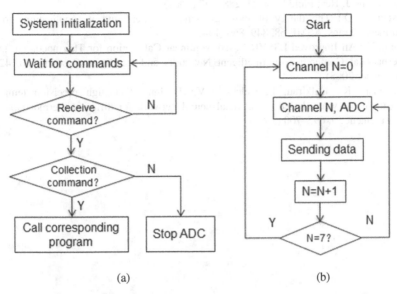

Fig. 5. The single chip flow charts of main program (a) and subprogram (b)

5   Conclusion

A multiple temperature measurement system is designed to be applied to laser bonding temperature field measurement based on K-type thermocouple and AD595. The measurement accuracy of the system reaches ± 1 °C using the single chip MSP430F149 with 12-bit ADC module. The real-time temperature curves are displayed on PC and each maximum temperature value of eight channels is obtained. The operator interface programmed by Visual Basic is suitable for user's operation. The system has a high accuracy in a wide range of 0 to 1000 °C and can be applied to the future temperature control of laser bonding.

Acknowledgments. This work was supported by a grant from the National Basic Research Program of China (NO.2011CB013103).

References

1. Carmignani, C., et al.: Transient finite element analysis of deep penetration laser welding process in a singlepass butt-welded thick steel plate. Comput. Methods Appl. Mech. Eng. 179, 197–214 (1999)
2. Xue, Z.-M., Gu, L., Zhang, Y.-H.: Temperature field simulation of laser welding. J. Trans. China Weld. Inst. 24(2), 79–82 (2003)

3. Mahrle, A., Schmidt, J.: The influence of fluid flow phenomena on the laser beam welding process. Int. J. Heat Fluid Flow 23, 288–297 (2002)
4. Rosenthal, D.: The theory of moving sources of heat and its applications to metal treatments. Trans. ASME 68, 849–866 (1946)
5. Wang, X.: An Improved LSSVR-Based Nonlinear Calibration for Thermocouple. In: First International Conference on Intelligent Networks and Intelligent Systems, pp. 421–424 (November 2008)
6. Danisman, K., Dalkiran, I., Celebi, F.V.: Design of a high precision temperature measurement system based on artificial neural network for different thermocouple types. Measurement 39, 695–700 (2006)

Modeling of Electromagnetic Interference Noise Mechanism for Magneto-Rheological Damper

Wei Yan[1], Enrong Wang[1,*], Yang Zhao[1], Rakheja Subhash[2], and Chunyi Su[2]

[1] School of Electric and Automation Engineering, Nanjing Normal University,
Nanjing 210042, China
erwang@njnu.edu.cn
[2] Department of Mechanical Engineering, Concordia University,
Montreal H3G 1M8, Canada

Abstract. The magneto-rheological (MR) damper has been widely explored in the study of vibration suppression for vehicle suspension and constructional systems, etc. Aiming at semi-active controllable hysteretic nonlinear property of the MR damper depending on direct magnetic field, the generation mechanism of conducted and radiated electromagnetic interference (EMI) noises for intelligent vehicle system with MR dampers are initially proposed in this paper, which includes strong nonlinearities arisen from the semi-active control strategy, road surface shock excitations, high-frequency devices in control circuit, environmental electromagnetic (EM) field coupling to excitation coil, and excitation coil impedance mismatch of the MR damper. Upon above studies, both the conducted EMI noise model and the radiated EMI noise model are generally proposed for the MR damper and its control system, and the far field characteristic of radiated EM field generated from excitation coil of the MR damper is further analyzed. The results of simulation and experiment show correctness of the proposed EMI noise models, which will play an important role in future application study for the EMI noise suppression of intelligent vehicle suspension design with MR dampers.

Keywords: magneto-rheological (MR) damper, electromagnetic interference (EMI), excitation coil, noise mechanism, model.

1   Introduction

The new magneto-rheological (MR) damper has been widely applied in vibration suppression studies of intelligent vehicle suspension and constructional systems, and the controllable MR damper depending on direct magnetic field and semi-active control strategy is an important way for realizing intelligent vehicle suspension, which can ideally improve the ride comfort, handling stability and safety of road vehicles [1-2]. Whereas, MR suspension system can yield a great amount of electromagnetic interference (EMI) noises, which are mainly divided into two

---

* Corresponding author.

C.-Y. Su, S. Rakheja, H. Liu (Eds.): ICIRA 2012, Part II, LNAI 7507, pp. 153–163, 2012.

categories of conducted and radiated EMI noises, arising from the MR damper, controller, sensors and detection circuits, etc. On the one hand, the peculiar semi-active control strategy, road surface shock excitations, and environmental electromagnetic (EM) field coupling to the excitation coil can generate serious EMI noises, due to the nonlinear hysteretic and saturation properties of the MR damper depending on direct magnetic field. On the other hand, the high-frequency electronic devices in controller of the MR damper and in the sensors and detection circuits can also generate such EMI noises. The above-mentioned EMI noises would bring about harmful effect on operation reliability for the MR damper control and other electronic equipments installed in the vehicle.

In recent years, scientists have carried out a lot of researches on magnetic circuit design of excitation coil of the MR damper, by employing the finite element and numerical calculation methods and the EM field simulation software such as ANSYS, etc. [3-4]. However, few reports have been found about the EMI noise mechanism and modeling for the MR damper and its controller, while many application achievements have been obtained, aiming at the study on EMI noise mechanism and suppression for ordinary electronic equipments. Literatures [5-7] employ the artificial supply network and noise separation network to determine the conducted EMI noise mechanism by extracting the differential mode (DM) and common mode (CM) noises in the equipments under test, while literature [8] employs the near and far EM field impedances and literatures [9-10] apply the transformation between near and far EM fields, so as to determine the radiated EMI noise mechanism in the electronic equipments. Furthermore, literatures [11-13] propose reconstruction methods of the radiated EMI noise by utilizing the EM field analysis tool and the circuit parameter model. Above-mentioned methods are also suitable for studying the EMI noise generation mechanism of MR vehicle suspension system, which has significant theorem and application meaning in association with the particular properties, such as semi-active control strategy and strong hysteresis and saturation nonlinearity of the MR damper and shock excitations from road surface, etc.

In view of above analysis and on basis of the acquired achievements about semi-active control of MR vehicle suspension and EM compatibility of electronic equipments [8,14-18], the circuit and EM analysis methods are utilized initially to determine the EMI noise generation mechanism systematically for the MR vehicle suspension system. It is analyzed that such EMI noises arise from semi-active control strategy and road surface shock excitations, high-frequency devices in control circuit, environmental EM field coupling to excitation coil, and excitation coil impedance mismatch of the MR damper, and both the conducted and radiated EMI noise models are generally proposed for the MR damper and its control system, as well the far field characteristic of radiated EM field generated from excitation coil of the MR damper is further proposed, which are in keeping with the standards of ISO 11451 and ISO 11452, and establishes an important theoretic foundation for the future EMI noise suppression study of intelligent vehicle suspension design with MR dampers.

2   Conducted EMI Noise of the MR Damper

The MR intelligent vehicle suspension system consists of MR damper, controller, sensors and detection circuits, etc., wherein a great amount of radiated EMI noises can be yielded due to the high-frequency electronic devices such as single-chip microcomputer (SCM), DSP, A/D converter and crystal oscillator in the control circuit. Such EMI noises can form the conducted EMI noise in power supply through transmission line and form the radiated EMI noise spreading to space through excitation coil of the MR damper. In addition, the radiated EMI noise can be further enhanced by environmental EM field coupling to excitation coil of the MR damper, as shown in Fig.1.

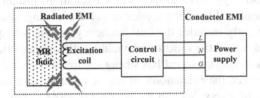

Fig. 1. EMI noise generation mechanism of the MR damper

It is not difficult to find that the conducted EMI noise comes from the following three sources, as shown in Fig.1.

(1) The first source yielding conducted EMI noise is the nonlinear high-frequency electronic devices in the MR damper controller, such as SCM, DSP and crystal oscillator. It can be analyzed through the artificial supply network and noise separation network, and suppressed by synthesizing a proper EMI filter.

(2) The second source yielding conducted EMI noise is the environmental EM field coupling to excitation coil of the MR damper, as shown in Fig.2. The radio frequency (RF) EM field can be yielded in surrounding of the wire due to random change with time of the wire signal, by coupling the noise to other transmission lines.

Employing the Maxwell's equation, the conducted EMI noise current coupling to excitation coil of the MR damper can be expressed as [8]

$$I = 2.632 \times 10^{14} \frac{nEr}{Af^2} \tag{1}$$

Where, I and f denote current and frequency of the conducted EMI noise, respectively. E expresses intensity of the environmental EM field, and r, A and n represent the measurement distance, equivalent area and coil turns of the excitation coil, respectively.

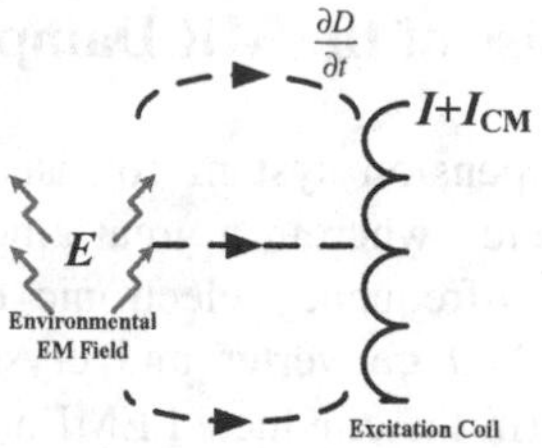

Fig. 2. Conducted EMI noise generated by the environmental EM field

(3) The third source yielding conducted EMI noise is the strong nonlinear transient property of control signal in excitation coil of the MR damper, which is caused by the semi-active control strategy, road surface shock excitation, instantaneous excitation such as road roughness, and handling modes of vehicle turning, starting and braking. The control signal mainly includes the low-frequency and high-frequency parts. The low-frequency signal serves the function of yielding direct magnetic field in the MR fluid, while the high-frequency signal has strong nonlinear transient property. Due to parasitic parameter effect, the excitation coil can be regarded as a number of sections, and the impedance of every section is hence not 50Ω. Thus, such impedance mismatch can lead to the conducted EMI noise through the wave transmission and reflection yielded by the high-frequency control signal. Employing the scatter parameter and normalized EM field intensity analysis methods, the total transmission wave of the excitation coil can be derived as [18]

$$\Gamma = \frac{T_{12}T_{23}e^{-\gamma t}}{1 - R_{21}R_{23}e^{-2\gamma t}} \tag{2}$$

Where, R_{ij} and T_{ij} denote transmission and reflection coefficients of EM field from the section i to section j ($i, j = 1, 2, 3$, and $i \neq j$). γ represents propagation constant of the coil material.

3 Radiated EMI Noise of the MR Damper

The radiated EMI noise comes from the following two sources, as shown in Fig.1.

(1) The first source yielding radiated EMI noise is control circuit of the MR damper, such as the signal transmission line, crystal oscillator and not-well grounding, etc. The mechanism of such radiated EMI noise can be diagnosed by applying the near EM field measurements, and has relationship with radiation line impedance and length, because the signal transmission line can be considered as a radiation antenna. Furthermore, the antenna radiation impedance can be determined by establishing Helmholtz equation upon the electric dipole model and the antenna radiation model, and the retarded potential of the EM field can be resolved by employing Lorentz condition, as well the closed resolution function can be derived by

applying functions of current density, energy flux density and power of the radiation line.

The radiation impedance of electric antenna can be expressed as [11]

$$R_E = \frac{2P}{I_0^2} = \frac{\pi}{6}\sqrt{\frac{\mu_0}{\varepsilon_0}}\left(\frac{l}{\lambda}\right)^2 = 197\left(\frac{l}{\lambda}\right)^2 \ \Omega \tag{3}$$

Where, R_E and P denote impedance and power of the electric antenna, respectively, I represents current in radiation line, μ_0 and ε_0 express vacuum permeability and permittivity, l and λ signify length of the radiation line and wavelength of the radiated EM field.

The radiation impedance of half-wave rod-shaped antenna can be thus obtained as

$$R_{HR} = 2.44 \times \frac{\mu_0 c}{4\pi} = 73.2\Omega \tag{4}$$

Where, R_{HR} denotes impedance of the half-wave rod-shaped antenna.

Concerned with non-half-wave rod-shaped antenna, the radiation impedance can be derived through retarded potential of EM field, radiated EM field intensity, average energy flux density and total radiation power of radiation line. It is formulated as

$$R_{NHR} = \frac{0.13\mu_0 c}{4k\pi\lambda}\left(\begin{array}{l} 0.62k\lambda + 0.92k\lambda\cos(kl) + 4.0k\lambda\cos(k(1-\lambda)) + 2.0k\lambda\cos(kl)Ci(-2k\lambda) \\ -16k\lambda\cos^2\frac{kl}{2}Ci(k\lambda) + 2k\lambda\cos(kl)Ci(2k\lambda) - 2k\lambda\cos(kl)\ln(-2k\lambda) \\ +8k\lambda\ln(k\lambda) + 6k\lambda\cos(kl)\ln(k\lambda) - 2\sin(kl) + 2\sin(k(1-2\lambda)) \\ +4\sin(k\lambda) - 8k\lambda\sin(kl)Si(k\lambda) + 4k\lambda\sin(kl)Si(2k\lambda) \end{array}\right) \tag{5}$$

Where, R_{NHR} denotes impedance of non-half-wave rod-shaped antenna, k is constant, $Si(\cdot)$ and $Ci(\cdot)$ are sine integral function and cosine integral function, formulated as $Si(x) = \int_0^x \frac{\sin(t)}{t}dt$ $Ci(x) = \int_0^x \frac{\cos(t)}{t}dt$, herein, x denotes independent variable of function, and t represents variable of the integration.

Due to difference of radiation impedance between electric dipole and non-half-wave rod-shaper antenna, the impedance of radiation line could be determined based on the length of radiation line and equivalent wavelength of noise current in radiation line. In practice, five steps are introduced as follows.

Step 1: Determine the length of radiation line (l). Assuming the wavelength (λ) is quarter of l, the reference frequency (f) can be derived.

Step 2: Divide noise spectrum into two ranges f_1 and f_2. f_1 is lower than f, while f_2 is larger than f.

Step 3: In frequency range f_1, electric dipole model and Eq. (3) can be employed.

Step 4: In frequency range f_2, non-half-wave rod-shaped antenna model and f Eq. (5) can be applied.

Step 5: The radiated EMI noise generated from the MR damper can be calculated based on Step4 and Step 5, and intensity of radiated EM field can be thus derived as [11]

$$P = \oiint \frac{1}{2} \frac{|E|^2}{\eta_0} ds = \frac{4\pi r^2 |E|^2}{2\eta_0} \equiv \frac{1}{2} I^2 R \quad |E| \approx \sqrt{30R} \frac{I}{r} \tag{6}$$

Where, P and E denote power and intensity of the radiated EM field, respectively, η_0 represents wave impedance in free space ($120\pi \ \Omega$), R, r and I express impedance, measurement distance and noise current in the radiation line, respectively.

(2) The second source yielding radiated EMI noise is excitation coil. According to operation and regulation principle of the MR damper, the magnetic intensity and shear force of MR fluid in piston region can be thus regulated by control current signal in the excitation coil. Based upon EM field analysis of the MR damper, the magnetic intensity around the MR damper piston can be formulated as [3]

$$H = \frac{NI}{\pi\mu_{mrf} l (R_1 + R_2) \sum R_m} \tag{7}$$

Where, H denotes magnetic intensity in the MR damper piston region, N and I represent coil turns and control current in excitation coil, respectively. μ_{mrf} expresses relative permeability of the MR fluid, $\sum R_m$ expresses the total magnetic reluctance, and others are structure parameters of the MR damper.

Furthermore, the high-frequency signal generated from control circuit of the MR damper can be regarded as N segments magnetic dipoles. It can generate radiated EMI noise seriously, and the intensity of radiated EM can be derived as [8]

$$E = 2.632 \times 10^{-14} \frac{f^2 ANI}{r} \tag{8}$$

Where, E denotes intensity of the radiated EM field, I expresses control current in the excitation coil, A represents equivalent loop area of the excitation coil, and r is the measurement distance.

4   Simulation and Experiment Validation

When the MR damper operates in normal function, the control current signal has strong transient characteristic due to the semi-active control strategy, road surface shock and instantaneous excitations such as road roughness and handling modes of vehicle turning, starting and braking. Without loss of generality, control signal of the MR damper is expressed as Gauss distribution in direct current, as shown in Fig.3. The radiated model of the MR damper can be established as shown in Fig.4. Where, copper is used as the material of excitation coil, the relative permeability is 1 and the relative dielectric constant of the total excitation coil is 2.5.

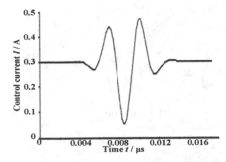

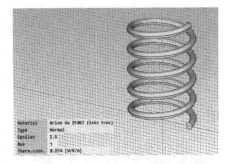

Fig. 3. Control signal in Gauss distribution   **Fig. 4.** Radiated model of the MR damper

According to ISO 11451 and ISO 11452, the frequency of radiated EMI noise is suggested in range of 30MHz to 1GHz (up to 6GHz). Herein, a radiated EM filed at 295MHz is taken as an example for analyzing the radiated EMI noise generated form the MR damper. Based on Eqs.(6) and (7), the EM field mode in excitation coil port of the MR damper is a transverse magnetic (TM) wave, and the normalized intensity of EM field in 3m, axial ratio, θ directivity pattern, φ directivity pattern, and φ/θ pattern can be obtained, as shown in Fig.5. The results illustrate that the intensity of normalized radiated EM field generated from the MR damper is uniform and non-directivity in 3m, as well the vertical component is larger than the horizontal component. Moreover, it is easily seen from Eq. (8) that the intensity of radiated EM field generated from the MR damper is enhanced with the increasing of control current, signal frequency and equivalent loop area.

Fig.6 shows a MTS for testing dynamic characteristic of the MR damper [14-17], in which one terminal of the MR damper is fixed on the frame and the other terminal is fixed on the hydraulic servo actuator. The MR damper is driven to take sinusoidal motion by the hydraulic servo actuator and its output instantaneous displacement and velocity can be measured by an acceleration sensor mounted on vibration exciter.

A MR damper candidate of MagneShock for the vehicle suspension is employed, which is tested under harmonic excitation with amplitude is 12.5mm at frequency 1.5Hz, and control current is in the range of 0A-0.4A. Fig.7 shows characteristics of the MR damper in function of damping force in relationship with displacement velocity of the damper piston and control direct current, which exhibits obvious hysteretic and saturation nonlinear properties. Besides, Figs.8 (a), (b) and (c) illustrate a set of smooth pulse excitations under different parameters of pulse stiffness, fundamental frequency and road surface roughness, which can reasonably emulate the road surface shock excitations, and Fig.8 (d) shows a typical control current signal of the MR damper, which has heavy transient sharp variations due to such road surface shock excitations and the semi-active control strategy [14-17].

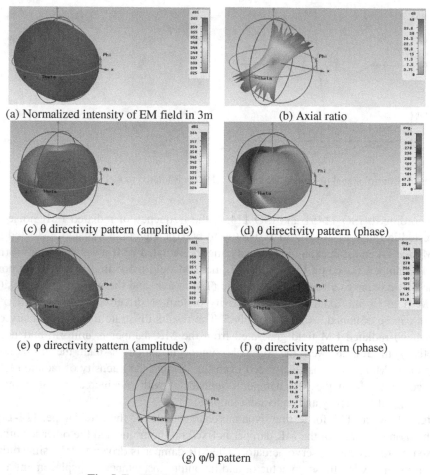

(a) Normalized intensity of EM field in 3m

(b) Axial ratio

(c) θ directivity pattern (amplitude)

(d) θ directivity pattern (phase)

(e) φ directivity pattern (amplitude)

(f) φ directivity pattern (phase)

(g) φ/θ pattern

Fig. 5. Far EM field characteristics of the MR damper

Fig. 6. MTS for MR damper test

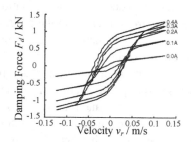

Fig. 7. Characteristics of tested MR damper

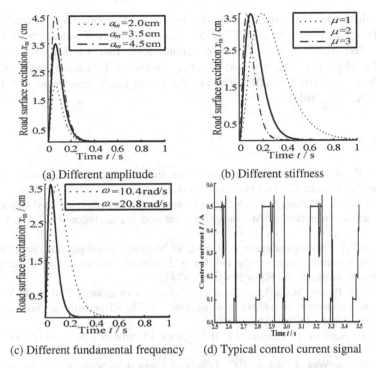

(a) Different amplitude   (b) Different stiffness

(c) Different fundamental frequency   (d) Typical control current signal

Fig. 8. Smooth pulse signals emulating road shock excitation

5   Conclusion

In this paper, the EMI mechanism generated from MR intelligence suspension system is analyzed, and the conducted and radiated EMI models of the MR damper are proposed, which establishes an important theoretic foundation for the future EMI noise suppression study of intelligent vehicle suspension design with MR dampers. Following conclusions are obtained.

(1) The EMI noise generation mechanism is systematically studied for the MR vehicle suspension system. It is analyzed that such EMI noises arise from semi-active control strategy and road surface shock excitations, high-frequency devices in control circuit, environmental EM field coupling to excitation coil, and excitation coil impedance mismatch of the MR damper.

(2) The conducted and radiated EMI noise models are generally proposed for the MR damper and its control system.

(3) The far EM field characteristic of the radiated EMI noise generated from excitation coil of the MR damper is further proposed, in which the normalized EM field intensity is uniform and non-directivity, and its vertical component is larger than its horizontal component.

Acknowledgments. This paper is supported by Project Supported by National Natural Science Foundation of China (51075215); Natural Science Foundation of Jiangsu Province (BK2011789); Foundation of State Key Lab of Millimeter Waves (K201106); High-tech Industry and Science Funds of Education Department of Jiangsu Province (JHB2011-20); Graduate Education Innovation Project of Jiangsu Province(CXZZ12_0404).

References

1. Daniel, F., Rolf, I.: Mechatronic semi-active and active vehicle suspension. Control Engineering Practice 12(11), 1353–1367 (2004)
2. Privandoko, G., Mailah, M.: Vehicle active suspension system using Skyhook adaptive neuro active force control. Mechanical System and Signal Processing 23(3), 855–868 (2009)
3. Tadisina, Z.R., Natarajarathinam, A., Gupta, S.: Magnetic tunnel junctions with Co-based perpendicular magnetic anisotropy multilayers. Journal of Vacuum Science & Technology A: Vacuum, Surfaces, and Films 28(4), 973–978 (2010)
4. Ala, G., Di Piazza, M.C., Tine, G., et al.: Evaluation of radiated EMI in 42-V vehicle electrical systems by FDTD simulation. IEEE Transactions on Vehicular Technology 56(4), 1477–1484 (2007)
5. See, K.Y.: Network for conducted EMI diagnosis. Electronics Letters 35(17), 1446–1447 (2002)
6. Wang, S., van Wyk, J.D., Lee, F.C.: Effects of interactions between filter parasitics and power interconnects on EMI filter performance. IEEE Transactions on Industrial Electronics 54(6), 3344–3352 (2007)
7. Jin, M., Weiming, M., Lei, Z., et al.: High Frequency Model of Conducted EMI for PWM Variable-speed Drive Systems. Proceedings of the CSEE 28(15), 141–146 (2008)
8. Wei, Y., Yang, Z., Enrong, W., et al.: Analysis and Suppression on Radiated EMI Noise for Radio Frequency Identification System. Proceedings of the CSEE 32(9), 161–166 (2012)
9. Zhang, W., Xing, Y., Cui, X.: Measurement system for near field electromagnetic radiation of power line communication networks. Proceedings of the CSEE 30(12), 117–121 (2010)
10. Hua, X., Jiang, J.: Study on novel numerical analysis of coupling electromagnetic inference. Process of the CSEE 27(30), 108–112 (2007)
11. Fu, Y., Hubing, T.H.: Analysis of Radiated Emissions From a Printed Circuit Board Using Expert System Algorithms. IEEE Transactions on Electromagnetic Compatibility 49(1), 68–75 (2007)
12. Manish, O., Kye-Yak, S., Weishan, S., et al.: Near-field to far-field prediction for high-speed board using an empirical approach. In: 2010 IEEE Electrical Design of Advanced Packaging & Systems Symposium (EDAPS), pp. 1–4 (2010)
13. Hernando, M.M., Fernandez, A., Arias, M., et al.: EMI Radiated Noise Measurement System Using the Source Reconstruction Technique. IEEE Transactions on Industrial Electronics 55(9), 3258–3265 (2008)
14. Wang, E.R., et al.: Semi-active control of vehicle suspension with MR-Damper: Part I-Controller Synthesis and Evaluation. Chinese J. of Mechanical Engineering 21(1), 13–19 (2008)

15. Wang, E.R., et al.: Semi-Active Control of Vehicle Suspension with MR-Damper: Part II-Evaluation of Suspension Performance. Chinese J. of Mechanical Engineering 21(2), 52–59 (2008)
16. Wang, E., Ying, L., Wang, W.: Semi-Active Control of Vehicle Suspension with MR-Damper: Part III-Experimental Validation. Chinese J. of Mechanical Engineering 21(4), 93–100 (2008)
17. Wang, W., Ying, L., Wang, E.: Comparison on Hysteresis Models of Controllable Magneto-rheological Damper. Journal of Mechanical Engineering 45(9), 100–108 (2009)
18. Yan, W., Zhao, Y., Wang, E., et al.: Investigation and Reduction on Conducted Electromagnetic Interference Noise Mechanism for Complex Power Electronics Systems. Proceedings of the CSEE (in press, 2012)

An Image Based Algorithm to Safely Locate Human Extremities for Human-Robot Collaboration

Johannes Höcherl and Thomas Schlegl

Regensburg University of Applied Sciences, Department of Mechanical Engineering, Galgenbergstr. 30, 93053 Regensburg, Germany
{Johannes3.Hoecherl,Thomas.Schlegl}@hs-regensburg.de
http://www.hs-regensburg.de

Abstract. For safe human-robot collaboration a technologically diverse and redundant sensor system is developed which comprises ultrasound sensors and two monocular camera systems. The sensor system recognizes human extremities in the collaboration area in which robot and human shall work together interactively. The robot controller calculates the shortest distance between the robot and a human operator. With the fused sensor data the controller determines how to adapt the robot behavior to avoid undesired physical contact with the human operator.

Keywords: functional safety, embedded systems, human-robot collaboration, monocular machine vision, infrared imaging, safe robotics.

1 Introduction

1.1 Project Framework and Related Work

The research project "ManuCyte" [1] focuses on the realization of an industrial scale cultivation platform for human cells and tissues. Within the project the team of the Laboratory for Material Handling Systems and Robotics realizes human-robot collaboration in a common working area – the Hybrid Workplace – by using a redundant sensor system consisting of cameras as well as ultrasound sensors.Both sensor systems are applied to recognize objects in their working area. The Machine Vision System (MV) is able to distinguish human extremities (HE) from other objects. Using the position of the extremities it is possible to calculate the distance between them and the robot. By making sure this distance never falls below a certain threshold value – combined with a fault-proof system architecture – collisions can safely be avoided. The software realization of the Machine Vision System will be discussed in detail within the scope of this paper. KUKA has developed the robots KR 3 SI and KR 5 SI [2] which can be used for human-robot collaboration. Compared to the comprised sensor system, however, the robot evasion strategy of KUKA is less flexible, since its path planning is based on ultrasound sensors only. On the other hand, the sensor system discussed in this paper applies the fused information from a machine vision and ultrasound

C.-Y. Su, S. Rakheja, H. Liu (Eds.): ICIRA 2012, Part II, LNAI 7507, pp. 164–175, 2012.
© Springer-Verlag Berlin Heidelberg 2012

sensor system to realize the same task. To form a collaborative environment, Pilz has developed a sensor system which can be combined with robots fulfilling the norms DIN ISO 10218-1 and 10218-2 as well as DIN EN ISO 13849. The system, called SafetyEye consists of several cameras which work together to form the necessary information [3]. This, however, is a static variant of collaboration, inasmuch as the robot is controlled/stopped by hand gestures or illegal area violation. Furthermore, it cannot be used in small area environments and thus it is not applicable here. Many other developments aim at potential analysis of collaboration between robot and human, but not at applicability in an industrial case. The SIMERO system [4], for example, is similar to the above one named SafetyEye. Others like the GRACE system [5] target interaction between robot and human, but not necessarily regarding a common working area. The approach proposed in this paper, however, aims at real-time operation of a system which is ready for industry.

1.2 Paper Organization

The paper is organized as follows. First, the hardware components are discussed, beginning from the overall system design and subsequently moving on to the Machine Vision part of the proposed sensor system in Section 2 in which the software design is discussed briefly. Then, Section 3 discusses the detection of the human extremities within images. Experimental results are shown and analyzed in Section 4 and finally Section 5 concludes the article and gives an outlook on future work.

2 System Design

The hardware and software design of the work is discussed in the following. To understand the developed Machine Vision System it is first necessary to outline the system enclosing it.

2.1 Hardware

Industrial PCs controlling the robot are situated inside of the robot's switching cabinet. In Figure 1 the *computer architecture* is shown. A Camera PC is gathering information from the camera via a CameraLink Base connection. The processed data is sent to a Control PC, where it is fused with the data gathered from the Ultrasound Sensor System connected to the Control PC. If necessary, the planned trajectory of the robot is adapted. All safety-relevant calculations are performed redundantly on both systems. In such a way, the Monitor PC cross-checks the computation results of the Control PC exchanged via a shared memory connection. If one of the systems identifies a difference between corresponding calculation results, both of them are capable of interfering the robot control up to bringing the robot to a safe halt. Figure 2 shows the *Object Recognition System* consisting of 18 ultrasound sensors and two CMOS cameras. Like

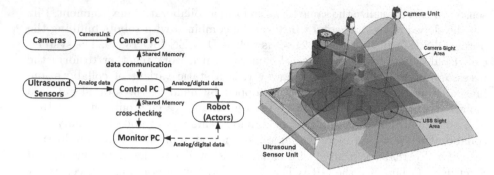

Fig. 1. Computer architecture for the Object Recognition System

Fig. 2. Schematics of the Object Recognition System

[6] in the scope of this work monocular vision processing is used to realize human robot collaboration. The figure shows how the two sensor systems are able to recognize objects in their sensing area. It is not possible to surveil the complete area of the Hybrid Workplace at minimum working distance (with reference to the camera), even if lenses with shortest available focal lengths are used. In order to ensure safe collaboration in the complete working area under such circumstances, the Machine Vision System is supported by laser scanners (not displayed) which guard the working area not surveyed by the Machine Vision System.

2.2 Software

Figure 3 illustrates the flow chart of the image processing algorithm running in part on the Camera PC and the Control PC in real-time. The algorithm is developed using Simulink in combination with the toolboxes Simulink Coder, xPC, Computer Vision System Toolbox and the third party programming library OpenCV. The image acquisition is done using two frame grabbers and cameras supported by the development software. Subsequently, the images are undistorted using OpenCV routines [12] and the human extremity is detected. Since the Ultrasound Sensor System (USS) is not able to distinguish different objects, it is necessary to provide the Control PC with the position of all objects, that is to say the human extremity and non-human objects (eliminated objects). Using this data, a plausibility check will be able to test, if USS and MV are referring to the same object. In case that both systems identify the same object positions – in a certain tolerance margin – it is assumed that neither of the two systems is malfunctioning. The depth determination computed next in the sequence is able to determine the distance of the human extremity referring to the camera using characteristic shape descriptors. This approach is similar to the mentioned *appearance based approaches* described by Garg [7] or the *single frame pose estimation* by Erol [8] respectively. If no hand is recognized, but still there is an unknown object in the surveillance area, it is assumed to be of infinite height. In such a way the algorithm obtains less precise, but safe results. After

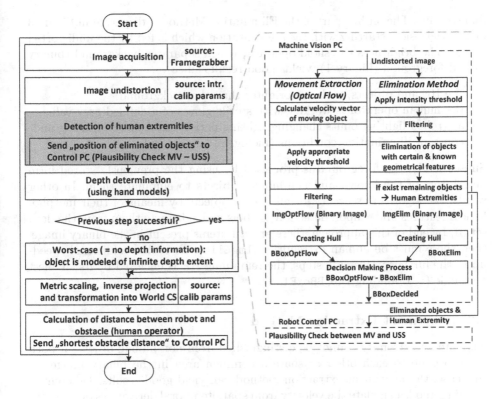

Fig. 3. Flow chart of image processing algorithm (HE detection in detail)

the isolation of significant points on the contour of the robot and human operator these candidates are transformed to the World Coordinate System, similar to [11]. Subsequently, the Euclidean distances between the robot and HE points are calculated. The shortest value is sent to the Control PC, where it is used to adapt the robot behavior from slowing down up to an evasive motion, if necessary.

3 Detection of Human Extremities

The detection of human extremities is based on two different procedures: The elimination of non-human objects (Elimination Method) and the differential based movement extraction (Movement Extraction Method). Both techniques are combined to achieve better and more stable results.

3.1 Elimination Method

At first, images of all objects utilized inside the Hybrid Workplace, e. g. tools, have to be taken. Their features (area, center of mass, eccentricity etc.) are extracted and stored for the usage in the algorithm. These first two steps are done off-line. The on-line part of the Elimination Method is displayed in Figure 3 on the right side, starting with the segmentation which is fed by the undistorted image. The brightness threshold operator, which separates background (binary 0) and foreground (binary 1), yields good results since

- the HE and objects/tools are brighter than the background,
- the human operator is working with sterile gloves of a defined grey value,
- a strobed lighting omits changing lighting performance due to heating and
- constant illumination conditions (biological laboratory)

Subsequently, the foreground is processed by using the previously stored form descriptors of the known and non-human objects to eliminate them. In other words, the algorithm searches for all known objects by means of their morphological features and – upon detection – labels and subtracts them from the data set. If, by end of this approach, there are still items present in the binary image, then these must be human extremities (`ImgElim`). To realize additional speed-up in the further processing steps, the remaining HE is enclosed by its smallest rectangle (= Bounding Box `BBoxElim`).

3.2   Movement Extraction Method

The human extremity cannot be distinguished from non-human objects if both are too close to each other or share a common area in the binary image. In this case, the movement extraction method can yield good results. Differential based methods calculate the velocity from spatiotemporal derivatives of intensity $I(\underline{x}, t)$ at location $\underline{x}$ within the image at time t. Based on

$$I(\underline{x}, t) = I(\underline{x} - \underline{v}t, 0) \tag{1}$$

with $\underline{v} = (v_x, v_y)^T$ and with the assumption of temporally constant intensity $\frac{dI(\underline{x},t)}{dt} = 0$ the gradient is defined by:

$$I_x \cdot v_x + I_y \cdot v_y + I_t = 0 \tag{2}$$

I_x, I_y and I_t are spatial and temporal gradients respectively; v_x and v_y the required horizontal and vertical velocity component. (2) is an under-determined system of equations which can be solved using the Simulink block "Optical Flow" of the Computer Vision System Toolbox incorporating the Horn-Schunk or the Lucas-Kanade method [13]. The first one provides an iterative solution to the optimization problem named in (2). However, the latter, implemented one solves the problem in a closed form. Tests show that this method runs 50 % faster with the used setup. (1) shows that the actual image $I(\underline{x}, t)$ is related to an older one, $I(\underline{x}, 0)$, using the implied movement $\underline{v}t$. If the velocity vector for every pixel has been calculated, that is to say (2) has been solved, the human extremity can be extracted utilizing an adequate velocity threshold. This can be done automatically (using a mean velocity threshold over time) or by applying a defined threshold which needs to be determined empirically through tests.

The latter one yields faster run-time characteristics accepting a possibly worse result at very slow movements of the object. Finally, the human extremity is also enclosed by a Bounding Box (`BBoxOptFlow`). The necessary steps of the Movement Extraction Method are represented in Figure 3.

3.3 Combination of Both Methods

In the block "Decision Making Process" in Figure 3 `BBoxElim` and `BBoxOptFlow` are compared with each other. If the latter one is a certain amount smaller than the first one, the Movement Extraction data is used in the following processing steps; otherwise the Elimination technique is applied to get the required results. The stability of the Elimination Method is fused with the higher precision in object overlapping cases of the Movement Extraction Method. By this means, the positive factors of both methods are conflated, while the negative ones can be omitted. After that, the binary image of the chosen method (`ImgElim` or `ImgOptFlow`) is utilized to determine the distance between the Object Plane and the human extremity in the block "Depth Determination". The shortest distance between object and imaging unit is 600 mm, while the farthest one is 900 mm, as can be seen in Figure 4. With the used optical system (data follows in Section 4) the captured area at the nearest Object Plane is (712 x 587) mm, while at farthest it is (1105 x 911) mm. When assuming that the human operator is situated at the nearest Object Plane but in reality is at the farthest one, a maximum scaling error of

$$\delta = \frac{1105\,\text{mm}}{712\,\text{mm}} = 1.55 \tag{3}$$

is committed, not taking into account the depth of the human extremity itself. In the end this means, that in worst case the robot would stay 1.55 times farther away from the HE than necessary which conforms to [6]. For safety issues this is not critical. A problem arises due to the requested redundant system architecture. It is practically impossible to perform a plausibility check of ultrasound

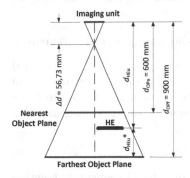

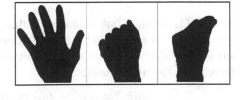

Fig. 4. Sketch of optical system used for depth determination

Fig. 5. Hand models (open, fist and pick respectively) for depth determination (similar to [9],[10])

sensor and machine vision system if the latter one is allowed to have a maximum scaling error of 1.55. The plausibility check, however, is critical, since it determines whether one of the sensor systems is malfunctioning by comparing both with each other. Thus, three possibilities have been identified to ascertain the distance between operator and imaging unit:

- Feature extraction: relating a significant feature of the HE to a taught one at a known pose;
- Intensity values: relating the extracted intensity values of the human extremity to a predefined distance (similar to a lookup table);
- Depth of field blur: calculating distance using the amount of image blur;

The first one is tested and will be discussed subsequently. Similar to the approaches of Shimada [9] and Kölsch [10], the developed algorithm is deployed to calculate required 3D information from the 2D appearance of the hand based on extracted feature information. This algorithm is provided with the contour of the human extremity by the object detection, with ImgElim or ImgOptFlow representing them in Figure 3. In this detail, the comprised approach alters from Shimada [9] and Kölsch [10], that is, the hand models are only used to extract the distance between human operator and camera. It is not necessary to make an estimation of the complete pose, since this is done by means of coordinate transformation equations. So far, only a reduced set of three distinct hand models, to be seen in Figure 5, has been introduced to evaluate this method. As every operator has a specific hand size, it is required to capture and store an image of every hand model prior to the algorithm at a certain, known distance referring to the imaging unit, e. g. at the bottom plate of the Hybrid Workplace. In the on-line application it is then necessary to relate the captured image (ImgElim or ImgOptFlow) to one of the three predefined hand models. A defined, unique feature, e. g. the diameter D of the captured hand D_{HE_u} is then extracted and related to the same feature of the stored hand D_{HE_k}. The ratio of both

$$s_{HE} = \frac{D_{HE_u}}{D_{HE_k}} = 1\ldots\delta = 1\ldots1.55 \tag{4}$$

can then be used to calculate the distance of the human extremity to the imaging unit

$$d_{HE_u} = \frac{d_{OP_f} - \Delta d}{s_{HE}} + \Delta d = \frac{(900 - 56,73)\,\text{mm}}{1\ldots1.55} + 56,73\,\text{mm} = (600\ldots900)\,\text{mm}. \tag{5}$$

The value Δd is actually not a constant value, but in the application an error of only $7.404 * 10^{-4}$ is committed if it is assumed to be constant. Since the value between farthest Object Plane and human extremity is easier to measure, this distance can be calculated using

$$d_{HE_u}{}^* = d_{OP_f} - d_{HE_u} = (0\ldots300)\,\text{mm}. \tag{6}$$

After the depth determination using the data from the Movement Extraction or the Elimination Method is finished, the related Bounding Box is scaled to correct size and described in the vector

$$\underline{h}_{HE} = \left(\begin{matrix} x_{HE} & y_{HE} & \Delta x_{HE} & \Delta y_{HE} & d_{HE_u}{}^* \end{matrix} \right)^T =$$

$$= s_{HE} \cdot \left(\begin{matrix} x_{HE_0} & y_{HE_0} & \Delta x_{HE_0} & \Delta y_{HE_0} & \frac{d_{HE_u}{}^*}{s_{HE}} \end{matrix} \right)^T , \tag{7}$$

where x_{HE} is the scaled (actual) position of the Bounding Box in x and x_{HE_0} the unscaled value. Furthermore, Δx_{HE} is the extent of the Bounding Box in x. The vector $\underline{h}_{HE}$ can be converted to the four corner points of the Bounding Box which can be transformed to the World Coordinate System.

4   Experimental Results

Since the facility makes use of an interactive monitor (changing background) and, furthermore, of the sensor system PS1080, better known as "Microsoft Kinect" system, the complete camera application is designed to work in the near in- frared (IR) spectrum (740 nm). Table 1 shows all necessary information about the setup of the system. The algorithm presented in Figure 3 has been tested experimentally in the RTOS, except for the function "Depth Determination". This function, however, has already been tested in real-time independently of the remaining algorithm. The software checks have been performed in an artifi- cial environment, with no glare and only a reduced set of tools. In the described setup, the HE has been recognized in all images. Further settings for the follow- ing measurements can be seen in Table 2. Task execution times (TET) of the algorithms are shown in Table 3. For a correct and precise representation of the

Table 1. Technical data for experimental results

CAE	Mathworks Matlab 2011b (32bit)	incl. toolboxes Simulink 7.8, Simulink Coder 8.1, Computer Vision System 4.1, DSP System 8.1, xPC 5.1, and third party libraries OpenCV 2.1
real-time op- erating system (RTOS)	Mathworks xPC 5.1	provided by xPC Toolbox; sample time ad- justable; multitasking possible
compiler	Microsoft Visual Studio C++ 2008 Pro	supported by Matlab 2011b
frame grabber	BitFlow NEON CLB	supported by RTOS xPC
camera	Photonfocus MV1- D1312i-80-CL-12	1312 x 1082 pixels; 55 fps; max. sensitivity @ 740 nm; supported by frame grabber
camera trigger	NI DAQ Board PCI-6221	supported by RTOS xPC; 5V I/O ports
lighting	self-developed	LEDs @ 740 nm; 9.24 W optical power
optics	Goyo Optical GMHR48014MCN-1	maximum distortion -1.6 %; transmission factor @740 nm = 0.75; f = 8 mm
optical filter	Midwest Optical Systems BP735-55.0	bandpass filter; central wavelength 735 nm; transmission factor @740 nm = 0.9427

Table 2. Settings of Vision System   **Table 3.** Execution times of image processing

exposure time	10 ms
image resize factor	25%
⇒ effective resolution	328 x 271

TET undist. & detect. (1 cam.)	71.9 ms
TET depth determ. (1 cam.)	50.0 ms
estimated total TET (2 cam.)	≈ 250 ms

human extremity in world coordinates the distance between Object Plane and imaging unit has to be known. Since the depth determination has not yet been incorporated in the presented algorithm, this value has been defined manually through measuring. For this test the operator works on a determined Object Plane with a known relation of pixel to metric units.Figure 6 illustrates the position of the human extremity measured with one ultrasound sensor ($_0y_{\text{HE,USS}}$) and with one camera ($_0y_{\text{HE,cam}}$) in a common coordinate system (0). Test circumstances are that the position of the robot is fixed, whereas the human operator is moving only one-dimensionally or perpendicularly to the robot respectively (here in y-coordinates). The ultrasound sensor is also adjusted perpendicular to the human extremity to be able to compare the results of both measurement systems. The y-coordinate of the point, plotted in Figure 6 is the one with the shortest distance between robot and human extremity over time. As the HE is approximated by a non-rotated rectangle, $_0y_{\text{HE,cam}}$ is the nearest of the two y-coordinates of its Bounding Box. The value of the ultrasound sensor, however, is the direct measured one. Both of them still have to be transformed into one common coordinate system so that they can be compared. The difference between the measurements of the Ultrasound Sensor and the Machine Vision System is due to the prototypic implementation of the robot and the Hybrid Workplace. Figure 7 illustrates the course of the shortest distance between robot and human operator d_{RHE} over time if both of them are allowed to move. Furthermore, the course is only based on the measurements of the MV system combined with the knowledge of the position of the robot. If the minimum distance $d_{\min}$ between human and robot is underrun, the robot stops or starts an evasive movement. The position of the robot is measured in a fast sample rate (1 ms), thus producing a smooth discrete course. The HE is measured by the Machine Vision System with 200 ms and therefore produces coarse discrete steps. As a result, d_{RHE} represented in Figure 7 shows a smooth course if only the robot is moving, a coarse one if only the hand of the human operator is moving and a mixed one if both of them are moving at the same time. The marked interval *approximation/removal of the human extremity → avoiding movement* in Figure 7 will be discussed subsequently. In this sector, the minimum distance is underrun. Immediately after this event, the robot starts an evasive movement. The course of the figure shows big jumps towards shorter distances in the slow sample rate and small ones towards longer distances in the fast sample rate, as anticipated. According to the international standards, mentioned in Section 1, the robot is only allowed to move with a maximum velocity of 0.250 $\frac{\text{m}}{\text{s}}$ in a collaborative environment. The human operator, however, is able to move with a maximum of 2.0 $\frac{\text{m}}{\text{s}}$, according to Thiemermann [14]. If the human operator is moving fast

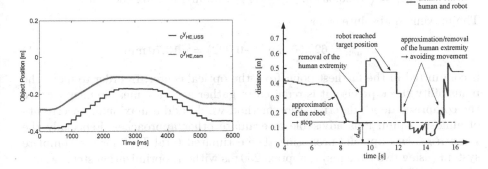

Fig. 6. Object position of the human extremity based on camera and ultrasound data (slow moving object)

Fig. 7. Shortest distance between robot and human extremity over time

towards the robot, the conclusion is that it cannot get beyond the minimum distance threshold. Yet, if the human operator tries hard to catch the robot, he/she will achieve it, since the robot is much slower. Figure 8 shows the results of the evaluation algorithm for the depth determination. A maximum positive uncertainty of 10 mm and a negative one of 16 mm is observed. With (6) and (5) it is possible to calculate the scaling factors for the actual s_{HE} and both maximum error values ($s_{HE_{neg}}$, $s_{HE_{pos}}$). Thus a relative error of

$$\delta_{neg} = \frac{s_{HE_{neg}} - s_{HE}}{s_{HE}} = \frac{1.125 - 1.150}{1.150} = -0.022 \tag{8}$$

and

$$\delta_{pos} = \frac{s_{HE_{pos}} - s_{HE}}{s_{HE}} = \frac{1.166 - 1.150}{1.150} = 0.014 \tag{9}$$

can be calculated. The imaged area at $d_{HE_u}{}^* = 110$ mm is (960.63×791.97) mm. By this means, the distance between the image center and the farthest point on the referred Object Plane is

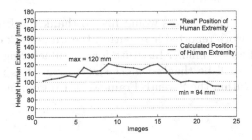

Fig. 8. Depth determination algorithm compared to real object

$$d_{far} = \sqrt{(960.63\,\text{mm}/2)^2 + (791.97\,\text{mm}/2)^2} = 622.50\,\text{mm}. \tag{10}$$

The maximum absolute error

$$\Delta_{max} = 622.50\,\text{mm} \cdot (-0.022) = -13.70\,\text{mm} \tag{11}$$

is committed in the farthest point from the optical center. In order to make the plausibility check precise, it is required to gather accurate measurements. Since the comprised depth determination method would add a maximum uncertainty of almost 14 mm, it is advisable to evaluate other approaches. Especially the *intensity values* appears promising. The estimated total TET for the complete system (using two cameras) is approx. 250 ms without optimization steps, as can be seen in Table 3.

5   Conclusions and Outlook

An algorithm for the detection of human extremities in monocular camera images has been developed. Furthermore, this article introduces an algorithm for the depth determination with a certain precision. The two discussed algorithms need to be combined in one real-time application and optimized regarding their runtime characteristics. Possible approaches are the usage of a region-of-interest (ROI) on the complete image processing algorithm or on certain parts of it and lookup tables for the image undistortion. For the determination of the ROI, the past position of the human extremity could be used. The aim is to achieve a total TET of under 50 ms. As already mentioned, the actual approach of the depth determination appears to be slow and rather imprecise. Therefore, the method of intensity values will be pursued in order to get a desired maximum position error of only 5 mm in less operational time. The higher accuracy, in particular, is required to increase the performance of the plausibility check. The entire algorithm also has to be tested under the real conditions of the finalized system. That is, the real environmental conditions must be applied, which will increase glare due to the integrated high reflective metal surfaces. A possible 90° cross-polarization of lighting and camera has been tested (yet not documented in the scope of this article) to get better image quality regarding reflections.

Acknowledgments. The authors would like to thank the European Community for funding the work reported here within the framework of the ManuCyte Project (see [1]). The "Fraunhofer Institute for Manufacturing Engineering and Automation (IPA)" shall be thanked most sincerely as it is the leader of this project consortium within the Seventh Framework Programme (FP7).

References

1. ManuCyte: Modular Manufacturing Platform for Flexible, Patient-Specific Cell Cultivation. Fraunhofer Institute for Manufacturing Engineering and Automation (IPA). Nobelstr. 12, D-70569 Stuttgart, http://www.manucyte-project.eu/

2. Heiligensetzer, P.: Aktuelle Entwicklungen bei Industrierobotern im Bereich der Mensch-Roboter Kooperation. Technical Report, Tag der Arbeitssicherheit in Fellbach (2009)
3. Frey, S., Fuchs, L., Kramer-Wolf, T., Kurth, M., Maibach, J., Merx, J., Schwarz, M., Stark, T., Skaletz-Karrer, S., Wimmer, M.: Dreidimensionale Sicherheit. Mensch und Automation 03, 3 (2011)
4. Gecks, T., Henrich, D.: SIMERO: Camera Supervised Workspace for Service Robots, Technical Report, 2nd Workshop on Advances in Service Robotics, Fraunhofer IPA (2004)
5. Simmons, R., Goldberg, D., Goode, A., Montemerlo, M., Roy, N., Sellner, B., Urmson, C., Bugajska, M., Coblenz, M., Macmahon, M., Perzanowski, D., Horswill, I., Zubek, R., Kortenkamp, D., Wolfe, B., Milam, T., Maxwell, B.: GRACE: An Autonomous Robot for the AAAI Robot Challenge. AI Magazine 24, 51–72 (2003)
6. Ebert, D.: Bildbasierte Erzeugung kollisionsfreier Transferbewegungen für Industrieroboter. Dissertation, University of Bayreuth (2003)
7. Garg, P., Aggarwal, N., Sofat, S.: Vision Based Hand Gesture Recognition. Engineering and Technology 49, 972–977 (2009)
8. Erol, A., Bebis, G., Nicolescu, M., Boyle, R., Twombly, X.: A Review on Vision-Based Full DOF Hand Motion Estimation. In: IEEE Computer Society Conference on Computer Vision and Pattern Recognition, CVPR (2005)
9. Shimada, N., Kimura, K., Shirai, Y.: Real-time 3D hand posture estimation based on 2D appearance retrieval using monocular camera. In: ICCV Workshop on Recognition, Analysis, and Tracking of Faces and Gestures in Real-Time Systems, pp. 23–30 (2001)
10. Kölsch, M., Turk, M.: Robust Hand Detection. In: International Conference on Automatic Face and Gesture Recognition, Seoul, Korea, pp. 614–619 (2004)
11. Heikkilä, J., Silven, O.: A Four-step Camera Calibration Procedure with Implicit Image Correction. In: IEEE Computer Society Conference on Computer Vision and Pattern Recognition, pp. 1106–1112 (June 1997)
12. OpenCV Reference Manual v2.1, Open Source/Willow Garage (March 2010)
13. Barron, J.L., Fleet, D.J., Beauchemin, S.S.: Performance of Optical Flow Techniques. International Journal of Computer Vision 12, 43–77 (1994)
14. Thiemermann, S.: Direkte Mensch-Roboter-Kooperation in der Kleinteilmontage mit einem SCARA-Roboter. Dissertation, Faculty Mechanical Engineering – University Stuttgart (2005)

Research of a Multi-DOF Pathological
Sampling Flexible Robot

Hangfei Zhou[1], Jian Fei[2], Gen Pan[1], Weixin Yan[1], Zhuang Fu[1,3], and Yanzheng Zhao[1]

[1] State Key Lab of Mechanical System and Vibration, Shanghai 200240, China
[2] Ruijin Hospital Affiliated to Shanghai Jiao Tong University, Shanghai 200240, China
[3] State Key Lab of Robotics and System, Harbin 150080, China
feijian@hotmail.com, {zhfu,xiaogu4524,yzh-zhao}@sjtu.edu.cn

Abstract. Robot assisted medical system has become one of the most important directions among robot studying field. This paper records a research on Multi-DOF pathological sampling flexible robot system which can be used in minimally invasive surgery. The main work includes: Overall structure design based on some special requirements, mathematical modeling and analysis, system hardware and software building, movement experiment and simulation capture experiment. Result of the experiments shows that the Multi-DOF pathological sampling flexible robot can fulfill the prospective design requirements and be capable for sampling and detecting.

Keywords: multiple degrees of freedom(multi-DOF), flexible robot, pathology, sampling.

1   Introduction

Technique of micro operating system is in widespread use in medical field. The most prospective application is intervened minimally invasive treatment, which has improved the health quality of patients because of its advantages: small-wound, shorter healing time, quicker recovery, shorter hospital stays and so on [1]. The existing catheter technique is not so suitable for sampling of pathological tissues in post-operation. Surgeons have to manually exteriorize the pathological tissues after the high-strung surgery; If a surgeon performs surgeries twice a day or more, he or she will be extremely tired, gaunt, even has a serious headache. Furthermore, manual operation has some disadvantages: big cuts and longer surgery time. So robots are necessary in surgery to assist or replace surgeons [4].

At present, many achievements on the intervene system for master-slave surgery are achieved [5-7]. Some catheters are installed SMA for servo actuator on the front, and some are installed sensors on account of catheter operating system [8-9]. But these projects may be expensive or encountered precision problems. This paper develops a new MDOF micro operating robot for automatic pathological tissue sampling. With this robot platform, surgeons can intuitively control the robot's position, velocity and buckling according to prompt of the far-end. This robot

C.-Y. Su, S. Rakheja, H. Liu (Eds.): ICIRA 2012, Part II, LNAI 7507, pp. 176–185, 2012.

platform is suitable for minimally invasive surgery because it is capable to simplify the surgery operation and greatly shorten the sampling time.

2   Operation Requirement and Ensemble Design

Figure 1 shows the system structure of the MDOF pathological tissue sampling robot platform. It consists of nounmenon, control system, hand shank and sensor testing system. Control system collects information from the hand shank, controls the motions of motors by system internal arithmetic and then detects the actual running state by sensor testing system to perform closed-loop control and so the precise control of the robot achieves.

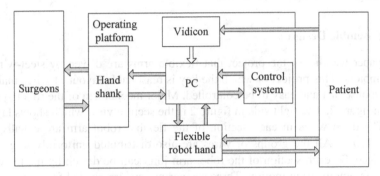

Fig. 1. Flexible robot system chart

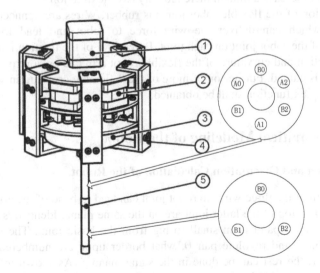

Fig. 2. Mechanical diagram of the robotic system(5. multi-level flexible robot   4.   skeleton   3. the bottom assembly   2. the middle assembly   1. the upper assembly)

2.1   Operation Requirement

Index of the MDOF flexible pathological tissue sampling robot:

1) Diameter: Less than 12mm.
2) Amount of DOFs: More than 6.
3) Positioning precision: Less than 0.1mm.

In addition, the robot system, which should be easily disinfected to ensure the operation safety, shall possess the function of off-line simulation. On the basis of requirements above, it is designed to be guided by neither outside magnetic field nor driving force from the robot head. Guided by driving force from the robot head the intervene device volume will be too big, while interference is hard to control if outside magnetic field guide is chosen.

2.2   Ensemble Design

In this paper we choose the project that flexible arms are driven by steel-wires and stepper motors. This project of which the key is reasonable layout of wires makes the robot response fast and easy to be controlled. Major mechanism of the robot system is shown in figure 2. The right side in figure 2 is the section view which shows layout of wires. The three wires in each section of the flexible robot arm are equally at the angle of 120°. All the groups of wires are also distributed uniformly to get better concordance. So each section of the robot arm joint can be driven by the three wires to complete omnibearing motion. Three stepper motors are needed for each section to drive the three wires. The motors are equipped on a rotatable flat and then DOFs of the mechanism increase although there are only two flexible joints.

Composition of the flexible robot joints is rubber. Wires are connected through a head cover which can deliver the wire force to robot and lead to controllable deformation of the robot joint on each joint. By control of the traction length of wires, bending direction and curvature of the flexible robot arm can be controlled and the 2-DOF-control is gained. Further on, if more of these flexible arms are in series, a robot arm with complex function shall be obtained.

3   Mathematical Modeling of the Robot

3.1   Position and Orientation Calculation of the Robot

Traction length of the three wires in robot joint can lead to bend of the arm. Bottom of the fore joint and top of the latter joint are on the same plane. Identifiers of each joint and revolute pair expand from small to big from the basic joint. The foundation is numbered joint 0 and revolute pair 0, what border upon are numbered joint 1 and revolute pair 1, the rest can be done in the same manner. As shown in figure 2, the upper joint is joint 1 and revolute 1, transformation matrix from the upper joint to lower joint is numbered matrix 1.

Suppose base coordinate system of the first joint is $o_0x_0y_0$, the after $o_ix_iy_i$ means coordinate system of the joint i+1. P_i is pose matrix of joint i, transformation matrix from joint i-1 to joint i is $A_i=Trans(l,0,0)Rot(y, \varphi_i)Rot(z, \theta_i)$ which can be expressed as the fourth dimension matrix below:

$$A_i = \begin{cases} \cos\theta_i\cos\varphi_i & -\cos\varphi_i\sin\theta_i & \sin\varphi_i & L \\ \sin\theta_i & \cos\theta_i & 0 & 0 \\ -\cos\theta_i\sin\varphi_i & \sin\sin\varphi_i & \cos\varphi_i & 0 \\ 0 & 0 & 0 & 1 \end{cases} \tag{1}$$

Transformation matrix from point in joint i to the base coordinate system is T_i, which satisfy the equation below:

$$T_i=A_1A_2 \bullet \bullet \bullet A_i. \tag{2}$$

It can be expressed as:

$$P_i=P_{i-1}A_i. \tag{3}$$

The total Transformation matrix is:

$$P_i=P_0T_i. \tag{4}$$

If the tip coordinate of the last joint is $M_i(l_i,0,0,0)^T$, while l_i is the length of tip sensor or other device, coordinate of the tip is:

$$M=P_0T_i M_i. \tag{5}$$

3.2   Calculation of the Wire Length Alteration and Angle

Suppose the wires are rigid, that is to say, elastic deformation in stretching is not considered. Alteration of wire length therefore correlate with rotation angle of joint.

Suppose the length alteration of the three wires are $|AA_1|$, $|BB_1|$, $|CC_1|$, which can be calculated by the method as follows. Take calculation of $|AA_1|$ for example:

As it is shown in figure 3, location of A_1 is A_1' before the joint rotation, $A_1'(d/2,$ $r\cos\alpha, r\sin\alpha, 0)^T$.

d is the joint length, r is the joint radius. After the joint rotation, equations are gained as follows:

$$T=Trans(l,0,0)Rot(y, \varphi)Rot(z, \theta). \tag{6}$$

$$A_1=TA_1'. \tag{7}$$

$$\Delta d = |AA_1|-d. \tag{8}$$

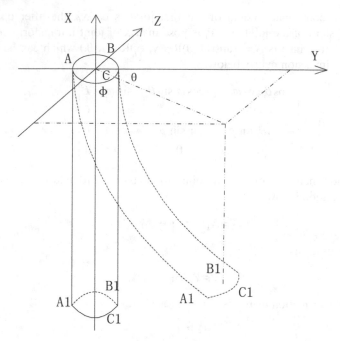

Fig. 3. Flexible robot joint alternation

Alteration of wire length is accumulation. So alteration summation of wire length in joint 1 is

$$D=\Delta d_1+\Delta d_2+\cdot\cdot\cdot+\Delta d_i .\qquad(9)$$

Needed rotating angular of motors can be calculated through the alteration summation of wire length. So we can control the alteration of wire length to achieve accurate motion of flexible robot fingers by controlling rotating angular of motors.

4   Control System Design of the Robot

4.1   Hardware Structure Design of Control System

In this research, two phase four wire 39 stepper motors of which the step angle 1.8 and torque 0.21 are chosen to ensure that the robot has considerable accuracy and is easy to control. Furthermore, the resolution ratio of stepper motor should be magnified for controlling accuracy. In the design we choose the chip TB6560 as driver. With 16 subdivision capability of this chip, the actual step angle shall be transferred to be 0.1125 degrees and the resolution ratio of the robot is therefore greatly improved.

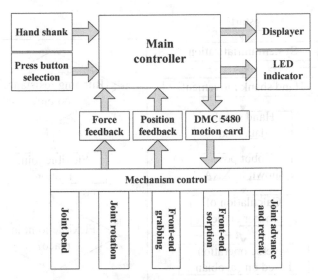

Fig. 4. Flexible robot control system chart

The cybernetics core of the robot is motion control card DMC5480, which is on the basis of PCI. It has strong real-time processing ability because its specialized motion control chip ASIC, CPU and RAM. It is able to control up to 4 stepper motors. 16 digital inputs and outputs enable it to read signals from sensors and feed it back to main controller which handled the signals and feed the force signals back to operating hand shank; then, graphic signals is fed back to operator by the displayer.

In this research, 7 stepper motors that are able to control motions of robot in every direction and axis are provided to drive the flexible 6-DOF robot which is able to grab or absorb things extensively.

4.2   Software Structure Design of Control System

C# is used to design the control system programs. XNX platform which is helpful for intuitionistic debug work is used to debug the software. Control system that the prototype refers to mainly contains: main program module, pulse sending module, controlling module, force feedback and graphic feedback module.

Figure 5 shows the system program tree. Motion of operating hand shank will change the coordinates in the virtual environment, meanwhile, virtual control system in computer will synchronously collect these data and feed it back to virtual environment established by XNA. Computer virtual environment will show the robot motions in actual environment according to the motion parameters of virtual telecontrol hand shank, then the motions of flexible robot in virtual environment are used to calculate distance-which each motor should rotate-by formulas deduced by the mathematic models before. Then relevant pulses are sent to actual flexible robot fingers controlling motors by motor driving board. By procedures above, data as virtual environment can be shown in actual environment.

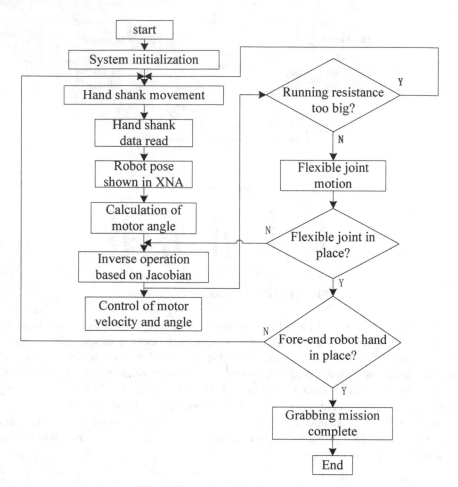

Fig. 5. System program flow chart

5   Experiment and Conclusion

We carried out virtual experiment(figure 7) and grabbing experiments(figure 8) through the built system on the designed robot experiment platform(figure 6) with a ping pong which was used to imitate pathological tissue. Multi-axial linkage interpolation algorithm was used to achieve accurate motion control. In the experiments, the imitated pathological tissue was laid in the experiment platform randomly, then the flexible robot was operated by operating hand shank to move to the position of pathological tissue and grab it. After that, the tissue was moved to a appointed position. In the procedure of repeated experiments, attitude of robot was changed by program control(figure 9) and was able to accurately complete grabbing mission in which the grabbing and reset time was controlled within 30 seconds each time.

Fig. 6. Micro operating robot system

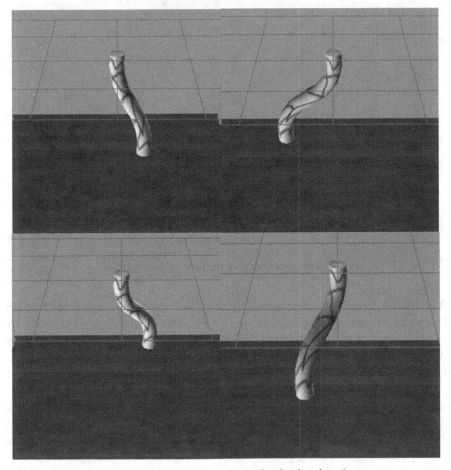

Fig. 7. All directions of motion of the robot in virtual environment

Fig. 8. Grabbing experiment

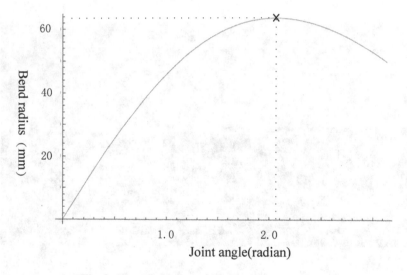

Fig. 9. Simulation results of the joint angle and radius

The MDOF minimally invasive surgery automatic sampling micro robot platform in this paper will greatly help surgeons to pick up pathological tissues and reduce the possibility of surgeons' misoperation. Results of the experiment and simulation show that the platform which can be conveniently applied in observation and sampling of pathological tissues has considerable application value.

Acknowledgments. This work was partially supported by the Research Fund of State Key Lab of MSV, China (Grant No. MSV-MS-2010-03), the State Key Laboratory of Robotics and System (HIT) (Grant No. SKLRS-2010-ZD-06), and the National Natural Science Foundation of China under Grant No. 61075086, 60875058.

References

1. Ju, H.: Research on Control System for the Laparoscopic Minimally Invasive Surgery Robot. Nankai University (2009)
2. Breindel, B.: The catheter business: How much? Who? Where? BCC Research, HLC019B (2004)
3. Chen, Y., Chang, J.H., et al.: Multi-turn, Tension-stiffening Catheter Navigation System. In: ICRA, Anchorage, Alaska, USA, pp. 5570–5575 (2010)
4. Guo, J., Xiao, N., Guo, S., Tamiya, T.: A Force Display Method for a Novel Catheter Operating System. In: ICRA, Harbin, China, pp. 782–786 (2010)
5. Arai, F., Tanimoto, M., Fukuda, T., Shimojima, K., Matsuura, H., Negoro, M.: Distributed Virtual Environment for Intravascular Tele-Surgery Using Multimedia Telecommunication. In: Proceedings of VRAIS 1996 (1996)
6. Tanimoto, M., Arai, F., Fukuda, T., Negoro, M.: Augmentation of Safety in Teleoperation System for Intravascular Neurosurgery. Advanced Robotics, 323–325 (1998)
7. Preusche, C., Ortmaier, T., Hirzinger, G.: Teleoperation concepts in minimal invasive surgery. Control Engineering Practice, 1245–1250 (2002)
8. Wang, J., Guo, S., Kondo, H., Guo, J., Tamiya, T.: A Novel Catheter Operating System with Force Feedback for Medical Applications. International Journal of Information Acquisition, 83–91 (2008)
9. Guo, S., Guo, J., Xiao, N., Tamiya, T.: Force Sensors-based a Novel Type of Catheter Operating System. In: IEEE, Kobe, Japan, pp. 11–16 (2010)

Control by 3D Simulation – A New eRobotics Approach to Control Design in Automation

Juergen Rossmann, Michael Schluse,
Christian Schlette, and Ralf Waspe

Institute for Man-Machine Interaction, RWTH Aachen University
Ahornstrasse 55, 52074 Aachen, Germany
{rossmann,schluse,schlette,waspe}@mmi.rwth-aachen.de
http://mmi.rwth-aachen.de

Abstract. This paper introduces new so-called control by 3D simulation concepts which are the basis for the simulation based development of complex control algorithms e. g. in the field of robotics and automation. Now, a controller design can be developed, parameterized, tested and verified using so called Virtual Testbeds until they perform adequately in simulation. Then a stripped down version of the same simulation system uses the same simulation model and the same simulation algorithms on the real hardware implementing a real-time capable controller. This results in an integrated development approach, which brings simulation technology on the real hardware to bridge the gap between simulation and real world operation. In this way, Virtual Testbeds and control by 3D simulation provide major building blocks in the emerging field of eRobotics to keep manageable the ever increasing complexity of current computer-aided solutions.

Keywords: Rapid Control Prototyping, Virtual Testbed, Multi Robot Control.

1 Introduction

The research field of eRobotics is currently an active domain of interest for scientists working in the area of "eSystems engineering" [1]. The aim of the corresponding developments is "to bring robotics technology into the computer" providing a comprehensive software environment to address various robotics-related issues. Starting with user requirements analysis of system design, support for the development and selection of appropriate hardware, the programming of algorithms and mechanisms, system and process simulation, control design and implementation, and encompassing the validation of developed models and programs, eRobotics provides a continuous and systematic computer support throughout the entire life-cycle of robotic systems. In this way, the ever increasing complexity of current computer-aided robotic solutions will be kept manageable, and know-how from completed work is electronically preserved and made available for further applications.

C.-Y. Su, S. Rakheja, H. Liu (Eds.): ICIRA 2012, Part II, LNAI 7507, pp. 186–197, 2012.
© Springer-Verlag Berlin Heidelberg 2012

The development of such complex systems usually can not be done individually for each subcomponent, but requires a holistic development approach, also regarding their interplay under varying conditions and in changing target scenarios. That is why we developed the Virtual Testbed methodology, one of the key concepts in the field of eRobotics. Virtual Testbeds provide an integrated simulation framework (see Figure 1) comprising not only system, environment and simulation models as well simulation methods, but also control and data processing algorithms, the inner and outer dependencies of the digital prototype, as well as interfaces to real systems. This way, a Virtual Testbed contains everything necessary to simulate a dynamic system, e. g. geometric models, actuator and sensor models, control algorithms, but also means for visualization and interaction.

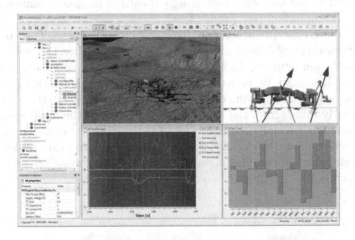

Fig. 1. The Virtual Crater Testbed ([2]), one example for various Virtual Testbeds realized so far, integrates all aspects necessary for the development of mobile legged robots like dynamics, actuators, sensors, terra-mechanics, hardware interfaces, etc. (robot model ©DFKI Bremen)

The result is an integrated simulation based development process based on one single comprehensive knowledge base, the simulation model. But what is missing now is the step into reality. If it would now be possible to use the control and data processing part of the simulation model to control or supervise the real system directly, one could bridge the gap between developments for simulation and real hardware resulting into one single, comprehensive and truly concurrent development approach.

At first glance, the methods for this are well known. Concepts from the field of "Computer Aided Control System Design" [3] are well established for enabling simulation based control design in automation using "hardware in the loop" or "software in the loop" scenarios (see Figure 2). In this context "Rapid Control Prototyping" approaches first model, simulate and test a control design with a

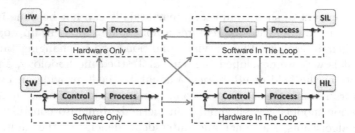

Fig. 2. Established concepts for Computer Aided Control System Design

dedicated simulation system [4]. In a second step, the resulting control algorithms are transferred to the hardware platform by means of manual reimplementation or automatic compilation (see Figure 3, A).

However, these concepts practically have specific drawbacks. They mainly focus the development of "classical" control systems and therefore rely on block oriented simulation systems. To use the models to control or supervise real systems, the models must be converted making on-line modifications as well as visualization or debugging difficult. Because of the fact, that the target environment greatly differs from the simulation environment, the integration of user defined algorithms normally requires a lot of extra work. Also, these approaches lack an overall semantic model of the environment, an important building block for the development of complex algorithms, for use in simulation, as well as in the real controller.

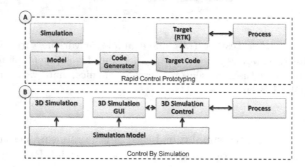

Fig. 3. Comparison of the "classical" Rapid Control Prototyping and the Control-By-Simulation approaches

One could overcome these limitations if it would be possible to directly use the simulation framework in the real controller itself. The only necessary action in this case would be to switch off the simulated sensors and actuators, connect the real sensors and actuators to the control and data processing algorithms of the overall simulation model and load the result into a real-time capable version of the simulation system. That is exactly the approach we will present in this paper (see Figure 3, B).

The challenge now is to find a simulation system which could act as the basis of the Virtual Testbed on the one hand and - at the same time - is able to run under real-time restrictions to realize the real controller. To fulfill the manifold requirements by Virtual Testbeds concerning simulation technology we have already developed a new architecture for 3D simulation systems, which is highly configurable for a large variety of different applications. This system has been built on a real-time database and is modular enough to strip away unnecessary parts, so it can be made real-time capable and can process selected control algorithms in real-time. It is based on scalable approaches in distributed simulation, concepts which can be used for the implementation of distributed control, visualization and user interfaces and enable a bidirectional transfer of functionality between simulation and real hardware control.

This way, this simulation system enables and supports the realization a new simulation based control design paradigm for automated systems we named "control-by-simulation", a concept which is rooted in well established methods in control theory.

This contribution is organized as follows: In section 2, we give an overview of the current developments in control system design and selected fields of applications. In section 3, we introduce the micro kernel architecture of our simulation system. The resulting system is highly modular and scalable to support on the one hand the Virtual Testbed concept as described in section 4, as well as the new simulation based control design paradigm "control-by-simulation" as introduced in section 5. The validity of our concept is demonstrated for two scenarios in section 6.

2   State of the Art

In the following paragraphs a few examples are given, which illustrate the many development flows that are all categorized as rapid control prototyping. The abbreviations used in this section are shown as yellow markers in Figure 2. In general the aim of rapid prototyping is to develop a functioning hardware component. Rapid prototyping is mostly done by using block oriented development tools such as *Matlab/Simulink* [5]. Often third party solutions such as *dSpace* [6] are used, which provide I/O hardware components that are connected to the process hardware and are capable of running code compiled from the Matlab/Simulink model.

In [7] a hardware in the loop prototyping using dSapce directly leads to a hardware solution for the control (HIL - HW). [8] is concerned with the development of power electronics controls using real time enabled hardware in the loop solutions. He inserts an extra step in the development chain, by implementing a Virtual Testbed, a pure software solution in which algorithms are developed before they are transfered to the HIL stage (SW - HIL - HW). Others add a further software in the loop step into the development chain. [9] develops a helicopter control using dSpace utilizing an integrated (SIL - HIL- HW) approach, while [10] adds a further simulation step (SW - SIL - HIL -HW). It is also possible to use rapid control prototyping without a intermediate "in-the-loop" step, as shown in the development of a robot control by [11] (SW - HW). Also the development of a dedicated hardware controller is not always the goal of the process. [12] uses SIL only, while [13] switches between pure simulation (SW) and SIL to develop control algorithms for an automation system. [14] uses the term "control by simulation" for a similar scenario.

Virtual Testbeds are used in a variety of application areas like network simulation [15] or building simulation [16]. They are also used for testing algorithms for space robotics as described in [17], a Virtual Testbed for the development of rovers used in extraterrestrial exploration. Virtual Testbeds do not necessarily include a block oriented algorithm development. However the may benefit from HIL or SIL capabilities, which are used to fine tune the simulation to give realistic results.

What is still missing so far is a fully integrated approach using 3D simulation technology even on the hardware controller to realize even complex controllers e.g. in the field of robotics (see section 6). That is the focus of this paper.

3   The Real-Time Simulation Database

One key aspect of every simulation system is its internal (real-time) database, which provides a certain data schema describing the data, contains the data itself on which the simulation is performed and provides methods for data storage and representation. For the simulation performance it is important how the data can be accessed and manipulated by the simulation algorithms. Ideally database management itself should be very time efficient and ready for real-time operation, thus leaving computing power available to the simulation routines. A general purpose simulation system should be able to flexibly adopt new data scheme for its internal database, without additional programming. It must be possible to easily add new simulation algorithms or enhance existing methods, while guaranteeing stability and performance of the system.

To fulfill these requirements and to eliminate unnecessary dependencies we developed a new architecture for 3D simulation systems, as shown in Figure 4. It is based on a small kernel, the *Versatile Simulation Database* (VSD). The VSD provides the essential data types and functionalities of the database, which is enhanced by a system of numerous application specific simulation plugins. The VSD is called *active*, since it is not only a static data container, but also allows for containing, activating and connecting algorithms to process data directly in the database. In order to manage and maintain this integration of data and algorithms, the VSD is an object oriented graph database (see [18]), consisting of nodes and extensions. The nodes constitute the basic element of the graph database and extensions can be attached to nodes in order to add new functionalities or properties to existing types of nodes.

The VSD also provides essential functionalities for parallel and distributed simulation. Depending on the application, the performance of the simulation or

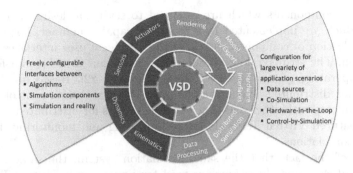

Fig. 4. The micro-kernel architecture of our simulation system

the controller can thus be enhanced by being parallelized on multi-core processors or distributed in a network of computers. In addition, the mechanisms for distribution allow for separating real-time processes from graphical user interfaces and monitoring tools (see Figure 3, B).

4   Virtual Testbeds

Using the concepts illustrated above we are now able to simulate complex systems with all relevant system components and their interdependencies. The result is a comprehensive development and testing environment based on simulation technology, a Virtual Testbed, which acts as a central focal point in multi-disciplinary development projects. Since Virtual Testbeds already offer a comprehensive set of simulation methods to model e.g. kinematics and dynamics of automated environments and systems, they can be interpreted as a virtual substitute for physical testbeds which offers sophisticated tools for detailed monitoring, rapid prototyping and control design.

For the development of various Virtual Testbeds in research and industry, our simulation system has been extended by specific modules for 3D simulation and rendering, dynamic [19], kinematic [20] and sensor simulation [21], but also State Oriented Modeling techniques or Geo Information Systems.

5   Control by Simulation

The underlying simulation framework not only allows for the design, prototyping, test and verification of control algorithms using Virtual Testbeds up to the point when the control is ready to be applied to real world applications, they also support the application of 3D simulation techniques to control actual hardware itself using control-by-simulation concepts. For this, only minor reconfigurations of the simulation system are necessary "to bring the simulation framework on the real hardware", because its micro kernel architecture allows for the detailed selection of the active simulation modules. Thus, the system can be stripped down to the components which are essential to set up a desired control system and which are implemented in a real-time capable manner. For example, a typical selection of components exclude the graphical user interfaces and 3D visualization. The stripped down simulation system can then be transferred to real-time operating systems such as QNX Neutrino [22]. Based on the functionalities for distributed simulation, stripped down real-time control systems can communicate with other real-time control systems for distributed control or with full-featured Virtual Testbeds for commanding and monitoring, but also supportive simulations.

Because of the fact, that the same simulation system, the same real-time database and the same algorithms are used for simulation in Virtual Testbeds, as well as for real-time operation on the real hardware, identical models are the basis for simulation as well as for the controller implementation. The transfer of the controller design is carried out without the drawback of manual reimplementation or automatic compilation. In addition, the transfer is bidirectional, because the lossless transfer back to the simulation is also available.

In its final stage, a comprehensive Virtual Testbed models and simulates the physical behavior of automated environments and systems and also incorporates the necessary control algorithms to simulate the individual automated components as well as their interdependencies. After the control algorithms perform adequately in the simulation, the simulation model is simply enhanced by the interfaces to the real automation components. The 3D simulation now acts on real world data and is able to control the real hardware. In this manner simulation and control can be developed in parallel without additional work, because the interfaces, programs and control algorithms are all completely described in the simulation model. An example will be given in section 6.1.

6   Applications

This section will show two examples of the integrated simulation based development of control or supervisor design introduced in this paper.

6.1   Self Localization Of Mobile Robots

In the first example, the Virtual Testbed and control-by-simulation concepts are used to develop new localization methods for mobile systems using fused sensor data - on planetary surfaces as well as in the woods. Here, a Virtual Testbed has been used to develop the localization algorithms at first. To parameterize, test and verify the developments, the simulation model has been extended by a virtual, fully operable and interactive forest harvester/exploration rover, which is equipped e. g. with virtual laserscanners (the blue components in Figure 5) and actuators. After having successfully verified the supervisor, interfaces to the real sensors are added to the simulation model and connected to the supervisor (the green components in Figure 5). At the end, the entire model is loaded into the simulation system on the on-board computer of the harvester/exploration rover to localize the real machine. The resulting "VisualGPS" framework not only uses the control-by-simulation concepts, but also the simulation model for environment modeling and map management, the user interface, the communication infrastructure, as well as manifold data processing algorithms for the framework implementation.

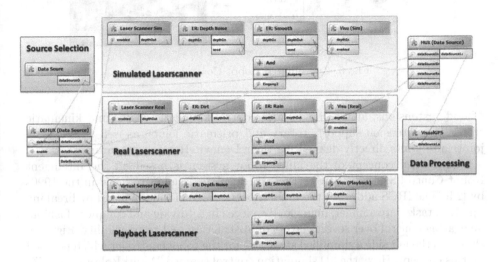

Fig. 5. A block oriented view on an excerpt of the simulation model of a new localization system integrating simulation, real world operation as well as playback mode into one single simulation model [21]

The foundation of our self localization approach is the fusion of sensor data with information of landmarks, calculated beforehand from aerial survey data. In the 3D simulation control a local landmark map (tree map) is generated using the data of the mounted laser scanners. Object extraction algorithms determine relevant features in this sensor data, according to the position and orientation of the laser scanners. With a correct parametrization of the object extraction algorithms, trees are detected as landmarks. Using the collected information, a local landmark map of trees can be generated. In [23] it is shown how this local map is then matched to a global tree map of the area, which has previously been extracted from aerial survey data, thus localizing the forest harvester/exploration rover.

6.2   Coordinated Robot Control

In the second example, these concepts are the basis for the development of the overall control system of the multi-robot workcell depicted on the right of Figure 6 consisting of two redundant 8-axis robots (linear axis plus a 7-axis robot). For robot control the database of our simulation system is extended with new types

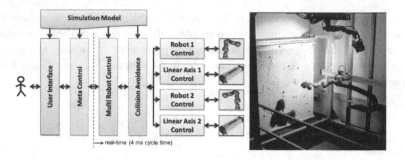

Fig. 6. Coordinated Robot Control System

of node extensions, able to model and control kinematic chains and kinematic trees. The extension supports rotary and prismatic joints, as well as universal joints and joints directly defined via their Denavit-Hartenberg parameters.

The control concept of the multi robot system is based on the Intelligent Robot Control System (IRCS) structure, developed and introduced in the 1990s by [24]. The IRCS addresses the main aspects of multi robot control by breaking up given tasks into smaller, manageable pieces in a "divide and conquer" fashion, delegating control over several layers of abstraction and responsibility. Figure 6 shows on the left side a simplified structure for the robot controller which is based on this concept. Here, the 3D simulation control (named "Multi Robot Control") acts as a coordinator of the vendor specific robot control units by implementing the control by simulation concept. To communicate with the physical devices, the Ethernet based Fast-Research-Interface (FRI) is used for the KUKA Light-Weight-Robots, while a Profibus-Interface is used for the linear axes.

The user interaction via a "User Interface" and the real-time robot coordination "Multi Robot Control" is performed on different computers, both running the same simulation system, though with different configurations on different operating systems (Windows and QNX). Both simulations use the same model, which is kept in sync between the computers by distribution methods provided by the core database. This demonstrates the coexistence of simulation and control in our approach. The 3D simulation normally controls the motions of a simulated robot. In our kinematic robot control, the same controller now generates motion increments to command a physical robot. Thus, new motions can be programmed and tested in simulation, before they are executed on the physical robots, allowing for a faster and safer implementation of new tasks. Besides the pure robot control, components for a so called "Meta Control" layer (action generation and distributed using algorithms from the field of artificial intelligence) as well as for on-line "Collision Avoidance" will be implemented exactly the same way using the same simulation framework and the same control-by-simulation concepts, so that the entire IRCS is build on the simulation technology presented in this paper.

7   Conclusion

As the applications demonstrate, the concept of control-by-simulation is able to offer new insights and new accesses to simulation based control design and concurrent engineering. While Virtual Testbed concepts focus on the holistic simulation of complex systems, control-by-simulation provides the necessary concepts for the transition between simulation and reality. Both concepts are major building blocks of the "eRobotics" developments which now provide all the methods necessary for the systematic development of simulations of robots resp. automated systems (which virtually cover every aspect of their functioning as well as their environment ranging from kinematics and dynamics to sensors and control systems), as well as for the control of such systems.

The technical realization of control-by-simulation is fully based on the capabilities of our simulation system. The seamless direct transition from SW to SIL is only possible because of the features of its highly modular and scalable, active simulation database and its built-in support for distributed simulation and distributed control. Now, we carry out control design in a Virtual Testbed which provides a comprehensive simulation of the individual automated components in the context of their complex environment. To gain a real-time capable control system, we strip the Virtual Testbed down to the most essential components. The control system is then ready to be carried out in separate real-time tasks or on dedicated real-time operating systems, while it is still fully based on the identical simulation system, models and algorithms.

Based on the close coupling of control-by-simulation to Virtual Testbeds, we are also able to address the most sensitive aspect of the whole concept which is calibration. Of course, the validity of the transition between SW and SIL is highly dependent on the accuracy of the representation of the automated system in the simulation and the quality of the resulting control design is only as good as the simulation of the process, too. Here, the structure of Virtual Testbeds allows for calibrating subsystems step by step, using small, focused and affordable physical testbeds for each group of component. In addition, the modular approach of our simulation system enables us to systematically build up libraries of reliable, calibrated components which will finally yield modeling complex automated systems "off-the-shelf".

The described approach has been implemented and thoroughly tested within the VEROSIM® framework. VEROSIM® is a commercial 3D virtual reality and simulation system which, through its flexible architecture, served as an ideal basis for the test and application of the presented concepts.

In the next step, we plan to extend the concept of control-by-simulation to new applications and scenarios of control design. Beyond the further development of the IRCS components like Meta Control or Collision Avoidance, one major direction of our future developments will be to directly include predictive 3D simulations in robot controllers. The idea is sketched in Figure 7. Beyond well established methods in motion control and path planning, here control-by-simulation provides the basis to use of 3D dynamics simulations for the prediction of physical consequences of robot motions, e.g. the reaction of objects to contact.

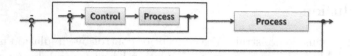

Fig. 7. Predictive 3D Simulation

Such predictions and evaluations allow to tackle robotic problems similar to the way a human handles interaction with his environment: Think, imagine different alternatives, choose the best and act. Control-by-simulation provides the basis to also develop and evaluate different alternatives in simulation before the best solution is applied to the physical system. Thus the control-by-simulation approach has the potential to turn artificial intelligence know-how and software into "embodied artificial intelligence" [25] applications.

References

1. Rossmann, J., Schluse, M.: Virtual robotic testbeds: A foundation for e-robotics in space, in industry - and in the woods. In: Developments in E-systems Engineering, DeSE 2011 (2011)
2. Yoo, Y.H., Jung, T., Römmermann, M., Rast, M., Rossmann, J., Kirchner, F.: Developing a virtual environment for extraterrestrial legged robot with focus on lunar crater exploration. In: Proceeding of 10th International Symposium on Artificial Intelligent, Robotics and Automation in Space (2010)
3. Brdyś, M., Malinowski, K.: Computer Aided Control System Design: Methods, Tools, and Related Topics. World Scientific (1994)
4. Abel, D., Bollig, A.: Rapid Control Prototyping. Springer, Heidelberg (2006)
5. The MathWorks, I.: Simulink - simulation und model-based design (2012), http://www.mathworks.de/products/simulink/ (accessed April 24, 2012)
6. dSpace GmbH: dspace prototyping systems (2012), http://www.dspace.de/shared/data/pdf/catalog2011/dSPACE-catalog2011_PrototypingSystems.pdf (accessed April 24, 2012)
7. Isermann, R., Schaffnit, J., Sinsel, S.: Hardware-in-the-loop simulation for the design and testing of engine-control systems. Control Engineering Practice 7, 643–653 (1999)
8. Lu, B., Wu, X., Figueroa, H., Monti, A.: A low-cost real-time hardware-in-the-loop testing approach of power electronics controls. IEEE Transactions on Industrial Electronics 54, 919–931 (2007)
9. Busch, C., Lambeck, S.: Rapid control prototyping of a controller for a experimental helicopter set-up used in control engineering courses. In: 2010 IEEE International Conference on Control Applications, CCA (2010)
10. Thiel, S., Derichsweiler, F.: Petri net based verification of causal dependencies in electronic control unit test cases. In: 2011 IEEE 35th Annual Computer Software and Applications Conference Workshops, COMPSACW (2011)
11. Chen, C.H., Tsai, H.L., Tu, J.C.: Robot control system implementation with rapid control prototyping technique. In: 2004 IEEE International Symposium on Computer Aided Control Systems Design (2004)

12. Jang, J., Han, S., Kim, H., Ahn, C.K., Kwon, W.H.: Rapid control prototyping for robot soccer. Robotica 27, 1091–1102 (2009)
13. Bonivento, C., Cacciari, M., Paoli, A., Sartini, M.: Rapid prototyping of automated manufacturing systems by software-in-the-loop simulation. In: 2011 Chinese Control and Decision Conference, CCDC (2011)
14. McConnell, P.G., Medeiros, D.J.: Real-time simulation for decision support in continuous flow manufacturing systems. In: Proceedings of the 24th Conference on Winter Simulation (1992)
15. Volvnkin, A., Skormin, V.: Large-scale reconfigurable virtual testbed for information security experiments. In: 3rd International Conference on Testbeds and Research Infrastructure for the Development of Networks and Communities, TridentCom 2007 (2007)
16. Wetter, M.: Co-simulation of building energy and control systems with the building controls virtual test bed. Journal of Building Performance Simulation 4, 185–203 (2011)
17. Schaefer, B., Gibbesch, A., Krenn, R., Rebele, B.: Verification and validation process on 3D dynamics simulation in support of planetary rover development. In: Proceedings of the 10th ESA Workshop on Advanced Space Technologies for Robotics and Automation (2008)
18. Gyssens, M., Paredaens, J., van den Bussche, J., van Gucht, D.: A graph-oriented object database model. IEEE Transactions on Knowledge and Data Engineering 6, 572–586 (1994)
19. Jung, T.: Methoden der Mehrkörperdynamiksimulation als Grundlage realitätsnaher Virtueller Welten. PhD thesis, Institue For Man-Machine Interaction, RWTH Aachen University, Germany (2011)
20. Rossmann, J., Schlette, C., Schluse, M., Eilers, K.: Simulation, programming and control of kinematics and other articulated mechanisms based on a uniform framework. In: Proceeding of 10th WSEAS International Conference on Signal Processing (2011)
21. Rossmann, J., Hempe, N., Emde, M.: New methods of render-supported sensor simulation in modern real-time vr-simulation systems. In: Proceedings of the 15th WSEAS International Conference on Computers (2011)
22. Limited, Q.S.S.: Qnx neutrino rtos (2012), http://www.qnx.com/products/neutrino-rtos/index.html (accessed April 24, 2012)
23. Rossmann, J., Schluse, M., Schlette, C., Buecken, A., Krahwinkler, P., Emde, M.: Realization of a highly accurate mobile robot system for multi purpose precision forestry applications. In: International Conference on Advanced Robotics, ICAR 2009. IEEE (2009)
24. Freund, E., Rossmann, J.: Systems approach to robotics and automation. In: Proceedings of the 1995 IEEE International Conference on Robotics and Automation (1995)
25. Pfeifer, R., Scheier, C.: Understanding Intelligence. Bradford Books, MIT Press (2001)

Human Intention Estimation Using Time-Varying Fuzzy Markov Models for Natural Non-verbal Human Robot Interface

Peter Liu* and Chang-En Yang

Department of Electrical Engineering, Tamkang University
No. 151, Ying-Chuan Rd. Tamsui,
New Taipei city, Taiwan 25137
pliu@ieee.org

Abstract. In this paper, we establish a time-varying fuzzy Markov model to estimate human intention for natural non-verbal human robot interface. Based on human posture information, we change the probability between states to improve the accuracy of estimation of human intention. The advantages of the approach are three fold: i) non-verbal information is core of natural interaction; ii) time-varying probability improves estimation accuracy; and iii) fuzzy inference consider practical human experience.

1 Introduction

The ultimate goal for human robot interface (HRI) design is to achieve natural interactivity between the human and robot. In other words, the human must feel as if they were interacting with an actual human being. Core to achieving natural interactivity is the ability to provide a response before the actual command is given. To achieve this ability efficiently, we need to estimate human intention accurately. Conventional human intention research has focused on using: i) image tracking of the human posture or gesture analysis, see the works [1–3] applied to smart homes [4–6]; ii) context awareness (CA) and belief-desire-intention (BDI) inference system define the human intention [7,8]. Especially, the work [9] proposes context-aware estimation using semantics to help the elderly lead independent lives; iii) human posture information to control the robot [10–12]; iv) electromyography (EMG) sensor analysis to control a meal assistance robot [13]; v) analysis on human generated sounds to help people during internet communication [14,15].

From the above, both verbal and non-verbal analysis was used to estimate human intention. From the works [16–18], we find that verbal content only accounts for 7% of interaction information, while voice and facial expressions accordingly

---

* This work was supported by National Science Council, R.O.C., under grant NSC 100-2221-E032-024.

C.-Y. Su, S. Rakheja, H. Liu (Eds.): ICIRA 2012, Part II, LNAI 7507, pp. 198–206, 2012.

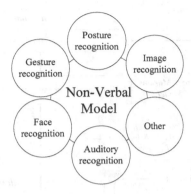

Fig. 1. Non-verbal system concept map

account for 38% and 55%, adding to a total of 93% for non-verbal communication. Therefore, we find the importance in researching the complex problem of analyzing non-verbal interactions to construct an accurate human intention model. The conceptual non-verbal model, from a human eye point of view, includes recognition of image, posture, gesture, face and auditory as shown in Fig.1.

In this paper, we propose a time-varying fuzzy Markov model to estimate human intention for natural non-verbal human robot interface. This model improves on the conventional Markov model of human intention [19–22] where probability is constant. We take into consideration that states of human behavior varies with time. In addition, we introduce a In this paper, fuzzy inference system to define the initial intention state, where fuzzy weights change the Markov probability matrix. The final model generates an estimation of human intention with the largest probability.

2   Methodology

The work [23] introduced the human decision mechanism and intention flow chart. Based on a similar concept, we use the time-varying fuzzy Markov model to estimate the meaning of human posture which leads to the actual intention. We define here the human posture as the hand to body distance range. The overall intention estimation is carried out in three steps shown in Fig. 2. In details, we first define the body range and initial Markov probability matrix of human intention, and use a fuzzy system to analyze the hand to body distance to get the weights to adjust the probability of intention. In the second step, we create the time-varying model by modifying intention probability during daytime. In the final step, we summate the first and second fuzzy weights to adjust the Markov probability matrix of human intention.

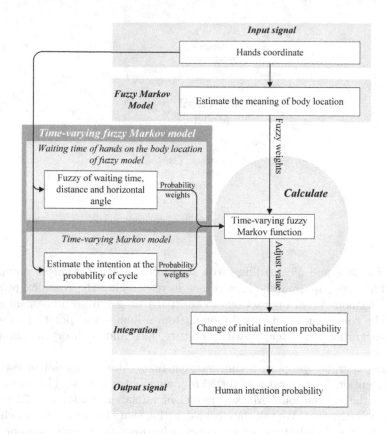

Fig. 2. System flow chart

In the upcoming sections, we will compare and explain the differences between the initial Markov probability model, fuzzy Markov model and time-varying Markov model.

2.1   Initial Markov Probability Model

We use psychology statistics and human experience to define the initial probability. The target of is the achieve similarity between human thinking and observation. This model is shown in Fig. 3.

The initial Markov model of intention has ten states: thinking(S1), headache(S2), suffocation(S3), wait(S4), asthma(S5), heart disease(S6), belly ache(S7), repose(S8), need medication(S9) and cry for help(S10), etc. This model then links the second model's fuzzy system analysis with the body location and the meaning of behavior. As a result, we can real-time get the weights of probability of intention state. For example, when both hands are placed on the head, there is a probability of thinking and headache, which then defines the initial probability.

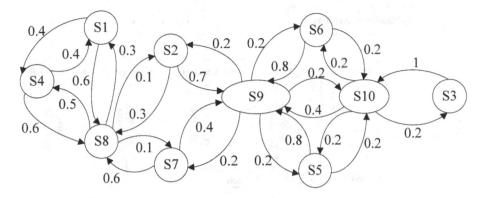

Fig. 3. Initial of intention markov model

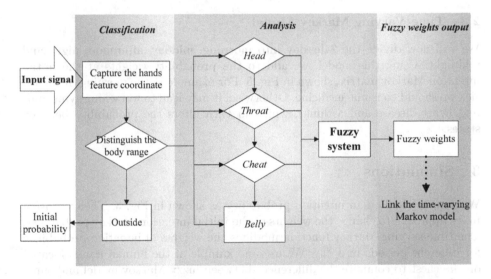

Fig. 4. Fuzzy markov system flow chart of body range of probability weights

2.2   Fuzzy Markov Model

We use the feature points on the body location using fuzzy analysis to change the probability as shown in Fig. 4. In this flow chart, we will classify the various hand body coordinate. We then analyze the different body range using fuzzy system, to obtain the fuzzy weights of intention probability.

Although the intention probability is obtained in real time, human behavior varies in time. For example, the intention of hands placed near the heart location varies over time. During night-time the probability of sickness or a cry for help is more probable. Therefore, in the upcoming section, we propose time-varying Markov model.

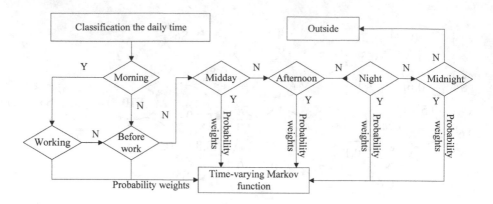

Fig. 5. Time-varying model flow chart

2.3 Time-Varying Markov Model

We will now divide the 24hr day into morning, midday, afternoon, night and midnight. Using this model, we add to the probability weights at the initial intention Markov matrix, shown in Fig. 5. For example in the morning, if we feel sick we should consume medicine. Otherwise, it may lead to worsening symptoms (ex. heart disease and asthma), which in turn alters the probability between states.

3 Simulations

We assume the human intention probability as shown in Fig. 3. Then we use a fuzzy approach to change the weights of the initial intention Markov probability. The time-varying Markov function modifies the weights of intention probability for different periods in a day. We use an example of the human hands located on the chest to compare the differences between fuzzy Markov model and time-varying fuzzy Markov model.

3.1 Time-Varying Markov Model

We used the time-varying Markov model to modify the intention initial probability at time-varying life environment. In the light of [24], we now define the Markov model shown in the following function:

$$H_j(t) = \sum_{i=1}^{s} P_{ij}(t) H_i(t-1) \tag{1}$$

where $H_j(t)$ is the adjust probability $(j = 1, 2, 3, \ldots, s)$ at time t, and $P_{ij}(t)$ is the probability $(i = 1, 2, 3, \ldots, s)$ of changing from state i at time $t-1$ to state

Situation	Time	Weight / h	State1-1	State1-2	State2-1	State2-2	State3-1	State3-2	State4-1	State4-2
Initial probability			0.4	0.6	0.6	0.4	0.6	0.4	0.5	0.4
Morning	05:00~09:00		0.28	0.72	0.48	0.52	0.48	0.52	0.38	0.52
	09:00~12:00		0.4	0.6	0.58	0.42	0.58	0.42	0.48	0.42
Midday	12:00~14:00		0.4	0.6	0.52	0.48	0.52	0.48	0.42	0.48
Afternoon	14:00~17:00	0.02	0.4	0.6	0.62	0.38	0.62	0.38	0.52	0.38
Night	17:00~21:00		0.4	0.6	0.56	0.44	0.56	0.44	0.46	0.44
	21:00~00:00		0.4	0.6	0.66	0.34	0.66	0.34	0.56	0.34
Midnight	00:00~05:00		0.34	0.66	0.6	0.4	0.6	0.4	0.5	0.4

Fig. 6. Numerical analysis using time-varying Markov model of intention probability

j at time t. This process of the element of $H_j(t)$ and the rows of $P_{ij}(t)$ must sum to 1 in every period:

$$\sum_{i=1}^{s} H_j(t) = 1 \tag{2}$$

$$\sum_{i=1}^{s} P_{ij}(t) = 1 \tag{3}$$

From the above, we define the time-varying transition probability in the following function:

$$P_{ij}(t) = f_{ij}(z(t), \beta_{ij}) \tag{4}$$

where $z(t)$ is the human experience variables at daily time t and β_{ij} is the human hands waiting on the body location of time parameters $(i, j = 1, 2, \ldots, s)$. Then, the time-varying fuzzy Markov calculation function:

$$H_j(t) = \sum_{i=1}^{s} f_{ij}(z(t), \beta_{ij}) H_i(t-1) \tag{5}$$

We will use the above of function to adjust the human intention probability. Then the variable $z(t)$ will adjust according to fuzzy analysis, and β_{ij} will denote the time the hands are on the body. In the upcoming Subsection 3.2, we will simulate the human intention during the day. The calculation process generates the time-varying Markov probability weights at t shown in Fig. 6.

3.2 Differences Between Fuzzy Markov Model and Time-Varying Fuzzy Markov Model

In this simulation, in both Figs. 7 and 8, subfigure A is the human body range with the asterisk symbol representing the human hands on the chest location. The Figs. 7 and Fig. 8 subfigure B, represents the estimation of intention probability between state probability and waiting time(sec) of hands on the heart location. The figure includes three states: i) the asterisk line represents the waiting state; ii) the circle line represent the asthma state; iii) the fork symbol line

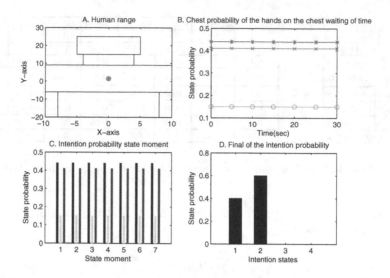

Fig. 7. Using fuzzy Markov model to simulation the human intention probability of chest

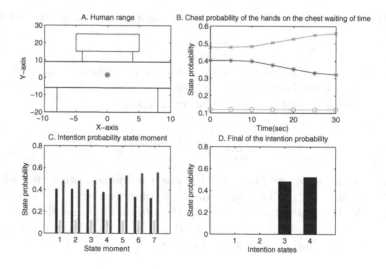

Fig. 8. The initial intention probability of hands on the heart using time-varying fuzzy Markov model at working time

represent the heart disease state. The Fig. 7 and Fig. 8 subfigure C, represent the intention probability state moment, this picture have three probability states: i) the left bar is the waiting state; ii) the middle bar is the asthma state; iii) the right bar is the heart disease state. In the Fig. 7 subfigure D, represent two intention probability: i) probability of human in thinking state is 40%; ii) probability of human need in repose state is 60%. The Fig. 8 subfigure D, this result represent the intention states: i) the human need medicine probability is 48%; ii) represent the human have danger so need cry for help probability is 52%. From these results, we can observe the difference between Figs. 7 subfigures B, C, D and Fig. 8 subfigures B, C, D where the latter human intention probability varies with time.

Through the time-varying fuzzy Markov model analysis and estimate the meaning of the feature points of human hands location. We will used this model at future understand the human intention probability then help people at real time. As a result, the robot decision-making will be similarity the human behavior.

4   Conclusions

We have proposed a time-varying fuzzy Markov model estimate the meaning of nonverbal human intention. The main concept of this model is to modify the probability of human intention at various periods in a day. As a result, the intention probability is more accurate. The proposed estimation methodology may be used as the core of human robot interfaces to achieve natural non-verbal interactions.

References

1. Matsumoto, Y., Sasao, N., Suenaga, T., Ogasawara, T.: 3D model-based 6-dof head tracking by a single camera for human-robot interaction. In: IEEE International Conference on Robotics and Automation, ICRA 2009, pp. 3194–3199 (May 2009)
2. Yu, E., Aggarwal, J.: Human action recognition with extremities as semantic posture representation. In: IEEE Computer Society Conference on Computer Vision and Pattern Recognition Workshops, CVPR Workshops 2009, pp. 1–8 (June 2009)
3. Juang, C.F., Chang, C.M., Wu, J.R., Lee, D.: Computer vision-based human body segmentation and posture estimation. IEEE Transactions on Systems, Man and Cybernetics, Part A: Systems and Humans 39(1), 119–133 (2009)
4. Ho, Y., Shibano, T., Sato-Shimokawara, E., Yamaguchi, T.: The information providing system by using human motion recognition. In: 2011 4th International Conference on Human System Interactions (HSI), pp. 110–116 (May 2011)
5. Ye, Y.: Design and implementation of a real-time image processing based e-home robot (2003)
6. Chen, Y.H., Lu, C.H., Hsu, K.C., Fu, L.C., Yeh, Y.J., Kuo, L.C.: Preference model assisted activity recognition learning in a smart home environment. In: IEEE/RSJ International Conference on Intelligent Robots and Systems, IROS 2009, pp. 4657–4662 (October 2009)
7. Dey, A.: Understanding and using context. Personal and Ubiquitous Computing 5(1), 4–7 (2001)
8. Oyama, K., Jaygarl, H., Xia, J., Chang, C., Takeuchi, A., Fujimoto, H.: A human-machine dimensional inference ontology that weaves human intentions and requirements of context awareness systems. In: 32nd Annual IEEE International Computer Software and Applications, COMPSAC 2008, July 28-August 1, pp. 287–294 (2008)

9. Chang, C., Yi Jiang, H., Ming, H., Oyama, K.: Situ: A situation-theoretic approach to context-aware service evolution. IEEE Transactions on Services Computing 2(3), 261–275 (2009)

10. Koo, S., Kwon, D.S.: Recognizing human intentional actions from the relative movements between human and robot. In: The 18th IEEE International Symposium on Robot and Human Interactive Communication, RO-MAN 2009, September 27-October 2, pp. 939–944 (2009)

11. Kuan, J.Y., Huang, T.H., Huang, H.P.: Human intention estimation method for a new compliant rehabilitation and assistive robot. In: Proceedings of the SICE Annual Conference 2010, pp. 2348–2353 (August 2010)

12. Han, J.H., Kim, J.H.: Human-robot interaction by reading human intention based on mirror-neuron system. In: 2010 IEEE International Conference on Robotics and Biomimetics (ROBIO), pp. 561–566 (December 2010)

13. Zhang, X., Wang, B., Wang, X., Sugi, T., Nakamura, M.: Human intention extracted from electromyography signals for tracking motion of meal assistance robot. In: IEEE/ICME International Conference on Complex Medical Engineering, CME 2007, pp. 1384–1387 (May 2007)

14. Morency, L.P.: Modeling human communication dynamics [social sciences]. IEEE Signal Processing Magazine 27(5), 112–116 (2010)

15. Kwak, K.C., Kim, S.S.: Sound source localization with the aid of excitation source information in home robot environments. IEEE Transactions on Consumer Electronics 54(2), 852–856 (2008)

16. Krauss, R., Fussell, S.: Social psychological models of interpersonal communication. In: Social Psychology: Handbook of Basic Principles, pp. 655–701 (1996)

17. Mehrabian, A.: Nonverbal communication. Aldine (2007)

18. Navarro, J., Marcin Karlins, P.: What every body is saying: An Ex-FBI Agent's Guide to Speed-Reading People (2009)

19. Awad, M.A., Khalil, I.: Prediction of user's web-browsing behavior: Application of markov model. IEEE Transactions on Systems, Man, and Cybernetics, Part B: Cybernetics PP(99), 1–12 (2012)

20. Ge, H., Asgarpoor, S.: Reliability evaluation of equipment and substations with fuzzy markov processes. IEEE Transactions on Power Systems 25(3), 1319–1328 (2010)

21. Tamura, Y., Sugi, M., Ota, J., Arai, T.: Deskwork support system based on the estimation of human intentions. In: 13th IEEE International Workshop on Robot and Human Interactive Communication, ROMAN 2004, pp. 413–418 (September 2004)

22. Baldwin, D., Baird, J.: Discerning intentions in dynamic human action. Trends in Cognitive Sciences 5(4), 171–178 (2001)

23. Kowalczuk, Z., Czubenko, M.: Model of human psychology for controlling autonomous robots. In: 2010 15th International Conference on Methods and Models in Automation and Robotics (MMAR), pp. 31–36 (August 2010)

24. MacRae, E.: Estimation of time-varying markov processes with aggregate data. Econometrica: Journal of the Econometric Society, 183–198 (1977)

Influence of Human Driving Characteristics on Path Tracking Performance of Vehicle

Siavash Taheri, Subhash Rakheja, and Henry Hong

Concordia University, Mechanical and Industrial Engineering, 1515 St. Catherine St. West, Montreal, Quebec, Canada
si_taher@encs.concordia.ca, rakheja@alcor.concordia.ca, henry.hong@Concordia.ca

Abstract. This study aims to contribute to improved road safety through development of a directional driver model. A comprehensive driver model incorporating path preview, prediction, muscular system dynamic, neural process, processing and sensory time delay, is formulated and coupled with a yaw-plane vehicle model. The coupled driver/vehicle model is analyzed to investigate path tracking performance and steering effort of human driver through variation of driving characteristics. Thus, a composite performance index which closely describes the tracking performance of the vehicle and driver's steering effort has been formulated and minimized to obtain the control measures of human driver. The results illustrate that drivers with different driving skill could effectively reduce the path tracking error to a safe threshold level by minimizing the defined performance index. The results further suggest that drivers with higher level of driving skill employ less steering effort while performing a path tracking task.

Keywords: Coupled vehicle/driver system, pursuit-compensatory control, muscular dynamic, human reaction time, perception time, path preview.

1   Introduction

Human driving characteristics are complex combinations of physical and mental processes in response to perceived motion, visual and acoustic cues. Using different motion perceptions, the driver performs as a controller to satisfy key guidance and control requirements for the vehicle system. It has been vastly reported that the human driver employs visual cues to look ahead and obtain path information [1]. It has been hypothesized that a small amount of visual information could effectively satisfy the guidance requirement of driving task [2,3]. Thus, a number of reported driver models employ a single preview point to obtain required path information [4,5]. However, recent driving simulator studies illustrate that the human driver benefits from more than a single preview point ahead of the vehicle [6-9]. It has been illustrated by Land and Horwood [3] that viewing the path through two horizontal apertures, defined as near and far preview points, would result in steering performance which is indistinguishable from unrestricted whole scene observation. The concept of two distinct preview points could be traced to Donges' two-level

C.-Y. Su, S. Rakheja, H. Liu (Eds.): ICIRA 2012, Part II, LNAI 7507, pp. 207–216, 2012.

driver model [6], which constitutes: (i) an anticipatory level (far-range process); and (ii) a stabilization level (short-range process). The anticipatory level represents the guidance level of steering and involves the perception of the future path curvature in an open-loop manner. Further, the stabilization level attempts to compensate the instantaneous deviation from the intended path in a closed-loop manner. This steering concept, however, shows two main limitations: (i) using anticipatory control that aims to satisfy the guidance requirement in an open-loop manner; and (ii) using the curvature information of the previewed path. Two-level driver models is, in general, developed based on the hypothesis that the human driver has the capability to perform the driving task in an open-loop manner, quite literally with closed eyes, and employ the compensatory closed-loop control to correct the perceived errors. However, it has been experimentally illustrated that even skilled drivers have significant limitations to perform well-practiced steering tasks without any sensory feedback [10]. In addition, experimental studies have shown that human driver cannot accurately estimate the previewed path curvature [11]. Further, it has been suggested that the vehicle drivers effectively benefit from the perceived lateral position and orientation error of the vehicle, which is directly obtained through the visual cues information [12,13].

In this study, a comprehensive driver model is described to assess the effect of variation of driving parameters on path tracking performance of the coupled driver/vehicle system and steering effort of human driver. The proposed driver model relies directly on the direct perceivable information of the preview path to satisfy the guidance requirement of the driving task.

2   Mathematical Model of Human Driver

The human driver attempts to minimize the perceived error between the predicted vehicle path and previewed path and also eliminate environmental disturbances to satisfy the control and guidance requirements of a driving task. The structure of a control driver model coupled with a vehicle has been achieved based on an extensive review of the literature on the steering task of driving. The overall structure of a control driver model involves various elements of the human driver, namely, perception, preview, prediction and neuromuscular dynamic system (Fig.1).

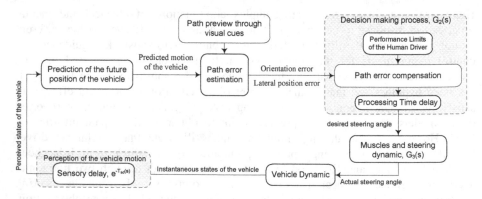

Fig. 1. The overall structure of coupled driver/vehicle system

With reference to Fig. 1, vehicle motion states are perceived by the driver with considerations of the sensory delays. This time delay varies with various environmental factors and sensory channels and ranges from 0.1 to 0.2 s [14,15]. The prediction process reflects the human driver capability of predicting future behavior of the vehicle on the basis of the instantaneous perceived vehicle motion, such as lateral position, forward speed and orientation of the vehicle. The path preview process represents the visual aspects of the human driving to obtain the path information. Using the previewed path and predicted behavior of the vehicle, the driver estimates the error between the previewed and predicted states of the vehicle. Further, the driver converts the perceived error into the vehicle's inputs such as steering wheel angle with consideration of the performance and control limits, processing time delay and muscular dynamic.

The human driver capability to look ahead and obtain the path information has been referred as the driver preview process. The primary issue in the preview process is how far ahead of the vehicle the driver may look to obtain the path information. In general, the distance between the vehicle and the driver's preview point ahead of the vehicle is defined as the preview distance. It is widely accepted that the preview distance increases almost linearly with forward speed [5]. The high influence of forward speed on the preview distance has led to introduce the preview time, which defines the time interval between the vehicle and the preview point ranging from 0.5 to 2 s [5]. In this study, the preview process of human driver to obtain the path information is characterized in two distinct processes: (i) near preview, which associates with the lateral position error to maintain the central lane position; and (ii) far preview process, which associates with the orientation error of the vehicle to account for the upcoming roadway. With reference to Fig. 2, the near preview point is obtained by intersecting a virtual circle with the radius of preview distance, L_p, which is centered at the c.g. of the vehicle, and the centerline of the path (Point A in Fig. 2). The vehicle driver has the capability to predict future behavior of the vehicle on the basis of the instantaneous motion states of the vehicle and thereby undertake desirable corrective actions to achieve minimal path tracking error [16-18]. Assuming constant forward speed and heading angle of the vehicle in the preview interval the predicted lateral position of the vehicle can be estimated by (Point B in Fig. 2):

$$Y(t + T_p) = Y(t) + T_p V_x \sin \psi(t) \tag{1}$$

where $Y(t + T_p)$ is the predicted lateral position of the vehicle. Preview time, T_p, is the estimated time to traverse the preview distance with constant forward speed of V_x. $Y(t)$ and $\psi(t)$ are the instantaneous lateral position and orientation of the vehicle, respectively. Using the previewed path information, attained through visual perception of the driver, and predicted behavior of the vehicle, the driver estimates the lateral position error of the vehicle with the previewed path, which is referred as ε_y, is defined as (Fig. 2):

$$\varepsilon_y(t) = Y(t + T_p) - Y_P(t) \tag{2}$$

where $Y_P(t)$ is the lateral position of the near preview point and $Y(t+T_p)$ is the predicted position of the vehicle.

A novel technique, inspired by experimental studies of Land et al. [3] and Robertshaw et al. [2], has been used to determine the position of the far preview point. In this technique the tangent point on the inside edge of the road ahead of the vehicle is determined and extended to intersect with the centreline of the path to obtain the far preview point of the vehicle driver (Point C in Fig. 2). The orientation error is defined as the angle between the direction of vehicle heading and the far preview point, given as:

$$\varepsilon_\psi(t) = \psi_v(t) + \psi(t) \tag{3}$$

where $\psi(t)$ and $\psi_v(t)$ are respectively the instantaneous orientation of the vehicle, and the angle between the far preview point and the reference horizontal line respect to the fixed coordinate (Fig. 2).

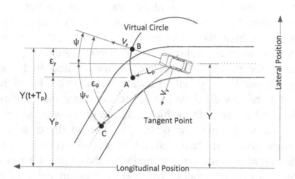

Fig. 2. Estimation of the lateral position and orientation error

The vehicle driver converts the estimated lateral position and orientation errors into the corrective control action with consideration of the control limits and muscular dynamic. The central nervous system thus aims to compensate the orientation and lateral position error of the vehicle in the following manner:

$$G_2(s) = \left(K_1 \frac{T_L s + 1}{T_I s + 1} \varepsilon_y + K_2 \varepsilon_\psi \right) e^{-T_d s} \tag{4}$$

where K_1 and K_2 are proportional gain constants associated with the lateral position and orientation error, respectively. T_L and T_I are respectively the lead and lag time constants. T_d is the processing time delay of central nervous system. The processing time delay defines the interval between sensation of the path error and sending the control signal to the muscular system that vary with depth of required mental processing and decision-making abilities ranging from 0.1 to 1.5 s [5,14,16,19].

A systematic assessment of human driving behavior in path tracking task, necessitates understanding of the dynamic interaction between the vehicle's steering system and the driver's muscular system. The muscular system causes the limb motion in response to the actuation signal of the central nervous system. A number of early and recent studies attempts to simplify the muscles dynamic by pure time delay or first-order lag which denotes as movement time and ranges from 0.1 to 0.3 s [20,21]. However, simplified muscular dynamic models, which are primarily formulated for small magnitude of arm's movement, are not accurate for using in vehicle driver steering control models [5]. Some recent studies thus aim to obtain the mathematical modeling of vehicle drivers' muscular dynamic through driving simulator measurements [22]. Based on these studies, the dynamic response of the coupled driver's arms and steering dynamics can be represented by a second-order system dynamics, such that:

$$G_s(s) = \frac{\theta_{sw}(s)}{T_{demand}(s)} = \frac{1}{(J_{dr}+J_{st})s^2+(B_{dr}+B_{st})s+(K_{dr}+K_{st})} \tag{5}$$

where θ_{sw} is the steering wheel angle of the coupled arm-steering system to the driver's torque demand T_{demand}. J_{dr}, B_{dr} and K_{dr} are respectively the inertia, damping and stiffness of the arm, and J_{st}, B_{st} and K_{st} are those of the vehicle steering system, respectively. It has been suggested that two different commands are generally involved in the control of muscle's movements (Fig. 3). One is a position command through reflex system, which indicates the desired length of muscle, and a torque command through reference model [22]. The reflex dynamic system, $H_r(s)$, defines the demanded torque to minimize the difference between the desired and actual steering angle, such that:

$$H_r(s) = \frac{\omega_c(sB_r+K_r)e^{-s\tau_r}}{s+\omega_c} \tag{6}$$

where B_r, K_r and ω_c are respectively the damping and stiffness constants of the reflex system, and cut-off frequency which is set at 30 rad/s. τ_r is the transport lag in sending messages to and from the spinal cord, which is approximated as 0.04s [22]. Further, the torque command of the reference model is an estimation of the demanded torque based on the learnt inverse internal model of the steering and arm dynamics.

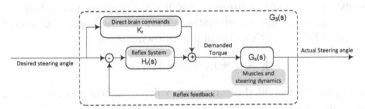

Fig. 3. The overall structure of muscles' dynamic system

3   Yaw-Plane Vehicle Model

Existing vehicle analytical models vary from simplified constant speed linear yaw plane models to comprehensive three dimensional variable speed models. The choice of vehicle model relies mostly on the analysis objectives. In this study a simple model of the vehicle has been employed to facilitate its integration with the proposed driver model. Thus, a simplified directional vehicle model which incorporates lateral and yaw velocities of the vehicle, has been formulated with the following assumptions:

- Small steering angle and small slip angles;
- Neglecting longitudinal tire forces and variation of longitudinal velocity;
- Neglecting roll, pitch and bounce motion of the vehicle;
- Neglecting the lateral load transfer on the tires in the absence of roll motion;

Using the hypothetical model parameter of an SUV vehicle, the proposed model has been validated by comparing its directional response with measured data [23]. Open-loop simulation of the proposed yaw-plane model illustrates that the directional responses are comparable with those observed from the measured data (Fig. 4).

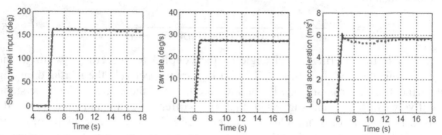

Fig. 4. Comparison of directional response of the vehicle model, subject to a step steer input at a constant speed of 43 km/h (solid line), with the measured data (dotted line)

4   Coupled Driver/Vehicle System

The human driver acts as a controller which attempts to compensate the path tracking error in a stable and well-damped manner. Although the mathematical representation of human driving behavior is quite complex, the control characteristics of the driver may be analyzed using a defined performance index which is described by the path tracking performance and driver's steering effort [19]. This performance index could serve as a qualification measure to determine the effectiveness of the proposed driver model strategy. A composite performance index has been formulated by integrating the normalized lateral deviation, orientation error, steering angle and steering wheel rate as a measure of the driver's effort in the following manner:

$$J_t = J_y + J_\psi + J_\delta + J_{\dot{\delta}} \tag{7}$$

where J_y and J_ψ are the weighted mean square value of lateral position and orientation error, respectively, given by:

$$J_y = \frac{1}{T} \int_0^T \left[\frac{(y(t) - y_d(t))}{\Delta y_{th}} \right]^2 dt \quad , \quad J_\psi = \frac{1}{T} \int_0^T \left[\frac{(\psi(t) - \psi_d(t))}{\Delta \psi_{th}} \right]^2 dt \tag{8}$$

where $y_d(t)$ and $\psi_d(t)$ are the lateral coordinate and orientation of the desired path, respectively. $y(t)$, $\psi(t)$ and T are the instantaneous lateral position and orientation of the vehicle, and simulation time, respectively. Δy_{th} and $\Delta \psi_{th}$, are defined as the maximum allowable deviation of the lateral position and orientation errors between the previewed and resulting paths, which is selected as 1 m and 5 deg, respectively. These have been selected on the basis of geometrical specification of the path and the vehicle to satisfy safe path tracking performance. The terms J_δ and $J_{\dot{\delta}}$ describe the magnitude and rate of steering and thus the driver's steering effort, given by:

$$J_\delta = \frac{1}{T} \int_0^T \left[\frac{\delta}{\Delta \delta_{th}} \right]^2 dt \quad , \quad J_{\dot{\delta}} = \frac{1}{T} \int_0^T \left[\frac{\dot{\delta}}{\Delta \dot{\delta}_{th}} \right]^2 dt \tag{9}$$

where δ and $\dot{\delta}$ are steering angle and steering rate of the steering wheel. $\Delta\delta_{th}$ and $\Delta\dot{\delta}_{th}$ represent the maximum human capabilities of steering and rate of steering, which is selected as 187 deg and 746 deg/s. [24].

It is assumed that the human driver determines the essential driver model parameters by minimizing the defined performance index such that these parameters lie within the specified ranges, which are reported in the literature (Table 1) [14,16,19,25]. It should be noted that the threshold values for the compensatory gains significantly depend upon the steering system and vehicle design characteristics.

Table 1. Control performance limit of human driver

Human driver parameter	Range	Unit
Lead time constant	0.05 - 1.40	s
Lag time constant	0.02 - 0.48	s
Lateral position compensation gain	0.10 - 1.40	rad/m
Orientation compensation gain	0.02 - 0.32	rad/rad

The analysis of coupled driver/vehicle model is performed with three sets of driver parameters, which represent three different driving characteristics of vehicle driver. Human driving characteristics are simplified and expressed in terms of near preview distance and processing time delay (Table 2). The driver "A" exhibits a novice driver, as described by highest processing time and least preview time, while driver "C" represents a driver with superior driving skill.

Table 2. Three driver model parameters representing different driving characteristics

Driver	Near preview time (s)	Processing time (s)
A	1.0	0.3
B	1.2	0.2
C	1.5	0.1

In the coupled driver/vehicle simulation all the other driving parameters such as parameters associated with human arm and vehicle steering system are determined on the basis of the reported literature and held fixed through simulation (Table 3).

Table 3. Driver model parameters which are held fix through simulation [14,22]

Human driver parameter	Value	Unit
Steering ratio of the vehicle	22	
Sensory time delay	0.1	s
Steering stiffness, K_{st}	1.0	N m/rad
Steering damping, B_{st}	0.9	N m s/rad
Steering inertia, J_{st}	0.17	Kg m^2
Arm stiffness, K_{dr}	5.0	N m/rad
Arm damping, B_{dr}	0.9	N m s/rad
Arm inertia, J_{dr}	0.104	Kg m^2
Reflex system stiffness, K_r	10	N m/rad
Reflex system damping, B_r	1.0	N m s/rad

5   Results and Discussion

The coupled driver/vehicle model adopted to perform a standard double lane change maneuver with a constant forward speed of 54 km/h. This maneuver necessitates a high demand on the driver's abilities and steering effort. The performance index is minimized subject to limit constraints for the driver model parameters. Figure 5 illustrates a comparison of path tracking and steering response of two drivers with different driving skill derived under a double lane change maneuver. The resulting values of desirable driver parameters, which are obtained for the three drivers, are shown in Table 4 and are discussed in the following subsections.

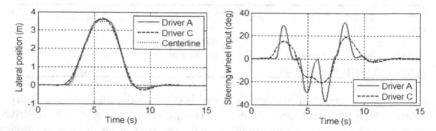

Fig. 5. Path tracking and steering response of the coupled driver/vehicle system subject to a standard double lane change maneuver

Table 4. Desirable driver parameters which are attained by minimizing the performance index

Driver	Desirable driver parameters			
	K_1 (rad/m)	K_2 (rad/rad)	T_L (sec)	T_I (sec)
A	0.645	0.025	0.254	0.023
B	0.514	0.051	0.106	0.034
C	0.344	0.128	0.060	0.177

The results show that different drivers with varying skill levels adopt their control measures to achieve best control performance. For instant, driver "A" with least skill level, exhibit highest lateral position compensatory gain and least orientation compensatory gain. It may thus be concluded that drivers with relatively poor driving skill more rely on lateral position feedback of the vehicle, while skilled drivers more benefit from orientation feedback. The results also illustrates that the driver "C" with higher level of driving skill obtained least lead time constant and highest lag time constant, which are translated as less mental workload during the path tracking task. The various component of driver's performance index are summarized in Table 5.

Table 5. Various components of performance index

Driver	Performance Indices				
	J_t	J_y	J_ψ	J_δ	$J_{\dot{\delta}}$
A	0.0241	0.0053	0.0099	0.0023	0.0066
B	0.0316	0.0068	0.0199	0.0008	0.0041
C	0.0558	0.0134	0.0389	0.0003	0.0031

The results reveal that driver "C" with relatively higher preview time can effectively minimize the steering effort at the expense of decreasing the path tracking performance. However, driver "A" attempts to follow the exact centerline of the path, which yields significant increase of the steering effort. The results of the analyses clearly demonstrate that variation of preview time and processing time could significantly affect dynamic performance of the coupled driver/vehicle system and steering effort of the driver. Thus, it has illustrated that higher preview time and lower processing time of human driver, which is generally translated to higher level of focus on driving task, could significantly decrease mental workload and steering effort of human driver. It should be emphasized that the human driver control measures and driving characteristics is strongly dependent upon the vehicle design characteristics, the forward speed of the vehicle and maneuver chosen.

6   Conclusion

A simplified vehicle model is developed, validated and coupled with a comprehensive model of the human driver. The proposed driver model incorporates the path preview, prediction, central nervous system, muscular dynamic, processing time and sensory time delays. Three sets of driving parameters, which represents different driving skill level of vehicle driver, have been defined. Subsequently, a performance index including the path deviation, orientation error and steering effort has been developed and minimized to obtain the control measures of the human driver. The closed-loop simulation results clearly demonstrate that drivers with superior driving skill could effectively minimize the steering effort while reducing the lateral deviation of the vehicle to a safe threshold level in a stable and well-damped manner. In addition, drivers with higher perception time and lower preview time, which generally translate to novice drivers, tend to minimize the path tracking performance at the expense of higher mental and steering effort. The results also illustrate that the proposed concept of coupled driver/vehicle system could effectively represent human driving behavior.

References

1. Cloete, S., Wallis, G.: Visuomotor Control of Steering: The artifact of the matter. Experimental Brain Research 208(4), 475–489 (2010)
2. Robertshaw, K.D., Wilkie, R.M.: Does gaze influence steering around a bend? Journal of Vision 8(4), 1–13 (2008)
3. Land, M., Horwood, J.: Which Parts of the Road Guide Steering? Nature 377, 339–340 (1995)
4. Macadam, C.: An Optimal Preview Control For Linear Systems. ASME Journal of Dynamic Systems, Measurement and Control 192, 188–190 (1980)
5. Plöchl, M., Edelmann, J.: Driver Models in Automobile Dynamics Application. Vehicle System Dynamics 45, 699–741 (2007)
6. Donges, E.: A Two-level Model of Driver Steering Behavior. Human Factors 20(6), 393–413 (1978)

7. Menhour, L.: Steering Control Based on a Two-Level Driver Model: Experimental Validation and Robustness Tests. In: IEEE Multi-Conference on Systems and Control, Saint Petersburg, Russia (2009)

8. Mitschke, M.: Driver-Vehicle-Lateral Dynamics Under Regular Driving. Vehicle System Dynamics 22, 483–492 (1993)

9. Sentouh, C., Chevrel, P., Mars, F., Claveau, F.: A Sensorimotor Driver Model for Steering Control. In: IEEE International Conference on Systems, Man, and Cybernetics, TX, USA, pp. 2462–2467 (2009)

10. Wallis, G., Chatziastros, A., Bülthoff, H.: An Unexpected Role for Visual Feedback in Vehicle Steering Control. Current Biology 12(4), 295–299 (2002)

11. Fildes, B., Triggs, T.: The Effect of Changes in Curve Geometry on Magnitude Estimates of Road-Like Perspective Curvature. Perception and Psychophysics 37(3), 218–224 (1985)

12. Myers, J.: The Effects of Near and Far Visual Occlusion upon a Simulated Driving Task. A Master's Thesis (2002)

13. Salvucci, D.: A Two-Point Visual Control Model of Steering. Perception 33(10), 1233–1248 (2004)

14. Evans, L.: Traffic Safety and the Driver. Van Nostrand Reinhold, New York (1991)

15. Teichner, W.H., Krebs, M.L.: Laws of the Simple Visual Reaction Time. Psychology Review 79 (1972)

16. Macadam, C.: Understanding and Modeling The Human Driver. Vehicle System Dynamics 40(1-3), 101–134 (2003)

17. Guo, K.: Modelling of Driver/Vehicle Directional Control System. Vehicle System Dynamics 22, 141–184 (1993)

18. Yoshimoto, K.: Simulation of Driver/Vehicle System Including Preview Control. Journal of Mechanics Society Japan 7 (1968)

19. Yang, X., Rakheja, S., Stiharu, I.: Structure of the driver model for articulated vehicles. International Journal of Heavy Vehicle Systems 9(1), 27–51 (2002)

20. Barrett, G., Kobayashi, M., Fox, B.: Feasibility of Studying Driver Reaction to Sudden Pedestrian Emergencies in an Automobile Simulator. Human Factors: The Journal of the Human Factors and Ergonomics Society 10(1), 19–26 (1968)

21. Davies, B., Waits, J.: Preliminary Investigation of Movement Time Between Brake and Accelerator Pedals in Automobiles. Human Factors: Journal of the Human Factors and Ergonomics Society 11(4), 407–410 (1969)

22. Pick, A.J., Cole, D.J.: A Mathematical Model of Driver Steering Control Including Neuromuscular Dynamics. Journal of Dynamic Systems, Measurement and Control 130 (2008)

23. Salaani, M.K., Heydinger, G.J.: Model Validation of the 1997 Jeep Cherokee for the National Advanced Driving Simulator. SAE Paper No. 2000-01-0700

24. Breuer, J.: Analysis of driver-Vehicle-Interactions in an Evasive Manoueuvre-Results of Moose Test Studies. In: Int. Technical Conference on ESV (1998)

25. Horiuchi, S., Yuhara, N.: An Analytical Approach to the Prediction of Handling Qualities of Vehicles with Advanced Steering Control System Using Multi-Input Driver Model. Journal of Dynamic Systems, Measurement and Control 22(3), 490–497 (2000)

Single Machine Oriented Match-Up Rescheduling Method for Semiconductor Manufacturing System[*]

Fei Qiao, Li Li, Yumin Ma, and Bin Shi

School of Electronics & Information Engineering,
Tongji University, 4800 Cao'an Road,
201804 Shanghai, China
{fqiao,lili,ymma,icycastle}@tongji.edu.cn

Abstract. Due to the high uncertainty of semiconductor manufacturing system, its rescheduling problems are extremely difficult to solve. In this paper, we investigate a novel single machine oriented match-up rescheduling (SMUR) method that implement the partial repair rescheduling in a dynamic manufacturing environment. Both of SMUR principle and algorithm are discussed. Its effectiveness has been verified by a simulation study. Computational results show that the proposed method has better stability and efficiency compared with the right-shift rescheduling method.

Keywords: Match-up rescheduling, Right-shift rescheduling, Semiconductor manufacturing system, Rescheduling algorithm.

1 Introduction

Manufacturing scheduling has been extensively researched, and a great number of optimal scheduling methods have been proposed [1-2]. However, most practical manufacturing industry, especially semiconductor manufacturing systems operate in dynamic environments where unpredictable events usually occur. These uncertain disturbances may upset the pre-established schedule, and even cause previously feasible schedule infeasible. In this case, rescheduling is necessary to react to disturbances. That is to say, manufacturers should not only create the best schedules but also react quickly to disturbances and revise original schedules in small computational cost [3].

According to static scheduling and dynamic scheduling categories of scheduling philosophy, rescheduling belongs to the dynamic scheduling, which pays more

[*] This work was supported in part by the National Natural Science Foundation of China (No. 61034004, 50905129), the Science and Technology Commission of Shanghai (No. 10DZ1120100, 09DZ1120600, 11ZR1440400), the Program for New Century Excellent Talents (No. NCET-07-0622), the major national S&T program (No. 2011ZX03005-004-01) and the Shanghai Leading Academic Discipline Project (No. B004).

C.-Y. Su, S. Rakheja, H. Liu (Eds.): ICIRA 2012, Part II, LNAI 7507, pp. 217–226, 2012.
© Springer-Verlag Berlin Heidelberg 2012

attention to the needs of practical environments, and attempts to make a schedule more applicable. Dynamic scheduling has been defined under three categories: robust pro-active scheduling [4-5], completely reactive scheduling [6], and predictive-reactive scheduling [1]. In this paper, we employ the predictive-reactive scheduling strategy and focus on its rescheduling method for dynamic manufacturing environments.

Present researches on production rescheduling mainly consist of rescheduling determination, rescheduling implementation and rescheduling evaluation [7]. *Rescheduling determination* triggers rescheduling. *Rescheduling implementation* generates and/or updates production schedules in response to a disruption. *Rescheduling evaluation* analyzes both rescheduling performance and its impact on the original schedule.

Based on the literature review [3, 8-9], the predictive-reactive rescheduling strategies can take account of both optimization and flexibility by a scheduling/rescheduling procedure. A partial repair rescheduling method is superior to generation rescheduling in its potential to maintain schedule stability with reasonable computational cost. Hence, we investigate a novel single machine oriented match-up rescheduling (SMUR) method that implements the partial repair rescheduling for semiconductor manufacturing system.

First, the basic idea of SMUR approach is proposed compared with the classical right-shift rescheduling method in Section 2. Then the algorithm of SMUR method is discussed in Sections 3. Section 4 presents the simulation results, and Section 5 is the conclusion of whole paper.

2   Single Machine Oriented Match-Up Rescheduling Principle

2.1   Right-Shift Rescheduling

Being a classical type of partial rescheduling method, right-shift rescheduling (RSR) updates the initial schedule by simply postponing each remaining operation by the repair duration [10]. Suppose an example production line, including two machines and four jobs, is running following a pre-generated schedule as shown in Fig. 1(a). At disturbing time T_d, machine M1 breaks down while processing the first production step of job A. It is estimated to be fixed and back to work at time T_r. The repair duration is T_r-T_d. The updated schedule according to RSR is given in Fig. 1(b). As shown, not only the completion time of operation A1 is delayed by T_r-T_d, all remaining operations, of which start processing time is later than T_d , are all delayed by T_r-T_d.

RSR repairs the disrupted initial schedule after a disturbance event occurs, while keeps the initial schedule as much as possible in terms of its order. RSR results in the delay of all operations which start after disturbing time T_d. Actually there usually exists idle time in the schedule that comes from the waiting for an immediate predecessor production step's completion or synchronization according to production flow. This work tries to find a mechanism to make use of these segments of idle time by proposing a new match-up rescheduling method.

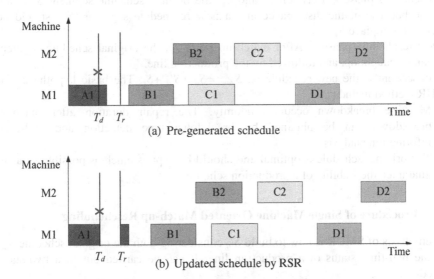

(a) Pre-generated schedule

(b) Updated schedule by RSR

Fig. 1. Example of Right-shift Rescheduling

2.2   Single Machine Oriented Match-Up Rescheduling

The basic idea of the proposed single machine oriented match-up rescheduling (SMUR) is to make full use of the idle time in the original schedule of the breakdown machine to absorb the impact from unexpected disturbance and try to find a time point till which all impact has been absorbed and the original schedule can be followed again. We call this time point match-up point (T_p).

To illustrate the procedure of SMUR approach, we divide a schedule scenario (S) into three phases as shown in Fig. 2. by the disturbing time point T_d and the match-up point T_p. Obviously, the recovery time is later than the disturbing time and earlier than the match-up point $T_d < T_r < T_p$.

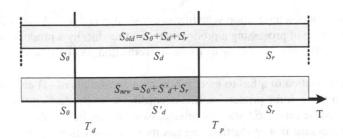

Fig. 2. Sketch map of the match-up rescheduling

Pre-reschedule phase -- Before a disturbance event occurs, a production line runs according to the original schedule, denote as S_0 ;

Reschedule phase -- Between T_d and T_p, the original schedule segment S_d is not feasible because of the disturbance and a new reschedule segment (S'_d) should be generated to replace S_d;

Post-reschedule phase -- After match-up point T_p, the original schedule segment (S_r) can be caught up, and followed by the production line.

Consequently, the new schedule is: $S_{new} = S_0 + S'_d + S_r$. The basic hypotheses for SMUR method include:

a) Machine breakdown occurs randomly. The repair duration after machine breakdown can be obtained by breakdown type detection and real-time information analysis;

b) The original schedule is optimal and should be kept as much as possible so as to guarantee the stability of a production schedule.

2.3   Procedure of Single Machine Oriented Match-up Rescheduling

The emphasis of SMUR is how to build S'_d considering both the original schedule S_{old} and the real-time status of a production line. It can be carried out in a two-stage procedure.

Search match-up point is a determination stage to evaluate if the disturbance can be completely absorbed within a restricted time span. If so, the set of production tasks to be rescheduled, denoted as ζ, is defined simultaneously. If not, it implies that the match-up rescheduling cannot be adopted. In this case we can simply employ RSR method to adjust the disrupted schedule.

Update schedule is to rearrange the tasks in ζ before T_p, and obtain a new schedule S'_d. There are two kinds of tasks in set ζ. One is principal tasks related to the breakdown machine M_K, denoted as ζ_K, which is directly impacted by the disturbance. Another is subordinate tasks related to other machines except for the breakdown one, denoted as ζ_k, $k{\neq}K$. Thus, $\zeta = \cup\zeta_k$, $k=1,...,m$. Here, m denotes the number of machines in system.

3   Single Machine Oriented Match-Up Rescheduling Algorithm

The basic element of a production schedule is a task, denoted as i. A task can be done by a production job of processing a production item (e.g. lot) by a production resource (e.g. machine). We use $q_{(i,\ k)}$ or q to express production job of task i processed by machine k.

The implementation of q has to meet production constraints of (1) each production item must run through the production line according to its production flow. Each job of an item must be processed after its predecessor job and before the successor one; and (2) each machine in a production line has its own production capacity. Task i can be scheduled on machine k after and only after machine k finished its last production task. Fig. 3 gives the flowchart of SMUR.

As shown in Fig. 3, the existence of a match-up point is the pre-condition to employ SMUR to rescheduling. Otherwise, only other rescheduling method such as

RSR fits (Fig. 3D). Next, the two parts of SMUR algorithm, determine match-up point and reschedule task set (Fig. 3A,B) and update start time of each task (Fig. 3C) will be discussed respectively.

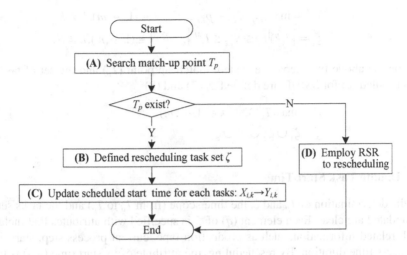

Fig. 3. Flowchart of SMUR

3.1   Determine Match-Up Point and Reschedule a Task Set

To search T_p and to determine ζ can be implemented simultaneously after disturbance occurs. While system is running according to the original schedule, each task has its pre-scheduled start time $X_{i,k}$, and given process time $p_{i,k}$. There are total m machines in the system: M_k, $k\in(1,...,m)$. Suppose machine M_K breakdown at time T_d, and its estimative repair time is T_r. The determination of T_p and ζ_K starts from evaluating each task with $X_{i,k} \geq T_d$. According to the above mentioned principal tasks and subordinate tasks classification. The evaluation can be executed separately:

First, to determine match-up time point of the breakdown machine (T_K^M) and the principal reschedule task set (ζ_K) of breakdown machine M_K.

- Selecting possible impacted tasks in the original schedule of M_K; and sequence them in ascending order;

$$O^{[1]} = \min_{\forall i}(X_{i,K}|X_{i,K} \geq T_d) \tag{1}$$

- Searching the last task be impacted by M_K breakdown. The serial number of such task q satisfies (2);

$$T_r + \sum_{i=1}^{q}(p_{i,K} - X_{q+1,K}) \leq 0 \tag{2}$$

- Defining T_K^M and ζ_K as (3) and (4)

$$T_k^M = X_{q+1,K} \tag{3}$$

$$\zeta_K = \left\{ O^{[1]}, O^{[2]}, \cdots, O^{[q]} \right\} \tag{4}$$

Second, to determine match-up point (T_k^M) and the set of subordinate tasks to be rescheduled (ζ_k) of other machines, M_k, $k \neq K$, except for the breakdown machine M_K.

$$T_k^M = \max_{i=\zeta_K} X_{i,k} + p_{i,k}, \qquad k \in (1, \cdots, m), k \neq K, \tag{5}$$

$$\zeta_k = \left\{ (i,k) \middle| T_d \leq X_{i,k} \leq T_k^M \right\}, \qquad k \in (1, \cdots, m), k \neq K, \tag{6}$$

Based on the above two steps, the system match-up point (T_p) and the set of tasks to be rescheduled (ζ) for SMUR are defined as (7) and (8).

$$T_p = \max(T_k^M), \qquad k \in (1, \cdots, m) \tag{7}$$

$$\zeta = \zeta_1 \cup \zeta_2 \cup \cdots \cup \zeta_m \tag{8}$$

3.2   Update Task Start Time

After the determination of T_p and ζ, the time scope (from T_d to T_p) and the tasks set (ζ) to be updated are clear. Each element (q) of ζ, is specified with attributes that includes all task related information, such as production type, current process step, start time, and process time duration. By rescheduling, the attribute of its start time $(X_{i,k})$ is to be updated.

According to production constraints, the earliest start time of the next task at a machine is the larger one of the following two values: (a) earliest available time of the machine; and (b) earliest arrival time of the item to the machine.

The procedure of updating task start time is designed to be an iterative one as shown in Fig. 4.

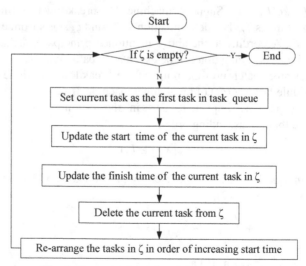

Fig. 4. The procedure of updating task start time

4   Case Study

In order to verify the proposed SMUR method, a case study based on a typical Minifab model with 5 machines (Fig. 5) that is derived from a semiconductor production line is given. There are 3 production types: A, B and C. They have the same production flows from Step 1 to Step 6, but different production parameters. Table 1 describes the detail of their production flows.

Table 1. Production flows of Minifab (unit: minute)

flow	Step 1		Step 2		Step 3	Step 4		Step 5		Step 6
	Ma	Mb	Mc	Md	Me	Mc	Md	Ma	Mb	Me
A	225	240	30	35	55	50	55	255	250	10
B	225	240	35	30	60	45	50	255	250	15
C	225	240	32	25	65	55	40	255	250	12

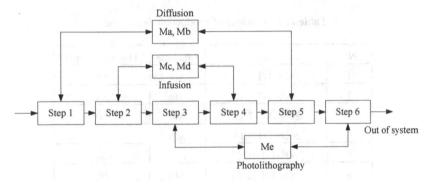

Fig. 5. Minifab model

4.1   **Evaluation Index**

(a) Stability
Stability is defined as the degree of similarity of a new schedule and the original one. In our research, the index of stability is defined based on the deviation of the start time of each task as given in (9).

$$Stab(S_0, S_{new}) = \frac{\sum_{i=1}^{n} |ST_{new,i} - ST_{0,i}|}{n} \tag{9}$$

Here, S_0 and S_{new} are the original and new schedules respectively; n is the number of tasks in set ζ; $ST_{0,i}$ and $ST_{new,i}$ are start time of task i in the original and new schedules respectively. The smaller the value $Stab(S_0, S_{new})$ is, the better stability performance the new schedule has.

(b) Efficiency
Efficiency evaluates the effect of a selected objective function after rescheduling. This work selects the equipment utilization as the objective function, and defines

efficiency as the deviation of mean equipment utilizations under new and original schedules as (10).

$$Util(S_0, S_{new}) = \sum_{k=1}^{m} \lambda_k \frac{P_{new,k} - P_{0,k}}{P_{0,k}} \qquad (10)$$

Here, $P_{0,k}$ and $P_{new,k}$ are utilization of machine k under the original and new schedules respectively. λ_k is the weight coefficiency which can distinguish the importance of different machines. The bigger the value in (10) is, the better efficiency performance the reschedule has.

4.2   Simulation and Analysis

Each simulation running duration is set to be 24 hours. Suppose there are 8 breakdowns at different machines at different disturbing time points as listed in Table 2. The duration of each breakdown is also given. With different rescheduling methods, the RSR, and the proposed SMUR, simulation results are shown in Figs. 6. and 7.

Table 2. Test sample of production disturbance

No	Td	Machine	Duration (min)
1	2008-1-1 3:13	Ma	55
2	2008-1-1 5:13	Mc	34
3	2008-1-1 7:13	Me	60
4	2008-1-1 9:13	Mb	40
5	2008-1-1 10:25	Md	40
6	2008-1-1 12:51	Ma	68
7	2008-1-1 14:21	Mc	68
8	2008-1-1 18:04	Me	39

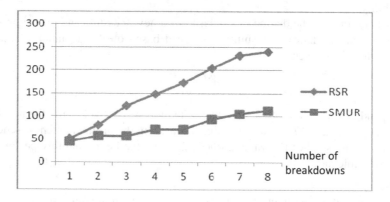

Fig. 6. Comparison of rescheduling stability

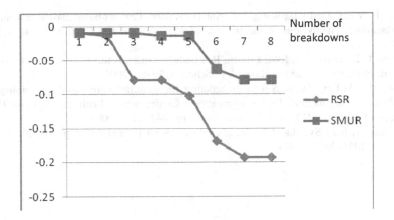

Fig. 7. Comparison of rescheduling efficiency

Figs. 6. and 7. show that SMUR is prior to RSR in performance of both stability and efficiency. And with the increase of disturbance frequency, the improvement of SMUR than RSR becomes higher.

5   Conclusion

Rescheduling allows manufacturers to react to disturbances and revise schedules. In this paper, breakdown machine oriented match-up rescheduling approach is proposed. A representative semiconductor production example line, Minifab model, is used to validate the proposed methods by simulation. Comparison results show that the rescheduling stability and utilization performances can be improved.

References

1. Ouelhadj, D., Petrovic, S.: A survey of dynamic scheduling in manufacturing systems. J. Sched. 12, 417–431 (2009)
2. Qiao, F., Li, L., Wu, Q.D.: Colored Petri net based hierarchical scheduling model for semiconductor production line. In: 5th World Congress on Intelligent Control and Automation, Spain, pp. 3014–3018 (2004)
3. Cheng, M., Sugi, M., Ota, J.: A fast rescheduling method in semiconductor manufacturing allowing for tardiness and scheduling stability. In: Proc. of the 2006 IEEE Int. Conf. on Automation Science and Engineering, Shanghai, China, pp. 100–105 (2006)
4. Liu, L., Gu, H.Y., Xi, Y.G.: Robust and stable scheduling of a single machine with random machine breakdowns. Int. J. Adv. Manuf. Technol. 31, 645–654 (2007)
5. Nasr, A.H., ElMekkawy, T.Y.: Robust and stable flexible job shop scheduling with random machine breakdowns using a hybrid genetic algorithm. Int. J. Production Economics 132, 279–291 (2011)
6. Dominic, P.D.D., Kaliyamoorthy, S., Kumar, M.S.: Efficient dispatching rules for dynamic job shop scheduling. Int. J. Adv. Manuf. Technol. 24, 70–75 (2004)

7. Qiao, F., Wu, Q.D., Li, L., Wang, Z.T., Shi, B.: A fuzzy Petri net-based reasoning method for rescheduling. Transactions of the Institute of Measurement and Control 33(3-4), 435–455 (2011)
8. Vieira, G.E., Herrmann, J.W., Lin, E.: Rescheduling manufacturing systems: a framework of strategies, policies, and methods. J. of Sched. 6, 39–62 (2003)
9. Mustapha, M.F.B., Deris, S.B.: Rescheduling for manufacturing based on ontology and problem solving method. In: 8th International Conference on Intelligent Systems Design and Applications, ISDA 2008, Taiwan, vol. 2, pp. 444–449 (2008)
10. Abumaizar, R.J., Svestka, J.A.: Rescheduling job shops under disruptions. Int. J. Prod. Res. 35, 2065–2082 (1997)

Sub-regional Flank Milling Method

Yunfei Dai[1,*], Xiaoming Zhang[1], Han Ding [1], Haikuo Mu[1], and Chunjing Wang[2]

[1] State Key Laboratory of Digital Manufacturing Equipment and Technology,
Huazhong University of Science and Technology, Wuhan 430074, China
dyf502@126.com
[2] First Aeronautic college of the PLAAF, Xinyang 464000, China

Abstract. In the field of CNC machining, comparing with point milling, flank milling has a significant advantage in terms of processing efficiency. However, for machining of complex surfaces or large ruled surface, we have to divide the whole surface into different regions and then the flank milling is employed. With the method of sub-regional flank milling, we can achieve those goals. In this paper, iso-parametric method is used for dividing ruled surface into sub-regions and the LBM method for the tool path generation. In order to test and verify the accuracy of the proposed method, the tool path error is calculated by comparing the nominal surface with the one enveloped by the tool movement. Envelope theory of two-parameter family of spheres was used to get the envelope surface. Tool path error can be calculated by signed distance between the ruled surface and the envelope surface.

Keywords: ruled surface, flank milling, sub-regional, envelope surface, error analysis.

1   Introduction

Ruled surface machining has attracted interest due to the fact that complex surfaces can be approximated using piecewise ruled surface. Also, ruled surface is widely used in power-driven devices, such as impellers and blades. The quality of ruled surface plays an important role in the whole device, especially on the aerodynamic characteristics and operational reliability.

Compared with traditional point milling, flank milling takes the advantages of its high material removal rates. Researchers have proposed many methods to tool path generation for flank milling of ruled surface. Liu[1] presented double point offset (DPO) method. Two points on a rule are offset by a distance, which equals to the tool radius. The tool axis orientation can be defined by joining the two points. Redonnet et al.[2] proposed a method in which they positioned a cylindrical cutter tangent to the ruled surface at three points: two points on two directrices, and one point on a ruling. The method is accurate but complex on computation and time consuming. Bedi[3] developed a method sliding the cutter along two rails, keeping the cutter tangent to

---

* Corresponding author.

C.-Y. Su, S. Rakheja, H. Liu (Eds.): ICIRA 2012, Part II, LNAI 7507, pp. 227–234, 2012.
© Springer-Verlag Berlin Heidelberg 2012

both curves at every parameter value. Chiou[4] proposed a swept envelope approach to determine tool position for five-axis ruled surface machining. The initial tool positional are located to contact with two directrices of a ruled surface. The swept profile of the tool is then determined based on the tool motion. By comparing the swept profile with the ruled surface, the tool positions are corrected to avoid machining errors. However, the method does not reduce the total machining error. Gone [5] proposed three points offset(TPO) strategy to approximate the offset surface.

Generally speaking, flank milling cannot be employed directly to machining of complex surfaces. When finishing a complex surface or a large ruled surface, people have to divide the whole surface into different sub-regions. For these reasons, in this paper, we approach the problems of dividing the whole ruled surface into sub-regional with a new perspective. Iso-parametric method has been used for dividing ruled surface.

We begin with dividing the whole surface into many sub-region surfaces by iso-parametric method, then generate tool path for flank milling of sub-region surfaces by the LBM method[6]. Next, envelope theory of two-parameter family of spheres[7, 8] was used to obtain analytical expressions of envelope surfaces. Finally, the tooth path errors can be calculated by signed distance[9] between the ruled surface and the envelope surface.

2   Generation of Tool Path and Envelope Surface

2.1   The Generation of Tool Path

In this section, we discuss the generation of tool path for ruled surface with the method of sub-regional in details. As shown in Fig. 1, the ruled surface can be described as:

$$S(u,v) = (1-v)B(u) + vT(u) \tag{1}$$

A conical tool is tangential to the two guiding rails $T_r(u)$ (top rail) and $B_r(u)$ (bottom rail), and the two tangency points are selected at the same parametric value u. The top circle center C_T and the bottom circle center C_B on the conical tool are calculated to determine the tool orientation and position. The radius of top and bottom circles are R_T and R_B, respectively. An appropriate frame should be selected to develop the mathematical relationships between the ruled surface and the conical tool. As the conical cutter is tangential to $T_r(u)$ and $B_r(u)$, the axis $\overline{T}_t$, $\overline{T}_m$ and $\overline{T}_b$ in the frame at $T_r(u)$ is defined as follows:

$$\overline{T}_1 = \frac{\partial T(u)}{\partial u}, \ \overline{T}_t = \frac{\overline{T}_1}{|T_1|}, \ \overline{T}_m = \frac{\overline{T}_1 \times (T(u) - B(u))}{|\overline{T}_1 \times (T(u) - B(u))|}, \ \overline{T}_b = \overline{T}_m \times \overline{T}_t,$$

Similarly, the frame $\vec{B}_t$, $\vec{B}_b$ and $\vec{B}_m$ at $B_r(u)$ can also be determined. $\overrightarrow{T_b}$ and $\overrightarrow{T_m}$ is perpendicular to $\overrightarrow{T_t}$. C_T lies in the plane spanned by $T_r(u)$, $\overrightarrow{T_b}$ and $\overrightarrow{T_m}$, and $T(u) - C_T$ is perpendicular to $\overrightarrow{T_t}$. The angle between the vector from $T_r(u)$ to C_T and $\overrightarrow{T_m}$ is θ, and the angle between the vector from $B_r(u)$ to C_B and $\overrightarrow{B_m}$ is β. We can obtain the following equations by the geometric relationship in Fig.1.

$$C_T - T_r(u) = R_T \cos(\theta)\overrightarrow{T_m}(u) + R_T \sin(\theta)\overrightarrow{T_b}(u) \tag{2}$$

$$C_B - B_r(u) = R_B \cos(\beta)\overrightarrow{B_m}(u) + R_B \sin(\beta)\overrightarrow{B_b}(u) \tag{3}$$

$$(C_T - C_B) \cdot (C_T - T_r(u)) = 0 \tag{4}$$

$$(C_T - C_B) \cdot (C_B - B_r(u)) = 0 \tag{5}$$

From Eqs.2-5, we can get the following equations:

$$\vec{l} \cdot (\cos(\theta)\overrightarrow{T_m} + \sin(\theta)\overrightarrow{T_b}) + R_T = 0 \tag{6}$$

$$\vec{m} \cdot (\cos(\beta)\overrightarrow{B_m} + \sin(\theta)\overrightarrow{B_b}) + R_B = 0 \tag{7}$$

where:

$$\vec{l} = T_r(u) - B_r(u) - R_B \cos(\beta)\overrightarrow{B_m} - R_B \sin(\beta)\overrightarrow{B_b} \tag{8}$$

$$\vec{m} = T_r(u) - B_r(u) - R_T \cos(\beta)\overrightarrow{T_m} - R_T \sin(\beta)\overrightarrow{T_b} \tag{9}$$

With the Eqs.6-7, the unknowns θ, β and R_T can be solved. C_T and C_B can be calculated with Eqs.2-3, and the tool position and orientation can be obtained.

The simplest way to divide a surface is the iso-parametric method[10]. Specifically, when parameter v equals 0.5, we can get a curve $D_r(u)$ (divided rail) in the middle of the whole surface. The curve $D_r(u)$ is bottom rail with curve $T_r(u)$ and top rail with curve $B_r(u)$. The whole ruled surface has been divided into two sub-regions. The tool path generation of each sub-regional is separated. To avoid interference we could machining the surface like Fig.2 shows.

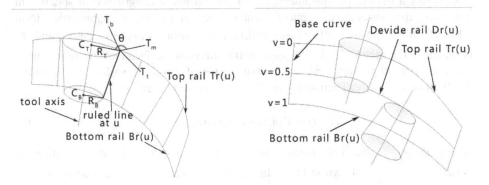

Fig. 1. Example position of conical tool on ruled surface   **Fig. 2.** Example position of conical tool of sub-regional flank milling method

2.2   The Generation of Cutter Envelope Surface

Theoretically the cutting error is inevitable when machining a non-developable ruled surface using the flank milling method. So the crucial problem of flank milling is to calculate cutter error and analysis it on the whole ruled surface. In this section analytical expressions of envelope surface by movement of conical cutter can be obtained with the help of envelope theory of two-parameter family of spheres. So we can calculate cutter error by signed distance between the ruled surface and the envelope surface. Meanwhile, the relationship between envelope surface and cutter axis can be obtained. That means the envelope surface shape control can be transformed into the control of tool axis, thus providing the foundation for optimizing tool axis in the future work.

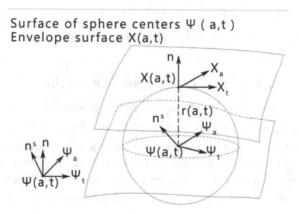

Fig. 3. Envelope of the two-parameter family of spheres

Consider a smooth two-parameter family of spheres, a congruence of spheres, in 3D. Let the surface of sphere centers be given in a parametric form $\{\Psi(a,t) \in R^3, r(a,t) > 0 \in R\}$, where $\Psi(a,t)$ is the surface of sphere centers, and R is radius of the sphere. In the tangency point, envelope surface and the sphere have the same normal vectors, and the normal vector of envelope surface is the radial direction of the sphere. Therefore, the $\Psi(a,t)$ is expressed as:

$$X(a,t) = \Psi(a,t) + r(a,t)n(a,t) \tag{10}$$

where $n(a,t)$ is the unit normal vector of the envelope in the direction of $X(a,t) - \Psi(a,t)$, as shown in Fig.2. In Eqs.10, calculating the partial derivatives to parameters a and t respectively, we have:

$$X_a = \Psi_a + r_a n + r n_a, X_t = \Psi_t + r_t n + r n_t \qquad (11)$$

X_a, X_t is perpendicular to n, so

$$\Psi_a \cdot n = -r_a, \Psi_t \cdot n = -r_t \qquad (12)$$

The normal vector n can be expressed in terms of the Gauss frame of the surface $\Psi(a,t)$ as

$$n = \alpha \Psi_a + \beta \Psi_t + \gamma n^s \qquad (13)$$

Taking the dot product of Eq.11 with Ψ_a and Ψ_t, we have

$$g_{11}\alpha + g_{12}\beta = -r_a, g_{21}\alpha + g_{22}\beta = -r_t \qquad (14)$$

where, $\begin{bmatrix} g^{11} & g^{12} \\ g^{21} & g^{22} \end{bmatrix} = \begin{bmatrix} g_{11} & g_{12} \\ g_{21} & g_{22} \end{bmatrix}^{-1}$.

Substituting Eq.14 into Eq.10, and taking the dot product of the resultant equation with n, we have

$$\gamma = \pm\sqrt{1 - (r_a^2 g^{11} + 2r_a r_t g^{12} + r_t^2 g^{22})} \qquad (15)$$

Finally, analytical expressions of envelope surface $X(a,t)$ can be obtained by substituting Eq.13 into Eq.10.

For conical tool, the surface of sphere centers is $\Psi(a,t) = al(t) + p(t)$, the surface of sphere radius is $r(a,t) = R\cos\varphi + a\sin\varphi$, where $p(t) \in R^3$ is the curve of tool tip point, $l(t) \in S^2$ is the direction curve of tool axis, φ is the half cone angle of the tool, $t \in [t_0, t_1]$, $(a,t) \in [R\tan\varphi, H/\cos^2\varphi + R\tan\varphi] \times [t_0, t_1]$.

Select the LBM paper's data[6] to simulate the ruled surface, the two rail $Tr(u)$ and $Br(u)$ are Bezier curves, and the control points are demonstrated in Table 1. The conical tool parameters are: tip radius $R_0 = 3.175$ mm, length of cut $L = 60mm$, tool half angle $15°$.

Table 1. The control points of the two rails

	T_0	T_1	T_2	B_0	B_1	B_2
Concave	(65,15,-5)	(30,30,-5)	(0,60,-5)	(60,9,-35)	(30,30,-35)	(15,75,-35)
Convex	(60,9,-5)	(45,45,-5)	(15,75,-5)	(65,15,35)	(45,45,-35)	(0,60,-35)

We get 30 individual tool positions and orientations with the two-rail method. Envelope surface can be calculated with the tool positions and orientations. We pick up 100×100 disperse points on the ruled surface. The envelope surfaces generated by whole surface and sub-regional are showed in fig.4.

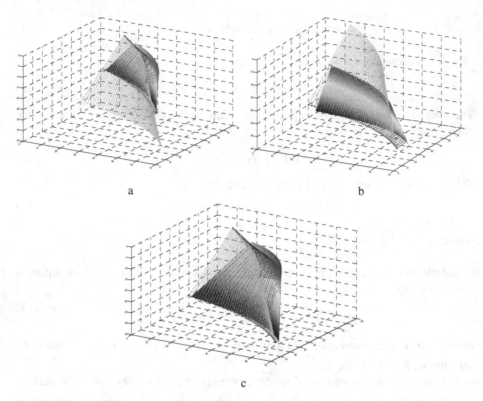

Fig. 4. The generation of tool path and envelope surface of whole surface and sub-regional.
(a) Upper sub-regional. (b) Lower sub-regional. (c) The whole surface.

3   Cutting Error Analysis

For non-developable ruled surfaces, from mathematics point of view, it is impossible
to flank milling of workpiece exactly, so the cutting error analysis is crucial. In this
section, we calculate the cutter error by signed distance theory.

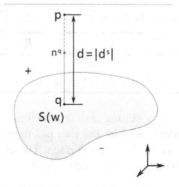

Fig. 5. The function of signed distance

The only foot point of point p is point q which is on the surface $S(w)$, signed distance from point p to surface $S(w)$ is defined as

$$d^s(p,w) = (p-q) \cdot n^q \tag{16}$$

where point q belongs to $S(w)$, n^q is unit normal direction of point p, the positive and negative value represents whether it point to p or the opposite, the normal direction of point q pass through point p. Fig.5 gives an illustration.

Positive and negative of the signed distance represents undercut and overcut, respectively. We calculate the cutter error and obtain the error distribution in the whole surface, as show in Fig.6, and we get maximum overcut, undercut and mean

Table 2. Cutting errors of milling the whole surface and sub-regional(mm)

	Overcut$_{max}$	Undercut$_{max}$	Mean error
Flank mill whole surface	0.8771	0.1115	0.1510
Flank mill upper sub-regional	0.1282	0.0169	0.0213
Flank mill lower sub-regional	0.1031	0.0373	0.0207

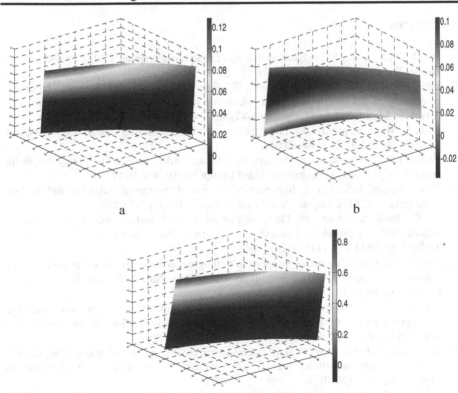

Fig. 6. The cutting error distributions of the whole surface and sub-regional. (a) Upper sub-regional. (b) Lower sub-regional. (c) The whole surface.

error as show in Table 2. It can be seen that the error is reduced by a great value with the sub-regional flank milling method.

4   Conclusions and Future Work

In this paper, sub-regional flank milling method has been preliminary studied. We propose an iso-parametric method to divided the rule surface. Tool path is generated, and envelope surface is generated by movement of the tool. The cutter error has been discussed. It can be seen the error is reduced greatly with the sub-regional flank milling method.

The future work is to optimize the tool path and do further research about how to divided the ruled surface.

Acknowledgments. This work was partially supported by the National Basic Research Program of China (Grant No.2011CB706804) and the National Natural Science Foundation of China (Grant No.51005087).

References

1. Liu, X.W.: Five-axis NC cylindrical milling of sculptured surfaces. CAD Computer Aided Design 27(12), 887–894 (1995)
2. Redonnet, J.M., Rubio, W., Dessein, G.: Side milling of ruled surfaces: Optimum positioning of the milling cutter and calculation of interference. International Journal of Advanced Manufacturing Technology 14(7), 459–465 (1998)
3. Bedi, S., Mann, S., Menzel, C.: Flank milling with flat end milling cutters. CAD Computer Aided Design 35(3), 293–300 (2003)
4. Chiou, J.C.J.: Accurate tool position for five-axis ruled surface machining by swept envelope approach. CAD Computer Aided Design 36(10), 967–974 (2004)
5. Gong, H., Cao, L.X., Liu, J.: Improved positioning of cylindrical cutter for flank milling ruled surfaces. CAD Computer Aided Design 37(12), 1205–1213 (2005)
6. Li, C., Bedi, S., Mann, S.: Flank milling of a ruled surface with conical tools-an optimization approach. International Journal of Advanced Manufacturing Technology 29(11-12), 1115–1124 (2006)
7. Zhu, L.: Modeling the surface swept by a milling cutter by using the envelope theory of two-parameter family of spheres. Jixie Gongcheng Xuebao/Journal of Mechanical Engineering 46(5) (2010)
8. Zhu, L.M., et al.: Analytical expression of the swept surface of a rotary cutter using the envelope theory of sphere congruence. Journal of Manufacturing Science and Engineering, Transactions of the ASME 131(4), 0410171–0410177 (2009)
9. Zhu, L.M., et al.: Geometry of signed point-to-surface distance function and its application to surface approximation. Journal of Computing and Information Science in Engineering 10(4) (2010)
10. Loney, G.C., Ozsoy, T.M.: NC machining of free form surfaces. Computer-Aided Design 19(2), 85–90 (1987)

Robotics for the Benefit of Footwear Industry

Iñaki Maurtua, Aitor Ibarguren, and Alberto Tellaeche

IK4-TEKNIKER, Av. Otaola 20
20600 Eibar, Spain
{imaurtua,aibarguren,atellaeche}@tekniker.es

Abstract. This paper presents the initial results achieved by the ROBOFOOT project aimed at contributing to the introduction of robotics in the Footwear Manufacturing Industry. In particular, user requirements, operations selected and technical achievements reached so far are described. Visual servoing solution developed for shoe pose identification is described with deeper detail. The introduction of this technology allows the coexistence of current working practices and robotic solutions, with minor changes in the production means already existing in most companies. This has been identified as one of the requirements by the end-users taking part in the project.

Keywords: Footwear, Force Control, Visual Servoing, Programming.

1 Introduction

With more than 26.000 companies and almost 400.000 employees footwear industry is still relevant in Europe [1]. However trend shows a clear decline on business figures; low cost countries are becoming an obvious threat for the future of the sector.

Fashion Footwear production is currently mainly *handcrafted*. Some manufacturing processes are assisted by specialized machinery (last manufacture, cementing and cutting) and there exist highly automated lines in mass production of technical shoes (i.e. safety footwear). But most production is still handmade, being especially true in the case of *high added value shoes* production, where Europe maintains its leadership.

The introduction of intelligent *robotics may contribute to overcome the complexity in the automation of the processes of this industry* that accounts for some of the shortest production runs to be found (eight pairs of shoes is the average order size). The main reasons that justify this lack of automation and extensive labor demand are:

- High number of products *variants*. On the one hand, a minimum of two different collections (summer & winter) of shoes are developed to be presented to the customers every year. As an average, more than 200 different *models* are manufactured for the two seasons. On the other hand, it is necessary to adapt each model to at least six different *sizes* and two sides (left and right).

  Finally, we have to take into account that each model can be manufactured in different *leather qualities and colors*.

C.-Y. Su, S. Rakheja, H. Liu (Eds.): ICIRA 2012, Part II, LNAI 7507, pp. 235–244, 2012.
© Springer-Verlag Berlin Heidelberg 2012

- *Complex manufacturing process.* For each model it is necessary to develop and manufacture the last (the rough form of a human foot used in shoemaking to provide the fit and style of the shoe), to produce the list of components (sole, heel, sock, strap, inner parts, etc.), to cut the inner and outside parts, to stitch different part to form the upper.
- *Complex assembly process.* The assembly process is very laborious (up to 25 different operations) and especially complex in fitting operations due to the non uniformity and the different elasticity of the natural leather as well as the non-rigid nature of the components. Finally each pair of shoes requires a final inspection (small spots or color differences in the leather, correct alignment of parts, etc.) and they are packaged.

Fig. 1. Semi-automatic assembly operation

Although some companies in this sector tried to incorporate robotic solutions, they did not succeed in the objective except for the injection process. The EU co-funded *ROBOFOOT* project is developing different solutions to facilitate the introduction of robotics in traditional footwear industry.

This paper presents some initial results, starting with the user requirements presented in Section 2 and the Operation selection in Section 3. First technical results are described in Section 4 with more detailed information on visual servoing achievements. Finally Section 5 summarizes the re-design of the manufacturing process.

2   Robots in Footwear Industry: User Requirements

The project consortium has done a deep analysis of current practices and main needs of Footwear Industry. The process has included reviewing several studies, the internal analysis of the two end-user partners, ROTTA and PIKOLINOS, and the contribution of the rest of partners that visited both manufacturing plants and participated in the decision making process providing their technical background. In summary, the main requirements identified are the following:

- *Quality*: introduction of robots shouldn´t increase the number of shoes that need some kind of retouching at the end of the line (currently an average of 80%). On the contrary, as most of these small faults are due to the low stability of some processes, it is expected that the use of robots will contribute to reduce these retouching operations.
- *Impact in current production process*: A basic requirement is the possibility to combine current production procedures with the robotized solutions proposed by ROBOFOOT. This includes the coexistence of manual operations with robotized ones and the reuse of existing production means.
- *Efficiency*: reduction of manufacturing time. It should be taken into account that the robotized production has to be integrated in current production. So, reduction of individual operation time cannot be considered an objective unless we consider combining two operations.
- *Production flexibility.* Two business trends demand new and more flexible manufacturing technologies [2]: on the one hand, higher flexibility and adaptability at a process level: Due to changes in the habits and behaviours of (both industrial and private) consumers, product life cycles are getting shorter and more product variants have to be offered. On the other hand, demand for higher flexibility and adaptability at plant and supply chain level: Shoe manufacturing companies have to be able to shortly react on changes on the market.
- ROBOFOOT has to guarantee the production flexibility, handling a wide variety of models/sizes coexisting in the production line and allowing frequent model changes
- *Reduction of costs.* Although it is not the main reason for introduction of robotics in this sector, it will allow some workers to do tasks with higher added value and overcome the lack of skilled workers for some operations.
- *Working conditions.* Currently there are several operations that involve potential risk for workers (dust, use of solvents, rotating parts, effort...). Introducing robots has to help in reducing the potential risk of those operations to the minimum.
- *Usability and maintainability.* The system has to be easy to use and maintain by no specialists.

3   Operation Selection

The criteria used for operation selection have been:

- Has it a positive impact on initial requirements?
- Does it mean an innovation in the process?
- Is the operation applied in most shoe types?
- Are there many variants in the way of doing the process? Can we cope with most of them?
- Is the solution proposed suitable to be used in other operations?
- Does it seem feasible to be done in the timeframe of the project?
- Is it suitable to be introduced in a demonstrator?

According to the criteria established and the analysis of operations, it has been established a ranking of operations, grouped in three prototypes:

- *Basic prototype*. It includes individual operations: Roughing, Gluing, Inking, Polishing, Last Manufacturing.
- *Intermediate prototype*. They correspond to some operations that can be combined in the same robotic cell: Roughing+ Gluing; Inking+ polishing+ last removal. Inspection will be included as well, in order to detect the presence of nails, assess gluing and roughing processes and to identify defects on the shoe.
- *Final prototype*: It corresponds to the most challenging operation, i.e. packaging. A complete robotized cell has been designed, although only some of the sub-operations will be implemented in the context of ROBOFOOT.

4   Technologies for Robotic Footwear Production

4.1   Robot Programming and Controlling

The general approach for robot programming and controlling is presented in the picture below. The starting point is the 3D information of the shoe. It can be obtained from the CAD or from a digitalization of the shoe mounted on the Last (not all companies use 3D CAD system for shoe designing).

Technicians define the trajectories for the different operations, including technological features (1).

The resulting file is the input for the postprocessor that generates the robot program in PDL2 language, specific for the COMAU robots used in the project (2).

To overcome the problem of minor misalignments between the Grasping Device and the last it is necessary the correction of the resulting program (3). Finally, real time adjustment of trajectories is needed for several operations, such as roughing (4).

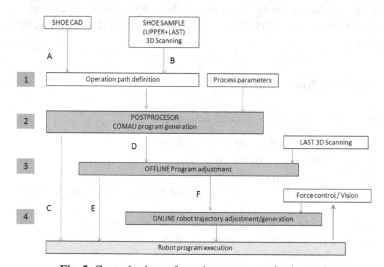

Fig. 2. General scheme for trajectory generation/control

Automatic Robot Part Program Generation from Digital Data

A CAM system has been developed by INESCOP to define the tool-path that has to be followed by the robot as well as process parameters.

The geometry is imported from the virtual model or from a digitalized model. Based on that, the user can define the area to be processed and the parameters to be used. After post-processing the resulting file it is generated the executable program.

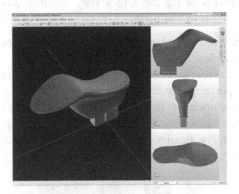

Fig. 3. Off-line robot programming (INESCOP)

However even a small assembly error between the GD and the last may lead to a significant difference between the theoretical and real tool trajectory – especially at shoe tip.

To overcome this problem it has been developed a system for online adaptation of off-line robot program.

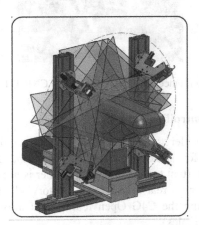

Fig. 4. 3D scanning for off-line program adjustment (CNR-ITIA)

On-Line Smart Adaptation of Off-Line Automatic Robot Part Program

CNR-ITIA has developed an innovative solution for on-line smart adaptation of off-line automatic robot part program generated from digital data (CAD/CAM) through the use of on-line sensors, namely a new generation of modular, scalable and reconfigurable 3D laser scanner. It allows fine-tuning the program generated in the previous step by adding the real positioning of the GD with respect the Last.

Manual Guidance Device

This wireless device can be place anywhere after the sixth axe of the robot. Operators can control the movements of the robot in a very intuitive way using the MGD. It offers the following benefits to end-users:

- It represents an innovative and smart way to program robot movements in an intuitive way at a very low cost.
- The design of the device is such that it is made out of low-cost parts, without losing focus on the performance of the system.
- The device will allow operators (even unskilled ones) to save time during the robot movement programming, without losing the quality of the trajectory definition.
- The device is extremely flexible as it can be positioned on the robot tool (or mounted on the robot flange) regardless of the robot type.

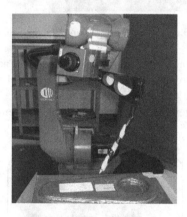

Fig. 5. Manual guidance device (Developed by CNR-ITIA for COMAU)

Sensor Based Robot Controlling

Finally, we have to consider that it is needed to correct or to generate the robot trajectory in real time for some operations. This is the case of operations like roughing, where it is important to guarantee that leather is not damaged.

CNR-ITIA is developing a real time robot trajectory adaptation mechanism based on force control and using the C4G Open feature that allows real-time parameters change (robot system variables).

On the other hand, visual servoing control has been developed to identify the pose of the shoes in the manovia and generate the robot trajectory to pick them up. To this aim, a vision system in an eye-in-hand configuration has been introduced.

Visual Servoing

Shoes go from one working station to the next one on trolleys that are placed in the Manovia. For each shoe on the trolley, the robot has to take it, manipulate it in the workstation (roughing, gluing,...) and leave it back on the trolley. Due to the fact that we are combining manual and robotized operations, it is not guaranteed an accurate positioning of the shoe on the trolley by workers.
Some colors show up very poorly when printed in black and white.

To overcome this problem and achieve a precise shoe grasping, a visual servoing system has been developed. The system uses images to estimate the pose of the Grasping Device attached to the shoe (external metallic element that allows a reliable grasping) and based on those estimations the robot corrects its pose until the desired position is reached. It is necessary to perform the grasping task with a precision of around 1 millimetre and 1-2 degrees in each axis to avoid damages in the shoe. The manoeuvre should not take more than 5-6 seconds to maintain the production time cycle.

The pose identification is difficult due to the industrial nature of the scenario; problems like the poor illumination of those environments, the metallic nature of the Grasping Device which makes difficult a proper illumination, as well as the wax and ink used during the shoe making process that can be adhered to the Grasping Device. All the above facts make it difficult to acquire good quality images to estimate the pose of the shoe.

TEKNIKER has developed a 6DOF visual servoing system using a dynamic look-and-move approach, including a particle filter to deal with the uncertainties (illumination, dirt in the Grasping Device...) of the image acquisition process. The process is as follows:

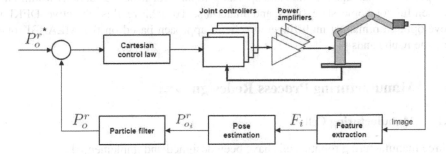

Fig. 6. Visual servoing schema

- *Feature extraction* from the image. In this step the image is analyzed, trying to find features of the Grasping Device, such as holes and edges. Even so, due to the uncertainties of the images it is difficult to determine exactly the position and dimensions of those features. To overcome this problem, different hypothesis have been extracted for each feature, determining possible positions and dimensions of the holes and edges.

- *Pose estimation* of all possible hypotheses. Based on the features extracted in the previous step, different poses are estimated, each of them related with a hypothesis.
- *Fusion of those hypotheses by means of the particle filter* to get the final pose estimation. The particle filter uses the estimated poses to determine which of the particles (hypothesis) are the most suitable for the given state and uses this distribution to improve the estimations in further steps.
- *Robot movement* based on the estimated pose. The robot moves in the workspace, trying to correct orientation and distance errors.

Based on the described loop, the system corrects iteratively the robot position until the desired one is achieved, as shown in Fig. 5. The experiments show good performance of the system, reaching high success rate and fitting in the time constraints previously explained.

4.2   Manipulation

In ROBOFOOT two different problems are considered: manipulation with Last and manipulation without Last, just the shoe.

In the first case it has been necessary to modify the current Lasts by introducing an external element, the Grasping Device (GD) that allows grasping the last with the required rigidity and repeatability. This modification has been done in such a way that Lasts are compatible with existing manufacturing machines at end-users facilities. Some colors show up very poorly when printed in black and white.

The vision system makes possible the identification of the pose of the lasts both on the manovia and when they lie on the exit of a chiller.

In the second scenario (shoes without Lasts) the deployment of a simple parallel gripper would damage the shoe and special grippers (for instance suction) would only be helpful for some shoe types and materials. To achieve this objective DFKI is developing a bimanual multifingered robotic approach based on the AILA [3] robot and the iCub hands [4].

5   Manufacturing Process Redesign

5.1   Manufacturing Cells

Three manufacturing robotic cells have been designed and implemented:

- *Roughing, gluing and last milling*: A multifunctional robotized cell for bottom and side roughing, gluing and last milling has been conceived by QDESIGN. Attention has been paid on how the roughing and gluing activities are actually performed by ROTTA.
- *Polishing, inking and last removal*: A robotic cell has been designed by AYCN. This cell integrates a robot that takes the shoes from the exit of the chiller, does the inking and polishing processes and, finally, opens the last for manual removal of the shoe by the operator. Inking is carried out in a conventional cabinet where painting guns are placed at fixed positions. Polishing operations are carried out

using a roller similar to those used in the conventional process, but the frame has been adapted to allow force monitoring.

- *Packaging*: it includes all the phases needed to pack a pair the shoes.

5.2   Quality Assessment

Quality inspection is currently done by workers at the end of the manufacturing process, just before packaging. These operators are in charge of doing manual reworking of shoes to repair small defects (80% of shoes require this kind of task). Due to this fact, it was decided that quality assessment supported by robots had to be implemented to verify the goodness of intermediate operations to ensure the final quality of the shoe. Specifically it was decided implementing visual inspection techniques in roughing, gluing and nail removing steps. Surface defects (cuts, scars, colour irregularities, etc.) will be tackled as well.

The robot manipulates the shoe inside inspection cabinet, where the following operations are verified:

- *Roughing*: There are two different objectives: to control the boundaries of the roughed area and to verify that the leather has not been damaged due to over-roughing. Different machine vision approaches, including thermography, are under dvelopment.
- *Nail removing*: the aim is to detect that there are not nails left on the sole (their removal is done manually by an operator). The proposed approach is to search the position of nails initially (once they are hammered in the last, although not necessarily just after this operation) and restrict the search space to those locations after the nail removal operation to guarantee that all of them have been removed.
- *Gluing*: To detect the excess (or lack) of glue in the shoe an additive sensible to ultraviolet light is added to the glue, making it easier to detect the presence of such excess or lack of glue. Using the correct lighting a simple threshold algorithm allows glue detection.
- *Texture analysis*: 2D vision will be used to detect marks, patterns and color changes on the leather surface.

6   Future Work and Acknowledgments

The project will last until February 2013. The last months will be devoted to experimental validation of the robotic solutions for each operation and the implementation of the packaging system.

Acknowledgments. This work has been performed within the scope of the project "ROBOFOOT: Smart robotics for high added value footwear industry ". ROBOFOOT is a Small or Medium- scale focused research project supported by the European Commission in the 7th Framework Programme (260159). For further information see http://www.robofoot.eu.

References

1. EU Commission, European Industry in a Changing World-Updated Sectoral Overview 2009 (2009)
2. Bessey, E., et al.: Research, Technology and Development for Manufacturing. In: The ManuFuture Road: Towards Competitive and Sustainable High-Adding-Value Manufacturing. Springer (2009)
3. Lemburg, J., de Gea Fernandez, J., et al.: AILA - design of an autonomous mobile dual-arm robot. In: IEEE International Conference on Robotics and Automation (ICRA), pp. 5147–5153 (2011)
4. Schmitz, A., et al.: Design, realization and sensorization of the dexterous iCub hand. In: 10th IEEE-RAS International Conference on Humanoid Robots (Humanoids), pp. 186–191 (2010)

Application of Grey Based Taguchi Method to Determine Optimal End Milling Parameters

Shasha Zeng and Youlun Xiong

State Key Laboratory of Digital Manufacturing Equipment and Technology,
Huazhong University of Science and Technology, Wuhan 430074, China
zengshasha316@163.com

Abstract. A multi-objective optimization problem has been proposed and developed in determination of the optimal combination of end milling process parameters. Experiments have been designed with five input cutting process parameters at five different levels. The values of surface roughness in both down milling process and up milling process are the required objective parameters. The Taguchi optimization technology coupled with Grey relational analysis has been applied for solving the proposed multi-objective optimization problem to achieve the desired machined surface quality characteristics. Simulation experiments give the optimal parametric combination. Furthermore, the modeling of machined surface topography on the texture profiles along the feed direction is formulated as a nonlinear programming problem with constrained conditions. Simulation experiments for the machined surface topography with the initial and optimal combination of end milling process parameters are implemented and the simulation results verify the feasibility of the proposed model and method.

Keywords: Process parameter optimization, Taguchi method, Grey relational analysis, Surface topography simulation.

1   Introduction

As a basic machining process, end milling is one of the most important and widely used metal removal processes in manufacturing and engineering industries. One of the essential criterions for selecting a proper manufacturing process is the functional performance of machined surface [1]. Surface topography of machined surface is significant for their functional performance. Three-dimensional topography of the machined surface is very important when surface functions are taken into consideration [2]. Among many parameters to characterize the surface topography, surface roughness is one of the most important parameters for evaluating the technological quality of a product. Accordingly, how to enhance the quality of the machined surface has been become an essential issue in the field of optimizing machining process parameters.

The machined surface topography is one of the most important indexes for evaluation of machining quality. There are many research works on this topic. Elbestawi et al. [3] proposed a surface topography model to examine the surface

C.-Y. Su, S. Rakheja, H. Liu (Eds.): ICIRA 2012, Part II, LNAI 7507, pp. 245–254, 2012.

topography characteristics of steel workpieces in finish machining. Toh [4] evaluated cutter path orientations and provided an in-depth understanding on the surface texture, with conclusion that milling in a single direction vertical upward orientation gives the best workpiece surface texture. Antoniadis et al. [5] proposed a novel simulation model to determine the surface produced and the resulting surface roughness for ball-end milling. Zhang et al. [6] developed a new and general iterative algorithm for simulating the machined surface topography in multi-axis ball-end milling.

The common methods to tackle the problems of process parameter optimization in metal cutting processes include statistical regression analysis, artificial neural network, response surface methodology, mathematical programming, and Taguchi method [7]. Experiments designed by means of the Taguchi orthogonal array show great success in process optimization [8-12]. The Taguchi method is a very powerful tool for solving process parameters optimization problems in the field of manufacturing and engineering industries [9], which provides a simple and efficient approach to optimize the design parameters. However, the traditional Taguchi method cannot be used for solving multi-objective optimization problems. To overcome this problem, the Taguchi method coupled with Grey relational analysis [13] is adopted in this study. In addition, the topography of the machined surface is simulated to validate the effectiveness of the proposed method.

2   End Milling Parameters Optimization

2.1   End Milling Surface Topography Formulation

As illustrated in Fig. 1 the frame configuration in the milling process, a set of coordinate frames are established to describe the relative motion relationship between the cutter edge and the workpiece. The Cartesian coordinate systems $O_W X_W Y_W Z_W$, $O_A X_A Y_A Z_A$, $O_C X_C Y_C Z_C$, $O_C X_E^j Y_E^j Z_E^j$, $O_F X_i^f Y_i^f Z_i^f$ represent the workpiece

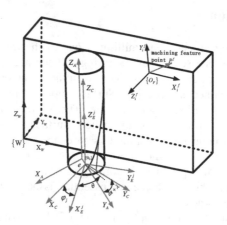

Fig. 1. Frame configuration in the milling process

coordinate frame, the main shaft coordinate frame, the cutter coordinate frame, the local coordinate frame attached to the jth cutting edge, the local coordinate frame whose origin is located at a sample point $P_i^f = (p_{ix}^f, p_{iy}^f, p_{iz}^f)^T$, respectively. φ_j is the angle between the axis $O_C X_C$ and axis $O_C X_E^j$. The vector $\mathbf{f} = (f_x, 0, 0)^T$ represents the feed rate vector.

The coordinates of a given point $P_i^e = (x_{E_{ij}}^P, y_{E_{ij}}^P, z_{E_{ij}}^P)^T$ on the jth cutting edge with respect to the coordinate frame $O_C X_E^j Y_E^j Z_E^j$ can be formulated as

$$\begin{pmatrix} x_{E_{ij}}^P \\ y_{E_{ij}}^P \\ z_{E_{ij}}^P \end{pmatrix} = \begin{pmatrix} R\cos(\theta_{ij}^P) \\ R\sin(\theta_{ij}^P) \\ R\theta_{ij}^P / \tan\beta \end{pmatrix} \tag{1}$$

where R represents the radius of the cutter, θ_{ij}^P is location angle of the jth cutting edge point in the ith cutter flute, and β is the helix angle of the cutter. In order to transform the motion of points on the cutting edge with respect to the workpiece coordinate frame into the motion of points on the cutting edge with respect to the machining feature points, the transformation matrix can be constructed as follows:

$$^C\mathbf{T}_E(\varphi_j) = \begin{bmatrix} \cos\varphi_j & -\sin\varphi_j & 0 & 0 \\ \sin\varphi_j & \cos\varphi_j & 0 & 0 \\ 0 & 0 & 1 & 0 \\ 0 & 0 & 0 & 1 \end{bmatrix} \tag{2}$$

where $\varphi_j = \varphi_0 + \dfrac{2\pi(j-1)}{N_t}$ represents the position angle of the jth cutting edge relative to the cutter coordinate frame with φ_0 the initial position angle and N_t the number of the cutter tooth. Analogously, the transformation matrix between the cutter coordinate frame and the main shaft coordinate frame can be constructed as follows:

$$^A\mathbf{T}_C(t) = \begin{bmatrix} \cos(\omega t + \lambda) & -\sin(\omega t + \lambda) & 0 & -e\cos(\omega t + \lambda) \\ \sin(\omega t + \lambda) & \cos(\omega t + \lambda) & 0 & -e\sin(\omega t + \lambda) \\ 0 & 0 & 1 & 0 \\ 0 & 0 & 0 & 1 \end{bmatrix} \tag{3}$$

where ω represents the angular speed of the end mill, λ represents the initial angle between the axis $O_C Y_C$ and axis $O_C Y_A$, t is the time of cutter traveling the workpiece, and e represents the run-out of the cutter body due to the misalignment between the cutter axis and the spindle axis. The transformation matrix of the main shaft coordinate frame with respect to the workpiece coordinate frame can be described as

$$^W\mathbf{T}_A(t) = \begin{bmatrix} 1 & 0 & 0 & f_x t + p_x^s \\ 0 & 1 & 0 & R + e + p_y^s \\ 0 & 0 & 1 & p_z^s \\ 0 & 0 & 0 & 1 \end{bmatrix} \tag{4}$$

where $\mathbf{P}_S = (p_s^x, p_s^y, p_s^z)^T$ represents the initial position vector of the axis of the cutter. The workpiece coordinate frame with respect to the local coordinate frame whose origin is located at a sample point $P_i^f = (p_{ix}^f, p_{iy}^f, p_{iz}^f)^T$ can be expressed as

$$\mathbf{T}_W^{Pf}(t) = \begin{bmatrix} 0 & 0 & -1 & p_{iz}^f \\ 1 & 0 & 0 & -p_{ix}^f \\ 0 & -1 & 0 & p_{iy}^f \\ 0 & 0 & 0 & 1 \end{bmatrix} \tag{5}$$

By combining Eqs. (1)-(5), an explicit, kinematical trajectory expression of cutting edge point with respect to machining feature point can be formulated as

$$\begin{cases} x_{E_{AP}}^{F_{AP}}(R,\omega,N_t,e,\lambda,\varphi_j,\theta_{ij}^p,t) = -\dfrac{R\theta_{ij}^p}{\tan\beta} + p_z^s + p_{iz}^f \\ y_{E_{AP}}^{F_{AP}}(R,\omega,N_t,e,\lambda,\varphi_j,\theta_{ij}^p,t) = R\cos(\omega t + \lambda - \varphi_j - \theta_{ij}^p) - e\cos(\omega t + \lambda) + f_x t + p_x^s \\ z_{E_{AP}}^{F_{AP}}(R,\omega,N_t,e,\lambda,\varphi_j,\theta_{ij}^p,t) = R\cos(\omega t + \lambda - \varphi_j - \theta_{ij}^p) + e\sin(\omega t + \lambda) - (R + e) - p_y^s + p_{iy}^f \end{cases} \tag{6}$$

Since the cutting edge trajectories along the feed direction are cycloid as a result of the combination of both translational motion and rotational motion of the end mill, based on the geometrical characteristics of the cutting edge and the tool path, the surface topography corresponds to the values of $z_{E_{AP}}^{F_{AP}}$ with θ_{ij}^p and t satisfying the condition that the cutting edge always contacts with the machined surface, then the contact constraint equation system can be derived. To find the minimum from a set of trochoidal motion of the cutter tooth with respect to the machining feature, the problem can be formulated as a nonlinear programming problem with constrained conditions as follows:

$$\text{Minimize}\left\{\Omega(\theta,t) = (x_{E_{AP}}^{F_{AP}}(R,\omega,N_t,e,\lambda,\varphi_j,\theta_{ij}^p,t))^2 + (y_{E_{AP}}^{F_{AP}}(R,\omega,N_t,e,\lambda,\varphi_j,\theta_{ij}^p,t))^2\right\}$$

$$\text{Subject to}\begin{cases} \left| y_{E_{AP}}^{F_{AP}}(\theta_0,t_0) \right| \le \dfrac{N_t f_t}{2} \\ \dfrac{\partial^2 z_{E_{AP}}^{F_{AP}}(R,\omega,N_t,e,\lambda,\varphi_j,\theta_{ij}^p,t)}{\partial\theta^2} > 0 \\ \dfrac{\partial^2 z_{E_{AP}}^{F_{AP}}(R,\omega,N_t,e,\lambda,\varphi_j,\theta_{ij}^p,t)}{\partial t^2} > 0 \end{cases} \tag{7}$$

The initial values satisfy the following conditions :

$$
\left\{
\begin{aligned}
t_0 &= \frac{1}{\omega}\left\{ k\pi + \arctan\left[\frac{e - R\cos\left(\varphi_0 + \dfrac{2\pi(j-1)}{N_t} + \dfrac{z_{Ei}^{P_{ij}}\tan\beta}{R} \right)}{R\sin\left(\varphi_0 + \dfrac{2\pi(j-1)}{N_t} + \dfrac{z_{Ei}^{P_{ij}}\tan\beta}{R} \right)} \right] - \lambda \right\} \\
\theta_0 &= \frac{1}{\omega}\left[k\pi + \arcsin\left(\frac{1}{\tan\beta} \right) + \varphi_0 + \frac{2\pi(j-1)}{N_t} - \lambda \right]
\end{aligned}
\right.
\tag{8}
$$

By means of solving this nonlinear programming problem with constrained conditions described in Eq. (7), the values of θ_{ij}^P and t during the milling process can be derived. By substituting the derived values of θ_{ij}^P and t into the expression $z_{E_{AP}}^{F_{AP}}(R,\omega,N_t,e,\lambda,\varphi_j,\theta_{ij}^P,t)$, the corresponding minimal values can be extracted so as to construct the surface topography as well as the texture profile.

2.2   Grey Based Taguchi Method for Optimization of End Milling Parameters

Generally speaking, classical process parameters design [14] is complicated and not convenient to implement with increasing number of process parameters. In order to solve this problem, Taguchi [15] proposed a standard orthogonal array to reduce the time required for experimental investigation. A loss function is developed to measure the deviation of the performance characteristic from the desired value. The value of the loss function is then converted to the signal-to-noise ratio (S/N ratio). It is true that a larger S/N ratio means a better performance characteristic when optimize a single performance characteristic. However, when optimize multiple performance characteristics, there is a problem that the higher S/N ratio for one performance characteristic may be the lower S/N ratio for another performance characteristic. To overcome this problem, the Grey relational analysis is adopted in this study.

In the Grey relational analysis, the first step is the generation of Grey relational, that is, normalize the S/N ratio ranging from zero to one and calculate the Grey relational coefficient to express the correlation between the desired and actual S/N ratios. In this study, the normalized values of surface roughness, corresponding to the lower-the-better characteristics criterion, can be expressed as

$$
x_i(k) = \frac{\max y_i(k) - y_i(k)}{\max y_i(k) - \min y_i(k)}
\tag{9}
$$

where $x_i(k)$ is the value after the Grey relational generation, $\min y_i(k)$ and $\max y_i(k)$ are the smallest value and the largest value of $y_i(k)$ for the kth response, respectively. The Grey relational coefficient $\xi_i(k)$ can be formulated as

$$\xi_i(k) = \frac{\Delta_{\min} + \psi \, \Delta_{\max}}{\Delta_{0i}(k) + \psi \, \Delta_{\max}} \tag{10}$$

where $\Delta_{0i} = \|x_0(k) - x_i(k)\|$ is the absolute value of the difference between the ideal sequence $x_0(k)$ and $x_i(k)$, ψ is the distinguishing coefficient satisfying $0 \le \psi \le 1$. $\Delta_{\min}$ and $\Delta_{\max}$ are the smallest value and the largest value of Δ_{0i}, respectively. By averaging the Grey relational coefficients, the Grey relational grade can be given as

$$\gamma_i = \frac{1}{n} \sum_{k=1}^{n} \xi_i(k) \tag{11}$$

where n is the number of process responses. The evaluation of overall performance characteristic depends on the Grey relational grade. Using this method, the optimization of multiple performance characteristics can be converted to optimize a single Grey relational grade, since the optimal combination of process parameters is achieved corresponding to the highest Grey relational grade.

3   Verification

3.1   Experimental Design and Simulation Result

Various cutting process parameters affect the machined surface topography and the surface roughness, which are indexes of importance for evaluating the machining quality. In the experiment, five cutting process parameters at five different levels each have been taken into consideration, namely, the cutter diameter, the cutter helix angle, the feed per tooth, the axial depth of cut, and the spindle speed. Process parameters during the simulation experiment with their symbols and values at different levels are listed in Table 1. The initial cutting process parameter settings are marked with asterisks in Table 1. The setting values of the number of cutter tooth , the radial depth of cut and the spindle run-out error are 4, 0.5mm and 5μm, respectively. The spindle run-out error refers to the run-out of the cutter body due to the misalignment between the cutter axis and the spindle axis. The design matrix is selected according to the Taguchi's orthogonal array design, which consists of 25 sets of coded conditions.

The surface roughness is usually quantified by the vertical deviations of a real surface from its ideal form. The commonly used three surface roughness parameters are Ra, Ry and Rz. Ra represents the arithmetical mean deviation of the profile. Ry represents the maximum height of the profile. Rz represents the mean roughness depth. Here, only Ra and Ry are considered in both down milling process and up milling process. The mean Gray relational grade for each cutting process parameter at levels 1, 2, 3, 4 and 5 have been listed in Table 2. It can measure the effect of each cutting process parameter at different levels. Fig. 2 shows the graphical representation of the S/N ratio for the overall Gray relational grade, where the dashed line represents the value of the total mean S/N ratio. According to the large-the-better criterion and Fig. 2, the optimal combination of the cutting process parameters can be determined, that is A5 B3 C1 D5 E5, where A, B, C, D and E represent the corresponding cutting process parameters showed in Table 1.

Table 1. Cutting process parameters and their levels

Symbol	Cutting process parameters	Level 1	Level 2	Level 3	Level 4	Level 5
A	cutter diameter (mm)	12*	14	16	18	20
B	cutter helix angle (degree)	30°*	32°	35°	40°	45°
C	feed per tooth (mm/tooth)	0.06	0.07	0.08*	0.09	0.10
D	axial depth of cut (mm)	6*	7	8	9	10
E	spindle speed (rpm)	2000*	3000	4000	5000	6000

* represents the initial cutting process parameter settings.

Table 2. Response table (mean) for overall Grey relational grade

Process parameters	Grey relational grade					
	Level 1	Level 2	Level 3	Level 4	Level 5	Max-Min
cutter diameter	0.45642	0.51756	0.56450	0.61894	0.69260	0.23618
cutter helix angle	0.54738	0.57734	0.59788	0.56996	0.55746	0.05050
feed per tooth	0.80970	0.66366	0.53388	0.44724	0.39554	0.41416
axial depth of cut	0.58210	0.55702	0.55690	0.56504	0.58896	0.03206
spindle speed	0.55200	0.56630	0.56088	0.58046	0.59038	0.03838

Total mean Grey relational grade = 0.57000

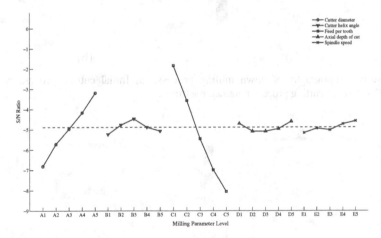

Fig. 2. S/N ratio plot for overall Gray relational grade

3.2   Simulation of End Milling Surface Topography

With the derived optimal end milling parameters in section 3.1, this section mainly concentrates upon predicting the topography of the machined surface in the case of both optimal cutting process parameter settings and initial cutting process parameter settings for testing and verifying the evaluated optimal parameters. In each case, both down milling process and up milling process are studied. The simulation results have been shown in Fig. 3 and Fig. 4, where ft represents the parameter feed per tooth, e represents the run-out of the cutter body due to the misalignment between the cutter axis and the spindle axis, and β represents the cutter helix angle. Fig. 3(a) and Fig. 3(b) show the predicted surface topography of down milling process for initial and optimal cutting process parameter settings, respectively. Fig. 4(a) and Fig. 4(b) show the predicted surface topography of up milling process for initial and optimal cutting process parameter settings, respectively.

Some conclusions can be drawn by comparing and analyzing Fig. 3 and Fig. 4. The results obviously show that the values of the machined surface roughness in the case of down milling process are much smaller than that of in the case of up milling process. Besides, Fig. 3 and Fig. 4 indicate that down milling take on convex ridge

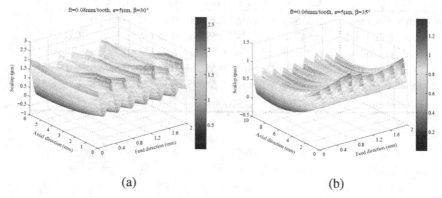

(a)   (b)

Fig. 3. Surface topography of down milling process. (a) Initial cutting process parameter settings. (b) Optimal cutting process parameter settings.

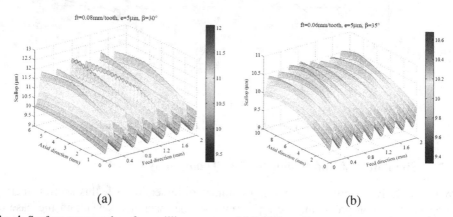

(a)   (b)

Fig. 4. Surface topography of up milling process. (a) Initial cutting process parameter settings. (b) Optimal cutting process parameter settings.

while up milling take on concave ridge. The quality characteristic of the machined surface with optimal combination of the cutting process parameters is better than that of the machined surface with initial cutting process parameter settings by comparing Fig. 3(a) and Fig. 3(b) as well as Fig. 4(a) and Fig. 4(b). Furthermore, the values of the machined surface roughness with optimal cutting process parameter settings are obviously smaller than that of with initial cutting process parameter settings. This further demonstrates the foregoing optimal combination of the cutting process parameters is reasonable.

4   Conclusions

The present study concentrates on the application of Taguchi optimization technology coupled with Grey relational analysis for solving the multi-objective optimization problem in the field of end milling process. The detailed methodology of Grey based Taguchi optimization technology is applied for evaluating the optimal combination of the cutting process parameters in end milling process so as to achieve the desired quality characteristics of the machined surface. Furthermore, the problem formulation for the topography of the machined surface is proposed and developed in detail. Simulation experiments of machined surface topography are implemented in the case of both down milling process and up milling process with the initial and optimal cutting process parameter settings. The experimental results indicate that the machined surface quality is improved after the optimization of the milling process parameters, which further verify the evaluated optimal parameters are reasonable and acceptable.

Acknowledgements. This work is supported by the National Natural Science Foundation of China (Grant No. 50835004).

References

1. Tönshoff, H.K., Arendt, C., Amor, R.B.: Cutting of Hardened Steel. CIRP Ann. 49(2), 547–566 (2000)
2. Waikar, R.A., Guo, Y.B.: A Comprehensive Characterization of 3D Surface Topography Induced by Hard Turning versus Grinding. J. Mater. Process. Technol. 197(1-3), 189–199 (2008)
3. Elbestawi, M.A., Ismail, F., Yuen, K.M.: Surface Topography Characterization in Finish Milling. Int. J. Mach. Tools Manuf. 34(2), 245–255 (1994)
4. Toh, C.K.: Surface Topography Analysis in High Speed Finish Milling Inclined Hardened Steel. Precis. Eng. 28(4), 386–398 (2004)
5. Antoniadis, A., Savakis, C., Bilalis, N., Balouktsis, A.: Prediction of Surface Topomorphy and Roughness in Ball-end Milling. Int. J. Adv. Manuf. Technol. 21, 965–971 (2003)
6. Zhang, W.H., Tan, G., Wan, M., Gao, T.: A New Algorithm for the Numerical Simulation of Machined Surface Topography in Multiaxis Ball-end Milling. ASME J. Manuf. Sci. Eng. 130(1), 1–11 (2008)

7. Mukherjee, I., Ray, P.K.: A Review of Optimization Techniques in Metal Cutting Processes. Comput. Ind. Eng. 50(1-2), 15–34 (2006)
8. Sayuti, M., Sarhan, A.A.D., Fadzil, M., Hamdi, M.: Enhancement and Verification of a Machined Surface Quality for Glass Milling Operation Using CBN Grinding Tool-Taguchi Approach. Int. J. Adv. Manuf. Technol. 60(9-12), 939–950 (2012)
9. Yang, W.H., Tarng, Y.S.: Design Optimization of Cutting Parameters for Turning Operations Based on the Taguchi Method. J. Mater. Process. Technol. 84, 122–129 (1998)
10. Hu, Y., Rao, S.S.: Robust Design of Horizontal Axis Wind Turbines Using Taguchi Method. J. Mech. Des. 133(11), 111009-1–111009-15 (2011)
11. Pontes, F.J., Paiva, A.P., Balestrassi, P.P., Ferreira, J.R., Silva, M.B.: Optimization of Radial Basis Function Neural Network Employed for Prediction of Surface Roughness in Hard Turning Process Using Taguchi's Orthogonal Arrays. Expert. Syst. Appl. 39(9), 7776–7787 (2012)
12. Al-Refaie, A., Al-Tahat, M.D.: Solving the Multi-response Problem in Taguchi Method by Benevolent Formulation in DEA. J. Intell. Manuf. 22(4), 505–521 (2011)
13. Datta, S., Bandyopadhyay, A., Kal, P.K.: Gray-based Taguchi Method for Optimization of Bead Geometry in Submerged Arc Bead-on-plate Welding. Int. J. Adv. Manuf. Technol. 39, 1136–1143 (2008)
14. Dean, A., Voss, D.: Design and Analysis of Experiments. Springer, New York (1999)
15. Taguchi, G.: Introduction to Quality Engineering. Asia Productivity Organization, Tokyo (1990)

Force Prediction in Plunge Milling of Inconel 718

KeJia Zhuang[*], XiaoMing Zhang, XiaoJian Zhang, and Han Ding

State Key Laboratory of Digital Manufacturing Equipment and Technology,
School of Mechanical Science and Engineering,
Huazhong University of Science and Technology,
Wuhan 430074, China
zkj26971@163.com

Abstract. In manufacturing, plunge milling is one of the most effective methods and widely used for material removal in rough and semi-rough machining while machining hard material. The cutting force in milling is very difficult and complex to predict, especially in plunge milling since there are many parameters acting as the design variables in the cutting force formulation. In this paper, an empirical formula is used for reference and a new cutting force model is developed in plunge milling of Inconel 718. The coefficients in the new formula are calibrated by the plunge milling cutting test, then an experiment is designed to confirm the new model. By using the proposed model, it's easy to predict the cutting force in plunge milling with considerable accuracy. Furthermore, the new model provides advice for the selections of machining parameters, machine tools and cutters to ensure the safety and high-quality of manufacturing process.

Keywords: plunge milling, average cutting force prediction, Inconel 718.

1 Introduction

Nickel-base alloy containing a niobium age-hardening addition takes advantages of very high strength, good ductility and anti-fatigue. The alloy can be used at temperatures from -217°to 700°with non-magnetic, oxidation- and corrosion-resistant [1]. It is called GH4169 in China and also known as Inconel 718 in US. The alloy is widely used in the manufacturing of components of liquid rockets parts, aircraft turbine engines, and cryogenic tankage. The challenges arise in the cutting of Nickel-base alloy, such as high cutting force, cutting tool abrasiveness, low thermal properties leading to high cutting temperatures, the surface of the workpiece is easy to damage, so the new approach to manufacturing Nickel-base alloy are needed. The chemical composition of this material is shown in table 1. The hardness of this workpiece is 412 HBD [2,3].

Since the strategy is more vibration free than in plane milling operations, plunge milling operation is used for roughing cavities and walls in moulds and dies, also used in rough of hard material such as Inconel 718 for remove excess material rapidly. Sample plunge milling operation is illustrated in Fig. 1, and a 2D picture shows

---

[*] Corresponding author.

C.-Y. Su, S. Rakheja, H. Liu (Eds.): ICIRA 2012, Part II, LNAI 7507, pp. 255–263, 2012.
© Springer-Verlag Berlin Heidelberg 2012

Nomenclature			
n	spindle speed	V_c	speed of cut
a_e	width of plunge milling	K	coefficient of the model
a_s	step of plunge milling	$F_i(i=x,y,z)$	force of plunge milling
F	federate of plunge milling	$F_{ia}(i=x,y,z)$	average force of plunge milling
fz	feed per tooth	$K_{Fi}(i=x,y,z)$	Coefficient of average force model

different kinds of plunge milling operation in Fig. 2. Figs. 2(a)-(c) show that the plunge milling can be used in rough, slotting large hole and enlarging small holes, respectively.

There are many difficulties in plunge milling operations that limits the use of this strategy. Most of the previous works concentrated on the design of cutter geometry and the chatter stability of the plunge milling. Wakaoka et al. [4] studied the intermittent plunge milling process to make vertical walls by focusing on the tool geometry and motion. Li et al. [5] presented a plunge milling method to create complex chamfer patterns and estimated cutting forces while neglecting the structural dynamics of the system. The remaining literatures belong to the commercial tool catalogs, which present only the dimensions and shape of the plunge milling cutters. Ahmed et al. has done some work in cutting Inconel 718 and the modeling of plunge milling operation. Ahmed and Mohamed Elbestawi et al. [6] proposed a horizontal approach to compute the chip area to consider the contribution of the main and   side edge in the cutting zone and to deal with any geometric shape of the insert. M. Al-Ahmad et al. [7] proposed a cutting model that included the determination of tool geometry (radial engagement, chip thickness) and the evaluation of the cutting forces. Yusuf Altintas et al. [8,9] has proposed time domain modeling of mechanics and dynamics of plunge milling, also he and his colleagues presented a frequency domain, chatter stability prediction theory for plunge milling by regenerative the chip thickness. But the previous papers did not take into account the role of cutting step and in experiments we found that this parameter plays an important role in the cutting force of plunge milling.

In this paper a new force model is used with milling parameters which include cutting width, feed in axial position, cutting step and cutting velocity to predict the average cutting force in milling Inconel 718 with plunge milling method shown in Fig. 2(a). With this new empirical formula, the average plunge milling force can be predicted with the known parameters, then a suitable machine as well as the plunge cutter for the strategy will be chosen.

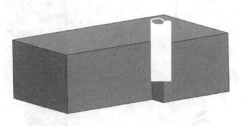

Fig. 1. Plunge milling operation

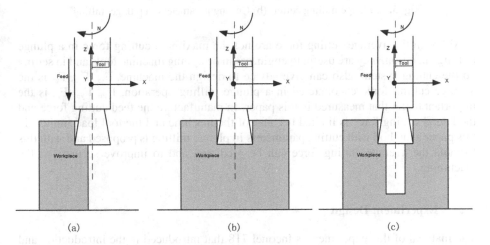

Fig. 2. Plunge milling process configuration: (a) intermittent plunge milling process to make vertical wall or conduct rough cutting, (b) plunge milling process for making large hole, (c) plunge milling process to enlarge a hole

2   Force in Plunge Milling

2.1   Mechanics of Plunge Milling

Fig. 3(a) shows the basic geometry of the plunge milling cutter, where axes X, Y are the horizontal coordinates, axis Z is the direction of the feed direction. For convenience of study, the cutting force is divided into lateral and feeding direction component. The lateral forces include F_x, F_y and feed direction force includes F_z. Fig. 3(b) shows the parameters that have influence on the cutting force prediction of plunge milling. Each factor in plunge milling has different influence on the cutting force, and to calculate the influences of different factors is an important work. The cutting force acting on the tool are shown in Fig.4, where F_x, F_y, F_z are the instantaneous cutting force in different directions of tool.

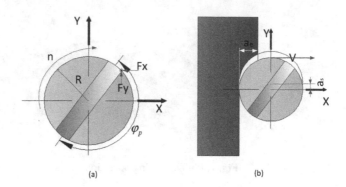

Fig. 3. (a)Plunge milling cutter, (b) Cutting parameters in plunge milling

Although the average cutting force are not the maximum cutting force in a plunge milling operation, they are useful to engineers in designing machine tools and in setting up the cutting system, also can give advice to design the machine. F_{xa}, F_{ya}, F_{za} is the average cutting force encountered in a plunge milling operation, F_{xa}, F_{ya}, F_{za} is the important target that measured in this paper. In manufacture the feed cutting force and the lateral cutting force is limited because of the machine and the tool load limiter. In this paper a method with cutting parameters in plunge milling is proposed and with this formula the average cutting force can be predicted and to improve security of the machining.

2.2   Experiment Design

The material of this experiment is Inconel 718 that introduced in the introduction and the mechanical is shown in table 1.

Table 1. The chemical composition of the workpiece

C	Mn	Si	P	Ni	Cr	Mo	Ti	Nb	Co	B	Mg	Al	Fe
0.03	0.02	0.09	0.003	52.48	18.94	3.03	0.98	5.13	0.02	0.003	0.002	0.51	other

The size of rectangle block is 83×76×30mm. The experiments were performed on a 5-axis high speed milling machine and the type is MIKRON DURO UCP 800 milling machine with a Heidenhain numerical control system. Test cutter is SECO plunge milling cutter (brand: MM06-06004-R10 -PL-MD02 F30M) with tool holder (brand:MM06-12070.3-0005), as shown in Fig. 4. Coolant is used to decrease the temperature and to lubricate the plunge milling cutter. Cutting force in three directions (X, Y, Z) are measured by using a three component force measurement dynamometer whose type is Kistler 9253B23. The dynamometer is connected to a series of charge amplifiers type which in turn is connected to an industrial personal computer (IPC) to collect the signals of current. In the cutting tests the cutter runout and vibration are ignored.

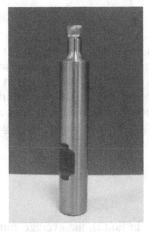

Fig. 4. Cutting tool

Fig. 5. Cutting force measurement

It has been verified that feed rate [10-14] and spindle speed [10,11,15-16] have great effects on the cutting force in milling. To confirm that whether other cutting parameters in plunge milling operation have influence on cutting force or not, a single-factor experiment cutting test as shown in table 2 is conducted. When the parameters that have influence on the plunge milling cutting force are found, a new experimental frame shown in table 3 with the use of orthogonal test design to decrease the test group is used to measure the average cutting force in plunge milling of Inconel 718.

Table 2. Single element cutting test & Verification tests form

Run	n(r/min)	a_e(mm)	F(mm/min)	a_x(mm)	F_x(N)	F_y(N)	F_z(N)
1	1200	0.50	120	3	167.9	110.3	201.7
2	1200	0.75	120	3	196.9	129.5	216.8
3	1200	1.00	120	3	212	154.5	220.3
4	1200	1.25	120	3	212.6	180.5	232.7
5	1200	1.50	120	3	223.1	195.5	244.9
6	1200	1.75	120	3	230.9	221.5	237.4
7	1200	2	120	1	173.5	122	234.6
8	1200	2	120	2	258.5	188.7	230.8
9	1200	2	120	3	318.4	216.4	234.8
10	1200	2	120	4	378.9	246.9	251

Table 3. Cutting test design with orthogonal test design

Run	n(r/min)	F(mm/min)	a_e(mm)	a_x(mm)	F_x(N)	F_y(N)	F_z(N)
1	800	80	0.5	1	109.9	51.0	131.3
2	800	100	1	2	208.9	80.0	110.0
3	800	120	1.5	3	371.3	223.8	142.2
4	1000	80	1	3	246.4	139.2	157.8
5	1000	100	1.5	1	105.0	54.4	168.1
6	1000	120	0.5	2	156.7	60.0	102.2
7	1250	80	1.5	2	211.6	166.1	237.9
8	1250	100	0.5	3	305.5	201.2	219.9
9	1250	120	1	2	193.3	106.0	246.4

3   Force Prediction and Model Analysis

In the milling, predicting the cutting force is a difficult and complex work, Eq.(1) is a former of the empirical formula in index model to predict the average cutting force which was widely used in manufacturing. When the meaningful parameters in the plunge milling has been found thought the cutting test shown in table 2, a new empirical formula (the former shows in Eq.(2)) which adds the cutting step called a_s in this paper in plunge milling is proposed to predict the average cutting force in plunge milling.

$$F = K\, a_e^{a_1} f_z^{a_2} v_c^{a_3}$$
(1)

$$F = K\, (a_e a_s)^{a_1} f_z^{a_2} v_c^{a_3}$$
(2)

With the empirical formula of the cutting force shown in Eq.(2), the average cutting force in plunge milling can be formulated as follows

$$F_{xa} = K_{F_x} (a_e a_s)^{a_1} f_z^{a_2} v_c^{a_3}$$

$$F_{ya} = K_{F_y} (a_e a_s)^{b_1} f_z^{b_2} v_c^{b_3}$$
(3)

$$F_{za} = K_{F_z} (a_e a_s)^{c_1} f_z^{c_2} v_c^{c_3}$$

Eq.(2) is a nonlinear expression for predicting the average cutting force in plunge milling. To calculate the factors and coefficients of Eqs.(3), first linearization the expression is needed and then using linear regression analysis soft such as statistical product and service solutions (SPSS) in this paper to calculate the factors and coefficients in the Eqs.(3). In this paper, experiments were done as shown in table 2 to confirm the useful parameter in plunge milling. With the measured forces shown in table 2, cutting step in plunge milling is relevant to cutting force as well as cutting width in plunge milling. Then a new cutting test shown in table 3 with the use of orthogonal test design to decrease the test group is used to calibrate the coefficients of Eqs.(3), the formulas of the cutting force in plunge milling can be written as Eqs.(4), while only cutting width used to predict the cutting force, the formulas can be written as Eqs.(5).

$$F_{xa} = 292.415(a_e a_s)^{0.468} f_z^{0.286} v_c^{0.044},$$

$$F_{ya} = 5.272(a_e a_s)^{0.647} f_z^{-0.223} v_c^{0.677},$$
(4)

$$F_{za} = 1.285(a_e a_s)^{0.112} f_z^{-0.325} v_c^{1.314},$$

$$F_{xa} = 390.84 a_e^{0.155} f_z^{0.542} v_c^{0.285},$$

$$F_{ya} = 7.980a_e^{0.356} f_z^{0.132} v_c^{1.016},$$ (5)

$$F_{za} = 1.340a_e^{0.197} f_z^{-0.264} v_c^{1.372},$$

A verification cutting test should be used to compare and analyze the given formulas. To reduce the test groups, experimental groups show in table 2 are used to verification this formula. With the average cutting forces that measured in table 2, the predicted cutting forces with Eqs.(4) and Eqs.(5) were plot in the Fig. 6.

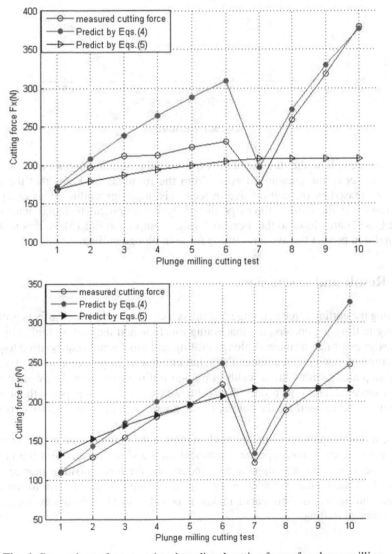

Fig. 6. Comparison of measured and predicted cutting forces for plunge milling

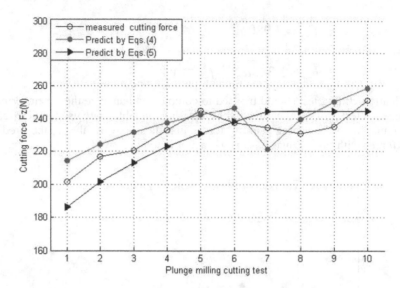

Fig. 6. (*continued*)

The pictures show that the formulas(Eqs.(4)) using cutting step as well as cutting width is closer to the measured forces. From the formulas we know that the cutting force is increased by the cutting area in feed axis in plunge milling. This comparison also shows that the cutting forces predicted by the empirical formulas with cutting step in Eqs.(4) are closer to the measured value compare to Eqs.(5), so this method is meaningful in predict the average cutting force in plunge milling.

4   Result and Discussion

Predicting the cutting force in plunge milling is a critical work, which affects greatly on choosing milling parameters, the machining machine and the cutting tool. This paper provides an empirical formula in plunge milling and this formula can be used to predict the average of cutting force under the same conditions in plunge milling. Using the cutting step along with cutting width in plunge milling to predict the average cutting force is more accuracy than only the width was used. In this paper orthogonal test design was used to decrease the cutting test compare with the signal-factor experiment design.

Since it is a complex and difficult work to predict the cutting force in plunge milling, the formulas given in this paper are empirical ones and not perfect. But the proposed model gives rise to the new approach to understand the mechanism of plunge milling process. It is shown that the average cutting forces have a closed form to the cutting step and cutting width. This paper makes it possible to identify the average cutting force of plunge milling.

Acknowledgments. This work is partially supported by the National Key Basic Research Program (Grant 2011CB706804), the National Natural Science Foundation of China (Grant 50835004).

References

1. Smithberg, D.: Inconel 718 machining manual. Manufacturing Research and Development, Boeing Commercial Airplane Company. Report 6M59–559 (1987)
2. Galimberti, J.M.: Improved metal removal rates for difficult-to-machine alloys. Creative Manufacturing Seminar, ASTME. SP 63–194 (1962-1963)
3. Shaw, Nakayama, M.K.: Machining high strength materials. CIRP Annals-Manufacturing Technology 15(1), 45–59 (1967)
4. Wakaoka, S., Yamane, Y., Sekiya, K., Narutaki, N.: High-speed and high-accuracy plunge cutting for vertical walls. Journal of Materials Processing Technology 127(2), 246–250 (2002)
5. Li, Y., Liang, S.Y., Petrof, R.C., Seth, B.B.: Force modelling for cylindrical plunge cutting. The International Journal of Advanced Manufacturing Technology 16(12), 863–870 (2000)
6. Damir, A., Ng, E.G., Elbestawi, M.: Force prediction and stability analysis of plunge milling of systems with rigid and flexible workpiece. The International Journal of Advanced Manufacturing Technology 54(9), 853–877 (2011)
7. Al-Ahmad, M., Acunto, A.D., Lescalier, C., Bomont, O.: Modelling of cutting forces in plunge milling. In: 7th International Conference on Advanced Manufacturing Systems and Technology, Udine, Italy, pp. 9–10 (2005)
8. Ko, J.H., Altintas, Y.: Time domain model of plunge milling operation. International Journal of Machine Tools and Manufacture 47(9), 1351–1361 (2007)
9. Altintas, Y., Ko, J.: Chatter stability of plunge milling. CIRP Annals-Manufacturing Technology 55(1), 361–364 (2006)
10. Jang, D.Y., Choi, Y.G., Kim, H.G., Hsiao, A.: Study of the correlation between surface roughness and cutting vibrations to develop an on-line roughness measuring technique in hard turning. International Journal of Machine Tools and Manufacture 36(4), 453–464 (1996)
11. El-Wardany, T., Gao, D., Elbestawi, M.: Tool condition monitoring in drilling using vibration signature analysis. International Journal of Machine Tools and Manufacture 36(6), 687–711 (1996)
12. Youn, J.W., Yang, M.Y.: A study on the relationships between static/dynamic cutting force components and tool wear. Journal of Manufacturing Science and Engineering 123(2), 196–205 (2001)
13. Sarhan, A., Sayed, R., Nassr, A., El-Zahry, R.: Interrelationships between cutting force variation and tool wear in end-milling. Journal of Materials Processing Technology 109(3), 229–235 (2001)
14. Elbestawi, M., Papazafiriou, T., Du, R.: In-process monitoring of tool wear in milling using cutting force signature. International Journal of Machine Tools and Manufacture 31(1), 55–73 (1991)
15. Lee, L., Lee, K., Gan, C.: On the correlation between dynamic cutting force and tool wear. International Journal of Machine Tools and Manufacture 29(3), 295–303 (1989)
16. Toh, C.K.: Evaluation of Cutter Path Strategies and Orientations When High Speed Milling Hardened H13 Steel AISI. Ph.D. Thesis, University of Birmingham, Birmingham (2003)

Dynamic Cutter Runout Measurement with Laser Sensor

XiaoJian Zhang[1], CaiHua Xiong[1,*], and Ye Ding[2]

[1] State Key Laboratory of Digital Manufacturing Equipment and Technology,
School of Mechanical Science and Engineering, Huazhong University of Science
and Technology, Wuhan 430074, China
[2] State Key Laboratory of Mechanical System and Vibration, School of Mechanical
Engineering, Shanghai Jiao Tong University, Shanghai 200240, China
quiet1016@yeah.net, chxiong@mail.hust.edu.cn

Abstract. The cutter runout is very common in machine milling and has a great effect on the surface accuracy. In this paper, a measurement of radial cutter runout in revolving milling tool is proposed by using the laser sensor. A laser beam is projected onto the milling tool edge and subsequently reflected. The diffuse reflection is captured by the sensor and the displacement between the cutter and the laser sensor is obtained. Based on the dynamic displacement, the cutter runout is calculated. The experimental results show that the radial cutter runout is dynamically varying in the constant rotation speed and the runout fluctuation largens with the increasing speed.

Keywords: dynamic cutter runout, milling tool, laser sensor, surface accuracy, high speed milling.

1   Introduction

The cutter radial runout is commonly encountered in the practice of milling. It occurs when the geometric axis of the milling cutter differs from the rotation axis and causes both the actual radius and feed to be distributed unequally among the cutting teeth, so the chip load and cutting force for each tooth is different. Preliminary analysis indicate that the cutter runout affects the cutting force [1], the vibrations frequencies during machine tool chatter [2], surface accuracy and surface location error of machined workpiece [3], the stability prediction of cutting processes [4], etc. Schmitz et al. [3] examined the effect of cutter runout on surface topography, surface location error and stability in end milling based on time-domain simulation. Insperger et al. [2] showed that the effect of the tool runout can sometimes prevent the proper determination of stability, and used the vibration signals and the corresponding Poincare section to determine whether chatter vibrations happened. Recently, Zhang et al. [4] discovered the milling stability lobes change greatly with the cutter runout variation by simulation, that the total trend of the milling stability domain is increasing, but some stable zone is

---

* Corresponding author.

C.-Y. Su, S. Rakheja, H. Liu (Eds.): ICIRA 2012, Part II, LNAI 7507, pp. 264–272, 2012.
© Springer-Verlag Berlin Heidelberg 2012

decresing with the increased runout offset. Plentiful works demonstrated that the cutter radial runout is an important factor for surface texture and stability prediction. Therefore, it is very necessary to measure the cutter runout with an accurate and efficient method in practice.

The cutter runout can be obtained by different methods, such as measured by dial gauge offline, analyzed by surface topography of the machined workpiece [5], and mostly based on calibration procedures using the measurement of cutting forces [6-9] because the value of cutter offset in cutting is real and it may be different from the one measured off-line. However, such cutting force based methods also have following disadvantages:

▪   The expensive dynamometer is essential for the cutting force measurement.
▪   Such operation is difficult especially in an industrial environment.
▪   The stiffness of the machining system is changed with the mounted dynamometer.
▪   The cutting force signal is distorted in high speed spindle rotation due to the constraint of the sampling bandwidth of the dynamometer (2~3kHz).

Since most modern machine tool is equipped with laser sensors, we propose an efficient method for the cutter runout measurement by using the laser beam. The cutter runout has two parts: the radial cutter runout and the axis tilt which are characterized by ρ, θ, τ, ϕ. In this paper, only the radial runout is considered.

In the previous researches, whether the cutter runout is measured offline or calibrated by the sampled cutting forces, or obtained by other methods, almost all the researchers assumed that the cutter runout is hold still whether the spindle is rotating or not. Herein, we abandon the assumption and assume that the radial cutter runout is not a constant, but dynamically varies with the spindle rotations. The remainder of this paper is detailed to verify such idea by the measurement with the contactless laser sensor. The experimental measuring configuration is described and the dynamic displacement signal between the revolving cutter and laser sensor is shown in Section 2. Then, the displacement data is optimized based on the linear search optimization model to obtain the dynamic cutter runout, which is detailed in Section 3. When the spindle revolving speed is varied, the runout fluctuation is given in Section 4, and some discussions are made. The conclusions are drawn in the last section.

2   Experimental Setup and Measurement

The laser sensing system configuration is shown in Fig.1. The setup briefly consists of the revolving spindle and the laser beam sensor supported by a stiffness clamping. Technique parameters of the sensor are 30 μm of spot size, 50 k Hz sampling rate and 0.05 μm repeat displacement accuracy. The laser beam is projected onto the rotating center of the spindle and the laser spot is located on the bottom of the new cutter for

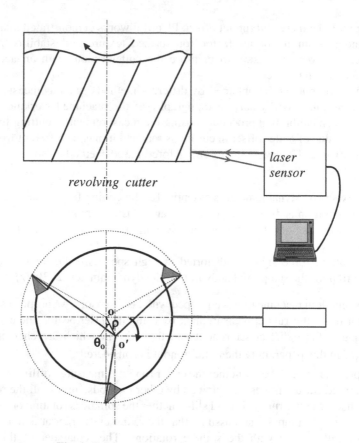

Fig. 1. Configuration of the laser sensing system

testing cutter runout in free cutting, as shown in Fig.1. An Industrial Personal Computer (IPC) is connected to the laser sensor and simultaneously converts and saves the dynamic displacement signals.

When the spindle is rotating, the profile of the cutter section with offset is measured and recorded, and the dynamic displacement measured is shown in Fig.2. When the local zone is magnified, the profile curve of the cutting tooth is conveniently distinguished. The displacement of the tooth point, which is usually the local highest point, is used to calculate the cutter runout.

By using some filtering and signal extraction technique, the peaks of each tooth are easily obtained, which is shown in Fig.3. It is shown that the peaks are almost periodic and its period is equals to the spindle rotation period. In the next section, the peak difference of tooth points between the adjacent teeth is used for calculation of the runout.

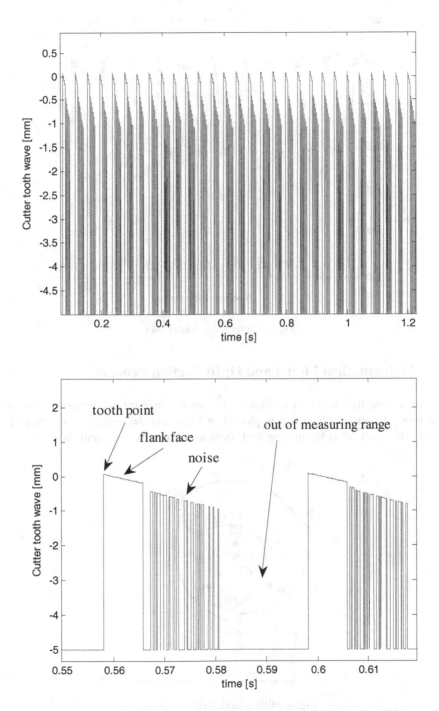

Fig. 2. Cutter profile curve measured with laser sensor at spindle speed n=500 rpm

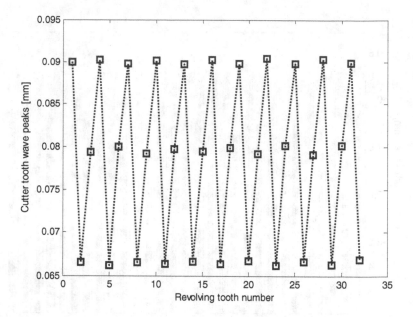

Fig. 3. Cutter tooth wave peaks

3   Mathematical Model and Optimization Process

Herein, a three-flute end-mill is illustrated as an example for mathematical modeling. The rotating cutter with runout is plotted in Fig.4 and the geometric relationship is given. The point 'o' is the milling tool section geometric center, and the point 'o'' is

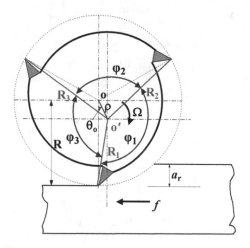

Fig. 4. Milling model with radial runout

the rotational center of the tool. The displacement between the geometric center and the rotational center equals the cutter axis offset ρ. The runout angle is supposed to be the angle from the direction of the axis offset to the nearest tooth clockwise (tooth 1 in Fig.4), so the runout angle satisfies $\theta_0 \in [0, 2\pi/3]$.

The length differences of radius between the adjacent teeth are denoted as h_1, h_2, h_3, respectively, which are equal to the height difference of cutter wave peaks in Fig.3. The actual cutting radii for each tooth are:

$$R_1 = \sqrt{R^2 + \rho^2 - 2R\rho\cos(\theta_0)},$$
$$R_2 = \sqrt{R^2 + \rho^2 - 2R\rho\cos(2\pi/3 - \theta_0)},$$
$$R_3 = \sqrt{R^2 + \rho^2 - 2R\rho\cos(2\pi/3 + \theta_0)},$$

where the runout offset $\rho \in [0, \max(|h_1|, |h_2|, |h_3|)]$, the diameter of the end-mill is 8 mm, so the radius R=4 mm. The cutter runout optimization solution is defined as the minimization of the following object function while respecting the limits of runout offset ρ and runout angle θ_0.

$$\min \ f = (R_3 - R_1 - h_1)^2 + (R_1 - R_2 - h_2)^2 + (R_2 - R_3 - h_3)^2$$
subject to $\rho \in [0, \max(|h_1|, |h_2|, |h_3|)]$, $\theta_0 \in [0, 2\pi/3]$.

4   Experimental Results and Discussions

After optimization, the cutter runout is obtained, as shown in Fig.5. It is shown that the cutter runout in practice fluctuates with the spindle rotating. When such variation is described in the polar coordinate, it is clearer.

When the spindle revolving speed is changed from 500 rpm to 12000 rpm, the cutter runout in free cutting is also varying. It fluctuates around the initial geometrical runout, as shown in Fig.6. It is not a constant vector anymore even in the constant spindle rotation speed. In the low spindle speed ($n<2000$ rpm), the cutter runout may be still regarded as a constant, but in the higher spindle speed ($n>2000$ rpm), the fluctuation of the runout enlarges. In Fig.6, when $n=12000$ rpm, the dynamic range of runout offset is from 11.7 μm to 18.1 μm, and the dynamic range of runout angle is from 11.5 degree to 48.4 degree. As a whole, it can be seen that the trend of the distribution range of the runout value enlarges with the increasing speed.

The enlarged dynamic range of the cutter runout will make the cutting process in high speed machining much more complicated, which maybe means that 1) the trajectory of the cutting tooth is not an cycloid curve or approximated as a circle any more, especially in high speed rotation, 2) the dynamic stiffness of the bearing is decreasing with the increasing speed, 3) the dynamic behavior of the cutter-holder-spindle system is more complex and the cutting process is more complex than in low spindle rotation speed.

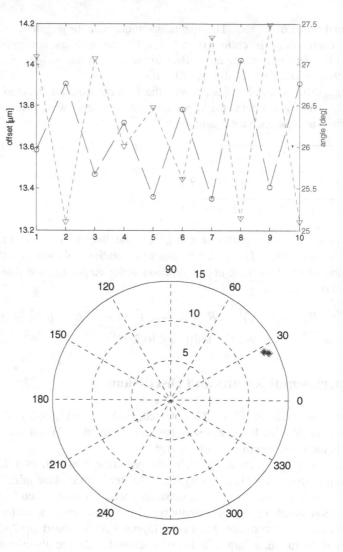

Fig. 5. Cutter radial runout distribution at n=500rpm

It's hard to say the dynamic cutter runout in free cutting is almost same with that in cutting, which needs further experimental research, especially in the cutting process. When the cutting force has small effect on the cutter-holder-rotor dynamics, the measurement of cutter runout in free vibration can be used as a substitute for prediction of the surface feature and vibration stability.

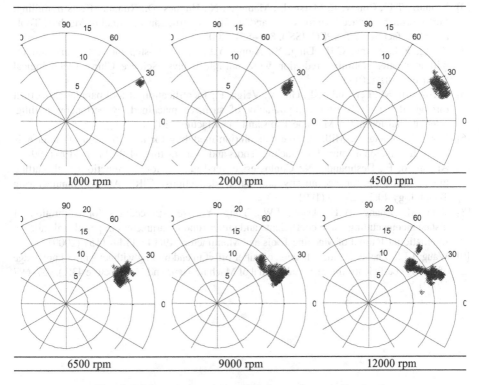

Fig. 6. Cutter runout variation with increasing spindle speed

5   Conclusions

In this work, a laser sensor is adopted to measure the dynamic displacement to investigate the actual cutter radial runout in milling. The linear search optimization method is used to obtain the cutter runout. It is found that the previous assumption that the cutter runout is a constant fails, especially in high speed milling. The cutter runout is not a constant any more in spindle rotating. When the revolving speed increases, the dynamic range of fluctuation enlarges, which will make the cutting process in high speed milling more complicated.

Acknowledgments. This work is partially supported by the National Key Basic Research Program (grant 2011CB706804), the National Natural Science Foundation of China (Grant 50835004).

References

[1] Kline, W., DeVor, R.: The effect of runout on cutting geometry and forces in end milling. International Journal of Machine Tool Design & Research 23(2-3), 123–140 (1983)
[2] Insperger, T., Mann, B.P., Surmann, T., Stepan, G.: On the chatter frequencies of milling processes with runout. International Journal of Machine Tools and Manufacture 48(10), 1081–1089 (2008)

[3] Schmitz, T.L., Couey, J., Marsh, E., Mauntler, N., Hughes, D.: Runout effects in milling: Surface finish, surface location error, and stability. International Journal of Machine Tools and Manufacture 47(5 SPEC. ISS.), 841–851 (2007)

[4] Zhang, X.J., Xiong, C.H., Ding, Y., Xiong, Y.L.: Variable-step integration method for milling chatter stability prediction with multiple delays. Science China Technological Sciences, 1–18 (2011)

[5] Arizmendi, M., Fernandez, J., Gil, A., Veiga, F.: Identification of tool parallel axis offset through the analysis of the topography of surfaces machined by peripheral milling. International Journal of Machine Tools and Manufacture (2010)

[6] Liang, S., Wang, J.: Milling force convolution modeling for identification of cutter axis offset. International Journal of Machine Tools and Manufacture 34(8), 1177–1190 (1994)

[7] Armarego, E., Deshpande, N.: Computerized end-milling force predictions with cutting models allowing for eccentricity and cutter deflections. CIRP Annals-Manufacturing Technology 40(1), 25–29 (1991)

[8] Wan, M., Zhang, W.H., Dang, J.W., Yang, Y.: New procedures for calibration of instantaneous cutting force coefficients and cutter runout parameters in peripheral milling. International Journal of Machine Tools and Manufacture 49(14), 1144–1151 (2009)

[9] Wang, J.J.J., Zheng, C.: Identification of cutter offset in end milling without a prior knowledge of cutting coefficients. International Journal of Machine Tools and Manufacture 43(7), 687–697 (2003)

Structure and Electromagnetic Actuation Systems of Microrobot

Shuqiang Zhu, Lina Hao[*], Bo Wang, Zhong Li, and Jie Dong

School of Mechanical Engineering & Automation, Northeastern University,
Shenyang 110819, China
haolina@me.neu.edu.cn,
{mishaw.chu,wb1987816,anymisshui,jiedong.neu}@gmail.com

Abstract. According to the feature of the magnetic actuation principle, now there are mainly three driving methods: one is alternating magnetic field, another is stationary gradient magnetic field and the last one is rotating magnetic field. This paper provides a detailed insight into the present-day state of microrobot technology and development on structure and electromagnetic actuation (EMA) systems. Firstly, the microrobot based on the three actuation methods is selectively elaborated respectively and the structure of EMA systems, microrobot characteristics and actuation principle are all analyzed and compared; finally some of the critical aspects of microrobot and EMA system design are considered. This paper shows that rotating magnetic field will be the most actuation promising method in the future biomedical application.

Keywords: Electromagnetic Actuation Systems, Microrobot, Helmholtz coils, Maxwell coils.

1 Introduction

Microrobot is a kind of robot with overall dimension of range from 10 to 100μm, and it is fabricated with the bulk micromachining technology by assembling micro actuator, micro sensor and signal processing circuit into a silicon slice [1]. Because microrobot can work in a narrow space where people and macro robots cannot get, and MEMS technology, LIGA technology and micro fabrication technology have achieved great progress in recent years, microrobot is attracting more and more attention [2-3]. In order to accomplish some special task in some special environments, it is a key development direction recently that utilizing external field for supplying energy, achieving actuation and precise control of microrobot. Microrobot can get power and propulsion in no physical connection methods, such as light, microwave, magnetic field and ultrasonic field, etc. So once microrobot is driven wirelessly, the disadvantages of the power supply method of microrobot using cables or micro battery can be overcome [4]. Of these methods, magnetic field, as a novel method that has fewer side effects and harm to human being and has a large operating environment and applied range, has been a main research subject now.

---

[*] Corresponding author.

C.-Y. Su, S. Rakheja, H. Liu (Eds.): ICIRA 2012, Part II, LNAI 7507, pp. 273–280, 2012.

In a general way, external magnetic field can be divided into three kinds of magnetic field——alternating magnetic field, stationary gradient magnetic field and rotating magnetic field [5]. In fact, because of its widely biomedical application in the targeted diagnosis and therapy of cardiovascular disease, actuation and control of microrobot in external magnetic field has attracted great attention among research institutions and universities and some actuation systems for test have been designed and equipped out in some labs. This paper will discuss the present-day state of microrobot technology and development on structure and electromagnetic actuation (EMA) systems.

2   Three Kinds of Electromagnetic Actuation Methods

2.1   Microrobot Driven by Alternating Magnetic Field

The direction of magnetic vector sum varies in a given angle range, and the angle generally is less than 180°. Flexible body begins to alternate motion under the actuation of the external ever-changing magnetic moment and microrobot will move forward in the liquid environment. This motion method is similar to fish swimming. In a word, the microrobot using this actuation method must have a fin-like mechanism and magnet, and complex structure will limit unavoidably the size decrease of microrobot, so the kind of robot generally reaches millimeter scale.

S. Park et al designed and produced a tadpole type microrobot [6]. The microrobot consists of an acrylic body, rotating axis, a cylinder type magnet and a silicone fin; structure and motion principle diagram are shown in fig1.

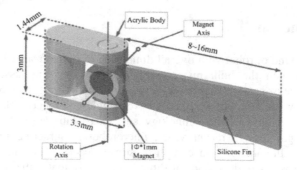

Fig. 1. Isometric view of microrobots motion

The electromagnetic actuation (EMA) system, which mainly is used to control and navigate for microrobot, consists of two pairs of Helmholtz coils. Two pairs of Helmholtz coils generate uniform magnetic flux intensity respectively along the X-axis and Y- axis between the coils and the vector sum of the magnetic fields can be adjusted by current flowing in the Helmholtz coils. With the direction of vector sum of the magnetic fields changing alternately at certain a frequency, the cylinder type magnet generates alternating motion at the same frequency, and that will push tail fin swing back and forth, so the tadpole type microrobot can move forward smoothly. The experiment result has shown that the swing angle, the swing frequency, and the fin length have large effect on the swimming velocity of the microrobot, and the swing angle is the largest one. Meanwhile, the microrobot with about 12 mm of the fin length shows the best velocity and stable swimming motion.

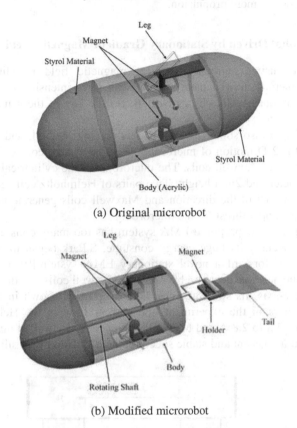

(a) Original microrobot

(b) Modified microrobot

Fig. 2. Microrobots based paddle motion

Like S. Park, Guo et al was inspired by paddling motion and proposed a new paddling type of microrobot that can move in human organs such as intestines, even blood vessel [7]. As it is shown in fig2, the microrobot is 55mm in length, 40mm in width; head consists of styrol material and tail cylindrical body acrylic. To bend the legs in the microrobot, a cylindrical magnet with dimensions of φ4×2mm and magnetic flux density of 330mT is assembled. Encouraged by magnetic moment, the rotational oscillation of the permanent magnet induces the bending motion on the robot tail. And the fin is connected with the head, so it also starts doing the same movement. During bending motions of the tail film, the robot tail presses backwards against the water or glycerol, in this way, the propelling force can be generated, and the robot can move forward while adjusting the frequency of input current. The pushing force of the microrobot is easy to change by controlling the frequency of inputted current. However, when the current signal is sine, triangle, and pulse, the relationship between input frequency and the force is not linear as we hope. Based these advantage and disadvantage, Guo improved the structure of the tail of the microrobot, as shown in fig 2(b). The fin of the improved microrobot is fastening to the end of the tail. Compared with the previous, and it has good balance with fin and legs and can generate more propulsion.

2.2   Microrobot Driven by Stationary Gradient Magnetic Field

The method of using stationary gradient magnetic field has little demand to microrobot. Generally, a permanent magnet with large intensity of magnetization is enough, and material usually choses NdFeB. So the key of the actuation method is EMA system design.

S.Park et al had also some research to this driving method, and he proposed an EMA system for 2-D motion of microrobot [8]. The system consists of two pairs of Helmholtz coils and Maxwell coils. The microrobot is the cylindrical NdFeB magnet with 2mm diameter and 2mm height. Two pairs of Helmholtz coils generate uniform magnetic flux to control the direction and Maxwell coils generate uniform gradient magnetic flux to supply thrust for the microrobot.

Considering that this proposed EMA system has too many coils and takes up too much space, especially its huge energy consume, S.Park began to transform to the structure, and put forward a novel stationary EMA system [9]. Compared to the previous one, the new one decrease by a pair of Maxwell coils and the coils are placed along with the z-axis. Its structure schematic diagram is shown in fig 3. As to the specific parameters in the experiment, the current flow in the Helmholtz coils is regulated from −2.8 to 2.8 A and Maxwell coils is 2A. Controlled microrobot can be easy to move at a constant and stable speed on the dish filled with silicone oil of high

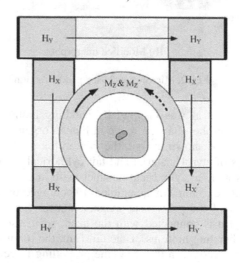

Fig. 3. The latest EMA system designed by S. Park team

viscosity (350 cp). The new EMA system will have remarkably less energy consume and the microrobot will be easier to be controlled. In their experiment, motion position of the microrobot can be measured in time through the CCD camera, and to ensure microrobot aligned in the desired direction, compiled program and manual operational joystick have been prepared.

Metin Sitti et al also designed a microrobot based stick–slip motion [10]. The microrobot with dimensions of 250μm×130μm×100μm is made of NdFeB material and reaches to 5×10^5A/m magnetization. Metin Sitti used five coils to control the microrobot. The direction and gradient of the horizontal magnetic field are controlled by four coils placed upright, and the remanent is placed below the work plane for electromagnetic clamping. When steady current flow accesses to four upright coils and the clamping coil is pulsed with a sawtooth waveform, the microrobot begins to stick-slip motion. According to the difference of coils pulsed with sawtooth waveform current signal, Metin Sitti have two different methods, that is, In Plane Pulsing (IPP) and Out Plane Pulsing (OPP). The experiment has demonstrated that robot velocity seems to be linear at low frequencies for both IPP and OPP control, and compared to IPP control, the OPP control method has much higher linear velocities, exceeding 2.8 mm/s with a 70 Hz drive signal. The result will have an important application, that is, OPP can be used for coarse robot motion and IPP can be used for fine adjustment in a particular possibility micro-manipulation task in future. Fig 4 is the Photograph of the EMA system designed and Fabricated by Metin Sitti.

Magnetic medium is capable of getting magnetic force in a nonuniform external magnetic field. In order to make microrobot move steady and controlled easily, uniform gradient magnetic field will be the best choice for us. So Maxwell coils are came to because the coils can generate uniform gradient field in bigger space compared to other kinds of coils. As to the direction control of microrobot, scientists generally use Helmholtz coils. Helmholtz coils have same advantage with Maxwell coils, so in the actuation method using stationary gradient magnetic field, Helmholtz coils and Maxwell coils will be the most common combination way. Scientists have not much demand for microrobot; a magnet of large magnetization intensity can

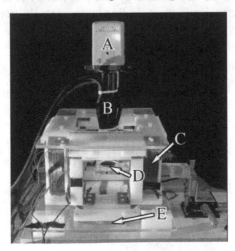

Fig. 4. Photograph of the EMA system

satisfy and it generally is cylinder. However, this method has too much energy consumption, furthermore, microrobot can generate fiction with human blood vessels and that will have seriously damage to human being. So this actuation needs to solve plentiful technique problems before true medical application

2.3   Microrobot Driven by Rotating Magnetic Field

There are two methods to generate rotating magnetic field: flowing in a certain wavelike current signal to magnet coils or directly rotating magnet. Magnet can get magnetic moment in a rotating magnetic field. Given an appropriate rotating frequency, microrobot will rotate at a certain angular velocity and that can generate propulsion force in liquid environment. The dimensions range of microrobot in liquid environment is up to dozens of micron, and it has some advantage, like simple structure, motion steady, high actuation efficiency and easy manipulation. So this method will be extremely promising and has huge application potential in medical diagnosis and biomedical engineering.

K.Ishiyama et al proposed a microrobot based snake-like mechanism and locomotion [11]. Snake-like microrobot has eight sections, 85mm length in all and NdFeB magnet is used for the joint in between the two adjacent sections, silicone tube and acrylic fibers respectively are used for artificial backbones and ribs as shown in fig 5. In their experiment, three-axis Helmholtz coil system provides a simple structure and dynamic actuation of the magnetic robots, and robot velocity can reach to 57mm/s at a 4Hz rotating magnetic field frequency. K.Ishiyama also compared alternating and rotating magnetic field actuation ways and the latter will be more range of application.

Bradley J. Nelson et al successfully designed a kind of microrobot assembling artificial bacterial flagella [12-13]. Entire robot has about 50μm length and can be divided into two parts: a helical nanobelt tail resembling the dimensions of a natural bacterial flagella and a thin soft-magnetic "head" on one end. The fabrication of the helical nanobelt tail is the key technology and that mainly is self-scrolling technique. The image of the microrobot is shown in fig 6(a) through electron microscope. Fig 6(b)

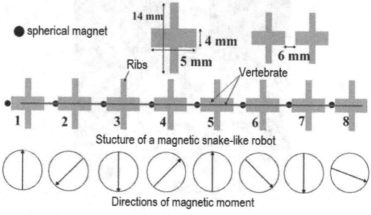

Fig. 5. Snake-like microrobot

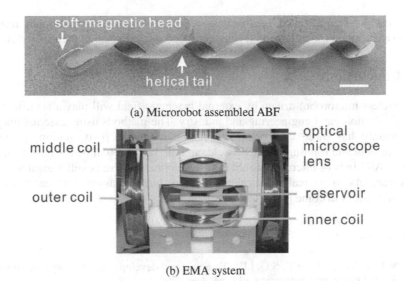

(a) Microrobot assembled ABF

(b) EMA system

Fig. 6. Microrobot and MEA system designed by ETH Zurich

is the EMA system for the microrobot, which consist of three pair of orthometric electromagnetically coils. In liquid environment, microrobot can generate propulsion because of self-propelled structure using a low-strength rotating magnetic field. Through a series of experiments, Nelson found a linear relationship between the frequency of the applied field and the translational velocity when the frequency is lower than the step-out frequency of the artificial bacterial flagella. And when the rotating magnetic field strength is 2mT, microrobot has its maximum velocity 18μm/s.

3   Issues about Microrobot and EMA System

The microrobot driven by external magnetic field is still at laboratory research stage and lots of problems eagerly need to be solved. Of course, some research institutions and universities all over the world have fabricated some EMA systems for experiment test, and the microrobot scale is enough micro to apply in organism, but many work, such as feedback of microrobot location, turning performance of microrobot and structure optimize of microrobot, is still at the early stage or don't begin to research.

In detail, some key points must be considered as follow: firstly, in order to achieve high efficiency, more propulsion and easily control, novel coils distribution of EMA system should be designed. Nowadays, most research teams use circular coil like Helmholtz coils and Maxwell coils, but this type of coils must meet many problems in the future biomedical application. A new type of coils, which can be suit for application body parts, must be designed. Secondly, how to achieve 3-DOF motion of microrobot and accurately control is also required. The novel structure of microrobot is helpful to this and there are also a lot of works to do in electromagnetic actuation principle to achieve it. Thirdly, that is how to get accurate control to microrobot in the liquid environment. Turning performance is an essential evaluation index for microrobot motion and many researchers have much achievement about it. Other one is feedback system. Visual feedback system and ultrasound positioning feedback system are applied in the lab and it achieved good performance in their experiment.

4   Conclusions

The wireless microrobot driven by external magnetic field will play a significant role in medical, biological engineering and industry. The methods using external magnetic field mainly has three categories: alternating magnetic field, stationary gradient magnetic field and rotating magnetic field, and the last one will be the most promising method. All kinds of microrobots are in research phase; there is still a great way to go for researchers to its real practical application, but fundamental researches are an essential process to come true.

References

1. SUN, L.N., LIU, P.K, WU, S.Q, LIU, T.: Status and development of in-pipe micro robot .J. Optics and Precision Engineering, v11, n4, Aug. (2003)
2. SONG, X.F., TAN, S.l.: Development and Research State of Micro-robot at Home and Abroad .J. Machine Tool & Hydraulics, Aug.(2004)
3. CAI, H.G.: Robot Will be a Hot Spot of Technological Development in the Twenty First Century .J. CHINA MECHANICAL ENGINEERING, (2001)
4. FU, G.Q., MEI, T., KONG, D.Y., ZHANG, Y.: Status quo and future development of microrobot field driving technology .J. Optics and Precision Engineering, v11, n4, Aug.(2003)
5. Kim, S.H., Hashi, S., Ishiyama, K.: Magnetic Actuation Based Snake-Like Mechanism and Locomotion Driven by Rotating Magnetic Field .J. IEEE TRANSACTIONS ON MAGNETICS. VOL. 47. NO. 10, OCTOBER (2011)
6. Byun, D., Choi, J., Cha, K., Park, J., Park, S.: Swimming microrobot actuated by two pairs of Helmholtz coils system .J. Mechatronics, v21, n1, p 357-364, February (2011)
7. Pan, Q.X., Guo, S.X.: A Paddling Type of Microrobot in Pipe. In: Proceedings of 2009 IEEE International Conference on Robotics and Automation (ICRA2009), Kobe, Japan, pp. 2995-3000, (2009)
8. Choi, J., Choi, H., Cha, K., Park, J., Park, S.: Two-dimensional locomotive permanent magnet using electromagnetic actuation system with two pairs of stationary coils. In:2009 IEEE International Conference on Robotics and Biomimetics (ROBIO 2009), p 1166-71, (2009)
9. Choi, H., Choi, J., Jeong, S., Yu, C., Park, J., Park, S.: Two-dimensional locomotion of a microrobot with a novel stationary electromagnetic actuation system .J. Smart Materials and Structures, v 18, n 11, (2009)
10. Floyd, S., Pawashe, C., Sitti, M.: An untethered magnetically actuated micro-robot capable of motion on arbitrary surfaces. In: IEEE Int. Conf. on Robotics and Automation 2008, pp 419–24, (2008)
11. Kim, S.H., Hashi, S., Ishiyama, K.: Magnetic Actuation Based Snake-Like Mechanism and Locomotion Driven by Rotating Magnetic Field .J. IEEE Transactions on Magnetics, v 47, n 10, p 3244-7, Oct. (2011)
12. Zhang, L., Abbott, J.J., Dong, L.X., Peyer, K.E., Kratochvil, B.E., Zhang, H.X, Bergeles, C., Nelson, B.J.: Characterizing the swimming properties of artificial bacterial flagella .J. Nano Letters, v 9, n10, p 3663-3667, October 14, (2009)
13. Zhang, L., Abbott, J.J., Dong, L.X., Kratochvil, B.E., Bell, D.J., Nelson, B.J.: Artificial bacterial flagella: fabrication and magnetic control .J.   Appl. Phys. Lett., 94 .064107,(2009)

Modeling of Rate-Dependent Hysteresis for Piezoelectric Actuator with MPI Model-Based Hammerstein System

Yongxin Guo[1,2], Yufeng Wang[2], Gang Sun[2], and Jianqin Mao[1]

[1] School of Automation Science and Electrical Engineering,
Beihang University,
100191, Beijing, P.R. China
[2] Dalian Air Force Communication NCO Academy,
116600, Dalian, P.R. China
gyx1979_1999@yahoo.com.cn

Abstract. In this paper, a Hammerstein system is proposed to describe the rate-dependent hysteresis nonlinearity of a piezoelectric actuator. In this system, a MPI model represents the nonlinear static block and a second order linear system represents the linear dynamic block. The parameters identification method for the system is given. Comparison between the outputs of the system and experiment shows that the system can describe the rate-dependent hysteresis nonlinearity of the piezoelectric actuator in a wide range.

Keywords: piezoelectric actuator, rate-dependent hysteresis, MPI model, Hammerstein system.

1 Introduction

Piezoelectric actuators (PEAs) have nanometer resolution in displacement, high stiffness, and rapid response. They are widely used in the field of ultra-high-precision positioning [1-4], micro-manipulation [5], micro-robot arm [6], and vibration active control [7]. However, PEAs have inherent drawbacks, such as nonlinear hysteresis behavior, creep phenomena and high frequency vibration. As the uppermost nonlinear characteristics, hysteresis behavior could cause inaccuracy and oscillations in the system response, and could lead to instability of the closed system. So, the hysteresis limits the development of PEA applications. What's more, the hysteresis nonlinearity is rate-dependent, that is, the output displacement of a PEA depends on the rate of the input signal, as depicted in Fig.1, which poses a significant challenge in analysis and design.

Many models have been used to describe the nonlinear hysteresis of PEAs, such as Preisach model [8], Duhem model [9], Maxwell slip model [10], Bouc-Wen model [11-12], Prandtl-Ishlinskii model [13], intelligent modeling method [14-15], etc. On the modeling of rate-dependent hysteresis for the PEAs, Some researchers focused on the Preisach model by including the speed of the input in the density functions [16-17], some researchers developed rate-dependent Prandtl-Ishlinskii model through formulations of rate-dependent play operator and density functions [18], some researchers used neural networks [19-21].

C.-Y. Su, S. Rakheja, H. Liu (Eds.): ICIRA 2012, Part II, LNAI 7507, pp. 281–290, 2012.
© Springer-Verlag Berlin Heidelberg 2012

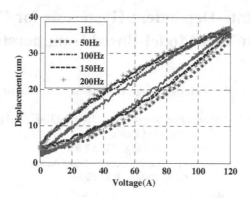

Fig. 1. Rate-dependent hysteresis loops of PEA

A Hammerstein system is a block-oriented nonlinear system which was introduced in 1930 by A. Hammerstein which involves a static nonlinear function $N(\cdot)$ followed by a linear dynamic subsystem $G(z)$, as depicted in Fig.2. The static nonlinear function block $N(\cdot)$ can be in various forms such as polynomials, series expansion, piecewise linear mapping, neural network, Least Square-Support Vector Machine, fuzzy cluster method and so on. The Hammerstein system have proved to be able to describe a wide variety of nonlinear systems, e.g., chemical process, electrically stimulated muscles, power amplifiers, electrical drives, thermal micro-systems, physiological systems, sticky control valves, solid oxide fuel cells, and magneto-rheological dampers [22]. However, to the best of our knowledge, few researchers have used MPI model to estimate the nonlinear block of the Hammerstein system and few researchers have used the MPI model-based Hammerstein system to describe the rate-dependent hysteresis nonlinearity of a PEA.

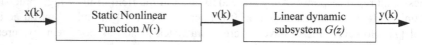

Fig. 2. The structure of a Hammerstein system

In this paper, a Hammerstein system is proposed to describe the rate-dependent hysteresis nonlinearity of a piezoelectric actuator. In this system, a MPI model represents the nonlinear static block and a second order linear system represents the linear dynamic block. The parameters of the MPI model are determined by least squares method with constraints and those of the second order linear system are determined by least squares method. Comparison between the outputs of the system and experiment shows that the system can describe the rate-dependent hysteresis nonlinearity of the piezoelectric actuator in a wide range.

The paper is organized as follows: Section 2 introduces the MPI model. In Section 3, the Hammerstein system with MPI model is proposed to model the rate-dependent hysteresis of a PEA, parameters identification method for the Hammerstein system is proposed. In Section 4, modeling results are given. Section 5 concludes this paper.

2   MPI Model

2.1   MPI Model Review

The Modified Prandtl-Ishlinskii (MPI) model was presented in [23]. It consists of weighted superposition of inner operators and outer operators.

The inner operators applies the weighted superposition of many play (or backlash) operators to model the real complex hysteresis nonlinearities. The play operator H_r is depicted in Fig.3 (a) and is defined as:

$$y_p(t) = H_r[x](t) = \max\{x(t) - r_h, \min\{x(t) + r_h, y_p(t)\}\} \tag{1}$$

where $x(t)$ and $y_p(t)$ are input and output of the play operator, $r_h \in R_0^+$ is the threshold. Then the PI model can be defined as:

$$y(t) = \mathbf{w}_h^T \cdot \mathbf{H}_{r_h}[x, \mathbf{y}_0](t) \tag{2}$$

where vectors $w_h = [w_{h0} \cdots w_{hn}]^T$ and $r_h = [r_{h0} \cdots r_{hn}]^T$ are the weights and thresholds of play operators respectively.

The outer operators are one-sided dead-zone operators which are memory-free, non-convex and negatively odd symmetric as depicted in Fig.3 (b). It is defined as:

$$y_d(t) = S(x(t), r_s) = \begin{cases} \max\{x(t) - r_s, 0\}, & r_s > 0 \\ x(t), & r_s = 0 \\ \min\{x(t) - r_s, 0\}, & r_s < 0 \end{cases} \tag{3}$$

where $x(t)$ and $y_d(t)$ are the input and output of the one-sided dead-zone operator, $r_s \in R_0^+$ is the threshold.

Consequently, the MPI model is expressed as:

$$y(t) = \Gamma[x](t) = w_s^T \cdot S_{r_s}[w_h^T \cdot H_{r_h}[x, y_0]](t) \tag{4}$$

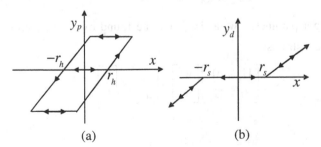

(a)   (b)

Fig. 3. (a) The play operator (b) The one-sided dead-zone operator

2.2   Parameters Identification of MPI Model

When the weights of the play and dead-zone operators satisfy some constraints, the inverse model of $\Gamma[x](t)$ exists and is given by [23]:

$$\Gamma^{-1}[x](t) = \mathbf{w}_h'^T \cdot \mathbf{H}_{r_h'}[\mathbf{w}_s'^T \cdot \mathbf{S}_{r_s'}[y, \mathbf{y}_0']](t) \tag{5}$$

where vector $\mathbf{w}_h'$ and r_h' are the weights and thresholds of the inverse play operators, vector $\mathbf{w}_s'$ and r_s' are the weights and thresholds of the inverse one-sided dead-zone operators, vector $\mathbf{y}_0'$ is the initial states of the inverse play operator. The parameters of the MPI model and its inverse can be found by the following:

$$r_{hi} = \frac{i}{n+1} \|x(t)\|_\infty \; ; i = 0\ldots n, \tag{6}$$

$$r_{s0}' = 0, \tag{7}$$

$$r_{si}' = \frac{i - \frac{1}{2}}{l} \max\{y(t)\}; i = 1\ldots l, \tag{8}$$

$$r_{si}' = \frac{i + \frac{1}{2}}{l} \min\{y(t)\}; i = -l\ldots-1 \tag{9}$$

Equation (5) can be changed into

$$\left(\mathbf{w}_h^T \quad \mathbf{w}_s'^T\right) \cdot \begin{pmatrix} \mathbf{H}_{r_h}[x, \mathbf{y}_0](t) \\ -\mathbf{S}_{r_s'}[y](t) \end{pmatrix} = 0 \tag{10}$$

For simplicity, the initial states are initialized to zero, that is

$$\mathbf{y}_0 = [y_0 \cdots y_{0n}]^T = [0 \cdots 0]^T \tag{11}$$

Then, the weight parameters $\mathbf{w}_h^T$ and $\mathbf{w}_s'^T$ can be found by least squares method with the following constrains:

$$\begin{bmatrix} \mathbf{U}_h & 0 \\ 0 & \mathbf{U}_s \end{bmatrix} \begin{bmatrix} w_h \\ w_s' \end{bmatrix} - \begin{bmatrix} u_h \\ u_s \end{bmatrix} \le \begin{bmatrix} 0 \\ 0 \end{bmatrix} \tag{12}$$

where

$$\mathbf{U}_h = \begin{pmatrix} -1 & 0 & \cdot & \cdot & 0 \\ \cdot & -1 & \cdot & \cdot & 0 \\ \cdot & & \cdot & & \cdot \\ \cdot & & & \cdot & \cdot \\ 0 & 0 & \cdot & \cdot & -1 \end{pmatrix} \quad \mathbf{u}_h = \begin{pmatrix} -\varepsilon \\ 0 \\ \cdot \\ \cdot \\ 0 \end{pmatrix} \tag{13}$$

and

$$\mathbf{U}_s = \begin{pmatrix} -1 & \cdots & -1 & -1 & 0 & \cdots & 0 \\ \vdots & \ddots & \vdots & \vdots & \vdots & \cdot & \vdots \\ 0 & \cdots & -1 & -1 & \cdots & & 0 \\ 0 & \cdots & 0 & -1 & \cdots & & 0 \\ 0 & \cdots & 0 & -1 & -1 & \cdots & 0 \\ \vdots & \cdot & \vdots & \vdots & \vdots & \ddots & \vdots \\ 0 & \cdots & 0 & -1 & -1 & \cdots & -1 \end{pmatrix} \quad \mathbf{u}_s = \begin{pmatrix} -\varepsilon \\ \vdots \\ -\varepsilon \\ -\varepsilon \\ -\varepsilon \\ \vdots \\ -\varepsilon \end{pmatrix} \tag{14}$$

Parameters r_s and w_s can be found by the following (15)-(18):

For $r_s \in \Re^+$

$$r'_{si} = \sum_{j=0}^{i} w_{sj}(r_{si} - r_{sj}); \qquad i = 0,1,\ldots l \tag{15}$$

$$w'_{si} = -\frac{w_{si}}{(w_{s0} + \sum_{j=1}^{i} w_{sj})(w_{s0} + \sum_{j=1}^{i-1} w_{sj})}; \quad i = 1,2\ldots l \tag{16}$$

For $r_s \in \Re^-$

$$r'_{si} = \sum_{j=i}^{0} w_{sj}(r_{si} - r_{sj}); \qquad i = -l\ldots0 \tag{17}$$

$$w'_{s0} = \frac{1}{w_{s0}}, \quad w'_{si} = -\frac{w_{si}}{(w_{s0} + \sum_{j=i}^{-1} w_{sj})(w_{s0} + \sum_{j=i+1}^{-1} w_{sj})}; \quad i = -l\ldots-1 \tag{18}$$

3   Modeling Based on Hammerstein System

The rate-dependent hysteresis model for a PEA has the same structure as depicted in Fig. 2. The static block is represented by a MPI model. $x(k)$ and $y(k)$ denote the input and output of the PEA respectively at the *kth* sampling time. $v(k)$ is the corresponding unmeasured internal variable. The modeling steps of the PEA are as follows:

Step 1: Given an input sinusoidal signal at low frequency (1Hz) to the PEA. With the input-output experimental data $(x(k), y(k))$, $k = 1, 2, ...M$, the parameters of the MPI model can be identified through (6)-(18). Then the MPI model is fixed and used to approximate the nonlinearity part of Hammerstein system.

Step 2: A sinusoidal scan signal is used to excite the PEA, and the corresponding input-output experimental data $(x(k), y(k))$ can be obtained. According to *Step 1*, the internal variable $v(k)$ is the output of the MPI model. Then data $(v(k), y(k))$ is the input and output of the linear dynamic subsystem. The linear dynamic subsystem can be identified by the least squares method.

Through above two steps, we could obtain the parameters of the Hammerstein system of the PEA.

4   Model Validation

4.1   Experimental Setup

In the experiment, the hysteresis loops at different frequencies of the PEA will be measured by an experimental setup. The schematic diagram of experiment for data acquisition is shown in Fig.4 (a), while the photograph of the whole experimental setup is shown in Fig.4 (b). The whole experimental system includes a PEA produced by PIEZOMECHANIK GmbH, a piezoelectric ceramics power amplifier, an eddy current sensor (85745) and the DSPACE (DS1103) controller installed in an industrial control computer (IPC) which is used to realize the real-time input/output data acquisition with a sampling frequency 20 kHz.

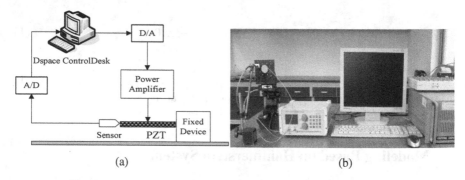

(a)   (b)

Fig. 4. Experimental setup (a) The schematic diagram (b) photograph

4.2   Model Validation

All the data used are from above experiments. Comparisons between the outputs of the MPI model and the experiment at 1Hz are depicted in Fig.5. The accuracy of the model is measured in terms of Root Mean Square Error (RMSE) and Relative Error (RE) defined as:

$$\text{RMSE} = \sqrt{\sum_{i=1}^{M}\left(\hat{y}^{i} - y^{i}\right)^{2} / M}, \quad \text{RE} = \sqrt{\sum_{i=1}^{M}\left(\hat{y}^{i} - y^{i}\right)^{2} / \sum_{i=1}^{M}\left(y^{i}\right)^{2}} \qquad (19)$$

where $\hat{y}^{i}$ is the output of the model, y^{i} is the output of the PEA, M is the number of data pairs. According to (19), the RMSE and RE between MPI model output and experiment at 1Hz are 0.3056 and 0.0131.

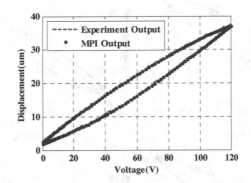

Fig. 5. Outputs of MPI model and experiment at 1Hz

The sinusoidal scan signal is generated with a MATLAB function "idinput" to identify the linear dynamic system. A linear dynamic subsystem is identified as:

$$G(z) = \frac{1.1994(z - 0.9569)}{(z + 0.9667)(z - 0.5185)} \qquad (20)$$

Then the modeling of the PEA based on Hammerstein system is complete. The block diagram is as shown in Fig. 6.

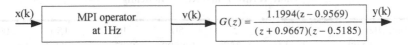

Fig. 6. The Hammerstein system of the PEA

The Hammerstein system of the PEA is tested with the input frequency at 1Hz, 5Hz, 50Hz, 100Hz, 150Hz and 200Hz respectively. Comparisons between the rate-dependent hysteresis loops simulated based on the Hammerstein system and those measured by experiments are depicted in Fig.7. The RMSE and RE are listed in Table 1. As can be seen from Fig.7 and Table 1 that the MPI model itself can't describe the

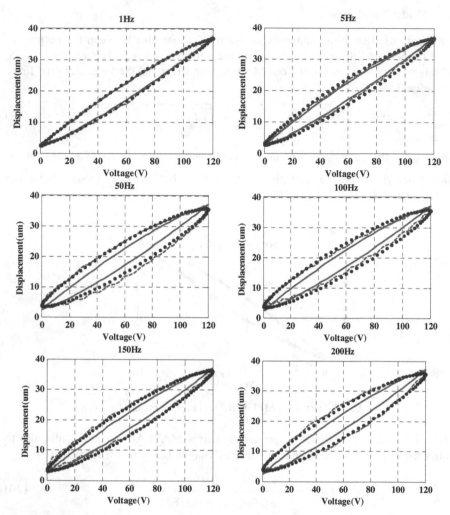

Fig. 7. Model Validation (dot blue: output of Hammerstein system; solid green: output of MPI model; dashed red: output of PEA)

Table 1. RMSE and RE of Modeling

Frequency (Hz)	1	5	50	100	150	200
Hammerstein RMSE(μm)	0.4425	0.7579	0.8592	0.8712	0.7482	0.5991
Hammerstein RE	0.0190	0.0326	0.0385	0.0380	0.0323	0.0258
MPI RMSE(μm)	0.4802	0.6126	2.7688	1.7302	1.9141	2.3393
MPI RE	0.0207	0.0263	0.1240	0.0755	0.0825	0.1009

rate-dependent hysteresis because it is rate-independent, but the Hammerstein system proposed in this paper can describe the rate-dependent hysteresis from 1Hz to 200Hz well.

5   Conclusions

The main contribution of this paper is to propose a Hammerstein system with MPI model for the rate-dependent hysteresis modeling of a PEA. The MPI model is used to approximate the nonlinear part of the Hammerstein system. An identification method for the system is given. Comparison between the outputs of Hammerstein system and experiment shows that the system proposed in this paper can describe the rate-dependent hysteresis of the PEA well in the range 1Hz-200Hz.

Acknowledgement. This work is supported by the National Natural Science Foundation of P. R .China (91016006) and the Fundamental Research Funds for the Central Universities.

Yufeng Wang contributed equally to this paper and she is the co-first author.

References

1. Lin, C.J., Yang, S.R.: Precise Positioning of Piezo-Actuated Stages using Hysteresis-Observer Based Control. Mechatronics 16, 417–426 (2006)
2. Chen, K.: A Novel Piezo-driven Micro-jet Injection System for Transdermal Drug Delivery. In: Proceedings of ASME 2009 4th Frontiers in Biomedical Devices Conference, BioMed 2009, Irvine, California, USA, June 8-9 (2009)
3. Croft, D., Shed, G., Devasia, S.: Creep, Hysteresis, and Vibration Compensation for Piezoactuators: Atomic Force Microscopy Application. Journal of Dynamic Systems, Measurement and Control 123/35 (March 2001)
4. Kobayashi, T., Tsaur, J., Maeda, R.: Development of 1D Optical Micro Scanner Driven by Piezoelectric Actuators. In: Proceedings of IPACK 2005 ASME Inter, PACK 2005, San Francisco, California, USA, July 17-22 (2005)
5. Goldfarb, M., Celanovic, N.: Modeling Piezoelectric Stack Actuators for Control of Micromanipulation. IEEE Control Systems Magazine 17(3), 69–79 (1997)
6. Simu, U., Johansson, S.: Evaluation of a Monolithic Piezoelectric Drive Unit for a Miniature Robot. Sensors and Actuators A: Physical 101, 175–184 (2002)
7. Viswamurthy, S.R., Ganguli, R.: Modeling and Compensation of Piezoceramic Actuator Hysteresis for Helicopter Vibration Control. Sensors and Actuators A: Phys. 135(2), 801–810 (2007)
8. Ge, P., Jouaneh, M.: Generalized preisach model for hysteresis nonlinearity of piezoceramic actuators. Precision Engineering 20(2), 99–111 (1997)
9. Xie, W., Fu, J., Yao, H., Su, C.Y.: Observer Based Control of Piezoelectric Actuators with Classical Duhem Modeled Hysteresis. In: 2009 American Control Conference Hyatt Regency Riverfront, St. Louis, MO, USA, June 10-12 (2009)
10. Goldfarb, M., Celanovic, N.: Modeling Piezoelectric Stack Actuators for Control of Micromanipulation. In: International Conference on Robotics and Automation, Minneapolis, MN (April 1996)

11. Jouaneh, M., Tian, H.: Accuracy enhancement of a piezoelectric actuator with hysteresis. In: Japan/USA Symposium on Flexible Automation, vol. 1. ASME (1992)
12. Gomis-Bellmunt, O., Ikhouane, F., Montesinos-Miracle, D.: Control of a piezoelectric actuator considering hysteresis. Journal of Sound and Vibration 326, 383–399 (2009)
13. Ru, C., Sun, L.: Hysteresis and creep compensation for piezoelectric actuator in open-loop operation. Sensors and Actuators A: Physical 122(1), 124–130 (2005)
14. Zhang, X., Tan, Y., Su, M.: Modeling of hysteresis in piezoelectric actuators using neural networks. Mechanical Systems and Signal Processing 23, 2699–2711 (2009)
15. Wang, R., Mao, J.: Research and Application of Dynamic Hysteresis Modeling Based on LS-SVM. In: Proceedings of Chinese Intelligent Automation Conference 2009 (2009)
16. Yu, Y., Xiao, Z., Naganathan, N.G., Dukkipati, R.V.: Dynamic Preisach modeling of hysteresis for the piezoceramic actuator system. Mech. Mach. Theory 37(1), 75–89 (2002)
17. Ben Mrad, R., Hu, H.: A model for voltage-to-displacement dynamics in piezoceramic actuators subject to dynamic-voltage excitations. IEEE Trans. Mech. 7(4), 479–489 (2002)
18. Al Janaideh, M., Rakheja, S., Su, C.-Y.: Experimental characterization and modeling of rate-dependent hysteresis of a piezoceramic actuator. Mechatronics 19, 656–670 (2009)
19. Dong, R., Tan, Y., Chen, H., Xie, Y.: A neural networks based model for rate-dependent hysteresis for piezoceramic actuators. Sensors and Actuators A 143, 370–376 (2008)
20. Zhang, X., Tan, Y., Su, M.: Modeling of hysteresis in piezoelectric actuators using neural networks. Mechanical Systems and Signal Processing 23, 2699–2711 (2009)
21. Zhang, X., Tan, Y., Su, M., Xie, Y.: Neural networks based identification and compensation of rate-dependent hysteresis in piezoelectric actuators. Physica B 405, 2687–2693 (2010)
22. Giri, F., Bai, E.W. (eds.): Block-oriented Nonlinear Systems Identification. Springer (June 2010)
23. Kuhnen, K.: Modeling, Identification and Compensation of Complex Hysteresis Nonlinearities, a Modified Prandtl-Ishlinskii Approach. European Journal of Control 9(4), 407–418 (2003)

Identification of Prandtl-Ishlinskii Hysteresis Models Using Modified Particle Swarm Optimization

Mei-Ju Yang, Guo-Ying Gu, and Li-Min Zhu*

State Key Laboratory of Mechanical System and Vibration,
School of Mechanical Engineering, Shanghai Jiao Tong University,
Shanghai 200240, China
{yangmeixianglian,guguoying,zhulm}@sjtu.edu.cn

Abstract. A modified particle swarm optimization algorithm (MPSO) is proposed in this paper. The algorithm is implemented to identify the parameters of the hysteresis nonlinearity, which is described by a modified Prandtl-Ishlinskii model. This new algorithm redefines the global best position and personal best position in the traditional PSO algorithm by an effective informed strategy, in order to balance the exploitation and exploration of the algorithm. Furthermore, a mutation operator is employed to increase the diversity of the particles and prevent premature convergence. Experiments have been conducted to verify the effectiveness of the proposed method. The comparisons with other variants of the PSO demonstrate that the identification of hysteresis based on the MPSO is effective and feasible.

Keywords: Identification, Particle Swarm Optimization, Hysteresis, Prandtl-Ishlinskii Model.

1 Introduction

Piezoelectric actuators (PEA) have been widely used in a variety of applications such as scanning probe microscopes [1],atomic force microscopes [2], and micromanipulation [3]. The advantages of piezoelectric actuators are fast frequency response, high positioning precision, high electrical mechanical coupling efficiency, small size and small thermal expansion during actuation. However, the main drawback of the PEA is the hysteresis nonlinearity, which can cause the positioning inaccuracy, even lead to instability of the closed system.

The direct solution to deal with the hysteresis effect is inverse compensation, aiming to cancel the hysteresis effect by constructing the inverse of a hysteresis model. To describe the hysteresis nonlinearity, a number of hysteresis models are available in the literature [4–10]. However, no matter what kind of models, there must be some errors between the simulated model and the actual model because

---

* Corresponding author.

C.-Y. Su, S. Rakheja, H. Liu (Eds.): ICIRA 2012, Part II, LNAI 7507, pp. 291–300, 2012.

of assumptions and approximations made in modeling [11]. In order to accurately describe the hysteresis, parameter identification of the hysteresis model is of great importance. For this purpose, many efforts have been made in the literature. The least mean square algorithm [12] is a simple and robust algorithm to identify hysteresis, however, it relies on the derivative of the object function. The genetic algorithm was used to identify hysteresis in [4, 13, 14], however, it usually caused premature convergence and low calculation efficiency. Recently, the particle swarm optimization was proposed to improve the performance of the hysteresis identification [5, 15].

Particle swarm optimization(PSO), developed by Eberhart and Kennedy in 1995 [16], is a swarm intelligence optimization algorithm according to the observations of the social behavior such as bird flocking and fish schooling. There are many researches about improving the performance of PSO. In order to balance the global and local search ability, a parameter called inertia weight was introduced into the original PSO algorithm. A linear reduction strategy of inertia weight (PSO-w) was designed by Shi and Eberhart [17]. By analyzing the convergence behavior of the PSO, a PSO variant with a constriction factor (PSO-cf) was introduced by Clerc and Kennedy [18]. Li et.al [11] proposed an effective informed adaptive PSO algorithm (EIA-PSO), however, the adoption of the BFGS local search strategy required derivative calculations of the objective function and cost much more time for massive problems.

In this paper, a modified particle swarm optimization (MPSO) is proposed, on the basis of PSO-cf because of its fast convergence rate. An effective informed strategy is introduced to increase the diversity of the equilibrium points and balance the exploration and exploitation of the algorithm. In order to prevent premature convergence, the diversity of the particles is increased by a mutation operator. Finally, the MPSO is implemented on the Matlab software to identify the parameters of a Prandtl-Ishlinskii (PI) hysteresis model and experimental results demonstrate the effectiveness of the proposed MPSO.

The rest of the paper is organized as follows: Section 2 describes the modified Prandtl-Ishlinskii hysteresis model and parameter identification problem; Section 3 presents the proposed MPSO method; the experimental setup and validation are presented in Section 4; and Section 5 concludes the paper.

2   Hysteresis Modeling and Parameter Identification

2.1   Hysteresis Modeling

In this paper, the Prandtl-Ishlinskii (PI) model is selected to describe the hysteresis nonlinearity due to its simple structure and analytical inverse. The play operator is the primary operator in the PI model as follows [9]:

$$
\begin{aligned}
F_r[v](0) &= \max\{v(0) - r, \min\{v(0), 0\}\} \\
F_r[v](t) &= \max\{v(t) - r, \min\{v(t), F_r[v](t - T)\}\}
\end{aligned}
\tag{1}
$$

where $v(t)$ is the control input, $F_r[v](t)$ is the operator output, r is the input threshold of the play operator, and T is the sampling period.

The loop generated by the classical PI model is symmetric, but in fact, most of the real actuator hysteresis loops are not symmetric. In this paper, a modified Prandtl-Ishlinskii (PI) model is employed to describe the hysteresis, which is the combination of a weighted classical one-side play operator and a polynomial input function as follows:

$$y(t) = g(v(t)) + \sum_{i=1}^{N} p_i F_{r_i}[v](t) \tag{2}$$

where $g(v(t)) = a_1 v^3(t) + a_2 v(t)$ is a polynomial input function with constants a_1 and a_2, p_i denotes the weighting value of the play operator with the threshold value r_i, satisfying $p_i > 0, i = 1, 2, ..., N$, which is generally calculated from the experimental data, N is the number of the play operator, and $y(t)$ is the displacement of the piezoelectric actuators.

Generally, the larger the number of play operators, the better the precision of the model is. However, the expense is that much more effort must be made . Therefore, the number of play operators N is set to 10 in this work. The fixed thresholds are determined as:

$$r_j = \frac{j}{N} \|v(t)\|_\infty, j = 0, 1, 2, ..., N - 1 \tag{3}$$

with $\|v(t)\|_\infty = 1$ in the normalized case.

2.2   Parameter Identification

From the hysteresis model described in (2), it can be known that there are 12 parameters to be identified, that is: $X = [p_1, p_2, ..., p_{10}, a_1, a_2]$. Since the PI hysteresis model is nonlinear and non-differential, the gradient matrix can not be formulated by explicit expressions. Therefore, the parameter identification can be considered as a nonlinear discontinuous optimization problem. Although this problem can be handled by the direct search algorithm, such as the Nelder-Mead simplex algorithm, it relies on a good stating point heavily and may fall into a local optimum solution. As a global search algorithm , the MPSO is proposed in this paper to identify the parameters of the hysteresis. The key point in the application of MPSO is the selection of the fitness function (or object function), which has an important influence on the identified results [19]. In this paper, the fitness function is chosen as follows:

$$F(X) = \frac{1}{n} \sum_{i=1}^{n} (y_i - y_i^a)^2 \tag{4}$$

where n denotes the total number of the experimental data, y_i and y_i^a are the simulated data and the experimental data at the ith sampling time, respectively. Therefore, the minimize optimization problem can be formulated as follows:

$$\min_{X} F(X) = \frac{1}{n} \sum_{i=1}^{n} (y_i - y_i^a)^2$$

s.t.

$$\begin{cases} F_{r_i}[v](t) = \max\{v(t) - r_i, \min\{v(t), F_{r_i}[v](t-T)\}\} \\ y(t) = a_1 v^3(t) + a_2 v(t) + \sum_{i=1}^{N} p_i F_{r_i}[v](t) \\ p_i \geq 0, \quad i = 1, 2, ..., N. \end{cases} \tag{5}$$

3   Modified Particle Swarm Optimization(MPSO)

3.1   PSO Algorithm

In PSO, a swarm is composed of m particles. Each particle i is associated with two vectors: the position vector $x_i = [x_i^1, x_i^2, ..., x_i^n]$ and the velocity vector $v_i = [v_i^1, v_i^2, ..., v_i^n]$, where n refers to the dimension of the search space. The velocity and position of each particle are initialized by random vectors within the corresponding ranges. All the particles are evaluated according to the predefined fitness function. Comparing the fitness value, each particle records its personal best experienced position as $pbest_i$, and the global best experienced position as $gbest$. Then the velocity and position of the ith particle on dimension d are updated as [18]:

$$\begin{cases} v_i^d = \chi(v_i^d + \varphi_1 r_1(pbest_i - x_i^d) + \varphi_2 r_2(gbest - x_i^d)) \\ x_i^d = x_i^d + v_i^d \end{cases} \tag{6}$$

where r_1 and r_2 are two random numbers in the range of [0,1], φ_1 and φ_2 are acceleration coefficients. χ is a so-called constriction factor and is defined below:

$$\chi = \frac{2}{\left|2 - \varphi - \sqrt{\varphi^2 - 4\varphi}\right|} \tag{7}$$

where $\varphi = \varphi_1 + \varphi_2$, satisfying $\varphi > 4$. According to [18], the parameters are chosen as $\chi = 0.7298, \varphi_1 = \varphi_2 = 2.05$.

3.2   MPSO Algorithm

The MPSO is on the basis of the PSO-cf. The flowchart of the MPSO is given in Fig. 1. In order to improve the performance of the PSO, two strategies are proposed in the MPSO algorithm.

The first strategy is the effective informed strategy. As in the PSO algorithm, the equilibrium point, which decides the accuracy of the algorithm, depends on $pbest_i$ and $gbest$. Thus, bad choice of $pbest_i$ and $gbest$ can result in the fast convergence and make the particles trapped in the local optimum. In order to solve this problem, an effective informed strategy [11] is employed to improve the quality of the equilibrium point. Firstly, all of the particles are sorted in an

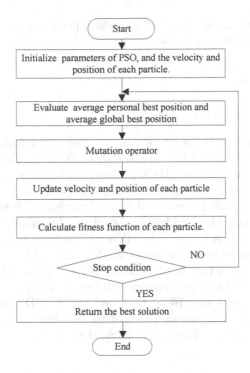

Fig. 1. The flowchart of the MPSO

ascending order of fitness value. Then, *gbest* is replaced by the weighted average p_g of the top s particles. $pbest_i$ is replaced by the weighted average p_a of $pbest_{i-1}$ and $pbest_i$. They are expressed as follows:

$$\begin{cases} p_g = \sum_{j=1}^{s} \mu_j pbest_j \\ \mu_j = \frac{1}{F_j} \Big/ \sum_{k=1}^{s} \frac{1}{F_k} \\ p_a = (F_i pbest_{i-1} + F_{i-1} pbest_i)/(F_i + F_{i-1}) \end{cases} \tag{8}$$

where μ_j is the weighted constant and F_j is the fitness value corresponding to the particle optimal location.

The second strategy is an introduction of the mutation operator. In the PSO algorithm, the particles always easily converge to the local optimum solution because of the lack of population diversity. Particularly, the global best solution may remain unchanged with the generation increases during the later period of the optimization. In order to solve this problem, a mutation operator [20] is introduced here, which works as the mutation operator in the genetic algorithm. If the global best solution is not improving when the generation increases, a particle is selected randomly, and then a random perturbation is added to the velocity vector of the selected particle by a predefined probability, called mutation probability. In this paper, the random perturbation is set proportionally to the maximum allowable velocity.

4   Experiments

4.1   Experimental Setup

The experimental setup is shown in Fig. 2. The setup includes a preloaded piezoelectric stack actuator (PPSA) (PSt 150/7/100 VS12, Piezomechanik, Germany), a high-voltage amplifier (HVA), a high-resolution strain gauge position sensor (SGPS), a position servo-control module (PSCM), a dSPACE-DS1103 rapid prototyping controller board and a one-dimensional flexure hinge guiding nano-positioning stage. The PPSA is used to drive the stage with the maximum displacement of 75 μm. It is driven by HVA with a fixed gain of 15, which provides excitation voltage to the actuator in the range of $0 - 150V$. The SGPS is used to measure the actual displacement. Then, the PSCM is used to transfer the actual displacement to analogue voltage in the range of $0 - 10V$. The dSPACE board equipped with 16-bit D/A and 16-bit A/D is hosted by the personal computer. The D/A converter is used to send the excite signal generated by the computer to the amplifier, and the A/D converter is used to sample the displacement data.

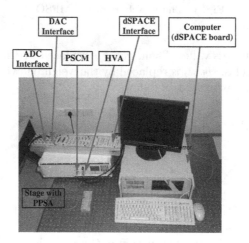

Fig. 2. The experiment platform

4.2   Experimental Validation

According to the experiment data, the identification algorithm is implemented on the Matlab software. The input voltage is chosen as the complex harmonic wave as shown in Fig. 3(a). Fig. 3(b) shows a comparison of the hysteresis loops

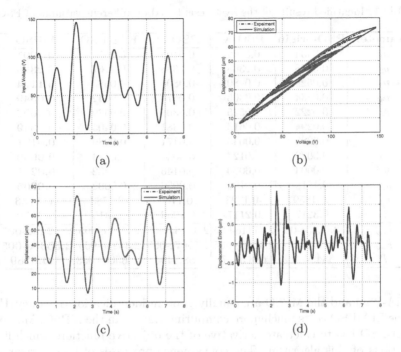

Fig. 3. Identified results based on MPSO: (a)the input voltage; (b)comparison of hysteresis loops; (c)comparison of transient response; (d)comparison of transient errors

between the experimental results and the simulative results. Fig. 3(c) shows a comparison of the transient response between the experimental results and the simulative results. The transient error between them is shown in Fig. 3(d). The maximum error is less than $1.35\mu m$, 1.8% of the full range of the stage.

In order to further verify the superiority of the MPSO, the parameter identification of the PEA is also implemented by PSO-origin, PSO-w, PSO-cf and EIA-PSO. In all experiments, the population size is set to 60, the maximum number of the generation is 1000, and the run number is 5. All the algorithms are run on the same computer with the same object function and the same search ranges. The parameters of the PSO-origin are that $c_1 = c_2 = 2$. The parameters of the PSO-w are that $c_1 = c_2 = 2$, and the inertia weight linearly decreases from 0.9 to 0.4. The parameters of the PSO-cf are that the constriction factor is 0.7298, and $c_1 = c_2 = 2.05$. The parameters of the EIA-PSO are that $E = 50, R = 100, s = 9$, and the inertia weight is in the range of [0.4,0.9].

The identified results of all the algorithms are listed in Table 1. In the table, F_{op} is the smallest optimum solution during the five tests, and F_{av} is the average optimum solution of the five tests. In order to compare the convergence rate, the iteration time T is also recorded and listed in the table. From the table, it is clearly observed that the MPSO is superior to the PSO-origin, the PSO-w, and the PSO-cf in the aspects of convergence rate and identification accuracy.

Table 1. Identified results of the hysteresis based on different variants of PSO

Parameters	PSO-origin	PSO-w	PSO-cf	EIA-PSO	MPSO
p_1	0.3434	0.5162	0.5103	0.2675	**0.4091**
p_2	0.3478	0.2368	0.2688	0.2767	**0.2305**
p_3	0.0528	0.0980	0.0806	0.0580	**0.1124**
p_4	0.0564	0.0305	0.0670	0.0642	**0.0349**
p_5	0.0222	0.0525	0.0306	0.0529	**0.0602**
p_6	0.0294	0.0613	0.0381	0.0405	**0.0349**
p_7	0.0283	0.0046	0.0171	0.0089	**0.0121**
p_8	0.0029	0.0124	0.0044	0.0114	**0.0060**
p_9	0.0003	0.0030	0.0146	0.0062	**0.0211**
p_{10}	0.1318	0.0198	0.0056	0.0002	**0.0005**
a_1	-0.1859	-0.1723	-0.1740	-0.1783	**-0.1733**
a_2	0.3217	0.2117	0.1959	0.4415	**0.3150**
F_{op}	3.5513e-05	2.3711e-005	2.3943e-005	2.2944e-005	**2.3249e-005**
F_{av}	4.1768e-05	2.4608e-005	2.5567e-005	2.3324e-005	**2.3538e-005**
T	684.5741	688.5517	688.3494	1.6856e+003	**644.0789**

The EIA-PSO and the MPSO are equally good in identification accuracy. However, the EIA-PSO costs much more computing time than the MPSO. Moreover, the EIA-PSO has to calculate derivative of the objective function, which limits applications of this algorithm. The convergence processes of the average optimum value based on the five different algorithms are plotted in Fig. 4. It can be observed that the MPSO and the EIA-PSO algorithm have better convergence results than the other three methods after the 30th generation.

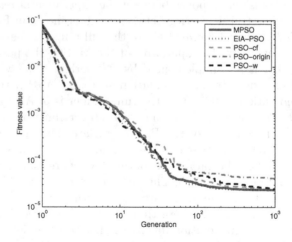

Fig. 4. Convergence of the average optimum value for different methods

5 Conclusion

The main objective of this paper is to propose a new identification method for the hysteresis nonlinearity described by a modified Prandtl-Ishlinskii model. An effective informed strategy and a mutation operator are incorporated with the traditional particle swarm optimization in the MPSO algorithm. Then, a complex harmonic wave is generated and input to the stage to drive the actuator. Based on the experimental data, parameter identification of the PEA is implemented by the the proposed MPSO algorithm as well as some other PSO algorithms on the MATLAB software. The results demonstrate that the hysteresis identification based on the MPSO method is feasible.

Acknowledgement. This work was supported in part by the National Natural Science Foundation of China under Grant 91023047, the Science and Technology Commission of Shanghai Municipality under Grant 11520701500, and the Shu Guang Project supported by Shanghai Municipal Education Commission under Grant 10SG17.

References

1. Salapaka, S.M., Salapaka, M.V.: Scanning Probe Microscopy. IEEE Control Systems 28(2), 65–83 (2008)
2. Leang, K.K., Devasia, S.: Design of hysteresis-compensating iterative learning control for piezo-positioners: Application to atomic force microscopes. Mechatronics 16(3-4), 141–158 (2006)
3. Gu, G.Y., Zhu, L.M.: High-speed tracking control of piezoelectric actuators using an ellipse-based hysteresis model. Review of Scientific Instruments 81(8), 0851041–0851049 (2010)
4. Ha, J.L., Kung, Y.S., Fung, R.F., Hsien, S.C.: A comparison of fitness functions for the identification of a piezoelectric hysteretic actuator based on the real-coded genetic algorithm. Sensors and Actuators A: Physical 132(2), 643–650 (2006)
5. Xu, Q., Li, Y.: Dahl Model-Based Hysteresis Compensation and Precise Positioning Control of an XY Parallel Micromanipulator With Piezoelectric Actuation. Journal of Dynamic Systems, Measurement, and Control 132, 041011 (2010)
6. Bernard, Y., Mendes, E., Bouillault, F.: Dynamic hysteresis modeling based on Preisach model. IEEE Transactions on Magnetics 38(2), 885–888 (2002)
7. Kuhnen, K.: Modeling, Identification and Compensation of Complex Hysteretic Nonlinearities A modified Prandtl-Ishlinskii Approach. European Journal of Control 9(4), 407–418 (2003)
8. Al Janaideh, M., Rakheja, S., Su, C.Y.: An Analytical Generalized Prandtl-Ishlinskii Model Inversion for Hysteresis Compensation in Micropositioning Control. IEEE/ASME Transactions on Mechatronics 16(4), 734–744 (2011)
9. Jiang, H., Ji, H., Qiu, J., Chen, Y.: A modified prandtl-ishlinskii model for modeling asymmetric hysteresis of piezoelectric actuators. IEEE Transactions on Ultrasonics, Ferroelectrics and Frequency Control 57(5), 1200–1210 (2010)
10. Gu, G.Y., Zhu, L.M.: Modeling of rate-dependent hysteresis in piezoelectric actuators using a family of ellipses. Sensors and Actuators: A. Physical 157(2), 303–309 (2011)

11. Li, Q., Chen, W., Wang, Y., Liu, S., Jia, J.: Parameter Identification for PEM Fuel-Cell Mechanism Model Based on Effective Informed Adaptive Particle Swarm Optimization. IEEE Transactions on Industrial Electronics 58(6), 2410–2419 (2011)
12. Ru, C., Chen, L., Shao, B., Rong, W., Sun, L.: A hysteresis compensation method of piezoelectric actuator: Model, identification and control. Control Engineering Practice 17, 1107–1114 (2009)
13. Chan, C.H., Liu, G.: Hysteresis identification and compensation using a genetic algorithm with adaptive search space. Mechatronics 17, 391–402 (2007)
14. Fung, R.F., Hsu, Y.L., Huang, M.S.: System identification of a dual-stage XY precision positioning table. Precision Engineering 33, 71–80 (2009)
15. Kao, C.C., Fung, R.F.: Using the modified PSO method to identify a Scott-Russell mechanism actuated by a piezoelectric element. Mechanical Systems and Signal Processing 23, 1652–1661 (2009)
16. Eberhart, R., Kennedy, J.: A new optimizer using particle swarm theory. In: Proceedings of the 6th International Symposium on Micro Machine and Human Science, MHS 1995, pp. 39–43 (1995)
17. Shi, Y., Eberhart, R.: A modified particle swarm optimizer. In: The 1998 IEEE International Conference on Evolutionary Computation Proceedings, IEEE World Congress on Computational Intelligence, pp. 69–73 (1998)
18. Clerc, M., Kennedy, J.: The Particle Swarm Explosion, Stability, and Convergence in a Multidimensional Complex Space. IEEE Transactions on Evolutionary Computation 6(1), 58–73 (2001)
19. Qu, J., Huang, G.: Influence of Objective Function on Parameter Identification Result. In: International Conference on Electric Information and Control Engineering, pp. 2274–2277 (2011)
20. Ratnaweera, A., Halgamuge, S.K., Watson, H.C.: Self-organizing hierarchical particle swarm optimizer with time-varying acceleration coefficients. IEEE Transactions on Evolutionary Computation 8(3), 240–255 (2004)

Wireless Electrical Power to Sub-millimeter Robots

Robert A. Nawrocki[1,*], Dominic R. Frutiger[2], Richard M. Voyles[1],
and Bradley J. Nelson[2]

[1] Department of Computer Engineering, University of Denver, Colorado, USA
[2] Institute of Robotics and Intelligent Systems, ETH Zürich, Switzerland
{Robert.Nawrocki,RVoyles}du.edu, {DFrutiger,BNelson}ethz.ch

Abstract. A sub-millimeter scale coil is investigated as an alternative means to power electronics for small-scale robots. The AC voltage is induced by time-varying magnetic field. FEM analysis of employing magnetic field concentrators to increase the field density is carried out, concluding with their ineffectiveness to offset the occupied space. The choice of conductive versus non-conductive photoresist is investigated. The coil fabrication process is based upon three-dimensional, two-photon-absorption photolithography. Additional steps include metal sputtering, microlaser patterning and wire-bonding. The steps detailing the entire design process are described. With the coil occupying a volume of 0.45 pico m^3, the maximum AC voltage of approximately 84 nV, with power density of about 1.96 mW per meter cube were measured. The study concludes with proposing ways to increase the induced voltage to a useable voltage of 2 V.

Keywords: microfabrication, microrobotic manipulation, power generation.

1 Introduction

Currently most untethered, sub-millimeter scale robots do not possess any on-board information processing. A form of cognition is typically located external to the robot, on a full-scale computer. Commonly, in a system such as the microrobotic MagMite platform [1], or Magnetic Micro-Robot [2] the only form of control comes from visual feedback provided by the operator. These systems would benefit from the ability to process information locally, for instance from a sensor. Any proposed forms of on-board cognition, such as a Synthetic Neural Network [3], would rely on electrical elements to realize this functionality.

1.1 Related Work

Recently, a number of new technologies emerged that allow for power storage or power generation on a sub-millimeter scale. One example of the former is a thin-film battery. In this power storage technology, a device commonly consists of multiple, layered components, typically cathode, cathode current collector, anode, anode

---

[*] Corresponding author.

C.-Y. Su, S. Rakheja, H. Liu (Eds.): ICIRA 2012, Part II, LNAI 7507, pp. 301–312, 2012.
© Springer-Verlag Berlin Heidelberg 2012

current collector, and electrolyte. The entire structure, normally less than 5 μm thick, is then encapsulated by a protective coating [4]. Voltages as high as 4 V have been reported [5]. A major advantage of such a solution to power on-board electronics is the fact that they can be formed or deposited on a flexible substrate and often stacked to multiple layers [6]. Their disadvantage lays in the need to have them periodically recharged. Also, their general dimensions are in the range of a few to a few tens of millimeters, which renders them impractical in microrobotic application.

Radioisotope-powered generators have been recently reported in the literature. In one such example [7], a piezoelectric generator relies on the electrical charge generated by a mechanical beam from a radioactive thin film. The charge is then converted into electricity by a piezo element. An advantage of such technology is the exceedingly long lifetime of radioactive elements, such as nickel-63 or tritium. Its disadvantage, however, is due to relatively low power density and radioactivity of the electricity-generating layer.

Another possibility for generating electrical power on the sub-millimeter scale is the use of piezo generators. For instance [8] proposed a design consisting of a flexible PET vibration substrate, piezoelectric zinc oxide thin film, design of lump structures, and electrodes. The piezoelectric thin film acts as a transducer and converts the mechanical energy stored in the spring into electrical energy. The generated voltage was reported as high as 2.25 V with power density of 0.276 W per centimeter square.

Other, more conventional methods of on-board energy storage or generation, such as a solar cell [9] or a millimeter-scale capacitor [10], have been demonstrated as viable methods for millimeter-scale robots. However, scaling these technologies to the micrometer scale still remains several years away and is presently not a viable option.

1.2 Coils and Solenoids

An alternative for providing continuous electrical power is via electromagnetic induction. Faraday's law states that a voltage can be induced in any conductive surface by a changing magnetic field. This can be accomplished by inserting a moveable magnetic rod inside a coil or by placing a stationary coil in a changing magnetic field. The latter is a more desirable solution to the problem as it would allow for continuous, wireless power delivery to sub-millimeter scale robots inside the magnetic field.

On the sub-millimeter scale all forms of power generation or storage, including the thin-film battery and piezo generator, suffer from scaling effects [11]. The voltage and power density decreases dramatically on the micrometer scale. Electromagnetic induction, as outlined later, has several advantages over alternative solutions.

Very few examples in which millimeter or sub-millimeter scale coils for generating energy have been demonstrated. In [12] a coil, assembled using a wire bonder, was demonstrated to generate an output voltage of 10.4 mV with an output power of 0.62 μW. The coil occupied a large volume of 0.46 cm³, rendering it infeasible for sub-millimeter scale robots. In another study an array of micro-coils with 0.2 mm diameters was shown to generate output of < 500 μV [13]. However, even though individual coils were of a micron size, the array occupied a much larger area.

Our intention is to deploy the microcoil demonstrated here on a surface of a MagMite [1], a micro robot, for the purposes of powering electronics located on the robot. This study focused on a new form of microfabrication which can lead to a better integration with micro robots. Fig. 1(a) shows a proposed concept of the coil.

2   Theory and Simulation

Faraday's Law of Induction states that the electromotive force (EMF) produced by a changing magnetic field is proportional to the rate of change of the magnetic flux through any surface bounded by that path. The EMF is equal to the time rate of change of the magnetic flux perpendicular to the surface of the closed path [14], where V is the voltage generated, N is the number of loops, B is the strength of the magnetic field, A is the area perpendicular to the magnetic field, and f is the frequency of the changing magnetic field.

$$V = -Nf\Delta(BA). \tag{1}$$

2.1   Helmholtz Coils

A magnetic field density, produced by a single coil, is inversely proportional to the square root of the distance between the coil and the point of interest. A fairly uniform field can be achieved by a pair of coils assembled into a Helmholtz configuration. The arrangement is such that the centers of both of the coils, connected in series, are separated by the distance equal to their radii. This ensures a greater uniformity of the field density and simplifies the FEM analysis.

2.2   Field Concentrators

A field concentrator (FC) is a block of ferromagnetic material that diverts and concentrates the magnetic flux lines. Positioning two such bodies, for instance made from *Ni* or *NiCo*, with their shorter sides facing each other, results in a larger and more uniform magnetic field inside the gap. This, via Eq. 1, will result in a larger induced voltage. Fig. 1(a) demonstrates the basic setup of the FCs with the microcoil placed inside the gap. Fig. 1(b) shows an FEM snapshot indicating the increase in flux density around the ferromagnetic bodies. In the simulation, the bodies were modeled of *Ni* with a relative permeability of 600.

Our intention is to deploy the microcoil on a micro robot. Hence, there is a constraint of maximum area that the setup, the microcoil and possibly FCs, can occupy. Therefore, given the finite amount of space, we needed to understand if the FCs would offset their required space that would otherwise be occupied by the microcoil.

In order to elucidate the efficacy of the FCs, FE analysis was conducted in COMSOL Multiphysics. Table 1 shows the average increased strength of the magnetic field inside the FC gap for different gap sizes from 40 µm through 300 µm.

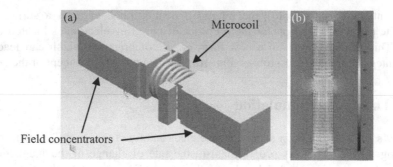

Fig. 1. Field concentrators used to increase the strength of the magnetic field. (a) Proposed design with microcoil placed inside the gap. (b) Snapshot from FEM (COMSOL Multiphysics).

Table 1. Average magnetic flux density between concentrators (mT)

		Gap (µm)						
		40	60	80	90	100	200	300
	5	24.5	19.2	16.3	15.3	14.3	10.2	8.7
B (mT)	10	48.3	38.4	32.8	30.4	28.6	20.4	17.4
	20	95.8	76.5	65.0	60.8	57.2	40.8	34.8
	40	194.4	154.7	130.1	121.2	114.4	81.6	69.6
Magnification		**4.9**	**3.8**	**3.3**	**3.0**	**2.9**	**2.0**	**1.7**

It can be seen that, for a given gap size, the increase of the flux density is linear (it does not factor the material's saturation effect) and an average *magnification* factor can be extrapolated. For instance, for a 40 µm gap the factor is 4.9, while for a 300 µm gap the factor is 1.7. Intuitively, this factor is going to approach the value of 1, implying no magnifying effect, at infinity.

As seen in Fig. 2, with the increase of the gap inside the FCs the number of microcoil loops increases linearly, however, the beneficial effect of the FCs (termed *magnification* in Table 1) decreases logarithmically. Therefore, in Eq. 1, the leading factor is going to be N and the total number of loops is going to outgrow the benefits of the FCs. The conclusion is that it is better not to include the FCs but use all of that area for the largest microcoil (greatest number of loops).

2.3   Flux Density

Eq. 2 is used to compute the strength of a magnetic field produced by a Helmholtz coil [15], where μ_0 is the permeability constant (equal to $1.257 \cdot 10^{-6}$ T·m/A), n is the number of loops, I is the current through the coil, and R is the coil radius. It can be seen that, in a fixed setup (loop count and coil size), the field only depends on the current through the coil.

$$B = (0.7155\mu_0 nI)/R. \tag{2}$$

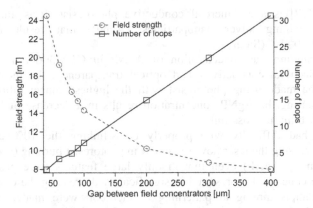

Fig. 2. With the use of field concentrators, the number of microcoil loops that can fit inside the gap increases linearly while the flux density decreases exponentially, reaching the unmagnified value (in this case the value of 5 mT) at infinity.

3   Fabrication

3.1   Photolithography Process

Fabricating a microcoil is a challenge. Planar coil, fabricated with a conventional two-dimensional photolithography process, is relatively easy. However, the coil loops need to be positioned not horizontally but perpendicular to the surface (the voltage induced is proportional to the area perpendicular to the magnetic field). Therefore, a true three-dimensional photolithography process is desirable.

3.1.1   Nanoscribe
Nanoscribe (Nanoscribe GmbH, Germany) is a company that produces table-top laser lithography system that allows for creating three-dimensional micro structures in a wide variety of commercially available photoresists [16]. The system is based on direct laser writing with two-photon absorption. In this system a laser beam is split into two streams, each being at an energy level that does not result in photoresist being cross-linked. Photoresist is cross-linked at a point where the two streams cross each other. This point, known as voxel, is not a perfect sphere, but rather oblong (the height is about 3 times its width). This feature has an effect on the final product. All of the designs are patterned on a glass wafer 170 μm-thick.

3.1.2   Photoresist
Nanoscribe allows working with any positive or negative photoresists. From the process perspective, two possibilities exist for creating the induction microcoil. The first is the use of a conductive photoresist. The second option is a non-conductive photoresist that would then require covering it with conductive material. Because the use of a conductive photoresist is a single-step process and, hence, more straightforward, this choice was investigated first.

GCM3060 [17] is a commercial conductive photoresist. It is an SU-8–based photoresist containing silver nanoparticles (AgNP) that result in electrical conductivity of 10^3-10^6 ($S \cdot cm^{-2}$).

When determining the concentration of AgNP in GCM3060, the trade-off is between the electrical conductivity and optical transparency; the most conductive design could be made using photoresist with the highest concentration of AgNP. However, increasing the AgNP concentration results in a decrease of UV exposure and eventual inability to cross-link.

Nanoscribe had difficulty with properly cross-linking the 10% concentration photoresist. Increasing the laser power resulted in photoresist burning (possibly due to heat absorption by AgNP) even though only large features were properly made. Decreasing the concentration resulted in significantly decreasing the conductivity. A number of attempts aiming at patterning a microcoil were made. All of them, however, failed. As a result an alternative was investigated, that of creating the microcoil from a non-conductive photoresist followed by metal sputtering.

Nanoscribe provides two proprietary, non-conductive photoresists, called IP-L ("L" stands for "liquid") and IP-G ("G" stands for "gel"), both specifically formulated for three-dimensional photolithography. Compared to SU-8, both of these photoresists are easy to use and allow for very fine features to be made. Additionally, IP-L does not require pre- nor post-baking while IP-G only requires pre-baking. The disadvantage of this non-conductive photoresist is that it necessitates the addition of two extra steps. The first step is the need to cover the coil with a thin film of conductive material (i.e. copper). The second step is the need to pattern conductive pads around the support structures and the individual microcoil loops for the current to flow along the microcoil and not across the substrate. (Electroless plating was investigated. However, it did not result in a sufficiently thick layer of metal for a sufficiently small electrical resistance).

3.1.3   Critical Point Dryer

During the development, it became apparent that the surface tension during the drying process would become an issue. A common procedure used to partially or fully alleviate this effect is the use of a critical point dryer (CPD), which exploits the phenomenon known as supercritical region.

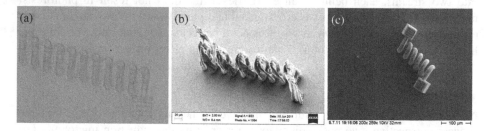

Fig. 3. Two prototype coils used for testing the surface tension hypothesis. It can be seen that before (a) the development the coil is patterned correctly. However, after developing (b) the individual loops collapse together due to surface tension. (c) Coil dried using CPD. It can be seen that all of the coil loops are free standing and are not touching any of the adjacent loop.

Fig. 3(a-b) show an example of a coil prepared without CPD. Before the development (a), it can be clearly seen that all of the microcoil loops are separated from one another. However, after the development (b), due to the surface tension during the drying process, the individual loops are attracted to loops immediately adjacent, resulting in structure collapse.

CPD was subsequently used during the development process. While CPD does not alleviate all of the surface tension during the drying, it ensures a significantly greater success rate. All successful coils were fabricated using CPD (Fig 3(c)).

3.2   Microcoil Process

The following outlines the entire 9-step process needed to successfully create the coil.

1. Create the design (microcoil) using CAD software, such as NX Unigraphics.
2. Export the design into a STereoLithography (STL) file format.
3. Converted file into a file format for use with 3D photolithography (General Writing Language, or GWL).
4. Three-dimensional photolithography (i.e. Nanoscribe).
5. Dry using Critical Point Dryer.
6. Because the created microcoil is non-conductive, it needs to be covered by a layer of electrically conductive metal (0.5 μm of copper was used to bridge a gap between the glass substrate and supports).
7. As sputtering indiscriminately covers the microcoil and the glass substrate, the individual loops and the connecting pads need to be separated (see Fig. 4 and Fig. 5). This can be accomplished by micro-laser patterning.
8. Glass wafer needs to be trimmed and glued to PCB.
9. Finally, the conductive pads need to be connected to pads on PCB using a wire bonder. Such a chip can then be placed inside a Helmholtz coil and tested inside Faraday cage to avoid signal interference from external sources.

4   Experiments and Results

4.1   Induction Setup

All of the measurements were performed using the following setup. The equipment used included a waveform generator (BK Precision 4070A), a current amplifier (Violin VIO-15/60), a pair of Helmholtz coils (R = 25 cm, N = 70), and a nanovolt meter (Lock-in amplifier, SRS830). The magnetic field was measured using a magnetometer from Metrolab (THM1176).

4.2   Flux Density Measurements

As previously stated, the strength of the magnetic field produced by the Helmholtz coils depends on the current flowing through the coils. Because of the physical characteristics of the current amplifier, for smaller frequencies (a few hundred Hz), the current produced was larger than for larger frequencies (greater that one kHz).

Table 2 shows measured magnetic field produced by the Helmholtz coils. Because the field depends on the current supplied, the measured values are significantly higher for lower frequencies than for higher frequencies.

Table 2. Empirical magnetic field (mT) produced by Helmholtz coil

| | | \multicolumn{8}{c}{Frequency (Hz)} | | | | | | | |
		151	305	500	706	978	1208	1428	1821
V (V)	1	5.2	3.4	3.3	1.8	1.4	1.6	1.1	0.7
	1.5	7.6	6.6	4.7	2.6	1.7	1.4	1.7	0.8
	2	10.5	8.9	5.5	3.6	1.9	2.1	1.9	0.8
	2.5	12.4	10.5	6.5	4.3	2.3	2.5	2.5	0.8
	3	14.4	12.1	7.4	5.2	2.4	2.9	2.9	0.9
	3.5	14.9	13.9	7.9	6.0	2.4	3.3	3.3	0.9

4.3   Induced Voltage Measurement

In the initial attempt, the microcoil was positioned on a probe station with easy access to the connection pads. The probe station tips were then positioned to touch these pads (Fig. 4). The output of the coil was measured using a lock-in amplifier (measuring RMS values) that was externally synchronized to the sinusoidal signal sent to the Helmholtz coils. The output signal (the signal from the microcoil) was verified by observing a significant decrease in the strength at slightly different frequencies from the input signal (frequency shift was used as an indication of maximum amplitude). For example, the 151Hz signal was checked at 150.5Hz and 151.5Hz). A significant decrease in signal strength was observed for the change in the frequency of the input signal. Additionally the noise level, also measured by the lock-in amplifier, was observed as being less than 8% of the measured quantity.

In this setup, the measured values were in the millivolt range, or several orders of magnitude stronger than the expected values. This significant variation was attributed to the electromagnetic interference from the setup. The power cables, measurement cables, along with other metal object contributed to the signal being measured.

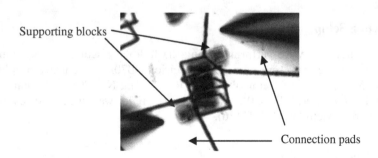

Supporting blocks

Connection pads

Fig. 4. Snapshot of the sub-millimeter coil with two probe tips connected to the supporting structures being shown

In order to measure the signal of interest and not the noise, it was necessary to eliminate any external interference. Therefore, it was necessary to completely isolate all of the components that were susceptible to electromagnetic interference. This included the Helmholtz coils, the microcoil and all of its connectors (previously micro-manipulators and probe tips), as well as all of the cables. Consequently the substrate with the microcoil was trimmed to a small chip that was subsequently glued onto a small printed circuit board (PCB). The coil pads were connected to PCB pins using wire bonder. A small box was turned into Faraday cage by lining it with multiple layers of industrial aluminum foil. The Helmholtz coils, along with the centrally placed chip and all of the wires, were then placed inside the box. The recorded values were in the nanovolt range, which was within the expected bounds. Table 3 lists the average of three voltage measurements.

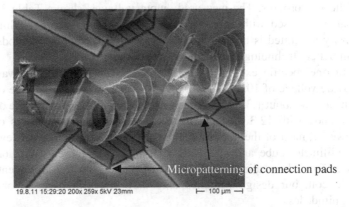

Micropatterning of connection pads

19.8.11 15:29:20 200x 259x 5kV 23mm   ⊢ 100 μm ⊣

Fig. 5. Scanning-electron micrograph of a helical microcoil. It can be seen that the loops of the microcoil are stretched along the Z-axis. This is due to the shape of the voxel.

In this study, the volume occupied by a coil can be considered to be a cylinder with R_1 and R_2 equal to 60 μm and 30 μm, respectively, and 80 μm in height, or 0.45 pm^3 (picometer cube). Its resistance was measured to be about 8 Ω. Based on the observed values of induced voltage, the coil achieved the maximum power density of about 1.96 mW per meter cube.

Table 3. Empirical induced voltage (nV) with insulation and chip on PCB

		Frequency (Hz)							
		151	305	500	706	978	1208	1428	1821
V (V)	1	12.1	16.0	25.7	20.1	20.5	29.1	28.8	19.8
	1.5	17.9	32.2	36.6	29.1	26.2	26.7	36.5	21.7
	2	24.5	41.6	40.9	38.1	28.5	36.5	41.8	21.6
	2.5	29.3	49.2	50.2	45.4	29.7	46.0	53.5	23.8
	3	36.2	63.2	63.1	62.5	39.2	60.2	71.2	26.1
	3.5	41.1	79.4	74.5	78.7	45.1	75.1	83.9	28.7

5   Discussion

A number of successful three-dimensional helical microcoils with varying height, radius, pitch, and thickness were created. Fig. 5 shows one such example. It can be seen that individual loops are elongated along the Z-axis. This, as already discussed, is due to the shape of the voxel. This difference in shape, however, is not critical, as long as there is a looped path between two connection pads. Also, the micropatterning of the metallic surface can be seen on the surface of the chip.

The general intention for this study was to provide electrical power for on-board information processing for sub-millimeter scale robots, in a form of electronic circuit. Such a circuitry would undoubtedly be created, either via printing [18] or some other photolithographic process, such as electron beam lithography, directly on the surface of the microrobots. The measured output voltages, shown Table 3, are currently too small to be used with commercial electronics components. Additionally, the power density generated is noticeably smaller compared to other methods, such as the thin film battery technology or the piezo generator.

In one specific example, the millimeter-scale coil in [11] was demonstrated to provide voltage of 10.4 mV with 0.62 μW of power from volume of 0.46 cm^3, which translates to about 1.35 W per meter cube. This is compared to the design presented in this study with 12.3 mW per meter cube, or about two orders of magnitude less. However, most of the published alternatives occupy volume of few tens or hundreds of millimeter cube and all of the alternative power generation or storage methods suffer from the scaling factor [11]. Compared with the aforementioned millimeter-scale coil, our design occupies only 0.58 pm^3 of space, or about six orders of magnitude less.

5.1   Voltage Amplification

Values displayed in Table 3 were obtained using standard equipment that was readily available in our laboratory. A number of changes to the demonstrated microcoil and the driving equipment should result in increasing the voltage, and the power density, to a level suitable to power currently available low-power electronics.

These changes can be grouped into two categories: change in the driving setup, and change in the microcoil. Increase in the field density could be obtained by increasing the driving current and a change to the Helmholtz coils. The output voltage could also be boosted by patterning a larger coil with a greater number of loops. The limiting factors are the overall size of the microcoil, as it is intended to be on a sub-millimeter scale, as well as the increase in stress generated by the increased size of the microcoil. Proposed changes, outlined in Table 4, should result in increasing the maximum induced voltage, by a factor of $24 \cdot 10^6$, from 84 nV to about 2 V.

One major advantage of the coil, compared to other solutions for power generation or power storage, is that it provides for a continuous voltage delivery without the need of recharging. Also, as indicated, the reported voltages and power densities can be increased without the change in the technology itself, but by modifying the driving setup (for instance with the use of stronger current amplifier). Its disadvantage is the

Table 4. Proposed method(s) to increase induced voltage

	Present	Proposed	Increase
Loop count[1]	5	15	3x
Loop count[2]	70	350	5x
Coil area[2]	$4.8 \cdot 10^{-9} \, m^2$	$19.2 \cdot 10^{-9} \, m^2$	4x
Current[1]	3 A	6 A	2x
Frequency[1]	1.5 kHz	300 MHz	$2 \cdot 10^5$

[1] refers to Helmholtz coils
[2] refers to voltage-inducing microcoil

fact that the generated voltage is AC and would have to be rectified as most of today's electronics relies on DC voltage. It should also be noted that the voltage measurements were conducted with the microcoil being placed perpendicular to the magnetic field. However, a microrobot does not necessarily operate with a constant orientation. This would further decrease the induced voltage.

Consideration also has to be given to the fact that, at present, the microcoil was assembled on a transparent glass wafer with a diameter of 3 cm (facilitated by the Nanoscribe system's requirement). This necessitates additional steps needed to place the microcoil atop a microrobot. A possible workaround to this hindrance would be to directly pattern the micro coil on a chip precut to the dimensions comparable to that of the microrobot for a subsequent microassembly.

6   Conclusion

With the help of a new fabrication method called direct laser writing, we have been able to demonstrate a possible solution of generating electrical power on a sub-millimeter scale via electromagnetic induction of voltage by a microcoil placed inside time-varying magnetic field. Magnetic field concentrators were shown as not viable to offset the space requirement. We described the investigation of the various conductive and non-conductive photoresists as possible materials as well as the experimental setup used for the testing. The size of the coil was about 60 µm in diameter with 5 loops. Voltages as high as 84 nV were reported with a maximum power density of about 1.96 mW per meter cube. Possible solutions to increase the generated voltage were proposed.

Acknowledgement. This work was sponsored in part by NSF grants OISE-1053249 and CNS-0923518 as well as SNF grant 200020-12521/2. We would like to acknowledge the help of all of our colleagues at ETHZ, specifically Li Zhang, Hsi-Wen Tung, Famin Qiu, Salvador Pané i Vidal, and Felix Beyeler from IRIS, as well as David Borer from the Institute of Fluid Dynamics and Klaus Marquardt from University of Zürich.

References

1. Frutiger, D.R., Vollmers, K., Kratochvil, B.E., Nelson, B.J.: Small, Fast, and Under Control: Wireless Resonant Magnetic Micro-agents. IJRR 29(5), 613–636 (2010)
2. Pawashe, C., Floyd, S., Sitti, M.: Modeling and Experimental Characterization of an Untethered Magnetic Micro-Robot. IJRR 28(8), 1077–1094 (2009)

3. Nawrocki, R.A., Shaheen, S.E., Voyles, R.M.: A Neuromorphic Architecture From Single Transistor Neurons With Organic Bistable Devices For Weights. In: Proc. IEEE IJCNN, pp. 450–456 (2011)

4. http://www.excellatron.com/advantage.html
(last accessed August 31, 2011)

5. Jeea, S.H., Leeb, M.J., Ahnc, H.S., Kimc, D.J., Choid, J.W., Yoond, S.J., Name, S.C., Kime, S.H., Yoon, Y.S.: Characteristics of a new type of solid-state electrolyte with a LiPON interlayer for Li-ion thin film batteries. Solid State Ionics 181(19-20), 902–906 (2010)

6. Peckerar, M., Dilli, Z., Dornajafi, M., Goldsman, N., Ngu, Y., Proctor, R.B., Krupsaw, B.J., Lowy, D.A.: A novel high energy density flexible galvanic cell. Energy & Environmental Science 4, 1807–1812 (2011)

7. Lal, A., Duggirala, R., Li, H.: Pervasive power: A radioisotope-powered piezoelectric generator. IEEE Pervasive Computing 4, 53–61 (2005)

8. Pana, C.T., Liua, Z.H., Chenb, Y.C., Liu, C.F.: Design and fabrication of flexible piezo-microgenerator by depositing ZnO thin films on PET substrates. Sensors and Actuators A 159, 96–104 (2010)

9. Hollar, S., Flynn, A., Bellew, C., Pister, K.S.J.: Solar powered 10 mg silicon robot. In: IEEE Micro Electro Mechanical Systems, pp. 706–711 (2003)

10. Churman, W.A., Gerratt, A.P., Bergbreiter, S.: First leaps toward jumping microrobots. In: IEEE IROS, pp. 1680–1686 (2011)

11. Arnold, D.P.: Review of Microscale Magnetic Power Generation. IEEE Trans. on Magnetics 43(11), 3940–3951 (2007)

12. Cepnik, C., Wallrabe, U.: A micro energy harvested with 3D wire bonded microcoils. Transducers, 665–668 (2011)

13. Mack, B., Kratt, K., Stürmer, M., Wallrabe, U.: Electromagnetic Micro Generator Array Consisting of 3D Micro Coils Opposing a Magnetic PDMS Membrane. In: Transducers 2009, pp. 1397–1400 (2009)

14. Brauer, J.R.: Magnetic actuators and sensors, p. 20. John Wiley and Sons (2006)

15. Yeadon, W.H., Yeadon, A.W.: Handbook on small electric motors, p. 1.67. McGraw-Hill (2001)

16. http://www.nanoscribe.de/ (August 31, 2011)

17. http://www.gersteltec.ch/userfiles/1197841690.pdf
(August 31, 2011)

18. Sheats, J.R., Biesty David, D., Noel, J., et al.: Printing technology for ubiquitous electronics. Circuit World 36, 40–47 (2010)

A Digital Lock-In Amplifier Based Contact Detection Technique for Electrochemical Nanolithography

Shi-Yu Zhou, Lei-Jie Lai, Guo-Ying Gu, and Li-Min Zhu[*]

State Key Laboratory of Mechanical System and Vibration,
School of Mechanical Engineering,
Shanghai Jiao Tong University, Shanghai 200240, China
zhulm@sjtu.edu.cn

Abstract. This paper presents a digital lock-in amplifier (DLIA) based technique to detect the template-substrate contact in electrochemical nanolithography. This technique is applied to a specially designed electrochemical nanolithography system for verification. The system adopts a macro-micro positioning setup consisting of a fine stepping motor to drive the macropositioning stage and a PZT(lead zirconate titanate, $Pb[Zr_xTi_{1-x}]O_3$) actuator to drive the micropositioning stage. The template is mounted on a force-displacement sensing module which is attached to the PZT actuated micropositioning stage and the substrate is mounted on a holder which is merged in the solution. When the template approaches the substrate, it is controlled to oscillate at a certain frequency. Two capacitive displacement sensors are used to measure the template oscillation. Afterwards, a digital lock-in amplifier is adopted to separate the oscillation information from the raw signal. The contact is determined by monitoring the separated oscillation information. Finally, experiment tests are conducted to verify the effectiveness of the digital lock-in amplifier. Experimental results demonstrate that the developed DLIA technique makes the template-substrate contact to nanometer accuracy.

Keywords: nanolithography, contact detection, force-displacement sensing module, digital lock-in amplifier.

1 Introduction

Recently, electrochemical lithography has become popular in the field of nanolithography due to its advantages of high efficiency, large processing area and high resolution [1], [2]. For electrochemical nanolithography, the most important problem that limits its extensive use is the fine determination and adjustment of the distance between the template and the substrate. This problem comprises two aspects, accurate determination of the initial template-substrate gap in the first place and fine adjustment of the displacement afterwards. Since micropositioning stages with high-

---

[*] Corresponding author.

C.-Y. Su, S. Rakheja, H. Liu (Eds.): ICIRA 2012, Part II, LNAI 7507, pp. 313–322, 2012.
© Springer-Verlag Berlin Heidelberg 2012

resolution displacement sensors have been adopted to realize the fine adjustment of the displacement [3], [4], the poor accuracy of initial gap determination comes to be the major problem. Therefore, it is necessary to establish the template-surface contact within nanometer accuracy and determine the initial template-substrate gap accurately before the processing.

Several methods have been proposed to solve this problem. Gao has employed a modulation technique to establish a tool-sample contact within a sub-nanometer range [5]. This technique needs the sample to be mounted on a capacitive displacement sensor. In electrochemical nanofabrication, the substrate should be merged in working solution where sensors like capacitive displacement sensor cannot be setup. For Randall's nanoindentation tester [6], the slight change in the contact stiffness, which is the slope of the linear fit of the proceeding and succeeding 30 data points from the force sensor, is used to detect the contact of the indenter. In Ferreira's paper [7], the force obtained by the deflection of the cantilevered stamp is used to detect the stamp-substrate contact.

In this paper, a digital lock-in amplifier (DLIA) is developed as an efficient technique to detect the template-substrate contact. This technique eliminates the thermal drift effect of the structure and performs much better than common filters in noise suppression. To apply this technique in electrochemical nanolithography, a compact design with a force-displacement sensing module attached to a PZT actuated micropositioning stage is developed.

The remainder of the paper is organized as follows. The electrochemical nanofabricating system is introduced in Section 2. The principles of this technique, including the basic lock-in amplifier theory and the determination of the initial template-substrate gap, are addressed in Section 3. The experimental setup and the contact detection experiment are presented in Section 4 and Section 5 respectively. Finally, Section 6 concludes the paper.

2   System Description

The electrochemical nanofabrication system consists of a macro-micro dual driven positioning stage, a force-displacement sensing module and a visual sensing module. The overall schematic diagram is depicted in Fig. 1. The macro-micro dual driven positioning stage is comprised of a macropositioning stage driven by a fine stepping motor and a micropositioning stage driven by a PZT actuator. The micropositioning stage is composed of a PZT actuator, a double compound flexure mechanism and a high-resolution capacitive displacement sensor. The force-displacement sensing module fixed on the micropositioning stage consists of a double compound flexure mechanism and a capacitive sensor. The template is mounted on the moving platform of the sensing module and the substrate is fixed on the bottom of the electrolyzer. The contact force between the template and the substrate is obtained by detecting the elastic deformation of the flexure mechanism on the sensing module. The whole system is mounted on a granite bridge base. The granite is suitable for stable structure due to its low thermal expansion coefficient, high stiffness and damping ratio.

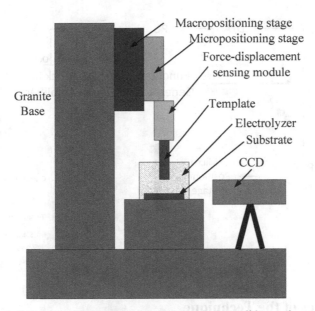

Fig. 1. Schematic diagram of the electrochemical nanolithography system

The template-substrate contact is accomplished in two steps: the fast approaching step driven by the macro positioning stage with the visual feedback and the successive approaching step using macro-micro dual driven stage. In the successive approaching step, the micropositioning stage firstly moves the template towards the substrate for 6 μm at a speed of 1 nm/ms. During this process, the force-displacement sensing module keeps monitoring if the contact happens. Once the module detects the contact, the stage stops moving. Otherwise, the micropositioning stage retracts 6 μm and the macro positioning stage extends 5 μm. This process is repeated until the contact is accomplished.

When detecting the template-substrate contact, the accuracy is mainly determined by the sensitivity of the capacitive sensor. Although the employed sensor possesses sub-nanometer precision, the output is influenced by environmental mechanical vibrations, thermal drift and electronic noise. To reduce such influences, a digital lock-in amplifier (DLIA) based technique is proposed in this work. The schematic diagram is shown in Fig. 2. In the approaching process, the micropositioning stage drives the force-displacement sensing module towards the substrate surface while oscillating with amplitude of 1nm and frequency of 50 Hz. Since the force-displacement sensing module is attached to the micropositioning stage, the output contains an AC component with the same frequency. This AC component can be detected by the lock-in amplifier. Once the tip of the template comes into contact with the substrate, the amplitude of the AC component will increase. When the amplitude increases beyond the threshold value, which is determined based on the statistical characteristics of the oscillation amplitude, the template-substrate contact is established.

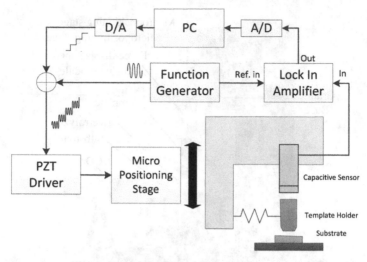

Fig. 2. Schematic diagram for contact detection

3   Principles of the Technique

3.1   Basic Lock-In Amplifier Theory

The lock-in amplifier is a useful instrument in research and development laboratories. It can be used to measure small sinusoidal signals, even when these signals are masked by noise [8], [9]. Fig. 3 shows the basic lock-in amplifier (LIA) configuration (internal source). It is composed of one internal source, one phase shifter, two multiplier stages and two low pass filters.

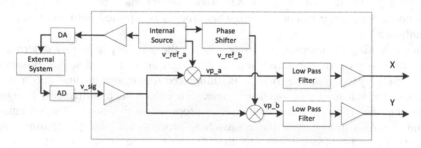

Fig. 3. Basic lock-in amplifier

For simplicity, quantization noise introduced by both ADC and DAC is not considered in the analysis. The reference signal generated by the LIA internal source is

$$v\_ref\_a = \sin\left(\Omega_{ref} n\right) \tag{1}$$

where Ω_{ref} is the discrete reference frequency, n is the time.

The phase shifter adds a $\dfrac{\pi}{2}$ phase difference to v_ref_a, which yields

$$v\_ref\_b = \sin\left(\Omega_{ref}n + \frac{\pi}{2}\right) \tag{2}$$

The system response signal is expressed as

$$v\_sig = V_{sig}\sin\left(\Omega_{sig}n + \theta_{sig}\right) + \eta_n \tag{3}$$

where V_{sig} is the amplitude response, Ω_{sig} is the frequency response, θ_{sig} is the phase response, η_n is the zero-mean additive discrete stochastic process (Gaussian) with noise power σ_n^2.

The output of the two multiply stage is obtained as

$$vp\_a = v\_ref\_a \cdot v\_sig \tag{4}$$

$$vp\_b = v\_ref\_b \cdot v\_sig \tag{5}$$

$$vp\_a = \frac{V_{sig}}{2}\cos\left[\left(\Omega_{sig} - \Omega_{ref}\right)n + \theta_{sig}\right] - \frac{V_{sig}}{2}\cos\left[\left(\Omega_{sig} + \Omega_{ref}\right)n + \theta_{sig}\right] + \eta_n\sin\left(\Omega_{ref}n\right) \tag{6}$$

$$vp\_b = \frac{V_{sig}}{2}\cos\left[\left(\Omega_{sig} - \Omega_{ref}\right)n + \theta_{sig} - \frac{\pi}{2}\right] - \frac{V_{sig}}{2}\cos\left[\left(\Omega_{sig} + \Omega_{ref}\right)n + \theta_{sig} + \frac{\pi}{2}\right] + \eta_n\sin\left(\Omega_{ref}n + \frac{\pi}{2}\right) \tag{7}$$

These signals are then applied to low pass filters. The cut off frequency is set by the user, aiming at removing higher frequencies components. The output of the low pass filters can be expressed as

$$X = \frac{V_{sig}}{2}\cos\left[\left(\Omega_{sig} - \Omega_{ref}\right)n + \theta_{sig}\right] + \eta_n' \tag{8}$$

$$Y = \frac{V_{sig}}{2}\cos\left[\left(\Omega_{sig} - \Omega_{ref}\right)n + \theta_{sig} - \frac{\pi}{2}\right] + \eta_n' \tag{9}$$

The noise power is affected by the sinusoidal signals and the modulus of the filter response, and the noise mean remains unaffected. Thus, the noise can be replaced by a new random variable η_n'. The frequencies of the system response and reference signals are equal. Hence the output signals can be expressed as

$$X = \frac{V_{sig}}{2}\cos\theta_{sig} + \eta_n' \tag{10}$$

$$Y = \frac{V_{sig}}{2}\cos\left(\theta_{sig} - \frac{\pi}{2}\right) + \eta_n' = \frac{V_{sig}}{2}\sin\theta_{sig} + \eta_n' \tag{11}$$

In order to measure the amplitude response V_{sig} and the phase response θ_{sig} of the input signal, the equations (10) and (11) can be rewritten as

$$V_{sig} = 2\sqrt{\left[\left(X - \eta_n'\right)^2 + \left(Y - \eta_n'\right)^2\right]} = 2\sqrt{X^2 + Y^2 - 2X\eta_n' - 2Y\eta_n' + 2\sigma_n'^2} \tag{12}$$

$$\theta_{sig} = \tan^{-1}\left(\frac{Y - \eta_n'}{X - \eta_n'}\right) = \tan^{-1}\left(\frac{Y}{X}\left(1 + \frac{\eta_n'}{X} - \frac{\eta_n'}{Y} + \frac{\eta_n'^2}{XY}\right)\right) \tag{13}$$

For simplicity, the cut off frequency of the low pass filter is chosen to be low enough to drive a severe attenuation of the noise interference. Hence the noise power can be neglected. Besides, the noise η_n' is a zero-mean variable. Thus, the measured signal parameters can be expressed as functions of the output signals of the low pass filters.

$$V_{sig} = 2\sqrt{X^2 + Y^2} \tag{14}$$

$$\theta_{sig} = \tan^{-1}\left(\frac{Y}{X}\right) \tag{15}$$

3.2   Determination of the Initial Gap

Both the micropositioning stage and the template are kept oscillating in the approaching process. When the contact is detected, the system stops oscillating. In this case, there is still a gap between the template and the substrate. This initial gap should be determined.

In practice, the micropositioning stage is controlled to oscillate at a certain frequency with a given amplitude. The oscillation with respect to the basement can be expressed as follows

$$X_{10} = S_{10}(t) + A_1 \sin \omega t \tag{16}$$

where A_1 is the amplitude and ω is determined by the frequency. $S_{10}(t)$ represents the instantaneous position of the micropositioning stage with respect to the stage base, which can be captured by the capacitive displacement sensor.

Since the force-displacement sensing module is attached to the micropositioning stage, its flexure platform should oscillate at the same frequency with respect to the stage. Hence, the oscillation of the template (mounted on the flexure platform) with respect to the micropositioning stage is obtained as

$$X_{21} = S_{21}(t) + A_2 \sin(\omega t + \phi) \tag{17}$$

where A_2 is the oscillation amplitude and ϕ is the phase difference between X_{10} and X_{21}. $S_{21}(t)$ is the position of the template with respect to the micropositioning stage when the system is not operating.

The oscillation of the template with respect to the stage base should be the summation of X_{10} and X_{21}. Thus, it can be expressed as follows.

$$X_{20} = X_{10} + X_{21} = S_{10}(t) + S_{21}(t) + A_1 \sin(\omega t) + A_2 \sin(\omega t + \phi) \qquad (18)$$

This equation (18) can be rewritten as

$$X_{20} = S_{10}(t) + S_{21}(t) + A_{template} \cdot \sin(\omega t + \phi') \qquad (19)$$

$$A_{template} = \sqrt{A_1^2 + A_2^2 + 2A_1A_2 \cos\phi} \qquad (20)$$

where $A_{template}$ is the oscillating amplitude of the template. Thus, when the system detects the contact, the instantaneous gap between template and substrate can be recorded as $A_{template}$, that is the initial gap.

4   Experimental Setup

To verify the developed technique, an experimental platform is built to detect the template-substrate contact. Fig. 4 shows the experimental setup. For the macro positioning stage: a motion control card (PCI-4P from HIWIN) is used to drive the stepping motor. For the micropositioning stage: A PZT (P-840.30 from PI) is adopted to drive the micropositioning stage through a corresponding PZT amplifier (E-503.00 from PI); two capacitive displacement sensors (D-100.00 from PI) are used to measure the displacement of the micropositioning stage and the force-displacement sensing module respectively; a 16-bit data acquisition card (PCI-6221 from NI) is used to acquire the voltage of the capacitive sensors (0-10V) and to apply the control voltage (0-10V) to the PZT amplifier. The application of the experiment is developed in the environment of LabVIEW 2010.

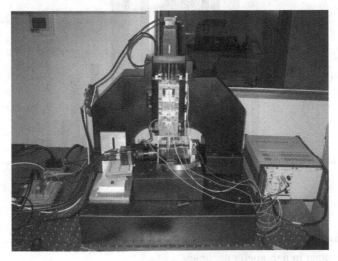

Fig. 4. Photograph of the experimental setup

5   Contact Detection Experiment

In the contact detection experiment, the oscillation frequency is chosen as 50Hz to avoid resonance and the oscillation amplitude of the micropositioning stage is chosen as 5nm. The approaching speed is set to be 0.4 μ m per second. Before the template contacts the substrate, it oscillates freely and stably. Fig. 5 shows the statistical characteristics of the amplitude. The mean value is 1.20 nm and the standard variance is 0.61 nm. Hence, the threshold value can be set as 3.10 nm($\mu+3\sigma$). Fig. 6 depicts amplitude and phase of the oscillation during the contact detection. Before contact, the amplitude remains stable but the phase changes from 0 to π randomly . As the template comes into contact with the substrate, the amplitude increases rapidly and the phase becomes stable. After the amplitude increases beyond the threshold value, the system stops approaching and the initial gap can be determined by equation (20) .

$$A_{template} = \sqrt{A_1^2 + A_2^2 + 2A_1A_2\cos\phi} \qquad (21)$$

where A_1 is 5 nm, A_2 is 1.20 nm and ϕ is π. Thus, the initial gap is obtained as 3.80nm.

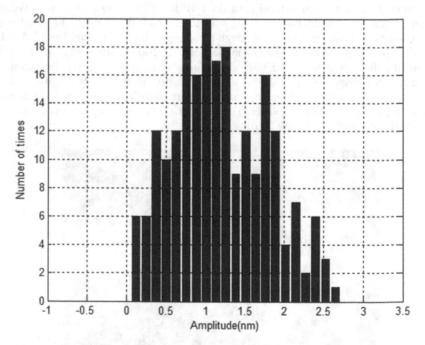

Fig. 5. Statistical characteristics of the amplitude

This experiment verifies the proposed technique and demonstrates its ability to establish a contact in nanometer accuracy.

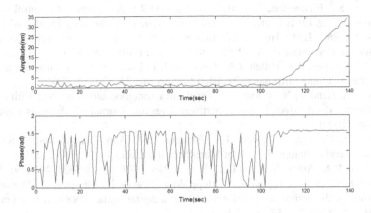

Fig. 6. Amplitude and phase during the contact detection

6   Conclusions

A new contact detection technique has been introduced and verified in this paper. This technique is applied to a specially designed electrochemical nanolithography system for verification. The system adopts a macro-micro positioning setup to realize the approaching process. During this process, the micropositioning stage is controlled to oscillate at a certain frequency and the oscillation of the template is measured by two capacitive displacement sensors. By utilizing a digital lock-in amplifier, the oscillation information is separated from the raw signal. Thus, the contact can be easily determined by monitoring the oscillation information. Finally, experiment tests are conducted to verify the effectiveness of the digital lock-in amplifier. Experimental results demonstrate that the developed DLIA technique makes the template-substrate contact to nanometer accuracy.

Acknowledgements. This work was supported by the National Natural Science Foundation of China under Grant No. 91023047, and the "Shu Guang" project supported by Shanghai Municipal Education Commission under Grant No. 10SG17, and the Science and Technology Commission of Shanghai Municipality under Grant No. 11520701500.

References

1. Simeone, F.C., Albonetti, C., Cavallini, M.: Progress in Micro- and Nanopatterning via Electrochemical Lithography. The Journal of Physical Chemistry C 113, 18987–18994 (2009)
2. Zhang, L., Ma, X.Z., Zhuang, J.L., Qiu, C.K., Du, C.L., Tang, J., Tian, Z.W.: Microfabrication of a Diffractive Microlens Array on n - GaAs by an Efficient Electrochemical Method. Advanced Materials 19, 3912–3918 (2007)

3. Devasia, S., Eleftheriou, E., Moheimani, S.O.R.: A survey of control issues in nanopositioning. IEEE Transactions on Control Systems Technology 15, 802–823 (2007)
4. Gu, G.Y., Zhu, L.M.: High-speed tracking control of piezoelectric actuators using an ellipse-based hysteresis model. Review of Scientific Instruments 81, 085–104 (2010)
5. Gao, W., Hocken, R.J., Patten, J.A., Lovingood, J., Lucca, D.A.: Construction and testing of a nanomachining instrument. Precision Engineering 24, 320–328 (2000)
6. Nohava, J., Randall, N., Conté, N.: Novel ultra nanoindentation method with extremely low thermal drift: Principle and experimental results. Journal of Materials Research 24, 873–882 (2009)
7. Ahmed, N., Carlson, A., Rogers, J.A., Ferreira, P.M.: Automated micro-transfer printing with cantilevered stamps. Journal of Manufacturing Processes 14, 90–97 (2012)
8. Remillard, P.A., Amorelli, M.C.: Lock-in amplifier. US Patent. US5210484 (1993)
9. Gaspar, J., Chen, S.F., Gordillo, A., Hepp, M., Ferreyra, P., Marqués, C.: Digital lock in amplifier: study, design and development with a digital signal processor. Microprocessors and Microsystems 28, 157–162 (2004)

Optimization of a Compliant Mechanical Amplifier Based on a Symmetric Five-Bar Topology

John Michael Acob, Vangjel Pano, and Puren Ouyang

Department of Aerospace Engineering,
Ryerson University, Toronto, Canada
pouyang@ryerson.ca

Abstract. When combined with a piezoelectric actuator, a mechanical amplifier can achieve high resolution and long range motion. In this paper, a previously proposed compliant mechanical amplifier based on a symmetric five bar structure was studied for performance optimization. The amplifier was optimized based on its most significant design parameters with goals of large amplification ratio and high natural frequency. The design was also optimized for various load cases and over a range of input displacements. The optimization procedure validated the variability of the amplification based both on applied load, structure, and input displacement.

Keywords: Compliant Mechanism, Amplifier, Piezoelectric Actuator, Optimization, Finite Element Analysis.

1   Introduction

The combination of a mechanical displacement amplifier with a piezoelectric (PZT) actuator has great potential in various industrial and medical applications. PZT actuators feature small, efficient sizes and the ability to produce high displacement resolution with low strain and high-force output [1]. Unfortunately, their relatively small range of motion makes PZT actuators inadequate for most engineering applications. Displacement amplification mechanisms are employed to overcome that disadvantage.

The idea of using compliant mechanical amplifiers (CMA) is not a new one [2-15]. Several designs of varying shapes and purposes have been proposed and analyzed [7-17].The main design objective of a CMA is to achieve a large amplification ratio (AR). This, however, may compromise the structure's generated force and natural frequency (NF) [12]. Nevertheless, the large force output of PZT actuators makes the generated force reduction tolerable. Xu *et al.* [9] have provided a good summary of existing designs and have drawn conclusions on the limitations of CMA's such as low natural frequency and the presence of undesirable lateral displacement.

Mottard *et al.* [13] suggests that aligned hinges provide better performance than simple parallel configurations, and Kim *et al.* [14] introduced multiple bridge configurations in order to achieve greater stiffness and tolerance to external static loads. In [15], an increase in flexural hinge thickness was found to decrease the

C.-Y. Su, S. Rakheja, H. Liu (Eds.): ICIRA 2012, Part II, LNAI 7507, pp. 323–332, 2012.
© Springer-Verlag Berlin Heidelberg 2012

amplification ratio and increase the natural frequency. Additionally, the design of a CMA has to be a compromise between the conflicting objectives of the structure's flexibility and stiffness [16]. Therefore, the two most important design goals of an amplification mechanism are large amplification ratio and high natural frequency.

Ouyang *et al.* [17] introduced a CMA based on a symmetric five-bar topology and discussed some design parameters affecting the AR. In this paper, an optimization analysis was performed which includes all parameters found to significantly affect the performance of the CMA.

2   Compliant Mechanical Amplifier

2.1   Five-Bar Topology

The CMA that will be optimized is based on the topology proposed in [17], shown in Fig. 1. This topology is designed to be symmetric in configuration with two driving links that simultaneously rotate in opposite directions. The input displacement is provided by a PZT such that the output displacement is constrained to only one direction. This topology can be viewed as a combination of a symmetric four-bar topology and a lever arm topology, which have been reported several times in literature and have been used extensively in industrial applications [7-17]. The advantages of this topology in comparison with a double symmetric four-bar topology are the high natural frequency and large amplification ratio while maintaining a compact size [17]. Fig. 1(a) shows the direction of displacements for the five-bar topology, while the pseudo-rigid body model (PRBM) [2] of this topology is shown in Fig. 1(b).

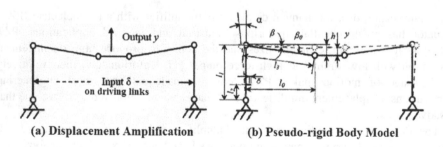

(a) Displacement Amplification   (b) Pseudo-rigid Body Model

Fig. 1. Symmetric five-bar topology

2.2   Geometry and Design Parameters

The schematic of the proposed geometry of the CMA, based on the five-bar topology, is shown in Fig. 2. A key parameter of this geometry is the initial height of the middle bar from the top of the two driving links, which corresponds to the parameter h in Fig. 1(b). Some other key parameters include the thicknesses of the flexure hinges of the CMA.

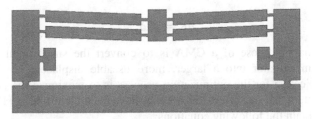

Fig. 2. CMA based on symmetric five-bar topology

The notation used in this paper to define the parameters for the proposed geometry is shown in Fig. 3. It should be noted that this figure shows only half of the actual geometry as the amplifier is symmetric about the vertical axis.

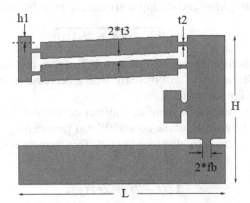

Fig. 3. Notation used for CMA parameters

Table 1. Dimensions of the initial geometry of the CMA

L [mm]	H [mm]	h1 [mm]	fb [mm]	t2 [mm]	t3 [mm]
32.2	22.5	1.0	0.6	0.5	0.5

The notations for the shown parameters are among those that were used to define the geometry in ANSYS Mechanical APDL, a software that uses the finite element method (FEM) of analysis [18]. The initial parameters of the CMA are listed in Table 1. It should also be noted that the CMA has a uniform thickness of 5 [mm].

3   Optimization

3.1   Significant Parameters

The ratio of the output displacement, y, and the input displacement, δ, shown in Fig. 1 (a), can be defined as the amplification ratio of this CMA:

$$AR = y/\delta \tag{1}$$

Since the primary purpose of a CMA is to convert the small input displacement provided by an actuator into a larger, more useable displacement. Therefore, an appropriate objective for the optimization process is to maximize the AR. There are several parameters that can affect the AR that have been identified in [17]. From Fig. 1(b), we can obtain the following equations:

$$l_3 \sin \beta = h - y$$
$$l_3 \cos \beta = l_0 + k\delta \tag{2}$$

where $k = l_1/l_2$. The output displacement can be written in terms of the dimensions of the PRBM of the amplifier and the input displacement as follows:

$$y = h - \sqrt{h^2 - (k\delta + 2l_0)k\delta} \tag{3}$$

The derivation of this formula can be found in [17]. From this formulation it can be seen that the amplification ratio will increase with a decrease in initial height, h, and an increase in the design parameter k.

Another parameter that has a significant effect on the AR is the stiffness of the flexure hinges. The stiffness, K, of the corner-filleted flexure hinges used in this CMA can be calculated using the formula given in [19]. This formula is given as follows:

$$K = \frac{Ebt^3}{12(l - 2r + 2rf(\gamma))} \tag{4}$$

where

$$\gamma = \frac{2r}{t} \tag{5}$$

and

$$f(\gamma) = \frac{(2\gamma + 1)(3\gamma^2 + 2\gamma + 1) + 3\gamma(\gamma + 1)^2\sqrt{2\gamma + 1}\tan^{-1}(\sqrt{2\gamma + 1})}{(\gamma + 1)(2\gamma + 1)^3} \tag{6}$$

These formulas show that the parameter that has the greatest effect on the stiffness of a corner-filleted flexure hinge is the thickness of the hinge, t.

Table 2. Allowable ranges for design variables

Design Parameter	Range
h1	$3.0 \times 10^{-4} \sim 2.25 \times 10^{-3}$ [m]
t2	$3.0 \times 10^{-4} \sim 6.0 \times 10^{-4}$ [m]
t3	$3.0 \times 10^{-4} \sim 1.0 \times 10^{-3}$ [m]
fb	$5.0 \times 10^{-4} \sim 2.25 \times 10^{-3}$ [m]

Examining Fig. 3, obvious selections for design variables are $h1$, $t2$, and fb. These correspond to the parameters shown in the PRBM and those used in Equations (1 to (4) and are precisely the variables that were selected for the optimization process. Another parameter that affects the thicknesses of the upper flexure hinges is $t3$, and was also chosen as a design variable. The range of allowable values for the design variables can be found in Table 2.

3.2   Optimization Setup and Constraints

To optimize the proposed CMA, a number of scenarios were considered. Simulations were first run without applied loads while subsequent simulations had loads incorporated. To simulate the loads experienced by the CMA, two equal downward forces were applied at two points on the top surface of the middle bar. It is intuitive that applying such a load causes a downward displacement of the top surface. A static analysis with only this force applied was conducted where the negative displacement of the top surface was recorded and denoted as dy_0.

A static analysis was then performed which included the input displacements from the PZT actuator on the driving links. The displacement of the top surface was then recorded from which dy_0 was subtracted. The difference in displacements was recorded as the total output displacement and its ratio with the input displacement was defined as the amplification ratio. For the cases without an applied load, dy_0 was set to zero.

For each scenario, a number of constraints were applied for the optimization process. A typical function for a CMA is to function as the base for each leg of a hybrid macro-micro system. As such, the base of the amplifier itself is constrained with no displacement being allowed in both the vertical and horizontal directions. In terms of the kinematics of the CMA, at the point where the axes of the coupler links and the center bar become aligned in space, there exists a singularity. For this reason, the coupler links were not allowed to reach a horizontal position.

Another constraint applied on the proposed design was the maximum von Mises stress of the structure. This was not allowed to exceed 276 [MPa], the yield stress of Aluminum 6061-T6 alloy. The material properties of this alloy were used for the FEA. As the natural frequency of a structure has a significant effect on its fatigue performance, the natural frequency of the CMA was not allowed to fall below 450 [Hz]. This value was deemed appropriate for this analysis based on results from literature [17].

Finally, the force required to produce the desired input displacement was not allowed to exceed the push load capacity of the PZT actuator. The PZT actuator to be used for the proposed CMA is the Newport NPA25-D, which has a maximum push load capacity of 1000 [N] . The force required to produce a desired input displacement, including the inherent stiffness of the actuator, was subtracted from the push load capacity of the PZT actuator and the remaining available force (RAF) was not allowed to fall below zero.

For each case (both with and without applied forces), ANSYS was used to perform a first-order optimization for a series of input displacements ranging from 5[μm] to 10[μm] at each driving link. Each combination of applied force and input displacement produced a different set of optimized parameters. Although the ideal design would produce the largest displacement, a sufficient goal was to maximize the amplification ratio of each case since the input displacement is held constant for each optimization. As the goal was to maximize the AR, the objective function was set to its inverse, $1/AR$. By minimizing this parameter, the maximum AR may be obtained. As was previously mentioned, for the cases with an applied load, two static solutions were produced, one with and one without the input displacement, before the optimization was carried out.

4   Results and Discussion

Five different loading scenarios were employed: $0\,[N]$, $2\,[N]$, $4\,[N]$, $6[N]$, and $8\,[N]$, resulting in a total of 30 (6x5) designs. For each load case, the design that produced the largest output displacement was selected. Static analyses were then performed on each of the selected designs over the entire range of input displacements for their respective loading scenarios. This way, the behavior of each design over the entire projected working range of the PZT actuator was observed. Furthermore, the selected designs were subjected to the entire range of applied loads while holding the input displacement at the maximum ($10 \times 10^{-6}\,[m]$). Based on these results, an final optimal design was produced.

4.1   Initial Optimizations

For the sake of brevity, the notation used for the optimized design for each case refers to the applied load and input displacement combination for which it was optimized. For instance, the design resulting from an optimization with applied load of $8\,[N]$ and input displacement of $6 \times 10^{-6}\,[m]$ is referred to as design 8.6. Several significant parameters of the design for each of the optimization cases are shown in Fig. 4.

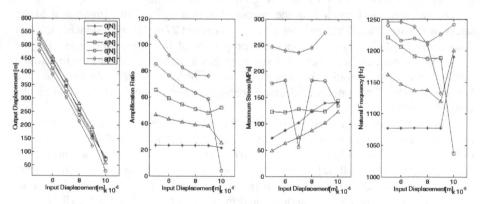

Fig. 4. Several key parameters of the optimized designs for each case

As expected, the results of the optimizations with no applied loads did not produce significant changes in the design. This was mostly due to the low values of the maximum stress experienced by the structure, which was the factor with the greatest effect on the optimization procedure. The AR was kept relatively constant, as shown by the slope of the input output displacement. Similarly, the NF, the decrease of the RAF and the optimization variables kept relatively constant values. The last optimization showed a considerable change, which corresponds to the case with the maximum input displacement. Although the difference in results is not large, design 0.10, which produced an output displacement of 215.06×10^{-6} $[m]$ and had a NF of 1190.32 $[Hz]$, was chosen as the best one from this scenario.

The results of the optimization scenario for 2 [N] loads show that with an increasing flexural hinge thickness, $t2$, the AR decreases while the NF increases. This is in agreement with the analysis from Section 3. The best design, 2.9 had an output displacement of 342.98×10^{-6} $[m]$ $(AR = 38.1)$ and a NF of 1119.74 $[Hz]$. Although the stress experienced by this design was one of the highest seen, it is still far below the yield stress of the material. Under 4 [N], the changes in the optimization variables became more visible and significant. The increase in AR and NF is larger than those of the previous load cases. Design 4.10 produced an output of 522.46×10^{-6} $[m]$ $(AR = 52.25)$ and a NF of $1036.97[Hz]$. Although, its frequency is the lowest of this load case, it is still far above 450 $[Hz]$.

The optimal design for the 6 [N] load case was found to be design 6.9 which featured an output of 526.48×10^{-6} $[m]$ $(AR = 58.5)$ and a NF of $1226.17[Hz]$. In the 8 [N] load scenario, the optimization for an input of 10 $[\mu m]$ did not produce a feasible result. As it is also shown in Figure 8, this scenario was the only one that reached the limits of allowable stress and it showcased the effect of the optimization variables on the amplifier clearly. The best design was found to be 8.9 with an output of 686.02×10^{-6} $[m]$ $(AR = 76.22)$ and a NF of $1132.07[Hz]$. The dimensions of the designs that produced the largest output displacements are summarized in Table 3.

Table 3. Optimized parameters for varying loadings

Design	h1 [mm]	fb [mm]	t2 [mm]	t3 [mm]	NF [Hz]	Output Displacement [μm]
0.10	1.654	0.5444	0.4576	0.5005	1190.32	215.0594
2.9	1.770	0.6521	0.3002	0.4896	1119.74	342.9809
4.10	1.610	0.5422	0.3002	0.5679	1036.97	522.4753
6.9	1.984	0.6101	0.3003	0.5016	1226.17	526.4849
8.9	1.831	0.5004	0.3052	0.4761	1132.07	686.0241

4.2   Input Displacement Variation

In this stage, the selected designs were subjected to the full spectrum of the input displacements. The applied load for each design was kept the same as the case for which it was optimized. The results indicate that design 8.9 consistently featured the largest output displacement and therefore the largest AR.

As seen in Fig. 5(a), the average amplification ratio changed depending on the loads applied on the structure. In fact, the AR increased with an increase in load. This can be explained by Equations (2) and (3). Large applied loads cause greater β angles that leads to a greater output displacements for the amplifier. Additionally, the average amplification ratio for the optimized design is slightly larger than the AR given by the optimization without applied load. This is justified by the non-linear relationship that exists between the input and output displacements as indicated by Equation (3). Therefore, the amplification ratio of the amplifier changes in value depending on applied loads as well as the input displacement of the actuator. Interestingly, the RAFs for each load case were quite similar in value, with the exception of the zero load case. This can be explained by the relatively small differences between the optimization variables of the selected designs. Having similar geometries, all the designs exhibited similar reaction forces under the same inputs.

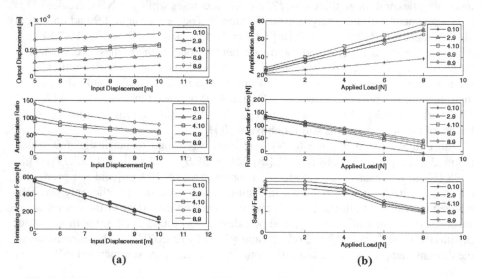

(a)   **(b)**

Fig. 5. (a) Results from varying input displacement (b) Results from varying applied load

4.3   Varying Loads

In this section the selected designs were subjected to the maximum input displacement (10 [μm]) and under various loads from 0 [N] to 8 [N]. The AR and RAF results followed the expected trend, with AR increasing as the load increased and RAF decreasing. Although design 8.9 was optimized for the highest loads, design 6.9 has a greater safety factor, and therefore a better structural behavior than 8.9. This can be explained by looking at the fb parameter for both designs. The base fillets in the amplifier always exhibit the highest stresses in the structure along with the hinge thickness $t2$.   Design 6.9 features a thicker base fillet ($fb = 0.61$ [mm]) than design 8.9 ($fb = 0.50$ [mm]) and therefore in this case experiences lower stresses in that region. The rest of the designs, behaved in as expected with 2.10 having a better safety factor that 2.9 and 0.10.The best design was considered to be 6.9 since it exhibited the largest AR values for every load case.

Looking at the performance of each design, 4.10 was the one with the largest AR. This is due to its more flexible structure having been optimized for lower loads that 6.9 or 8.9. However, the stresses experienced by the design were too high, as seen by its safety factor, and in fact its structure failed to support 8 [N] loads. Therefore, the best design is considered to be 8.9.

4.4   Optimal Design

Having been considered the best design for both scenarios, 8.9 is chosen the optimal design for the CMA.   The following table summarizes its structural properties.

Table 4. Optimal design parameters

Natural Frequency [Hz]	h1 [mm]	fb [mm]	t2 [mm]	t3 [mm]
1132.7	1.831111	0.500457	0.305195	0.476068

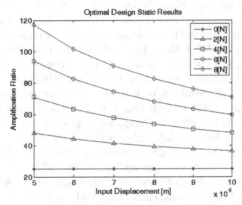

Fig. 6. Performance of optimal design over a range of input displacements and applied forces

As seen in Fig. 6, the amplification ratio changed depending on the loads applied on the structure. In fact, the AR increased with an increase in load. This can be explained by Equations (2 and (3. High applied loads cause greater β angles which lead to a greater output displacements for the amplifier. Additionally, the average amplification ratio for the optimized design is slightly larger than the AR given by the optimization. This is justified by the non-linear relationship that exists between the input and output displacements as indicated by Equation (3. Therefore, the amplification ratio of the amplifier changes in value depending on applied loads as well as the input displacement of the actuator. It is interesting to note that for all designs, if the applied forces are removed, the relationship between the input and output displacements is roughly linear. This leads to a near-constant AR for all input displacements.

5   Conclusion

In this paper, the symmetric five-bar compliant mechanical amplifier introduced in [17] was studied and a new optimized design was found. First-order FEM optimization was performed for various loading scenarios over a range of input displacements. The optimal design was found based on its combination of average amplification ratio, natural frequency, and maximum experienced stress. It was concluded that the pre-load has a significant effect on the amplification ratio. Finally, further FEA simulations on the optimal design validated the nonlinearity between the input and output displacements of the amplifier.

Acknowledgments. This research is supported by the Natural Sciences nd Engineering Research Council of Canada (NSERC) through a Discovery Grant awarded to the third author.

References

1. Ouyang, P.R., Tjiptoprodjo, R.C., Zhang, W.J., Yang, G.S.: Micro-motion Devices Technology: The State of Arts Review. Int. J. Adv. Manuf. Technol. 38(5-6), 463–478 (2007)
2. Howell, L.L.: Compliant Mechanisms. Wiley and Sons, New York (2001)
3. Timoshenko, S.P., Gere, J.M.: Theory of Elastic Stability. McGraw-Hill, New York (1961)
4. Lu, K.J., Kota, S.: Topology and Dimensional Synthesis of Compliant, Mechanisms Using Discrete Optimization. ASME J. Mech. Des. 128(5), 1080–1091 (2006)
5. Hull, P.V., Canfield, S.: Optimal Synthesis of Compliant Mechanisms, Using Subdivision and Commercial FEA. ASME J. Mech. Des. 128(2), 337–348 (2006)
6. Su, H.J., McCathy, J.M.: Synthesis of Bistable Compliant Fourbar Mechanisms using Polynomial Homotopy. ASME J. Mech. Des. 129(10), 1094–1098 (2007)
7. Kota, S., Rodgers, M.S., Hetrick, J.A.: Compliant Displacement-Multiplying Apparatus for Microelectromechanical Systems, U.S. Patent No.6,175,170 (2001)
8. King, T., Xu, W.: The Design and Characteristics of Piezomotors Using Flexure-Hinged Displacement Amplifiers. Part. Syst. Charact. 19(2), 189–197 (1996)
9. Xu, W., King, T.: Flexure Hinges for Piezoactuator Displacement Amplifiers: Flexibility, Accuracy, and Stress Considerations. Precis. Eng. 19(1), 4–10 (1996)
10. Lobontiu, N., Garcia, E.: Analytical Model of Displacement Amplification and Stiffness Optimization for a Class of Flexure-Based Compliant Mechanisms. Comput. Struct. 81(32), 2797–2810 (2003)
11. Su, X.P.S., Yang, H.S.: Design of Compliant Microleverage Mechanisms. Sens. Actuators, A 87(3), 146–156 (2001)
12. Choi, K.B., Lee, J.J., Hata, S.: A Piezo-driven Compliant Stage with Double Mechanical Amplification Mechanisms Arranged in Parallel. Sensors and Actuators A161, 173–181 (2010)
13. Mottard, P., St-Amant, Y.: Analysis of Flexural Hinge Orientation for Amplified Piezo-driven Actuators. Smart Materials and Structures 18(3), 1–9 (2009)
14. Kim, J.H., Kim, S.H., Kwak, Y.K.: Development and Optimization of 3-D Bridge-type Hinge Mechanisms. Sensors and Actuators A116, 530–538 (2004)
15. Ma, H.W., Yao, S.M., Wang, L.Q., Zhong, Z.L.: Analysis of the Displacement Amplification Ratio of Bridge-type Flexure Hinge. Sensors and Actuators A132, 730–736 (2006)
16. Ananthasuresh, G.K., Saxena, A.: On an Optimal Property of Compliant Topologies. Structural Multidisciplinary Optimization 19, 36–49 (2000)
17. Ouyang, P.R., Zhang, W.J., Gupta, M.M.: A New Compliant Mechanical Amplifier Based on Symmetric Five-Bar Topology. Journal of Mechanical Design 130(10), 104501.1–104501.5 (2008)
18. ANSYS, Inc., Ansys Mechanical APDL Programmer's Manual Release 13.0, Canonsburg, United States of America (2010)
19. Lobontiu, N., Paine, J.S.N., Garcia, E., Goldfarb, M.: Corner-Filleted Flexure Hinges. ASME J. Mech. Des. 123(3), 346–352 (2001)

Hybrid Potential Field Swarm Optimization Based Novel Targeted Drug Delivery System Using Drug Loaded Nano Carriers

Syed Hassan and Jungwon Yoon

School of Mechanical and Aerospace Engineering, Gyeongsang National University
660701 Jinju, South Korea
{hassan,jwyoon}@gnu.ac.kr

Abstract. While treating the disease using the targeted drug delivery method, the effectiveness of a drug primarily depends on the disease affected area, targeted particles and drug control release of the drug. In this paper, an optimum or near optimum real time targeted drug delivery system is proposed. Targeted path planning algorithm for ferromagnetic nano particles based on particle swarm optimization approach and artificial magnetic field concepts used as virtual MRI (magnetic resonance Imaging) is proposed to solve the obstacle free targeted drug delivery process in a 3d virtual environment. At first stage 3d path planning scheme based on attractive and repulsive artificial potential field for obstacle free path in certain blood vessels is used. Later, an optimization process for all the discovered trajectories by combining particle swarm optimization algorithm is performed to generate an optimal path. Simulation results showed that proposed algorithm has higher success rate in targeting the drugs with a faster convergence rate towards the optimal solution.

Keywords: PSO, Virtual Reality, Nano particles, Targeted drug delivery.

1   Introduction

The nano particles (NP's) are very small objects, less that 1/1,000 the width of an average human hair, which can interact with individual human cells, proteins and even single molecules. Nano particles (NP's) can also be modified in their shape, size and surface properties to remain in the bloodstream long enough to accumulate mostly in tumor tissues, which have leakier blood vessels than normal tissues. NP's are thus excellent candidates for the transport of drugs to sites of disease. [1]. Magnetic NP's have been investigated for biomedical applications for more than 30 years. In medicine they are used for several approaches such as magnetic cell separation or magnetic resonance imaging (MRI). Goya et al. [2] mentioned that the common feature of all NP based cancer therapies is the need of specific NPs for achieving the desired therapeutic effect. They emphasized that the NP function is activated using an external agent (magnetic fields, light, radiation, etc) that interacts with the NPs.

NP's can offer several advantages over more traditional drug delivery methods, including improved drug solubility, stability, and the ability to simultaneously target

C.-Y. Su, S. Rakheja, H. Liu (Eds.): ICIRA 2012, Part II, LNAI 7507, pp. 333–343, 2012.
© Springer-Verlag Berlin Heidelberg 2012

multiple different molecules to particular cell or tissue types. Kovochich et al. experimentally demonstrated the ability of nano-technological approaches to provide improved methods for activating latent HIV and provide key proof-of-principle experiments showing how novel delivery systems may enhance future HIV therapy. [3]. Jurgons et al. [4] ,in an experimental cancer model, performed targeted drug delivery and used magnetic iron oxide nano particles, bound to a chemotherapeutic agent, which were attracted to an experimental tumor in rabbits by an external magnetic field (magnetic drug targeting). Complete tumor remission is claimed to be achieved.

Wang et al. [5] commented that the power of nano-medicine, a subfield of nanotechnology that uses nano-materials for the diagnosis and treatment of diseases, stems from ability to tailor the properties of materials. They mentioned that the promise of nano-medicine is unlikely to arrive until we can selectively deliver nano-materials to particular sites of interest, with minimal accumulation in off-target regions. Von Maltzahn et al. [6] report a giant leap forward with their development of NP's that can communicate to enhance cancer targeting. Nano-materials can be directed to the tumor through both passive- and active-targeting mechanisms [7] Wang et al. presented a system comprising 'signalling' and 'receiving' modules, where the receiving module circulating in the bloodstream is directed to the tumor by a cascade triggered by the signaling module, improves the targeting effect of a nano-medicine.

Particle swarm optimization (PSO) is an artificial intelligence (AI) technique that can be used to find approximate solutions to extremely difficult or impossible numeric maximization and minimization problems. Particle Swarm Optimization (PSO) algorithm was proposed by James Kennedy and R. C. Eberhart in 1995, motivated by social behavior of organisms such as bird flocking and fish schooling. PSO algorithm is not only a tool for optimization, but also a tool for representing socio-cognition of human and artificial agents, on principles of social psychology [8]. Cancer chemotherapy is a complex treatment mode that requires balancing the benefits of treating tumors using anti-cancer drugs with the adverse toxic side-effects caused by these drugs. Some methods of computational optimization, genetic algorithms in particular, have proven to be useful in helping to strike the right balance [9]. Petrovski et al. In their study compared three algorithms - Genetic Algorithms, global best PSO, and local best PSO. The comparison was done on the problem of multi-drug cancer chemotherapy optimization. In their experiment, they showed that the PSO algorithms find the feasible region in the solution space of chemotherapeutic treatments faster than Genetic Algorithms.

Similarly Petrovski et al [10] comment that the problem of chemotherapy optimization necessitates the use of multi-objective optimization methods. The techniques based on swarm intelligence have certain features that make them applicable and effective in addressing multiple treatment objectives of cancer chemotherapy. [11] Demonstrated the adaptive capabilities of particle swarm optimization (PSO) that enables this bio-inspired meta-heuristic to carry out an efficient search for both effective and versatile chemotherapy treatments. Zhang et al. [12] proposed a new global path planning approach based on particle swarm optimization (PSO) for a mobile robot in a static environment. Simulation results were provided to verify the effectiveness and practicability of this approach.

Our prior work has focused on combined genetic algorithm (CGA) and ant colony algorithm (ACO) for path planning simulations in virtual environment frameworks [13-15]. However, when performing simulation for medical engineering a real time environment is required to perform the simulation process, especially in case of targeted drug delivery system the highest priority of the researchers is to well target the doze towards the affected cell. Hence, an urge for improvement in optimal path planning algorithm utilizing magnetic potential field scheme as virtual MRI (magnetic resonance Imaging) concept was required. A process that can adequately perform quick optimization in complex swarms to get real time path deflection result.

In response to the above problem, this paper proposes distinct intelligent targeted drug delivery method based on the advantages of artificial potential field (APF) and particle swarm optimization (PSO) combined to find the optimal drug delivery path in a 3d virtual environment. The proposed method supports the PSO swarm population directing towards the goal using the attractive forces, whereas, to avoid collision of NP's with obstacles the artificial magnetic repulsive forces are used. Evaluation between the proposed nano particle swarm optimization algorithm (NAPSO) and existing traditional PSO in a similar 3d environment showed a higher performance in terms of convergence rate and time for the proposed approach.

2   Preparation and Characterization of Nano-carriers

The drug loaded NP's used in this study were prepared using biopolymer method in spherical shape followed by CAD modeling of the particles. In order to investigate the morphology of the prepared NPs, AFM observations were conducted. Fig. 1(a) and 1(b) shows typical non-contact AFM images of the P(3HV-co- 4HB)-b–mPEG NPs, respectively. The AFM images show that the NPs formed as a result of solvent evaporation were discrete amorphous shaped and smooth in surface morphology, in the range with an average 100 to 200 nm in the diameter. Using the AFM (Atomic force Microscopy) images, CAD models for the nano particles were developed with similar physical appearance to perform studies in virtual environment as shown in fig. 2 (spherical x particle).

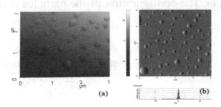

(a)   (b)

Fig. 1. Morphology of the copolymer NPs, AFM images of P(3HV-co- 4HB)-b–mPEG with a scan size of 4µm x 4µm

3   Artificial Potential Field

Artificial potential field [14] is a path planning technique based on obstacles as repelling force sources, and goals as attracting force sources. Potential field approach has been successfully applied to various problems to find an obstacle free path [15]. An object is driven by the accumulation of the two forces; the artificial attractive and repulsive forces, virtual MRI (Magnetic Resonance Imagining) technology scheme was used for attractive and repulsive force generation in virtual environment as shown in fig. 2. In 2(a), the blue magnet rays having high repulsive forces for the particle whereas, in 2(b) the white magnets have medium attractive forces to signal and attract particles toward the destination. This method is also known as local path planning. The white magnets played an important role in signaling (by attracting) the particles towards the final position. The blue labeled magnets contrarily worked as artificial repulsive forces (an obstacle) to push the particles away from undesired paths.

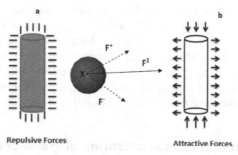

Repulsive Forces   Attractive Forces

Fig. 2. F- is a repulsive force applied to the particle "x" while F+ is an attractive force towards the destination (a) The blue magnet rays having high repulsive forces for the particle (b) The white magnets having medium attractive forces to signal and attract particles

Targeted drug delivery is a process to find a 3d trajectory for the swarm of NP's from its initial position to the final position. Given a 3d environment, each particle is defined in a plane by geometrical shapes and an origin (O) representing the center of the particle. The bounding box technology is used to draw bounding boxes around the NP's to highlight the boundary of the particle as shown in fig. 3. The positions of a particle and its bounding box in a frame O_1 with respect to the reference frame O_0 can be represented as the transformed points of particles vertex using a 3d homogenous transformation matrix (1). The configuration of the particles is represented by q = [dxi dyi dzi θi].

$$
\begin{bmatrix}
cos\theta_i cos\varphi_i & cos\theta_i sin\varphi_i sin\psi_i - sin\theta_i cos\psi_i & cos\theta_i sin\varphi_i cos\psi_i + sin\theta_i sin\psi_i & d_{xi} \\
sin\theta_i cos\varphi_i & sin\theta_i sin\varphi_i sin\psi_i + cos\theta_i cos\psi_i & sin\theta_i sin\varphi_i cos\psi_i - cos\theta_i sin\psi_i & d_{yi} \\
-sin\varphi_i & cos\varphi_i sin\psi_i & cos\varphi_i cos\psi_i & d_{zi} \\
0 & 0 & 0 & 1
\end{bmatrix}
\tag{1}
$$

Where, d_{xi}, d_{yi}, d_{zi} is translation along the x-axis, y-axis and z-axis of the workspace coordinate.

Considering the general laws of potential field, in our virtual environment the particles from its start position to the final position moves with an attractive force, this attractive force pulls the particles to its final position. In case the path is blocked by an obstacle; each obstacle has its own repulsive force that repels the particle from the obstacle avoiding collision of particle and obstacle. As the particle reaches its final position from initial to final a 3d trajectory is formed.

The attractive and repulsive forces are represented as:

If $\rho(\text{oi(q)}) \leq \rho_0$

$$F_{rep}(q) = -\eta \left[\frac{1}{\rho(\text{oi(q)})} - \frac{1}{\rho_0} \right] \delta \tag{2}$$

$$\delta = \frac{1}{\rho^2(o_i(q))} \nabla \rho(o_i(q))$$

$$If \rho(o_i(q)) > \rho_0$$

$$F_{rep}(q) = 0$$

$$If \left| o_i(q) - o_i(q_f) \right| \leq d$$

$$F_{att} = -\zeta (o_i(q) - o_i(q_f)) \tag{3}$$

$$If \left| o_i(q) - o_i(q_f) \right| > d$$

$$F_{att} = -d\zeta \frac{(o_i(q) - o_i(q_f))}{|o_i(q) - o_i(q_f)|} \tag{4}$$

Where q_f is final configuration of a particle at its final position, d is evaluation value of distance from the current position to the final position, ζ is scale factor, F_{att} is attractive forces, q is configuration of the particles, F_{rep} is repulsive forces, ρ_0 is repulsive force radius, $o_i(q)$ is point on the workspace, ηi is scale factor, I is index of the ith particle. The repulsive force has a provisional value $\rho(o_i(q))$, which is the distance from the center of a particle to the center of an obstacle. The summation of the attractive and repulsive forces gives the direction for movement as a normalized vector as follows:

q = [qx , qy, qz θ]

$$\vec{f} = \Delta q \frac{F_{att} + F_{rep}}{||F_{att} + F_{rep}||} S \tag{5}$$

Where q is coordinates of the NP's, force applied to move the particle, S is step size between path points. This 3d path planning process based on 3d potential field method is further assisted by the PSO for optimization process in finding optimal path. Within the context of path planning via APF, the avoidance of local minima has been addressed in many different ways; in particular, dynamic search characteristics are employed to avoid local minima by various researchers. One of the finest techniques having swarm behavior was proposed by researchers [16-17-18].

In potential field scheme only valid path is planned and it is not considered as optimal as in an environment there can be many paths from initial to final position. Therefore, in order to deal with this scenario swarm optimization as suggested by many scientists [4-6] is opted to perform optimization among all available valid paths resultant by applying potential field concepts.

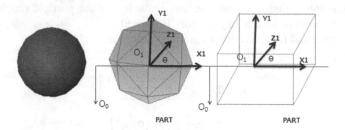

Fig. 3. The orientation & configuration of a drug loaded particles q = [d_{xi} d_{yi} d_{zi} Θ_i] and the bounding box calculation

4   Particle Swarm Optimization

PSO algorithm was introduced by Kennedy and Eberhart in 1995 [19]. Since then, PSO algorithm has been successfully applied to many optimization problems, such as learning of artificial neural networks (ANN) model predictive control [20]. The traditional PSO algorithm [10] comes from the simulation of the social behavior of the birds seeking for food. The best strategy for one bird to reach the destination is to pursue the bird that is nearest to the food. The solutions of the optimization problems are viewed as the birds which are called particles. The optimization process of the problems is regarded as the progressive paths of the particles seeking for the food. Each particle has a fitness computed by the fitness function.

The particle direction and distance of each particle are subject to its velocity. All the particles are pursuing the best particle owning the optimum fitness until the optimal or near-optimal solutions are obtained. The particles are commenced with stochastic initializations and the optimal or near-optimal solutions are generated by iterative computations. Each particle renews its own solution based upon two best solutions in each computation time step, i.e. the current individual best solution searched by it and the global best solution searched by the particle colonies, which are represented as **pbest** and **gbest**, respectively. To improve the computation efficiency, a portion of the whole particles are selected for comparison and the global best solution can be replaced by the local best solution if the population size of the particles is too large. For multivariable optimization problems, the best solutions **pbest** and **gbest** will be substituted with the vectors **pbest** and **gbest** respectively as shown in fig 4. The next velocity vector and solution vector of each particle are updated according to formulae (4) and (5) [19] after the two current best solution vectors are calculated.

$$\mathbf{V}_i^{k+1} = w\mathbf{V}_i^k + c_i(\boldsymbol{pbest}_i - s_i^k) + c_i(\boldsymbol{gbest} - s_i^k) \tag{6}$$

$$\mathbf{w} = \mathbf{w}Max - [(\mathbf{w}Max - \mathbf{w}Min)\,\text{Iter}]/Max\text{Iter} \tag{7}$$

$$s_i^{k+1} = s_i^k + \mathbf{V}_i^{k+1} \tag{8}$$

Where, $\mathbf{v}_i^k$ is velocity of agent i at iteration k, w is weighting function, c_i is coefficient of weighting factor such that $c_1 \in [0, 1]$ and $c_2 \in [1, 2]$, s_i^k is current position of agent i at iteration k, ***pbest***$_i$ is the current optimal solution of the particle i, ***gbest***$_i$ is global optimal solution of the group, wMax is initial weight, wMin is final weight, MaxIter is maximum iteration and iter is current iteration number. APF method [17] has the particular characteristics, such as the collision avoidance and attraction towards goal, which can enhance the diversity of the particles and actuate the particles to move out from the local near-optimal solutions. Therefore, the traditional PSO algorithm can be improved and be modified using APF planner support to meet the applied demands of the complex optimization problems. The adverse situations are considered to be lowered after the APF method is combined with the traditional PSO algorithm.

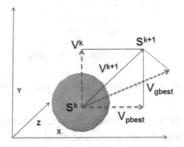

Fig. 4. Nano particles modifying the searching point in targeted delivery mode using PSO

5   Proposed Hybrid Path Planning Algorithm

Our proposed approach Nano Artificial potential field particle swarm optimization (NAPSO), which is a hybrid algorithm of artificial potential field and PSO [15], the premature convergence of the traditional PSO algorithm, is undermined and the convergence rate is also accelerated. Furthermore, the performance to accomplish the global optimization is also improved with subject to the optimization method. First, the principal drug delivery process constraints are specified and the optimization model of virtual blood vessels taking these constraints into account is presented. The APF path planner initially investigates and optimizes the magnetic ratio of attractive and repulsive forces presented in eq (2-4) to generate obstacle free path. Secondly, the principles of the traditional PSO algorithm forming the swarm and performing the optimization of path are outlined.

The artificial potential field (AFP) algorithm is implemented as primary path planning algorithm that generates a path from initial to final position. Applying APF algorithm can result in more than one path as a solution. Therefore, the APF path planning algorithm is combined with particle swarm optimization (PSO) technology to derive the optimal solution. The flowchart of the proposed algorithm is shown in fig 5. In particle swarm optimization the drug loaded virtual NP's were considered as swarm particles and their moving velocity was based on the attractive and repulsive forces generated by the particles and obstacles in the environment.

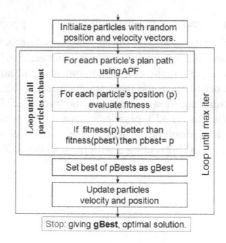

Fig. 5. Flow chart of NAPSO finding optimal path in virtual environment

The proposed algorithm performs obstacle free path planning initially by loading the 3d CAD models of NP's with their initial and final position, where all the NP's are placed on the starting point and random velocity (V_i^k) is initialized for every particle. In adhesion, velocity update rule was followed based on equation 6. When the particle reaches the final position its *gbest* is calculated and a list of path value is maintained for each particle. The process starts by placing the particles on their initial position. The movement of the particles is affected by $\overrightarrow{F_V}$ as shown in Eq. 9, which is accumulation of two types of forces, the attractive forces F_{att} and the repulsive forces F_{rep}.

$$\overrightarrow{F_V} = \Delta t \frac{F_{att} + F_{rep}}{\|F_{att} + F_{rep}\|} S \tag{9}$$

Hence, proposed algorithm is derived from equation (6) and (7) is presented as:

$$F_{V_i}^{k+1} = wF_{V_i}^{k} + c_1 (\textbf{\textit{pbest}}_i - s_i^k) + c_2 (\textbf{\textit{gbest}} - s_i^k) \tag{10}$$

$$s_i^{k+1} = s_i^k + F_{Vi}^{k+1} \tag{11}$$

$$F(i) = \Sigma i^{k+1} {}^{\wedge} c_i \tag{12}$$

Where i is number of total particles and F(i) is the fitness function which takes real numbers. The attractive force pulls the NP's towards its final position while the repulsive force repels the NP's from a collision with the obstacles. If the NP's reaches the final position the *gbest* of the path is reported as optimal solution. If the *pbest* of the path is greater than the previous *pbest*, the new *pbest* value is ignored. The loop mechanism in traditional PSO for updating *gbest* and *pbest* were used. When numbers of max iterations are performed the *gbest* is considered as shortest and optimal path.

6   Results and Discussion

The simulator (targeted drug delivery Path Planner) is based on two aspects first the APF based obstacle free path generating of the NP's and second optimizing the obstacle free path. The virtual targeted drug delivery path planner system reported in this paper as shown in Fig. 6(a) the complete view of virtual blood vessel and heart model and (b) virtual blood vessel model with particle swarm flow inside, utilizes a pc based application and general-purpose hardware for interaction. The graphical interface was designed in C++ to let the user interact with the virtual environment. The presented experiment was done using the C++ platform and Open Inventor for 3d virtual environment. A single computer with a Pentium (2.14 GHz-D'Core) CPU and 2 GB ram is used to run the simulations NP's and blood vessels with a total weight of 644627 faces. The computed workspace was (4.0x4.0x4.0 cm) environment as it can be seen in fig. 6. Once the optimal path for the single NP is obtained the swarm algorithm builds the swarm and searched for the optimal path as shown in fig. 6(b).

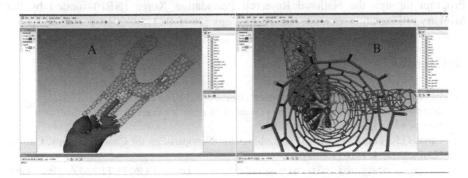

Fig. 6. The virtual targeted drug delivery path planner system

Two different experiments were performed with similar parameters. In the first environment normal flow blood vessels were considered with a blood flow velocity with no blockage in the vessels. In second experiment the velocity parameter was lowered down for the blood flow imitating blockage in the blood vessels caused due to blood clots present inside vessel. It was observed that the environment in the second environment became more complex and ideal for the swarm searching because of slow velocity and complex obstacle presence (blood clot). The comparative experiment and its convergence result are detailed in table 1.

Table 1. Results comparison between two experiments

Experiment	Fitness value	Success rate	CPU Time	Targeted particles
A normal flow	0.881	100%	1200 min	12 NP's
B obstacle flow	0.512	100%	2600 min	24 NP's

7   Conclusion

In this paper, a novel targeted drug delivery path planning optimization framework is developed and tested that allows operators to determine an optimal or near optimal path planning solution for targeted drug delivery towards the affected cells. The proposed algorithm is based on improved particle swarm optimization using potential field concepts for path planning. For comparison with existing traditional PSO, the path planning parameters were measured in terms of convergence rate and computation time. The results obtained from the virtual simulation demonstrated that the proposed algorithm converges faster to the optimal or near optimal path having low cost and consumes less computation Our proposed future work will consist of utilizing the path trajectory results as guidance to real-time MRI based Invivo targeted drug delivery process.

Acknowledgment. This work was supported by ReCAPT, Priority Research Centers Program through the National Research Foundation Korea (NRF) funded by the Ministry of Education, Science and Technology (2011-00313832010-0029690).

References

1. http://blogs.scientificamerican.com/guest-blog/2011/07/08/learning-from-insect-swarms-smart-cancer-targeting (last cited January 2012)
2. Goya, G.F., Grazú, V., Ibarra, M.R.: Magnetic Nanoparticles for Cancer Therapy. Current Nanoscience 4, 1–16 (2008)
3. http://www.ncbi.nlm.nih.gov/pmc/articles/PMC3071729/ (last cited January 2012)
4. Jurgons, R., Seliger, C., Hilpert, A., Trahm, L., Odenbach, S., Alexiou, C.: Drug loaded magnetic nanoparticles for cancer therapy. Journal of Physics: Condensed Matter 18(38) (September 2006)
5. Wang, Y., Brown, P., Xia, Y.: Swarming towards the target. Nature Materials 10 (July 2011)
6. von Maltzahn, G., et al.: Nature Mater. 10, 545–552 (2011)
7. Petros, R.A., DeSimone, J.M.: Nature Rev. Drug Discov. 9, 615–627 (2010)
8. http://www.cis.syr.edu/~mohan/pso/ (last cited January 2012)
9. Petrovski, A., Sudha, B., McCall, J.: Optimising Cancer Chemotherapy Using Particle Swarm Optimisation and Genetic Algorithms. In: Yao, X., Burke, E.K., Lozano, J.A., Smith, J., Merelo-Guervós, J.J., Bullinaria, J.A., Rowe, J.E., Tiňo, P., Kabán, A., Schwefel, H.-P. (eds.) PPSN VIII. LNCS, vol. 3242, pp. 633–641. Springer, Heidelberg (2004)
10. http://www.aisb.org.uk/convention/aisb09/proceedings/evolutionary/files/petrovskia.pdf
11. Alksne, J.F., Fingerhut, A., Rand, R.: Magnetically controlled metallic thrombosis of intracranial aneurysms Surgery 60, 212–218 (1966)

12. Zhang, Q., Li, S.: A global path planning approach based on particle swarm optimization for a mobile robot. In: Proceedings of the 7th WSEAS International Conference on Robotics, Control & Manufacturing Technology, ROCOM 2007 (2007)
13. Hassan, S., Yoon, J.: Haptic based optimized path planning approach to virtual maintenance assembly/ disassembly (MAD). In (IROS) IEEE/RSJ International Conference on Intelligent Robots and Systems, pp. 1310–1315 (2010), doi:10.1109/IROS.2010.5653600
14. Hassan, S., Yoon, J.: Virtual maintenance system with a two-staged ant colony optimization algorithm. In: IEEE International Conference on Robotics and Automation, ICRA 2011, pp. 931–936 (2011)
15. Christiand, Yoon, J.: Assembly simulations in virtual environments with optimized haptic path and sequence. Robotics and Computer-Integrated Manufacturing 27(2), 306–317 (2011)
16. Abdel Wahid, M.H.M., McInnes Colin, R.: Wall following to escape local minima for swarms of agents using internal states and emergent behavior. In: International Conference of Computational Intelligence and Intelligent Systems, ICCIIS (2008)
17. Zou, X.-Y., Zhu, J.: Virtual local target method for avoiding local minimum in potential field based robot navigation. Journal of Zhejiang University - Science A (2003)
18. Liu, C., Marcelo, A., Hariharan, K., Ser, Y.L.: Virtual Obstacle Concept for Local-minimum-recovery in Potentialfield Based Navigation. In: Proceedings of the 2000 IEEE International Conference on Robotics & Automation (2000)
19. Kennedy, J., Eberhart, R.: Particle swarm optimization. In: Proceedings of the IEEE International Conference on Neural Networks, pp. 1942–1948 (1995)

The CSUF Unmanned Utility Ground Robotic Vehicle

Jidong Huang and Michael Yeh

California State University Fullerton, Fullerton, California, USA

Abstract. The goal for the California State University, Fullerton (CSUF) Unmanned Utility Ground Robotic Vehicle (UUGRV) project is to create a fully autonomous multi-functional modular robotic platform to experiment various possible applications in the area of ground based robotics. To achieve full automation in both indoor and outdoor environment, the robot is equipped with Differential Global Positioning System, Inertial Measurement Unit, Laser Measurement Scanner, and a X-box Kinect for indoor application. The robot's mechanical design features two independently driven wheels and pivoting casters to achieve differential drive. Speed reduction is achieved by using chain drives to allow flexibility in gear ratio for different applications. Currently, the robot is being constructed as an autonomous lawn mower and has won the 2012 ION (Institute of Navigation) robotic lawn mower competition in the static category. In the future, more hardware and software for different applications will be developed on this platform.

Keywords: Ground Robot, Unmanned Vehicle, Autonomous Robot, Robot Navigation.

1 Introduction

Today, robots are assigned to perform many different tasks that are dangerous or repetitive to human beings. There are large amounts of robots used in factory assembly line and military applications. However, a lot more possible robotic applications for daily use are yet to be discovered. With the Unmanned Utility Ground Robot Vehicle (UUGRV) at California State University, Fullerton (CSUF), students can experiment and design many applications for the robot to provide daily convenience. Currently the robot is being designed as an autonomous lawn mower as shown in figure 1; therefore this paper will focus the robot's design as a lawn mower.

Our team has studied works from universities with successful autonomous lawn mower, such as Ohio University, Case Western Reserve University and Wright State University [1][2][3][4]. The main difference between our design and designs by other universities is that our robot is designed to have a wide range of applications with add-on modules. The figures below show some other application that we are planning to develop: a robotic street cleaner and a robotic personal transport for hospital use.

This Paper is divided into five sections, with each section describing the subsystems or features of the robot. Section two gives an overview on the robot's design which includes mechanical design, electric machine and electronic integration.

C.-Y. Su, S. Rakheja, H. Liu (Eds.): ICIRA 2012, Part II, LNAI 7507, pp. 344–353, 2012.

Section three describes the robot's software algorithms, mainly focusing on navigation, path planning and obstacle detection and avoidance algorithms. Section four brings discussions regarding the results of testing the robot. The conclusion is given in section five which summarizes our work and discusses future improvements and concepts.

Fig. 1. CSUF UUGRV (as lawn mower)

Fig. 2. Possible applications for UUGRV (lawn mower, street cleaner and personal carrier)

2   Design Overview

2.1   Hardware Overview

As shown in figure 3, the CSUF UUGRV features a differential drive system to ensure its dexterity in a wide range of applications. The robot consists of two drive motors to independently drive two wheels through a series of sprockets and chains to achieve gear reduction. The control of these two drive motors are done through the use of a Roboteq HDC2450 Controller with encoder feedback [5].

By using chains, as shown in figure 4, the reduction ratio can be adjusted easily to change the driving characteristic of the robot. As a lawn mower, the robot has a 21:1 ratio between the motor and wheel to achieve precise control over the wheel. In addition, encoders on the wheel allow the robot to know the current position on each wheel for precision speed control. The blade module on the robot to cut grass is an off-the-shelf electric motor-and-blade assembly from a battery powered push mower; and it is controlled by a 24v speed controller.

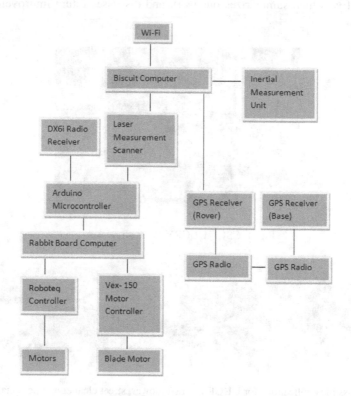

Fig. 3. Electronic hardware block diagram

Fig. 4. Reduction gear and driver motor

To control these motor controllers, we are using a versatile microcontroller called BL4S200 Rabbit board [6]. The rabbit board consists of 32 digital interfaces which can be used for serial interface; or pulse width signal outputs. The rabbit board also receives signals from a radio controlled receiver which changes the inputs and output of the microcontroller. The microcontroller is then connected to a single-board biscuit computer via serial port. The single-board biscuit computer receives outputs from the sensors and sends out command signals to the microcontroller.

2.2   Safety

Due to the weight and power of the robot, safety is one of our main design concerns. There are three ways to trigger emergency stop to the robot during a hazardous event. Firstly, the software on the computer can be interrupted by sending stop command to motion control through Wi-Fi using a remote laptop. Secondly, a radio transmitter can send out a logic-level signal to the microcontroller for issuing stop command to the motor controllers. Lastly, a mushroom switch on the top of the robot serves as a circuit breaker to all the motors, once pressed, all circuits with direct connection to the motor will be opened from their power supplies.

3   Software Design

The robot consists of multiple software algorithms to perform various tasks. The three main functions included in our software design are: Navigation, Path Planning, and Obstacle Avoidance, which are all executed on the biscuit computer. The biscuit computer integrates the data from several sensors and takes appropriate action in appropriate condition. As shown in figure 5, the autonomous operation of the robot primarily relies on the use of three sensors, GPS, Inertial Measurement Unit (IMU) and Laser Measurement Scanner (LMS).

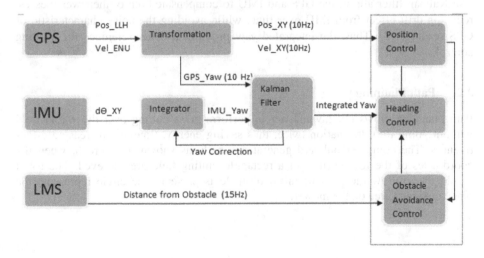

Fig. 5. Sensor integration block diagram

3.1   Navigation

GPS. The GPS outputs position and velocity data in geographical frame, which our computer transforms and maps into a local frame in terms of X and Y coordinates on the field. The heading (yaw) of the robot can be derived from position and velocity in the local frame in terms of degrees. These position and velocity data are then taken into consideration by the position control algorithm to ensure the robot is inside the field boundary and on track per path planning requirements. The GPS set we used on the robot are manufactured by Navcom Technology, a John-deere company [7]. It is able to provide centimeter-level positioning accuracy under the Real-Time Kinematic (RTK) mode.

IMU. The IMU outputs data in the form of angular velocity. Through integration, the heading of the robot can be obtained from the IMU at a high rate of 76 Hz. However, there are two major disadvantages when a system uses IMU alone for navigation. First, the initial heading of the mower has to be known precisely in order to obtain an accurate heading data for successive accumulations in the local frame. For instance, if the initial heading is not parallel to the Y axis, the IMU will assume the wrong heading as zero degree, which will negatively affect the navigation algorithm due to this misalignment error. Second, the IMU yaw is obtained from cumulated yaw rate, thus errors in the yaw reading will cumulate over time, which will also provide the mower with wrong heading information.

Kalman Filter. To reduce these negative effects, a Kalman filter is used to take the readings from IMU and combine it with the GPS heading to form an integrated yaw. The Kalman filter allows the GPS and IMU to compensate both of their weaknesses, reducing drift effect from IMU over time, while avoiding the noisy characteristic of GPS readings [8]. Thus, the integrated yaw provides a better reference for heading control.

3.2   Path Planning

Path planning allows our lawnmower to perform grass cutting over the whole field without going to a destination twice, thus saving energy, time and increasing effectiveness. The computer onboard generates a path, as shown in figure 6, when the coordinates of the four corners of a rectangle cutting field are surveyed. The robot would then follow the path when no obstacle is present. The circle represents the blade coverage area on the mower.

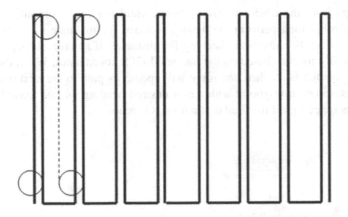

Fig. 6. Path generated after surveying the 4 corners of a rectangle field

3.3   Obstacle Avoidance

To detect and avoid obstacles, a Laser Measurement Scanner is used on the robot [9]. When an obstacle is detected, the predefined path will be modified based on the GPS coordinates at the moment the robot detects the obstacle. The robot will then perform a three step move to navigate away from the obstacle, drive past the obstacle from the side and return to designated path as shown below in figure 7. The current obstacle algorithm is done by adding a few additional motion command based on the GPS coordinates received during an event of obstacle detection. This method is dynamic since obstacle avoidance can be achieved without knowing the location of the obstacle. However, it is not intelligent since the robot does not avoid obstacle based on its shape and size, so the dimension of the obstacle has to be known in order to perform obstacle avoidance successfully.

Fig. 7. Three step obstacle avoidance

3.4   Navigation Algorithm

The figure below shows the navigation software process when the robot is moving at an outdoor environment. During initialization, the robot calibrates IMU and waits for valid readings from the LMS and GPS. When valid readings from all sensors are obtained, the robot then perform the heading control for maintaining on the predefined path, while at the same time checking for obstacles. If an obstacle is present, the robot will modify its path based on the last valid GPS coordinates. When the current destination waypoint is reached, the robot will update its path to the next one. In that case, a new destination waypoint with a new desired heading will be loaded; and the entire process repeats until the final destination is reached.

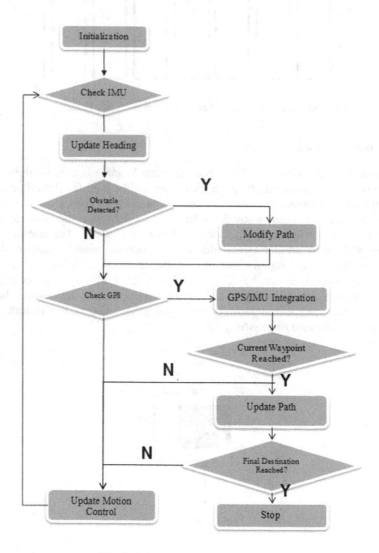

Fig. 8. Outdoor navigation algorithm

4   Results

The CSUF UUGRV has been tested for its robotic functions at different occasions, for both indoor and outdoor. The following shows the outdoor testing result as an autonomous lawnmower from the 9th Institution of Navigation (ION) Robotic Lawn-mower Competition (RLC) held in June 2012 at Dayton, Ohio [10].

Fig. 9. The photograph of running CSUF UUGRV from 2012 ION RLC

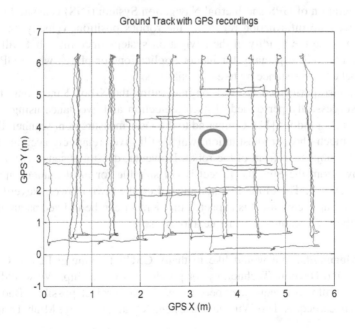

Fig. 10. Ground Track from GPS data during the competition run

Shown in figure 10 is the ground track recorded by the GPS onboard the robot for the competition run. The blue lines represent the path taken by the robot; and the red circle represents the approximate location of the obstacle. There is a two-meter buffer zone outside of the cutting zone to allow some error tolerance. As seen in the graph, the mower performed consistently throughout the entire run within the given boarder. The centimeter-level positioning accuracy from Differential GPS has given the robot very precise positioning information to follow its desired path. The obstacle avoidance maneuver also appeared consistent every time the robot saw the obstacle, although the avoidance maneuver appeared on the bottom left of the graph is the result of the laser scanner detecting an object from the ground. For readers who are interested, please refer to http://www.youtube.com/watch?v=p2OMPVi-e2o&feature=plcp

5   Conclusion

This project is still at its early state since we have now only developed and tested our lawnmower module. However, through this module, we have successfully integrated multiple sensors on board the robot to achieve autonomous guidance, path planning and obstacle avoidance capabilities with respectable precision.

5.1   Future Development

A tight integration of GPS and Inertial Navigation System (INS) is desired for obtaining more accurate information regarding the robot's position, velocity and heading. This will increase the rigidity of the navigation system since the robot will decrease its reliance on GPS, especially for indoor applications or places where GPS signals may be blocked, for instance by trees or buildings.

We have also performed research on integrating the X-box Kinect onto the robot; and have successfully performed obstacle detection and avoidance using Kinect for running the robot indoor [11]. Compared to the laser measurement scanner, the X-box Kinect is a much cheaper substitution, which still gives relatively accurate depth information for objects in front of the robot. However, due to its sensitivity to ambient infrared rays from the Sun, the Kinect is not suitable for most outdoor applications during the daytime. Therefore, it is not utilized on the lawn mower. Nevertheless, for indoor robotic applications, it is expected that Kinect can be utilized as an alternative choice for the laser scanner to generate a local map.

Acknowledgements. We would like to thank CSUF Intramural Funds, CSUF ASI IRA Funds, and Navcom Technology for providing sponsorship. We would also like to thank the following team members to make this project possible: Bao Nguyen, Martin Dean Larocque, Tuo Wu, Jianzhi Chen, Riyad El-Laithy, Minh Tran, and Vy Phung.

References

1. Bates, D., Van Grass, F.: GPS-Guided Autonomous Lawnmower with Scanning Laser Obstacle Detection. In: Proceedings of ION GNSS 2006, Fort Worth, TX (September 2006)
2. Baine, N.A., Rattan, K.S., Gallagher, J., Thomas, S.: Design and Implementation of a Robotic lawnmower. In: Proceedings of ION GNSS 2007, Fort Worth, TX (September 2007)
3. Snow, H.H., Hughes, B.E., Smith, A.D., Hall, J.R., Kreinar, E.J., Quinn, R.D., Green, J.M.: CWRU Cutter IV: Case Western Reserve University's Autonomous Lawn Mower Design and Performance Review. In: Proceedings of ION GNSS 2011, Portland, OR (September 2011)
4. Huang, J., Yeh, M.: The CSUF Robotic Lawnmower: Lessons Learned from Modifying a Riding Lawn mower. In: Proceedings of ION ITM 2012, Newport Beach, CA (January 2012)
5. Roboteq, "HDC2450 User Manual", http://www.roboteq.com
6. Digi International Inc, "BL4S200 Product Manual", http://www.digi.com
7. NavCom Technology, "SF-3050 GNSS Product User Guide", http://www.navcomtech.com/
8. Grewal, M.S., Weill, L.R., Andrews, A.P.: Global Positioning System, Inertial navigation, and Integration, 2nd edn. Wiley Interscience (2007)
9. SICK USA, "Quick Manual for LMS communication setup", http://www.sick.com
10. Institute of Navigation, ION Robotic Lawnmower Competition, http://www.automow.com
11. El-Laithy, R., Huang, J., Yeh, M.: Study on the Use of Microsoft Kinect for Robotics Applications. In: Proceedings of IEEE/ION PLANS 2012, Myrtle Beach, SC (April 2012)

Guaranteed Mobile Robot Tracking Using Robust Interval Constraint Propagation

Marco Langerwisch and Bernardo Wagner

Leibniz Universität Hannover, Real Time Systems Group (RTS),
Appelstr. 9A, D-30167 Hannover, Germany
{langerwisch,wagner}@rts.uni-hannover.de

Abstract. The paper presents an approach for localizing a mobile robot in a feature-based map using a 2D laser rangefinder and wheel odometry. As the presented approach is based on set membership methods, the localization result consists of sets instead of points, and is guaranteed to contain the true robot position as long as the sensor errors are absolutely bounded and a maximum number of measurement outliers can be assumed. It is able to cope with a multitude of measurement per time step compared to previous approaches. Moreover, the approach is capable of identifying and marking outlier points in the laser range scan. A real world experiment, where a mobile robot is moving in a structured indoor environment with previously unmapped static and dynamic obstacles shows the feasibility of the approach. It is shown that the true robot pose is always included in the solution set, which is computed in real time.

Keywords: Mobile robot localization, tracking, set membership, constraint propagation, outlier detection.

1 Introduction

To localize a mobile robot, a combination of proprioceptive and exteroceptive sensors can be used. Proprioceptive sensors, like wheel odometry or gyrometers, induce cumulative errors when estimating the robot pose. Therefore, exteroceptive sensors, like radar or laser rangefinders, can be used to correct and improve the estimation, when a map of the environment is known.

Sensor data are always influenced by measurement errors, resulting from imprecision on the hardware layer and possible occlusions or dynamic objects in the environment. This results in an uncertain measurement of the real value to be measured. Algorithms trying to localize a mobile robot in a map have to model this induced uncertainty. When the error around the actual value can be assumed to be absolutely bounded, an attractive alternative class of methods can be applied: the bounded-error, or set-membership approaches [1][2]. As the calculation is done with absolute and guaranteed values, the result is also guaranteed and consistent.

Conventional approaches for modelling the uncertainty in sensor measurements handle the measurement as a stochastic distribution around the actual

C.-Y. Su, S. Rakheja, H. Liu (Eds.): ICIRA 2012, Part II, LNAI 7507, pp. 354–365, 2012.

value, usually normally distributed. See the sensor beam model in [3] for example. Well-known solutions based on the (Extended) Kalman Filter [4] have very few memory and runtime requirements. They apply linearizations in case of non-linear system equations and assume the sensor noise to be Gaussian. This can lead to divergence in the localization result. Moreover, these approaches are not capable of calculating with multiple localization hypotheses, and result in one (possibly divergent) single distribution. Particle filtering techniques like the Monte Carlo Localization [5] overcome these drawbacks by avoiding linearization and by calculating with multiple solutions (samples) in parallel. The outcome of each localization step is the single position estimate with the highest probability, or a weighted mean over all samples (or a subset), without any measure on the quality of the result. There is no guarantee that this estimate is correct or at least near the true position. The results of current set membership approaches are guaranteed in that way, that the true position is, by all means, included in the computed sets.

When possible sets are aligned along the axes of a coordinate system, the combined sets result in boxes [6]. Various approaches deal with the localization of mobile robots based on sensor uncertainty modelling with sets and boxes. In [7] the authors use algorithms called SIVIA and IMAGESP [8] to localize a mobile outdoor vehicle. The results are position estimates that are more pessimistic than the results of an applied particle filter, but are, in contrast to the latter, guaranteed to contain the true position during the whole test run.

To localize a mobile robot in a known (feature-based) map, Seignez et al. [9] use SIVIA applied to ultrasonic sensor measurements. Their approach is robust to a certain number of outliers, but deals with only a small number of measurements (ten) at each time step. [10] applies a version of SIVIA based on constraint propagation that is robust against outliers, called RSIVIA, to the localization of an underwater robot equipped with a sonar sensor. The sonar sensor rotates and measures one distance value per time step. Both approaches were not tested explicitly in case of static or dynamic obstacles in the environment.

In this paper, we present an approach for mobile robot tracking (localization) in a known (structured) indoor environment using wheel odometry and a rotating laser rangefinder. The main contribution of our work is to apply RSIVIA based on constraint propagation when a feature-based map of the environment is available, and a rotating laser rangefinder with a multitude of measurements per time step is used. The increase in the number of measurements compared to existing approaches results in a potentially more segmented solution space, representing a guaranteed position estimation set. To overcome a possibly heavily segmented solution space, we suggest several filters for use in a post-processing step. Finally, our approach is capable of detecting and marking outliers in the laser rangefinder scan in real time. A real world experiment will show the applicability in structured environments with previously unmapped static and dynamic obstacles.

The paper is organized as follows. The following chapter will introduce the concept of intervals and some basic notions. In Sec. 3, the applied models are explained. The implementation of prediction and correction steps, and the main localization algorithm are introduced in Sec. 4. Experimental results will be presented in Sec. 5. This paper ends with a conclusion and an outlook on future work.

2   Interval Analysis

In this section, we will briefly recapitulate the basics of interval analysis and some techniques based on it and used in this paper.

2.1   Basic Notions

A closed and connected subset of $\mathbb{R}$ is an interval

$$[x] = [x^-, x^+] = \{x \in \mathbb{R} | x^- \leq x \leq x^+\}. \tag{1}$$

The width of an interval is $w([x]) = x^+ - x^-$. A scalar $a \in \mathbb{R}$ can be seen as point interval $[a] = [a, a]$. The set of all intervals is denoted as $\mathbb{IR}$. A box $[\mathbf{x}] \in \mathbb{IR}^n$ is the cartesian product of n intervals: $[\mathbf{x}] = [x_1] \times [x_2] \times \ldots \times [x_n]$. The width of this box is $w([\mathbf{x}]) = \max_{1 \leq i \leq n} w([x_i])$.

As the image of an interval by a function is not necessarily again an interval, the notion of inclusion function has been introduced. The interval function $[\mathbf{f}] : \mathbb{IR}^n \to \mathbb{IR}^m$ for a real-valued function $\mathbf{f} : \mathbb{R}^n \to \mathbb{R}^m$ is an inclusion function for $\mathbf{f}$ if $\mathbf{f}([\mathbf{x}]) \subset [\mathbf{f}]([\mathbf{x}]), \forall [\mathbf{x}] \in \mathbb{IR}^n$. Basic elementary arithmetic operations like $+$, $-$, $*$ and $\div$, functions like sin, tan or exp, and common operations on sets like $\subset$, $\cap$ or $\cup$ are easily extended to the interval domain (see [8]).

A set of non-overlapping interval boxes, also called subpaving [8], is defined as

$$\mathbb{X} = \{[\mathbf{x_1}], [\mathbf{x_2}], \ldots\}. \tag{2}$$

$\mathbb{X}_i$ is the ith interval box $[\mathbf{x}_i]$ of $\mathbb{X}$.

2.2   Interval Constraint Propagation

A Constraint Satisfaction Problem (CSP) is a system of m equations (constraints) linking n variables. Each variable belongs to a finite domain. The equations have the form $f_j(x_1, \ldots, x_n) = 0$, $j = 1, \ldots, m$, rewritten in a vectorized form $\mathbf{f}(\mathbf{x}) = 0$. A possible solution to the CSP $\mathcal{C}$ satisfies all constraints and is an assignment of values from its domains to each variable. If the domains of the variables are intervals [11], the CSP $\mathcal{C}$ can be noted as

$$\mathcal{C} : (\mathbf{f}(\mathbf{x}) = 0 | \mathbf{x} \in [\mathbf{x}]). \tag{3}$$

The solution set of $\mathcal{C}$ is

$$\mathbb{S} := \{\mathbf{x} \in [\mathbf{x}] | \mathbf{f}(\mathbf{x}) = 0\}. \tag{4}$$

To gain a box containing the solution set, contractors are applied to the CSP. A contractor is defined as an operator that contracts the prior domain [**x**] to a new box [**x'**] ⊂ [**x**] such that $\mathbb{S} \subset [\mathbf{x'}]$.

Different contractors exist. Taking advantage of the redundancy existing in the sensor data, an adaption of Waltz's contractor [12] to real interval domains [11] has been used. The idea of this contractor is to decompose all constraints in primitive constraints, and to propagate changes in the interval domains forward and backward until no contraction is gained any more. This *Forward Backward Propagation (FBP)* results in locally consistent solution sets [13]. A detailed overview can be found in [8]. See [14] for an illustrating example.

Please note, that the order of the constraints may contain cycles and thus may not be optimal [13]. According to Waltz [12], FBP can be iterated until no more contraction is obtained. If the domain of any variable gets empty during calculation, the CSP has no solution.

3 Models

Our approach considers the localization of a mobile robot in a two-dimensional environment. Therefore, a robot pose is represented as an interval vector, or interval box respectively, $[\mathbf{x}] = ([x], [y], [\theta])^T$. The width of this box represents the uncertainty in the pose. A set of pose boxes is defined as $\mathbb{X} = \{[\mathbf{x}_1], [\mathbf{x}_2], \dots\}$. This set is guaranteed to contain the true location of the robot.

State estimation for robot localization usually consists of two steps, prediction and measurement update. In terms of set membership, the prediction equation can be defined as follows:

$$[\mathbf{x}_k] = \mathbf{f}([\mathbf{x}_{k-1}], [\mathbf{u}_{k-1}]), \tag{5}$$

where [**u**] is the control vector, deduced from the proprioceptive sensor data. **f** will be derived in the following section. The measurement update equation

$$[\mathbf{y}_k] = \mathbf{g}([\mathbf{x}_k]) \tag{6}$$

will be defined in Sec. 3.4. **y** is the measurement vector. As described in the following sections, process and measurement noise are modelled implicitly by interval uncertainty.

3.1 Kinematic Model

The mobile robot is equipped with wheel odometry measuring the revolutions per minute (rpm) for each of the two driving wheels. It has a differential drive, steering by differential revolutions on both wheels. The origin of the robot pose is located in the middle of the driving wheel axis. The time-discrete kinematic model of the vehicle displacement can be formulated as

$$[\mathbf{x}_k] = \begin{pmatrix} [x_{k-1}] + [\triangle x] \cdot \cos\left([\theta_{k-1}] + \frac{[\triangle \theta]}{2}\right) \\ [y_{k-1}] + [\triangle x] \cdot \sin\left([\theta_{k-1}] + \frac{[\triangle \theta]}{2}\right) \\ [\theta_{k-1}] + [\triangle \theta] \end{pmatrix} . \tag{7}$$

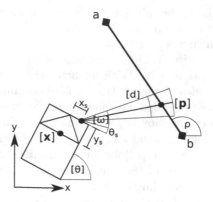

Fig. 1. Sensor and map model

As the wheel odometry measures the revolutions per minute, the actual left and right rpm measurements $\hat{v}_L$ and $\hat{v}_R$ with their maximal error err_v calculate to $[v_L] = [\hat{v}_L - err_v, \hat{v}_L + err_v]$ and $[v_R] = [\hat{v}_R - err_v, \hat{v}_R + err_v]$, respectively. The longitudinal $[\triangle x]$ and rotational motion $[\triangle \theta]$ are calculated as follows:

$$[\triangle x] = \triangle t \pi \left([v_L][r_L] + [v_R][r_R]\right) \text{ and}$$
$$[\triangle \theta] = \triangle t \frac{2\pi}{[w]} \left([v_L][r_L] - [v_R][r_R]\right),$$

$$(8)$$

where $[r_L]$ and $[r_R]$ are the left and right wheel radii, and $[w]$ is the wheel base. Wheel radii und wheel base are assumed to be not perfectly known, hence having a small interval-modelled error.

3.2   Laser Rangefinder Model

The sensor model of the laser rangefinder has to cover several possible sources of imprecision induced during the measurement process. In this work, errors induced by the hardware, uncertainties due to unexpected and missed objects, and random measurements are modelled. Unexpected objects, missed objects, and random measurements are referred to as outliers. Section 4.2 covers the consideration of outliers.

It is assumed that the uncertainties of the laser rangefinder hardware can be covered by two modelled sensor errors, longitudinal and angular imprecision. Furthermore, it is assumed that these errors are absolutely bounded, and that these boundaries can be determined. The sensor model is drawn in Fig. 1.

If $\hat{d}_i$ is the distance reading and $\hat{\omega}_i$ is the angle of sensor reading i, the corresponding interval domains calculate to $[d_i] = [\hat{d}_i - err_d, \hat{d}_i + err_d]$, and $[\omega_i] = [\hat{\omega}_i - err_\omega, \hat{\omega}_i + err_\omega]$ respectively, having err_d and err_ω as the maximum longitudinal and angular fault. The sensor is located relative to the robot coordinate system, with offsets x_s, y_s and θ_s. These offsets are assumed to be exactly known and hence represented as scalars. With $[\mathbf{x}]$, $[d_i]$, $[\omega_i]$, x_s, y_s and θ_s, the interval box of a sensor measurement in global coordinates calculates to

$$[\mathbf{p}_i] = \begin{pmatrix} [x] + (x_s \cdot [\cos]([\theta])) - (y_s \cdot [\sin]([\theta])) + ([d_i] \cdot [\cos]([\theta] + \theta_s + [\omega_i])) \\ [y] + (x_s \cdot [\sin]([\theta])) + (y_s \cdot [\cos]([\theta])) + ([d_i] \cdot [\sin]([\theta] + \theta_s + [\omega_i])) \end{pmatrix}. \tag{9}$$

The correct values for err_d and err_ω are taken from the technical specification of the sensor, or have to be measured in advance.

3.3   Map Model

A map consists of m simple line features. Each line feature consists of two coordinates a and b that are connected and thus build the start and end point of the feature:

$$a = (a_x, a_y)^T \text{ and}$$
$$b = (b_x, b_y)^T \tag{10}$$

(see Fig. 1). As the correctness of the map is assumed, the coordinates are represented as pairs of real scalars. Here, a map feature will be represented by its conxev hull

$$[\mathbf{m}] = \begin{pmatrix} [\min(a_x, b_x), \max(a_x, b_x)] \\ [\min(a_y, b_y), \max(a_y, b_y)] \end{pmatrix}. \tag{11}$$

A map $\mathbb{M}$ consists of m features:

$$\mathbb{M} = \{[\mathbf{m}_1], [\mathbf{m}_2], \dots, [\mathbf{m}_m]\}. \tag{12}$$

3.4   Measurement Update

The measurement update equation for sensor reading i can be defined as follows:

$$[d_i] = \mathbf{g}(\mathbb{M}, [\omega_i], [\mathbf{x}]). \tag{13}$$

$\mathbf{g}$ calculates the distance, given the map features, the sensor reading angle and the current position of the robot. As the map can be assumed as static, and the sensor reading angle is independent of the actual measurement process, (13) simplifies to

$$[d_i] = \mathbf{g}_i([\mathbf{x}]). \tag{14}$$

4   Mobile Robot Tracking

To implement the mobile robot localization algorithm, we adapted the IMAGESP and *Relaxed Set Inverter Via Interval Analysis* (RSIVIA) algorithms. The following sections present the realization of prediction and update steps, including the dealing with outliers. Sec. 4.3 describes the complete relaxed set inversion localization algorithm. The subsequent sections explain the suggested filters and the detection and marking of outliers in the laser scan.

4.1 Prediction Step

The purpose of the prediction step is to predict the current robot pose based on a previous robot pose, here a set of poses. Therefore, the prediction equation (7) is applied to all boxes of the current pose set. Because the computed boxes might be overlapping, a subpaving has to be calculated before the measurement update step.

This procedure is similar to the application of IMAGESP [8]. In contrast to IMAGESP, we dispense with the mincing step, and continue directly with the image evaluation. To regularize the solution set afterwards, we apply an algorithm similar to BUILDSP [15], which is an recursive algorithm computing a subpaving. Because our localization is dedicated to be executed on an embedded PC running a real time operating system, a recursive algorithm might let the memory stack grow boundless by recursive procedure calls. Therefore, we modified BUILDSP to an iterative algorithm, keeping the stack size constant.

If there are more proprioceptive than exteroceptive sensor measurements per time step, the prediction step is repeated several times before computing one update step.

4.2 Update Step

The update step is necessary to correct possible errors induced during prediction. In terms of set membership localization, its purpose is to reduce the uncertainty in the predicted pose estimate.

Considering the measurement update equation (14), the previous pose $[\mathbf{x}_k]$, and n distance measurements, the problem of localizing a mobile robot in a known (feature-based) map can be seen as the problem of finding the smallest box enclosing

$$[\mathbf{x}_{k+1}] = [\mathbf{x}_k] \cap \bigcap_{i \in \{1,\dots,n\}} \mathbf{g}_i^{-1}([d_{k,i}]).$$ (15)

When dealing with outliers in the measurements, the problem changes to the q-relaxed problem

$$[\mathbf{x}_{k+1}] = [\mathbf{x}_k] \cap \bigcap_{i \in \{1,\dots,n\}}^{q} \mathbf{g}_i^{-1}([d_{k,i}]).$$ (16)

The q-relaxed intersection $\bigcap^q$ describes the intersection of all except q arbitrary intervals [10].

To solve the inverse measurement update equation (14), a CSP will be defined and solved by *Forward Backward Propagation (FBP)* as follows.

First, the intersection of the map $\mathbb{M}$ and the sensor measurement box $[\mathbf{p}_j]$ (see (9)) has to be calculated:

$$[\mathbf{q}_j] = \bigsqcup (\mathbb{M} \cap [\mathbf{p}_j])$$ (17)

The interval hull operator $\sqcup$ calculates the convex hull of all its operands [8]. The CSP follows directly from (9) and (17):

$$
\mathcal{C} : \begin{pmatrix} x + (x_s \cdot \cos(\theta)) - (y_s \cdot \sin(\theta)) + (d_i \cdot \cos(\theta + \theta_s + \omega_i)) - q_x = 0 \\ y + (x_s \cdot \sin(\theta)) + (y_s \cdot \cos(\theta)) + (d_i \cdot \sin(\theta + \theta_s + \omega_i)) - q_y = 0 \\ (x, y, \theta) \in [\mathbf{x}], d_i \in [d_i], \omega_i \in [\omega_i], (q_x, q_y) \in [\mathbf{q}_i] \end{pmatrix},
$$

$$
i = 1, \ldots, n. \quad (18)
$$

Having the CSP $\mathcal{C}$, a FBP as described in Sec. 2.2 can be applied. It is able to contract the domains of the CSP and to deal with the strong non-linearities contained in it.

4.3 Localization Algorithm

Taking into account the prediction and update steps, RSIVIA with the q-relaxed intersection [10], and the formulated CSP (18), the localization algorithm can be stated as in Alg. 1.

Algorithm 1. ROBUST MOBILE ROBOT LOCALIZATION

1: **procedure** LOCALIZATION(in: $[\mathbf{x}]$, out: $\mathbb{X}_{out}$)
2:     $\mathbb{X} = \{[\mathbf{x}]\}$
3:     **while** true **do**
4:         **repeat**
5:             $\mathbb{X} = \mathbf{f}(\mathbb{X}, [\mathbf{u}])$
6:         **until** laser measurements available
7:         $\mathcal{L} = \text{BUILDSP}(\mathbb{X})$
8:         **while** allocated time did not elapse and $\mathcal{L} \neq \emptyset$ **do**
9:             $[\mathbf{x}] = \text{PULL}(\mathcal{L})$
10:             **repeat**
11:                 **for all** $i = 1$ to n **do**
12:                     $[\mathbf{x}_i] = [\mathbf{x}] \cap \mathbf{g}_i^{-1}([d_i])$
13:                 **end for**
14:                 $[\mathbf{x}] = \left[\bigcap_{i \in \{1, \ldots, n\}}^q [\mathbf{x}_i] \right]$
15:             **until** contraction of $[\mathbf{x}]$ is smaller than threshold
16:             **if** $[\mathbf{x}] \neq \emptyset$ **then**
17:                 bisect $[\mathbf{x}]$ and push subboxes into $\mathcal{L}$
18:             **end if**
19:         **end while**
20:         $\mathbb{X} = \text{ID}(\mathcal{L})$
21:         $\mathbb{X}_{out} = \text{FILTER}(\mathcal{L})$
22:     **end while**
23: **end procedure**

$\mathcal{L}$ is a list of non-overlapping interval boxes, implemented as a *FIFO*-queue. First, $\mathbb{X}$ is initialized with the initial search box. The whole algorithm consists of a never-ending localization loop, returning the localization result $\mathbb{X}_{out}$ at the end of each cycle (line 26). Lines 4 to 6 apply the robot displacement, or the prediction step respectively, until a new measurement of the laser rangefinder is available. Afterwards, a subpaving is calculated as described above, before starting the update step. The condition in line 8 is supposed to guarantee a maximum computation time when required. When computation time is not an issue, a criterion regarding the box sizes should be applied. Thereafter, a box is pulled out of $\mathcal{L}$. In lines 11 to 13 the inverse measurement update equation is calculated for each measurement as described in the previous section. Line 14 calculates the interval hull containing the q-relaxed intersection of all previously calculated $[\mathbf{x}_i]$. If the q-relaxed intersection is not the empty set, the box is bisected and pushed into $\mathcal{L}$. Finally, the interval box set $\mathbb{X}$ is reinitialized with the boxes of $\mathcal{L}$ (see Sec. 4.4 for the ID-Filter). Before output the localization result, one of the possible filters described in Sec. 4.4 is applied in line 21.

4.4   Filtering the Resulting Interval Box List

Depending on the previous pose set and the environment, the resulting list $\mathcal{L}$ of non-overlapping pose boxes might be heavily segmented. Therefore, we suggest the following four filters (ID, MERGE, CLUSTER, and HULL) that can be applied to the resulting list $\mathcal{L}$ to calculate a resulting subpaving $\mathbb{X}_{out}$.

The simplest filter function ID returns the list $\mathcal{L}$ as a subpaving $\mathbb{X}_{out}$. It might result in a very large interval box set and should be avoided.

The MERGE filter merges all boxes that are equal in two dimensions and have a non-empty intersection in the remaining dimension. Typically, recently bisected boxes and boxes that do not contract anymore are merged. This is the simplest reduction step and should always be applied.

Applying the CLUSTER filter, all interval boxes closer than a certain threshold in all dimensions will be merged. This results in clustering dense regions of possible solution boxes. Experiments have shown that the CLUSTER filter is a good trade-off between accuracy and reduction.

A filter that has been used in the RSIVIA of [10] is the HULL filter. It returns the smallest box enclosing all boxes of $\mathcal{L}$. The advantage is the guaranteed outcome of a single interval box, at the possibly high costs of induced additional imprecision.

Because the filters are subsets of each other, only one filter should be applied. The subset order is as follows:

$$\text{ID} \subseteq \text{MERGE} \subseteq \text{CLUSTER} \subseteq \text{HULL}. \tag{19}$$

4.5   Online Detection of Outliers

When the localization result is a small pose box after applying a reduction filter, we propose to use information of the q-relaxed intersection as a side-effect to identify outliers in the laser scan. All measurements that are not part of the resulting q-relaxed intersection are certain outliers. Please note, that on the other side, not all measurements part of the q-relaxed intersection have to be correct.

Figure 2 shows 2D laser scans of the experiment presented in Sec. 5, where outlier scan points have been marked in red. These outlier points result from static and dynamic obstacles. The information about outlier points could be used to detect dynamic objects in the environment, for example.

5   Experimental Results

To show the ability of our approach to localize a moving mobile robot in dynamic and structured indoor environments, a real world experiment will be presented. The map of the environment was known in advance. In addition, static obstacles like unexpected opened or closed doors, and dynamic obstacles (up to two simultaneously moving people) were present in the environment. The robot followed a path on a typical office floor while localizing itself in real time using our presented approach, and pure odometry for comparison.

The experiment was conducted on a mobile robot platform equipped with a 2D laser scanner SICK LMS200 and an embedded PC running a small Linux distribution with the Xenomai real time extension and our robotic framework RACK. A full 2D scan consisted of 180 measurements with an opening angle of 180°. The distance measurement and angular accuracy was assumed to be ±50mm, and ±0.125°, respectively. At each iteration step, one third of the laser measurements were chosen randomly for the localization, from which in turn one third were allowed to be outliers.

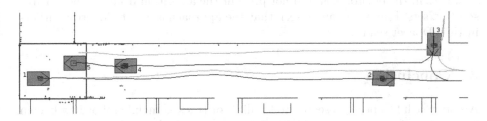

Fig. 2. Results of the localization experiment. Trajectory of the robust localization approach in black, pure odometry in green. Localization boxes of five exemplary situations painted in blue, the initial search box is the larger box on the left side of the map. 2D laser points of situations 1 and 4 projected into the map; valid points marked in blue, detected outliers in red.

The results are depicted in Fig. 2. The initial search box is the larger blue box on the left side, enclosing the gray robot marked with a '1'. Calculated localization trajectories are painted in black and green. The black trajectory was created by applying the HULL filter to the resulting pose box list computed by our approach, and taking the center of the hull, while the green trajectory was calculated relying only on wheel odometry. Five exemplary situations are depicted in Fig. 2, together with their current localization box sets in blue. Note, that the ID filter has been applied to the localization result to visualize the resulting box set. Situation 1 is the start position, situation 5 the goal position. Table 1 presents the intervals $[x]$ and $[y]$ of the hulls of the localization boxes together with their actual values $\hat{x}$ and $\hat{y}$, measured by hand. Moreover, the scan points taken by the 2D laser rangefinder at positions 1 and 4 are projected into the map. Blue scan points are regular, red scan points are detected as outliers by our approach. The robot was able to compute its position in real time while following the trajectory.

Table 1. Localization results of experiment [mm]

	$\hat{x}$	$[x]$	$\hat{y}$	$[y]$
1	850	[780 949]	830	[757 988]
2	790	[719 943]	15770	[15566 15818]
3	2230	[2153 2318]	17910	[17776 18063]
4	1350	[1286 1499]	4500	[4346 4660]
5	1470	[1421 1621]	2330	[2185 2442]

Obviously, our approach was able to keep track of the robot during the whole experiment. Moreover, at five exemplary points, the true robot position was guaranteed to be inside the localization result. We expect to proof this guarantee for the whole track in future experiments. Compared to the odometry-based trajectory, our approach does not suffer from drift. The static and dynamic obstacles in the environment did not prevent the algorithm from finding feasible solution sets. Finally, it can be seen that the approach is able to identify outliers in the 2D laser scan.

6   Conclusion

An approach has been presented to localize, or track, a mobile robot in a known feature-based map using a rotating 2D laser rangefinder and wheel odometry. Belonging to the class of set membership approaches, the proposed localization algorithm results in guaranteed robot pose sets when the initial assumptions about sensor error boundaries are met. The approach is capable to deal with a certain number of outliers in the sensor data, and identifies outliers in the laser range scan.

A real world experiment in a typical office floor showed the feasibility of the approach. A mobile robot following a path in the floor was able to localize itself in real time during the whole path. It has been shown, that the true robot position was guaranteed to be in the calculated position boxes. The approach could cope with measurement outliers as well as with occlusions by static and dynamic obstacles in the environment, as long as the maximum outliers assumption was met.

Future work will deal with further experiments to verify that the true robot position is contained in the localization result all the time. Moreover, we will have a deeper look on issues regarding the computation time, and on the effects of the different suggested filters on the returned pose estimation set.

References

1. Hanebeck, U., Schmidt, G.: Set theoretic localization of fast mobile robots using an angle measurement technique. In: Proc. IEEE International Conference on Robotics and Automation, vol. 2, pp. 1387–1394 (1996)
2. Sabater, A., Thomas, F.: Set membership approach to the propagation of uncertain geometric information. In: Proc. IEEE International Conference on Robotics and Automation, vol. 3, pp. 2718–2723 (1991)
3. Thrun, S., Burgard, W., Fox, D.: Probabilistic Robotics. Intelligent robotics and autonomous agents. MIT Press (September 2005)
4. Kalman, R.E., Bucy, R.S.: New results in linear filtering and prediction theory. Transactions ASME, Series D, J. Basic Eng. 83, 95–108 (1961)
5. Dellaert, F., Fox, D., Burgard, W., Thrun, S.: Monte carlo localization for mobile robots. In: Proc. IEEE International Conference on Robotics and Automation, vol. 2, pp. 1322–1328 (1999)
6. Milanese, M., Vicino, A.: Estimation theory for nonlinear models and set membership uncertainty. Automatica 27(2), 403–408 (1991)
7. Lambert, A., Gruyer, D., Vincke, B., Seignez, E.: Consistent outdoor vehicle localization by bounded-error state estimation. In: Proc. IEEE/RSJ International Conference on Intelligent Robots and Systems, pp. 1211–1216 (2009)
8. Jaulin, L., Kieffer, M., Didrit, O., Walter, E.: Applied Interval Analysis. Springer, London (2001)
9. Seignez, E., Kieffer, M., Lambert, A., Walter, E., Maurin, T.: Real-time bounded-error state estimation for vehicle tracking. Int. J. Rob. Res. 28(1), 34–48 (2009)
10. Jaulin, L.: Brief paper: Robust set-membership state estimation; application to underwater robotics. Automatica 45(1), 202–206 (2009)
11. Davis, E.: Constraint propagation with interval labels. Artificial Intelligence 32(3), 281–331 (1987)
12. Waltz, D.: Understanding line drawings of scenes with shadows. In: The Psychology of Computer Vision, pp. 19–91. McGraw-Hill (1975)
13. Benhamou, F., Goualard, F., Granvilliers, L., Puget, J.F.: Revising hull and box consistency. In: Proc. International Conference on Logic programming, pp. 230–244. Massachusetts Institute of Technology, Cambridge (1999)
14. Gning, A., Bonnifait, P.: Constraints propagation techniques on intervals for a guaranteed localization using redundant data. Automatica 42(7), 1167–1175 (2006)
15. Seignez, E., Lambert, A.: Complexity study of guaranteed state estimation for real time to robot localization. Journal of Automation, Mobile Robotics & Intelligent Systems 5(2), 12–27 (2011)

Trajectory Tracking of Wheeled Mobile Robot with a Manipulator Considering Dynamic Interaction and Modeling Uncertainty

Guoliang Zhong, Yukinori Kobayashi, Takanori Emaru, and Yohei Hoshino

Graduate School of Engineering, Hokkaido University, Kita 13, Nishi 8, Kita-ku, Sapporo, 0608628 Hokkaido, Japan
zhglxtt@mech-hm.eng.hokudai.ac.jp

Abstract. This paper proposes an adaptive control strategy for trajectory tracking of a Wheeled Mobile Robot (WMR) which consists of a suspended platform and a manipulator. When the WMR moves in the presence of friction and external disturbance, the trajectory can hardly be tracked accurately by applying the backstepping approach. For addressing this problem, considering the dynamic interaction, a dynamic model of the system is constructed by using Direct Path Method (DPM). An adaptive fuzzy control combined with backstepping approach based on the dynamic model is proposed. To track the trajectory accurately, a fuzzy compensator is proposed to compensate modeling uncertainty such as friction and external disturbance. Moreover, to reduce the approximation error and ensure the system stability, a robust term is added to the adaptive control law. Simulation results show the effectiveness and merits of the proposed control strategy in the counteraction of modeling uncertainty and the trajectory tracking.

Keywords: wheel mobile robot, trajectory tracking, adaptive control, interaction, uncertainty.

1 Introduction

Recently, the tread of academic research has directed towards the development of autonomous mobile robot, especially the Wheeled Mobile Robot (WMR) [1], since the application of mechanical automation is extended to agricultural, industrial and service sectors. Over the last several years, there has been considerable interest in the design of advanced system for motion control of WMR. The problem of motion control addressed in the literatures can be classified into three groups: 1) *point stabilization*, where the goal is to stabilize a robot at a given target point with a desired orientation; 2) *path planning*, where the robot is required to converge to and follow a desired path without any temporal specifications; 3) *trajectory tracking*, where the robot is required to track a time parameterized reference.

From the above classification and definitions, path following problem can be regarded as a special case of trajectory tracking problem. These problems have been investigated by several researchers. Tsai and Wang [2] proposed the simultaneous

C.-Y. Su, S. Rakheja, H. Liu (Eds.): ICIRA 2012, Part II, LNAI 7507, pp. 366–375, 2012.

point stabilization and trajectory tracking method via backstepping approach. Yang and Red [3] constructed an on-line Cartesian trajectory control of mechanism along complex curves and Red [4] presented a dynamic optimal trajectory generator for Cartesian path following. However, they did not cope with the trajectory tracking of platform and manipulator simultaneously, or rather, the interaction between platform and manipulator was neglected. Furthermore, the issues of modeling uncertainty from friction and external disturbance were not considered.

The WMR with a manipulator is extensively used in tasks such as welding, paint spraying, accurate positioning systems and so on [1]. In these practical applications, to follow some given path or to track the obtained optimal trajectory, the interaction between platform and manipulator cannot be neglected because it causes the sliding inevitably [5, 6]. Yamamoto and Yun [7, 8] have discussed the effect of the dynamic interaction between mobile platform and manipulator of a mobile manipulator on the task performance. Meghdari et al. [9] investigated the dynamic interaction between a one D.O.F. manipulator and vehicle of the mobile manipulator for a planar robotics system. Moosavian and Papadopoulos [10] utilized Direct Path Method (DPM) for deriving the dynamics of a space robotic system equipped with multiple arms which has been shown that the DPM concept has fewer computations compared to other criteria. Eslamy and Moosavian [11] presented a dynamic model of a multiple arm wheeled mobile platform equipped with a suspension system by introducing DPM. To obtain an explicit dynamic model of the WMR with a manipulator, this useful method will be extended in this paper.

It is relevant to point out that most of the results mentioned above only considered the nominal model of the system. Only a few authors have tackled the control problems considering modeling uncertainty [12, 13]. Actually, robotic manipulator is inevitably subject to structured and unstructured uncertainty which is very difficult to model accurately. Motivated by these considerations, the goal of this paper is to put emphasis on using adaptive controllers to achieve the trajectory tracking for a WMR with a three-link manipulator in the presence of modeling uncertainty. An adaptive fuzzy controller with backstepping approach [2, 14] is designed to deal with the trajectory tracking of WMR. To track the trajectory accurately, a fuzzy compensator [15, 16] is added to counteract the modeling certainty such as friction and external disturbance, and a robust term is introduced to reduce the approximation error and ensure the system stability.

2   System Modeling

The main configuration of the Wheeled Mobile Robot (WMR) is a modular manipulator mounted on the suspended platform and the platform is supported by two rear driving wheels and one front caster wheel as shown in Fig. 1. The two rear wheels are actuated by independent motors and the caster wheel is free to attain any orientation according to the motion of the robot. In the modeling of the WMR system, the following assumption should be adopted: wheels, platform and each link of manipulator are rigid.

In order to take account of the interaction between platform and manipulator, the Direct Path Method (DPM) is introduced to obtain the dynamic model. DPM is a concept which relies on taking a point on the base platform (preferably its center of mass) as the representative point for the translational motion of the system. As seen in Fig. 2, the kinematics of the WMR system can be developed by using a set of body-fixed geometric vectors to formulate the position and velocity with respect to a representative point p. The motion of the center of mass (CM) is used to describe the system translation with respect to an inertial frame of reference, $O_g\text{-}X_gY_gZ_g$. The CMs of each body are defined as c_*, the joints are defined as j_*, and the rest of the definitions are described in Fig. 2.

The inertial position of the representative point p is R_p which can be written as

$$R_p = R_{c_b} + r_{p/c_b}, \qquad i = 1,2,3,b. \tag{1}$$

$$r_{p/c_b} = r_{p/c_i} + r_{c_i/c_b}, \qquad i = 1,2,3 \tag{2}$$

$$r_{c_i/c_b} = \begin{cases} r_{c_b/c_b} = 0, & i = b. \\ r_{c_i/c_b} = r_{j0/c_b} - r_{j_{i-1}/c_i} + \sum_{k=1}^{i-1}\left(r_{j_k/c_k} - r_{j_{k-1}/c_k}\right), & i = 1,2,3. \end{cases} \tag{3}$$

Substituting Eq. (3) into Eq. (2) yields

$$r_{p/c_b} = \begin{cases} r_{p/c_b}, & i = b. \\ r_{p/c_i} + r_{j0/c_b} - r_{j_{i-1}/c_i} + \sum_{k=1}^{i-1}\left(r_{j_k/c_k} - r_{j_{k-1}/c_k}\right), & i = 1,2,3. \end{cases} \tag{4}$$

Substituting Eq. (4) into Eq. (1) completes the position analysis and yields

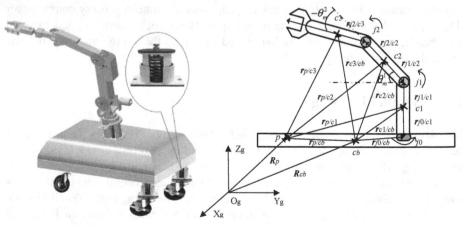

Fig. 1. WMR system   **Fig. 2.** Vector diagram for DPM

$$
\boldsymbol{R}_p = \begin{cases} \boldsymbol{R}_{c_b} + \boldsymbol{r}_{p/c_b}, & i = b. \\[2mm] \boldsymbol{R}_{c_b} + \boldsymbol{r}_{p/c_i} + \boldsymbol{r}_{j_0/c_b} - \boldsymbol{r}_{j_{i-1}/c_i} + \sum_{k=1}^{i-1} \left(\boldsymbol{r}_{j_k/c_k} - \boldsymbol{r}_{j_{k-1}/c_k} \right), & i = 1,2,3. \end{cases} \tag{5}
$$

Then the inertial velocity is derived as follows:

$$
\dot{\boldsymbol{R}}_p = \begin{cases} \dot{\boldsymbol{R}}_{c_b} + \boldsymbol{\omega}_b \times \boldsymbol{r}_{p/c_b}, & i = b. \\[2mm] \dot{\boldsymbol{R}}_{c_b} + \boldsymbol{\omega}_b \times \boldsymbol{r}_{j_0/c_b} + \boldsymbol{\omega}_i \times \left(\boldsymbol{r}_{p/c_i} - \boldsymbol{r}_{j_{i-1}/c_i} \right) + \sum_{k=1}^{i-1} \left\{ \boldsymbol{\omega}_k \times \left(\boldsymbol{r}_{j_k/c_k} - \boldsymbol{r}_{j_{k-1}/c_k} \right) \right\}, & i = 1,2,3. \end{cases} \tag{6}
$$

To express the dynamics of the WMR system, the Lagrange approach is used together with DPM concept. To derive equation of motion for the WMR system, the Lagrange equation of the second kind can be written

$$
\frac{d}{dt}\left(\frac{\partial T}{\partial \dot{q}_i}\right) - \frac{\partial T}{\partial q_i} + \frac{\partial U}{\partial q_i} + \frac{\partial U_F}{\partial \dot{q}_i} = Q_i \qquad i = 1,\cdots,N, \tag{7}
$$

where T, U and U_F are the robotic system's kinetic, potential and dissipated energies. Here, N describes the degree-of-freedom (DOF) of the system. And q_i, $\dot{q}_i$ and Q_i are the i-th element of the vector of the generalized coordinates, speeds, and forces, respectively.

The generalized coordinate is defined as below:

$$
\boldsymbol{q} = \{\boldsymbol{R}_b, \boldsymbol{\Theta}_b, \boldsymbol{\Theta}_m\}^T, \tag{8}
$$

where $\boldsymbol{R}_b = (x_G, y_G, z_G)^T$ and $\boldsymbol{\Theta}_b = (\theta_y, \theta_p, \theta_r)^T$ describe position vectors of the CM of the suspended platform and its Euler angles. The vector of joint angles for the manipulator is represented by $\boldsymbol{\Theta}_m = (\theta_m^0, \theta_m^1, \theta_m^2)^T$. And x_G, y_G, z_G are the CM position of the platform with respect to the inertial O-XYZ coordinate axes; $\theta_y, \theta_p, \theta_r$ are the yaw angle, pitch angle and roll angle, respectively; $\theta_m^0, \theta_m^1, \theta_m^2$ denote the angle of each joint.

After deriving the terms of kinetic, potential and dissipated energy, the dynamic model can be obtained as

$$
M(q)\ddot{q} + C(\dot{q},q)\dot{q} + G(q) = Q. \tag{9}
$$

where $M(q)$, $C(\dot{q},q)$, $G(q)$ and Q denote the inertial matrix, Coriolis force, gravity component and torque matrix, respectively.

3   Adaptive Backstepping Control with Fuzzy Compensator Based on Dynamics

In a general way, in kinematic level, the immediate cause of sliding is velocity deviation. However, in dynamic level, the root causes of sliding are the friction and the interaction between platform and manipulator. Therefore, in this section, an adaptive backstepping controller which takes account of the interaction effects is designed, and a fuzzy compensator is added to counteract the friction and disturbance.

According to Section 2, consider the dynamic model rewritten as

$$M(q) \cdot \ddot{q} + C(\dot{q}, q) \cdot \dot{q} + G(q) + F(\dot{q}, q) = Q, \tag{10}$$

where $F(\dot{q}, q)$ denotes the modeling uncertainty which includes the friction and external disturbance. In order to compensating for $F(\dot{q}, q)$, the sliding surface $s = 0$ is chosen as a hyper plane

$$s = \dot{\tilde{q}} + \Lambda \tilde{q}, \tag{11}$$

where Λ is a positive-definite matrix whose eigenvalues are strictly in the right-half complex plane and $\tilde{q}$ is the tracking error vector. Let us define

$$\dot{q}_r = \dot{q}_d - \Lambda \tilde{q}, \tag{12}$$

where $\dot{q}_d$ is the derivative of desired trajectory.

The Lyapunov function candidate is chosen as

$$V(t) = \frac{1}{2} \left(s^T M s + \sum_{i=1}^{n} \tilde{\Theta}_i^T \Gamma_i \tilde{\Theta}_i \right), \tag{13}$$

where $\tilde{\Theta}_i = \Theta_i^* - \Theta_i$ is the i-th column vector of the optimal parameter matrix and Γ_i is a strictly positive real constant. Differentiating $V(t)$ with respect to time yields

$$\dot{V}(t) = -s^T (M\ddot{q}_r + C\dot{q}_r + G + F - Q) + \sum_{i=1}^{n} \tilde{\Theta}_i^T \Gamma_i \dot{\tilde{\Theta}}_i, \tag{14}$$

where $F(q, \dot{q})$ is a completely unknown nonlinear function vector. Therefore, we replace $F(q, \dot{q})$ by a MIMO fuzzy logic system which is in the form of $\hat{F}(q, \dot{q}|\Theta)$.

Let us define the control law as

$$Q = M\ddot{q}_r + C\dot{q}_r + G + \hat{F}(q, \dot{q}|\Theta) - K_D s, \tag{15}$$

where $K_D = diag(K_i)$, $K_i > 0$, $i = 1, 2, \cdots, n$, and

$$\hat{F}(q, \dot{q}|\Theta) = \begin{bmatrix} \hat{F}_1(q, \dot{q}|\Theta_1) \\ \hat{F}_2(q, \dot{q}|\Theta_2) \\ \vdots \\ \hat{F}_n(q, \dot{q}|\Theta_n) \end{bmatrix} = \begin{bmatrix} \Theta_1^T \xi(q, \dot{q}) \\ \Theta_2^T \xi(q, \dot{q}) \\ \vdots \\ \Theta_n^T \xi(q, \dot{q}) \end{bmatrix}. \tag{16}$$

Letting the optimal parameter matrix of the fuzzy logic system Θ^*, we can define the minimum approximation error vector

$$w = F(q, \dot{q}) - \hat{F}(q, \dot{q}|\Theta^*). \tag{17}$$

Substituting Eq. (15) into Eq. (14), $\dot{V}(t)$ can be rewritten as

$$\dot{V}(t) = -s^T \left(F(q,\dot{q}) - \hat{F}(q,\dot{q}|\Theta) + K_D s \right) + \sum_{i=1}^{n} \tilde{\Theta}_i^T \Gamma_i \dot{\tilde{\Theta}}_i$$

$$= -s^T K_D s - s^T w + \sum_{i=1}^{n} \left(\tilde{\Theta}_i^T \Gamma_i \dot{\tilde{\Theta}}_i - s_i \tilde{\Theta}_i^T \xi(q,\dot{q}) \right),$$

(18)

where $\tilde{\Theta} = \Theta^* - \Theta$ and $\xi(q,\dot{q})$ is fuzzy basis function. Therefore, the adaptive laws are

$$\dot{\Theta}_i = -\Gamma_i^{-1} s_i \xi(q,\dot{q}), \qquad i = 1, 2 ; \cdots, n.$$

(19)

Then

$$\dot{V}(t) = -s^T K_D s - s^T w \leq 0.$$

(20)

It satisfies the Lyapunov theorem of stability.

Because Eq. (18) contains the term "$s^T w$" which is the order of the minimum approximation error, from the universal approximation theorem, it is expected that w should be very small. Therefore, to reduce the approximation error and ensure the system stability, a robust term is added to the adaptive control law (Eq. (15)) as

$$Q = M\ddot{q}_r + C\dot{q}_r + G + \hat{F}(q,\dot{q}|\Theta) - K_D s - W \operatorname{sgn}(s),$$

(21)

where $W = diag[w_{M_1} \quad w_{M_2} \quad \cdots \quad w_{M_n}], w_{M_i} \geq |w_i|, i = 1, 2, \cdots, n$.

Substituting Eq. (21) into Eq. (14), $\dot{V}(t)$ can be rewritten as

$$\dot{V}(t) = -s^T K_D s \leq 0.$$

(22)

The structure of the proposed control scheme is shown in Fig. 3.

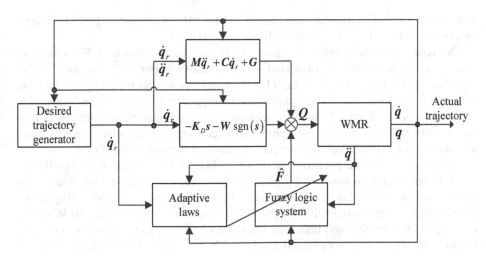

Fig. 3. Structure of control scheme

4   Results and Discussion

A Wheeled Mobile Robot (WMR) system is considered as shown in Fig. 1. In order to illustrate more clearly and simply, the rotation of the first joint j_0 from the posture shown in Fig. 2 does not be considered. In this case, the manipulator becomes a two-link mechanism. Parameters of the WMR, which is a prototype robot designed for a future experimental study, are given in Table 1. In this simulation, dynamics of the mobile platform and the manipulator are considered simultaneously.

Considering the dynamic model Eq. (10), we set a desired trajectory of joint 1 and joint 2 of the manipulator as $\theta_{md}^1 = \theta_{md}^2 = 0.5\sin t$. The desired trajectory of platform is designed like "∞" which can be described by $x_d = \cos 0.5t$, $y_d = \sin t$, and the initial configuration of WMR is given as $P_s = \begin{bmatrix} 1 & 1 & 0 \end{bmatrix}$. The membership function of fuzzy logic system is defined by

$$\mu_{A_i}(x_i) = \exp\left(-\left(\frac{x_i - \bar{x}_i}{\pi/24}\right)^2\right), \tag{23}$$

when $i = 1, 2, 3, 4, 5$, $\bar{x}_i = -\pi/6, -\pi/12, 0, \pi/12, \pi/6$, respectively. Fuzzy set A_i is defined by NB (Negative Big), NS (Negative Small), ZO (Zero), PS (Positive Small), and PB (Positive Big). According to coulomb model of friction, the frictions of joint 1, joint 2, left wheel and right wheel can be set as a vector

$$F(\dot{q}) = \begin{bmatrix} 5\dot{\theta}_m^1 + 0.2\mathrm{sgn}(\dot{\theta}_m^1) & 5\dot{\theta}_m^2 + 0.2\mathrm{sgn}(\dot{\theta}_m^2) & 10v_L + 0.5\mathrm{sgn}(v_L) & 10v_R + 0.5\mathrm{sgn}(v_R) \end{bmatrix}^T, \tag{24}$$

where v_L, v_R are the linear velocities of the left and right wheels. The disturbance terms of joint 1, joint 2, left wheel and right wheel are defined by

$$\boldsymbol{\tau}_d = \begin{bmatrix} 0 & 0 & 0.05\sin(20t) & 0.1\sin(20t) \end{bmatrix}^T. \tag{25}$$

The parameters of controller are chosen as $\varLambda = 10I$, $K_D = 20I$ (where I is unit matrix), $\varGamma_1 = \varGamma_2 = \varGamma_3 = \varGamma_4 = 0.0001$, $W = diag[0, 0, 2, 2]$.

The results of manipulator are shown in Figs. 4-6. As shown in Eq. (25), the disturbance of joints is not considered in the simulation. For this case, we use the adaptive control law defined by Eq. (15). Figure 4 shows the trajectory tracking of each joint. As seen in Fig. 4, each joint of the manipulator tracks the desired trajectory at a high precision. Figure 5 shows the friction and its compensation. From Fig. 5, it is obvious that the fuzzy compensator provides the convergent estimation of the friction. The time histories of control input torques for each joint are shown in Fig. 6.

The results of mobile platform are shown in Figs. 7-10. For the mobile platform, the disturbance of each wheel is considered. Therefore, the adaptive control law with robust term defined by Eq. (21) is employed. Figure7 shows the path following of the mobile platform, and reveals that the proposed controller is able to force the WMR to converge to the desired path under the influence of friction and external disturbance. Figure 8 shows the trajectory tracking in X and Y directions. As shown in Fig. 8, the trajectory tracking of platform is accurately after controlling by using the adaptive control law with robust term. Figure 9 reveals the friction, disturbance and their compensation. The time histories of control input torques for each wheel are shown in Fig. 10.

As indicated in these results, the proposed adaptive controller which is designed in the dynamic level can track the desired trajectory accurately not only for platform but also for manipulator. This is really because that the friction and disturbance can be counteracted by applying the fuzzy compensator and robust term.

Table 1. Values of the parameters

Symbol	Parameter	Value
M_b	Mass of the platform	20.00 kg
$M_m^2 = M_m^3$	Mass of the 2nd and 3rd link of the manipulator	2.00 kg
$l_m^1 = l_m^2 = l_m^3$	Length of each link of the manipulator	0.2 m
I_b	Moment of inertia of the platform	0.37 kg·m²
$I_2 = I_3$	Moment of inertia of the 2nd and 3rd link	0.06 kg·m²
$k_L = k_R$	Stiffness coefficient of left and right suspension	2.50 kN / m
$c_L = c_R$	Damping property of left and right suspension	5.00 N / m / s

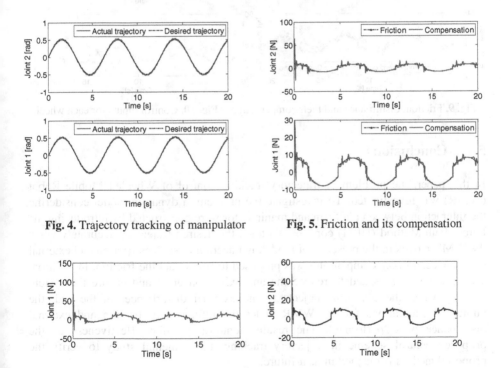

Fig. 4. Trajectory tracking of manipulator   **Fig. 5.** Friction and its compensation

Fig. 6. Control inputs for manipulator

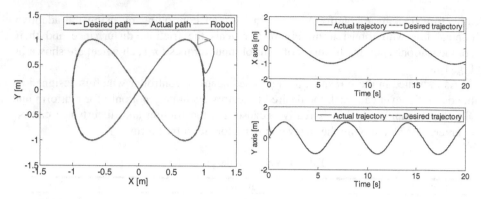

Fig. 7. Path following of mobile platform   **Fig. 8.** Trajectory tracking in X and Y directions

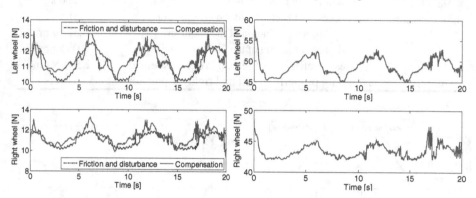

Fig. 9. Friction, disturbance and their compensation   **Fig. 10.** Control inputs for each wheel

5   Conclusions

In this paper, the problem of trajectory tracking control of Wheeled Mobile Robot (WMR) was investigated. To investigate the problem, a dynamic model considering the interaction between platform and manipulator were constructed by introducing the Direct Path Method (DPM) concept. To track the desired trajectory accurately when the WMR moves in the presence of modeling uncertainty such as friction and external disturbance, a fuzzy compensator was proposed to counteract the friction. In addition, a robust term was added to reduce the approximation error and ensure the system stability when the platform subjects to the external disturbance. In the end, the numerical simulations for the WMR under the influence of friction and external disturbance were performed. The results demonstrated the effectiveness of the proposed control scheme in trajectory tracking. Experimental study to verify the proposed method is planned in near future.

Acknowledgment. The authors thank the China Scholarship Council and Hokkaido University for the support of this work.

References

1. Siegwart, R., Nourbakhsh, I.R.: Introduction to Autonomous Mobile Robots. Prentice-Hall of India, New Delhi (2005)
2. Tsai, C.C., Wang, T.S.: Nonlinear Control of an Omnidirectional Mobile Robot. In: Proceedings of Int. Conf. on Automatic Technology, New York, USA, pp. 727–732 (2005)
3. Yang, Z., Red, E.: On-line Cartesian Trajectory Control of Mechanism along Complex Curves. Robotica 15, 263–274 (1997)
4. Red, E.: A Dynamic Optimal Trajectory Generator for Cartesian Path Following. Robotica 18, 451–458 (2000)
5. Wang, D., Low, C.B.: Modeling and Analysis of Skidding and Slipping in Wheeled Mobile Robots: Control Design Perspective. IEEE Trans. on Robotics 24(3), 676–687 (2008)
6. Wang, D., Low, C.B.: An Analysis of Wheeled Mobile Robots in the Presence of Skidding and Slipping: Control Design Perspective. In: IEEE Int. Conf. on Robotics and Automation, Roma, Italy, pp. 2379–2384 (2007)
7. Yamamoto, Y., Yun, X.: Effect of the Dynamic Interaction on Coordinated Control of Mobile Manipulators. IEEE Trans. on Robotics and Auto. 12(5), 816–824 (1996)
8. Yamamoto, Y., Yun, X.: Modeling and Compensation of the Dynamic Interaction of a Mobile Manipulator. In: IEEE Int. Conf. on Robotics and Automation, San Diego, California, USA, pp. 2187–2192 (1994)
9. Meghdari, M., Durali, M., Naderi, D.: Investigating Dynamic Interaction Between the one D.O.F. Manipulator and Vehicle of a Mobile Manipulator. J. Intell. Robot. Syst. 28, 277–290 (1997)
10. Moosavian, S.A., Papadopoulos, E.: Explicit Dynamic of Free Flyers with Multiple Manipulator via SPACEMAPLE. J. Adv. Robotic 18(2), 223–244 (2004)
11. Eslamy, M., Moosavian, S.A.: Dynamics and Cooperative Object Manipulation Control of Suspended Mobile Manipulators. J. Intell. Robot Syst. 60, 181–199 (2010)
12. Aguiar, A.P., Hespanha, J.P.: Trajectory-Tracking and Path-Following of Underactuated Autonomous Vehicles with Parametric Modeling Uncertainty. IEEE Trans. on Auto. Cont. 52(8), 1362–1379 (2007)
13. Kim, M.S., Shim, J.H., Hong, S.G.: Designing a Robust Adaptive Dynamic Controller for Nonholonomic Mobile Robots under Modeling Uncertainty and Disturbances. Mechatronics 13(5), 507–519 (2003)
14. Dovgobrod, G.M., Klyachko, L.M.: Simplified Derivation of Control Law Providing for a Vehicle's Motion on a Nonlinear Path. Gyroscopy and Navigation 3(1), 35–40 (2012)
15. Chen, W., Mills, J.K., Chu, J., Sun, D.: A Fuzzy Compensator for Uncertainty of Industrial Robots. In: IEEE Int. Conf. on Robotics and Automation, Seoul, Korea, pp. 2968–2973 (2001)
16. Liu, S., Ma, C., Luo, C., Wang, X.: Adaptive Control of Free-Floating Space Robot with Disturbance Based on Robust Fuzzy Compensator. In: 2nd. Int. Conf. on Intelligent Human-Machine System and Cybernetics, Nanjing, China, pp. 23–28 (2010)

Proposal and Evaluation of Integer Inverse Kinematics for Multijoint Small Robot

Takeshi Morishita and Osamu Tojo

Toin University of Yokohama, Department of Robotics
1614 Kugogane-cho Aoba-ku Yokohama, Japan
morishita@cc.toin.ac.jp

Abstract. In this paper, we propose an integer inverse kinematics method for multijoint robot control. The method reduces computational overheads and leads to the development of a simple control system as the use of fuzzy logic enables linguistic modeling of the joint angle. A small humanoid robot is used to confirm via experiment that the method produces the same cycling movements in the robot as those in a human. In addition, we achieve fast information sharing by implementing the all-integer control algorithm in a low-cost, low-power microprocessor. Moreover, we evaluate the ability of this method for trajectory generation and confirm that target trajectories are reproduced well. The computational results of the general inverse kinematics model are compared to those of the integer inverse kinematics model and similar outputs are demonstrated. We show that the integer inverse kinematics model simplifies the control process.

Keywords: Inverse Kinematics, Integer, Fuzzy, Multijoint Robot, Control.

1 Introduction

Small robots are gradually becoming a common feature in the daily living environment of modern societies. They are often subject to cost constraints, and this, along with their size, makes the mounting of large-scale devices difficult. As a countermeasure, the control software for small size microcomputers requires a degree of ingenuity and an efficient algorithm.

Many robots actively work with limbs constructed from links and joints. These joints, e.g., robot arms and legs, often have one or more degrees of freedom (DOF). Forward and inverse kinematics for controlling the limb positions of the target machine are used to relate the controlled object to the coordination system. This is a standard approach to robot control. Naturally, the mathematics involved in this level of control usually includes trigonometric functions and matrix techniques based on real numbers. In addition, higher the number of joints of the robot, more complex and nonlinear is the inverse kinematics equation. Such mathematical functions are computationally expensive and a burden on small processors.

C.-Y. Su, S. Rakheja, H. Liu (Eds.): ICIRA 2012, Part II, LNAI 7507, pp. 376–386, 2012.

To solve the problem of multijoint control, many authors have proposed a control approach based on fuzzy logic for simplifying trajectory generation and extending the range of application [1], [2], [3]. Fuzzy logic deals with intermediate values via a membership function, in contrast to traditional binary logic. The membership function expands the range of the defined function from {0,1} to [0,1]. The function specifies the degree to which an input is included in the set and the numerical value grade. When explaining the theory and mathematical logic using an intermediate value, the grade is often normalized to aid understanding and use. This is natural fuzzy logic, and is a general method for quantifying ambiguity [4]. However, normalization is not necessarily needed for computational calculations for fuzzy logic, because it can be calculated by only four arithmetic operations in some defined method of membership function.

In this paper, we propose a simplifying method to implement inverse kinematics using only integer arithmetic. In addition, we show how this approach can be applied to experiments with an actual self-contained multijoint robot, and evaluate the reproducibility of the orbit to produce the integer inverse kinematics.

2   Integer Inverse Kinematics Model

2.1   Extended Range of Fuzzy Set

Fuzzy logic can accommodate an unnormalized definition function. We define a fuzzy set A of the universal set X consisting of integer multiples in the 1 byte range:

$$\mu_A : X \rightarrow [0,255] \tag{1}$$

where, $\mu_A(x)$ is the membership function of A with $x \in X$ and is an integer value in the closed interval [0,255].

2.2   Fuzzy Model for Multijoint Robot Control

A limb with n joints can be controlled using the following inverse kinematics control model based on fuzzy logic. The i-th control rule is given by the fuzzy relation Ri defined by the space (x, y, θ) where x and y are the coordinates of bicycle pedal and θ is the joint angle. Then, the fuzzy relations for the robot mechanism joints are given by

$$R_{ij} = (x, y, \theta_j) \tag{2}$$

where j denotes the specific joint, i.e., the hip, knee, or ankle joint.

The following four rule bases use the sentence connective "also":

$$R_{HP} = \bigcup_{i=1}^{n} R_{iHP} \quad \text{or}$$

$$R_{HR} = \bigcup_{i=1}^{n} R_{iHR} \quad \text{or}$$

$$(3)$$

$$R_{KN} = \bigcup_{i=1}^{n} R_{iKN} \quad \text{or}$$

$$R_{AN} = \bigcup_{i=1}^{n} R_{iAN}$$

Here, *HP*, *HR*, *KN*, and *AN* denote the hip pitch, hip roll, and knee and ankle joints, respectively.

A measurement values input (x^0, y^0) gives the output joint angle B_j^0 (θ_j). The input membership function $\mu_{i1}(x)$ of the x coordinate and the input membership function $\mu_{i2}(y)$ of the y coordinate are defined as

$$\omega_i = \mu_{i1}(x) \wedge \mu_{i2}(y) \tag{4}$$

where ω_i is the grade of the i-th rule. The maximum grade for this system is 255, and the value is truncated to yield an integer. In general, the fuzzy relation between the input and the output membership function $B_{ij}(\theta_j)$ is

$$B_j^o(\theta_j) = \bigvee_{i=1}^{n} \left[\omega_i \wedge B_{ij}(\theta_j) \right] \tag{5}$$

We aim to increase the joint control performance with a lightweight algorithm, and, therefore, we apply a center of gravity (COG) defuzzification method using a singleton-type output membership function:

$$\theta_j = \frac{\sum_{i=1}^{n} \omega_i B_{ij}}{\sum_{i=1}^{n} \omega_i} \tag{6}$$

This fuzzy logic control model will be applied to multijointed robots. Thus, this logic can derive each joint angle from the tip coordinate of the limb. Moreover, since this algorithm is, by definition, an integer variable system, any decimal value obtained by division is rounded down according to the microprocessor specifications [5], [6].

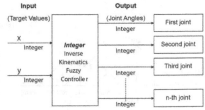

Fig. 1. Analysis of bicycle pedaling action using video images of a human subject

Fig. 2. Block diagram outlining the inverse kinematics controller

3   Analysis of Human Action

We have analyzed the bicycle pedaling action requiring the cooperative operation of two legs, as shown in Figure 1, using video images of a human subject. Four points (the hip joint, knee joint, ankle, and tip of the toe) were selected for the analysis, and the movement was recorded from two directions (side-on and from behind). In addition, we confirmed that humans do not consciously consider the angles of their joints. Moreover, we determined the following from the two types of sample images of the bicycle action: 1)There is little change in the yaw and roll of the hip, knee, and ankle joint angle or the ankle joint pitch angle. 2)Pedaling defines a trajectory that is approximately two-dimensional. We thus define the controlled object to be a single foot with 3 DOF.

4   Robot System Based on Human Model

4.1   Integer Inverse Kinematics Control Model

The controller utilizes the algorithm defined in section 2 to construct the quantification method for the behavior of the human subject and the formulation of linguistic rules. This algorithm easily describes the behavior of the human subject by the four arithmetic integer operations. In this way, we have realized a lightweight and flexible control process for a embedded computer system inside small robot.

The advantage of the fuzzy model is that human behavior models can be easily applied by the microprocessors inside small robots. To demonstrate, we applied the fuzzy controller to the legs of a small autonomous multijoint type robot. Figure 2 shows the system block diagram of the control section designed by the fuzzy logic.

4.2   Linguistic Quantification

Using the results of sample image analysis, we used fuzzy sets to quantify the (x, y) coordinates of the foot position on the bicycle pedal. Figure 3 shows the input membership functions, scaling factors, language labels, and fuzzy sets. The output membership functions are shown in Figure 4.

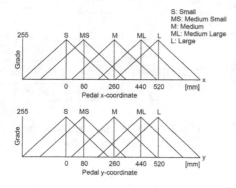

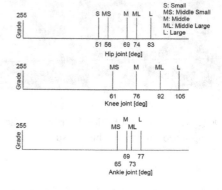

Fig. 3. Input membership functions based on human behavior analysis

Fig. 4. Singleton output membership functions based on human behavior analysis

The turning radius of the pedals, the input target object, is 250 mm and we use the (x, y) coordinates of eight points at 45 degree intervals on the circumference of this circle to define the center of each input membership function fuzzy set (Fig. 3). In a similar manner, the joint angles of the leg are allocated to the center of each output membership function fuzzy set. Here, the output membership functions are defined by singletons (Fig. 4). At the same time, fuzzy labels are defined for the fuzzy sets of all membership functions using the dynamic characteristic data from the human analysis.

4.3   Fuzzy Rule for Inverse Kinematics

Table 1 shows the fuzzy control rules that were obtained from the human action analysis. This shows the relationship between the language label and the corresponding joint angle dynamics. The rule constitutes the inverse kinematics model used to calculate the joint angles of the 3 DOF system by using fuzzy reasoning for the target coordinates. The inference algorithm uses the minimum-maximum composition method and a singleton type membership function.

Table 1. Fuzzy rules for the 3 DOF based on human behavior

| | | \multicolumn{5}{c}{Hip Joint} | \multicolumn{5}{c}{Knee Joint} | \multicolumn{5}{c}{Ankle Joint} |
| | | \multicolumn{5}{c}{X} | \multicolumn{5}{c}{X} | \multicolumn{5}{c}{X} |
		S	MS	M	ML	L	S	MS	M	ML	L	S	MS	M	ML	L
	S			S					L					L		
	MS		MS		S			L		ML			ML		ML	
Y	M	M				MS	ML				M	MS				ML
	ML		L		ML			M		MS			M		M	
	L			L					MS					MS		

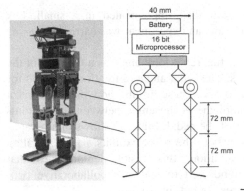

Fig. 5. The autonomous humanoid robot system

Table 2. Robot specifications

Microprocessor :	
	H8/300H CPU
	25 MHz
	RAM 8KB
Battery :	7.4 V Lipo
Actuator :	RC Servomotor x 10

Table 3. Calculation times

4DOF	8DOF	12DOF	24DOF
175μs	350μs	510μs	1040μs

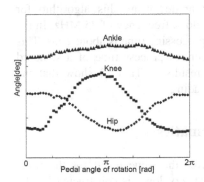

Fig. 6. Trajectories of robot joint angles during pedaling action

Fig. 7. Pedaling action performed by the biped autonomous robot

4.4   Robot Hardware Model

Figure 5 shows a photograph of the robot used in the experiment and the hardware configuration. The lower body is an autonomous 10 DOF humanoid robot with a 16-bit microprocessor. However, we have defined the leg to consist of 3 DOF, and, therefore, 6 DOF in total are controlled. The robot system specifications are shown in Table 2.

5   Reproducing Human Action

5.1   Bicycle Driving Experiment and Results

System checks were undertaken by initial simulations before the actual experiment was conducted. The coordinates of pedals were entered into the simulated integer inverse kinematics fuzzy control model, and the output results were confirmed to be the appropriate joint angles. The model was then implemented in a small, low performance 16-bit microprocessor, 25MHz and an experiment was carried out using the robot.

Figure 6 shows the trajectories of each actual robot joint angle as a function of the pedal angle over a sampling time of 100 ms. The pedal angle of rotation was used for the input data at intervals of 1 degree ($\pi/180$ rad). These results show that the control model, constructed from eight points, complements the angle between these points continuously and smoothly from the angle of the pedal. Figure 7 shows photographs of the bicycle operation performed by the robot. The robot exhibits a fluid pedaling action and good bicycle control. In addition, this result demonstrates that appropriately interpolated trajectories can be used to realize a collaborative two-legged cycling work system and is 180 degrees (π rad) phase difference.

5.2   Integer Inverse Kinematics Processing Capacity

Table 3 lists the calculation times of the joint angles using this algorithm for increasing DOF on a 16-bit microprocessor with a clock frequency of 25 MHz. In the case of a small humanoid robot with 24 DOF, the processing time is about 1 ms. This is equal to the pulse-width modulation (PWM) control process time of a standard commercial remote-controlled servo motor. The results in Table 3 show that the microprocessor can control all joints without overloading.

6   Evaluation of Integer Inverse Kinematics

The general inverse kinematics model always gives the same result for the same input. The integer inverse kinematics model with fuzzy logic is constructed by the membership functions and control rules based on three joint angles and movement from sampling image data of human behavior. Therefore, if we can construct an integer inverse kinematics model based on the behavior results from the general inverse kinematics model, then we can evaluate the motion trajectory generative capacities of this integer model.

6.1   Feature Extraction from General Inverse Kinematics

We first calculated the 3 DOF movement of the leg from a general inverse kinematics model. Figure 8 shows the simulation models of the real small humanoid behavior used in the experiment. Here, the angles θ_1, θ_2, θ_3, and θ_p represent the hip joint, knee joint, ankle joint, and pedal angles, respectively. The angle of the foot is kept constant at 20 degrees, and the posture for eight pedaling positions at 45 degree intervals is shown. The region of interest for this behavior is the hip, knee, and ankle with the sampling posture being the posture of the leg at pedal positions at 45 degree intervals (see Figure 8). The truncated integer joint angle for each posture is recorded in Table 4.

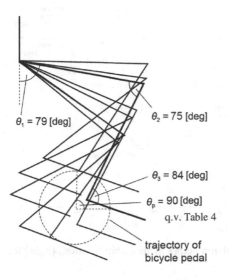

Table 4. Data analysis based on the general inverse kinematics

Pedal θ_p [deg]	Hip θ_1 [deg]	Knee θ_2 [deg]	Ankle θ_3 [deg]
0	81	48	57
45	88	59	77
90	79	75	84
135	67	86	82
180	54	89	73
225	50	81	61
270	54	63	46
315	63	53	45

Fig. 8. Simulation based on the general inverse kinematic model. The angles θ_1, θ_2, θ_3, and θ_p represent the hip joint, knee joint, ankle joint, and pedal angles, respectively.

6.2 Fuzzy Integer Inverse Kinematics Model Derived from General Inverse Kinematics

The membership functions and fuzzy control rules are derived from the behavior and joint angle characteristics. When the (x, y) coordinates of the pedal rotational position is input in 1 degree steps, the reproducibility of the integer inverse kinematics model can be demonstrated through a comparison with the calculated results of the general inverse kinematics model. In addition, x and y are used as inputs to express rotation in terms of integer coordinates. Figures 9 show the input and output membership functions constructed using the survey data of Table 4 and the general inverse kinematic model. The joint angles in Table 4 were sorted in descending order, assigned a label, and from this, the output membership functions and fuzzy control rules (Table 5) were developed. This result is shown in Figure 11.

7   Consideration of Integer Inverse Kinematics Model Reproducibility

We calculated the hip, knee, and ankle joint angles during the pedaling action using the x and y coordinates of the pedal position for both the general and integer inverse kinematics models. Figures 10 and 11 show the simulation results of the general and integer inverse kinematics models, respectively.

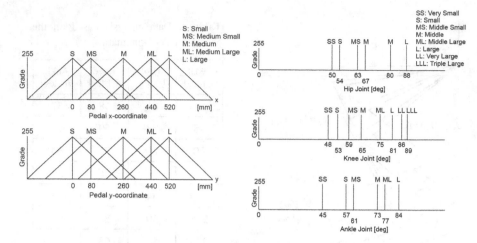

Fig. 9. Input membership functions (left) and singleton output membership functions (right) for the general inverse kinematics model

Table 5. Fuzzy rules for the 3 DOF based on general inverse kinematics

		Hip Joint					Knee Joint					Ankle Joint				
		X					X					X				
		S	MS	M	ML	L	S	MS	M	ML	L	S	MS	M	ML	L
Y	S			S					L					M		
	MS		SS		M			LLL		M			MS		L	
	M	S				ML	LL				S	SS				L
	ML		MS		L			ML		SS			SS		ML	
	L			ML					MS					S		

The results of the integer inverse kinematics model are very similar to the output of the general model. This demonstrates that the integer inverse kinematics model can reproduce the original behavior by only performing integer operations. From this results, the integer inverse kinematics model is confirmed to be a simplified method that can approximate traditional inverse kinematics. We note that Figures 8 and 14 show very similar results and pedaling action by the actual robot. This is also good bicycle control as fluid motion of Figure 7, thus, further confirm that this model approximates traditional methods well.

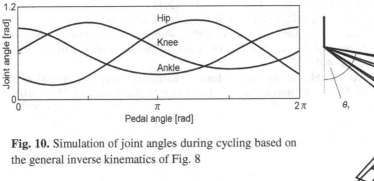

Fig. 10. Simulation of joint angles during cycling based on the general inverse kinematics of Fig. 8

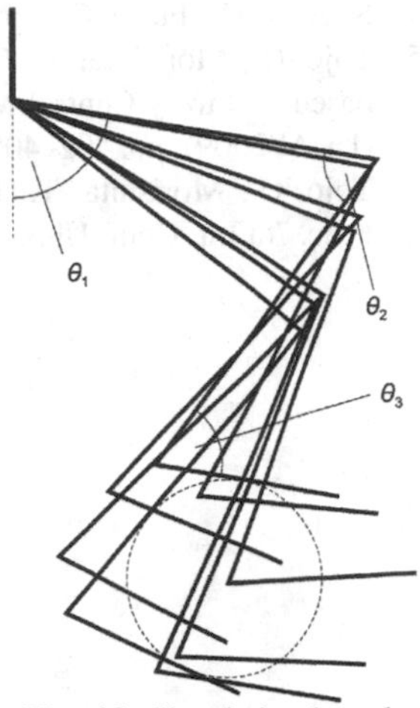

Fig. 12. Simulation based on the integer inverse kinematics model

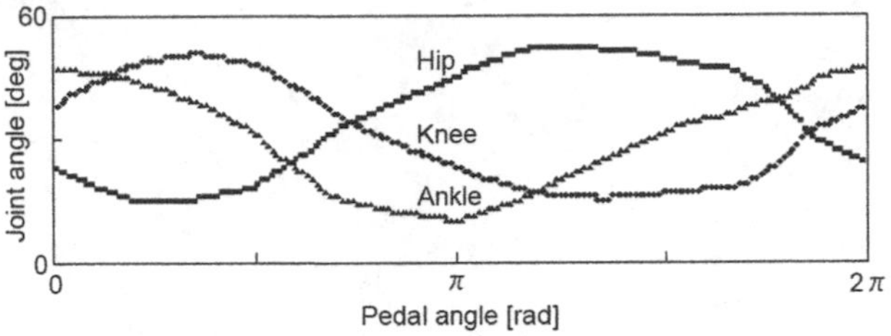

Fig. 11. Fuzzy inverse kinematics outputs defined by integer number and based on the general inverse kinematics

8   Conclusion

This paper has outlined an inverse kinematics model consisting of integer variables and proposed a method to realize inverse kinematics using integer input and output and integer arithmetic. We have also shown that the application of this model to an actual humanoid robot system reproduces the cycling behavior of a human very well. Furthermore, we have confirmed the reproducibility of this model based on the original target behavior when deriving this inverse kinematics model. We have also showed that it is possible to generate approximated behavior of the original motion. Moreover, the integer inverse kinematics model is shown to be a reduced and simplified calculation method that discretizes the real variables of a conventional robot joint control program.

References

1. Kumbla, K.K., Jamshidi, M.: Control of robotic manipulator using fuzzy logic. In: Proc. Third IEEE World Conf. Fuzzy Sys., vol. 1, pp. 518–523 (1994), doi:10.1109/FUZZY.1994.343731
2. Chen, C.-Y., Her, M.-G., Hung, Y.-C., Karkoub, M.: Approximating a Robot Inverse Kinematics Solution Using Fuzzy Logic Tuned by Genetic Algorithms. Int. J. Adv. Manuf. Technol. 20, 375–380 (2002), doi:10.1007/s001700200166

3. Piltan, F., Sulaiman, N., Nasiri, H., Allahdadi, S., Bairami, M.A.: Novel Robot Manipulator Adaptive Artificial Control: Design a Novel SISO Adaptive Fuzzy Sliding Algorithm Inverse Dynamic Like Method. Int. J. Eng. 5, 399–418 (2011)
4. Sugeno, M.: Fuzzy Control. Nikkan Kougyou Shinnbun, Tokyo (Japanese) (1988)
5. Tojo, O., Morishita, T.: Compact Autonomous Robot with Inverse Kinematics Algorithm based on Fuzzy Control Model. In: Proc. 6th Int. Conf. Ubiquitous Robots Ambient Intell. (URAI 2009), pp. 402–405 (2009)
6. Tojo, O., Morishita, T.: Method for Integer Inverse Kinematics and its Application. In: Proc. 7th Int. Conf. Ubiquitous Robots Ambient Intell. (URAI 2010), pp. 233–236 (2010)

Velocity Selection for High-Speed UGVs in Rough Unknown Terrains Using Force Prediction

Graeme N. Wilson, Alejandro Ramirez-Serrano,
Mahmoud Mustafa, and Krispin A. Davies

Department of Mechanical and Manufacturing Engineering, University of Calgary,
Calgary, Alberta, Canada
{wilsongn,aramirez,mmmustaf,kdavies}@ucalgary.ca

Abstract. Enabling high speed navigation of Unmanned Ground Vehicles (UGVs) in unknown rough terrain where limited or no information is available in advance requires the assessment of terrain in front of the UGV. Attempts have been made to predict the forces the terrain exerts on the UGV for the purpose of determining the maximum allowable velocity for a given terrain. However, current methods produce overly aggressive velocity profiles which could damage the UGV. This paper presents three novel safer methods of force prediction that produce effective velocity profiles. Two models, Instantaneous Elevation Change Model (IECM) and Sinusoidal Base Excitation Model: using Excitation Force (SBEM:EF), predict the forces exerted by the terrain on the vehicle at the ground contact point, while another method, Sinusoidal Base Excitation Model: using Transmitted Force (SBEM:TF), predicts the forces transmitted to the vehicle frame by the suspension.

Keywords: Unmanned Ground Vehicles, High Speed Terrain Traversal, Terrain Assessment.

1 Introduction

Autonomous traversal of unknown rough terrains at high-speeds is a challenging endeavor for Unmanned Ground Vehicles (UGVs). Information about unknown terrain must be gathered online using either proprioceptive or exteroceptive sensors to allow UGVs to avoid obstacles, achieve navigation goals, and maintain forces transmitted by the terrain on the vehicle at safe levels.

Proprioceptive detection of vehicle vibrations during terrain traversal has been used to classify terrain using trained probabilistic neural networks (PNNs)[1], [2] as well as using support vector machine (SVM) classifiers [3]. The problem with these methods is that significant offline training is required, they are dependent on the speeds at which the vehicles are trained, and they produce misclassifications of terrain during traversal. To resolve the speed dependency problem the frequency response of the terrain was obtained from the acceleration data using a transfer function in [4], but offline training is still required and misclassification of terrain still occurs. In addition to the previous stated problems, proprioceptive approaches are reactive, which means

C.-Y. Su, S. Rakheja, H. Liu (Eds.): ICIRA 2012, Part II, LNAI 7507, pp. 387–396, 2012.
© Springer-Verlag Berlin Heidelberg 2012

that large changes in terrain roughness may be undetected until after the vehicle encounters them.

To detect upcoming terrain changes exteroceptive sensors can be used. The combination of vibration and vision based classification using SVM has been used to classify upcoming terrain characteristics [5], [6]. These methods predict upcoming terrain at the expense of offline training. Online training methods using this combined approach have also been investigated; however, these approaches still present the potential for terrain misclassification which would damage the UGV [7], [8].

To prevent misclassification of terrain, methods have been developed which use geometric information about the terrain from stereo cameras and laser scanners [9–11]. Using a stereo camera a danger value is computed in [9] using terrain roughness, slope, and step height. While this work is useful for path planning it does not consider velocity selection for the UGV. In contrast, the authors in [10] present a fuzzy logic approach which outputs target velocity based on roughness and slope inputs. This approach allows for velocity control of UGV based on upcoming terrain; however, it does not guarantee that forces acting on the UGV are kept in a safe range.

Addressing the problem of maintaining safe forces, the work presented by [11] computes a Roughness Index (RI) based on the elevation of the terrain detected by a laser scanner. RI value is used to compute the allowable velocity for traversing upcoming terrain based on the predicted forces that the terrain will exert on the vehicle. While this approach solves many of the issues previously presented, the methods used in [11] to calculate the force exerted by the terrain produce aggressive velocity estimates which may still result in UGV damage.

To avoid UGV damage this paper presents three novel safer methods of predicting the force exerted by unknown terrain on a UGV. These new methods include two techniques that predict the base excitation force exerted by the terrain, and one technique predicting the force transmitted to the vehicle frame. These techniques use the assumption that elevation data follows a normal distribution; they thus calculate the worst case maximum terrain elevation from the RI. The potential for resonance in the suspension is even accounted for in the transmitted force model. These methods are designed to produce fast and safe values of maximum allowable velocity for rough unknown terrains.

2   Roughness Index

Developing force prediction models for high-speed UGVs requires a measure of the traversability of upcoming terrain. As described in [11] the Roughness Index (RI) can be used to provide a quantitative measure of terrain roughness from a 3D point cloud. In this approach the RI was described as a number ranging from 0 to 1, where 0 was the roughest perceived terrain. The problem with the approach proposed in [11] is that in many cases, such as a simple sinusoidal terrain profile, the RI becomes negative before the maximum terrain elevation exceeds the ground clearance of the vehicle. Since negative values of RI are considered untraversable in [11], certain terrain are falsely considered untraversable. To solve this problem the RI proposed in [11] is redefined here as shown in Eq. (1) where e represents the terrain elevation for each point in the 3D point cloud and h represents the vehicle ground clearance.

$$RI = STD\left(\frac{e}{h}\right) \tag{1}$$

The redefined RI is a number which ranges from 0 (smoothest terrain) to ∞ (roughest possible terrain). The RI at which the terrain is considered untraversable is a value which is defined separately for each application as it depends on the abilities of the vehicle being used. A comparison of the RI defined in this paper and the RI defined in [11] is shown in Fig. 1. In this figure the RI values are shown as calculated on a range of sinusoidal terrains with frequencies of 2π and amplitudes ranging from 0 to $0.1m$. The ground clearance of the vehicle was set at $0.1m$. For other values of ground clearance results will be similar except the slopes of the lines will decrease.

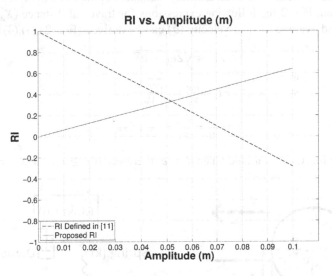

Fig. 1. Comparison of RI's – [11] vs. Proposed RI (Eq. (1))

From Fig. 1 the problem with the RI defined in [11] is clear since the RI becomes negative before the amplitude of the terrain reaches the ground clearance of the vehicle. With the newly proposed RI from Eq. (1) it can be seen that the RI starts at zero and becomes an ever increasingly positive number as terrain roughness increases. This behavior is more intuitive than the method from [11], therefore it is desirable to use the RI from Eq. (1).

3   Velocity Models

In the work presented in [11] a method for determining allowable velocity from a calculated RI and a known allowable excitation force was developed. In this model the calculations depend on an estimated maximum terrain frequency. As a result complications can arise in situations where the maximum terrain frequency exceeds the estimated maximum frequency. This can lead to situations where the predicted maximum velocity causes damage to the vehicle. In this paper three new methods are developed to prevent these problems, the first being the new Instantaneous Elevation Change Model, and the last two being variations on the new Sinusoidal Base Excitation Model.

3.1   Instantaneous Elevation Change Model

In the Instantaneous Elevation Change Model (IECM) the worst case scenario of a step change in the terrain elevation is considered (Fig. 2). In this scenario the maximum potential force that could be exerted on a vehicle by terrain of any given roughness can be calculated to an arbitrary statistical confidence to be selected by the designer. From Fig. 2 the following expressions for traversal distance (X_w), traversal time (Δt), and average vertical velocity $(\dot{e})$ can be derived (Eq. (2),(3),(4)).

$$X_w = \sqrt{2er - e^2} \tag{2}$$

$$\Delta t = \frac{X_w}{V_x} = \frac{\sqrt{2er-e^2}}{V_x} \tag{3}$$

$$\dot{e} = \frac{e}{\Delta t} = \frac{eV_x}{X_w} = \frac{eV_x}{\sqrt{2er-e^2}} \tag{4}$$

The value for X_w is saturated when $r = e$, therefore if $e \geq r$ then $X_w = r$.

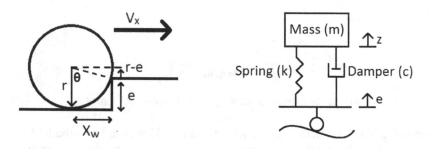

Fig. 2. IECM Model   **Fig. 3.** Simplified Quarter Car Model

Using this IECM model the excitation force acting on the vehicle can be derived from a simplified quarter car model (Fig. 3). The derived expression is shown in Eq. (5) where the constants ω_n, ζ, and m represent the natural frequency, damping ratio, and mass of the quarter car model respectively.

$$\hat{F} = \frac{F}{m \cdot \omega_n} = \frac{1}{\omega_n^2}\ddot{z} + \frac{2\xi}{\omega_n}\dot{z} + z = \frac{2\xi}{\omega_n}\dot{e} + e \tag{5}$$

Combining Eq. (4) and Eq. (5) an expression relating excitation force to velocity is derived:

$$\hat{F} = \left(\frac{2\xi V_x}{\omega_n X_w} + 1 \right) e \tag{6}$$

By rearranging Eq. (6) for V_x and substituting e_{max} for e, Eq. (7) is obtained.

$$V_x = \left(\hat{F} - e_{max} \right) \frac{\omega_n X_w}{2\zeta e_{max}} = \left(\hat{F} - e_{max} \right) \frac{\omega_n \sqrt{2 e_{max} r - e_{max}^2}}{2\zeta e_{max}} \tag{7}$$

The expression shown in Eq. (8) for e_{max} is obtained by assuming that the values for e obtained from a laser scanner follow a normal distribution with a mean of 0. With this assumption the cumulative distribution function is used to calculate the probability (P_e) that $e_{max} \leq$ z-score of e_{max}. The probability function P_e is then used to obtain Eq. (8).

$$e_{max} = \sqrt{2}\, erf^{-1}(2P_e - 1)(RI)\, h \tag{8}$$

Using Eq. (7) and (8) the allowable traversal velocity can be calculated to an arbitrary confidence, as defined by the designer, through assigning a value for P_e and substituting in an appropriate value for the maximum allowable excitation force $F_{max} = F$ as well as the vehicle and suspension properties.

3.2   Sinusoidal Base Excitation Model

With the new IECM the issue from [11] of estimated maximum terrain frequency being exceeded has been avoided. However, since vertical velocity of the terrain is calculated as the average of the vertical velocity during step traversal in IECM, there is the danger that the peak vertical velocity during step traversal could cause damage to the vehicle. To reduce this issue IECM is transformed into a Sinusoidal Base Excitation Model (SBEM) using the traversal time as the quarter period of the function (Fig. 4).

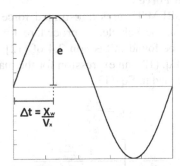

Fig. 4. Sinusoidal Base Excitation Model

With the same procedure used to derive Eq. (5), the equation for excitation force was obtained (Eq. (9)). The constants c and k represent the damping constant, and spring constant of the quarter car model respectively.

$$F(t) = m\ddot{z} + c\dot{z} + kz = ke \sin\left(\frac{\pi}{2\Delta t} t \right) + \frac{ce\pi}{2\Delta t} \cos\left(\frac{\pi}{2\Delta t} t \right) \tag{9}$$

Using this new model two new equations relating allowable velocity to the RI are derived in SBEM: Using Excitation Force (SBEM:EF), and SBEM: Using Transmitted Force (SBEM:TF).

SBEM: Using Excitation Force
The SBEM:EF method uses excitation force to define the maximum force that can be exerted on the vehicle. To determine the maximum allowable speed of the vehicle it is important to predict the maximum excitation force during obstacle traversal. To do this the derivative of Eq. (9) is set equal to zero $\left(\dot{F}(t)=0\right)$ and then the equation can be rearranged for time. As shown in Eq. (10) this enables the calculation of the time at which the maximum excitation force occurs (t_{max}) with respect to the start of the obstacle traversal.

$$t_{max} = \frac{2X_w}{\pi V_x} tan^{-1}\left(\frac{2kX_w}{\pi c V_x}\right) \tag{10}$$

Substituting Eq. (10) into Eq. (9) and using Eq. (8) for e, an expression representing the maximum excitation force is obtained (Eq. (11)).

$$F_{max} = \frac{\frac{2k^2 e_{max}X_w}{\pi c V_x} + \frac{\pi c e_{max}V_x}{2X_w}}{\sqrt{1+\frac{4k^2 X_w^2}{\pi^2 c^2 V_x^2}}} \tag{11}$$

As a result the maximum allowable velocity for the vehicle can now be obtained from Eq. (11) with a numerical method using the appropriate value for F_{max} as defined by the designer. In this paper Newton's Method was used to solve for the allowable velocity V_x.

SBEM: Using Transmitted Force
In contrast to SBEM:EF, SBEM:TF uses transmitted force to define the maximum force that can be exerted on the vehicle. A procedure for determining transmitted forces in general cases can be found in Section 2.4 of [12]. Adapting this procedure and using ω_b as defined in Eq. (12), an expression for the maximum transmitted force problem in this paper is obtained in Eq. (13).

$$\omega_b = \frac{\pi V_x}{2X_w} \tag{12}$$

$$F_{t\,max} = \frac{k e_{max} \pi^2 V_x^2}{4X_w^2 \omega_n^2}\left[\frac{1+\left(\frac{\pi \zeta V_x}{X_w \omega_n}\right)^2}{\left(1-\left(\frac{\pi V_x}{2X_w \omega_n}\right)^2\right)^2+\left(\frac{\pi \zeta V_x}{X_w \omega_n}\right)^2}\right]^{1/2} \tag{13}$$

As with the excitation force method, the maximum allowable velocity V_x is solved with a numerical method in Eq. (13) using the appropriate value for $F_{t\,max}$ as defined by the designer. As stated previously, Newton's Method was used in this paper.

4   Results

In this section the three force prediction methods for determining allowable maximum velocities derived in this paper are compared to each other (Eq. (7), Eq. (11), Eq. (13)) as well as to the method derived in [11]. The methods being compared are IECM, SBEM:EF, SBEM:TF, and Prev:BEM (Base Excitation Model from [11]).

To compare these methods vehicle properties for a typical large All-Terrain Vehicle were assumed to allow for simulation. The vehicle properties can be seen in Table 1. The terrain was simulated by one hundred different 2D sinusoidal profiles with properties also listed in Table 1. The sinusoidal amplitude of the terrain was set at one hundred different values evenly spaced between 0 and 0.1m. The sinusoidal profile was used to represent a typical 2D uniformly oscillating terrain profile.

Table 1. Vehicle/Terrain Properties

Quarter Mass m	Ground Clearance h	Wheel Radius r	Suspension Natural Frequency ω_n	Suspension Damping Ratio ζ
100 kg	0.1 m	0.1 m	3 rad/s	0.5

Confidence in e_{max} P_e	Maximum Allowable Excitation Force F_{max}	Maximum Allowable Transmitted Force $F_{t_{max}}$	Terrain Distance Frequency f	Terrain Amplitude
0.999999	5000 N	5000 N	1.5 Hz	-0.1 to 0.1 m

Using the vehicle properties defined in Table 1 the methods were compared graphically. As previously stated, one hundred unique amplitudes were used for the sinusoidal terrain profiles; therefore one hundred unique RI values were used for plotting. In Fig. 5 the calculated allowable velocities of the four methods are plotted against the RI of the terrain (calculated from the sinusoidal terrain profiles). In addition, the maximum velocity of the vehicle was considered to be $20\ m/s$ (consistent with a typical large All-Terrain Vehicle).

From Fig. 5 it can be seen that, as expected, the method derived in [11] produces the most aggressive velocity profile. Also as expected, the SBEM:EF and SBEM:TF models produced the safest velocity profiles. IECM had a more aggressive velocity profile than the two SBEM methods, which is consistent with expectations since it relies on the average vertical velocity during obstacle traversal, which as previously stated could lead to unsafe force predictions.

It can also be seen that SBEM:EF and SBEM:TF produced almost identical profiles. The transmitted force is very dependent on the frequency ratio ω_b/ω_n, where for high frequency ratios the transmitted force is generally higher than the excitation force. However, for low frequency ratios the transmitted force can be less than the excitation force [12]. The problem with low frequency ratios is that in this area resonance occurs as $\omega_b/\omega_n \to 1$; therefore these ratios are often avoided. In this case the transmitted and excitation force are approximately equal, which is generally the best case scenario when avoiding resonance by using high frequency ratios.

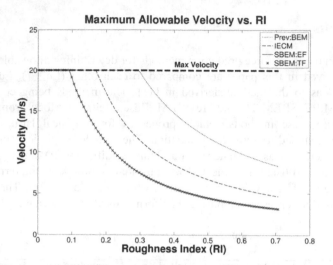

Fig. 5. Allowable Velocity vs. RI

To highlight the differences between SBEM:EF and SBEM:TF the vehicle properties in Table 1 have been manipulated to induce resonance where $\omega_n = 6\,rad/s$, $\zeta = 0.1$, and $F_{max} = F_{t\,max} = 1000\,N$. The graphs comparing these methods in the resonance case are shown in Fig. 6.

With resonance it can be seen that SBEM:TF deviates significantly from SBEM:EF, especially starting at $RI \approx 0.45$. This RI value is where resonance reaches full effect due to the nature of the sinusoidal terrain. It is easy to see that SBEM:TF is a much safer method than all other presented methods since it is very possible for transmitted forces to exceed the excitation force.

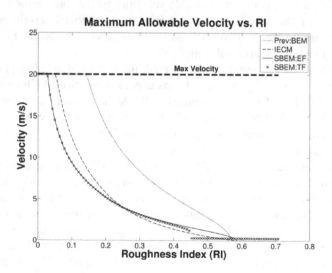

Fig. 6. Allowable Velocity vs. RI – Resonance Case

5   Conclusion

This paper presents three novel force prediction models for calculating allowable traversal velocity based on a 3D point cloud obtained from proprioceptive sensors. To achieve this a Roughness Index (RI) was used to create a quantitative measure of the upcoming terrain. With this RI three methods for predicting force were derived from the Instantaneous Elevation Change Mode (IECM) and the Sinusoidal Base Excitation Model (SBEM) developed in this paper. The SBEM force prediction was split into two methods, one which predicted the excitation force SBEM:EF, and one which predicted transmitted force SBEM:TF.

The three new methods were compared to each other as well as to the force prediction method developed in [11]. The comparison was done using sets of sinusoidal terrain with different amplitudes. In the comparison it was found that as expected the method developed in [11] produced very aggressive allowable velocities which could cause damage to the vehicle during traversal. The IECM produced the second most aggressive profile since the vertical velocity of the terrain was calculated as an average over the traversal of an obstacle. The SBEM methods produced almost identical results for the particular dynamics selected when resonance was not in effect, both predicting the safest velocity profile. When resonance is being avoided the frequency ratio ω_b/ω_n should be high; therefore it is expected that the transmitted force will be at least slightly greater than the excitation force. In the case of resonance it was seen that SBEM:TF produced much different results than SBEM:EF. When resonance frequency was encountered SBEM:TF demonstrated its ability to reduce the allowable velocity to maintain safe traversal speeds.

From the simulations it is expected that the SBEM:EF and SBEM:TF methods would be the safest techniques to use as it is suspected that both the method from [11] and the ICEM method could produce unsafe allowable velocities. In particular SBEM:TF seems like the most promising candidate since it accounts for resonance and also predicts forces transmitted to the vehicle frame, which are the most important for avoiding equipment damage.

For future work these methods will be tested experimentally on a vehicle platform in various rough terrains to verify simulated expectations. Also since suspension parameters may not always be available an adaptive online approach will be developed to eliminate the need for known suspension parameters. These techniques for determining allowable velocities will also be integrated into a navigation system that will allow UGVs to operate autonomously at high speeds in unknown rough terrains to accomplish predetermined navigation goals.

References

1. DuPont, E.M., Moore, C.A., Collins, E.G., Coyle, E.: Frequency response method for terrain classification in autonomous ground vehicles. Auton. Robot. 24(4), 337–347 (2008)
2. Sadhukhan, D.: Autonomous ground vehicle terrain classification using internal sensors. MIT Press (2004)

3. Ward, C.C., Iagnemma, K.: Speed-independent vibration-based terrain classification for passenger vehicles. Veh. Sys. Dyn. 47(9), 1095–1113 (2009)
4. Collins, E.G., Coyle, E.J.: Vibration-based terrain classification using surface profile input frequency responses. In: IEEE Int. Conf. on Robot. and Autom., pp. 3276–3283 (2008)
5. Mou, W., Kleiner, A.: Online Learning Terrain Classification for Adaptive Velocity Control. In: Int. Work. on Safety Security and Rescue Robotics, pp. 1–7 (2010)
6. Weiss, C., Tamimi, H., Zell, A.: A combination of vision- and vibration-based terrain classification. In: IEEE/RSJ Int.Conf. on Intell. Robots and Sys., pp. 2204–2209 (2008)
7. Stavens, D., Thrun, S.: A self-supervised terrain roughness estimator for off-road autonomous driving. In: Proc. of Conf. on Uncertainty in AI, UAI (2006)
8. Brooks, C.A.: Learning to Visually Predict Terrain Properties for Planetary Rovers. Massachusetts Institute of Technology (2009)
9. Chilian, A., Hirschmuller, H.: Stereo camera based navigation of mobile robots on rough terrain. In: IEEE/RSJ Int.Conf. on Intell. Robots and Sys., pp. 4571–4576 (2009)
10. Jin, G.-G., Lee, Y.-H., Lee, H.-S., So, M.-O.: Traversability analysis for navigation of unmanned robots. In: SICE Annu. Conf., pp. 1806–1811 (August 2008)
11. El-Kabbany, A., Ramirez-Serrano, A.: Terrain Roughness Assessment for High Speed Ugv Navigation in Unknown Heterogeneous Terrains. Int. J. of Inf. Acq. 7(2), 165 (2010)
12. Inman, D.J.: Engineering Vibration. In: Engineering Vibration, 3rd edn., pp. 130–139. Pearson Education Inc. (2008)

Modeling and Autonomous Control of Multiple Mobile Manipulators Handling Rigid Objects

Mahmoud Mustafa, Alejandro Ramirez-Serrano, Krispin A. Davies,
and Graeme N. Wilson

Department of Mechanical Engineering,
Schulich School of Engineering, University of Calgary,
Calgary, Canada
{mmmustaf,aramirez,kdavies,wilsongn}@ucalgary.ca

Abstract. This paper investigates a new method of modeling and simulation of a two wheeled Mobile Manipulators (MMs) system each equipped with a 6 DOF arm. Such system modeled in Matlab/Simulink (Simmechanic) environment is used to transport objects without explicit communication between the MMs. MMs cooperation control has received big interest in the last few years and has been suggested for various applications such as tasks involving hazardous environments, explosive handling, and space operations. However most research in MMs cooperation has been performed within 2D flat terrain environment. In this paper MMs are considered working in 3D space and we use the nonholonomic characteristics of the robotic manipulators which has been neglected in previous work. This paper describes a control algorithm for two MMs cooperation executing cooperation's tasks. The proposed approach uses common MM sensors. The paper includes the description of the proposed control mechanism that enables ground mobile manipulators to execute complex tasks in cooperation's.

Keywords: Mobile Manipulators, mobile manipulators cooperation, Matlab and Simmechanics simulation, intelligent fuzzy logic control, motion on rough terrains.

1 Introduction

A mobile manipulator (MM) is a robotic arm mounted on a ground, aerial or underwater mobile platform. The mobile platform (e.g., ground wheeled vehicle) increases the size of the manipulator's workspace, and as a result the increased degree of mobility enables better positioning of the manipulator in different configurations for efficient task execution [1]. In this paper we employ such increased capabilities to transport objects (considered rigid) from point "A" to point "B" via two MMs having implicit cooperation. Herein the proposed work in targeted for wheeled and tracked ground MMs but can potentially (with suitable changes) be applicable to other types of MMs including legged and aerial systems. Thus, in what follows when MMs refer to wheeled and tracked MMs. Despite their degree of mobility and their potential uses the complex physical structure of the robots, the highly coupled dynamics between the mobile platform and the mounted robot arm, and the potential (common)

C.-Y. Su, S. Rakheja, H. Liu (Eds.): ICIRA 2012, Part II, LNAI 7507, pp. 397–406, 2012.
© Springer-Verlag Berlin Heidelberg 2012

nonholonomic dynamics of the mobile base are some of the aspects that increases the difficulties of the system design and control. In this regard, the aim of this paper is to present a recently developed control architecture that enables MMs to cooperates and interact in static and dynamic heterogeneous outdoor rough terrain environments where current cooperation mechanism fail to provide an effective solution for the handling of rigid objects in 3D space (i.e. Translates and rotate objects in cooperation). Flexible objects can potentially be handled with the same approach but significant research still needs to be performed before this is effectively possible. In this paper we focus our attention to the cooperation control mechanisms between two MMs when handling a rigid object. In this scenario two MMs grasps the object by applying an intentional force/torque to the MM's end-effector. To achieve this, the goal is for the two MMs is to distribute the object handling tasks between the MMs, between its manipulator and its mobile base to achieve this one of the two MMs is considered the master while the other is considered the follower. MMs cooperation in this kind of task is particularly useful when heavy or big complex loads must be handled in both smooth and rough terrains. The master role of the task is assigned to the actor having better perception capabilities or to the MM which is in charge of the mission (e.g., guiding the cooperation task) [2]. By using reverse engineering principles, researchers have been trying to learn from nature on how cooperation should be performed. Few years ago, biologists noticed that coordinated motion of animal groups is an interesting and suggestive phenomenon in nature[2]. As a result coordinated controls of multiple mobile manipulators have attracted the attention of many researchers [3-7]. For independent tasks where no cooperation is needed researchers consider the control of the absolute position and orientation of the robots, while for cooperative tasks, we consider the control of the relative position, orientation, and contact force between the end effectors [8].The control of multiple mobile manipulators presents a significant increase in complexity over the single mobile manipulator case. The difficulties lie in the fact that when multiple mobile manipulators coordinate with each other, they form a closed kinematic chain mechanism. This imposes a set of kinematic and dynamic constraints on the position and velocity of coordinated mobile manipulators. As a result, the degrees of freedom of the whole system decrease, and internal forces are generated which need to be controlled [9]. Similar to the work described in this paper two issues are resolved simultaneously: i) the coordination between locomotion and manipulation, and ii) the task execution itself (e.g., transporting an object). In [10] the force control scheme is integrated with coordination algorithms. The force control part sustains the object while the coordination between the manipulator and the mobile platform is maintained at a position such that the manipulator does not fully extend or retract. Computer simulations provided in [11] show the efficacy of the proposed approach. Without a priori knowledge about the trajectory of the object, the mobile manipulator is able to keep up with the motion of the object, hence the motion of MM, while carrying objects. In addition, the coordinated motion control algorithm between the manipulator and the mobile base for each mobile manipulator is taken into consideration. By using these motion control algorithms, the coordination among multiple mobile manipulators is realized without using the geometric relations among robots. From the published approaches for MMs cooperation it is found that the existing methods are diverse. However, the existing literature only considers robot-robot interaction in 2D. Current approaches/mechanisms do not provide solutions to MMs cooperation in 3D (which will enable MMs to work on rough terrains, handle flexible objects while avoiding obstacles. This would be achieved by using effective 3D motion and the inherent redundancy of the nonholonomic manipulators). The MMs cooperative control algorithm presented in this paper seeks to fill this void. First the mathematical models used in this research are presented followed by the description of the proposed control mechanism. Following the work in [12, 13] Simmechanics are used in this paper here for multiple purposes including. i) model the MMs systems, ii) Handeling objects and iii) control the MMs within the Matlab/Simmechanics environment. The problem addressed in this paper is a very difficult field as stated in [7]. The work presented in this paper is a step forward in using MMs in complex dynamic rough terrain while handling flexible elements via non explicit communication.

2 Mobile Manipulator Modeling

2.1 Kinematics of the Wheeled Mobile Robot

The MM used in this paper is composed of a rigid platform with rigid wheels (i.e., tracks) where we neglect the complex terramechanics interactions between the wheels and the terrain. The two left wheels and the two right wheels are connected with a synchronous belt forming a traditional skid steering track locomotion system. As a result the mobile platform can be modeled as two wheels platform (Fig.1) where the configuration of the mobile robot is described by the following vectors and parameters.

$\theta = [\theta_r \quad \theta_l]^T$, $X_v = [x_b \quad y_b \quad \theta]^T$; $\dot{\theta}_l, \dot{\theta}_r$: Angular velocity of the left and the right wheel respectively; θ: Absolute rotation angle (heading angle) of the MM; x_b, y_b: Absolute position of the MM's center of mass, v_l, v_r: left/right wheel linear velocity, respectively. The vehicle linear velocity (v) and an angular velocity ($\dot{\theta}$) are obtained using Equations (1) and (2), respectively.

$$v = \frac{v_l + v_r}{2} = \frac{r(\dot{\theta}_l + \dot{\theta}_r)}{2} \tag{1}$$

$$\dot{\theta} = -\frac{r}{b}\dot{\theta}_l + \frac{r}{b}\dot{\theta}_r \tag{2}$$

As a result, the differential kinematics model of the robot (frame of reference {B})w.r.t the right and left wheel velocities can be represented in a matrix form as:

$$\begin{bmatrix} \dot{x}_B \\ \dot{y}_B \end{bmatrix} = \begin{bmatrix} \cos\theta & -\sin\theta \\ \sin\theta & \cos\theta \end{bmatrix} \begin{bmatrix} r/2 & r/2 \\ -l_B.r/b & l_B.r/b \end{bmatrix} \begin{bmatrix} \dot{\theta}_l \\ \dot{\theta}_r \end{bmatrix} \tag{3}$$

2.2 Kinematic Modeling of the Robot Arm

Based on the typical coordinate transformation concept, the frame of reference fixed on the MM platform can be transformed to the base frame of reference of the manipulator by two translational and one rotation matrices. The frames of reference of the manipulator under consideration are shown in Fig.1. The transformation matrix between the manipulator's frames for the employed 5 DOF manipulator is obtained using the well-known Denavit_Hartenberg method. As a result the final link transformation matrix with respect to the base of the manipulator is obtained as: $T05 = T01*T12*T23*T34*T45$.

Therefore the forward kinematics of the manipulator is formulated as:

$$T_0^5 = \begin{bmatrix} n_x & o_x & a_x & p_x \\ n_y & o_y & a_y & p_y \\ n_z & o_z & a_z & p_z \\ 0 & 0 & 0 & 1 \end{bmatrix} ;$$

where: $p_x = -d_2 s_1 + c_1(a_2 c_2 + a_3 c_{23} - d_5 s_{234})$;
$p_y = d_2 c_1 + s_1(a_2 c_2 + a_3 c_{23} - d_5 s_{234})$;
$p_z = d_1 - a_2 s_2 - a_3 s_{23} - d_5 c_{234}$;
$n_x = c_1 c_{234} c_5 + s_1 s_5$; $n_y = s_1 c_{234} c_5 - c_1 s_5$; $n_z = -s_{234} c_5$; $o_x = -c_1 c_{234} s_5 + s_1 c_5$; $o_y = -s_1 c_{234} s_5 - c_1 c_5$; $o_z = s_{234} s_5$; $a_x = -c_1 s_{234}$; $a_y = -s_1 s_{234}$; $a_z = -c_{234}$

In the above expressions: $c_i = cos(\theta_i)$; $s_i = sin(\theta_i)$; $s_{23} = sin(\theta_2 + \theta_3)$; $c_{23} = cos(\theta_2 + \theta_3)$; $c_{234} = cos(\theta_2 + \theta_3 + \theta_4)$; $s_{234} = sin(\theta_2 + \theta_3 + \theta_4)$ and θ_i for i=1 to 5 are the joint angles of the manipulator, as a result the linear velocity and angular Jacobians in matrix form can be written as: $J_v = [J_{v1} \quad J_{v2} \quad J_{v3} \quad J_{v4} \quad J_{v5}]$.

To find the manipulator's singularities the determinant of the jacobian is set to jacobian $Det(J) = 0$. Subsequently, the manipulability value of the arm, which is a critical parameter used in the proposed cooperation mechanism, can be calculated as: Manipulability= $Det(J) = (a_2 c_2 + a_3 c_{23})(a_3 a_2 s_3)$. In the proposed approach one of the important factors to achieve the cooperation on rough terrain is to model the F/T sensor by cooperating the motion of the robot as it moves on rough terrain. As a result the F/T values are a function of the robot's arm joint angles and the robot's roll, pitch and yaw measured by the Inertia Measurement Unit (IMU) sensor. The forces and moments sensed in a robot's wrist when the MM moves on rough terrain can be obtained using Equation (4):

$$J = \begin{bmatrix} -s_1(a_2 c_2 + a_3 c_{23}) & -a_2 c_1 s_2 - a_3 c_1 s_{23} & -a_3 c_1 s_{23} \\ c_1(a_2 c_2 + a_3 c_{23}) & -a_2 s_1 s_2 - a_3 s_1 s_{23} & -a_3 s_1 s_{23} \\ 0 & -a_2 c_2 - a_3 c_{23} & -a_3 c_{23} \end{bmatrix}$$

$$\theta_{weight} = \frac{\pi}{2} - (\emptyset + \theta_2 + \theta_3 + \theta_4); \quad F = mg = \sqrt{F_x^2 + F_y^2 + F_z^2} ; \tag{4}$$

$$F_x = F \sin \theta_{weight}; \quad F_y = F \cos \theta_{roll}; \quad F_z = F \cos \theta_{weight}$$

$\emptyset$: The pitch angle of the vehicle, θ_{roll}: The roll angle of the vehicle

where $\{m\}$ is the mass of the object being manipulated, $\{g\}$ the local acceleration of gravity and F_x, F_y and F_z are the sensed forces along the x, y and z direction of the F/T sensor frame of reference, respectively. For ease of explanation, here we neglect the moments, which should be considered to fully determine the effect of the object as the MM rolls, pitches and yaws as it interacts with the terrain. The end effector in world coordinate frame using the arm base point B and the mobile robot can be expressed as:

$$x_e = x_b + p_x = x_b + -d_2s_1 + c_1(a_2c_2 + a_3c_{23} - d_5s_{234})$$
$$y_e = y_b + p_y = y_b + d_2c_1 + s_1(a_2c_2 + a_3c_{23} - d_5s_{234}) \qquad (5)$$
$$z_e = z_b + p_z = z_b + d_1 - a_2s_2 - a_3s_{23} - d_5c_{234}$$

where: $z_b = vehicle\ height + rough\ terrain\ profile$

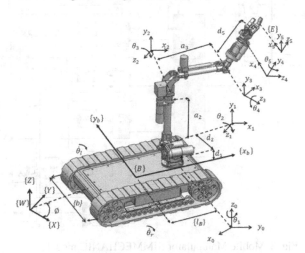

Fig. 1. Wheeled mobile manipulator robot model

3   Model of The MM Using SIMMECHANICS

SimMechanics software is a block diagram modeling environment for the engineering design and simulation of rigid multibody machines and their motions, using the standard Newtonian dynamics of forces and torques. With SimMechanics software, you can model and simulate mechanical systems with a suite of tools to specify bodies and their mass properties, their possible motions, kinematic constraints, and coordinate systems, and to initiate and measure body motions. You represent a mechanical system by a connected block diagram, like other Simulink models. You can also incorporate hierarchical subsystems. The visualization tools of SimMechanics software display and animate 3-D machine geometries, before and during simulation [14].The MM arm consist of five revolute joints and we have a motor attached to each joint. It's arranged to work in (6D Figure 2.). The model comprises a set of connected blocks (i.e., body, joint, actuator, sensors, constraint and driver and initial conditions) (Fig. 2). These blocks were defined using special forms available in the modeling environment and all bocks included the real MM's properties such as mass, and moments of inertia. In fig.3 the robot block is analysed so that we have 6 blocks express about the system. Each block has a sensor attached to it in order to measure its angular position, velocity and joint torques. For kinematics and dynamic simulation we give motion for the joints and the wheels by joint actuator see (Fig.2). Figure. 3 shows the SIMMECHANICS model of the two MMs handling a rigid object.

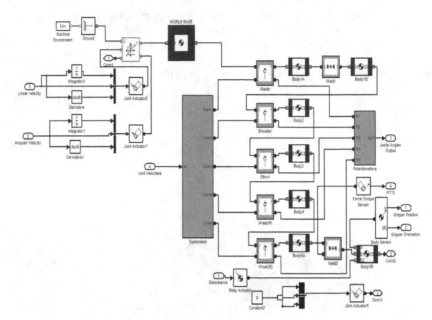

Fig. 2. Mobile Manipulator SIMMECHANIC model

4   Control Architecture

In order to address the problems found in current control mechanisms of cooperation between two MM's a new yet simple control approach is proposed herein [15]. The approach combines well known techniques in an attempt to maximize their advantages while reducing their disadvantages [15]. In this architecture two MM's cooperating for handling a rigid object in 3D. The end effectors of the MM's are rigidly attached to the rigid object so that there is no relative motion between the end effectors and the object [16]. For this, we consider the MM's as a coupled system carrying an object (assumed to be rigid so that the object cannot deformed under any forces) in cooperation. The process starts by initializing the system (i.e., the sensed changes in the force torque sensor values should be equal to zero. This is achieved by avoiding any disturbance to the manipulator). Subsequently, during cooperation there will be changes sensed in the F/T values. According to the value of such changes, Δ (F/T), the robot computes its motion by using resolved motion rate control method including using of pseudo inverse jacobian to avoid the singularity of the robot's arm (i.e., joint angle velocities) to eliminate any changes in the F/T values (i.e., make Δ (F/T) =0 at all times). Herein, we refer to this approach as a velocity feedback. The central controller will send the signal commands which include the robot's joints velocities and the wheel velocities for both MMs at the same time. The motion of the mobile base is subject to nonholonomic kinematics constraints, which renders the control of MM very challenging, especially when robots work in non-engineered environments. Figure (4) shows the detailed control algorithm represented in general form. The cooperation starts by initializing the robot. This includes placing the object to be manipulated on the robot's gripper and gathering all sensor data (at this point the robot holding the object by itself). Sensor data at initialization is considered the reference value. Once cooperation starts the initial sensor value, used as a reference, are update at all times.

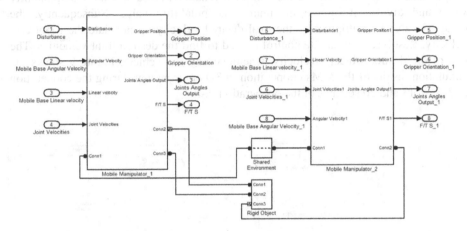

Fig. 3. Two Mobile Manipulator cooperating SIMMECHANIC model

5   Simulation and Results

The kinematics-dynamics simulation model of the robot was performed using SIMMECHANICS and the controller was implemented in SIMULINK. Figure 6 shows the results of one test showing the performance of the controller. In this test the MM's was placed on a flat terrain handling a rigid object and moving forward in a straight line (i.e., MMs was handling the object being transported). Thus the end-effector was aimed at tracking sinusoidal trajectory. Figure 5 shows the corresponding change in the joint arm positions. Figure 6 shows the joint velocity of the MM to compensate the changes in the F/T values. In this case there are two types of cooperation. The first is the cooperation between the MMs handling the object. The second is the cooperation between the arm and the mobile base to achieve the desired object's motion and minimize the error of the desired trajectory. Figure 7 shows the robot vehicle linear velocity and robot arm linear velocity. As seen in this figure, the end-effector converges (i.e., tracks) the desired motion accurately. The base also tracks the desired motion accurately with only small disturbances due to the oscillating motion of the end-effector. The vehicle is contributes to the motion in two dimensions (i.e., x and y velocities) while the arm contributes in 3D dimentions (i.e., x, y and z velocities). In this approach the manipulability is used to coordinate the motion between locomotion and manipulation of the MMs. The control mechanism measures the manipulability value and according to this change the control divides the desired velocity between the mobile base and the manipulator. Figure 8 shows the changes in the robot arm manipulability value. As can be seen when the manipulability value is maximum the robot's arm velocity is maximum and when the manipulability value is minimum the vehicle's velocity is maximum. During the cooperation between the MM's the control mechanism calculates the manipulability value and divides it by the maximum manipulability value. Subsequently, the obtained value is multiplied by the total desired velocity to calculate the robot arm velocity. Resolved motion rate control is used to find the desired joint velocities. The rest of the desired object's velocity is achieved by the vehicle. Figure 9 shows the simulation results of the MMs cooperation in 3D environment during the cooperation at 2, 7, 6, 13 and 20 seconds of the cooperation task.

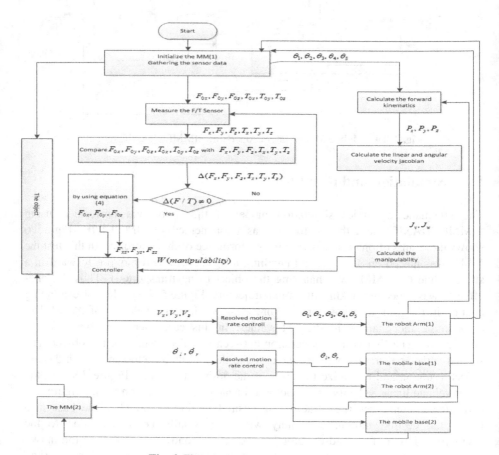

Fig. 4. Flowchart of the control algorithm

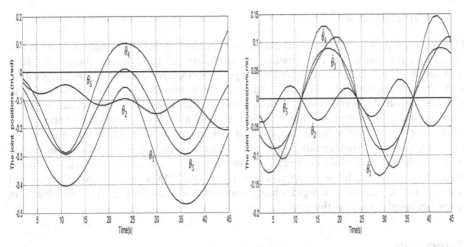

Fig. 5. Joint position of the MM(i), i=1,2   **Fig. 6.** Joint velocity of the MM (i), i=1, 2

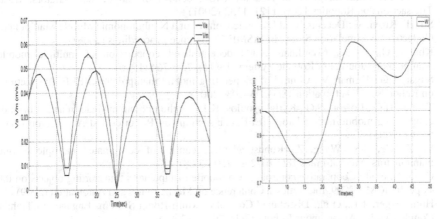

Fig. 7. Vehicle's and arm's linear velocities(i), i=1,2

Fig. 8. Changes of the arm's manipulability(i), i=1,2

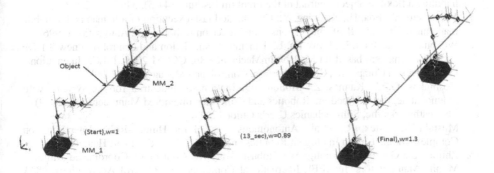

Fig. 9. Graphical time lapsed simulation results of MM

6   Conclusions

This research present a way of simulation and control of MMs systems in Matlab and Simmechanics based on the kinematics modeling of the system (based on D-H convention). This research achieved a simple yet effective control strategy/algorithm with the corresponding software, which enables two MMs to perform tasks in cooperation on flat terrains and achieved the desired trajectory. This is achieved by enabling the robot's arm and the vehicle's wheels to cooperate (on top of the robot-robot cooperation) to achieve the desired velocity that will accurately follow the desired trajectory. Another advantage of this control scheme is the MMs arm moves in 3D while the two MMs cooperate so we can use this to avoid obstacles in future work. In this research the cooperation between the MMs and the master was not targeted to be handling a rigid object (cooperation handling a flexible object in unknown rough terrain is the goal).

References

1. Sheng, L., Goldenberg, A.A.: Neural-network control of mobile manipulators. IEEE Transactions on Robotics 12(5), 1121–1133 (2001)
2. Su, H., Krovi, V.: Decentralized Dynamic Control of a Nonholonomic Mobile Manipulator Collective: A Simulation Study. In: ASME Conference Proceedings (2008)
3. Khatib, O., et al.: Coordination and decentralized cooperation of multiple mobile manipulators. Journal of Robotic Systems 13(11), 755–764 (1996)
4. Sugar, T.G., Kumar, V.: Control of cooperating mobile manipulators. IEEE Transactions on Robotics and Automation 18(1), 94–103 (2002)
5. Tanner, H.G., Loizou, S.G., Kyriakopoulos, K.J.: Nonholonomic navigation and control of cooperating mobile manipulators. IEEE Transactions on Robotics and Automation 19(1), 53–64 (2003)
6. Li, Z., Ge, S.S., Wang, Z.: Robust adaptive control of coordinated multiple mobile manipulators. Mechatronics 18(5-6), 239–250 (2008)
7. Chao, T., et al.: Cooperative control of two mobile manipulators transporting objects on the slope. In: ICMA 2009. International Conference on Mechatronics and Automation (2009)
8. Huntsberger, T.L., et al.: Distributed Control of Multi-Robot Systems Engaged in Tightly Coupled Tasks. Autonomous Robots 17(1), 79–92 (2004)
9. Su, H.: (Cooperative Control Of Payload Transport By Mobile Manipulator Collectives). Thesis The State University of New York at Buffalo
10. Al-Yahmadi, A.S., Abdo, J., Hsia, T.C.: Modeling and control of two manipulators handling a flexible object. Journal of the Franklin Institute 344(5), 349–361 (2007)
11. Yamamoto, Y., Eda, H., Xiaoping, Y.: Coordinated task execution of a human and a mobile manipulator. In: 1996 IEEE International Conference on Robotics and Automation (1996)
12. Wenbin, D., Jae-Won, L., Hyuk-Jin, L.: Kinematics simulation and control of a new 2 DOF parallel mechanism based on Matlab/SimMechanics. In: CCCM 2009. ISECS International Colloquium on Computing, Communication, Control, and Management (2009)
13. Vosniakos, G.-C., Kannas, Z.: Motion coordination for industrial robotic systems with redundant degrees of freedom. Robotics and Computer-Integrated Manufacturing (2009)
14. The mathworks.Inc, Simmechanics User's Guide (2011b)
15. Mustafa, M., Alex, R., et al.: Autonomous Control for Human-Robot Interaction on Complex Rough Terrain Intelligent Robotics and Applications. Springer, Heidelberg
16. Zhijun, L., Ge, S.S., Zhuping, W.: Robust Adaptive Control of Coordinated Multiple Mobile Manipulators. In: IEEE International Conference on Control Applications, CCA 2007 (2007)

A Mobile Robotic Platform for Generating Radiation Maps

Florentin von Frankenberg, Robin McDougall, Scott Nokleby, and Ed Waller

University of Ontario Institute of Technology
2000 Simcoe Street North, L1K1N2, Oshawa, Ontario, Canada
{florentin.vonfrankenberg,robin.mcdougall,
scott.nokleby,ed.waller}@uoit.ca
http://www.uoit.ca

Abstract. The use of mobile robots to collect the sensor readings required to generate radiation maps has the significant advantage of eliminating the risk of exposure that humans would otherwise face by collecting the readings by hand. In this work, a mobile robotic platform designed specifically to collect this information to synthesize radiation maps is presented. Details of the design are discussed, focusing in particular on the physical map generating capabilities of this new platform that are necessary to enable the generation of the radiation maps. The physical maps are generated using a laser range finder based implementation of Simultaneous Localization and Mapping (SLAM).

1 Introduction

Radiation maps show how a radiation intensity field varies in an area by overlaying radiation intensity values on a physical map. A number of approaches for their synthesis have been presented previously. Until now, these methods typically rely on taking radiation readings throughout the area being mapped and methodically transferring these values to a pre-existing physical map either using a previously placed network of static sensors [1–3], operators using hand-held sensors [4,5], or sensors mounted on mobile robots [6].

The most significant obstacle to current techniques are presented when barriers exist in the environment that make it impossible to position a radiation sensor throughout the entire area being mapped or if no physical map is available ahead of time. In these situations, generating reasonably accurate, usable radiation maps of the complete area will require using both predicted radiation intensity values for the inaccessible regions from an appropriately selected radiation model (calibrated with sensor readings from the accessible areas) and integrating this with a map-making capability to provide the geometrical or physical layout of the area under study. To this end, a strategy for generating probabilistic radiation maps from sparse sensor data was developed and tested in a simulation study with very encouraging results [7, 8]. The methodology comprises three main stages as shown in Figure 1.

C.-Y. Su, S. Rakheja, H. Liu (Eds.): ICIRA 2012, Part II, LNAI 7507, pp. 407–416, 2012.

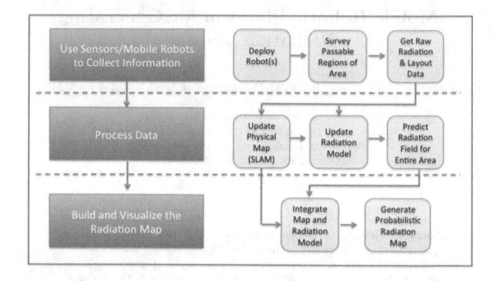

Fig. 1. Radiation mapping algorithm

This work focuses on the design and development of the mobile robotic platform that facilitates the testing of the radiation mapping algorithm of Figure 1. The platform, which has been named Radbot, is capable of creating a map of a previously unknown environment in a format understandable to humans. This physical map contains information about the physical layout of an area of interest. In contrast to this, the radiation map contains information about the radiation levels with respect to location. The problem of building a physical map by exploring an unknown environment is commonly known as SLAM (Simultaneous Localization and Mapping) [9–11]. To facilitate the testing of the radiation mapping algorithm, Radbot must also be capable of autonomously navigating through the environment as it creates the physical map.

The initial goal of this work is to establish a proof-of-concept of the radiation mapping system as a whole. It is intended in the future to replace the current robotic platform by a more robust one capable of operating outdoors with the same basic functionality. This follows the principle of modularity, in which specific modules must fulfill some purpose, but the degree to which they do and the performance at which they accomplish their task is dependent on the module, not the method. Radbot demonstrates that a real robot can move, navigate, map, and localize itself, thereby validating the functionality of the method in [7]. For real-world applications, a more robust robot which can operate in more difficult terrain could easily replace Radbot without affecting the feasibility of the overall method.

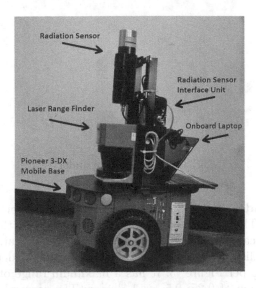

Fig. 2. Subsystems of Radbot

2   Mechanical Design

This section discusses the mechanical design of Radbot, including several of the subsystems labeled in Figure 2.

2.1   Mobile Base

A mobile platform capable of housing and transporting the radiation sensor and other hardware was required. The Pioneer 3-DX, an off-the-shelf solution, was chosen to fulfill this purpose. The selection criteria at this stage were primarily high reliability and ease of implementation. Using the Pioneer 3-DX has several advantages to building a custom robot base. No time and labour are required, and there is product support from the vendor. Also, due to its popularity in the field of academic mobile robots, many problems have been previously encountered and solved by the robotics community. Open source software for interfacing with the robot has been developed and is readily available.

The Pioneer 3-DX has an approximately circular footprint, which means that there is no risk of collisions when rotating on the spot. It is a two-wheeled differential drive robot with a rear caster wheel. It is capable of speeds of approximately 5 km/h and has a run time of 8-10 hours. The Pioneer 3-DX comes with built in high-resolution wheel encoders that are used to regulate wheel speeds and feed information into an odometry system.

2.2   Additional Sensors

This section discusses some additional sensors that are of particular importance to the operation of Radbot.

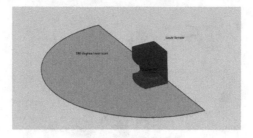

Fig. 3. 2D Laser range finder

Laser Range Finder. A Sick LMS 200 laser range finder is an add-on to the Pioneer 3-DX. This sensor is the primary sensor used by the SLAM system for building a physical map of the environment. This sensor gathers information about the relative distance between the sensor and objects detected in a two-dimensional scan as per Figure 3. It has a maximum range of 80 meters, and a selectable resolution of 0.25, 0.5, or 1 degree. The sensor has a 180 degree field-of-view and a refresh rate of up to 75 Hz (at 1 degree resolution).

Radiation Sensor. The radiation sensor package selected for the Radbot was a 3x3 NaI(Tl) scintillation detector coupled with a portable 4,096 channel MCA (Multi Channel Analyzer). The large volume scintillation detector was selected to provide omni-directional response to gamma rays and has good energy efficiency over a large range of gamma energies that may be encountered in harsh radiation environments. For radiation mapping, the detector will be used in scaler (count per second) mode, although the fact that the system is a spectrometer will allow for source identification through gamma peak analysis when required. The sensitivity can be increased by adding a larger volume detector, or, more detectors. The sensor is mounted directly between the two drive wheels, at the centre of rotation of the robot. This was done in order to allow the robot to rotate on the spot while accumulating radiation counts for a specific location. This allows the laser range finder to accumulate physical data of the environment and build a better map more quickly while taking radiation readings. Spinning on the spot also increases the accuracy of the localization system.

Video Camera. A forward-facing video camera is mounted on Radbot in order to provide a video feed to a remote user during operation. This allows the user to detect obstacles which are below or above the scan-height of the laser range finder.

3   Software

A laptop using the Ubuntu 11.10 operating system was chosen to run all of the software for Radbot. This was done primarily to allow the use of the tool set and codebase provided by ROS (Robot Operating System: www.ros.org). ROS is an open source software platform aimed at facilitating the development of robotic systems. It consists of a set of tools and libraries which help software developers create software. The primary goal behind ROS is to accelerate the research and development of robotic systems. This goal is accomplished by supporting code re-use and facilitating collaboration between researchers. Extensive code libraries are available which provide functionality for both low-level functions such as controlling actuators or reading sensors, as well as high level algorithms such as obstacle avoidance, or computer vision. By using the ROS platform, developers are able to work within a consistent framework for managing their software. Tasks such as passing information from one software module to another are managed by the ROS system. This makes it easy to re-use, build on, and adapt previous work to a particular purpose. In other words, less time is spent "reinventing the wheel".

3.1 SLAM

The task of localization and mapping was accomplished by selecting a pre-existing solution with proven reliability. The algorithm is known as GMapping and is described in [12]. The source code is available through the OpenSlam.org project. The algorithm uses a Rao-Blackwellized particle filter approach, which has been demonstrated to work particularly well with laser range finders, 2D mapping, and environments that are not unlimited in size. A wrapper was written for the algorithm by Brian Gerkey to integrate it with ROS [13].

The version of the algorithm available through ROS requires several data inputs to function. The first of these is a stream of laser scan data, essentially composed of a series of distance measurements accompanied by the angle of that measurement to the laser scanner. The measurements are the distances from the laser to the objects it detects. The second set of data required is an approximation of where the robot has traveled with respect to its previous position. This is typically supplied by an odometry system based on the wheel encoders of the robot. Lastly, it is required to know the transform of position and orientation of the laser scanner with respect to the centre of the robot. Additionally, there are numerous parameters which can be adjusted to tune the behaviour of the GMapping algorithm to work in various scenarios. These parameters include information about the expected error and range of the sensors, the desired map resolution, and the update frequency (which results in proportional computational load). The default values of these parameters were designed to work with the Sick LMS 200 laser range finder and typical wheel odometry performance, and so they were not modified.

The ROS wrapped GMapping algorithm was selected because of its ease of implementation and proven reliability. Additionally, the open-source nature of the software allows it to be modified and expanded if necessary to improve performance in three-dimensional, unstructured, or dynamic environments.

3.2   Navigation

The navigation task was also accomplished by using pre-existing solutions provided through ROS. A description on the system can be found in [14]. To use the navigation system, there are several pre-requisites which must be satisfied. The robot base must be able to accept velocity commands in component-form (x-velocity, y-velocity, and θ-velocity). A planar range-finding sensor such as a LIDAR (Light Detection And Ranging) is needed for obstacle detection and localization, and an odometry system is required to track the motion of the robot. Lastly, a physical map of the environment is required to navigate through. This map is commonly obtained by using SLAM to build one. Although the system is capable of determining the location of the robot on the map by comparing its current sensor information to features of the map, an initial pose estimate supplied by an operator allows the localization system to converge on the true location more quickly.

The navigation system allows a user or another algorithm to designate navigation destinations. The system will plot a path from the robot's current location to the destination, taking into account information from the map. The path which is generated uses a cost function which attempts to keep a user-specified distance away from walls and obstacles. In addition to this global path planning, the navigation system includes a local planner which takes into account temporary obstacles being picked up by the sensors. Currently, only the 2D laser range finder is used to detect obstacles, but the navigation system allows for the use of arbitrary other sensors, so long as the output of these sensors is formatted as a 3D point cloud. The point cloud represents the points in space at which the sensors detect obstacles. These obstacles may be moving and do not need to be present on the map. In this way, the path planning is robust to temporary obstacles such as human pedestrians. The local path planner attempts to stay close to the global path and the degree to which it does this is tunable through the parameters of the software.

3.3   Remote Control

An application called TeamViewer [15] was used to remotely access the laptop on board Radbot over a local wifi network. This was done so that a user can send navigation goals and view mapping information during use. The video feed of the on-board camera is also visible to the user by this method. The use of Teamviewer requires that both the laptop on board Radbot and the machine being used by the operator have internet access. However, this also means that control of Radbot can be accessible from anywhere globally, so long as there is internet access.

4   Results

The results of mapping and localization testing are displayed in Figures 4 and 5. In Figure 4, the map generated is displayed on the left and the building floor plan

Fig. 4. A map generated using the GMapping SLAM algorithm (left) and the building floor plan of the same area (right)

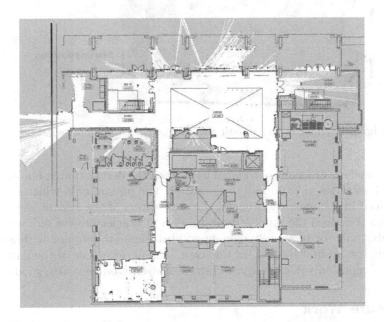

Fig. 5. Comparison of the map generated using SLAM and the building floor-plan

for the same area on the right. The white areas on the experimentally generated physical map represent explored, open space. The gray represents unexplored areas, and the black represents grid cells which are 90% likely to be occupied. Around the edges of the experimental map there can be seen some areas where the laser scanner has not fully swept or explored. These areas are due to windows, open doorways, and rooms which were not entered by the robot. Figure 5 shows the overlay of the building plans with the map that was generated. This was done by simply rotating and scaling the images by eye. It can be seen that there is a high degree of correspondence between the building plans and the experimental map. As indicated on Figure 4, some renovations were done to the building which are not shown on the original building plan. Also not shown on the building plan are benches and lockers along the walls, which can be seen in the experimental map.

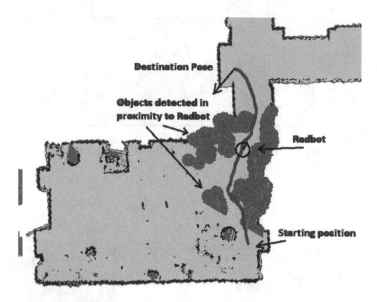

Fig. 6. Example of global path generated by path planning algorithm

Figure 6 shows an image of a global path, with the destination at one end, and the set of obstacles in proximity to the robot. The proximity in which obstacles are retained in the memory is one of the parameters of the system, and should depend on the speed the robot is operating at. Obstacles present on the map as well as dynamic (or previously unmapped obstacles) are retained within a four meter window around Radbot, in this case. The performance of the navigation was tested repeatedly in a dense and cluttered lab environment with good results.

5   Future Work

The test results demonstrate that the physical map generating and navigation capabilities of Radbot are operating correctly. As the next stage in this multi-stage project, the next task will be to perform tests using the radiation sensor and live radiation test sources. The algorithm previously developed in [7] will be used to predict the distribution of radiation levels throughout an area and the location of radiation sources. For real-world applications, a more robust mobile base will be required which is capable of operating in more difficult terrain. This should include such scenarios as disaster sites with various debris, handling of physical drop-off features, and in general unpredictable terrain. In accordance with this goal, generating a 3D map as opposed to a 2D one will be required. Potential improvements and augmentation to the SLAM system could include the use of computer-vision techniques. The use of a vision system could also be beneficial for the purpose of obstacle detection, as the current LIDAR method only provides a 2D slice of the world and cannot detect obstacles above or below the sensor height.

6   Conclusions

In order to help generate radiation maps in areas without pre-installed station-ary sensors, a system was required which could transport a radiation sensor and take readings, create a physical map of an unknown environment, and nav-igate autonomously within the environment. To accomplish this an off-the-shelf mobile robot base was selected and configured with the requisite sensors. Algo-rithms were selected and installed to perform SLAM, path planning, and obstacle avoidance. Radbot, the resulting system, is capable of generating highly accu-rate maps of the physical layout of an area in a format that is understandable to humans. A remote user is able to use these maps in conjunction with video feed from a camera on board Radbot to navigate through densely cluttered planar office environments. This demonstrates the feasibility of using a mobile robot to autonomoulsy collect radiation data as proposed in [7].

Acknowledgements. The authors would like to thank Cameco Corporation, the University Network of Excellence in Nuclear Engineering (UNENE), and the Natural Sciences and Engineering Research Council (NSERC) of Canada for their financial support of this work.

References

1. Kumar, A., Tanner, H.G., Kimenko, A.V.: Automated sequential search for weak radiation sources. In: IEEE Mediterranean Conference on Control and Automation, pp. 1–6 (2006)
2. Hou, J.: ZIB Structure Prediction Pipeline: Dynamic clustering for acoustic target tracking in wireless sensor networks. IEEE Transactions on Mobile Computing 3(3), 258–271 (2004)
3. Nemzek, R., Dreicer, J., Torney, D.: Distributed sensor networks for detection of mobile radioactive sources. IEEE Transactions on Nuclear Science 51(4), 1693–1700 (2004)
4. Borozdin, K.N., Klimenko, A.V., Priedhorsky, W.C.: Optimized Strategies for Smart Nuclear Search. In: IEE Nuclear Science Symposium Conference Record, pp. 926–928 (2006)
5. Ho, C.K., Robinson, A., Miller, D.R.: Overview of Sensors and Needs for Environ-mental Monitoring. Sensors 5(1), 4–37 (2005)
6. Cortez, R., Papageorgiou, X., Tanner, H.: Smart radiation sensor management. IEEE Robotics and Automation Magazine 15(3), 85–93 (2008)
7. McDougall, R., Nokleby, S., Waller, E.: Robotic Radiation Mapping from Sparse Data. In: CCToMM Symposium on Mechanisms, Machines, and Mechatronics (2011)
8. McDougall, R., Waller, E., Nokleby, S.B.: A Strategy for Creating Probabilistic Ra-diation Maps in Areas Based on Sparse Data. In: Proceedings of the 2010 American Nuclear Society (ANS), Las Vegas, USA (November 2010)
9. Thrun, S.: Robitic Mapping: A survey. Tech. Rep. CMU-CS-02-111 (2002)
10. Smith, R., Self, M., Cheeseman, P.: Autonomous Robot Vehicles. In: Estimating Uncertain Spatial Relationships in Robotics, pp. 167–193 (1990)

11. Leonard, J., Durrant-Whyte, H.: Mobile Robot Localization by Tracking Geometric Beacons. IEEE Transactions on Robotics and Automation 7(3), 376–382 (1991)
12. Grisetti, G., Stachniss, C., Burgard, W.: Improved Techniques for Grid Mapping with Rao-Blackwellized Particle Filters. IEEE Transactions on Robotics, 34–46 (2007)
13. A ROS Wrapper for the gmapping SLAM Algorithm,
    http://www.ros.org/wiki/gmapping
14. Marder-Eppstein, E., Berger, E., Foote, T., Gerkey, B.: The Office Marathon: Robust Navigation in an Indoor Office Environment. In: International Conference on Robotics and Automation (2010)
15. TeamViewer, http://www.teamviewer.com/en/index.aspx

Effect of Limiting Wheel Slip on Two-Wheeled Robots in Low Traction Environments

Ronald Ping Man Chan, Karl A. Stol, and C. Roger Halkyard

Mechanical Engineering Department, University of Auckland, New Zealand
ronalchn@gmail.com, {k.stol,r.halkyard}@auckland.ac.nz

Abstract. Ground traction is very important for balancing of two-wheeled robots. This paper examines whether limiting wheel slip to a nominal optimal value, as in conventional traction control, improves the performance of two-wheeled robots on low traction surfaces. For a particular robot and simulation conditions, comparing the baseline linear state feedback controller of the two-wheeled robot with and without traction control shows that conventional traction control is ineffective when stopping abruptly from a constant speed.

Traction control on a baseline controller decreases the maximum stable stopping speed on an ice-like surface. Compensating torque induced by traction control only partially recovers performance. On a hypothetical wet or lubricated surface with exaggerated Stribeck effect, traction control only slightly improves performance. Therefore traction control distinct from the balance and velocity LQR controller is ineffective, normally degrades overall performance, and motivates research for an alternative controller.

Keywords: Two-wheeled robot, traction control, wheel slip, friction, balancing.

1 Introduction

Robots are increasingly common today and actively stabilized two-wheeled robots are quite suited for unstructured environments, and though they must constantly rebalance, have unique advantages. Compared to statically stable robots, they can have a higher centre of mass, while being more stable on slopes, by tilting themselves to compensate for the incline. Even if it starts tipping, it can react and rebalance itself. Whereas statically stable robots tend to have low profiles with wide footprints, two-wheeled robots can have small footprints, fit through narrow corridors, and manoeuvre sharp turns. However, with limited ground traction, maintaining balance becomes difficult.

Fig. 1. Two-wheeled robot

Friction is generally modelled as a function of friction coefficient against wheel slip, increasing up to an optimal slip amount, after which it plateaus or declines.

C.-Y. Su, S. Rakheja, H. Liu (Eds.): ICIRA 2012, Part II, LNAI 7507, pp. 417–426, 2012.

Iagnemma and Dubowsky [1], for a many-wheeled robotic rover, control individual wheel forces to minimize wheel slip, by minimizing the maximum friction coefficient required. Abeykoon and Ohnishi [2] minimize the maximum wheel slip using a movable centre of mass. Conventional anti-lock braking systems (ABS) in automobiles increase or decrease braking pressure depending on whether wheel slip is above or below a threshold optimal slip.

More sophisticated controllers exist for traction control. Some aim to prevent the vibrations caused by rapid switching action in conventional ABS. They may model the friction-slip relationship [3-5] to generate a more appropriate controller output. Nyandoro et al. [3] show the effectiveness of feedback linearization in ABS braking.

They may search for the optimal slip, for example, sliding mode controllers in [6] by Drakunov et al. or [7] by Tan and Tomizuka, while a conventional implementation may assume an optimal slip threshold at a predetermined, fixed value [8].

2   The Two-Wheeled Robot Modelling and Simulation

The simulation models the two-wheeled robot in Fig. 1, and described by sub-models.

2.1   Motor Model

The drive wheel motors generally match the model of conventional DC motors, with some added non-linear terms. The model of the drive wheels can be described by

$$T = K_{t1}I + K_{t2}I\omega + K_{f1}\omega + K_{f2}\text{signum}(\omega)\left(1 - e^{-K_d|\omega|}\right), \tag{1}$$

$$V = K_e\omega + IR, \tag{2}$$

where the experimentally approximated parameters motor torque constant (K_{t1}, K_{t2}), friction constant (K_{f1}, K_{f2}), nonlinearity delay (K_d), and experimentally measured back EMF constant (K_e) and resistance (R) are:

$$[K_{t1}\ K_{t2}\ K_{f1}\ K_{f2}\ K_d\ K_e\ R] = [0.11\ -1.4 \times 10^{-5}\ -2.5 \times 10^{-4}\ -0.15\ 0.034\ 0.127\ 0.43], \tag{3}$$

describing motor torque (T) and voltage (V) in terms of current (I) and angular velocity (ω). The model is used to simulate motor saturation – otherwise a controller that could rebalance the robot from any state, even on frictionless ground surfaces.

There are un-modeled effects due to coulomb friction, motor cogging, and torque ripple on the order of 0.1Nm at the drive wheels.

The reaction wheel model used is identical to that found in Jones and Stol [9].

2.2   Platform Model

The simulation uses equations, as determined by Jones and Stol [9], with longitudinal motion only (no turning). Equations (4-6) explain the model without wheel slip, and the model given by equations (7-9) includes wheel slip, relating drive torque T_D and reaction wheel torque T_R to longitudinal position x, wheel angle ϕ, tilt angle θ.

$$\ddot{x} = \frac{aI_O\dot{\theta}^2 \sin\theta - a^2 g \sin\theta \cos\theta + T_D \frac{I_O}{r} + a\cos\theta(T_D+T_R)}{I_O m_O - a^2 \cos^2\theta}, \tag{4}$$

$$\ddot{\phi} = \frac{\ddot{x}}{r}, \tag{5}$$

$$\ddot{\theta} = \frac{-a^2\dot{\theta}^2 \sin\theta \cos\theta + am_O g \sin\theta - T_D \frac{a}{r}\cos\theta - m_O(T_D+T_R)}{I_O m_O - a^2 \cos^2\theta}. \tag{6}$$

$$\ddot{x} = \frac{a(\cos\theta + \mu\sin\theta)(T_D+T_R - ag\sin\theta) + aI_O\dot{\theta}^2(\sin\theta - \mu\cos\theta) + \mu g m_T I_O}{m_T I_O - a^2 \cos\theta(\cos\theta + \mu\sin\theta)}, \tag{7}$$

$$\ddot{\theta} = \frac{(\mu\cos\theta - \sin\theta)(a^2\dot{\theta}^2 \cos\theta - ag m_T) - m_T(T_D+T_R)}{m_T I_O - a^2 \cos\theta(\cos\theta + \mu\sin\theta)}, \tag{8}$$

$$\ddot{\phi} = \frac{T_D}{I_W} + \frac{r\mu}{I_W} \frac{(g m_T - a\dot{\theta}^2 \cos\theta)(a^2 - m_T I_O) - a m_T \sin\theta(T_D+T_R)}{m_T I_O - a^2 \cos\theta(\cos\theta + \mu\sin\theta)}. \tag{9}$$

The following platform parameters were estimated by measurement of the mass, centre of mass, and moment of inertia of its intermediate body, only some of which are the same as used in Jones and Stol [9]:

$$[a \quad m_O \quad r \quad I_O \quad m_T \quad I_W] = [8.55 \quad 54.5 \quad 0.196 \quad 2.95 \quad 49.9 \quad 0.178]. \tag{10}$$

2.3   Ground Surfaces

Two ground surfaces with wheel slip were tested in simulation. We consider the model by Jones [10], slip surface 1, an ice-like surface shown in Fig. 2, with a shape similar to most dry surfaces, while slip surface 2 is a modification with a greater drop-off after peaking, characteristic of wet, lubricated surfaces explained by the Stribeck effect.

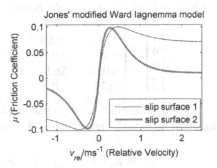

Fig. 2. Friction-slip for simulated surfaces

2.4   Reference Speed

We consider the manoeuvre of stopping abruptly from a constant speed to measure the stability of a controller. After a constant speed for 5 seconds, the reference speed to the reference tracking controller abruptly steps down to zero. If the robot remains upright after 5 seconds, it is stable. This was simulated at incrementally higher speeds (every 0.005m/s), until the speed at which the robot topples is found.

2.5   Controllers

For simplicity, we consider a two-wheeled robot (Fig. 1) with a simple linear, reference tracking controller, as a baseline. Linear state feedback controllers have been used by a number of other researchers [11-19].

Whether the controller fails depends on gain, determining how aggressively the controller will accelerate to match the reference speed. LQR is a common method [11-17] for obtaining the optimal gain which minimizes the cost function given by:

$$J = \int_0^\infty (x^T Q x + u^T R u)\, dt \ . \tag{11}$$

$$Q = \text{diag}([500 \quad 10 \quad 50 \quad 1]), R = [0.4]\ , \tag{12}$$

are selected for reasonable control performance, yielding the control law:

$$u = [T_D] = [35.4 \quad 39.6 \quad 142 \quad 25.1][\int \dot{x} - v_{ref} \quad \dot{x} - v_{ref} \quad \theta \quad \dot{\theta}]^T = K\vec{x}\ , \tag{13}$$

with reference speed v_{ref}, wheel torque T_D, speed $\dot{x}$, tilt angle θ and tilt rate $\dot{\theta}$.

Jacobian linearization of the either model (4-6) or (7-9) at equilibrium yields a controllable state-space model in the linear sense with LQR guaranteeing stability in the local region. Though they differ somewhat (because accounting for wheel slip makes some linear dynamics non-linear), both are controllable in the linear sense. Dynamics become uncontrollable far from equilibrium due to motor saturation rather than any other nonlinearity. For example, linearization of (7-9) yields

$$\begin{bmatrix} \ddot{x} \\ \dot{\theta} \\ \ddot{\theta} \\ \ddot{\phi} \end{bmatrix} = \begin{bmatrix} -14.1 & -9.69 & 0 & 2.76 \\ 0 & 0 & 1 & 0 \\ 40.8 & 56.5 & 0 & 7.99 \\ 389 & 0 & 0 & -76.2 \end{bmatrix} \begin{bmatrix} \dot{x} \\ \theta \\ \dot{\theta} \\ \phi \end{bmatrix} + \begin{bmatrix} 0.116 \\ 0 \\ -0.673 \\ 5.61 \end{bmatrix} T_D \ . \tag{14}$$

The slip controller is a high gain applied to limit wheel slip (v_{rel}) described by the function $s_{lim}(v_{rel})$, shown in Fig. 3, to limit wheel slip (v_{rel}). The new control law is:

$$T_D = K[\int \dot{x} - v_{ref} \quad \dot{x} - v_{ref} \quad \theta \quad \dot{\theta}]^T + s_{lim}(v_{rel}) \ . \tag{15}$$

The 1st term is the baseline or reaction wheel controller and the 2nd term is the slip controller, to yield the overall control law.

The reaction wheel controller corresponding to the baseline controller, but using the reaction wheel as well was tested. The control law, using gains found by LQR, where T_R is the reaction wheel torque, and ω is the angular velocity of the reaction wheel is:

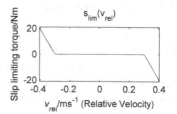

Fig. 3. −ve gain beyond 0.3ms^{-1}

$$\begin{bmatrix} T_D \\ T_R \end{bmatrix} = \begin{bmatrix} 32 & 36 & 135 & 24 & 0.47 & 0.289 \\ 30 & 29 & 63 & 13 & -2.0 & -0.94 \end{bmatrix} [\int \dot{x} - v_{ref} \quad \dot{x} - v_{ref} \quad \theta \quad \dot{\theta} \quad \int \omega \quad \omega]^T\ . \tag{16}$$

Limiting slip may actually be detrimental to balance, since the slip limiting controller may reduce the restoring torque required to rebalance. Therefore, a compensated slip controller was tested where any change in drive wheel torque is counteracted by an equal and opposite torque on the reaction wheel with control law:

$$\begin{bmatrix} T_D \\ T_R \end{bmatrix} = K\vec{x} + \begin{bmatrix} s_{\lim}(v_{rel}) \\ -s_{\lim}(v_{rel}) \end{bmatrix}. \tag{17}$$

The block diagram in Fig. 4 shows the configuration of the simulation. The baseline controller (or reaction controller) generates the primary actuator input signal. The traction control block may modify the actuator signal.

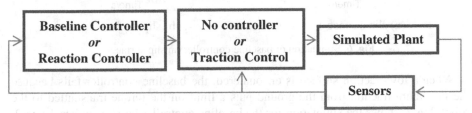

Fig. 4. Simulation block diagram

3   Results

3.1   Baseline Controller

First the results for the baseline controller (without the reaction wheel) on different surfaces are presented. Fig. 5 shows a simulation of the no slip surface.

The final cause of failure is motor saturation, because as the motor speed increases, there is increasing motor friction with current needed to overcome the motor friction increasing until it saturates at 20 amperes, seen in Fig. 5 showing voltage and current before failure. Although the motor does saturate in tests with lower speeds, with momentary periods of wheel slip, they remained recoverable until the finally, 20 amperes was insufficient to restore balance.

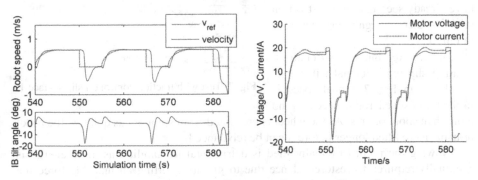

Fig. 5. Simulation of baseline controller on no slip surface

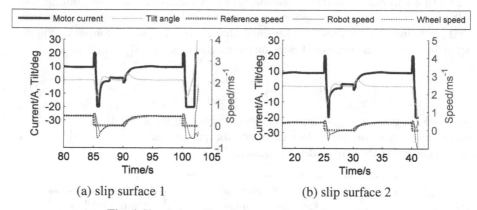

(a) slip surface 1   (b) slip surface 2

Fig. 6. Simulation of baseline controller on slip surfaces

When a low-traction surface is encountered, the baseline controller fails because the maximum traction from the ground puts a limit on the torque transmitted to the robot. Fig. 6 shows the simulation for the baseline controller on slip surface 1 and 2. On slip surface 1, although motor current does saturate, wheel speed is already much higher than robot speed before failure occurs. When wheel slip occurs, the controller continues to increase torque, further increasing slip. Meanwhile, the robot begins to tilt further and further, until it topples. Failure is similar for slip surface 2 (found in Fig. 6(b)). Therefore limited ground traction is clearly the main cause of failure.

The maximum speeds achieved by the baseline controller for each surface before failure is shown in Fig. 8, showing poorer performance for low-traction surfaces.

3.2   With Traction Control

Having established that performance suffers on surfaces with less traction, we would like to know whether limiting slip can recover performance. We have already seen that on low-traction surfaces, there is significant slip prior to failure.

Contrary to initial expectations, limiting slip tends to make it worse. As shown in Fig. 7, wheel speed is limited to exceed robot speed by no

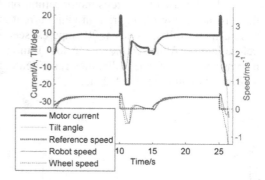

Fig. 7. Test with traction control on slip surface 1

more than about 0.3m/s. As the wheel is prevented from spinning as quickly, the robot remains more tilted longer before it can be rebalanced.

Allowing the robot to remain tilted is detrimental to stability, as more energy is eventually required to restore balance due to gravity exerting an unstable force the longer the robot is tilted. In effect, even if slip occurs, drive wheels can act as reaction wheels, which temporarily help to restore balance.

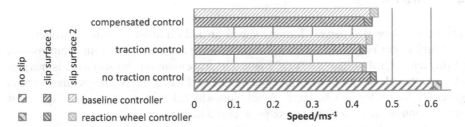

Fig. 8. Maximum reference speed to a successful stop – for each variation of controller, traction control and ground surface

Fig. 8 shows that traction control limiting wheel slip does not help, and the speed achieved before failure reduces, compared to without traction control for slip surface 1 – which is the more likely friction-slip curve. Traction control improves performance only marginally for slip surface 2, if friction coefficient versus wheel slip drops off very rapidly after peaking.

3.3 Compensated Baseline Controller

The slip controller above compromises performance, reducing drive wheel torque when they could by acting as reaction wheels, still temporarily provide relief.

However, if the drive wheels did not need to act as reaction wheels, it is probably better to limit wheel slip. We would like to know if using the reaction wheel more vigorously to compensate might improve overall performance. If the slip controller reduces drive wheel torque by 1Nm, it could increase reaction wheel torque by 1Nm.

The baseline linear state feedback controller does not use the reaction wheel for ordinary balancing purposes. As slowing down the reaction wheel is required over the long term to maintain actuation capacity, the baseline controller is slightly modified to do this – given by the control law:

$$\begin{bmatrix} T_D \\ T_R \end{bmatrix} = \begin{bmatrix} 35.7 & 39.6 & 142 & 25.1 & 0 & 0 \\ 0 & 0 & 0 & 0 & -2.24 & -1.07 \end{bmatrix} \vec{x} . \tag{18}$$

As shown in Fig. 8, although some performance is regained for slip surface 1, overall performance is still no better than without any traction control at all. For slip surface 2, further improvement is made, but overall improvement is still small, and surfaces with shape similar to this surface is unlikely (only some surfaces when wet).

3.4 Reaction Wheel Controller

With the reaction wheel controller, the speed achieved improves 0.015m/s almost uniformly with the same trends (shown in Fig. 8), therefore the best traction control strategy is unchanged, whether this controller or the baseline controller is used.

4   Discussion

The results show that naively limiting slip as an add-on to an existing controller does not improve performance in most low-traction environments, even with compensation of traction control torque. The performance improvement on slip surface 2 is marginal, even though the drop-off in traction of this surface is likely greater than what is generally found for wet surfaces. A solution which better manages stability versus acceleration is likely to yield a more pronounced improvement.

Unrecoverable states (due to motor saturation) can be reached even in the model without slip. Low-traction surfaces change the boundaries of unrecoverable states. A good controller should prevent the system becoming unrecoverable. Since this varies depending on traction, a good solution should to adapt to the traction available.

The baseline controller on a surface with no slip (infinite traction) can become destabilized simply because of the reference speed signal. This is caused by motor saturation, which occurs more readily at increasing motor speeds. It is not simple to limit the reference speed signal, as both the magnitude and derivative of the reference speed affects recoverability of a linear controller.

Motor saturation, and the effect of slip on the system, involves complex interaction making it difficult to prevent toppling as represented in Fig. 9. At the initial condition, there may be no problems. However, the state changes over time, in one case, without wheel slip, and in another case, with wheel slip (on a low-traction surface). It is only as the state changes (the exact path depending on the controller) that the motor begins to saturate. This is complicated by the reference speed, which changes the way the controller behaves – and thus, how the state changes.

The boundary of motor saturation is affected by system parameters. The design of a robot with regard to this can mitigate some of its limitations, including for use on low-traction surfaces. An increase in rotational inertia of the drive wheel system would reduce linear acceleration for the same force. Because all linear acceleration depends on traction with the ground, many parameters do not affect maximum linear acceleration. However due to torque reaction effects, rotational inertia may allow the robot to stabilize when there is little trac-tion. Motor saturation is greatly affected by motor friction and back EMF. This can be mitigated by decreasing the gearing ratio (which is 24 in this paper). This reduces the wheel torque available at equilibrium, but extends the speed range of the robot before saturation. In effect, for the purpose of stability, this makes the robot less sensitive to higher speeds, but more sensitive to larger tilt angles.

An increase in rotational inertia of the intermediate body by itself is not good, because long-term acceleration is the same for the same tilt. However, it

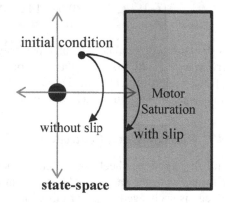

Fig. 9. Interaction between wheel slip and motor saturation

increases the torque required to stabilize the body, making motor saturation more likely for a disturbance in tilt angle. A higher centre of mass allows the robot to operate in a more linear region which is advantageous, as stabilizing in non-linear regions is more likely to cause motor saturation as larger motor torques is required to maintain stability.

5   Conclusion

A traction control solution separate from balancing does not improve performance, even when compensating traction control torques with a reaction wheel, compared to a simple baseline controller, which does not consider ground traction.

Independent traction control therefore appears to be a poor solution to the problem. Further research should focus more on maintaining and guaranteeing stability over an operating range, even when on low-traction surfaces. By recognizing the possible saturation of the motor, the robot may be able to remain balanced even when an unrealistic reference speed is used, with the controller only making a best effort to follow the reference without compromising stability. By guaranteeing stability within a region of attraction, with the boundaries being a function of ground traction, prevention of toppling on low-traction surfaces can be better managed.

Acknowledgements. We would like to recognize Rob Earl, Sarath Pathirana, Logan Stuart, Zareena Kausar and others involved with the two-wheeled robot at the University of Auckland.

References

1. Iagnemma, K., Dubowsky, S.: Traction Control of Wheeled Robotic Vehicles in Rough Terrain with Application to Planetary Rovers. The International Journal of Robotics Research 23, 1029–1040 (2004)
2. Abeykoon, A.M.H.S., Ohnishi, K.: Traction force improvement of a two wheel mobile manipulator by changing the centre of gravity. In: 3rd IEEE International Conference on Industrial Informatics (INDIN), pp. 756–760 (2005)
3. Nyandoro, O.T.C., Pedro, J.O., Dwolatzky, B., Dahuns, O.: State Feedback Based Linear Slip Control Formulation for Vehicular Antilock Braking System. In: World Congress on Engineering (2011)
4. Petersen, I.: Wheel Slip Control in ABS Brakes using Gain Scheduled Optimal Control with Constraints. Department of Engineering Cybernetics. Norwegian University of Science and Technology, Trondheim, Norway (2003)
5. Petersen, I., Johansen, T.A., Kalkkuhl, J., Lüdemann, J.: Wheel Slip Control in ABS Brakes Using Gain Scheduled Constrained LQR. In: European Control Conference (2001)
6. Drakunov, S., Ozguner, U., Dix, P., Ashrafi, B.: ABS control using optimum search via sliding modes. IEEE Transactions on Control Systems Technology 3, 79–85 (1995)
7. Tan, H.-S., Tomizuka, M.: An Adaptive Sliding Mode Vehicle Traction Controller Design. In: American Control Conference, pp. 1856–1862 (1990)

8. Chin, Y.-K., Lin, W.C., Sidlosky, D.M., Rule, D.S., Sparschu, M.S.: Sliding-Mode ABS Wheel-Slip Control. In: American Control Conference, pp. 1–8 (1992)
9. Jones, D.R., Stol, K.: Modelling and Stability Control of Two-Wheeled Robots in Low-Traction Environments. In: Australasian Conference on Robotics and Automation, ACRA (2010)
10. Jones, D.: Control of Two-Wheeled Robots in Low-Traction Environments. Mechanical Engineering, Masters of Engineering. University of Auckland, Auckland (2011)
11. Mokonopi, K.: Balancing a Two Wheeled Robot. Faculty of Engineering and Surveying, Bachelor of Engineering and Bachelor of Business (Mechatronics and Operations management). University of Southern Queensland (2006)
12. Ooi, R.C.: Balancing a Two-Wheeled Autonomous Robot. School of Mechanical Engineering, Degree in Mechatronics Engineering, pp. 56. The University of Western Australia, CRAWLEY (2003)
13. Kalra, S., Patel, D., Stol, D.K.: Design and Hybrid Control of a Two Wheeled Robotic Platform. In: Austraian Conference on Robotics and Automation (ACRA) (2007)
14. Coelho, V., Liew, S., Stol, K., Liu, G.: Development of a Mobile Two Wheel Balancing Platform for Autonomous Applications. In: 15th International Conference on Mechatronics and Machine Vision in Practice, M2VIP 2008 (2008)
15. Kim, Y., Kim, S.H., Kwak, Y.K.: Dynamic Analysis of a Nonholonomic Two-Wheeled Inverted Pendulum Robot. Journal of Intelligent and Robotic Systems 44, 25–46 (2005)
16. Charalambous, C.D., Lambis, A., Li, X.: Optimal control of a two-wheeled mobile robot via finite capacity communication channel. In: 2008 Mediterranean Conference on Control and Automation - Conference Proceedings, MED 2008, pp. 946–951 (2008)
17. Ha, Y., Yuta, S.I.: Trajectory Tracking Control for Navigation of Self-contained Mobile Inverse Pendulum. In: Proceedings of the IEEE/RSJ/GI International Conference on Intelligent Robots and Systems 1994. 'Advanced Robotic Systems and the Real World, pp. 1875–1882 (1994)
18. Grasser, F., D'arrigo, A., Colombi, S., Ruffer, A.: JOE: A Mobile, Inverted Pendulum. IEEE Transactions on Industrial Electronics 49, 107–114 (2002)
19. Han, J.H., Zhao, S.S., Li, J.S., Li, H.: Research on developed parallel two-wheeled robot and its control system. In: Proceedings of the IEEE International Conference on Automation and Logistics (ICAL), pp. 2471–2475 (2008)

Nao Robot Localization and Navigation Using Fusion of Odometry and Visual Sensor Data

Šimon Fojtů, Michal Havlena, and Tomáš Pajdla

Center for Machine Perception, Department of Cybernetics, FEE, CTU in Prague,
Karlovo náměstí 13, 121 35 Prague 2, Czech Republic
{fojtusim,havlem1,pajdla}@cmp.felk.cvut.cz
http://cmp.felk.cvut.cz/~fojtusim

Abstract. Nao humanoid robot from Aldebaran Robotics is equipped with an odometry sensor providing rather inaccurate robot pose estimates. We propose using Structure from Motion (SfM) to enable visual odometry from Nao camera without the necessity to add artificial markers to the scene and show that the robot pose estimates can be significantly improved by fusing the data from the odometry sensor and visual odometry. The implementation consists of the sensor modules streaming robot data, the mapping module creating a 3D model, the visual localization module estimating camera pose w.r.t. the model, and the navigation module planning robot trajectories and performing the actual movement. All of the modules are connected through the RSB middleware, which makes the solution independent on the given robot type.

Keywords: Structure from motion, Robot localization, Robot navigation, Nao humanoid robot.

1 Introduction

The intrinsic feature of a mobile robot is its ability to move in the surrounding environment. There are many types of robots from the motion point of view, starting from wheeled and ending with legged robots. Although the control of a two wheeled differential drive robot is relatively easy and precise, the more wheels and the more legs the robot has, the more complicated the task is. Humanoid robots, as the representatives of the legged ones, are known to be difficult to precisely navigate, since motion odometry is computed from the relative motion of legs, which often slip, and thus the odometry error is large and increases rapidly.

Nao humanoid robot, see Figure 1(a), is equipped with a bunch of various sensors. There are ultrasound sonars, microphones, IR transceivers, an inertial sensor, tactile and pressure sensors, and lastly two cameras. The head of the robot contains also a dual-core ATOM 1.6 GHz CPU, running Linux and firmware controlling the robot. Another CPU is also located in the robot torso. There is a lot of functionality already shipped within the firmware, such as face detection, Naomark detection, see Figure 1(b), walk and some other simple behaviours.

C.-Y. Su, S. Rakheja, H. Liu (Eds.): ICIRA 2012, Part II, LNAI 7507, pp. 427–438, 2012.

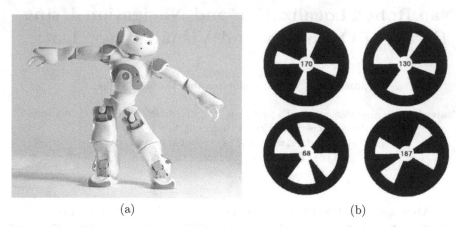

(a)   (b)

Fig. 1. (a) Nao robot. (b) Example of a Naomark. (courtesy of Ald. Robotics [1]).

The robot has a voice synthesizer and a simple speech recognition module. From our point of view, the most interesting sensors are the two cameras. Since the fields of view of the cameras do not overlap, they cannot be used as a stereo pair and thus we use only one of them. The top camera has 1.22 MPix with 61° HFOV and provides VGA resolution in rates slightly over 15 fps (on a Gigabit Ethernet connection). Higher resolution is available with reduced frame rate.

Naoqi, the firmware inside the robot, serves as an easy to use robotic framework that allows user modules to communicate with each other and also with various inbuilt modules. The modules can run directly on the robot or as remote applications from a PC. Although Naoqi is a useful framework, there might be needs for a more complex middleware that completely shields the Nao-specific interface from generic applications, such as Robot Operating System (ROS) [14] and Robotics Service Bus (RSB) [18]. We have decided for the latter one that, although being younger, presents an event-driven and message-oriented environment, interfaces with MATLAB and is ported to Nao. We have exploited the modular nature of the middleware to compose our navigation and localization system of separate modules, that can be extended or replaced as needed. The use of this middleware allows others to seamlessly build on our work.

In order to navigate a mobile robot, its pose w.r.t. some coordinate system needs to be known. One possible approach is to use artificial markers with known positions in the environment and localize the robot using e.g. a 3-point algorithm [7]. As mentioned above, the robot is equipped with an algorithm to automatically detect Naomarks, so these can be easily used as the artificial markers. This is a valid approach in many fields, e.g. industry [8], where the environment can be created with the robotic needs in mind. In a generic environment, on the other hand, the need for artificial markers of known poses limits the autonomy of the mobile robot and distracts people interacting with the robot.

An alternative approach that does not require artificial interventions to the scene is known as Simultaneous Localization and Mapping (SLAM). SLAM

combines mapping of surroundings and robot localization, by which it overcomes the classical chicken and egg problem. Impressive example of single camera
SLAM is presented by Davison et al. [4]. An example of Nao robot navigation
without artificial landmarks is given in the work of Osswald et al. [13]. They
improve robot odometry by detecting visual features on a wooden floor. The
disadvantage of their approach is the focus on the floor which means that the
surroundings are not perceived well.

2   Structure from Motion for Visual Odometry

Structure from motion (SfM) can be used to substitute the artificial markers for
the natural ones, i.e. the SURF [2] features automatically detected in the images
of the scene. In order to achieve efficient and accurate localization, we decided
to split the computation to mapping and visual localization.

The task of mapping is to build a 3D model of the environment by the means
of SfM methods, whereas the task of visual localization is to quickly estimate
robot pose w.r.t. the precomputed 3D model without updating it.

2.1   3D Model Construction

First, the lens distortion model along with internal camera calibration, which
facilitates the transformation from image pixel coordinates to unit direction
vectors, has to be obtained. Five images of a known calibration grid were used
to compute calibration matrix and two parameters of radial distortion according
to the polynomial model of degree two for the camera [10].

For constructing the model we have used Bundler [15], which accepts a bunch
of images and computes a sparse 3D point cloud model with camera poses.

Bundler detects and describes SURF [2] features on all input images and performs exhaustive pairwise feature matching. Promising image pairs are verified
w.r.t. epipolar geometry and the "best" image pair is chosen as the seed of the
reconstruction. Then, further cameras are added to the model, new 3D points are
triangulated [7], and the whole model is refined by sparse bundle adjustment [9]
in a loop until there are no feasible cameras left. To improve the quality of the
model, internal camera calibration can be fixed during the computation.

The sparse 3D point model, as received from Bundler, is transformed according to the user defined real world coordinate system and thus the localization
with respect to this model can be considered global. The world coordinate system is defined by assigning desired world coordinates to at least three 3D points
manually selected from the model and transforming all the model 3D points to
the new coordinates using the computed similarity transform [17].

2.2   Visual Localization

Visual localization makes use of the sparse 3D point cloud model created during the mapping phase. The visual localization estimating robot camera pose is

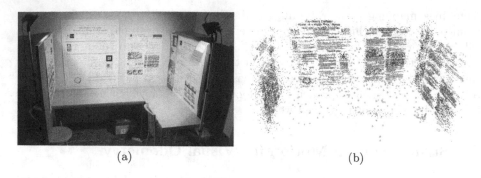

Fig. 2. Experimental workspace environment with drawings on the walls. (a) Overview of the environment. (b) 3D model resulting from Bundler. 502 estimated camera poses are denoted by red pyramids and 54,450 triangulated 3D points are drawn in real color.

performed in several steps. First, fast SURF [2] features are detected and described in an acquired image. Second, radial undistortion of the detected feature positions is achieved by computing the inverse of the radial distortion function.

Next, tentative feature matches w.r.t. the pre-computed 3D model loaded from a file are obtained using FLANN [11] approximate nearest neighbour search in the descriptor space. Finally, the camera pose is estimated from the 3D model by solving the 3-point camera pose problem for a calibrated camera [12] inside of a RANSAC [5] loop. Reprojection error [7] is used as the criterion for tentative match classification to inliers and outliers. Estimated camera pose is considered valid when the number of inliers exceeds a predefined threshold.

In some situations, visual localization does not output a valid result. This is caused by e.g. blurred images leading to an insufficient number of image-to-3D model point matches. This situation is dealt with during the fusion of data from visual localization and robot odometry.

3   Robot Pose Estimation and Navigation

Next, we investigate how to improve robot pose estimation by fusing visual localization results with robot odometry.

3.1   Robot Odometry

The odometry provided by robot firmware is computed from robot model, i.e. step length and walk angle only, no data from the inertial unit are used (although it is available on the robot). Robot poses output from odometry are relative to some starting point and so only the relative transformations to the previous poses are used in our localization system. The produced poses are known to be biased with an additive error, which is not negligible for legged robots. It was noted in the preliminary experiments that the odometry alone cannot be used

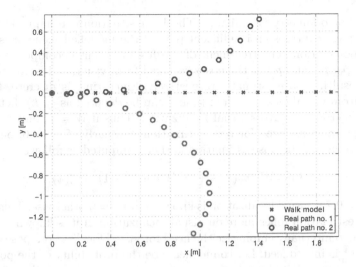

Fig. 3. Walk model error in two separate trials. Crosses denote the desired path and circles show the actual traversed path.

for reliable robot navigation, as the resulting robot pose deviates greatly from the ground truth, see Figure 3. Thus another source of robot pose is needed. We have decided to use the information from the robot camera.

3.2 Visual Odometry

The camera pose obtained by visual localization has 6 DOF (3DOF for position and 3DOF for rotation). The robot, on the other hand, has only 3DOF, i.e. it moves in a plane and rotates. The transformation from the general 6D space to 3D is as follows. Let the ground plane be the xy plane. The z axis points upwards and all the axes together form a right-handed coordinate system. Then the 6D to 3D transformation is the vertical projection along the negative z axis, see Figure 4. After this transformation is carried out, the transformation from camera to robot torso must be computed.

Since other modules controlling the robot are free to move its head, the transformation from the camera to robot body needs to be known. Currently, only the head yaw angle is used for the camera–body transformation because the distance from the camera center to torso center after projecting to the xy plane is in the order of centimeters and can be neglected.

With the knowledge of the overall transformation from 6D camera pose to 3D torso pose, we can now merge the two odometry sources in order to obtain more precise robot pose estimates.

3.3 Fusion of Robot and Visual Odometry

A weighted mean is used to fuse the two sources of pose estimates. During localization, two situations can occur. Either both measurements are available or only robot odometry is available. The later situation can happen when the received image captures an insufficient part of the modelled scene or is blurred due to robot motion. The treatment of the fusion is thus decomposed into two parts. Let p_v, p_o, and p_e be the poses received from visual and robot odometry and the resulting pose estimate, respectively. Since time is discrete, the pose obtained from visual localization in time k can be denoted as $p_v(k)$. Let W be a weighting factor that favors visual localization. Thus if $W = 1$, only data from the camera are considered for pose estimation. Similarly, if $W = 0$, only robot odometry is used. The pose estimation is then computed as follows

$$p_e(k) = W \cdot p_v(k) + (1 - W)(p_e(k - 1) + p_o(k)), \tag{1}$$

where $W = 0.7$ if visual localization is known and $W = 0$ otherwise. This ensures that pose estimation relies more on visual localization, if it is known.

In order to internally emphasize the need for visual localization, pose estimate confidence c is introduced. Let confidence c be the probability of the pose being confident, i.e. $c = 1$ if the robot is confident about the pose and $c = 0$ if it is completely unsure. From the comparison of the two sources of pose estimates, we would like to increase the confidence if both visual and robot odometry are known and decrease the confidence otherwise. For this purpose a Bayes filter, known from the occupancy grids in robotic mapping, is employed. The pose estimate confidence is computed according to the following update rule

$$c(k + 1) = \frac{p \cdot c(k)}{p \cdot c(k) + (1 - p)(1 - c(k))}, \tag{2}$$

where p is a parameter, which is set to 0.8 when both visual and robot odometry are known and to 0.2 if only robot odometry is available. Moreover, the confidence is limited by upper and lower bound, in order to speed up the change of confidence. The proposed update rule has the desired effect of increasing and decreasing the confidence according to the availability of visual localization.

3.4   Navigation

The purpose of navigation is to control the movement of a robot from one pose to another. After all, the term cybernetics stems from the Greek kybernētēs, i.e. steersman. Navigation combines trajectory planning with the execution of the plan, by monitoring the performed actions and adjusting control appropriately.

The robot coordinate system is defined as shown in Figure 4. Its origin is in the body center, x axis points ahead of the robot, and y axis points to its left.

Let us now focus on processing the fused pose estimates. In some situations, the confidence of robot pose estimate can drop below a predefined threshold c_θ, as described in Section 2.2. Navigation reacts to this event in the following way. First, it stops the movement of the robot in order to improve image quality. If this does not improve pose confidence, navigation starts turning robot's head in order to capture an image with a higher number of matches with the 3D model. Since the maximum yaw of the head is approximately 120°, it is not needed to

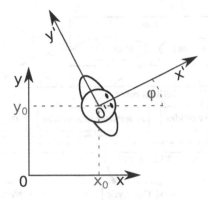

Fig. 4. Robot pose in world coordinates

turn the whole body. Moreover, with low confidence of the pose, it is not safe to move the whole robot since the robot can be close to an edge of the table or to an obstacle. Once the confidence increases above the threshold c_θ, the robot resumes its movement towards the target pose.

Although the working space of the robot is bounded by a polygon, it does not need to be convex and thus a more complex method than following a straight line is needed for safely navigating the robot on the table, e.g. for an L-shaped table a simple strategy with a *middle point* on the table, towards which the robot is walking unless the target pose is reachable along a straight line, can by chosen.

3.5   Simultaneous Localization and Mapping

If localization efficiency and accuracy was not the main concern, one could use also the method presented in [6], which makes use of the sequential Structure from Motion pipeline [16] implemented in MATLAB to construct a 3D model of the environment by the means of SLAM. The robot walks in a stop-and-go fashion capturing images and performing incremental 3D model construction. The direction of walk is continuously being refined by using robot odometry data and, once a partial 3D model is ready, also by visual localization. When needed, loop closing can be used to improve model consistency.

4   Implementation

This section covers the implementation details of the proposed method. Each module, implemented in C++ language, is running separately and can be easily replaced thanks to the employed RSB framework.

4.1   RSB

The RSB framework is basically a bus architecture, connecting various heterogeneous components via a hierarchical broadcast communication, separated into

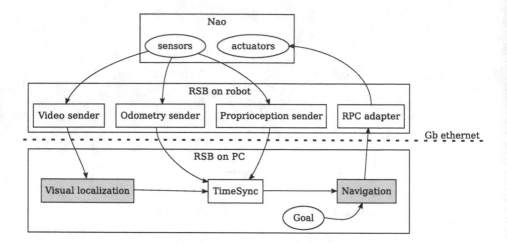

Fig. 5. Diagram of communication between individual modules and Nao

logical levels, rather than a huge number of peer-to-peer connections. Each module can act as a service provider or consumer and since all are connected via RSB, adding, replacing, or removing modules is seamless and does not interfere with the functionality of other modules [18].

Both visual localization and navigation modules are connected via RSB and communicate with other modules providing sensoric information and performing robot motion, see Figure 5.

4.2   Sensors, Actuators

The images taken by robot camera, joint angles, and robot odometry are all streamed in separate channels (scopes) using the modules distributed with RSB. The navigation module, which also performs odometry fusion should subscribe to all of these in order to receive all the necessary information for successful localization. Since the streams are asynchronous, we have employed an RSB TimeSync module. This module subscribes to several scopes and produces synchronized events via another scope. The navigation module thus subscribes to a single scope and receives all the input information, synchronized in such a way, that the time difference between the events in the original scopes is minimized.

The control of Nao is accomplished via an RSB Python RPC Adapter, which allows sending commands directly to NaoSDK without the need of having NaoSDK installed locally. The RPC adapter is employed for walking and turning of head.

4.3   Interface

Protobuf (Google data interchange format) is used for encoding data sent via RSB. Each datum type has its own protocol and the de-/serialization is perfomed by Protobuf. There are many protocol specifications common in robotics defined in Robotics Systems Types (RST) [3].

The visual localization module receives images from robot camera and outputs valid or invalid camera poses which are later synchronized with the output of other robot sensors. The world 3D point cloud and internal camera calibration (with optional radial distortion parameters) are read from a text file. There are several additional optional parameters (blob response threshold of SURF detector, maximum reprojection error for P3P in pixels, RANSAC confidence and maximum number of samples, and number of inliers required for a valid pose estimate), which can be set in order to balance the trade-off between efficiency, precision, and robustness.

The input to the navigation module consists of the synchronized sensory output, the description of the working polygon, and target poses. The working polygon is in the form of a sequence of points, denoting vertices, in such a way that consecutive vertices are connected with an edge stored in a text file. The interface for receiving target poses (controlling the robot) is based on a XTT-server architecture, so there is a blocking call to the navigation module, which gains control over the robot motion. Only one call can control the robot at a given time, which is desired. The return value of the call informs whether the target pose was reached or whether it was outside the working polygon of the robot. The two optional parameters are the maximum step size, i.e. the maximal distance between successive poses, and the precision of reaching the goal pose.

5 Experiments

Next, the proposed approach is validated by both the synthetic and real data experiments.

5.1 Synthetic Data

The synthetic experiment is aimed at the fusion of visual and robot odometry data using weighted mean and Bayes filter. The parameters are as follows: weight $W = 0.7$, $C_v = 0.8$, and $C_o = 0.2$, lower and upper bounds of pose confidence are set to 0.1 and 0.9, respectively. Robot odometry is modelled as a Gaussian variable with the mean equal to the true relative motion between single steps, the variance in position is equal to 0.02, and the variance in azimuth is equal to 0.03. Visual localization is modelled with the mean corresponding to ground truth and with the same variance as in the odometry model. Ground truth is chosen as 11 points along a straight line 0.1 m apart and the robot is starting at position $(0, 0)$, heading in the direction of the x axis. Three visual localizations are omitted in order to simulate unsuccessful visual localization and demonstrate the change in pose estimate confidence. The confidence decreases, when visual localization is not available (at steps 4, 6, and 7) and increases, as soon as the information is available again, see Figure 6.

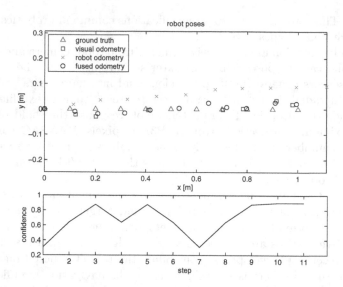

Fig. 6. Robot pose estimate and pose confidence. In positions 4, 6, and 7 the visual localization is missing—note the decrease in pose confidence.

5.2 Real Data

We used a simple RSB module to store all the images acquired by the top camera in PGM files and guided the robot manually through the scene in an approximately two minutes long sequence. Next, every fifth image of the sequence was selected giving raise to 504 VGA images of the scene. These were radially undistorted and passed to Bundler set in a way to use SURF features with threshold value 15 and known fixed internal camera calibration. The resulting 3D model obtained after 6.5 hours of computation consisted of 502 camera poses and 54,450 3D points, see Figure 2(b).

As a model with a relatively small number of high-quality 3D points is more suitable for subsequent localization than a model with a large number of medium-quality 3D points, we performed additional 3D point selection based on the number of verified 3D point projections to the images. Only 5,045 3D points having more than 15 verified projections were selected and exported to the resulting model file together with the SURF descriptors transferred from the images.

The actual experiment is performed on the real robot in order to demonstrate the ability to localize robot body w.r.t. the precomputed 3D model. The robot is placed in our workspace, shown in Figure 2(a), and moved manually along an L-shaped path, while the visual localization is running. The path is straight except for the beginning and the corner, where the robot turns 90° to the right. In Figure 7(a), the path starts at the lower part, with the robot facing down. Although the robot was moved by hand, the real trajectory deviates from a straight

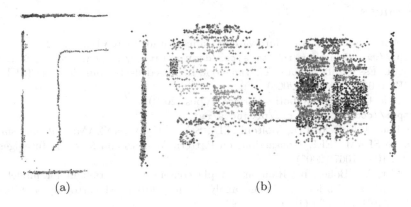

(a)   (b)

Fig. 7. Results of Nao localization w.r.t. the precomputed 3D model along an L-shaped path. Estimated camera locations for the head are denoted by red dots, the 5,045 3D points of the model are drawn in real color. (a) Top view. (b) Side view.

line at most by 1 cm. There is no ground truth available for this experiment but the reconstructed path is close to the true one, except for two obvious invalid localizations, which would be filtered out. The data shown in Figure 7 are directly from the visual localization, which works independently on each received image and uses no information about the desired trajectory or any motion model.

The process of visual localization is running at approximately 8 fps on a 64bit i5 laptop. The error of determining robot pose from visual odometry has a normal distribution around the true pose and thus nicely complements the additive error of pose estimation from robot odometry.

6 Conclusion

We have shown the possibility of enabling visual odometry of humanoid robot Nao using Structure from Motion without the need for artificial markers in the scene. Our approach improves robot pose estimation using fusion of odometry provided by robot firmware and visual localization by employing weighted mean and Bayes filter for updating pose confidence. The proposed modular implementation does not depend on any specific robot type thanks to the RSB middleware that connects all the components. The performance of our algorithm is demonstrated on synthetic and real experiments, showing the precision of visual localization and the improvement brought about by data fusion.

Acknowledgements. This work was supported by projects SGS12/187/OHK3/-3T/13, SGS12/191/OHK3/3T/13, and FP7-ICT-247525 HUMAVIPS.

References

1. Aldebaran Robotics: Nao Hardware Specification for SDK v1.12 (2012),
   http://www.aldebaran-robotics.com/documentation/nao/hardware/index.html
2. Bay, H., Ess, A., Tuytelaars, T., Van Gool, L.: Speeded-up robust features (SURF).
   CVIU 110(3), 346–359 (2008)
3. Bielefeld University: Robotics Service Types (2012),
   https://code.cor-lab.org/projects/rst
4. Davison, A.J., Reid, I.D., Molton, N.D., Stasse, O.: MonoSLAM: real-time single
   camera SLAM. IEEE Transactions on Pattern Analysis and Machine Intelligence
   29(6), 1052–1067 (2007)
5. Fischler, M., Bolles, R.: Random sample consensus: A paradigm for model fitting with applications to image analysis and automated cartography. Comm.
   ACM 24(6), 381–395 (1981)
6. Fojtů, Š.: Nao Localization and Navigation Based on Sparse 3D Point Cloud Reconstruction. Master's thesis, Czech Technical University in Prague (2011)
7. Hartley, R., Zisserman, A.: Multiple View Geometry in Computer Vision, 2nd edn.
   Cambridge University Press (2003)
8. Hu, H., Gu, D.: Landmark-based Navigation of Industrial Mobile Robots. Industrial
   Robot: An International Journal 27(6), 458–467 (2000)
9. Lourakis, M.I.A., Argyros, A.A.: SBA: A software package for generic sparse bundle
   adjustment. ACM Transactions on Mathematical Software (2009)
10. Mareček, P.: A Camera Calibration System. Master's thesis, Center for Machine
    Perception, K13133 FEE Czech Technical University, Czech Republic (2001)
11. Muja, M., Lowe, D.: Fast approximate nearest neighbors with automatic algorithm
    configuration. In: VISAPP 2009 (2009)
12. Nistér, D.: A minimal solution to the generalized 3-point pose problem. In: CVPR
    2004. pp. I:560–I:567 (2004)
13. Osswald, S., Hornung, A., Bennewitz, M.: Learning reliable and efficient naviga-
    tion with a humanoid. In: 2010 IEEE International Conference on Robotics and
    Automation (ICRA), pp. 2375–2380. IEEE (2010)
14. Quigley, M., Conley, K., Gerkey, B.: ROS: an open-source Robot Operating System.
    In: Open-Source Software workshop of the International Conference on Robotics
    and Automation, ICRA 2009 (2009)
15. Snavely, N., Seitz, S., Szeliski, R.: Modeling the world from internet photo collec-
    tions. IJCV 80(2), 189–210 (2008)
16. Torii, A., Havlena, M., Pajdla, T.: Omnidirectional image stabilization for visual
    object recognition. International Journal of Computer Vision 91(2), 157–174 (2011)
17. Umeyama, S.: Least-squares Estimation of Transformation Parameters Between
    Two Point Patterns. IEEE Transactions on Pattern Analysis and Machine Intelli-
    gence, 376–380 (1991)
18. Wienke, J., Wrede, S.: A Middleware for Collaborative Research in Experimental
    Robotics. In: 2011 IEEE/SICE International Symposium on System Integration,
    SII 2011, Kyoto, Japan, pp. 1183–1190 (2011)

A Graph-Based Hierarchical SLAM Framework for Large-Scale Mapping

He Zhang[1,2], Zifeng Hou[1,2], Nanjun Li[2], and Shuang Song[2]

[1] Institute of Computing Technology, GUCAS
fuyinzh@gmail.com
[2] Lenovo Group
{houzf,linj2,songshuang2}@lenovo.com

Abstract. In this paper, a graph-based hierarchical SLAM framework is proposed which ensures not only the high-speed operation of graph-based SLAM, but also feasibility of large-scale 3D map building. Both local and global level graph-based SLAM will be operated. They can be concurrently implemented in different computing units but must maintained communication which is called as a session. During each session, local level SLAM will create a pose-graph containing trajectory for mobile robot and information for local maps. To avoid communication congestion, raw density point cloud of each pose-node will be reduced into a sparser one by voxel grid filtering. When a session is closed, duo-graph strategy is executed to guarantee the consistency between successive local map. To associate massive local map information and closing loops in large-scale environment, graph-based algorithm will also be implemented in global level SLAM.

Two experiments are carried out in the real indoor environment. In the first experiment, SLAM process is greatly accelerated in this framework by distributing the whole SLAM task into different level SLAM entities: local level SLAM operated on robot and global on laptop. It shows that this framework is scalable and it can be implemented in CS(Client-Server) model. Second experiment is conducted in our biggest work office around which we control the robot traverse for three times. It demonstrates that this framework can simultaneously keep fast graph-based SLAM in local-end and generate consistent and convergent 3D map in global-end SLAM process.

1 Introduction

To perform tasks such as exploration, transportation, or searching, it is crucial for mobile robots to build large-scale 3D environment map for learning and navigating. In large-scale area, SLAM (Simultaneous localization and mapping) is more complex and remains to be solved. Many prior researches [1] concentrate on algorithms to speed up SLAM process. Others [2][3] focus on reducing the computational time and memory requirements using hierarchical SLAM framework. Besides, some independent submapping strategies [4], which enable robot to traverse in a limited local area, have also been explored. To generate more

C.-Y. Su, S. Rakheja, H. Liu (Eds.): ICIRA 2012, Part II, LNAI 7507, pp. 439–448, 2012.
© Springer-Verlag Berlin Heidelberg 2012

consistent and convergent global map, conditionally independent submapping algorithm is introduced [5]. In this paper, a fast graph-based hierarchical SLAM framework is presented which not only ensure high speed of the process of graph-based SLAM, but also capable of generating large-scale consistent and convergent 3D map.

In SLAM process, both frontend and backend have to be solved to ensure consistency of the map. The state of art graph-based SLAM algorithm [6][7] is recently well-known for efficiently nonlinear graph optimization in the backend.Deeply insights into the process of graph-based SLAM, it can be subtly divided into sequential steps: FE (Feature Extraction), FM (Feature Matching), ME (Motion Estimation), GO (Graph Optimization) and MB (Map Building). FE usually means extracting visual features [8][9] or geometry traits [10] from sensor observation. FM aims to find matched pairs of those similar feature points or patches of objects. Usually KD-tree structure is involved to speed this step. ME, based on those matched pairs, is normally to estimate the rigid body transformation using quaternion methods [11]. GO is an iterative process which commits to find a configuration of parameters or state variables that maximally accords to a set of measurements [6]. MB is to generate a global consistent and convergent 3D map. Because the pose-graph structure has to be sustained along with all these steps except the last one, this task can be transferred to global-end process.

When robot navigates in a large-scale environment which results in huge amount information of 3D scene, increasing requirement of computation and memory will dramatically decrease the efficiency of SLAM. Even if the robot repeatedly traverses over small place, the continuous increment of graph size will also attributes to undesirable SLAM performance. In this framework, both local and global SLAM are based on the graph-based algorithm, but with different meanings of nodes. The front end of local SLAM is similar to visual SLAM [12], where each node represents robot pose. In global SLAM, a node will be the aggregation of pose-nodes in a session, so it is called session-node. Therefore, the local SLAM graph is called pose-graph, while global SLAM one is session-graph. Both the backend of local and global SLAM depend on graph optimization [6].

2   Local Level Graph-Based SLAM

In graph-based SLAM, the poses of the robot are modelled by nodes in a graph and labelled with their positions in the environment. Its theory and solution have been fully illustrated in [6], thus only the details of duo-graph strategy is discussed below.

Duo-Graph strategy is operated in local level SLAM. The basic idea is simple: when the size of current graph arrives to certain threshold T_1, creates a back-up one by copying of the last several nodes; when the size of back-up graph becomes larger than threshold T_2, it will take place of the current one. As depicted in Figure 1, the blue nodes stand for the $n - 1$ th pose-graph, while the green ones for n th pose-graph. In the red circle of SLAM interval, those nodes will both be

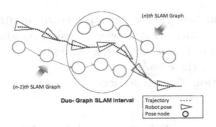

Fig. 1. Principle of Duo-Graph

added into the $n-1$ th pose-graph and n th. After the size of n th pose-graph grows big enough, the $n-1$ th one will firstly be reduced into a new super node containing all the information of local map, and then secondly registered into graph structure maintained in global SLAM process. The n th pose-graph will take place which will make sure of both consistency and efficiency of local level SLAM process.

Before graph switching, this whole process is called one "session" for global-end. Meanwhile, the super node mentioned before is thus called session-node. To simultaneously render 3D map in global-end, when a new pose-node is created in local-end, its information will be transmitted. Once small loop has been detected in local scene, updated trajectory will also be sent. All these work will be finished in a single session, during which global-end process will continuously communicate with local-end to build 3D map of current session. This is fully demonstrated in Algorithm 1.

3   Global Level Graph-Based SLAM

In the global-end process, three tasks have to be done in the SLAM process: 1) Register Session; 2) Map Builder; 3) Loop Closing. RS(Register Session) means to firstly reduce the whole session into a session-node, and secondly add it into the session-graph. MB(Map Builder) both build local map for current session and global map for the whole environment. LC(Loop Closing) monitors whether mobile robot enters the area that it has already visited. MB mainly concentrate on computation of transformation matrix and triangulation and LC will be discussed in 4.1. Thus, here RS is discussed below.

3.1   Reduce Session into a Single Session-Node

When session switch has occurred, it will reduce all the pose-nodes of current session into a session-node, add it into session-graph, and start a new session. Then, similar to [3], the whole hybrid map m can be notated as:

$$\mathbf{M} = \left(\{S_k\}_{k=1...n}, \{\Delta_{ab}\}_{\substack{a=1...n \\ b=1...n}} \right) \tag{1}$$

Each S_k stands for a single session, which has its own coordinate reference frame. Also, Δ_{ab} contains transformation between session S_a and S_b. In the session-graph, S_k will be reduced as a single session-node, and correspondingly $\{\Delta\}$ mean the edges between these nodes.

As discussed in section 2, each session contains the information of its pose-nodes, thus it can be presented as:

$$\mathbf{X_k} = \begin{pmatrix} X_{p_1}^B \\ \vdots \\ X_{p_n}^B \end{pmatrix}; \mathbf{L_k} = \begin{pmatrix} L_{f_1}^{p_1} & \cdots & L_{f_n}^{p_1} \\ \vdots & \ddots & \vdots \\ L_{f_1}^{p_n} & \cdots & L_{f_n}^{p_n} \end{pmatrix} \tag{2}$$

$X_{p_i}^B$ symbolizes each pose of robot in session S_k relative to the base reference frame, and $L_{f_i}^{p_i}$ stands for location of feature f_i relative to reference frame of pose $X_{p_i}^B$. The pose of the first node $X_{p_1}^B$ is deemed as the root pose R_k of session S_k, and then the locations of the features must be recalculated to the reference frame of R_k. Let $F_{p_i}^{p_j}$ stand for the set of features transformed from $L_f^{p_i}$ to $L_f^{p_j}$, F_k the union of feature set $F_{p_i}^{p_1}$ then:

$$F_{p_i}^{p_1} = L_{f_j}^{p_i} \oplus (X_{p_i}^B \ominus X_{p_1}^B) \qquad \text{for } j = 1 \ldots n \tag{3}$$

$$\mathbf{F_k} = \bigcup F_{p_i}^{p_1} \qquad \text{for } i = 1 \ldots n \tag{4}$$

$\oplus$ is pose composition operator while $\ominus$ the inverse pose composition operator. In the same way, each observation O_{p_i} can also be merged under the same coordinate system. Redundant features and points can be filtered according to their coordinates. Let F_k' and O_k' stand for filtered set of F_k and O_k respectively. Then session-node k can be simply represented as:

$$\mathbf{S_k} = \{R_k, F_k', O_k'\} \tag{5}$$

R_k is the root node of session-node S_k, that is X_{p1}^B.

3.2   Global Graph-Based SLAM Algorithm

Global-end process will not only build the local map for current session but also consistent global one. After receiving a new pose-node transmitted from local-end, global-end will update local map and then render it. When session switch occurs, firstly a new session-node is created as illustrated in 3.1; secondly, this session-node will be inserted into session-graph and matched with previous ones to close loop; thirdly, the global 3D map will be built after optimization of session-graph. Meanwhile, when loop is closed, it will find out which session robot enters and transmit this session-node to local-end. The process of global level SLAM algorithm is clearly illustrated in the following Algorithm 2:

Algorithm 1. Duo-Graph Local SLAM Algorithm

1: **function** DUOGRAPHSLAM
2:     **while** (*true*) **do**
3:         $SwitchSession \leftarrow false$
4:         $Ob_i \leftarrow getNewObservation()$ ▷ Get observation from external sensor
5:         $N_i \leftarrow createNewNode(Ob_i)$
6:         $Flag \leftarrow Graph.addNode(N_i)$ ▷ Add node to current pose-Graph
7:         **if** $Flag$ is false **then**
8:             *continue*
9:         **end if**
10:         $Trajectory \leftarrow Graph.Optimization()$
11:         **if** $Graph.size() > Threshold1$ **then**
12:             $Graph_{back}.addNode(N_i)$
13:             $Graph_{back}.Optimization()$
14:             **if** $Graph_{back}.size() > Threshold2$ **then**
15:   ▷ Whether the backup pose-Graph is reliable
16:                 $SwitchSession \leftarrow true$ ▷ Notice global-end
17:                 $Graph \leftarrow Graph_{back}$
18:                 $Graph_{back}.clear()$
19:             **end if**
20:         **end if**
21:         $SendInformation2GlobalEnd(N_i, Trajecotry, SwitchSession)$
22:                 ▷ Send Node, Trajectory and Switch Session Flag to global-end process
23:     **end while**
24: **end function**

4   Hierarchical Graph-Based Slam Frame Work

In this hierarchical frame work, the mobile robot will continuously implement local level SLAM, while another process finish global SLAM whose work is primarily global map registration. These two procedures can be executed simultaneously in a single robot, multi robots or one robot with a server. But reliable communication between them must be maintained.

4.1   Graph-Based Hierarchical Framework

As discussed in 1, graph-based SLAM process can be subdivided into small steps: FE, FM, ME, GO and MB. Because the pose-graph structure has to be sustained along with all these steps except the last one, this task can be transferred to global-end process. The whole frame work is shown in Figure 2, and it will be explained according to three mainly processes below:

Algorithm 2. Global SLAM Algorithm

1: Initialize: $LoopClosing \leftarrow false$
2: **function** GLOBALSLAM
3:    **while** ($true$) **do**
4:       **if** ($getInformation(N_i, Trajectory, SwitchSession)$) **then**
5:                       ▷ get Information from local-end process
6:         **if** $SwitchSession$ is false **then**   ▷ Current Session is active
7:            $S_{cur}.addNode(N_i)$
8:            $S_{cur}.updateTrajectory(Trajectory)$
9:            $MapBuilder(S_{cur})$
10:         **end if**
11:         **if** $SwitchSession$ is true **then**
12:            $S_i \leftarrow ReduceSession2node(S_{cur})$
13:            $S_{cur}.clear()$ ▷ clear current session
14:            $S_{cur}.addRootNode(N_i)$
15:                ▷ start new session, and set the first node as root node
16:            $Graph.addNode(S_i, LoopClosing)$
17:            $Graph.Optimization()$
18:            **if** $LoopClosing$ **then**
19:               $S_{cur}' \leftarrow Graph.findClosetSession(N_i)$
20:               $SendSession2LocalEnd(S_{cur}')$
21:                ▷ send this reentered session-node to local-end
22:            **end if**
23:         **end if**
24:       **end if**
25:    **end while**
26: **end function**

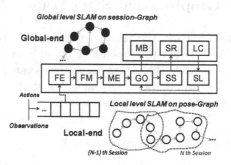

Fig. 2. Overview of Graph-based Hierarchical SLAM Framework

– *Local Level SLAM Process:* SLAM is divided into several subtle steps. The mobile robot will firstly read actions and observations from which features will be extracted. By matching features with previous ones, current pose will be estimated and a new pose-node will be created and added into pose-Graph. Its observation will be transmitted to global-end. Local-end will finish FE, FM, ME and GO while global-end MB.

- *Global Level SLAM Process:* When the current graph grows to its upper limitation, the back-up graph will take place and discard the current one which is called SS (Session Switch). Correspondingly, global-end will get this notification, construct a new session-node, and insert it into the session-graph. This is SR (Session Register) step.
- *Loop Closing Process:* It is common that the mobile robot will enter areas that it has visited before. Loop will be identified when the new session-node is matched with previous but not successive one. Then, by comparing root pose of each session and its feature points, the closest session can be found in which mobile robot most possibly enter. The corresponding session-node will be transmitted to local-end process. Then local-end process will rectify its pose-graph by matching its pose-nodes with this session-node. This action is called SL (Session Load).

5   Experiments

Two experiments in the real environment have been conducted to support those two claims:

- This hierarchy framework is scalable and can be applied in CS(Client-Server) model. In this way, high speed of local graph-based SLAM is guaranteed, when local and global level SLAM process being implemented synchronously in one robot with a global-end computer.
- In this framework, consistent and convergent large-scale 3D map can be built through simultaneously local and global graph-based SLAM.

We re-engineered Freiburg's rgbdslam [13] from Linux OS to Microsoft Windows OS and changed it following the process of local level SLAM in this framework. SURF [8] will be extracted from each frame, and graph optimization is based on Hogman [7] structure. Raw density point cloud is reduced by voxel grid filtering. Using self-developed C++ software, global level SLAM and communication module are realized following Client-Server model. The robot is a self-developed omni-directional wheels mobile system. It consists of a 3-wheel chassis, an onboard laptop, and a kinect.

5.1   Experiment 1

In the first experiment, the SLAM performance of three models is compared as:

- FreiburgSLAM: Mobile robot carries out Freiburg's rgbdslam [13]; 3D map is rendered using raw density point cloud.
- BIRSLAM: Both local and global SLAM are executed in mobile robot; 3D map is rendered using sparse point cloud with voxel size $4cm$.
- C2SSLAM: Mobile robot operates local SLAM with another laptop global SLAM; 3D map is rendered using sparse point cloud with voxel size $4cm$.

We control the robot traverse in the laboratory with 7m width, 13m length and 4.5m height using those three SLAM models. And to fully prove first claim, the threshold of SS is set big enough to fully compare the speed of SLAM process in one session. The 3D maps generated in these models are similar, while the performance of each step, and also of total SLAM will be compared.

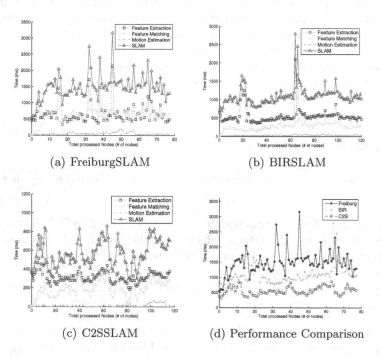

(a) FreiburgSLAM

(b) BIRSLAM

(c) C2SSLAM

(d) Performance Comparison

Fig. 3. Performance Analyse and Comparison of Freiburg, BIR, C2S SLAM

Because Hogman graph optimization actually takes little time when the size is under 100, so GO is not taken into consideration.Figure 3(a)-3(c) respectively displays the time consumed in each step and total SLAM process using FreiburgSLAM, BIRSLAM and C2SSLAM. In Figure 3(d), C2SSLAM cost nearly half of time than BIRSLAM, by separating MB from other steps. The reason that BIRSLAM is faster than FreiburgSLAM is that the former reduce the dense of point cloud by voxel grid filtering. Furthermore, in the process of experiment, because of slow SLAM calculation in FreiburgSLAM and BIRSLAM, the rate of failure of FM is much bigger than C2SSLAM. Then, we have to control the robot track back to find previous frames, that costs more time to explore.

5.2   Experiment 2

In the second experiment, we control the robot traverse three circles in our largest work office about 16m width, 19m length, and 4.5m height. In each circle, about

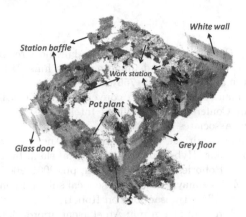

Fig. 4. Global 3D Map generated using this framework

Table 1. Time consuming for each step in Local level Slam process

Step	Mean Value (ms)	Standard Deviation (ms)
FE	450.3852	7.5981
FM	97.9956	5.5994
ME	24.5729	4.5792
SLAM	592.9537	8.4196

11 sessions are created and each one contains 50 nodes, thus total about 1650 nodes in this experiment.

Because there are many repeated scenes such as the same work station with green decoration products, without odometry's information, nodes are often mismatched in a single local pose-graph. This will result in such noisy information as overlapped glass door or multiple pot plants shown in Figure 4. Table 1 records time consumed in each subtle step of local level SLAM in experiment 2, and shows that it can be maintained high speed around 1.68fps.

6   Conclusion and FutureWork

In this paper, a hierarchical graph-based SLAM framework is proposed which not only ensures high speed of the process of local level graph-based SLAM, but also capable of building consistent and convergent 3D map in large-scale environment. This framework is scalable and can be applied by multi robots with many carrying out local-end process while another single one executes the global-end process. Furthermore, it may also enable robots to make use of the power of cloud computing if the global-end computer can be entitled to cloud service in the future. With the high bandwidth of internet and power of cloud computing, robots can support more powerful services to increase the quality of human life.

References

1. Guivant, J., Nebot, E.: Solving computational and memory requirements of feature-based simultaneous localization and mapping algorithms. IEEE Transactions on Robotics and Automation 19(4), 749–755 (2003)
2. Leonard, J., Newman, P.: Consistent, convergent, and constant-time slam. In: International Joint Conference on Artificial Intelligence, vol. 18, pp. 1143–1150. Lawrence Erlbaum Associates Ltd. (2003)
3. Blanco, J., Fernández-Madrigal, J., Gonzalez, J.: A new approach for large-scale localization and mapping: Hybrid metric-topological slam. In: 2007 IEEE International Conference on Robotics and Automation, pp. 2061–2067. IEEE (2007)
4. Huang, S., Wang, Z., Dissanayake, G.: Sparse local submap joining filter for building large-scale maps. IEEE Transactions on Robotics 24(5), 1121–1130 (2008)
5. Piniés, P., Paz, L., Tardós, J.: Ci-graph: An efficient approach for large scale slam. In: IEEE International Conference on Robotics and Automation, ICRA 2009, pp. 3913–3920. IEEE (2009)
6. Kummerle, R., Grisetti, G., Strasdat, H., Konolige, K., Burgard, W.: g2o: A general framework for graph optimization. In: 2011 IEEE International Conference on Robotics and Automation (ICRA), pp. 3607–3613. IEEE (2011)
7. Grisetti, G., Kummerle, R., Stachniss, C., Frese, U., Hertzberg, C.: Hierarchical optimization on manifolds for online 2d and 3d mapping. In: 2010 IEEE International Conference on Robotics and Automation (ICRA), pp. 273–278. IEEE (2010)
8. Bay, H., Tuytelaars, T., Van Gool, L.: SURF: Speeded Up Robust Features. In: Leonardis, A., Bischof, H., Pinz, A. (eds.) ECCV 2006. LNCS, vol. 3951, pp. 404–417. Springer, Heidelberg (2006)
9. Skrypnyk, I., Lowe, D.: Scene modelling, recognition and tracking with invariant image features. In: Third IEEE and ACM International Symposium on Mixed and Augmented Reality, ISMAR 2004, pp. 110–119. IEEE (2004)
10. Rusu, R., Marton, Z., Blodow, N., Beetz, M.: Learning informative point classes for the acquisition of object model maps. In: 10th International Conference on Control, Automation, Robotics and Vision, ICARCV 2008, pp. 643–650. IEEE (2008)
11. Horn, B.: Closed-form solution of absolute orientation using unit quaternions. JOSA A 4(4), 629–642 (1987)
12. Henry, P., Krainin, M., Herbst, E., Ren, X., Fox, D.: Rgb-d mapping: Using depth cameras for dense 3d modeling of indoor environments. In: the 12th International Symposium on Experimental Robotics, ISER (2010)
13. http://www.ros.org/wiki/rgbdslam/

LOCOBOT - Low Cost Toolkit for Building Robot Co-workers in Assembly Lines

Christian Wögerer[1], Harald Bauer[1], Martijn Rooker[1], Gerhard Ebenhofer[1],
Alberto Rovetta[2], Neil Robertson[3], and Andreas Pichler[1]

[1] PROFACTOR GmbH, Im Stadtgut A2, 4407 Steyr, Austria
[2] Politecnico di Milano, Via Lamasa 1, 20156 Milano, Italy
[3] Heriot-Watt University, Edinburgh, UK
christian.woegerer@profactor.at

Abstract. **LOCOBOT** (www.locobot.eu) is a European project funded in the first call of the "Factory of the future" in FP 7 (FoF.NMP.2010-1). LOCOBOT addresses strategic objective — Plug-and-Produce components for adaptive control. The 'Factories of the Future' public-private partnership (PPP) is a joint initiative of the European Commission and the private sector to promote research in advanced manufacturing across Europe. Launched in early 2009, this major European initiative has embarked upon its first 25 research projects which will achieve their final results in 2013 and 2014. 5 of these 25 projects are related to the Topic of robotics and LOCOBOT is one of this 5 projects. LOCOBOT is a system which reaches above and beyond what is currently available for those working in the automotive industry: it incorporates a flexible robotic assistant platform to support and increase manual production processes, as well as the engineering tools required for its setup. Further, this project aims to improve the ergonomics in industrial production processes.

Keywords: Plug and Produce, Intelligent sensing, Mobile Platforms.

1 Introduction

The European industry, especially the automotive industry and their component manufacturers are facing the biggest shift in their history. The transition from combustion engines to electric drives (e-vehicle) requires production facilities that can initially deal with low and varying production volumes and can quickly be up-scaled to large numbers at need. LOCOBOT provides a solution to this problem by developing a toolkit for building customized low cost robot co-workers for a broad spectrum of scenarios.

LOCOBOT does not only include the robot itself but also the engineering tools that are required for quickly building the robot, setting up its control structure and defining its tasks. Facing the demographic change, a further goal of LOCOBOT is the improvement of ergonomics in industrial production processes.

LOCOBOT will go beyond state-of-the-art in three important topics regarding a low-cost tool-kit for constructing robots:

C.-Y. Su, S. Rakheja, H. Liu (Eds.): ICIRA 2012, Part II, LNAI 7507, pp. 449–459, 2012.

- Plug-and-Produce robotic modules for robot assistants
- Self-optimizing and adaptive mechatronic systems
- Enhanced sensing and human activity interpretation including usability aspects

A group of key players in the automotive industry, in automation components, advanced robots and engineering software will be supported by a group of excellent researchers to solve the technical and scientific challenges in LOCOBOT.
The results will be demonstrated by setting up 3 typical and highly relevant use cases in a pilot production line of an Industrial End-user.

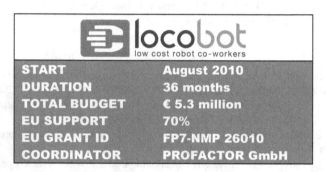

Fig. 1. LOCOBOT Facts

1.1   Consortium

The LOCOBOT consortium has 10 different partners from industry (Large Industry as well as SME´s) and research (University and research Centers) coming from 5 different counties with complementary Know How.

ID	Participant organization name	Type	Partner Acronym	Country
1	PROFACTOR GmbH (Coordinator)	High-Tech SME (SME)	PROF	Austria
2	Audi AG	OEM End User (IND)	AUDI	Germany
3	Heriot-Watt University	University (HE)	HWU	United Kingdom
4	Hochschule Ingolstadt	University (HE)	FHI	Germany
5	Politecnico di Milano	University (HE)	POLIMI	Italy
6	University of Edinburgh	University (HE)	UEDIN	United Kingdom
7	FerRobotics Compliant Robot Technology GmbH	Robot Manufacturer (SME)	FERRO	Austria
8	Festo AG	OEM Component Vendor (IND)	FESTO	Germany
9	Ridgeback sas	Human factors, Ergonomics, Work Psychology (SME)	RBK	Italy
10	Visual Components Oy	SME simulation software vendor (SME)	VIS	Finland

Fig. 2. LOCOBOT Consortium

2   Concept, LOCOBOTS Way of Thinking

The transition to-wards sustainable products and renewable energy poses new challenges to the European manufacturing industry in these times. This is particularly true for the automotive industry, which is facing the change from combustion engines to e-vehicles. The market for e-vehicle is growing and European companies need to

- secure profitability at initially low production rates and
- be able to quickly up-scale production if required.

2.1   Overall Concept

LOCOBOT addresses this need by creating a **tool-kit for low-cost robot assistants** built from a set of plug-and-produce kinematic modules with compliant, but precise actuators and intelligent sensing for man-machine cooperation. This tool-kit will provide higher flexibility, adaptively and scalability that are all required to meet these upcoming challenges.

The LOCOBOT **Toolkit** consists of the LOCOBOT Plug&Produce Components (HW-Modules) as well as the LOCOBOT Plug&Produce Robot Configurator Framework in order to configure, plan and set-up a robot application for robot co-workers that assist human workers (SW-Modules). The different modules can be used designing the Robot and the specific application.

- Plug&Produce Robot Modules (Hardware)
- Plug&Produce Sensing and Actuating
- Safety Concept and Safety Tools
- Rapid Engineering, reconfiguration, simulation and validation tools

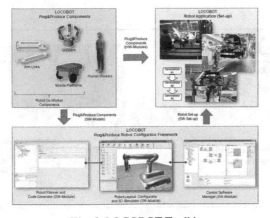

Fig. 3. LOCOBOT Toolkit

A Demonstration will be based on 3 different realistic scenarios at a pilot line of an industrial partner and will include the typical use cases, where robot assistant have a substantial impact on efficiency.

2.2 LOCOBOTS Way of Thinking

LOCOBOT is not only a project with the generic approach to realize the 3 defined scenarios with pre-defined components. These scenarios (down to earth examples) are to demonstrate and prove the generic approach of LOCOBOT. Nevertheless, the LOCOBOT **toolkit** has to be open for a wide variety of applications because there are a lot of scenarios benefitting from robotic assistance. One of the advantages of the LOCOBOT technology is the modularity of the Software Components. To reach the goal of plug&produce components well designed high level interfaces are necessary.

The principle of "separation of concern" is the basic of our component based development. That means an

- independent interface oriented development
- isolated component tested BEFORE system integration
- boosting the idea and the implementation of a toolkit

2.3 Initial Situation

Starting a LOCOBOT project is possible in almost each situation if there is a need for a robot application in the production environment. These could by various reasons, e.g. for improving the ergonomic situation in production environment or for the output increase of the production line to improving the economic situation of the production line. First of all a CAD modeling of production environment is necessary (LOCOBOT SW Tool). It must be specification of the scenario and the environment benefitting from a robotic assistant.

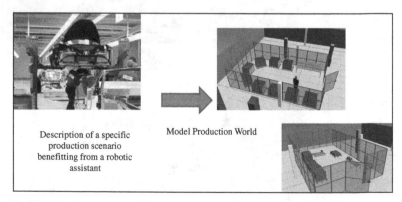

Fig. 4. Modeling the production World for using the LOCOBOT Toolkit

2.4   Design Your Own Low-COst_RoBOT

After the modeling of the Production world you are ready to design your own **LOw COst RoBOT**, a modular plug-and-produce robotic assistant platform, using the LOCOBOT Toolbox. This Robot will consist of a set of kinematic modules built upon a mobile platform. The single modules are lightweight and compliant to enable safe cooperation with humans. Furthermore the modules are mechanically standardized to allow the configuration of different kinematic structures. Simple electrical and software interface support a quick and easy re-configuration. Using available hardware components (platforms, grippers, arm…) a robot which is appropriate for the (already modeled) production environment is designed.

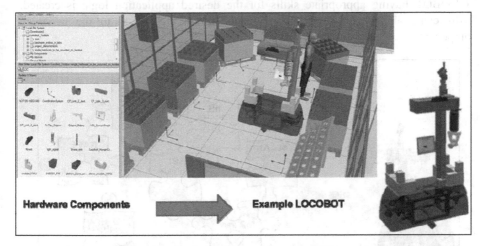

Fig. 5. Configuration using the toolkit

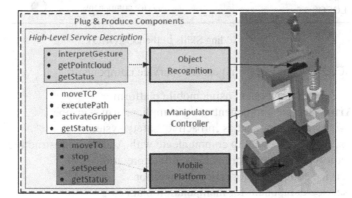

Fig. 6. Behind the scene

Behind the scene the LOCOBOT Developer Team has prepared service components in Advance. The Component models are linked to CAD components by attached XML specifications like functionality, behavior and communication. The execution is propagated to according service components and software components are implementing component models. Application designers are benefitting from well defined interfaces (Flexibility, Modularity and usage of same functionalities in different context).

Nevertheless LOCOBOT is designed for human robot collaboration, social aspects, usability and work psychology must be involved. Pre-requisite for enabling ´human robot collaboration´ requires a human robot interface and proposed (scenario-specific) interactions. Consequently, the robot will be equipped with a stereo camera system and audio components to acquire and process audio-visual information. This will be required for the robot to learn and to cooperate with human workers. These are also parts of the LOCOBOT Toolbox and can be added in the design phase. So a LOCOBOT having appropriate skills for the desired application logic is created. Skills came along with service components which are linked to the hardware components.

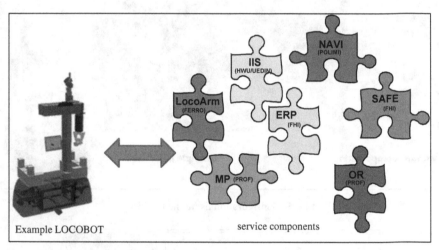

Fig. 7. Adding Skills to the LOCOBOT

Skills of LOCOBOT emerge from partner's service components

- **NAVI** – service component using mobile platform
- **LocoArm** – service component using compliant arm + gripper
- **SAFE** - service component as ‚proactive‘ safety system
- **ERP** - service component to communicate with AUDI's infrastructure
- **IIS** - audio/video system for interaction/interpretation
- **OR** - service component for object recognition
- **MP** – service component for manipulation planner

2.5   Design Your Specific Application

A Workflow Modeling Editor (WME) has been developed to enable simplified programming of a supervisory control application. The Workflow Specification is designed, based on modeled Plug&Produce service components that are extended with behavior information in 3D Create.

By using the implemented Code Generator an IEC 61499 compliant control application can be generated automatically. The resulting Function Block application is ready for execution on the target system (WEC)

Modelling Plug&Produce Components   Intuitive Workflow Model Construction

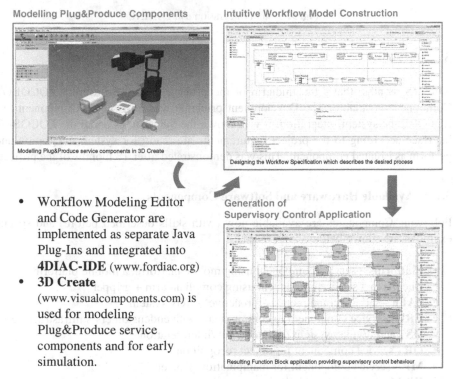

- Workflow Modeling Editor and Code Generator are implemented as separate Java Plug-Ins and integrated into **4DIAC-IDE** (www.fordiac.org)
- **3D Create** (www.visualcomponents.com) is used for modeling Plug&Produce service components and for early simulation.

Fig. 8. Workflow modeling environment and execution control

2.6 System Integration

After the high level workflow for the scenario has been modeled, the supervisory control application based on IEC 61499 is generated and firstly tested using the 3D simulation. Finally, the control application which has been tested in the simulation can be executed on the real system. For the system integration the Open source tool **4DIAC-IDE** (www.fordiac.org) is used. This tool enables code generation of function block network (IEC 61499) for LOCOBOT's supervisory control ,workflow execution control' (WEC). It enables an in initialization and coordination during runtime of (distributed) service components according to workflow modeling.

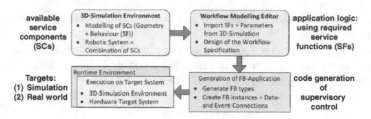

Fig. 9. System Integration using 4DIAC

3 Results

After 18 months, that's the midterm of the project, there are different LOCOBOT Components available. The Development principle was an isolated Component test BEFORE the system integration. It was shown the Subsystems using the LOCOBOT interface according to the project requirements are ready for system integration and perform as isolated component. This was demonstrated after 18 months of the project.

3.1 Available Hardware and Software Components

Following Components are available now (with skills described before) and special examples are shown below

- **Platforms** – service component using mobile platform, a mobile platform
- **LocoArm** – service component using compliant arm + gripper
- **SAFE** - service component as ‚proactive' safety system
- **ERP** - service component to communicate with endcustomers's infrastructure
- **IIS** - audio/video system for interaction/interpretation
- **OR** - service component for object recognition
- **MP** – service component for manipulation planner
- **WEM** – workflow modeling environment
- **WEC** – workflow execution control

Robotic Platform: The basic ideas on which the design of the platform is based are safety, low cost, autonomy, stability and re-configurability. The platform body is build up with all aluminum profiles. All the profiles and connections have been selected by the catalogue, to be as modular as possible at this development stage. The goal of a low cost module was reached by a very low number of components. The platform navigation is sustained by basic (always needed) sensors as well as by more advanced ones, to increase functionality during the next development stages.

The basic navigation uses 8 IR sensors and 8 sonars and controls 4 omnidirectional wheels. A platform prototype including basic movements and functionality of these sensors was shown.

Fig. 10. Realized platform prototype

Arms and Grippers: From the first requirements of having a compact "transport" position over the platform and a high range of motion on the other, and with regard to very common pick and place operations (with 3 DOF's) and human robot collaboration needs, a special arm kinematic was developed. It comprises a vertical elevation axis, a compliant modular arm operating horizontally (like a "scara" arm) and a "soft" actor/sensor element called active contact flange. Grippers for the three scenarios were developed. Simple construction is used for the first functional modules up to the evaluation of the precision of the whole system.

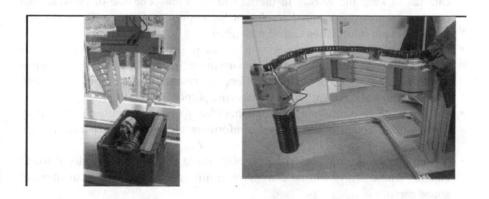

Fig. 11. Flexible gripper for scenario1 (left) and robot arm (right)

Human-Robot-Interaction Sensors (Audio+Video): The goal was designing an embedded network of audio-visual sensors dedicated to the acquisition of data for unforeseen Human-Robot Interaction (HRI) through speech and gestures. Two main practical issues to cope with have been identified: (i) the occlusion caused by the robotic arm in the field of view of cameras and (ii) the sound reverberation in the factory degrading the audio signal.

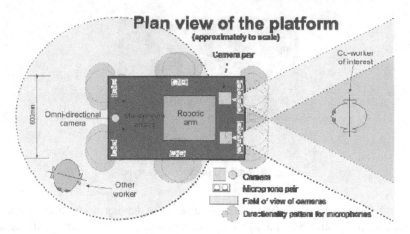

Fig. 12. Audio Visual sensor setup for HRI

The system is composed of:

- A pair of conventional cameras mounted on Pan-Tilt Units (represented as squares on the figure). The Pan-Tilt ability allows dynamically rotating the cameras to keep the worker in their Field Of View. The use of conventional cameras ensures the required resolution for gesture recognition. By using two cameras, depth information can be recovered.
- An omni-directional camera giving at each instant a 360o view of the surroundings. It is dedicated to environment monitoring by multi-human tracking. This type of camera offers a resolution less important than conventional ones, but sufficient for tracking purposes.
- An array of 8 directional microphones for speech recognition. The array configuration authorizes to apply beamforming algorithms and hence to cope with noise.
- 4 microphone pairs distributed on the platform to ensure omnidirectional sound caption. These arrays can be combined in different configurations to improve sound capture.

4   Further Development

Showing that LOCOBOT components work isolated it's now time for integration and Demonstration. This will be done at 3 defined scenarios at a side of one End-user. In parallel an Exploitation platform is set up to bring in other Components into the LOCOBOT Toolkit to provide a Toolkit with various Hard and Software Tools.

Acknowledgments. LOCOBOT project has been supported by the European Commission under the 7th Framework Program (FoF.NMP.2010-1-260101).

References

1. Stilman, M., Schamburek, J.U., Kuffner, J., Asfour, T.: Manipulation planning among moveable. In: ICRA, pp. 3327–3332. IEEE (2007)
2. Pichler, A., Vincze, M., Andersen, H.J., Madsen, O., Häusler, K.: A method for automatic spray painting of unknown parts. In: ICRA, pp. 444–449. IEEE (2002)
3. SMERobot. The European Robot Initiative for Strengthening the Competitiveness of SMEs in Manufacturing, http://www.smerobot.org
4. FLEXPAINT. Efficient Low Volume High Variant Robotized Painting,
   http://www.flexpaint.org
5. Maersk Mc-Kinney Moller Institute. SmartPainter demo,
   http://www.mip.sdu.dk/research/Smartpainter/help.html
6. Profactor. AHUMARI - Augmented based Human Robot Interaction (June 11, 2010),
   http://www.youtube.com/watch?v=Q2u_EiV2fmc,
   http://www.youtube.com/watch?v=U02wSsL9558
7. Pichler, A., Wögerer, C.: Towards Robot Systems for Small Batch Manufacturing. In: ISAM 2011, International Symposium on Assembly and Manufacturing, Tampere, Finland (IEEE Catalog Number: CFP11ATP-USB, ISBN: 978-1-61284-341-4), May 25-27 (2011)
8. Plasch, M., Pichler, A., Bauer, H., Rooker, M., Ebenhofer, G.: A Plug & Produce Approach to Design Robot Assistants in a Sustainable Manufacturing Environment. In: 22nd International Conference on Flexible Automation and Intelligent Manufacturing (FAIM 2012), Helsinki, Finland, June 10-13 (2012)

Model Identification and $\mathcal{H}_\infty$ Attitude Control for Quadrotor MAV's

Ole Falkenberg[1], Jonas Witt[1], Ulf Pilz[2], Uwe Weltin[1], and Herbert Werner[2]

[1] Hamburg University of Technology, Institute for Reliability Engineering,
Eißendorfer Str. 40, 21073 Hamburg, Germany
[2] Hamburg University of Technology, Institute of Control Systems,
Eißendorfer Str. 40, 21073 Hamburg, Germany
{ole.falkenberg,jonas.witt,ulf.pilz,weltin,h.werner}@tu-harburg.de

Abstract. This paper presents the results of modelling, parameter identification and control of the rotational axes of a quadrotor robot. The modelling is done in Newton-Euler Formalism and has been published before. Contrarily, our method uses a Grey-Box-based, iterative parameter identification approach, the results of which can easily be reproduced and offers great accuracy. By neglecting nonlinear and cross-coupling effects, only three to four parameters have to be identified per axis, depending on the order of the motor dynamics. Based on the achieved results we were able to design an aggressive $\mathcal{H}_\infty$ attitude controller, which shows superior performance to the normal PID-like controllers. With an anti-windup compensator based on Riccati–equations we are able to show exceptional input disturbance rejection, even with disturbances saturating the engines.

Keywords: micro unmanned aerial vehicle (MAV), robust control, system identification, quadrotor.

1 Introduction

Quadrotor robots are a popular research platform e.g. for autonomous navigation or multi-agent-control. Famous projects are located in the GRASP-laboratory at the University of Pennsylvania [1], the Flying Machine Area at the ETH Zürich [2] or the STARMAC II–project at the University of Stanford [3]. These projects rely on commercial quadrotors, except for the latter. The Hamburg University of Technology has developed an own quadrotor platform for research purposes, which shows exceptional research capabilities because of its insight to the lowest levels of interest. These insights reveal the drawbacks of common quadrotor controller designs. Especially the non–ideal performance of the common onboard MEMS–sensors in position estimation has driven many projects to use external camera systems, which provide great accuracy for the estimation of the quadrotors states, but also limits the operational area to the laboratory. Unlike those projects we do not rely on external camera systems, but only onboard sensors, onboard camera–vision and GPS, see [4]. Our research interest cover vision–based

C.-Y. Su, S. Rakheja, H. Liu (Eds.): ICIRA 2012, Part II, LNAI 7507, pp. 460–471, 2012.

navigation, formation control and aggressive manoevering. This paper focuses on linear parameter identification and attitude control, though. Attitude control is the most inner control loop and is crucial for a good overall flight performance. Therefore an advanced controller design scheme like $\mathcal{H}_\infty$-loopshaping should be favoured over traditional PID-control.

Beside the choice of a controller design scheme, an accurate model of the dynamics to be controlled is another crucial aspect for controller performance. The quadrotors physical equations of motion are well known and were published in e.g. [5] or [6]. But only few has been published about actual parameter identification based on real experiments. The reason for this absence is the unstable system dynamics of the quadrotor, which makes open-loop identification non-practical. Additionally, a bad signal to noise ratio and cross-coupling effects make for a challenging setup. The noise sources are mainly vibration and sensor noise.

Some first-order studies on aerodynamics have been done in [7] which have been extended in [3]. Infact, aerodynamics can have a major influence on attitude control. Especially the nonlinear variation of the induced velocity ν_i in forward flight, which effectively changes the relation of power P and thrust T, can lead to undesired behaviour. In [3], blade flapping is specified as another major source of nonlinearity causing undesired forces and torques. In this paper we present an advanced attitude control scheme, which is based on a linearized model, feasible in most common flight situations. Though its validity is limited:

- Nonlinearities caused by aerodynamics increase during forward flight with relative movement speed.
- During fast descent the quadrotor can enter the so-called vortex-ring-state, which cannot be estimated with normal momentum theory.
- The so-called Ground Effect augments thrust, if the quadrotor operates close to the ground ($\approx$ one rotor radius, see [5]).

However, it is obvious that a linear approach has advantages due to very powerful controller design and analysis tools. Using the linearized system dynamics we show that each quadrotor axis can be identified separately with a Grey-Boxed-based identification. With that model we have designed an aggressive $\mathcal{H}_\infty$-based attitude controller with anti-windup, which shows superior performance to a common PID-like controller. Particularly the robustness against input disturbances is considered, because main error sources in attitude control are aerodynamic torques and wind gusts.

2 Modelling

In various papers the quadrotor dynamics are derived, see [3], [6] or [5]. In this paper we are concerned with the results of our identification experiments in order to identify the dynamics that have an actual impact.

2.1 Quadrotor Dynamics

In figure 1, a schematic representation of a quadrotor is shown: Each motor produces a torque τ with respect to the center of gravity. By individually varying

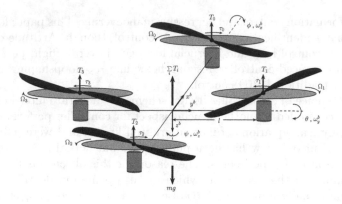

Fig. 1. Quadrotor forces T, torques τ, rotational velocities Ω, Euler–angles (ϕ, θ, ψ) and coordinate system

the produced thrust of the motors, the overall-torque will be non–zero, permitting the quadrotor to rotate about all three body-fixed axes with an angular velocity ω. If we assume a diagonal inertia matrix J (which is a quite good approximation, regarding the fact that the quadrotor is mechanically symmetric) and following the formalism of Newton-Euler, one gets the following model:

$$
\begin{aligned}
\dot{\omega}_x^b &= \frac{J_{yy} - J_{zz}}{J_{xx}} \omega_y^b \omega_z^b + \frac{1}{J_{xx}} \tau_x \\
\dot{\omega}_y^b &= \frac{J_{zz} - J_{xx}}{J_{yy}} \omega_x^b \omega_z^b + \frac{1}{J_{yy}} \tau_y \\
\dot{\omega}_z^b &= \frac{J_{xx} - J_{yy}}{J_{zz}} \omega_x^b \omega_y^b + J_R \dot{\Omega}_r + \frac{1}{J_{zz}} \tau_z
\end{aligned}
\tag{1}
$$

with

$$
\begin{aligned}
\Omega_R &= (\Omega_0 + \Omega_1 + \Omega_2 + \Omega_3) \\
\tau_x &= l(T_3 - T_1) \\
\tau_y &= l(T_0 - T_2) \\
\tau_z &= (\tau_0 + \tau_2 - \tau_3 - \tau_1)
\end{aligned}
\tag{2}
$$

The superscript b denotes the body frame. T_i is the thrust and τ_i the torque of the individual motors. The distance between the motors to the center of gravity is denoted as l, see figure 1.

2.2   Thrust and Torque

Motor thrusts T_i and torques τ_i are a direct result of the motors performing work on the air.

The input of the motor plant is a nondimensional number $b \in [0..1]$ which is sent via a digital interface to the motor controller, which actually performs the sensorless commutation for the brushless DC-motors. The output is the angular speed Ω. With the help of a simple experiment, one can identify the relation of Ω and b to be

$$\Omega(b) = a_0 \cdot b^{a_1} + a_2, \tag{3}$$

with scalar coefficients $a_0, a_1, a_2 \in \mathbb{R}$. The relation between motor speed and thrust/torque can be found by any introductory aerodynamic text to be

$$T = C_T \cdot \rho A R^2 \Omega^2 \tag{4}$$

$$Q = C_Q \cdot \rho A R^3 \Omega^2, \tag{5}$$

in which C_T and C_Q denotes the nondimensional thrust and torque coefficients, A the rotor disc area and R the rotor radius.

2.3 Motor Dynamics

We use brushless DC-motors with very low inductance. So the dynamics are approximated by a first-order ODE of the form

$$\dot{\Omega} = \kappa_1 \Omega + \kappa_2 V_{in}. \tag{6}$$

The coefficients κ_1 and κ_2 are motor specific. The motor dynamics are then modelled by the transfer-function

$$G_m = \frac{|p|}{s + p}. \tag{7}$$

Note that eq. (7) is normalized to 1, so it only covers the dynamics of the motor. Note also that $Q(\Omega)|_{\Omega_H} = Q(\Omega(b)|_{b_H})|_{\Omega(b_H)} = Q(\Omega(b_H)) + q\Gamma(b - b_H)$, where $q = 2C_Q \rho A R^3 \Omega_H$ is the linearization of eq. (5) around Ω_H and $\Gamma = a_0 a_1 b_H^{a_1 - 1}$ is the linearization of eq. (3) around b_H.

3 Model for Controller Design

Both quadrotor dynamics and force/torque generation are nonlinear, so we need to linearize if we want to use linear controller design techniques. We first have a look at quadrotor dynamics in eq. (1): As one can see, the nonlinear coupling terms only act, if the quadrotor rotates about at least two axis at a time. The moments of inertia for x and y are approximately the same, so the term for z cancels, while J_{zz} is slightly higher. Experiments show, that the nonlinear effects of the left over terms for x and y can be neglected in closed-loop operation, see [8]. Looking at the yaw-equation, one sees the additional linear term $J_r \dot{\Omega}$. This torque directly relates to the time derivative of angular momentum L

$$\dot{L} = M = J_r \dot{\Omega}, \tag{8}$$

with J_r being the combined inertia of the rotors and motors. That means when the motors change their speed, the time derivative of angular momentum will be nonzero, causing a torque about the z-axis. Once the speed change of the motors has stopped, L will be constant again. This results in a very fast response on yaw with a fast decay–time, comparable to the D-part of a PID-controller. By neglecting the nonlinear coupling terms and defining $(\boldsymbol{\Phi}, \dot{\boldsymbol{\Phi}})^T$ with output $\boldsymbol{\Phi} = (\phi, \theta, \psi)^T$, we get the following transfer function:

$$
\begin{pmatrix} \boldsymbol{\Phi} \\ \dot{\boldsymbol{\Phi}} \end{pmatrix} = \begin{pmatrix} \phi \\ \theta \\ \psi \\ \dot{\phi} \\ \dot{\theta} \\ \dot{\psi} \end{pmatrix} = \begin{pmatrix} \frac{1}{J_{xx}s^2} & 0 & 0 \\ 0 & \frac{1}{J_{yy}s^2} & 0 \\ 0 & 0 & \frac{(s+z)}{J_{zz}s^2} \\ \frac{1}{J_{xx}s} & 0 & 0 \\ 0 & \frac{1}{J_{yy}s} & 0 \\ 0 & 0 & \frac{(s+z)}{J_{zz}s} \end{pmatrix} \cdot \begin{pmatrix} \tau_x \\ \tau_y \\ \tau_z \end{pmatrix}
\tag{9}
$$

Now, let's have a look at the origin of the forces and torques: Equation (4) represents the equation of thrust in hover which depends quadratically on the angular rotor velocity Ω. By substituting eq. (3) in (4), (5) and linearizing about an operating point b_h one gets:

$$
T = \frac{C_T}{C_Q R} \tilde{\Gamma} + \frac{C_T}{C_Q R} q \Gamma \cdot b + \cdots \text{ and}
\tag{10}
$$

$$
Q = \tilde{\Gamma} + q \Gamma \cdot b + \cdots ,
\tag{11}
$$

with

$$
\tilde{\Gamma} = C_Q \rho A R^3 (a_0 b_H^{a_1} + a_2) [1 - 2(a_0 b_H^{a_1} + a_2) a_0 a_1 b_H].
\tag{12}
$$

By neglecting higher order terms, (10) and (11) become linear equations of the form $y = mx + c$.

With that we can write our torques in form of $\boldsymbol{\tau} = (\tau_x, \tau_y, \tau_z)^T = \boldsymbol{K}\boldsymbol{b} + const$. The overall model used for identification is then:

$$
\begin{pmatrix} \boldsymbol{\Phi} \\ \dot{\boldsymbol{\Phi}} \end{pmatrix} = \begin{pmatrix} \frac{1}{J_{xx}s^2} & 0 & 0 \\ 0 & \frac{1}{J_{yy}s^2} & 0 \\ 0 & 0 & \frac{(s+z)}{J_{zz}s^2} \\ \frac{1}{J_{xx}s} & 0 & 0 \\ 0 & \frac{1}{J_{yy}s} & 0 \\ 0 & 0 & \frac{(s+z)}{J_{zz}s} \end{pmatrix} \cdot \begin{pmatrix} K_x \frac{|p_0|}{s+p_0} e^{-sT_d} \cdot b_x \\ K_y \frac{|p_0|}{s+p_0} e^{-sT_d} \cdot b_y \\ K_z \frac{\tilde{K}_z |p_1|}{s+p_1} e^{-sT_d} \cdot b_z \end{pmatrix}
\tag{13}
$$

Note that we introduced an additional factor $\tilde{K}_z$ and that the engine pole for yaw is different than for roll and pitch. This is a direct result of the identification procedure: While fixing the pole at the same value as roll/pitch, the optimization process needs more variance to converge to a reasonable solution in form of a additional zero and pole. These can then be approximated by changing the fixed pole and gain, like denoted in eq. (13). A possible explanation is, that experiments for roll and pitch have been performed in a test rig, which only permits movement about one axis. In contrast, the experiment for yaw has been performed in free flight, which allows more vibration.

4   Grey–Box Parameter Identification

Due to unstable system dynamics of the quadrotor, the parameter identification has been performed in closed-loop. A Pseudorandom Binary Sequence (PRBS) γ of full length is used to excite the system. To improve the signal-to-noise ratio we averaged the experiments over ten periods, respectively. As stated before all three axes of the quadrotor have been identified separately. For that purpose we fixed the quadrotor in a test rig, allowing rotation only about one axis. The identification for the yaw–axis has been performed in free flight, though, because of the lack of an approriate test rig. Even though an operator is still required during free flight experiments for safety reasons, the operator can minimize possible noise introduced by reference steps, by limiting his commands to roll and pitch. Recall from eq. (1), that a reference step on roll/pitch influences yaw only through the nonlinear coupling term. Because of that it is also possible to average over several periods of γ, as stated above. The generic scheme of the identification process is depicted in figure 2. Note that the used PRBS-signal is persistently exciting of order $\gg 4$, which is sufficient for our purpose.

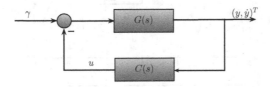

Fig. 2. Indirect closed–loop identification setup

The controller $C(s)$ used during identification is a simple stabilizing, hand-tuned PD-controller with known parameters. Using equation (13), the identification signal γ, the controller C and output data $(y, \dot{y})^T$, we can use non-linear optimization to estimate our parameter vector $\boldsymbol{\Delta}_{\phi,\theta} = (p, J, T_d)^T$ and $\boldsymbol{\Delta}_\psi = (p, z, J, T_d)^T$ respectively. Note that we excluded K from the parameter vector, because it can be calculated a–priori: The aerodynamic coefficients C_Q and C_T have been calculated using Blade Element Momentum Theory (BEMT), [9]. Note also, that you do not need this a–priori knowledge, even though you would not be able to distinguish between K and J in that case. See table 1 and 2 for results.

Figure 3 compares the simulation results of the identified models to a validation data set. For both, the simulation and the validation experiment, the same stabilizing controllers were used to close the unstable open–loop.

Table 1. Results of parameter estimation

	ϕ	θ	ψ
J	0.0181	0.0196	0.0273
p	-27.106	-26.963	-7.171
z	–	–	-2.434
T_d	0.024	0.028	0.016

Table 2. A-priori knowledge

l	$0.23m$
R	$0.127m$
C_T	0.0157
C_Q	0.0015
a_0	$701.2\frac{1}{s}$
a_1	0.8069
a_2	$-34.15\frac{1}{s}$
b_H	0.6

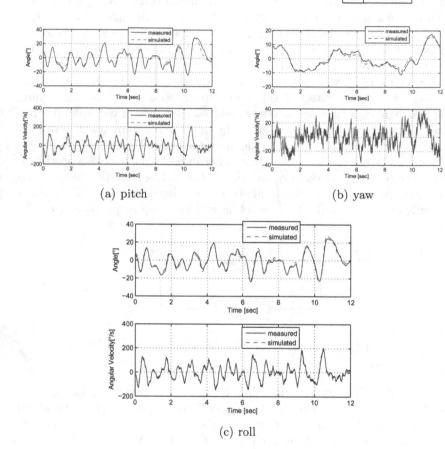

(a) pitch   (b) yaw

(c) roll

Fig. 3. Simulation of the final linear models for a validation data set for the pitch (a), yaw(b) and roll(c) axis. Due to unstable system dynamics simulation has been performed in closed-loop with the same stabilizing controller as used for identification.

5 Controller Design

We have designed three separate attitude controllers using $\mathcal{H}_\infty$-loop-shaping with the derived models of the quadrotors rotational axes from section 4. Recall that our models, which will be denoted as $G(s)$ respectively from now on, are single-input, multiple output (SIMO). Accordingly, our controllers $C(s)$ will be MISO. Our design goals are zero steady-state error, fast rise-time with little overshoot and good input-disturbance rejection.

The generalized plant used for the controller design is plotted in figure 4(a). To deal with input disturbances (e.g. wind gusts) we introduced an input d additionally to the reference input r. The prefilters V_d and $\mathbf{V_r}$ are scalar coefficients to weight between the channels with

$$\mathbf{V_r} = \begin{pmatrix} V_{r_1} & 0 \\ 0 & V_{r_2} \end{pmatrix}. \tag{14}$$

The shaping filters $W_K(s)$ and $\mathbf{W_S}(s)$ are first order transfer functions with

$$\mathbf{W_S}(s) = \begin{pmatrix} W_S(s) & 0 \\ 0 & 0 \end{pmatrix}. \tag{15}$$

The remaining filter $W_T(s)$ is only a static gain to reduce overshoot. The bandwidth of the controller has already been defined by $W_K(s)$ and $W_S(s)$.

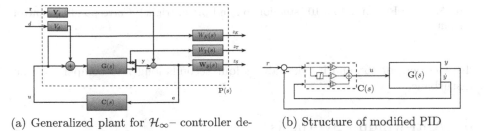

(a) Generalized plant for $\mathcal{H}_\infty$– controller design

(b) Structure of modified PID

Fig. 4. (a) Generalized plant for $\mathcal{H}_\infty$– controller design, (b) Structure of the modified PID-controller

For the evaluation of our controller performance, we have designed a modified PID controller, commonly used for quadrotor attitude control, see e.g. [10]. Its parameters are tuned by means of optimizing the simulated system response. Its generic structure is shown in figure 4(b). The main modification is the direct feedback of the time derivative $\dot{y}$ of the output y, because it can be measured directly, so there is no need for additional differentiation. Thus the D-part is just a static gain.

In figure 5 the results of a $10°$ reference step with the corresponding control inputs are plotted. It can be seen that both controllers have a rise time of $\approx 200ms$ with little overshoot, even though the PID-controllers have worse reference tracking. In figure 6 the results of an input disturbance of 10% of the maximum possible torque is shown. Here, our controller shows superior performance with a maximum displacement of only $4°$, whereas the PID goes up to a

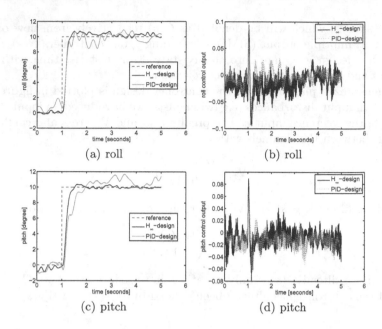

Fig. 5. (left): Response to a 10° step for roll and pitch. (right): Corresponding control output

displacement of 15° and it takes about four seconds longer to compensate the disturbance.

6   Anti-windup Synthesis

This section deals with the design of an anti-windup compensator that accounts for input saturation due to actuator constraints. For this purpose, the existing linear $\mathcal{H}_\infty$ controller is augmented with an anti-windup compensation scheme which becomes active only when saturation occurs. The augmentation technique also prevents a re-design of the existing control algorithm while limiting degradation of the closed-loop performance during saturation periods. The idea of the anti-windup synthesis using Riccati equations is taken from [11].

6.1   Design Procedure

Figure 7 shows the generic anti-windup scheme, where $G(s)$ is the plant given in section 4 and $K(s)$ is the $\mathcal{H}_\infty$ controller described in section 5 designed to stabilize the nominal plant while fulfilling desired performance specifications. The anti-windup compensator is given as $\Theta(s)$ which only becomes active once the actuators are saturated. Note that the compensator $\Theta(s)$ has one input $\tilde{u} = u - u_m$ and two outputs u_d and y_d which act on the controller output and the controller input, respectively. A parametrization of the anti-windup compensator

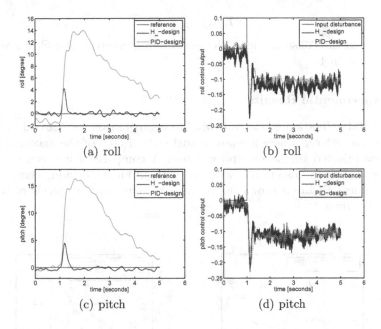

(a) roll

(b) roll

(c) pitch

(d) pitch

Fig. 6. (left): Response to a input disturbance equivalent to 10% of maximum engine thrust for roll, pitch. (right): Correspondig control output.

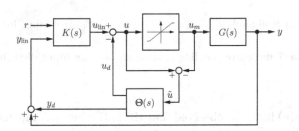

Fig. 7. Generic anti-windup scheme

which is completely independent of the controller $K(s)$ is given in [12]. A state-space representation for the anti-windup compensator is given as

$$
\Theta = \begin{bmatrix} \Theta_1 \\ \Theta_2 \end{bmatrix} \sim \begin{cases} \dot{x}_{aw} = (A + BF)\,x_{aw} + B\tilde{u} \\ u_d = F x_{aw} \\ y_d = (C + DF)\,x_{aw} + D\tilde{u}, \end{cases} \tag{16}
$$

where A, B, C, D are the state space matrices of the plant $G(s)$, F is a free parameter and $A + BF$ must be Hurwitz. The synthesis procedure is based on minimizing a scalar $\gamma > 0$ such that the induced 2-norm of the transfer function from the controller output u_{lin} to the compensator output y_d is smaller than a positive real scalar γ, or

$$\|\mathcal{T}_{y_d u_{\text{lin}}}\|_{i,2} \le \gamma. \tag{17}$$

The details of the construction of the anti-windup compensator $\Theta(s)$ are given in [11], Theorem 1.

6.2 Experimental Results

Experimental validation of the anti-windup compensator was carried out with the help of a test rig, where a input disturbance of 30% of the maximal motor power was injected to the quadrotor robot. A comparison between the $\mathcal{H}_\infty$-controller, described in section 5, with and without an anti-windup compensator was performed. Figure 8 shows the results of experiments in terms of the roll angle ϕ over time.

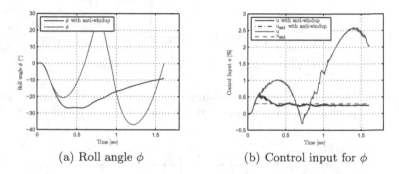

(a) Roll angle ϕ (b) Control input for ϕ

Fig. 8. Roll angle ϕ and corresponding control input of an input disturbance rejection experiment

From figure 8(a) it can be observed that the anti-windup compensation scheme is able to stabilize the quadrotor robot despite the input disturbance and to bring the roll angle ϕ asymptotically to the origin, whereas without anti-windup compensator unstable behavior occurs.

In figure 8(b), it is shown how the anti-windup compensator influences the control input such that the linear region is reached after an actuator saturation event has occured. After recovery from saturation, the control input always stays close below the saturation boundary which also indicates good disturbance rejection properties.

7 Conclusion

In this paper we have presented our results for linear model identification of the quadrotors rotational axes under real, non-ideal conditions. The derived models include a first-order transfer function for the motors, while aerodynamic co-efficients have been estimated using BEMT. The experimental results show a very good correlation with real data, which confirms the proposed Grey–Box approach. In addition to the model identification, we designed robust $\mathcal{H}_\infty$ attitude controllers. They have superior performance to commonly used modified PID controllers, particularly with regard to input disturbance rejections, but also to rise-time and reference tracking. Just to deal with input saturations, we augmented the attitude controllers with an anti-windup compensator based on Riccati-equations. This integrated anti-windup compensator leads to a further improvement of the performance, e.g. under harsh environmental conditions.

In the future we will account for nonlinear aerodynamic effects to especially optimize the control during forward flight.

References

1. Michael, N., Mellinger, D., Lindsey, Q., Kumar, V.: The GRASP Multiple Micro-UAV Testbed. IEEE Robotics & Automation Magazine 17(3), 56–65 (2010)
2. Lupashin, S., Schollig, A., Hehn, M., D'Andrea, R.: The Flying Machine Arena as of 2010. In: 2011 IEEE International Conference on Robotics and Automation (ICRA), pp. 2970–2971. IEEE (2011)
3. Hoffmann, G., Huang, H., Waslander, S., Tomlin, C.: Quadrotor Helicopter Flight Dynamics and Control: Theory and Experiment. In: Proceedings of the AIAA Guidance, Navigation, and Control Conference, vol. 4, p. 44 (2007)
4. Witt, J., Annighöfer, B., Falkenberg, O., Weltin, U.: Design of a High Performance Quad-Rotor Robot Based on a Layered Real-Time System Architecture. In: Jeschke, S., Liu, H., Schilberg, D. (eds.) ICIRA 2011, Part I. LNCS, vol. 7101, pp. 312–323. Springer, Heidelberg (2011)
5. Bouabdallah, S.: Design and Control of Quadrotors with Application to Autonomous Flying. Ecole Polytechnique Federale de Lausanne (2007)
6. Beard, R.: Quadrotor Dynamics and Control (2008)
7. Fay, G.: Derivation of the Aerodynamic Forces for the Mesicopter (2001)
8. Falkenberg, O.: Robuste Lageregelung und GPS/INS-Integration eines autonomen Quadrokopters. Hamburg University of Technology (2010)
9. Leishman, J.: Principles of Helicopter Aerodynamics. Cambridge Univ. Pr. (2006)
10. Tayebi, A., McGilvray, S.: Attitude Stabilization of a VTOL Quadrotor Aircraft. IEEE Transactions on Control Systems Technology 14(3), 562–571 (2006)
11. Sofrony, J., Turner, M., Postlethwaite, I.: Anti-Windup Synthesis Using Riccati Equations. International Journal of Control 80(1), 112–128 (2007)
12. Weston, P., Postlethwaite, I.: Linear Conditioning for Systems Containing Saturating Actuators. Automatica 36(9), 1347–1354 (2000)
13. Pilz, U., Gropengießer, W., Walder, F., Witt, J., Werner, H.: Quadrocopter Localization Using RTK-GPS and Vision-Based Trajectory Tracking. In: Jeschke, S., Liu, H., Schilberg, D. (eds.) ICIRA 2011, Part I. LNCS, vol. 7101, pp. 12–21. Springer, Heidelberg (2011)
14. Ljung, L.: System Identification: Theory for the User. Pearson Education (1998)
15. Witt, J.: Approximate Model Predictive Control for Nonlinear Multivariable Systems. In: Model Predictive Control, pp. 141–166. InTech (2010)

An Intelligent Approach to Hysteresis Compensation while Sampling Using a Fleet of Autonomous Watercraft

Abhinav Valada, Christopher Tomaszewski, Balajee Kannan,
Prasanna Velagapudi, George Kantor, and Paul Scerri

The Robotics Institute, Carnegie Mellon University
Pittsburgh, PA 15213, USA

Abstract. This paper addresses the problem of using a fleet of autonomous watercraft to create models of various water quality parameters in complex environments using intelligent sampling algorithms. Maps depicting the spatial variation of these parameters can help researchers understand how certain ecological processes work and in turn help reduce the negative impact of human activities on the environment. In our domain of interest, it is infeasible to exhaustively sample the field to obtain statistically significant results. This problem is pertinent to autonomous water sampling where hysteresis in sensors causes delay in obtaining accurate measurements across a large field. In this paper, we present several different approaches to sampling with cooperative vehicles to quickly build accurate models of the environment. In addition, we describe a novel filter and a specialized planner that uses the gradient of sensor measurements to compensate for hysteresis while ensuring a fast sampling process. We validate the algorithms using results from both simulation and field experiments with four autonomous airboats measuring temperature and dissolved oxygen in a lake.

Keywords: Adaptive sampling, Active learning, Multi-robot systems, Autonomous surface vehicle, Environmental monitoring.

1   Introduction

Recent advances in Autonomous Surface Vehicle (ASV) technology have enabled these systems to be used in missions that involve sampling large bodies of water for extended periods in order to monitor dynamic spatial and temporal phenomena with little or no human supervision. Monitoring water bodies is not only important for understanding the physiology of aquatic life but also for understanding how these systems are affected by both natural changes in the environment such as storms and volcanic eruptions as well as human activities such as surface run off from farms and industrial discharges. By collecting spatially distributed samples and analyzing the data it may be possible to predict how some of these processes work and potentially prevent adverse ecological effects such as eutrophication, oxygen depletion, and accelerated aging. ASVs are

C.-Y. Su, S. Rakheja, H. Liu (Eds.): ICIRA 2012, Part II, LNAI 7507, pp. 472–485, 2012.

a natural choice for this kind of application as they have the capability to sample large areas while providing real-time measurements. They have been successfully used for mapping applications both above and below the water surface [1], even at varying depths [2]. Cooperative fleets of ASVs have advantages over a single ASV in reliability, coverage and fault tolerance. Moreover intelligent sampling techniques can greatly improve the efficiency and quality of sampling by adaptively determining the next sampling locations based on the previously measured data.

A phenomenon known as hypoxia occurs in water bodies when oxygen saturation falls within the range of 1% to 30%, in which most types of fish and some invertebrates die due to insufficient oxygen. In the aquaculture industry, overstocking of fish increases susceptibility to hypoxia. Every year, this leads to millions of dollars worth of fish losses. The Fish and Wildlife Conservation Commission has recorded about 5114 incidents of fish kills from 1972 to 2012, where the number of fish lost at each incident ranged from hundreds to millions. There are several factors that lead to hypoxia, the most common being algae blooms, pollution, red tide, and rapid fluctuations in temperature. Water temperature in particular influences several aquatic processes such as the metabolic rates of organisms, level of dissolved oxygen and rate of photosynthesis, hence temperature fluctuations can not only drastically affect dissolved oxygen, but also cause severe imbalance in the aquatic ecosystem. Periodic monitoring of dissolved oxygen and temperature in aquacultural applications can help prevent such detrimental effects, as aerators can be deployed to replenish oxygen and heaters can be used to maintain the temperature. However, observed spatial and temporal variation patterns of dissolved oxygen and temperature are complex: they vary with the amount of dissolved solids, salinity and hydrodynamics of the water body, changing over the course of even a single day. Thus, these parameters must be sampled frequently in order to build accurate models.

In this paper, we describe our work on developing algorithms to adaptively sample dissolved oxygen and temperature using a fleet of autonomous watercraft. Initial experiments with autonomous sampling revealed that slow response of the polyethylene membrane used in dissolved oxygen sensors causes rate-dependent hysteresis, which significantly affects measurement accuracy. Similarly, with temperature sensors hysteresis is often caused by the introduction of some amount of strain or moisture penetrating inside the sensor. As these sensors are not specifically designed for dynamic measurements, a lag in the response of the sensor causes erroneous measurements if the vehicle travels at a rate that does not allow the sensor readings to stabilize. Developing a sensor model that predicts the rate of change is one potential solution, but even small errors in this estimate can dramatically affect the final measurement value. In our work we adopt an approach in which we use the time derivative of measurements, rather than the measurements themselves, to alter a pre-defined set of bounds that converge to the true value over time. The vehicle then plans its path based on the expected sensor value, range of the bounds, and the frequency with which the cell has been previously visited. To validate this approach we compare it to a suite of other sampling algorithms including random walks, lawn-mower patterns, level sets and maximum uncertainty sampling.

The rest of the paper is organized as follows. In Section 2 we formulate the problem in question and identify the associated related work in Section 3. We outline our our bounding filter solution for modeling the environment in Section 5 and apply it to the problem of multi-robot planning in Section 6. In Section 7 we outline comparative algorithms that we implemented for comparison against our bounded filter approach and subsequently analyze the performance results from the conducted experiments in Section 8. Finally, in Section 9, we conclude the paper with a summary of the results and an outline of future work directions.

2   Problem Formulation

In this work, we are interested in measuring a field which is continuous over $\mathbb{R}^\kappa$. Thus we can define a field mapping function:

$$\Psi : \mathbb{R}^n \to \mathbb{R}$$

We model a sensor with hysteresis as a process with internal state, based on a simple exponential average:

$$s(t+1) = \alpha^t \cdot \Psi(x) + (1 - \alpha^t) \cdot s(t)$$

In continuous time, this corresponds to a simple first-order differential process:

$$\frac{\partial s}{\partial t} = \log(\alpha)\left(\Psi(x) - s(t)\right)$$

Our objective is to estimate the value of $\Psi(x)$ at some set of points, $M \subseteq \mathbb{R}^n$. A simple method for doing so is simply to visit each point $x \in M$, and wait a certain amount of time for the sensor output s to approach $\Psi(x)$. However, α is small, $\frac{\partial s}{\partial t}$ is also small, meaning it can take a long time for s to approach $\Psi(x)$.

Additionally, there is a time cost associated with moving between the points in M. We define a distance function $D(x, y)$ which describes the amount of time necessary to travel from point $x \in M$ to $y \in M$. Then, we can describe our problem as one of traversing a minimum time path π over points in M such that we can estimate the value of $\Psi(x), \forall x \in M$ to within some accuracy, ϵ.

3   Related Work

Several intelligent sampling strategies have been developed for autonomous vehicles that aim to identify hotspots, reduce resource costs, optimize sampling coverage or more accurately measure environmental phenomena. The authors in [3] explored a sampling technique, using both a team of robotic boats and static sensor nodes, in which the sensing field is partitioned into sub regions either according to equal gains or equal area and each boat is assigned a specific sub area for sampling. The readings are gathered from the static nodes and paths are computed for the boat such that they reduce the integral mean squared error. In [4], the authors explore an approach based on model parameter estimation of a variable in which the physical parameter being measured is assumed to be linearly distributed across the field and the algorithm aims to minimize the measured uncertainty in the field distribution. The algorithm also has multiple secondary objectives such as to minimize the network utility of multiple AUVs by controlling the sampling location and sampling rate using a potential function that encapsulates the network model and minimizing the energy consumption by varying the speed of the vehicle according to the energy available.

Thermoclines are believed to be an important breeding zone for marine microorganisms and hence a considerable amount of work has been done on thermocline detection and monitoring using sensor networks, gliders and other AUVs [5,6]. Zhang in [7] used a wireless sensor actuator network and a robot mule to detect thermoclines using distributed binary search. In this algorithm the nodes were assigned regions to sample and could move vertically by altering their buoyancy. Each node first localized the temperature variation in its own region, then combined this data with that of children nodes, forwarded it to the parent node and so on, until the final bulk data was transferred to the user. They further improved the performance of the algorithm by using a mobile robot to collect data from an active node and communicate it to another.

Sampling of Phytoplankton has also gained popularity in recent years as it plays a very important role in ocean ecology. In [8] the authors used a Dorado AUV to describe a method to detect and collect water samples at peak chlorophyll fluorescence, taking into consideration the delay in measurement while detecting the peak. The AUV followed a yo-yo pattern and used gradient following to detect a peak in the ascend stage and successfully collected the peak chlorophyll fluorescence sample at the same depth in the descend cycle.

4 Watercraft Platform

The algorithms discussed in this paper were designed and implemented on the Cooperative Robotic Watercraft (CRW) platform [9]. CRW is a multi-robot autonomous surface vehicle, equipped with an Android smartphone that provides the inertial sensors and computing platform for the system. The CRW's design is similar to that of an airboat with a modified steering mechanism in which the entire propulsion assembly is actuated using servo motors, allowing for improved thrust vectoring, which enables sharper turns. The drive system and other electronics are interfaced to an Arduino microcontroller that communicates with the smartphone via Bluetooth. Most of the autonomy software resides on the phone while some of the application specific intelligence, such as the sampling algorithms, are implemented on a centralized operator interface that interacts with the individual vehicles via 3G or WiFi.

Water quality sensors such as dissolved oxygen, temperature, specific conductivity and pH, are mounted on the vehicle and interfaced to the system

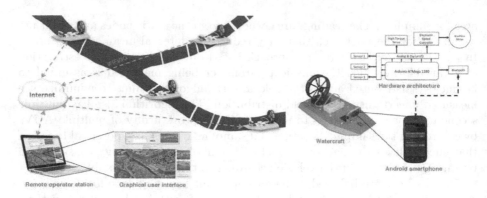

Fig. 1. Cooperative Robotic Watercraft platform

through the Arduino. The camera on the smartphone provides real-time situational awareness about the operating environment using a steady stream of images that are processed through an image queue and displayed on the operator interface. A water sampling mechanism on board each vehicle has the ability to collect physical samples on demand for more detailed analysis in the laboratory. A diagram depicting the operation of the entire system is shown in Figure 1.

5   Bounding Filter

Rate dependent hysteresis can be observed in several sensors and poses a very serious problem to autonomous sampling where a robot continuously collects measurements while moving through a large field to create models of a physical parameter. This phenomenon cannot be ignored in dynamic sensing applications as the lag between the input and output causes a delay in the responsiveness of the sensor: for a change in input, the output of the sensor slowly and consistently approaches the actual value. This effect is not as important in static sensing applications, where the rate of change of the physical parameter in the field is much slower than the hysteresis in the sensor. However, in our case the watercraft traverses through the water while simultaneously taking measurements, making compensating for the hysteresis effect critical. Within the suite of sensors on the CRW platform, we observe this effect significantly in both temperature and dissolved oxygen.

We propose an intelligent sampling solution to this problem in the form of a filter that accounts for this effect. Rather than recording the sensed value at a location, we maintain an upper and lower bound on the predicted value in each area and use the direction of change in the sensor measurement to adjust the bounds. For example, if the gradient is trending downwards, the actual value must be lower than the value reported by the sensor, hence the upper bound can be adjusted. The inverse holds when the values are trending upwards, allowing the lower bound to be increased.

While the gradients tend to be consistent and reasonably noiseless, we use a median filter to remove occasional noise in sensor measurements. The median value over a window of readings is computed and linear regression is used to find a gradient across a larger window over the median filtered values. The gradient is then used to change either the upper or lower bound in the area if it has an absolute value above a constant defined as ϵ. Based on our initial experiments with water quality sensors exhibiting hysteresis we made two practical design decisions on the filter. Firstly, a zero gradient is the most useful gradient as it could be used to bring the upper and lower bound to the current value, since the sensor must be at the true value. However, in practice we found that this was misleading in view of discretization in the sensor output, as the gradient might appear to be zero even when it is not. Therefore we choose to ignore gradients of zero, though these will be considered in future work. Conversely, at times a sensor measurement can oscillate between two discrete levels causing an apparent gradient even when there is none. To avoid the impact of these erroneous readings on the filter, we require the gradient be above ϵ which filters out very small gradients due to oscillations in the sensor output. ϵ can be determined by analyzing a small data set obtained from a sample run. The pseudo code for the filtering process is shown below.

```
function PROCESS(v)
    Data ← v_data
    Windows ← MedianFilter(Data)
    gradient ← LinearRegression(Windows)
    cell ← CellFor(v_position)
    if gradient > ε then
        if cell_lower < v_data thenbe
            cell_lower ← v_data
        end if
    else if gradient < ε then
        if cell_upper > v_data then
            cell_upper ← v_data
        end if
    end if
end function
```

6 Planning with Bounding Filter

Planning for information collection is a intriguing problem that has been extensively studied in recent years [10]. Adopting the bounding filter opens up new challenges and opportunities for developing a planning algorithm. The sensor measurement with which the watercraft enters a cell is important as a change in the measurement will in turn affect the bounds of that cell. Closer the measurement with which the watercraft enters a cell is to the mid-point of bounds of the current cell, the more valuable the collected data is likely to be, since a change in the measurement will lead to the biggest expected change in the filter. Planning using the bounding filter is a challenge as it needs to take into account what measurement the sensor might output along the path, even though it can only be estimated based on the current value of the upper and lower bounds of a cell.

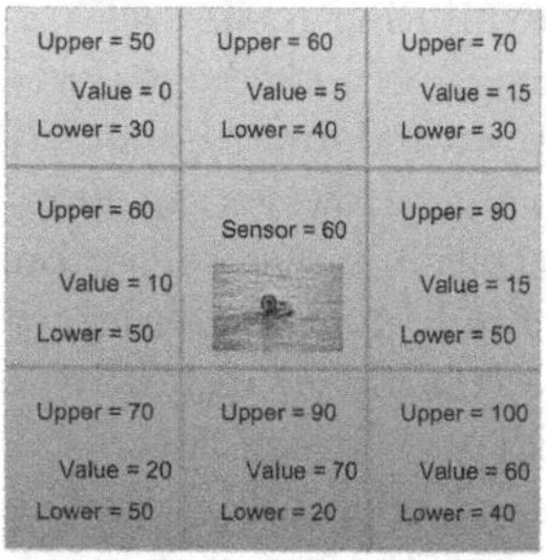

Fig. 2. Value of moving in different directions, given current sensor value and upper and lower bounds in adjacent areas. The bounded planner uses these values to create paths that maximize information gain

The approach we take is shown in Figure 2 where a tree is used to expand to the most promising nodes. As paths in the tree are expanded, an estimate of the sensor value is maintained as the mid-point between the upper and lower bounds of the filter, which is then used as the expected value of the sensor as the watercraft leaves the cell. The value of going into a cell is estimated as a function of how far the expected sensor measurement with which the watercraft enters the cell is from the mid-point between the upper and lower bounds of the cell, current difference between the upper and lower bounds and the number of times that cell has been previously visited on the path. The value of expanding a particular node in the search tree is a heuristic based on the current expansion depth and the rate that value has accumulated on the path so far. The aim of the heuristic is to encourage exploration of the paths that have the highest value.

function BOUNDED PLANNER
    $n.loc \leftarrow currentlocation$
    $n.value \leftarrow 0$
    $n.sensor \leftarrow currentsensorvalue$
    $queue.add(n)$
    while $expansions < maxExpansions$ **do**
        $n \leftarrow queue.poll$
        for $e \leftarrow getExpansions(n)$ **do**
            $e.value \leftarrow n.value + max(0.0, (e.cell.upper - e.cell.lower) - |((e.cell.upper + e.cell.lower)/2) - n.sensor)$
            $expectedSensorChange \leftarrow smaller((e.cell.upper + e.cell.lower)/2 - n.sensor, maxChange)$
            $e.sensor \leftarrow n.sensor + expectedSensorChange \ queue.add(e)$

    end for
  end while
end function

We evaluated the potential of our algorithm in a simulated environment partitioned into a ten by ten grid and created a model of the dissolved oxygen sensor
with mild hysteresis. The grid size is chosen based on the number of boats being
used in the experiment and the size of the sensing field. The more number of
grids, the better is the resolution but the longer it takes, therefore there is a
tradeoff between the sensing time and resolution of sensing. Two experiments
were performed to determine the utility of the filter and the planning approach.
In the first experiment, the value of each cell in the environment was drawn
from a uniform random distribution and in the second experiment, the value
of each cell in the environment was drawn from a mixture of Gaussians. The
results obtained using a simple averaging filter and the bounded filter along
with three different path planning algorithms: random walk, lawnmower pattern
and the bounded planner, are shown in Figures 3(a) and 3(b). In the bounded
filter, we measure the error from the mid-point of the filter which may not always be a good measure of the information in the filter. For example, one of the
bounds may get changed much earlier than the other due to gradients in the environment. The graphs represent the average result of 100 randomly generated
environments and one simulated boat. In both cases, random movement with
the bounded filter eventually leads to the lowest error. The difference is dramatically higher in the random environment as the random variation between the
cells makes the hysteresis effect more crucial and therefore makes the averaging
approach perform more poorly. The lawnmower pattern performs well initially,
in part because measurements are collected uniformly all over the field, in turn
significantly reducing the overall error. However, with the bounded filter, the
lawnmower approach asymptotes towards some non-zero error as the watercraft
enters cells from the same direction with the same hysteresis trend each time.
The bounded planner surprisingly does not perform better than random walk
over the long run, although it has an advantage for a short period. In early
stages, the good performance appears due to visiting a wider number of cells
and the reason for the poorer performance later on is not completely clear and
will be investigated in future work.

7   Other Algorithms

7.1   Adaptation of Level Set Approach

In some applications, a complete spatial map depicting the variation of a physical
variable in the field is not required, instead the interest might be to identify an
area where the concentration of that variable is above or below a certain value.
For example, a fish farmer is only interested in whether any part of his pond has a
dissolved oxygen level near or below what is required for the fish to survive. The
level set approach can also help us identify hotspots above a certain threshold
value. When only a certain level is of interest, we can adapt techniques that

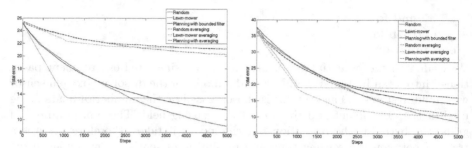

(a) Field with uniform random distribution (b) Field with mixed gaussian distribution

Fig. 3. Total error comparison in a simulated environment with different planning and filtering algorithms

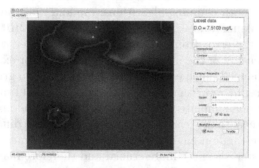

Fig. 4. CRW adaptive sampling interface showing the level set and boat markers

look specifically to find this level and isolate that area. Specifically, we have adapted an active learning approach developed by Bryan and Schneider[11]. In this approach, the observations collected to date are used to create a map of the environment and a polynomial interpolation scheme is used to estimate measurements at all locations, regardless of whether an observation has already been taken there. The marching squares algorithm is then used to generate a contour at the value of interest. Some locations along the contour may be purely based on estimates from the interpolation and some will be places where the observed values are not exactly the contour value, but the simplest contour that runs through that location.

Based on the interpolated values and estimated contour, we follow the approach by valuing points by looking at a function of uncertainty at a location and its distance to the value of interest (or contour). Given a contour value, C_v and a location value P_v, we value points as $e^{-|C_v - P_v|}$. Waypoints are assigned to locations with the highest valuation using this formula. When there is a fleet watercraft in the same environment, a centralized planner ensures that multiple watercraft are not sent to the same location.

7.2   Adaptation of Maximum Uncertainty

As shown in our previous work [9], a simple approach to intelligent sampling is to focus on areas with maximum uncertainty. Areas that have fewer observations or where the observations have a lot of noise are locations that are significant for collecting additional measurements. Our heuristic for collecting more observations in an area is based on the variance of observations measured in that area and the number of observations taken. Specifically, the value of an observation in an area is $v_{i,j} = \sigma^2 \times \alpha^c$, where σ is the variance in the cell, $\alpha < 1.0$ and c is the number of observations taken in that cell. Values of both the variables are used since some cells may have high variance across the cell and more observations may not be capable of bringing that uncertainty down. When the boats have completed a task, the next waypoint is assigned to the nearest location which has the highest value of this function and in cases where there are multiple boats in the same environment, the entire field is sub divided into regions based on the number of boats present and each boat is assigned a specific sub region for sampling.

8   Results

In order to evaluate the algorithms, we performed analysis both in simulation as well as by extensive field trials in a variety of operational scenarios and weather conditions. Our initial experiments on dissolved oxygen monitoring were performed at Shelby fish farm and the experimental validation of algorithms were performed at Panther Hollow lake using a fleet of four CRW. The CRW was equipped with dissolved oxygen sensors from Atlas-Scientific, along with specific conductivity and temperature sensors from Decagon Devices. In order to quantify the performance of the bounded filter and planner, we calculated the total error in estimation over a period of 30 minutes and compared the results with lawn-mower pattern and maximum uncertainty sampling algorithms. For these experiments, the field was subdivided in to a set of ten by 10 grid cells and the total estimation error was computed as the sum of difference between the values of cells obtained from the algorithms and values of cells from the ground truth where we consider the ground truth as the data collected from the lake from dawn to dusk for approximately about 14 hours. We assume that the field does not vary significantly within the 30 minutes of sampling. This is a reasonable assumption for temperature and dissolved oxygen as long as there is no drastic change in the climate such as rainfall or high winds which may cause a significant change in the distribution of the physical variable in the field.

The graph in Figure 5 shows the total error comparison from sampling water temperature across Panther Hollow lake with lawn-mower pattern, highest uncertainty and bounded filter sampling approaches using a fleet of four CRW as well as with one CRW. For the results obtained with one CRW it can be seen that the bounded filter approach has the lowest initial error followed by gradual steps caused by the bounds being tightened significantly after the end of each plan as the planner computes the next path such that the change in sensor value

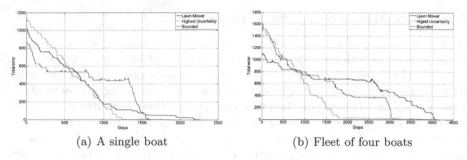

(a) A single boat   (b) Fleet of four boats

Fig. 5. Total error comparison while sampling temperature using lawnmower pattern, highest uncertainty and bounded algorithms

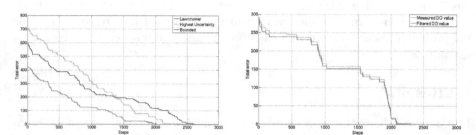

(a) Comparison between lawnmower, high- (b) Comparison between measured value
est uncertainty and bounded algorithms.   and filtered value from the bounded filter.

Fig. 6. Total error comparison while sampling dissolved oxygen using one boat

is not high enough for hysteresis to be significant. From 5(b) it can be seen that even with a fleet of CRW, the bounded filter approach has the fastest convergence to the final value, proving to scalable to various team sizes. The initial high error in the bounded planner in 5(b) is due to the selection of wider bounds in this experiment. Even though the highest uncertainty sampling has a large initial error in 5(a), the explorative nature of this algorithm forces the vehicle to sample new cells much faster and collect large amounts of samples in all the cells, therefore having the fastest convergence rate, but since the vehicle explores new cells one after the other, the hysteresis in the sensor affects the measurements in this approach considerably more, hence causing a prolonged error after the steep downward slope that can be seen in the both the plots 5(a) and 5(b). In the lawn-mower pattern sampling, as the vehicle traverses through the field in a uniform pattern, it takes a substantial amount of time for the error to reach the final convergence state as there is always the same amount of hysteresis in those specific order of cells that the vehicle follows, hence the error trend is in the form of long gradual steps.

Results from similar experiments using the dissolved oxygen sensor is shown in Figure 6(a). It can be seen that the bounded filter approach still has the lowest error compared to lawn-mower pattern and highest uncertainty sampling.

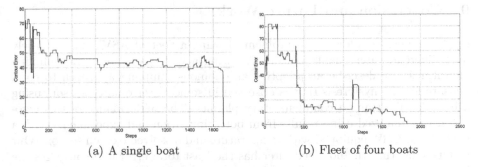

(a) A single boat   (b) Fleet of four boats

Fig. 7. Error in contour estimation

Fig. 8. Variation in dissolved oxygen observed in Panther Hollow lake

To further investigate the error trend of the bounded filter, a plot showing the comparison between the total error in field estimation using the bounded filter and the direct sensor output is shown in Figure 6(b). The bounded filter has a lower error throughout the sampling period and converges faster than the unfiltered output, validating the novelty of this approach.

Figures 7(a) and 7(b) show the error in contour estimation when using a single boat and four boats respectively to sample temperature in the same body of water for 30 minutes. The final measured temperature distribution is thresholded at the median of the distribution to produce a binary contour ground truth estimate. This process is repeated at each timestep to produce an intermediate contour estimate, after which a logical exclusive OR operation is applied with the ground truth integrated over the sampling area to calculate the error of the contour estimate at that timestep. As evidenced in the figures, a single boat has trouble producing a converging temperature contour estimate in 30 minutes whereas four boats can easily do so for the same sampling region. This illustrates one of the main advantages of the CRW system; the multi-agent nature of the system allows for models of environmental parameters, such as temperature, to be built for large areas more quickly and reliably.

9 Conclusion and Future Work

In this paper, we address the problem of using a fleet of ASV's to accurately map different water quality parameters using a variety of intelligent sampling algorithms. We describe an adaptive autonomous sampling approach to compensate for the hysteresis that is observed in some water quality sensors using a bounded filter and a complementary planner. The performance of this algorithm was analyzed using results from both simulation and experiments with a fleet of four CRW equipped with temperature and dissolved oxygen sensors. Our results show that the bounded filter has the least total error and converges the fastest when compared to a lawn-mower pattern and highest uncertainty sampling. Furthermore, a comparison of the results obtained with varying fleet sizes attests to the scalability of our approach consistently across experiments with both the sensors. We also describe an adaptive level set approach that can be used to identify hotspots given a certain threshold value. The error in contour estimation was computed and with four boats the error approached zero by the end of 30 minutes.

Future work on the bounded filter includes developing a method for using zero gradients to bring the bounds to the current measured value and creating a new metric that can be used to assign values to cells while evaluating the bounded filter, as currently we only take the midpoint of the bounds as the cell value at each timestep. The cooperation between the boats can also be improved by assigning the sampling location to each boat based on a heuristic such as the shortest distance to the sampling area. Investigation on the optimal fleet size to sampling region ratio, given specific convergence constraints will also be the subject of future work.

References

1. Leedekerken, J.C., Fallon, M.F., Leonard, J.J.: Mapping Complex Marine Environments with Autonomous Surface Craft. In: 12th International Symposium on Experimental Robotics 2010, New Delhi, Agra, India (December 2010)
2. Hitz, G., Pomerleau, F., Garneau, M.-E., Pradalier, C., et al.: Autonomous Inland Water Monitoring: Design and Application of a Surface Vessel. IEEE Robotics & Automation Magazine 19(1), 62–72 (2012)
3. Zhang, B., Sukhatme, G.S.: Adaptive Sampling for Field Reconstruction With Multiple Moblie Robots. In: The Path to Autonomous Robots, pp. 1–3. Springer (2009)
4. Popa, D.O., Sanderson, A.C., Komerska, R., Blidberg, R., et al.: Adaptive Sampling Algorithms for Multiple Autonomous Underwater Vehicles. In: IEEE/OES Autonomous Underwater Vehicles (June 2004)
5. Cruz, N.A., Matos, A.C.: Adaptive sampling of thermoclines with Autonomous Underwater Vehicles. In: Oceans 2010, pp. 1–6 (September 2010)
6. Petillo, S., Balasuriya, A., Schmidt, H.: Autonomous adaptive environmental assessment and feature tracking via autonomous underwater vehicles. In: Proc. IEEE Int. Conf. Oceans 2010, Sydney, Australia (May 2010)

7. Zhang, B., Sukhatme, G.S., Requicha, A.A.G.: Adaptive Sampling for Marine Microorganism Monitoring. In: IEEE/RSJ International Conference on Intelligent Robots and Systems, pp. 1115–1122 (2004)
8. Zhang, Y., McEwen, R.S., Ryan, J.P., Bellingham, J.G.: An Adaptive Triggering Method for Capturing Peak Samples in a Thin Phytoplankton Layer by an Autonomous Underwater Vehicle. In: Oceans, pp. 1–5 (October 2009)
9. Valada, A., Velagapudi, P., Kannan, B., Tomaszewski, C., Kantor, G., Scerri, P.: Development of a Low Cost Multi-Robot Autonomous Marine Surface Platform. In: The 8th International Conference on Field and Service Robotics, Japan (July 2012)
10. Low, K.H., Dolan, J.M., Khosla, P.: Active Markov Information-Theoretic Path Planning for Robotic Environmental Sensing. In: AAMAS 2011, pp. 753–760 (May 2011)
11. Bryan, B., Schneider, J.: Actively Learning Level-Sets of Composite Functions. In: Proceedings of the 25th International Conference on Machine Learning (July 2008)

Concept of a Biologically Inspired Robust Behaviour Control System

Tim Köhler[1], Christian Rauch[2], Martin Schröer[2],
Elmar Berghöfer[1], and Frank Kirchner[1,2]

[1] DFKI GmbH, Robotics Innovation Center
[2] University of Bremen, Robotics Research Group
Robert-Hooke-Straße 5, 28359 Bremen, Germany

Abstract. In safety-critical and in space applications, high demands are made on the reliability of the involved systems. As autonomy could increase both the efficiency and the reliability of such systems, a reliable autonomous system could be beneficial for several robotic scenarios.

In this paper, the concept of a biologically inspired, robust behaviour control system is presented. The system includes components for prediction of actions to be executed and the evaluation of the action consequences. In its design process, particularly the occurence of unexpected situations was taken into account. The paper concludes with a presentation of preliminary simulation results and the evaluation setup that will be used in future tests to demonstrate the model properties.

1 Introduction

1.1 Motivation

Robotic systems which are used in safety-critical or extraterrestrial applications need to meet special demands. This holds for materials, mechanics, and in robotics especially for software as the central component in the system. The control of actuators, the preprocessing and evaluation of sensor data, and the behaviour control are highly complex processes. However, strong demands are made on the reliability of an implementation, especially in safety-critical applications. This is particularly true for the behaviour of robots. An autonomous behaviour selection and execution can help to improve the efficiency of robot systems (e.g., in planetary missions). In extraterrestrial missions, command and data transfer latency, limited data bandwidth, and short communication time windows reduce the applicability of remotely operated systems. Autonomy could help to use the mission time more efficiently. The problem in such applications is that it needs to be ensured that autonomy does not impair the system's reliability.

With an appropriate behaviour control system, cooperative-adaptively behaving, reliable robot systems are feasible. Besides the control of single systems, the integration of the control system in a team of robots is especially interesting. Ideally, even a team of heterogeneous platforms can be run with the same behaviour control architecture in a loosely coupled way: The control system of

C.-Y. Su, S. Rakheja, H. Liu (Eds.): ICIRA 2012, Part II, LNAI 7507, pp. 486–495, 2012.

one robot recognizes the other systems, predicts their behaviours, and is able to adapt to them without the need for explicit communication.

In the following sections, the concept for a behaviour control system is presented which builds on a model of human automatic and willed action selection. One main property is a prediction system that allows to assess the quality of actions taken. This way, the impact of an action can be estimated. Based on that, the behaviour of an individual or a team could then be adapted accordingly. The system state may be adapted according to the error between the predicted and the measured environmental properties. Besides the system concept, the setup to be used for the planned system evaluation is described.

1.2   Biological and Psychological Basis

The range of basic publications to build on in a biologically inspired behaviour control system is twofold: While many specific questions and effects are well-studied in a number of biological and psychological publications, the overall behaviour control in vertebrates or specifically in humans was mainly studied and discussed just incipiently. Publications of both kinds have been taken into account for the proposed behaviour control system.

Examples of specific effects and questions that were studied up to the present are the generation and evaluation of expectations based on internal models of the sensorimotor loop (in biology, e.g., [1] and [2], in computational studies, e.g., [3] (review), and in robotic experiments, e.g., [4]). Furthermore, in cognitive psychology, plenty of distinct effects in cognition and task execution were studied and explained with effect-specific models (e.g. the Stroop effect [5], the Simon effect [6], and the Psychological Refracterior Period (PRP) in task selection and execution [7]).

Model architectures of overall behaviour control (i.e., task selection, attended task execution, unattended task execution, and the transition from attended to unattended execution (by learning)) were mainly discussed up to the 1980's. Switching between attended and unattended task execution can, for example, be explained with the architecture proposed by Norman and Shallice [8]. Another model was published by Shiffrin and Schneider [9].

1.3   Robotic Implementations

Robotic implementations based on psychologically inspired behaviour control architectures were published within the past decade. Gurney et al. [10] implemented the Norman and Shallice model with the application of autonomous vehicle control. The authors tested their system in simulations. Garforth et al. [11] chose the architecture proposed by Norman and Shallice, too. They tested their implementation in simple two-wheeled robot simulations. However, they tried to match the single function blocks of the architecture with specific regions of the human brain. Additionally, they compared data of brain lesions of human patients with simulation runs of their design with corresponding dysfunctions.

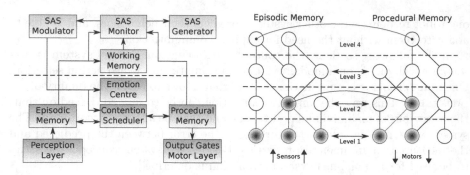

Fig. 1. *Left.* The architecture proposed by Garforth et al. (simplified sketch, adapted from [11]). The diagram does not show all connections. The relation between the model components and the assumed equivalent brain regions are given in the original sketch. *Right.* Connection of *Episodic* and *Procedural Memory* in the model proposed by Garforth et al.. Sensor data is processed by a neural network in the EM which can combine several features to an abstract one (gray shaded). EM and PM are connected on different hierarchical levels. On the PM side, there are primitive actions in the lowest level, and combined ones on higher abstraction layers (gray shaded). The basic concept of the figure is taken from [11].

Figure 1, *left* shows a simplified version of the model proposed by Garforth et al. [11]. Below the dashed line, the components needed in automatic (unattended) behaviour execution are located. As in the model published by Norman and Shallice, percepts can trigger one or multiple automatic reactions. The triggering on specific percepts is realized in the *Episodic Memory*. Direct connections to the *Procedural Memory* (sketched in Figure 1, *right*) lead to excitations of the respective actions. The *Contention Scheduler* compares the salient behaviours and selects the non-contradicting reactions for execution.

The components above the dashed line are needed for attended action selection. In particular, they realize the *Supervisory Attentional System* (*SAS*) of the Norman and Shallice model. The *SAS Monitor* supervises the automatic behaviour execution and compares it with the intended goals stored in the Working Memory. As long as both match, no influence from the upper to the lower part is exerted. If the automatic reactive behaviour does not match the intentions, the *SAS Monitor* triggers the *SAS Modulator* to bias the *Contention Scheduler*. The triggers for wanted behaviours are increased, the unwanted are attenuated. By this means, the *SAS* is able to let the system execute attended behaviours. The generation of automatic behaviours (i.e., learning of attended behaviours to execute them as unattended, reactive processes) is controlled via the *Limbic System* ("Emotion Centre").

Garforth et al. demonstrate their model in simple robot simulations. Thus, they need not care about sensor preprocessing, noise, and other problems of real application environments. Furthermore, they do not deal with the generation of new (attended) behaviours, i.e. the "*SAS Generator*" in Figure 1 is not implemented. Concerning the bottom end of the model, they mention spinal cord reflexes but do not integrate them. Finally, the generation of internal models and the comparison of expectations (predictions) and real percepts (especially the principle of efference copy) is not included in this architecture.

2   Reactive/Deliberative Behaviour Control System

2.1   System Structure

Many implementations of deliberative behaviour control systems are based on a task-driven model. That is, given a certain task, corresponding control variables are computed and fed to the system that is then converging to the desired output state by means of a feedback control system. In this kind of systems, if there is no current task to fulfill, the system may do nothing at all – it is idle.

Unlike this way of modelling, the system presented in this paper follows a different approach, based on a conception called the *Homeostasis*. This describes a state of general "well-being" of the system, e.g., the preservation of a certain functional and operational state of the system, even when there is no explicit task to be performed. In this conception, even if idle, that is, not executing a certain given task, the system is still monitoring and controlling sensor states, thus allowing it to instantaneously react to, e.g., environmental changes that – in contrast to the task-driven system models – do not have to be part of a certain task to be completed.

If, in contrast, there is actually a certain task given (i.e., to be performed), the changes in the system required for its execution can be understood as a shift to the point of homeostatic state within the model.

E.g., if a system using this kind of behavioural control model is standing at a slope, being idle, the preservation of the homeostatic state of the system would require the system to brake or even put some current on its locomotion actuators to retain its current position and not to start slipping / rolling down the slope. But if there is a task requiring to drive down the slope, this task's demands can be understood as being a shift to the point of homeostatic state within the system, thus allowing or even demanding the occurrence of a motion in the desired direction.

To fulfill the needs of this homeostatic concept, which indeed means to hold a state around a desired *Homeostasis*, a layered architecture is required that enables the system to *act* in its environment to pursuit its motivation for reaching its goal, and, at the same time, enables the system to *react* on unexpected external influences caused by other independent processes in the world.

In the following, we will consider such a layered architecture represented by the three-layered *Levels-of-Behaviour* (LoB) model shown in Figure 2. As noted, the main purpose of this architecture is to hold a state around the *Homeostasis*, and therefore it needs to act on different levels. Overall, the LoB architecture represents a hierarchical control system with a direct sensorimotor-loop in the lowest layer (*Reactive Layer*), and with two upper layers (*Deliberative Layer* and *Creative Cognition*) to modulate the execution of actions in the lowest layer.

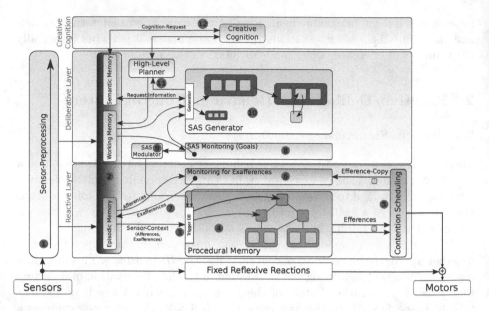

Fig. 2. Hierarchical LoB architecture. The lowest layer (*Reactive Layer*) contains the reactive behaviours and the access to the actuators. The middle layer (*Deliberative Layer*) contains the goal-following engine to modulate the behaviour of the lowest layer. The *Fixed Reflexive Reactions* block can be used to model, e.g., spinal reflexes. Components 1-12 are further described in the corresponding text.

The behaviour control system is meant to be used on different mobile robotic platforms. In order to allow that, several sensor types (e.g., stereo vision cameras, laser range finder, sonar, tactile sensors) in any combination can be attached to the architecture. They are further processed (see Figure 2: (1)) in a hierarchical manner, that first of all, very simple (primitive) features are extracted out of the raw sensor data. Based on these simple features, more generic shapes and combined features are extracted. This is comparable to the preprocessing of visual stimuli that takes place especially in the V1 (striate cortex) and V5/MT (middle temporal area) regions of the human brain [12]. Furthermore, these shapes can be combined to form prototypes of the world's objects that are then used to perform object detection.

Independent of the hierarchical level, only the current data is available after the preprocessing step. For further postprocessing and reasoning, the sensor data of each hierarchical layer needs to be stored in a memory (2). From several studies on humans, it is assumed that there are various areas of the brain that contain different types of memories [13]. Given the needed storage and computational effort to hold the data of all hierarchical levels, an abstraction over time is necessary. Therefore, the different types of memories hold data in a specific time frame with a certain level of detail, where the level of abstraction is increasing with increasing storage time span. In the *Episodic Memory* (EM) [14], a snapshot of current sensor data as well as a short period of past detailed sensor data is available. The *Working Memory* (WM) [15,16] stores the perception of the world as abstract shapes that are used to describe a state of the system, as well as the current goal of the system that is given by a planner. Finally, the *Semantic Memory* (SM) [17] stores valuable information about the world that is cumulated over long time by reasoning throughout the lifetime of the system. This data, which represents the most abstract and system-independent information, is used to describe the rules, the knowledge, and the world as it is known to the robot.

The selection of actions to be executed is solely done in the *Trigger Database* (*Trigger DB*) (3), based on the data given by the EM or by the motivation of the system defined at a higher level. Given a *Sensor Context*, which is a set of sensor values, the *Trigger DB* selects one or more assigned behaviours from the *Procedural Memory* (PM).

The *Procedural Memory* (4) holds all of the system's learned actions. Comparable to the sensor preprocessing in (1) they are hierarchically constructed. As with the features of sensor data, there are primitive actions, so-called *atomic actions*, and thereon build more generic actions, called *action sets*. Considering the *Procedural Memory* as a network of interconnected *atomic actions* and *actions sets*, which themselves can contain *atomic actions* or *actions sets*, this structure is comparable to Figure 1, *right*. In general, all kinds of actions will further be denoted as *behaviour*.

By selecting one or more behaviours depending on the *Sensor Context*, many *atomic actions* will be ready to be executed by the actuators (e.g. motors). The *Contention Scheduler* (5) recognizes atomic actions that try to access identical resources and selects that *atomic action* with the highest weight. *Atomic actions* that are not mutually exclusive can be run in parallel and, e.g, control different actuators.

A so-called *Efference-Copy* of the selected action (that is finally sent to the actuators) is given to the *Monitor for Exafferences* (6). The monitor is predicting the consequences of an action and compares them with the actual impacts of these actions (*Afferences*) coming from the sensors through the EM. Based on the discrepancy of both values, the so-called *Exafference* (see [1]) is computed.

These *Exafferences* (7) represent unexpected perceptions that can be caused by the impact of independent external processes of the world or wrongly predicted consequences of behaviours. The *Exafferences* are returned to the EM and processed additionally to regular sensor data by the *Trigger DB*, to be able to react on unexpected consequences of actions and to revert to a state where the system can continue to reach its goal. If it is not possible to solve the discrepancy that is caused by external processes, the *SAS Monitor* (8) needs to recognize that reaching the goal state was interrupted. Therefore, the *SAS Monitor* has access to the *Working Memory*.

Depending on the state difference from current state to goal state, the *SAS Generator* (10) is activated. If a plan has been executed once before which solved this task, it will be selected and executed again (by the *SAS Modulator* (9) directly affecting the *Trigger DB* (3)). If this is not the case, a new behaviour needs to be generated based on the already existing underlying actions and further knowledge stored in the SM. One way of behaviour generation (in case a plan could be generated) is the learning of a habit-like behaviour: When the *SAS Modulator* controls the action selection for some time (i.e., no appropriate behaviour is existing and the intended actions are repeated multiple times), a learning can be triggered (like proposed in [11]). The new behaviour is learned based on multiple repetitions of the intended actions. The sensory feedback during these repetitions can also be used to learn the sensorimotor model for the *Exafference* computation.

If knowledge from memory is not sufficient to generate new behaviours and to solve the problem, the *High-Level Planner* (11) can be activated to communicate with other robotic systems to exchange world models, to obtain new commands from a human operator, or it can use its *Creative Cognition* (12) to reason about the world with the knowledge of the SM or WM.

In the proposed design, the lower layers are still functional without the higher ones. The *Reactive Layer* alone can generate a successful reactive behaviour. And the *Reactive Layer* together with the *Deliberative Layer* can both show successful deliberative behaviour if the top layer is not functional. This independence of the separated layers is one helpful property to realize a robust system behaviour. For instance, if in the *Deliberative Layer* a plan has been generated based on false assumptions, the *Reactive Layer* can still save the system in critical situations (e.g., by invoking emergency reflexes). A second property to achieve a reliable behaviour is the system's adaptability. By that means it could even be possible to adapt to (e.g., environmental) changes that are not known at design time.

The functions of the single components as well as the whole-model behaviour need to be examined separately for two different initial conditions: The *Blank State* and the *Learned State*. In the *Blank State*, all memories, parameters, and learnable connections are empty, not existing, or have a random state. Reflexes, basic behaviours, and internal models are given just as little as possible (and as biologically plausible). Starting from this state, the system is supposed to gather all other needed informations (behaviours, models) on its own.

However, learning on a real system will take a lot of time – even in the very limited case of a simple robot platform and a simple use case (compare section 3). For that reason, a second state, the so-called *Learned State*, will be used for most of the evaluations. In the *Learned State* the system is supposed to have already learned several plans, reflexes, habits, and models. In a typical use case this gained knowledge is to be applied.

2.2   System Interfaces

To allow external monitoring and visualization (e.g., for a human operator in a multi-robot mission), certain interfaces are integrated in the system. To avoid any disturbance of the behaviour control system caused by the external monitoring, this monitoring is limited to only preprocessed, high-level, and low-bandwidth data like the current system state and the current behaviour selection. Through this high-level information, the operator is able to determine the overall state of the system (e.g., the current plan is successfully worked on, there were unexpected sensor states but the plan could be pursued, there is a persistent interruption of the plan execution).

Finally, to realize interfaces for robot-robot or human-robot communication, there are three different options possible: (1) integrated in the "Creative Cognition" component, i.e., modelled as reasoning, (2) integrated as artificial motor and sensor, thus, modelled comparable to vertebrate communication, and (3) integrated transparently to the model, e.g., the synchronization of different robots' world models in the *Working Memory* is performed by the underlying software framework.

3 Evaluation

The behaviour control system will be evaluated in simulation, on different robot platforms indoor, and on an outdoor robot. So far, switching between reactive behaviours and the interaction between *Deliberative Layer* and the *Reactive Layer* was tested in simulations. Figure 3 shows a model of a 3D simulator test track, where the robot has to pass a bottleneck. The reactive triggers in the *Trigger DB* are defined that way, that the robot holds a safety margin that is greater than the bottleneck. This forces the robot to stay within the starting area. To overcome the narrow bottleneck, a motivated behaviour (from the *SAS Modulator*) needs to surpass the reactive triggers. Figure 3 shows the weights of all actions (lower plot) and the distance to the goal point (upper plot). When the system is not approaching the goal further for some time (cycle 200 to 300), the weight for Forward is increased. When the weight for the Forward action gets higher than that one of the reactive turning behaviours, this action is selected and the robot passes the bottleneck. This can be seen in the plot by the decreasing distance to goal.

To test the behaviour control system with real data, a "SeekurJr" and up to two "Pioneer 3" robots[1] will be placed in a lunar environment. The environment is an indoor model of a lunar crater rim. It has a width of 9.5 m and a height of 4 m. The inclination ranges from 25° to 45°. The illumination can be set from total darkness to bright spots in direction to the robot cameras (compare Figure 4). Thus, it is possible to evaluate the behaviour control system in case a single sensor does not deliver any usable data for some regions (shadows in the camera images) or suddenly changes from usable to unusable data (blinded by the light). The "SeekurJr" platform (see Figure 4) is equipped with two cameras, a laser range finder (LRF), and an inertial measurement unit (IMU).

The planned test cases include sensor drop-out tests (for instance, illumination problems occuring in lunar missions) as well as robot-environment interaction and robot-robot interaction tests. Examples for robot-environment interaction tests are terrain changes that are not expected by the system: reaching a crater rim after having run on flat terrains only or entering an area of fine sandy soil from solid ground.

---

[1] The 'SeekurJr" and "Pioneer 3" systems are commercial research platforms of the manufacturer Adept MobileRobots.

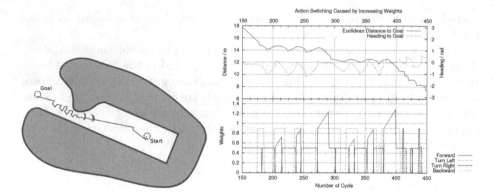

Fig. 3. *Left:* For the very first simulation tests, a bottleneck environment was used. In red the path the robot moved from start to goal is shown. *Right:* In the plot the behaviour activation levels (weights) and the distances (Euclidean and angular) can be seen.

Fig. 4. *Left:* As test environment a lunar crater model will be used. The illumination conditions can be controlled in a wide range, e.g., to create test situations where single sensors (the vision system) will fail. *Right:* The "SeekurJr" robot. This is one of two platform types to be used to evaluate the behaviour control system.

4 Conclusions

Proposed is a concept of a biologically inspired, robust behaviour control system that realizes pure-reactive and deliberative function layers. It is especially designed for missions in unknown environments. To achieve a robust behaviour under such conditions, two core properties were realized in the model: (1) a multi-layered architecture where, e.g., emergency reflexes can interrupt deliberative behaviours and (2) the combination of adaptation, learning, prediction, and self-evaluation to continuously compare and correct the internal world models with the actual sensor feedback and to react to unexpected situations.

As next steps, the current implementation of the model needs to be further evaluated in simulations. Afterwards, the system will be tested on different robotic platforms in the test environment described in Section 3.

Acknowledgment. Supported by the Federal Ministry of Economics and Technology on the basis of a decision by the German Bundestag, grant no. 50RA1113 and 50RA1114.

References

1. Holst, E., Mittelstaedt, H.: Das Reafferenzprinzip. Naturwissenschaften 37, 464–476 (1950), doi:10.1007/BF00622503
2. Sperry, R.W.: Neural basis of the spontaneous optokinetic response produced by visual inversion. Journal of Comparative and Physiological Psychology 43, 482–489 (1950)
3. Miall, R., Wolpert, D.: Forward models for physiological motor control. Neural Networks 9(8), 1265–1279 (1996); Four Major Hypotheses in Neuroscience
4. Schenck, W., Hoffmann, H., Möller, R.: Grasping of Extrafoveal Targets: A Robotic Model. New Ideas in Psychology 29(3), 235–259 (2011)
5. Dyer, F.: The stroop phenomenon and its use in the study of perceptual, cognitive, and response processes. Memory & Cognition 1, 106–120 (1973)
6. Richard Simon, J., Wolf, J.D.: Choice reaction time as a function of angular stimulus-response correspondence and age. Ergonomics 6(1), 99–105 (1963)
7. Pashler, H.: Dual-task interference in simple tasks: Data and theory. Psychological Bulletin 116, 220–244 (1994)
8. Norman, D.A., Shallice, T.: Attention to action: Willed and automatic control of behaviour. In: Davidson, R.J., Schwartz, G.E., Shapiro, D. (eds.) Consciousness and Selfregulation, vol. 4, pp. 1–18. Plenum Press (1986)
9. Schneider, W., Shiffrin, R.M.: Controlled and automatic human information processing: I. Detection, search, and attention. Psychological Review 84, 1–66 (1977)
10. Gurney, K., Hussain, A., Chambers, J., Abdullah, R.: Controlled and Automatic Processing in Animals and Machines with Application to Autonomous Vehicle Control. In: Alippi, C., Polycarpou, M., Panayiotou, C., Ellinas, G. (eds.) ICANN 2009, Part I. LNCS, vol. 5768, pp. 198–207. Springer, Heidelberg (2009)
11. Garforth, J., McHale, S., Meehan, A.: Executive attention, task selection and attention-based learning in a neurally controlled simulated robot. Neurocomputing 69(16-18), 1923–1945 (2006)
12. Beckers, G., Zeki, S.: The consequences of inactivating areas v1 and v5 on visual motion perception. Brain 118(1), 49–60 (1995)
13. Markowitsch, H.J.: Psychogenic amnesia. NeuroImage 20(suppl.1), S132–S138 (2003); Convergence and Divergence of Lesion Studies and Functional Imaging of Cognition
14. Tulving, E.: Episodic and semantic memory. In: Tulving, E., Donaldson, W. (eds.) Organization of Memory, pp. 381–402. Academic Press (1972)
15. Baddeley, A.: Working memory. Oxford psychology series. Clarendon Press (1986)
16. Baddeley, A.: The episodic buffer: a new component of working memory? Trends in Cognitive Sciences 4(11), 417–423 (2000)
17. Wheeler, M.A., Stuss, D.T., Tulving, E.: Toward a theory of episodic memory: The frontal lobes and autonoetic consciousness. Psychological Bulletin 121, 331–354 (1997)

MinPos : A Novel Frontier Allocation Algorithm for Multi-robot Exploration

Antoine Bautin, Olivier Simonin, and François Charpillet

INRIA Nancy Grand Est - LORIA Lab. - Université de Lorraine
`firstname.lastname@inria.fr`

Abstract. Exploring an unknown environment with multiple robots requires an efficient coordination method to minimize the total duration. A standard method to discover new areas is to assign frontiers (boundaries between unexplored and explored accessible areas) to robots. In this context, the frontier allocation method is paramount. This paper introduces a decentralized and computationally efficient frontier allocation method favoring a well balanced spatial distribution of robots in the environment. For this purpose, each robot evaluates its relative rank among the other robots in term of travel distance to each frontier. Accordingly, robots are allocated to the frontier for which it has the lowest rank. To evaluate this criteria, a wavefront propagation is computed from each frontier giving an interesting alternative to path planning from robot to frontiers. Comparisons with existing approaches in computerized simulation and on real robots demonstrated the validity and efficiency of our algorithm.

Keywords: frontier-based exploration, multi-robot exploration, coordinated multi-robot exploration, potential field, gradient methods, multi-robot task allocation, distributed robot systems.

1 Introduction

Exploration of unknown environments by autonomous mobile robots can be necessary in many real world situations, typically for areas where human access is difficult or hazardous. In exploration tasks, multiple robots systems are advantageous because, using an efficient coordination strategy, they are more accurate and/or faster to explore the environment than single robot systems [10]. Furthermore, multi-robot systems using a distributed algorithm are robust to failures, flexible and scalable [2]. Nevertheless collectively building a map with a team of robots also raises up some difficulties. Finding a good navigation strategy for each robot is not straightforward as the exploration policy of one robot strongly depends on the exploration policy of others. Another issue is the computational capabilities of the robots that are often limited when using multiple robots. Finally, in some cases, robots can negatively interact with each other, inducing blockage or avoidance maneuvers.

This work aims at providing an efficient method for assigning to each robot areas to visit within the environment in order to minimize the amount of time required to fully explore it. Frontiers are the boundaries between unexplored and explored empty/accessible areas. A robot "exploring a frontier" (moving towards a frontier) discovers new areas to add to the map and new frontiers. When complete exploration is

C.-Y. Su, S. Rakheja, H. Liu (Eds.): ICIRA 2012, Part II, LNAI 7507, pp. 496–508, 2012.

the objective, every frontiers should be explored. In this paper, we show that a good heuristic is for each robot to *go toward the frontier having fewer robots in its direction*.

The main contribution of this paper is a novel algorithm for the robot-frontier assignment problem. Each robot is assigned to the frontier for which it is in the best position i.e. the frontier where there is the fewest robots between the frontier and the robot to be assigned (in travel distance). Experimental results in simulation show that this algorithm gives significantly better results than a nearest frontier assignment and similar or better results to a greedy assignment while having a lower computation complexity. Cooperation is achieved by the robots sharing their location coordinates and the information gathered about the environment.

This paper is structured as follows. Section 2, next, defines the problem before introducing the notations used throughout the paper. Section 3 reviews the existing literature on the multi-robot exploration problem. Section 4 describes our exploration strategy. Finally, in section 5, we compare the performance of our algorithm with previously proposed algorithms by simulation in various environments, then we present first experimental results with real robots.

2   Problem Statement

The following presents the notations used and states formally the problem addressed. The fleet of robots is assumed to be homogeneous (identical robots) and equipped with exteroceptive sensors allowing them to build a map. To limit the scope of the problem, robot localization and mapping are not presented in this paper. It can either be done using an external localization system or by having the robots work with a common reference frame and using one of the Simultaneous Localization and Mapping (SLAM) algorithms in the literature (e.g. [11], [8]). Communication is critical for cooperation, therefore we use a wireless communication network (WiFi) which covers the full area to be explored by the robots. Exactly one frontier is assigned per robot for 2 reasons. First, a robot exploring a frontier generally pushes it back and fits the best for exploring that frontier, therefore it is unavailable to explore another frontier. Second, robots should not be left standing still if no frontier is available to them because other robots exploring frontiers are likely to discover new ones and require support to explore them.

Notations

- $\mathcal{R}$ the set of robots, $\mathcal{R} : \{\mathcal{R}_1...\mathcal{R}_n\}$ with $n = |\mathcal{R}|$ the total number of robots
- $\mathcal{F}$ the set of frontiers, $\mathcal{F} : \{\mathcal{F}_1...\mathcal{F}_m\}$ with $m = |\mathcal{F}|$ the number of frontiers
- $\mathcal{C}$ a cost matrix with $\mathcal{C}_{ij}$ the cost associated with assigning robot $\mathcal{R}_i$ to frontier $\mathcal{F}_j$
- $\mathcal{A}$ an assignment matrix with $\alpha_{ij} \in [0, 1]$ computed as follows :

$$\alpha_{ij} = \begin{cases} 1 & \text{if robot } \mathcal{R}_i \text{ is assigned to } \mathcal{F}_j \\ 0 & \text{otherwise} \end{cases}$$

The main objective is to minimize the overall exploration time. As the problem is dynamic - robots discovering an unknown environment - it is difficult to evaluate the final exploration duration during the system execution. Indeed, when selecting among different allocations, the impact of a given assignment on the global system performance is not known because no information about what is behind the frontiers is available. Consequently, optimization has to reevaluated at each time step or at least every time the robot observes the targeted frontier. The time for all assigned frontiers to be explored is determined by the maximum exploration time among all frontiers. The optimization criteria is therefore the minimization of the maximum cost :

$$C_{max}(\mathcal{A}) = \max_{\forall i} \sum_{j=1}^{m} \alpha_{ij} \, C_{ij} \tag{1}$$

The challenge of the frontier allocation lies in the number of possible assignments being equal to the number of permutations i.e. sequences without repetition. Therefore, in the best and most common case when $n \leq m$, it is equal to $\frac{m!}{(m-n)!}$. When $n > m$ it becomes even greater. These figures make the search for the optimal assignment intractable for large teams of robots and an approximation is therefore necessary.

3   State of the Art

In this section, we review previously proposed methods on multi-robot exploration strategies. These methods can be classified by their coordination method. First, implicit coordination that do not use communication for coordination. Then, the approaches which use communication to a central agent allocating an area to each robot or a decentralized decision making system.

3.1   Implicit Coordination : Nearest Frontier

In 1997, Yamauchi introduced the very popular frontier-based exploration algorithm for single robot [12]. He first referred to frontiers as the border between known free space and an unexplored area. A robot moving towards a frontier will therefore sense new areas of the map. Repeating this operation increases the size of explored environment until the entire environment is explored: when no frontiers are left. In its multi-robot extension [13] (see algorithm 1), robots share the gathered information so that they build a similar map resulting in a similar list of frontiers. Each robot moves towards its nearest frontier, makes an observation and broadcasts its results. This cooperatively built map is enough to achieve some coordination: when a frontier is explored by one robot, the information acquired is shared with the other active robots and the frontier will not be explored again by another robot. Coordination is said to be implicit because it is achieved only by sharing information gathered on the environment. No communication is necessary to coordinate the robots. This method is asynchronous, distributed and robust to robot failures.

This pioneering work put in evidence the central issue of assigning frontiers to each robot because, using this approach, several robots can be assigned to the same frontier not taking advantage of their number to explore different areas. Figure 1(a) illustrates a situation where two robots are assigned to the same frontier, leaving unexplored areas without robots (lines show the assigned robot-frontier pairs).

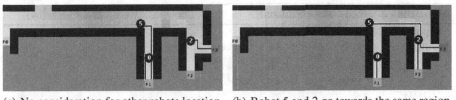

(a) No consideration for other robots location.   (b) Robot 5 and 2 go towards the same region.

Fig. 1. Resulting frontier assignment using the nearest frontier (a) and greedy (b) algorithms

---

Algorithm 1. Nearest frontier $O(m)$

Input: $\mathcal{R}_i$, $\mathcal{C}_i$ Cost Vector of $\mathcal{R}_i$
Output: α_{ij} assignment of robot $\mathcal{R}_i$ to frontier $\mathcal{F}_j$
begin

$\quad$ $\alpha_{ij} = 1$ with $j = \underset{\forall \mathcal{F}_j \in \mathcal{F}}{\operatorname{argmin}} \mathcal{C}_{ij}$

end

3.2 Coordination through Communication : Greedy Assignment

Greedy algorithms are commonly used for task allocation and the frontier assignment problem is a task allocation problem. At each iteration of the allocation loop, the robot-frontier pair with lowest cost is selected, the robot is assigned to the frontier, and both are removed from their respective list. This is repeated until all robots have an assigned frontier. The standard way of applying this greedy algorithm is centralized and synchronous. A centralizer assigns a frontier to each robot, robots travel to their frontier, share the information collected on the environment and wait for a new assignment. The centralizer can wait for all robots to arrive at their frontier to assign the new set of frontiers (synchronous) or whenever a robot reaches its frontier (asynchronous). For a fair comparison between algorithms a decentralized and asynchronous version of the greedy allocation algorithm is given in Algorithm 2. Each robot computes the allocation of the other robots until it finds its assignment. Because robots have the same information about the environment including other robots locations, a robot can assume that the allocation computed for another robot will be the same as the one computed by that robot. An example of a greedy assignment is illustrated on figure 1(b). Due to the robots considering the assignment of other robots, robots are evenly assigned to frontier. However, note that frontier $\mathcal{F}_0$ is not assigned while robots $\mathcal{R}_2$ and $\mathcal{R}_5$ go towards the same zone. Most frontier allocation approaches are greedy based [3], [9] [14].

3.3 Utility-Based vs Frontier-Based

Utility, proposed by Simmons et al. [9], refers to the difference or ratio between an estimated information gain and a cost. Evaluating it requires to estimate the expected area discovered from a target location reduced by the overlap in between robot sensed

---

Algorithm 2. Greedy (decentralized)   Complexity $O(n^2 m)$

Input: $\mathcal{R}_i, \mathcal{C}$ Cost Matrix
Output: α_{ij} assignment of robot $\mathcal{R}_i$ to frontier $\mathcal{F}_j$

while $\mathcal{R}_i$ *has no frontier assigned* **do**
      Find $k, j = \text{argmin } \mathcal{C}_{kj} \ \forall \mathcal{R}_k \in \mathcal{R}, \ \forall \mathcal{F}_j \in \mathcal{F}$
      $\alpha_{kj} = 1$
      $\mathcal{R} = \mathcal{R} \setminus \mathcal{R}_k, \mathcal{F} = \mathcal{F} \setminus \mathcal{F}_j$
      IF $\mathcal{F} = \varnothing$ THEN $\mathcal{F} = \mathcal{F}_{init}$
end

---

areas and the cost of reaching that target. Targets are greedily assigned on utility to robots thus maximizing information gain and minimizing the total cost. Utility-based approaches improves the frontier based approaches (see Burgard et al. [4]) but induces an extra computation load. However, regarding frontier-based approaches, contiguous frontiers cells can be grouped or identified into a unique frontier (Franchi et al. [7]) thus making their performances close to utility-based approaches. In this case, utility and frontier based approaches avoid sending several robots toward nearby frontier cells.

3.4 Centralized vs Decentralized Systems

In a centralized coordination scheme, one central agent decides which frontier each robot should explore [9]. Centralized coordination scheme represents a single point of failure and requires an additional computation and communication cost. In order to be decentralized, the utility based method was extended by Zlot et al. [14] by using a market based approach where robots bid on targets, thus negotiating their assignments. Existing bidding algorithms for frontier allocation usually work with the same principle as a greedy algorithm. Auctions systems can be centralized [9], one central agent receives bids from all robots and assigns frontiers to each robot, or decentralized as in [14] and [5], a robot discovering a frontier is auctioneer for this frontier. These approaches reduce the computation cost by making parallel computations of paths to frontiers and assignments but induce a communication overhead of $O(nm)$ because each robot sends a bid for each frontier.

4 Proposed Approach

Our approach to the frontier allocation problem is based on the distribution of robots among the frontiers. For this purpose, we do not only take into account the distance to frontiers. We consider the notion of position or rank of a robot towards a frontier, by counting how many robots are closer to the frontier. Before detailing the frontier allocation algorithm, we present the scheme of robots' behavior and the assumptions on the environnement representation.

Each robot performs repeatedly the four following steps :

1. Frontiers identification and clustering
2. Computation of the distances to frontiers
3. Assignment to a frontier
4. Navigation towards the assigned frontiers for a fixed time period.

The map representation used is an Occupancy Grid (OG) [6] which is a square tessellation of the environment into cells of the desired size, maintaining a probabilistic estimate of their occupancy state. This map is built from the robot perceptions and broadcasted maps of other robot. To reduce the computation cost, robots are assumed to have a circular shape and to be holonomic. The configuration space grid is then computed by enlarging obstacles (including other robots) by the size of the robot. This configuration space grid is then used for frontier identification and path planning.

Steps 1, 2 and 3 are detailed in the next sections.

4.1 Frontier Identification and Clustering

Each robot maintains a list of frontier cells updated with each information received or acquired. To reduce the distance computation step and avoid assigning robots to frontiers cells that will be observed with the same perception, contiguous frontiers cells are grouped. The size of groups of frontiers cells is thresholded with respect to the size of sensing areas.

4.2 Distances and Path Computation

To evaluate robots positions we use, as the other methods, a cost matrix. In order to compute the cost matrix we build a local minimum free artificial potential field from each group of frontier using the wavefront propagation algorithm (WPA) [1]. From each frontier cells in a group of frontiers, a monotonically increasing potential is built by iteratively propagating a wavefront through unoccupied cells in the Configuration grid. The result of the WPA gives for each cell in the environment the distance to the frontier using the shortest path. Building the cost matrix is then straightforward using the location information of each robot. In comparison, most approaches compute a path from each robot to each frontier (with a A* algorithm). Thus if a robot requires the cost for another robot, it needs to ask it to the other robot or to compute its path. The potential field grids is re-computed periodically, at least every time the robot is close to reaching the frontier, but ideally each time new information is significant enough to modify the configuration grid and could therefore affect the robot assignment.

4.3 Frontier Allocation

Frontier assignment is done in a decentralized way i.e. each robot autonomously decides which frontier it will explore next.

Our approach consists in assigning to a robot a frontier for which it is in best position, i.e. the frontier having the less robots closer than itself. Formally, we set $\mathcal{P}_{ij}$ the position of a robot $\mathcal{R}_i$ towards a frontier $\mathcal{F}_j$ as:

$$\sum_{\forall \mathcal{R}_k \in \mathcal{R},\ k \neq i,\ \mathcal{C}_{kj} < \mathcal{C}_{ij}} 1$$

which computes the cardinal of the set of robots closer to the considered frontier than the robot being assigned.

By reasoning on positions instead of distances, two close robots will be assigned on frontiers where they will be in first position whatever the distances, thus favoring a better spatial distribution of robots on frontiers. Figure 2 illustrates such an assignment. Robot $\mathcal{R}_5$ is assigned to frontier $\mathcal{F}_0$ instead of a closer frontier. Indeed robot $\mathcal{R}_5$ is in second position for frontiers $\mathcal{F}_1$, $\mathcal{F}_2$ and $\mathcal{F}_3$. This provides a well balanced direction assignment, which was not the case with the greedy approach (see fig 1(b)). The algorithm for assignment, called Minimum Position, is given in Algorithm 3.

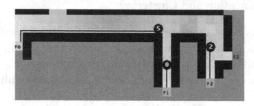

Fig. 2. Resulting frontier assignment using the MinPos algo. : directions taken are well balanced.

Algorithm 3. MinPos   Complexity $O(nm)$

Input: $\mathcal{R}_i$, $\mathcal{C}$ cost matrix
Output: α_{ij} assignment of robot $\mathcal{R}_i$

foreach $\mathcal{F}_j \in \mathcal{F}$ **do**
$\quad \mathcal{P}_{ij} = \sum_{\forall \mathcal{R}_k \in \mathcal{R},\ k \neq i,\ \mathcal{C}_{kj} < \mathcal{C}_{ij}} 1$
end
$\alpha_{ij} = 1$ with $j = \underset{\forall \mathcal{F}_j \in \mathcal{F}}{\operatorname{argmin}} \mathcal{P}_{ij}$
In case of equality choose the minimum cost among $\min \mathcal{P}_{ij}$

Wavefront Propagation Stopping. To limit the computation load, the propagation of a wavefront is stopped when it encounters the location of the robot computing its allocation. At this point all robots closer to frontiers have been reached by the wavefront. The robots not encountered are further to the frontier.

Parallel Computation of Wavefronts. Further reduction of the computation load can be obtained by computing wavefront propagation in parallel. Wavefronts are started simultaneously and propagate at the same speed. When a wavefront encounters a robot it is paused. Then two cases are considered :

- If the encountered robot is the robot computing its assignment then the process is finished. The robot is assigned to the frontier corresponding to this wavefront.
- If all wavefronts are paused on other robots, they are restarted sequentially from the lowest to the highest potential value in order to re-synchronize them. The whole process is repeated.

This process allows to synchronize the wavefronts propagation first on the number of encountered robots and second on the distance.

Figure 3 illustrates the result of a parallel wavefront computation.

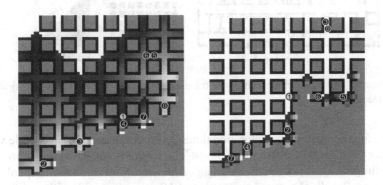

Fig. 3. Resulting potential values from the wavefront propagation algorithm when stopped on the robot computing its assignated frontier (left) and using the parallel wavefront computation (right). Robot computing its allocation is in yellow. Cell color is white when no potential value has been computed in this cell, otherwise it has the color of the frontier associated with minimum potential values computed in that cell.

4.4   Path or Trajectory Planning

The wavefront propagation algorithm allows to navigate to the frontier by descending the negative gradient. A different planner can be used to account for non-holonomic or dynamic constraints but a feasible trajectory may not exist.

Coordination in between robots is achieved only by cooperatively building the map and by sharing robots locations. This feature also applies to the decentralized versions of the greedy algorithms but in comparison the MinPos algorithm using the cost matrix is less complex. Furthermore, using the parallel wavefront computation, the cost matrix is not computed, only one complete path is computed: the one from the robot to its assigned frontier. In the next section, we show that this computation cost reduction does not compromise performances and can even improve them compared to state-of-the-art multi-robot exploration algorithms.

5 Experiments and Analysis

5.1 Simulation : Frontier Assignment Evaluation

Evaluation of the proposed method was carried out in a simulator specifically developed. Environment and time are discrete, the robot's size is set to the dimension of a cell. Robots know with certainty their location and can sense their neighborhood perfectly at 360° around them with a parameterized range. The simulated environments are buildings, randomly generated mazes and a regular grid (illustrated in figure 4). Exploration times are measured when robots have discovered every part of the environment.

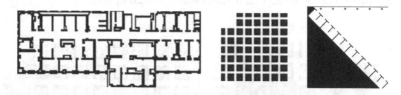

Fig. 4. Example of the environments used for the experiments: an hospital section, a regular grid, and a stable

Figure 5(a) compares the exploration times given in simulation steps, while varying the number of robots of different methods. The methods compared are nearest frontier, the Burgard et al. [4] greedy-based algorithm and MinPos on the hospital section environment. Results shown are an average of 60 runs of each algorithm with a given robot count. We observe that the Burgard et al. and Min Position algorithms are more efficient improving by 13% on average the number exploration steps required to fully explore the environment. On all the environments except the stable, when the number of robots is small (from 1 to 5 or 6 depending on the environment), the MinPos algorithm performs better. On the other hand, our implementation of the Burgard et al. algorithm has close but slightly better performance when the number of robots is large. Figure 5(b) compares a greedy allocation of frontiers with MinPos allocation on a more realistic simulator, exploration times are in seconds. On the environment named stable the MinPos algorithm is 18% more efficient on average, and this improvement remains true regardless the number of robots. Results on the mean number of steps and standard deviation on all the test environments show that the MinPos algorithm has less variability. This has been confirmed by an analysis of variance test run on the obtained data.

5.2 Analysis

As a tentative explanation of the results obtained we analyze, in this section, different assignments on static crossroad situations.

During system execution, an adequate dynamical behavior emerges that tends to separate grouped robots. For example, as shown in Figure 6(a), two robots following each other to reach the same frontier will separate as soon as the first one moves away from an unassigned frontier, when re-computing its assignment frequently and as soon as it

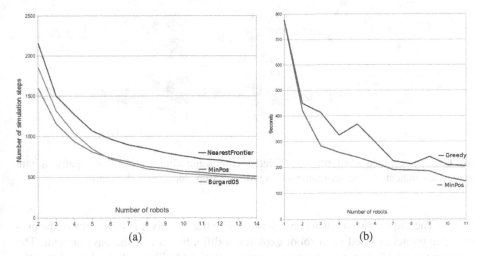

(a)

(b)

Fig. 5. Exploration results for simulations in the hospital (a) and stable (b) environment

reached the frontier otherwise. Indeed, the second robot is then in first position towards this frontier and therefore assigned to it. With the nearest frontier algorithm both robots would have continued exploring the area behind frontier $\mathcal{F}_1$, with a greedy algorithm robots would have initially been assigned to the different frontiers.

Compared to the greedy assignment of frontiers the MinPos algorithm does not only consider distances to frontiers but also directions to frontiers. This feature has the advantage of separating grouped robots in different directions. For example, in figure 6(b), the MinPos assignment will send robot $\mathcal{R}_1$ to frontier $\mathcal{F}_1$ which is further away than $\mathcal{F}_2$ and $\mathcal{F}_3$ but in a different direction whereas the greedy assignment will send $\mathcal{R}_3$ to $\mathcal{F}_2$ and $\mathcal{R}_1$ to $\mathcal{F}_3$. The MinPos assignment will lead to a shorter exploration time of all frontiers because once $\mathcal{R}_3$ has explored $\mathcal{F}_2$ it will then explore $\mathcal{F}_3$ to complete the exploration ($\mathcal{F}_2$-$\mathcal{F}_3$ are closer to each other than $\mathcal{F}_2$-$\mathcal{F}_1$).

A limit of the MinPos frontier assignment appears when, from a robot point of view, there is a direction with multiple frontiers and multiple robots in front. The robot will consider the robots in front even though the number of frontiers is larger than the number of robots, leaving unassigned frontiers. Figure 6(c) illustrates such a situation where $\mathcal{R}_3$ "sees" frontier $\mathcal{F}_1$ with 2 robots in front and will go towards $\mathcal{F}_4$ where it is in 2nd position. In these situations, a greedy assignment performs better. Nevertheless results show that the impact on performance are low.

5.3 Experiments with Robots

The MinPos algorithm was also tested with up to four robots. The robots used are MiniRex robot built in the LISA lab at the university of Angers France. For exploration, they are equipped with a Hokuyo utm-30lx laser range sensor and three ultrasound range sensors. The environment to explore, shown in Figure 7, is approximately $35m^2$ and features glass walls. Figure 7 shows the results of the exploration with 3

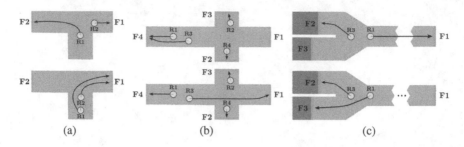

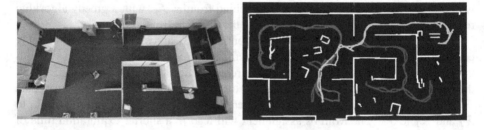

Fig. 6. (a) : two robots separating on a T intersection using MinPos; (b)(c) : comparisons with greedy assignment, frontier assignment using MinPos (top) and greedy (bottom)

robots. The trajectories of each robot demonstrate the validity and efficiency of the proposed approach, indeed each robot explored a different part of the environment. The comparison of MinPos with nearest frontier with the MiniRex robots showed that the exploration is faster with MinPos and generates less conflict in between robots.

Videos of an exploration of the arena can be seen at www.loria.fr/~bautin/outputfile.avi and www.loria.fr/~bautin/outputfile2.avi.

Fig. 7. Photo of the environment (left), map and trajectories resulting from an exploration (right)

6   Conclusion

We addressed the problem of exploring an unknown environment with multiple autonomous robots. A novel algorithm is proposed to assign frontiers that should be explored by each robots. This algorithm addresses the limitation of previous approaches in that it achieves a good coordination with a low complexity algorithm not requiring coordination with explicit communication.

The proposed algorithm is based on the concept of position of a robot toward a frontier, defined by the number of robots closer to the frontier than the robot evaluating its position. To cooperate, the robots share their location and local maps. Each robot then decides autonomously which frontier it will explore next.

Performance measures in simulation demonstrated that our approach is significantly more efficient in total exploration time than the nearest frontier assignment. Our algorithm performs better than a utility greedy assignment of frontier when the number of robots is small and has similar performances when the number of robots grows. Furthermore, the MinPos algorithm has a lower complexity than greedy algorithms and does not require to compute a path from each robot to every frontier beforehand. Indeed, distances to frontiers are computed using a wavefront propagation started from frontiers independently of the number of robots.

We have successfully used this approach during the french robotics challenge Carotte that has been won by deploying five robots in a $120m^2$ unkown 'appartement-like' environment. As future work, we are considering the use of a hybrid metric/topological map representation. We aim to further reduce bandwidth requirements by sharing only topological information in between robots exploring different parts of the environment. This should allow a more distributed and therefore scalable approach.

Acknowledgement. This work has been supported by the French National Research Agency (ANR) and Defence Procurement Agency (DGA) in the Cartomatic project of ANR Carotte.

References

[1] Barraquand, J., Langlois, B., Latombe, J.-C.: Numerical potential field techniques for robot path planning. In: Fifth International Conference on Advanced Robotics, ICAR 1991, Robots in Unstructured Environments, vol. 2, pp. 1012–1017 (June 1991)

[2] Bennet, D.J., McInnes, C.R.: Distributed control of multi-robot systems using bifurcating potential fields. Robot. Auton. Syst. 58, 256–264 (2010) ISSN 0921-8890

[3] Burgard, W., Moors, M., Schneider, F.: Collaborative Exploration of Unknown Environments with Teams of Mobile Robots. In: Beetz, M., Hertzberg, J., Ghallab, M., Pollack, M.E. (eds.) Plan-Based Control of Robotic Agents 2001. LNCS (LNAI), vol. 2466, pp. 52–70. Springer, Heidelberg (2002)

[4] Burgard, W., Moors, M., Stachniss, C., Schneider, F.E.: Coordinated multi-robot exploration. IEEE Transactions on Robotics 21(3), 376–386 (2005) ISSN 1552-3098

[5] Chaimowicz, L., Campos, M.F.M., Kumar, V.: Dynamic role assignment for cooperative robots. In: Proceedings of the IEEE International Conference on Robotics and Automation, ICRA 2002, vol. 1, pp. 293–298 (2002)

[6] Elfes, A.: Using occupancy grids for mobile robot perception and navigation. Computer 22(6), 46–57 (1989), doi:10.1109/2.30720, ISSN 0018-9162

[7] Franchi, A., Freda, L., Oriolo, G., Vendittelli, M.: The sensor-based random graph method for cooperative robot exploration. IEEE/ASME Trans. on Mechatronics 14(2), 163–175 (2009); Winner of the IEEE RAS ICYA Best Paper Award 2010

[8] Howard, A.: Multi-robot Simultaneous Localization and Mapping using Particle Filters. The International Journal of Robotics Research 25(12), 1243–1256 (2006)

[9] Simmons, R., Apfelbaum, D., Burgard, W., Fox, D., Moors, M., Thrun, S., Younes, H.: Coordination for multi-robot exploration and mapping. In: Proceedings of the AAAI National Conference on Artificial Intelligence, Austin, TX. AAAI (2000)

[10] Stachniss, C.: Exploration and Mapping with Mobile Robots. PhD thesis, University of Freiburg, Department of Computer Science (April 2006)

[11] Thrun, S., Liu, Y.: Multi-robot slam with sparse extended information filers. International Journal of Robotics Research, 254–266 (2005)

508   A. Bautin, O. Simonin, and F. Charpillet

[12] Yamauchi, B.: A frontier-based approach for autonomous exploration. In: Proceedings of the IEEE International Symposium on Computational Intelligence in Robotics and Automation, CIRA 1997, pp. 146–151 (July 1997)
[13] Yamauchi, B.: Frontier-based exploration using multiple robots. In: AGENTS 1998: Proceedings of the Second International Conference on Autonomous Agents, pp. 47–53. ACM, New York (1998)
[14] Zlot, R., Stentz, A., Dias, M.B., Thayer, S.: Multi-robot exploration controlled by a market economy. In: Proceedings of the IEEE International Conference on Robotics and Automation, ICRA 2002, vol. 3, pp. 3016–3023 (2002)

Experimental Validation of the Extended Computed Torque Control Approach in the 5R Parallel Robot Prototype*

Asier Zubizarreta[1], Itziar Cabanes[1], Marga Marcos-Muñoz[1],
and Charles Pinto[2]

[1] Automatics and System Engineering Department
[2] Mechanical Engineering Department
Faculty of Engineering of Bilbao
University of the Basque Country (UPV/EHU)
{asier.zubizarreta,itziar.cabanes,marga.marcos,charles.pinto}@ehu.es

Abstract. Parallel robots have become an interesting alternative to serial robots due to their capability to perform certain tasks at high speed
and precision. However, in order to fully exploit the theoretical capabilities of these mechanism, model-based, advanced control approaches
are required. In this paper, the Extended CTC control approach is introduced. This scheme is based on the introduction of the data of the passive
joint sensors on a CTC-based control law. Experimental validation on a
5R parallel manipulator prototype is provided in order to demonstrate
the effectiveness of the approach.

Keywords: Parallel Robots, Model Based Control, Redundant Sensors,Computed Torque Control, 5R robot.

1 Introduction

In the last decade, the interest of both academia and industry on parallel robots
[1] has increased due to the high properties of these mechanisms in terms of high
speed and accuracy. These capabilities are directly related to the structure of
these robots, which is composed by multiple kinematic chains that usually join a
mobile platform to a fixed one. This configuration provides higher stiffness than
the open-chain structure of serial robots, and allows to increase the load/weight
ratio, decrease the positioning errors of the Tool Center Point (TCP) and reduce
the moving mass of the mechanism in order to operate at high speed. Due to
these capabilities, these robots are considered to be the best solution for those
tasks that require high-speed, precision or heavy load handling.

However, the theoretical potential of these robots is also limited by their
own structure. The closed-chain structure, being more complex than the serial

* This work was supported in part by the Government of Spain under projects
DPI2009-07669 and DPI2011-22955, the Government of the Basque Country
(GV/EJ) under grant S-PE11UN110 and by UPV/EHU under grants GIU10/20
and UFI11/28.

C.-Y. Su, S. Rakheja, H. Liu (Eds.): ICIRA 2012, Part II, LNAI 7507, pp. 509–518, 2012.

open-chain structure, implies a more complex kinematic and dynamic model. Moreover, the interference and constraints imposed by each kinematic chain limits the movement of the robot, resulting in a smaller operational workspace than those offered by serial robots and the presence of internal singularities.

In order to give solution to these issues, in recent years extensive research has been done. However, this effort has not been balanced among the different areas of study. This way, while kinematics analysis, synthesis and workspace analysis have been the focus of a considerable number of research works, other areas such as calibration, control and dynamics have been less studied.

In the control area, most of the works that can be found in the literature apply the existing control approaches designed for serial robots directly to parallel robots, without considering the particularities of these mechanisms. Thereby, the control approaches in parallel robots fall into two categories: Local control approaches [2–7] and Model-based control approaches [8–12]. The first one is based on the use of simple PIDs to control each actuated joint of parallel robots independently from the rest. Thus, although its implementation is simple and easy, the independent joint control cannot compensate for the interferences caused by the high dynamic coupling of the mechanism. Therefore, local control approaches provide acceptable performance to execute low precision and speed tasks. On the other hand, model-based control approaches consider the whole robot dynamics and are suitable for high speed and precision tasks. Thus, the model-based control schemes seem the most suitable approaches for parallel robots, as they can theoretically exploit all the potential of these robots.

However, the latter approaches require the definition and identification of a proper kinematic and dynamic model, which is, in general, more complex to obtain. This issue, is even more critical in parallel robots due to two additional phenomena. First, in parallel robots, kinematic and dynamic calibration is still an open field, so the identification procedure of the model is a key issue. Second, as the precise location of the TCP of the mobile platform is difficult to be obtained, its pose has to be estimated using the data provided by the actuators attached to the active joints and the kinematic model [13]. This means that, due to the existence of the so-called passive joints, from the control point of view only the active joints are controlled and the rest of the mechanism is open-loop. These issues limit the performance of model-based approaches.

In previous works of the authors [14], a novel Computed Torque Control (CTC) based approach was introduced in order to reduce the effect of model parameter uncertainties and fully exploit the capabilities of parallel robots. The so-called Extended CTC approach combines the performance of model-based control approaches and the robustness of sensor redundancy. This way, the control law uses information from both active and some extra sensorized passive joints to calculate the control action, resulting in a better estimation of the pose of the TCP and increased control performance even when model parameter uncertainties are high.

In this paper, the simulation and experimental validation of the Extended CTC approach in a 5R parallel manipulator prototype is detailed. For that purpose, the rest of the paper is organized as follows: in section 2, the Extended CTC approach is introduced. In section 3, the 5R parallel robot prototype and its kinematic and dynamic models are detailed. Section 4 describes the experimental setup and results of the validation of the approach. Finally, the most important ideas are summarized.

2   The Extended CTC Approach

The Extended CTC approach is a generalization of the classical CTC approach widely analyzed in the literature. Thus, while the latter only uses the information provided by active joints, the first uses both active joint data and extra sensorized passive joint data to calculate the control action. The use of redundant sensor information provides better estimation of the unmeasured variables of the mechanism and the TCP. So, the direct feedback of the passive joint data allows better control of the mechanical structure.

As in the case of the classical CTC approach, the Extended CTC uses the Inverse Dynamic Model (IDM) to compensate the nonlinear dynamics of the robot. However, as the Extended CTC uses redundant information, this IDM is calculated in terms of the redundant coordinates, called *control coordinates* $\mathbf{q_c}$. The procedure to calculate this redundant dynamic model in a compact form is detailed in [15].

The Extended CTC approach can be implemented in both task and joint spaces. The task space implementation is shown in Fig. 1(a). As it can be seen, the redundant data, grouped in the control coordinates $\mathbf{q_c}$, is used implicitly in the model to estimate the task coordinates $\mathbf{x}$ and the nonsensorized passive joints $\mathbf{q_p}$. This way, in presence of model parameter uncertainties, this approach allows to calculate better estimates of the unmeasurable variables of the model, allowing a more accurate control. The control law of the Extended CTC in the task space is defined as,

$$\tau = \mathbf{D}\left(\ddot{\mathbf{x}}_{\mathbf{ref}} + \mathbf{K_v}\,\dot{\mathbf{e}}_{\mathbf{x}} + \mathbf{K_p}\,\mathbf{e_x}\right) + \mathbf{C}\,\dot{\mathbf{x}} + \mathbf{G} \tag{1}$$

where $\mathbf{K_p}$ and $\mathbf{K_v}$ are the position and velocity gains; $\mathbf{e_x} = \mathbf{x_{ref}} - \mathbf{x}$, $\dot{\mathbf{e}}_{\mathbf{x}} = \dot{\mathbf{x}}_{\mathbf{ref}} - \dot{\mathbf{x}}$ is the positioning and velocity error related to the task coordinates; $\ddot{\mathbf{x}}_{\mathbf{ref}}$, $\dot{\mathbf{x}}_{\mathbf{ref}}$ and $\mathbf{x_{ref}}$ are the task coordinates reference; and $\mathbf{D}$, $\mathbf{C}$ and $\mathbf{G}$ are the inertia, Coriolis and Gravity matrices, which are defined in terms of $\mathbf{x}$, $\mathbf{q_c}$ and $\mathbf{q_p}$, and their derivatives.

On the other hand, the joint space implementation (Fig. 1(b)) uses explicitly the redundant control coordinates $\mathbf{q_c}$ in the control law, providing direct control on all sensorized joints. This approach allows better control of the mechanism even in presence of model parameter uncertainties, as the controller will try to minimize errors in all sensorized joints. Note that in this approach the reference trajectories of the control coordinates $\ddot{\mathbf{q}}_{\mathbf{c_{ref}}}$, $\dot{\mathbf{q}}_{\mathbf{c_{ref}}}$, $\mathbf{q_{c_{ref}}}$ must be calculated from references of the task coordinates $\ddot{\mathbf{x}}_{\mathbf{ref}}$, $\dot{\mathbf{x}}_{\mathbf{ref}}$, $\mathbf{x_{ref}}$ using the Inverse Kinematic Model (IKM) of the robot. Thus, the control law is defined as,

$$\tau = \mathbf{D}\left(\ddot{\mathbf{q}}_{\mathbf{c_{ref}}} + \mathbf{K_v}\,\dot{\mathbf{e}}_{\mathbf{q}} + \mathbf{K_p}\,\mathbf{e_q}\right) + \mathbf{C}\,\dot{\mathbf{q}}_{\mathbf{c}} + \mathbf{G} \tag{2}$$

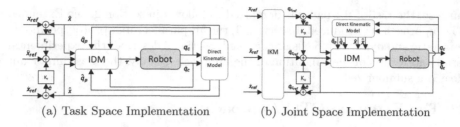

(a) Task Space Implementation   (b) Joint Space Implementation

Fig. 1. Extended Computed Torque Control approach

where $\mathbf{K_p}$ and $\mathbf{K_v}$ are the position and velocity gains and $\mathbf{e_q} = \mathbf{q_{c_{ref}}} - \mathbf{q_c}$, $\dot{\mathbf{e}}_{\mathbf{q}} = \dot{\mathbf{q}}_{\mathbf{c_{ref}}} - \dot{\mathbf{q}}_{\mathbf{c}}$ is the positioning and velocity error related to the control coordinates.

As demonstrated in previous works [14], the Extended CTC provides better control performance and tracking error reduction while maintaining stability.

3 The 5R Parallel Robot Prototype

In order to validate experimentally the proposed Extended CTC approach, a 5R parallel robot prototype has been built (Fig. 2(a)). The 5R is a two degrees-of-freedom parallel robot composed by 4 mobile links joined to a fixed base by means of 5 rotational (R) joints. Thus, the robot is composed by two active joints located in points $\mathbf{A_i}$, and three passive joints located in points $\mathbf{B_i}$ and $\mathbf{P}$. Point $P(x, y)$ reflects also the location of the TCP in the XY plane.

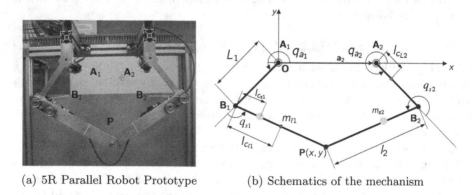

(a) 5R Parallel Robot Prototype   (b) Schematics of the mechanism

Fig. 2. 5R Parallel Robot

The prototype is mounted upside-down, so that the workspace lies on the negative subplane of axis Y. The mechanism is built entirely in aluminum and is actuated by two MAXON EC32 80W servomotors located in actuated joints $\mathbf{A_i}$.

The two passive joints of the robot located at points $\mathbf{B_i}$ are sensorized by means of two Wachendroff WDGA-36A absolute encoders. All devices are connected to a Labview RT based centralized controller using a CANOpen bus.

The dynamic model of the servomotors has been identified experimentally as a first order linear system composed by a inertia term I_m and a viscous friction term B_m,

$$\tau_m = I_m \dot{\omega}_m + B_m \omega_m = 0.16082 \dot{\omega}_m + 0.7736 \omega_m \, (\text{Nm}) \tag{3}$$

where τ_m is the motor torque and ω_m the angular velocity of the motor. Coulomb friction terms have been neglected.

In order to implement the Extended CTC approach, the dynamic model of the robot is defined in terms of all sensorized variables. These variables are grouped in the *control coordinates* $\mathbf{q_c} = \begin{bmatrix} \mathbf{q_a}^T & \mathbf{q_s}^T \end{bmatrix}^T$, where $\mathbf{q_a} = \begin{bmatrix} q_{a_1} & q_{a_2} \end{bmatrix}^T$ are the actuated joints and $\mathbf{q_{na}} = \mathbf{q_s} = \begin{bmatrix} q_{na_1} & q_{na_2} \end{bmatrix}^T$ are the nonactuated sensorized joints associated to points $\mathbf{B_i}$. The set of all joint variables is defined as $\mathbf{q} = \begin{bmatrix} q_a^T & q_s^T \end{bmatrix}^T$, and in this particular case $\mathbf{q} = \mathbf{q_c}$. The task coordinates $\mathbf{x} = \begin{bmatrix} x & y \end{bmatrix}^T$ are defined by the location of the TCP $\mathbf{P}(x, y)$.

3.1   Kinematic Model

Using these sets of variables, the kinematic and dynamic models can be derived. The direct and inverse position problems are calculated operating the loop closure equations of the mechanism,

$$\begin{bmatrix} x \\ y \end{bmatrix} = \mathbf{a_i} + L_i \begin{bmatrix} \cos q_{a_i} \\ \sin q_{a_i} \end{bmatrix} + l_i \begin{bmatrix} \cos(q_{a_i} + q_{s_i}) \\ \sin(q_{a_1} + q_{s_i}) \end{bmatrix}, \, i = 1, 2 \tag{4}$$

Thus, if all joint variables are sensorized, the task coordinates (x, y) can be easily obtained from (4). In order to provide more robustness to the estimation of the coordinates, the x and y coordinates are calculated as the mean of (4) applied to both diads. The inverse kinematic problem, on the other hand, can be easily obtained by operating (4), as detailed in [14].

The velocity relations and Jacobian matrices are calculated by differentiating the closure loop equations (4) with respect to time. Thus, the velocity equation that relates the velocity of the task coordinates $\dot{\mathbf{x}}$ and the control coordinates $\dot{\mathbf{q}}_{\mathbf{c}}$,

$$0 = \mathbf{J_x} \dot{\mathbf{x}} + \mathbf{J_q} \dot{\mathbf{q}}_\mathbf{c} \rightarrow \dot{\mathbf{q}}_\mathbf{c} = -\mathbf{J_q}^{-1} \mathbf{J_x} \dot{\mathbf{x}} = \mathbf{J_{qx}} \dot{\mathbf{x}} \tag{5}$$

The relation of the velocities of actuated and nonactuated joints is required in order to calculate the dynamic model [5]. Thus, combining each pair of equations of (4) and differentiating with respect to time,

$$0 = \mathbf{J_{q_a}} \dot{\mathbf{q}}_\mathbf{a} + \mathbf{J_{q_s}} \dot{\mathbf{q}}_\mathbf{s} \tag{6}$$

Using (6), the jacobian $\mathbf{T}$ can be calculated. This matrix relates the velocities of all joint coordinates $\mathbf{q}$ and the ones of active joints and is used to project the dynamic model into the actuator space,

$$\dot{\mathbf{q}} = \begin{bmatrix} \mathbf{I_2} -\mathbf{J_{q_s}}^{-1}\mathbf{J_{q_a}} \end{bmatrix}^T \dot{\mathbf{q}}_{\mathbf{a}} = \mathbf{T}\,\dot{\mathbf{q}}_{\mathbf{a}} \qquad (7)$$

The acceleration relations are obtained by differentiating the velocity relations.

3.2   Dynamic Model

Using the previously calculated kinematic relations and applying the Lagrangian formulation, the dynamic model of the 5R parallel manipulator can be calculated in terms of the control coordinates $\mathbf{q_c}$,

$$\boldsymbol{\tau} = \mathbf{T}^T \left(\mathbf{D}\,\ddot{\mathbf{q}}_{\mathbf{c}} + \mathbf{C}\,\dot{\mathbf{q}}_{\mathbf{c}} + \mathbf{G} \right) + \mathbf{I_m}\,\ddot{\mathbf{q}}_{\mathbf{a}} + \mathbf{B_m}\,\dot{\mathbf{q}}_{\mathbf{a}} \qquad (8)$$

where $\mathbf{I_m}$ and $\mathbf{B_m}$ define the actuator dynamics.

The inertia matrix $\mathbf{D} = [d_{ij}]$,

$$
\begin{aligned}
d_{11} &= m_{L_1} l_{c_{L1}}^2 + m_{l_1}\left(L_1^2 + l_{c_{l1}}^2 + 2L_1 l_{c_{l1}}\cos q_{s_1} \right) + m_{s_1}\left(L_1^2 + l_{c_{s1}}^2 + 2L_1 l_{c_{s1}}\cos q_{s_1} \right) \\
&\quad + m_c\left(L_1^2 + l_1^2 + 2L_1 l_1 \cos q_{s_1} \right) + I_c + I_{l_1} + I_{s_1} + I_{L_1} \\
d_{22} &= m_{L_2} l_{c_{L2}}^2 + m_{l_2}\left(L_2^2 + l_{c_{l2}}^2 + 2L_2 l_{c_{l2}}\cos q_{s_2} \right) + m_{s_2}\left(L_2^2 + l_{c_{s2}}^2 + 2L_2 l_{c_{s2}}\cos q_{s_2} \right) \\
&\quad + I_{l_2} + I_{s_2} + I_{L_2} \\
d_{33} &= m_{l_1} l_{c_{l1}}^2 + m_c l_1^2 + m_{s_1} l_{c_{s1}}^2 + I_{l_1} + I_c + I_{s_1} \\
d_{44} &= m_{l_2} l_{c_{l2}}^2 + m_{s_2} l_{c_{s2}}^2 + I_{l_2} + I_{s_2} \\
d_{13} &= d_{31} = m_{l_1}\left(l_{c_{l1}}^2 + L_1 l_{c_{l1}}\cos q_{s_1} \right) + I_{l_1} + m_{s_1}\left(l_{c_{s1}}^2 + L_1 l_{c_{s1}}\cos q_{s_1} \right) + I_{s_1} + \\
&\quad m_c\left(l_1^2 + L_1 l_1 \cos q_{p_1} \right) + I_c \\
d_{24} &= d_{42} = m_{l_2}\left(l_{c_{l2}}^2 + L_2 l_{c_{l2}}\cos q_{s_2} \right) + I_{l_2} + m_{s_2}\left(l_{c_{s2}}^2 + L_2 l_{c_{s2}}\cos q_{s_2} \right) + I_{s_2}
\end{aligned}
$$

the Coriolis matrix,

$$\mathbf{C} = \begin{bmatrix} h_1 \dot{q}_{s_1} & 0 & h_1(\dot{q}_{a_1} + \dot{q}_{s_1}) & 0 \\ 0 & h_2 \dot{q}_{s_2} & 0 & h_2(\dot{q}_{a_2} + \dot{q}_{s_2}) \\ -h_1 \dot{q}_{a_1} & 0 & 0 & 0 \\ 0 & -h_2 \dot{q}_{a_2} & 0 & 0 \end{bmatrix}$$

with,

$$
\begin{aligned}
h_1 &= -L_1 \sin q_{s_1}\left(l_{c_{l1}} m_{l_1} + m_c\, l_1 + m_{s_1}\, l_{c_{s1}} \right) \\
h_2 &= -L_2 \sin q_{s_2}\left(l_{c_{l2}} m_{l_2} + m_{s_2}\, l_{c_{s2}} \right)
\end{aligned}
$$

and the gravity vector $\mathbf{G} = \begin{bmatrix} g_1 & g_2 & g_3 & g_4 \end{bmatrix}^T$,

$$
\begin{aligned}
g_1 &= \left(m_{L_1} l_{c_{L1}} + m_{l_1} L_1 + m_{s_1} L_1 + m_c L_1 \right) g \cos q_{a_1} \\
&\quad + \left(m_{l_1} l_{c_{l1}} + m_{s_1} l_{c_{s1}} + m_c l_1 \right) g \cos\left(q_{a_1} + q_{s_1} \right) \\
g_2 &= \left(m_{L_2} l_{c_{L2}} + m_{l_2} L_2 + m_{s_2} L_2 \right) g \cos q_{a_2} + \left(m_{l_2} l_{c_{l2}} + m_{s_2} l_{c_{s2}} \right) g \cos\left(q_{a_2} + q_{s_2} \right) \\
g_3 &= \left(m_{l_1} l_{c_{l1}} + m_{s_1} l_{c_{s1}} + m_c l_1 \right) g \cos\left(q_{a_1} + q_{s_1} \right) \\
g_4 &= \left(m_{l_2} l_{c_{l2}} + m_{s_2} l_{c_{s2}} \right) g \cos\left(q_{a_2} + q_{s_2} \right)
\end{aligned}
$$

Equation (8) defines the IDM to implement the Extended CTC in the joint space (Fig. 1(b)). In order to implement the Extended CTC in the task space, the dynamic model (8) must be projected to the task coordinate space using the kinematic relation (5),

$$\boldsymbol{\tau} = \mathbf{T}^T \left(\mathbf{D_x}\,\ddot{\mathbf{x}} + \mathbf{C_x}\,\dot{\mathbf{x}} + \mathbf{G} \right) + \mathbf{I_m}\,\ddot{\mathbf{q}}_{\mathbf{a}} + \mathbf{B_m}\,\dot{\mathbf{q}}_{\mathbf{a}} \qquad (9)$$

where $\mathbf{D_x} = \mathbf{D}\,\mathbf{J_{qx}}$ and $\mathbf{C_x} = \mathbf{C}\,\mathbf{J_{qx}} + \mathbf{D}\,\dot{\mathbf{J}}_{\mathbf{qx}}$.

The identified parameters for each of the kinematic and dynamic parameters of the mechanical structure are summarized in Table 1. The nonredundant dynamic model of the 5R parallel robot used to implement the classical CTC controller can be found in [5].

Table 1. Identified model parameters in the 5R parallel robot prototype

Parameter	Value	Parameter	Value	Parameter	Value
$\mathbf{a_1}$	$\begin{bmatrix} 0 & 0 \end{bmatrix}^T$ (m)	$\mathbf{a_2}$	$\begin{bmatrix} 0.25 & 0 \end{bmatrix}^T$ (m)	L_1, L_2	0.15 (m)
$l_{c_{L1}}, l_{c_{L2}}$	0.075 (m)	l_1, l_2	0.25 (m)	$l_{c_{l1}}, l_{c_{l2}}$	0.125 (m)
$l_{c_{s1}}, l_{c_{s2}}$	0.05 (m)	m_c	0 (kg)	m_{L1}, m_{L2}	0.069 (kg)
m_{l_1}, m_{l_2}	0.159 (kg)	m_{s_1}, m_{s_2}	0.21 (kg)	I_{L_1}, I_{L_2}	$2.5\,10^{-4}$ (kg m^2)
I_{l_1}, I_{l_2}	$1.04\,10^{-3}$ (kg m^2)	I_{s_1}, I_{s_2}	$3\,10^{-5}$ (kg m^2)	I_c	0 (kg m^2)

4   Simulation and Experimental Validation

In order to demonstrate the effectiveness of the Extended CTC approach, the dynamic performance of the proposed control scheme will be compared with the one of the classical CTC approaches. For that purpose, two reference trajectories are defined in the task space: a circular one, characterized by a center in point $(0.125, -0.2965)$ (m) and a radious of 0.05 (m); and a spiral trajectory, characterized by a starting point $(0.125, -0.3665)$ (m) and center $(0.125, -0.2465)$ (m).

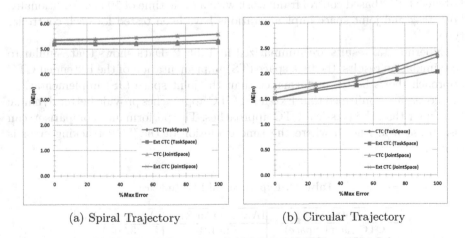

(a) Spiral Trajectory   (b) Circular Trajectory

Fig. 3. IAE index evolution

Both Extended and classical CTC have been tuned experimentally to achieve the best possible dynamic behaviour in the 5R prototype, i.e., the less trajectory tracking error. Thus, the position and velocity gains for both controllers have been tuned to achieve a maximum overshoot of 10% and a peak time of 0.3s ($k_p = 150$ and $k_v = 15$). Additionally, the reference trajectories will be executed by each controller defined in both joint and task space.

A set of simulation experiments has been carried out to analyze the dynamic behaviour of both Extended and classical CTC approaches when parameter uncertainty increases. For that purpose the aforementioned validation trajectories will be simulated for different parameter variations and the IAE (Integral of the Absolute Error) index will be measured. Model uncertainties will be simulated by modifying the parameters of the IDM used in the controller. The maximum parameter errors are 1mm for distance parameters, 0.01Kg for masses and 10% of the nominal inertia values.

Simulation results for a set of 250 random error variations are summarized in Fig. 3. As it can be seen, as model parameter deviation errors increase, the CTC approaches cannot compensate properly the nonlinear dynamics of the parallel robot, resulting in a decrease of the performance of the controller and increasing the IAE index of the TCP tracking error. However, in the Extended CTC approach, the effect of the model parameter uncertainties is lower due to the sensor redundancy, allowing a smaller increase ratio than the classical CTC approach. Thus, the data in Fig. 3 demonstrates that statistically, the Extended CTC approach present better dynamical behaviour that the traditional CTC approach when randomized error deviations are introduced in the IDM used by the controller.

These conclusions have been corroborated by a set of experiments carried out in the 5R parallel robot prototype. The controllers have been implemented on a Labview RT^{TM} based control framework with a cycle time of 10 ms. Additionally, both task and joint space implementations have been tested for each controller type.

Experimental results are summarized in Table 2. Data shows that, similar to the simulation results, the task space (TS) implementation of the Extended CTC approach shows better performance than the joint space (JS) implementation. Moreover, it is confirmed that Extended CTC approaches provide better dynamic behaviour than the classical CTC approaches. The performance comparison can also be seen in Fig. 4, where the time evolution of the TCP tracking error is shown.

Table 2. Experimental IAE Indexes

Controlador	IAE Circular Traj.	IAE Spiral Traj
CTC (Joint Space)	4.0101	3.7079
CTC EXT (Joint Space)	3.2123	3.6127
CTC (Task Space)	4.0304	3.0813
CTC EXT (Task Space)	2.0680	2.4325

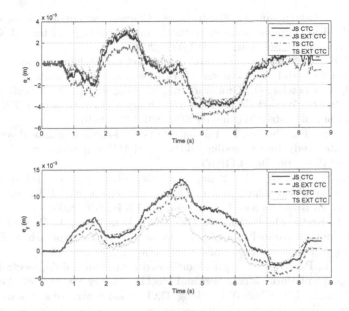

Fig. 4. Circular Trajectory Experimental Data

5   Conclusions

In this paper the advantages of the Extended CTC approach have been demonstrated experimentally on a 5R parallel robot prototype. The proposed approach combines the robustness provided by redundant sensors and the dynamic performance of the Computed Torque Control approach. The resulting control law allows to use the redundant data to increase the performance of the controller, providing better performance than the traditional CTC approaches even when parameter uncertainties arise.

The proposed controller is validated on the 5R parallel robot prototype by two complementary approaches. First, a simulation based performance analysis is carried out, in which randomly generated errors are introduced in the IDM used to implement both classical and Extended CTC approaches. Second, a experimental validation is carried out in a 5R parallel robot prototype, in which the performance of both controllers is analyzed. Results demonstrate that the Extended CTC provides better dynamic behaviour than the classical CTC approach, reducing the tracking error.

References

1. Merlet, J.P.: Parallel Robots, 2nd edn. Kluwer (2006)
2. Chiacchio, P., Pierrot, F., Sciavicco, L., Siciliano, B.: Robust design of independent joint controllers with experimentation on a high-speed parallel robot. IEEE Transactions on Industrial Electronics 40(4), 393–403 (1993)

3. Brecher, C., Ostermann, T., Friedrich, D.: Control concept for pkm considering the mechanical coupling between actuator. In: Proceedings of the 5th Chemnitz Parallel Kinematics Seminar, pp. 413–427 (2006)
4. Ghorbel, F.: Modeling and pd control of closed-chain mechanical systems. In: Proceedings of the 34th IEEE Conference on Decision and Control, pp. 549–542 (1995)
5. Ghorbel, F., Chételat, O., Gunawardana, R., Longchamp, R.: Modeling and set point control of closed-chain mechanisms: Theory and experiment. IEEE Transactions on Control System Technology 8(5), 801–815 (2000)
6. Gunawardana, R., Ghorbel, F.: Pd control of closed-chain mechanical systems: An experimental study. In: Proceedings of the 5th IFAC Symposium on Robot Control (SYROCO 1997), pp. 79–84 (1997)
7. Su, Y.X., Sun, D., Ren, L., Wang, X., Mills, J.K.: Nonlinear pd synchronized control for parallel manipulators. In: Proceedings of the 2005 IEEE International Conference on Robotics and Automation, pp. 1374–1379 (2005)
8. Pietsch, I., Krefft, M., Becker, O., Bier, C.C., Hesselbach, J.: How to reach the dynamic limits of parallel robots? an autonomous control approach. IEEE Transactions on Automation Science and Engineering 2, 369–380 (1995)
9. Davliakos, I., Papadopoulos, E.: Model-based control of a 6-dof electrohydraulic stewart-gough platform. Mechanism and Machine Theory 43(11), 1385–1400 (2008)
10. Lee, S.H., Song, J.B., Choi, W.C., Hong, D.: Position control of a stewart platform using inverse dynamics control with approximate dynamics. Mechatronics 13, 605–619 (2003)
11. Li, Q.: Error attenuation in the control of a parallel robot manipulator using a dual-model-based structure. Journal of Mechanical Engineering Science 217(2), 161–171 (2003)
12. Codourey, A.: Dynamic modeling of parallel robots for computed-torque control implementation. The International Journal of Robotics Research 17(12), 1325–1336 (1998)
13. Paccot, F., Andreff, N., Martinet, P.: A review on the dynamic control of parallel kinematic machines: Theory and experiments. The International Journal of Robotics Research 28(3), 395 (2009)
14. Zubizarreta, A., Cabanes, I., Marcos, M., Pinto, C.: Control of parallel robots using passive sensor data. In: Proceedings of the IEEE/RSJ 2008 International Conference on Intelligent Robots and Systems (2008)
15. Zubizarreta, A., Cabanes, I., Marcos, M., Pinto, C., Portillo, E.: Redundant dynamic modelling of the 3rrr parallel robot for control error reduction. In: Proceedings of the 2009 European Control Conference (2009)

Model-Free Robust Control for Fluid Disturbed Underwater Vehicles

Ricardo Pérez-Alcocer, Ernesto Olguín-Díaz, and L. Abril Torres-Méndez

Robotics and Advanced Manufacturing Group, Cinvestav-Unidad Saltillo
Carretera Saltillo-Monterrey, Km 13, Ramos Arizpe, C.P. 25900, Coahuila, México
{ricardo.perez,ernesto.olguin,abril.torres}@cinvestav.edu.mx

Abstract. We present a control scheme that does not require exact knowledge of the model of an underwater vehicle while maintaining robustness against both parameter uncertainties and environment disturbances. An important aspect of the proposed control is the relative simplicity of its implementation. To verify the effectiveness of the controller, we use an efficient simulator that takes into account the fluid velocity and acceleration without the explicit expression of the last term. Simulations shows the effectiveness of the proposed control law.

Keywords: Robust control, Stability, Simulator, Model-free control, Underwater Vehicles, Fluid disturbance.

1 Introduction

Substantial work has been dedicated on defining control schemes for underwater vehicles that provide good performance to the system. Although traditional adaptive controllers for robots in terrestrial environments work well, they do not have the expected performance in underwater vehicles. In general, the dynamics of underwater vehicles is highly nonlinear and strongly coupled. This is mainly due to the nonlinearities present in the dynamic and kinematic models as well as those prompted by actuator and thrusters characteristics when dealing with existing stochastic disturbances in the environment (e.g., currents), which alter the estimation of the exact dynamic parameters of the vehicle. Thus, the main challenge is to obtain a model that accurately describes the vehicle dynamics. We propose a control scheme that does not require exact knowledge of the model parameters of the vehicle while maintaining its robustness against disturbances present in the environment.

One of the control systems for underwater robots commonly used is the sliding mode control. This system is suitable for underwater control thanks to its robustness to uncertainty. In their work, Healey and Lienard [1] propose a multivariable sliding mode control based on state feedback and the results are quite satisfactory for the combined speed, steering and diving response of a slow speed AUV. More recently, Raygosa-Barahona et al. [2] present a non-linear model free high order sliding mode controller together with the backstepping and path planning techniques to solve the underactuated limitations of a remotely operated vehicle

C.-Y. Su, S. Rakheja, H. Liu (Eds.): ICIRA 2012, Part II, LNAI 7507, pp. 519–529, 2012.
© Springer-Verlag Berlin Heidelberg 2012

(ROV) and [3] describe an optimal integral-sliding-mode controller was designed for the AUV depth control system by constructing a sliding mode surface with quadratic optimization.

In addition to the sliding mode based control, there are other methods that provide robustness to the control when there exist uncertainty. For example, in [4] a fuzzy control system is applied to guide and control the AUV using a fuzzy modeling too and Teo et. al, in [5] show a robust autonomous underwater vehicle (AUV) docking approach that can handle unknown water currents, their simulation results demonstrated the inherent robustness of this designed fuzzy docking approach against unknown current disturbances, without any real-time velocity measurements. In [6] a hybrid (adaptive and sliding) controller is proposed. This controller consists of a switching term which compensates for uncertainties in the input matrix and an on-line parameter estimation algorithm. In other work, Park *et al.* [7] apply a nonlinear $\mathcal{H}_\infty$ optimal control to AUV, one feature of the control design is that it can deal with the robustness as well as the optimality. The problem is that it is complicated to calculate the control.

In this paper, a sub-optimal robust control for position tracking task of underwater vehicle is proposed, the design of the control law is based on the work presented in [8]. The main idea of this paper is to add to an existing PID lineal regulator, a nonlinear feedback loop to improve the robustness and performance of the resulting closed-loop system over the linear regulator. This passivity property of the system is used for control design, which ensures locally stable behavior when the desired velocities and accelerations of the vehicle are bounded as well as the position error, the velocity and acceleration of the fluid. We present simulation results on the NEROV model under different scenarios and simulator characteristics.

This article is organized as follows. Section 2 presents some aspects related with the project. The passive robust control approach is given in Section 3, the simulator description and the experimental results are presented in Section 4. Finally, some conclusions are given in Section 5.

2   Relevant Background

2.1   Dynamic Model

The underwater vehicle dynamics can be described from Kirchhoff's equations [9], where the total kinetic energy is given by an inertial term and the lumped parameter representation (added mass) of the fluid kinetic energy and the relative velocity between the underwater vehicle and fluid itself [10]:

$$K = \frac{1}{2}\boldsymbol{\nu}^T M_I \boldsymbol{\nu} + \frac{1}{2}\boldsymbol{\nu}_R^T M_a \boldsymbol{\nu}_R$$

Then the dynamics, where all external forces like fluid damping and gravity-buoyancy are included, becomes:

$$M\dot{\boldsymbol{\nu}} + C_v(\boldsymbol{\nu})\boldsymbol{\nu} + D_v(\boldsymbol{\nu}_R)\boldsymbol{\nu} + \boldsymbol{g}_v(\boldsymbol{q}) = \boldsymbol{F}_u + \boldsymbol{\eta}_v(\cdot) \tag{1}$$

$$\boldsymbol{\nu} = J(\boldsymbol{q})\dot{\boldsymbol{q}}, \tag{2}$$

where $q = (d^T, \vartheta^T)^T \in \mathbb{R}^6$ is the pose of the vehicle (position and orientation with respect to an inertial frame) that can be used as generalized coordinates vector, $\nu = (v^T, \omega^T)^T \in \mathbb{R}^6$ is the twist of the vehicle (linear and angular velocity) expressed in its own reference frame, $\zeta = (\zeta_v^T, 0)^T \in \mathbb{R}^6$ is the fluid velocity twist, expressed in the inertial frame, expressing a non rotational fluid, and $\nu_R = \nu - \mathcal{R}^T(q)\zeta \in \mathbb{R}^6$ is the relative fluid velocity twist where $\mathcal{R}(q) = diag\{R(\vartheta), R(\vartheta)\} \in SO(6)$ is an extended rotation matrix that transforms any 6D vector (like twists) from the vehicle frame coordinates to the inertial frame ones. The rest of the terms in (1)-(2) are as follows: $M = M_I + M_a = M^T > 0 \in \mathbb{R}^{6\times6}$ is the positive constant and symmetric inertia matrix which includes the inertial mass M_I and the added mass matrix M_a; $C_v(\nu) \in \mathbb{R}^{6\times6}$ is the twist dependent Coriolis matrix which may have multiple representation forms among some are skew symmetric (see [9]), and the product $C_v(\nu)\nu \in \mathbb{R}^6$ is the unique Coriolis vector, quadratic in velocity; $D_v(q, \nu, \zeta) > 0 \in \mathbb{R}^{6\times6}$ is the positive definite dissipative matrix, dependant in the magnitude of the relative fluid velocity that give rise the quadratic dissipative hydrodynamic effects of potential damping, and skin and viscous friction; $g_v(q) \in \mathbb{R}^6$ is the potential wrench (forces and torques) vector which includes gravitational and buoyancy effects; $F_u = (f_u^T, n_u^T)^T \in \mathbb{R}^6$ is the input wrench, expressed in the vehicle frame, produced by the vehicle's thrusters; $J(q) \in \mathbb{R}^{6\times6}$ is the operator that maps the generalized velocity (or pose tie derivative) to the vehicle twist; and $\eta_v(q, \nu, \zeta, \dot{\zeta})$ is the external disturbance wrench produced by the fluid currents, which is explicitly given as

$$\eta_v(q,\nu,\zeta,\dot{\zeta}) = M_a\mathcal{R}^T\dot{\zeta} + D_v(q,\nu,\zeta)\mathcal{R}^T\zeta(t) \tag{3}$$
$$- \left[M_a\Omega(\bar{\nu}) + \Omega^T(\nu)M_a \right] \mathcal{R}^T\zeta(t) \in \mathbb{R}^6.$$

The twist $\bar{\nu} = (0^T \ \omega^T)^T$ contains only angular velocity, and the operator $\Omega(\cdot)$ is defined as follows

$$\Omega(\nu) \triangleq \begin{bmatrix} [\omega\times] & [v\times] \\ 0 & [\omega\times] \end{bmatrix} \in \mathbb{R}^{6\times6}, \tag{4}$$

where $[a\times] \in SS(3)$ is the skew symmetric cross product operator. Notice that 1) one possibility of expressing the Coriolis Matrix is $C_v(\nu) = -\Omega^T(\nu)M$, which is not skew symmetric, but fulfills uniqueness of the Coriolis vector, i.e. $C_v(\nu)\nu = -\Omega^T(\nu)M\nu$; and 2) $\dot{\mathcal{R}} = \mathcal{R}\Omega(\bar{\nu})$.

In [11] is proven the existence of a single second order equivalence of the double first order differential equation set (1)-(2), in the absence of fluid velocity, where each one of its components fulfills all properties of Lagrangian systems (i.e. definite positiveness of inertia and damping matrices, skew symmetry property of the Coriolis matrix and appropriate bounds in all the terms). An extension including fluid velocity is derived directly using (2) in (1), yielding to

$$H(q)\ddot{q} + C(q,\dot{q})\dot{q} + D(\cdot)\dot{q} + g(q) = \tau_u + \eta_q(q,\dot{q},\zeta,\dot{\zeta}) \tag{5}$$

Where according to [10], all the terms are bounded for nonnegative constants $b_i \geq 0$ as follows:

$$\|H(q)\| \leq b_1 = \lambda_M\{H(q)\}$$
$$\|C(q,\dot{q})\| \leq b_2\|\dot{q}\|$$
$$\|D(q,\dot{q},\zeta(t))\| \leq b_3\|\dot{q}\| + b_4\|\zeta(t)\|$$
$$\|g(q)\| \leq b_5$$
$$\|\eta_q\| \leq b_6\|\dot{\zeta}\| + b_7\|\dot{q}\| \; \|\zeta\| + b_8\|\zeta\|^2$$

2.2   Control

In [12] and [13] it is proposed to use nonlinear regulators for linear plants based on an inverse optimal control problem. They describe the application of this methodology in the control structure of the type $PID + u_{NL}$, which is implemented in second-order mechanical systems subject to state disturbances and control input saturation. The problem of robustness is studied and the benefits of this control are analyzed. Later, in [8] a comparative analysis of applying the classical PID control and $PID + u_{NL}$ scheme in aquatic vehicles is presented. In this last work, they assume that the regulation problem of the system being controlled with a nonlinear PID controller can be written in the following state space description:

$$\dot{x} = Ax + B(\tau_{NL} + \gamma(x)), \tag{6}$$

where A is a Hurwitz matrix, induced by the linear controller, $x(t)$ is the system generalized error vector, $\gamma(x)$ is the state-dependent system disturbance provoked by nonlinear forces and inertia couplings, and τ_{NL} is the nonlinear component designed to compensate the effects of $\gamma(x)$. One possible solution is explicitly given to be the following:

$$\tau_{NL} = -2\beta(x^T P x)BPx \tag{7}$$

where β es una positive constant gain and P is the positive-definite matrix that fulfils the corresponding Lyapunov equation.

On the other hand, we also consider a passivity-based control scheme, that can be designed using the passivity properties of the Lagrangian model. A variety of studies have employed this philosophy, as described by [14], [15], [16]. In this scheme, the control input is defined as follows

$$u = \hat{H}(q)\ddot{q}_r + \hat{C}(q,\dot{q})\dot{q}_r + \hat{g}(q) - K_D s + u_0, \tag{8}$$

where $\hat{H}(q)$, $\hat{C}(q,\dot{q})$, and $\hat{g}(q)$, are nominal values related to the unknown parameters of $H(q)$, $C(q,\dot{q})$ and $g(q)$, where they can be obtained as approximations of real values. K_D is a positive definite, diagonal matrix, and u_0 is an additional control input. Finally the variables $s \triangleq \dot{q} - \dot{q}_r$ and $q_r \triangleq \dot{q}_d - \Lambda\tilde{q}$ are known as the extended error and reference trajectory respectively, where q_d is the desired trajectory that is obtained from a proper motion planner and Λ is a positive definite matrix. Therefore the extended error can also be defined as

$$s = \dot{\tilde{q}} + \Lambda \tilde{q}, \tag{9}$$

Both controllers are expected to have robustness properties because they do not rely on the exact cancelation of the robot nonlinearities. The control described in the following section makes a fusion of the two controls mentioned above, resulting in a simple scheme to implement while ensuring the system stability.

3   Sub-optimal Passivity-Based Robust Control

The control described in the following section makes a fusion of the two controls mentioned above, resulting in a simple scheme to implement while ensuring the system stability.

Consider the following control law to be applied to the dynamic system (1):

$$\boldsymbol{F}_u = \hat{M}\dot{\boldsymbol{\nu}}_r + \hat{D}_v \boldsymbol{\nu}_r - J^{-T}(\boldsymbol{q}) \left(K_s \boldsymbol{s} + K_i \int \boldsymbol{s}\, dt + \beta \|\boldsymbol{s}\|^2 \boldsymbol{s} \right), \tag{10}$$

with constant positive definite matrices $\hat{M}$, $\hat{D}_v$, K_s, K_i, and Λ and positive scalar β, with $\boldsymbol{s}$ defined as in (9) and the reference vehicle twist defined as

$$\boldsymbol{\nu}_r \triangleq J(\boldsymbol{q})\dot{\boldsymbol{q}}_r = J(\boldsymbol{q})(\dot{\boldsymbol{q}}_d - \Lambda \tilde{q}) = \boldsymbol{\nu}_d - J(\boldsymbol{q})\Lambda \tilde{q},$$

From the Kirchhoff-Lagrange equivalences, the control law (10) has the following Lagrange equivalence

$$\boldsymbol{\tau}_u = \hat{H}(\boldsymbol{q})\ddot{\boldsymbol{q}}_r + \hat{C}(\boldsymbol{q}, \dot{\boldsymbol{q}})\dot{\boldsymbol{q}}_r + \hat{D}(\boldsymbol{q})\dot{\boldsymbol{q}}_r - K_s \boldsymbol{s} - K_i \int \boldsymbol{s}\, dt - \beta \|\boldsymbol{s}\|^2 \boldsymbol{s}, \tag{11}$$

with the following relationships

$$\hat{H}(\boldsymbol{q}) \triangleq J^T(\boldsymbol{q})\hat{M}J(\boldsymbol{q}) > 0 \tag{12}$$
$$\hat{C}(\boldsymbol{q}, \dot{\boldsymbol{q}}) \triangleq J^T(\boldsymbol{q})\hat{M}\dot{J}(\boldsymbol{q}) \tag{13}$$
$$\hat{D}(\boldsymbol{q}) \triangleq J^T(\boldsymbol{q})\hat{D}_v J(\boldsymbol{q}) > 0 \tag{14}$$

that meet $\hat{C}(\boldsymbol{q}, \dot{\boldsymbol{q}}) + \hat{C}^T(\boldsymbol{q}, \dot{\boldsymbol{q}}) = \dot{\hat{H}}(\boldsymbol{q})$ which in turn is equivalent to the following property:

$$\boldsymbol{x}^T \left[\frac{1}{2}\dot{\hat{H}}(\boldsymbol{q}) - \hat{C}(\boldsymbol{q}, \dot{\boldsymbol{q}}) \right] \boldsymbol{x} = 0, \ \forall \boldsymbol{x} \neq 0. \tag{15}$$

On the other hand, consider that the first 3 terms in the left hand-side of (5) can be written in a regressor-like expression of the form $H(\boldsymbol{q})\ddot{\boldsymbol{q}} + C(\boldsymbol{q}, \dot{\boldsymbol{q}})\dot{\boldsymbol{q}} + D(\cdot)\dot{\boldsymbol{q}} = Y(\boldsymbol{q}, \dot{\boldsymbol{q}}, \ddot{\boldsymbol{q}})\boldsymbol{\theta}$, where $Y(\cdot) : \mathbb{R}^p \mapsto \mathbb{R}^n$ is the regressor made of known nonlinear functions of the generalized coordinates and its time derivatives, and $\boldsymbol{\theta} \in \mathbb{R}^p$

is the dynamic parametric vector of p unknown constant terms. The difference with an estimate version, expressed as $Y(\cdot)\tilde{\theta}$, would be explicitly given as

$$Y(\cdot)\tilde{\theta} = [H(q) - \hat{H}(q)]\ddot{q} + [C(q,\dot{q}) - \hat{C}(q,\dot{q})]\dot{q} + [D(q,\dot{q},\zeta) - \hat{D}(q)]\dot{q},$$

where $\tilde{\theta} = \theta - \hat{\theta}$ is the estimate error of the dynamic parameters, and which, after Lagrangian properties, is bounded as

$$\|Y(\cdot)\tilde{\theta}\| \leq c_1\|\ddot{q}\| + c_2\|\dot{q}\|^2 + c_3\|\zeta\|\|\dot{q}\| \tag{16}$$

for positive constants c_1, c_2 and c_3.

Given the above, we can state the following result:

Theorem 1. *Consider the open-loop system* (1)-(2) *with bounded signals $\dot{\nu}$, $\zeta(t)$ and $\dot{\zeta}(t)$. Then, for the input control law* (10), *there always exist positive gains* $(\beta, K_s, K_i, \Lambda)$, *such that close-loop regime is locally stable, i.e.* $s \to 0$, *provided that the feedback signals ν_d, $\tilde{q}$ are bounded. In consequence, both errors $\tilde{q}$ and $\dot{\tilde{q}}$ are also locally stable.*

The first step to prove Theorem 1 is to find the closed-loop dynamics. This is achieved by substituting the Lagrangian equivalent control law (11) in the Lagrangian equivalent open loop system (5), resulting in the following expression:

$$\hat{H}(q)\dot{s} + \hat{C}(q,\dot{q})s + \hat{D}(\cdot)s + K_s s + K_i \int s\, dt = -\beta\|s\|^2 s - Y(\cdot)\tilde{\theta} - g(q) + \eta_q(\cdot) \tag{17}$$

Secondly, consider the following Lyapunov candidate function

$$V(x) = \frac{1}{2}s^T \hat{H}(q)s + \frac{1}{2}\tilde{a}^T K_i^{-1}\tilde{a}, \tag{18}$$

where $\tilde{a} \triangleq a_0 - K_i\int s\, dt$ for a given constant vector $a_0 \in \mathbb{R}^n$. The time derivative of $V(x)$ becomes

$$\dot{V}(s) = s^T \hat{H}(q)\dot{s} + \frac{1}{2}s^T \dot{\hat{H}}(q)s + \tilde{a}^T K_i^{-1}\dot{\tilde{a}}$$

$$= s^T \hat{H}(q)\dot{s} + \frac{1}{2}s^T \dot{\hat{H}}(q)s - s^T a_0 + s^T K_i \int s\, dt,$$

with $\dot{\tilde{a}} = -K_i s$, which, after using the close-loop expression (17), property (15), and some manipulation, it yields

$$\dot{V}(s) = -s^T[\hat{D}(\cdot) + K_s]s - \beta s^T\|s\|^2 s - s^T a_0 + s^T\left(\eta_q(\cdot) - Y(\cdot)\tilde{\theta} - g(q)\right) \tag{19}$$

Assuming that $\dot{\nu}$ is bounded implies that both $\dot{q}$ and $\ddot{q}$ are also bounded. Then together with the assumption that $\dot{\zeta}$ and ζ are also bounded, it yields $\|\eta_q\| + \|Y(\cdot)\tilde{\theta}\| \leq k_1 + k_1\|\dot{q}\| + k_2\|\dot{q}\|^2..$ By substituting $\dot{q} = s - \dot{q}_r$, and taken into account that the reference trajectory is bounded since both ν_d and $\tilde{q}$ are assumed to be themselves bounded, last expression becomes

$$\|\eta_q\| + \|Y(\cdot)\tilde{\theta}\| \leq \mu_0 + \mu_1\|s\| + \mu_2\|s\|^2.$$

Finally, including the gravity vector bounds, last term in (19) is majored as

$$\|\boldsymbol{\eta}_q(\cdot) - Y(\cdot)\tilde{\boldsymbol{\theta}} - \boldsymbol{g}(\boldsymbol{q})\| \leq \|\boldsymbol{\eta}_q\| + \|Y(\cdot)\tilde{\boldsymbol{\theta}}\| + \|\boldsymbol{g}(\boldsymbol{q})\|$$
$$\leq \mu_0 + b_5 + \mu_1\|\boldsymbol{s}\| + \mu_2\|\boldsymbol{s}\|^2$$

Also, let $\boldsymbol{a}_0 \triangleq (\mu_0 + b_5)\boldsymbol{e}_6$, where $\boldsymbol{e}_6 \in \mathrm{I\!R}^6$ is a vector of ones, such that $\|\boldsymbol{a}_0\| = (\mu_0 + b_5) > 0$.

Then, by substituting these bounds in expression (19), it yields a majored version as

$$\dot{V}(\boldsymbol{s}) \leq -\lambda_{DK}\|\boldsymbol{s}\|^2 - \beta\|\boldsymbol{s}\|^4 + \mu_2\|\boldsymbol{s}\|^3 + \mu_1\|\boldsymbol{s}\|^2 \qquad , \qquad (20)$$

where λ_{DK} is the maximum eigenvalue of matrix $[\hat{D}(\cdot) + K_s]$.

For $\dot{V} \leq 0$, we have two cases to analyze. For the first case, when $\|\boldsymbol{s}\| \geq 1$, the two conditions that must be satisfied are $\lambda_{DK} > \mu_1$ and $\beta > \mu_2$. For the case when $\|\boldsymbol{s}\| < 1$, there is only one necessary condition to satisfy, being $\lambda_{DK} > \mu_1 + \mu_2$. Then, under the global conditions

$$\lambda_{DK} > \mu_1 + \mu_2,$$
$$\beta > \mu_2.$$

The time derivative of (18) is $\dot{V}(\boldsymbol{s}) < 0$ negative definite, which in turn implies that

$$\lim_{t\to\infty} \|\boldsymbol{s}\| \to \boldsymbol{0}, \qquad (21)$$

and, a direct consequence of this is that

$$\lim_{t\to\infty} \|\tilde{\boldsymbol{q}}\| \to \boldsymbol{0}. \qquad (22)$$

Therefore, the stability for the system is proved.

4   Simulation Results of Applying the Model-Free Robust Control

The system simulation was performed using the NEROV vehicle dynamic model, the parameters can be found in [17]. The implementation of this model in

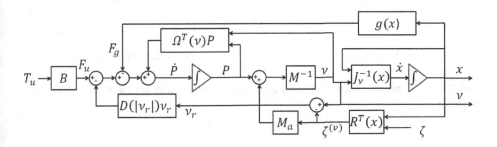

Fig. 1. Block diagram for underwater vehicle dynamic implementation

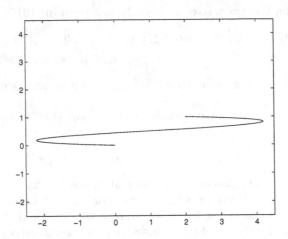

Fig. 2. Path followed by the robot on the X-Y plane

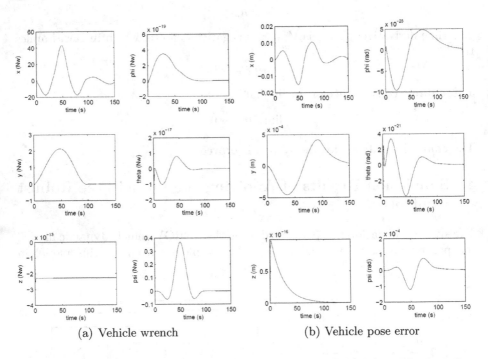

(a) Vehicle wrench   (b) Vehicle pose error

Fig. 3. forces and moments (left) and error curves for vehicle position and orientation (right)

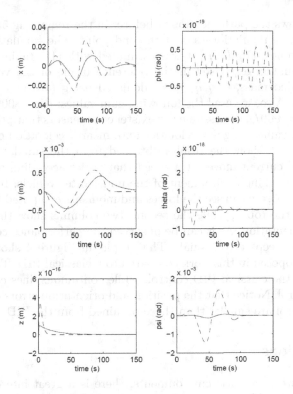

Fig. 4. Comparative graph of the performance of a classical PID control (dotted line) vs. the proposed robust control (solid line)

Simulink was performed based on an antisymmetric representation, and we get the dynamic model as

$$\dot{P} - \Omega^T(\nu)P + D(\cdot)\nu_r + g(q) = F_u, \tag{23}$$

where $P = \frac{\partial K}{\partial \nu} = M\nu - M_a \mathcal{R}^T \varsigma$, $\Omega(\nu)$ as was defined in (4), and input wrench $F_u = BT_u$ is made by the projection of the Thrusters vector via a Input matrix B. The importance of using this representation to implement the simulator is that it is easier to implement the perturbations in the environment and reduces the number of operations. Figure 3 shows a block diagram implementation of the dynamics of the AUV using this representation. It is important to mention that using this representation of the dynamics of the AUV, the required calculations to obtain the Coriolis matrix are reduced considerably, and thus significantly optimizes the performance of the simulator.

The evidence of sub-optimal robust control performance in the simulator described above was made in an environment where there is a fluid moving in x direction of the vehicle with a sinusoidal behavior. The task for the underwater vehicle consists of moving on the plane $x - y$ along the path shown in Figure 2. The simulation runs during 150 seconds, of which the first 100 seconds the vehicle follows the path mentioned before. In the remaining 50 seconds, the control performs a regulation task at the end point. The simulation tests used the following values. For $\hat{H}(q)$, it was estimated with (12) taking the diagonal of the inertia matrix expressed in the reference frame of the vehicle, not including the added mass, $\hat{C}(q, \dot{q})$ was calculated using (13) and $\hat{D}(q)$ was the identity matrix. Also, we used the following gain values: $\beta = 180000$, $\Lambda = 2.5I_6$, $K_i = 40I_6$, $K_s = 900I_6$. We assume the existence of sensors that provide position and orientation values, angular velocities and linear acceleration of the vehicle.

Figures 3 and 4 show the results obtained from the simulation of control when the added current moves at a speed that varies according to a sinusoidal function in the working environment of the underwater vehicle. In the first two columns of Figure3, we can see the forces and moments computed by the control and applied to the robot, while the second two columns show the error of the position and orientation. As it can be observed the performance control is quite good because it keeps errors small. The graphs in Figure 4 show the control performance proposed in this work compared to a classical PID. The dotted line corresponds to the classical PID control, while continuous lines corresponds to the robust control. Notice that the position and orientation errors obtained with the robust control are smaller than those obtained from the PID.

5   Conclusions

Given the nature of aquatic environments, there is a great interest on having reliable AUV's. In this paper, we have presented a simple control scheme for underwater vehicles. The control scheme is robust against uncertainties in the parameters of the dynamic model and to disturbances present in the environment. The scheme includes the stability analysis. In order to evaluate the performance of the control, some simulation tests were carried on using the NEROV vehicle. The obtained results have shown good performance in the task of position regulation, and compared to the classic PID control our robust control is better. Future work consists of applying this control scheme on an experimental platform for physical verification.

Acknowledgments. The authors thank the financial support of CONACYT, Mexico.

References

1. Healey, A.J., Lienard, D.: Multivariable sliding mode control for autonomous diving and steering of unmanned underwater vehicles. IEEE Journal of Oceanic Engineering 18(3), 327–339 (1993)
2. Raygosa-Barahona, R., Parra-Vega, V., Olguín-Díaz, E., Muñoz Ubando, L.: A model-free backstepping with integral sliding mode control for underactuated ROVs. In: 8th International Conference on Electrical Engineering Computing Science and Automatic Control (CCE), pp. 1–7 (October 2011)

3. Tang, Z., Zhou, J., Bian, X., Jia, H.: Simulation of optimal integral sliding mode controller for the depth control of auv. In: Proceedings of IEEE International Conference on Information and Automation, pp. 2379–2383 (June 2010)
4. Hassanein, O., Anavatti, S.G., Ray, T.: Fuzzy modeling and control for autonomous underwater vehicle. In: 5th International Conference on Automation, Robotics and Applications, pp. 169–174 (December 2011)
5. Teo, K., An, E., Beaujean, P.-P.J.: A robust fuzzy autonomous underwater vehicle (auv) docking approach for unknown current disturbances. IEEE Journal of Oceanic Engineering, 143–155 (April 2012)
6. Fossen, T., Sagatun, S.: Adaptive control of nonlinear underwater robotic systems. In: IEEE International Conference on Robotics and Autanatim, vol. 1, pp. 1687–1995 (April 1991)
7. Park, J., Chung, W., Yuh, J.: Nonlinear $\mathcal{H}\infty$ optimal PID control of autonomous underwater vehicles. In: Proceedings of the 2000 International Symposium on Underwater Technology, UT 2000, pp. 193–198 (2000)
8. Perrier, M., de Wit, C.C.: Experimental comparison of PID vs. PID plus nonlinear controller for subsea robots. Autonomous Robots 3, 195–212 (1996)
9. Fossen, T.I.: Guidance and Control of Ocean Vehicles. John Wiley and Sons Ltd. (1994)
10. Olguín-Díaz, E., Parra-Vega, V.: On the force/posture control of a constrained submarine robot. In: 4th International Conference on Informatics in Control, Robotics and Automation (May 2007)
11. Sagatun, S.I., Fossen, T.I.: Lagrangian formulation of underwater vehicles' dynamics. In: IEEE Intl. Conf. on Systems, Man, and Cybernetics, vol. 2, pp. 1029–1034 (October 1991)
12. de Wit, C.C., Williamson, D., Bachmayer, R.: Performance-oriented robust control for a class of mechanical systems: a study case. In: Proc. of Intl. Conf. on Systems, Man and Cybernetics, vol. 4, pp. 51–56 (October 1993)
13. Williamson, D., de Wit, C.C.: Performance oriented robust control for a class of nonlinear systems. In: Proceeding of the European Control Conference (1995)
14. Kelly, R., Ortega, R.: Adaptive control of robot manipulators: an input-output approach. In: Proceedings of the 1988 IEEE International Conference on Robotics and Automation, vol. 2, pp. 699–703 (April 1988)
15. Slotine, J.-J.E., Weiping, L.: Adaptive manipulator control: A case study. IEEE Transactions on Automatic Control 33(11), 995–1003 (1988)
16. Messner, W., Horowitz, R., Kao, W.-W., Boals, M.: A new adaptive learning rule. IEEE Transactions on Automatic Control 36(2), 188–197 (1991)
17. Fossen, T.I., Balchen, J.G.: The nerov autonomous underwater vehicle. In: Proceedings of the Ocean Technologies and Opportunities in the Pacific for the 90's', OCEANS 1991, pp. 1414–1420 (October 1991)

Sliding-Mode Observer Based Flux Estimation
of Induction Motors

Yong Feng[1,2], Minghao Zhou[1], and Xinghuo Yu[2]

[1] Department of Electrical Engineering, Harbin Institute of Technology, China
yfeng@hit.edu.cn, zhouminghaopeter@yahoo.com.cn
[2] School of Electrical and Computer Engineering, RMIT University,
Melbourne, VIC3001, Australia
{yong.feng,x.yu}@rmit.edu.au

Abstract. This paper proposes a sliding-mode observer based rotor flux estimation scheme for induction motors. The sliding-mode observer is designed to track the stator currents and the control signals of the observer are used to estimate the rotor flux. The proposed rotor flux estimation scheme utilizes the stator currents, but does not need the stator voltage. It has significant advantages in practical applications, especially for sensorless Field Oriented Control (FOC) of induction motors. Some simulations are carried out to validate the proposed rotor flux estimation scheme.

Keywords: Observer, induction motors, sliding-mode, parameter estimation.

1 Introduction

FOC has emerged as an important approach to the control of induction motors (IMs). It is a torque-flux decoupling technique applied to IM control and can realize high-performance IM control [0]. It is well known that IMs have been extensively used in various applications due to its simply construction, lower repair and maintenance costs, high reliability and relatively low manufacturing cost [1]. With the development of power electronics, control theory and electrical technique, IMs have been used in high-performance servo systems.

There are mainly three methods for the control of IMs: the scalar control, the direct torque control (DTC) and FOC. The latter two methods can be utilized to implement the high-performance IM servo systems. In DTC based IM servo systems the stator flux and the torque are regulated respectively using the bang-bang control strategies. This control method may lead to the torque ripple. If the motor runs at low speed, the performance of the motor will become poorer, and the range of the speed regulation of the motor will be limited. While in FOC-based IM servo systems, the stator flux and the torque of the motor are continuously controlled. Based on field orientation, that is Clarke-Park transformation, three-phase currents of an IM in a three-dimensional stationary reference frame (a-b-c) can be converted to two currents a two-dimensional rotating reference frame (d-q). The d-axis current represents the

C.-Y. Su, S. Rakheja, H. Liu (Eds.): ICIRA 2012, Part II, LNAI 7507, pp. 530–539, 2012.
© Springer-Verlag Berlin Heidelberg 2012

rotor flux and the q-axis current represents the torque. The decoupled rotor flux and the torque of the IMs can be separately controlled like as DC motors. Consequently it is possible to achieve good static and dynamic performance of IMs [3,4]. However, the accurate information on both the magnitude and the position of the rotor flux are needed by FOC for the transformation between the rotating and the stationary reference frames. The information on the rotor flux can be obtained using the direct measurements or the indirect estimation. But special sensors are needed in direct measurements, which is difficult for practical applications. Now indirect estimation methods are widely used to obtain the rotor flux [5]. These methods use the stator current, stator voltage and the motor speed to estimate the magnitude and the position of the rotor flux. A lot of flux estimation methods have been proposed, such as Luenberger observer based methods [6],[7], model reference methods[8],[9], Karlman filter based methods [10],[11], and neural networks [12].

Since the most important requirement of the flux estimation of IMs is the practical feasibility of implementation, it should be given priority to the robustness of the methods. Sliding-mode control method has outstanding advantages of low sensitivity to the system parameter variations [13],[14] and strong robustness to disturbances. Sliding-mode observer can be applied to the estimation of the rotor flux of IMs with the equivalent control signal [15].

This paper proposes a sliding-mode observer based rotor flux estimation scheme for IMs. It can be used in FOC of IMs for achieving high-performance of IM systems. A sliding-mode observer to the stator currents is designed. Its control signals are used to estimate the rotor flux. Some simulations are carried out to validate the proposed rotor flux estimation scheme.

2   Dynamic Model of Induction Motors

The mathematical model of an IM system in the two axis stationary frame reference frame (α-β) can be described as follows [11]:

$$
\begin{cases}
\dfrac{di_{\alpha s}}{dt} = K(u_{\alpha s} - R_s i_{\alpha s}) + K(\eta \phi_{\alpha s} + \omega_r \phi_{\beta s}) - \dfrac{\eta}{\sigma} i_{\alpha s} - \omega_r i_{\beta s} \\[2mm]
\dfrac{di_{\beta s}}{dt} = K(u_{\beta s} - R_s i_{\beta s}) + K(-\omega_r \phi_{\alpha s} + \eta \phi_{\beta s}) + \omega_r i_{\alpha s} - \dfrac{\eta}{\sigma} i_{\beta s} \\[2mm]
\dfrac{d\phi_{\alpha s}}{dt} = u_{\alpha s} - R_s i_{\alpha s} \\[2mm]
\dfrac{d\phi_{\beta s}}{dt} = u_{\beta s} - R_s i_{\beta s}
\end{cases}
\tag{1}
$$

where $\sigma = 1 - L_m^2 /(L_s L_r)$, $K = 1/(\sigma L_s)$, $\eta = 1/T_r = R_r/L_r$. $u_{\alpha s}$ and $u_{\beta s}$ are the stator voltages in α-β axes, $i_{\alpha s}$ and $i_{\beta s}$ the stator currents in α-β axes, $\phi_{\alpha s}$ and $\phi_{\beta s}$ the stator fluxes in α-β

axis respectively, ω_r the electric angle velocity of the rotor, R_s the stator resistor, L_r, L_s, and L_m the rotor inductance, the stator inductance, and the mutual inductance between the stator and the rotor, T_r the time constant of the rotor.

In the dynamic model of an IM system (1), only the stator fluxes, $\phi_{\alpha s}$ and $\phi_{\beta s}$ are involved. But FOC of an IM needs the rotor fluxes, therefore the relationship between the rotor fluxes and the stator fluxes should be built as follows [12]:

$$\begin{cases} \phi_{\alpha r} = \dfrac{L_r}{L_m}(\phi_{\alpha s} - \sigma L_s i_{\alpha s}) \\ \phi_{\beta r} = \dfrac{L_r}{L_m}(\phi_{\beta s} - \sigma L_s i_{\beta s}) \end{cases} \tag{2}$$

where $\phi_{\alpha r}$ and $\phi_{\beta r}$ are the rotor fluxes in α-β axis.

The model of an IM system can be rewritten as the following form from (1):

$$\begin{cases} \dfrac{di_{\alpha s}}{dt} = K(\dot{\phi}_{\alpha s} + \eta \phi_{\alpha s} + \omega_r \phi_{\beta s}) - \dfrac{\eta}{\sigma} i_{\alpha s} - \omega_r i_{\beta s} \\ \dfrac{di_{\beta s}}{dt} = K(\dot{\phi}_{\beta s} - \omega_r \phi_{\alpha s} + \eta \phi_{\beta s}) + \omega_r i_{\alpha s} - \dfrac{\eta}{\sigma} i_{\beta s} \end{cases} \tag{3}$$

The purpose of the paper is to estimate the rotor fluxes $\phi_{\alpha r}$ and $\phi_{\beta r}$ using the measurements of the stator currents, $i_{\alpha s}$ and $i_{\beta s}$.

3   Flux Observer of Induction Motors

A typical block diagram of the sliding-mode observer based vector control system of an IM is shown in Fig.1. The rotor speed is asymptotically decoupled from the rotor flux and depends linearly on the torque current [2]. The observer is used to estimate the rotor flux. Its inputs are the stator currents of the motor.

3.1   Estimation of the Stator Flux

For the dynamic model of an IM system (3), a sliding-mode observer can be designed as follows:

$$\begin{cases} \dot{\hat{i}}_{\alpha s} = K v_{\alpha s} - \dfrac{\eta}{\sigma} \hat{i}_{\alpha s} - \omega_r \hat{i}_{\beta s} \\ \dot{\hat{i}}_{\beta s} = K v_{\beta s} + \omega_r \hat{i}_{\alpha s} - \dfrac{\eta}{\sigma} \hat{i}_{\beta s} \end{cases} \tag{4}$$

where $\hat{i}_{\alpha s}$ and $\hat{i}_{\beta s}$ are the estimates of the stator currents $i_{\alpha s}$ and $i_{\beta s}$, $\hat{\phi}_{\alpha s}$ and $\hat{\phi}_{\beta s}$ the estimates of the stator fluxes $\phi_{\alpha s}$ and $\phi_{\beta s}$, $v_{\alpha s}$ and $v_{\beta s}$ the control signals of the observer.

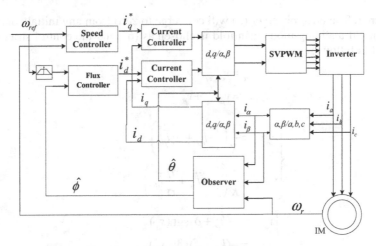

Fig. 1. IM vector control system

From the model of an IM system (3) and its sliding-mode observer for the stator currents (4), the error observer equations, describing the estimation errors between the stator currents and their estimations can be obtained:

$$\begin{cases} \dot{\bar{i}}_{\alpha s} = K v_{\alpha s} - K(\dot{\bar{\phi}}_{\alpha s} + \eta \bar{\phi}_{\alpha s} + \omega_r \bar{\phi}_{\beta s}) - \dfrac{\eta}{\sigma} \bar{i}_{\alpha s} - \omega_r \bar{i}_{\beta s} \\ \dot{\bar{i}}_{\beta s} = K v_{\beta s} - K(\dot{\bar{\phi}}_{\beta s} - \omega_r \bar{\phi}_{\alpha s} + \eta \bar{\phi}_{\beta s}) + \omega_r \bar{i}_{\alpha s} - \dfrac{\eta}{\sigma} \bar{i}_{\beta s} \end{cases} \tag{5}$$

where $\bar{i}_{\alpha s} = \hat{i}_{\alpha s} - i_{\alpha s}$ and $\bar{i}_{\beta s} = \hat{i}_{\beta s} - i_{\beta s}$ are the estimation errors of the currents in α-β axis, $\bar{\phi}_{\alpha s} = \hat{\phi}_{\alpha s} - \phi_{\alpha s}$ and $\bar{\phi}_{\beta s} = \hat{\phi}_{\beta s} - \phi_{\beta s}$ the estimation errors of the stator fluxes in α-β axis.

A sliding-mode surface for the error observer (5) is designed as follows:

$$s = \begin{bmatrix} s_\alpha \\ s_\beta \end{bmatrix}. \tag{6}$$

where $s_{\alpha s}$ and $s_{\beta s}$ are defined as follows:

$$\begin{cases} s_\alpha = \bar{i}_{\alpha s} \\ s_\beta = \bar{i}_{\beta s} \end{cases}. \tag{7}$$

For designing the control strategies of the observer, it is assumed that the following assumption holds:

$$\begin{cases} \dot{\bar{\phi}}_{\alpha s} + \eta \bar{\phi}_{\alpha s} + \omega_r \bar{\phi}_{\beta s} < k_\alpha \\ \dot{\bar{\phi}}_{\beta s} - \omega_r \bar{\phi}_{\alpha s} + \eta \bar{\phi}_{\beta s} < k_\beta \end{cases}. \tag{8}$$

where k_α and k_β are positive constants.

Theorem 1. The error observer (5) will converge to zero from any initial condition in finite time, if a sliding-mode manifold is chosen as (6), and the control strategies are designed as follows:

$$\begin{cases} v_\alpha = v_{as\_eq} + v_{as\_n} \\ v_\beta = v_{\beta s\_eq} + v_{\beta s\_n} \end{cases}. \tag{9}$$

$$\begin{cases} v_{as\_eq} = \dfrac{1}{K}\left(\dfrac{\eta}{\sigma}\bar{i}_{as} + \omega_r \bar{i}_{\beta s}\right) \\ v_{\beta s\_eq} = \dfrac{1}{K}\left(-\omega_r \bar{i}_{as} + \dfrac{\eta}{\sigma}\bar{i}_{\beta s}\right) \end{cases}. \tag{10}$$

$$\begin{cases} v_{as\_n} = -(k_\alpha + \delta)\operatorname{sgn}(s_\alpha) \\ v_{\beta s\_n} = -(k_\beta + \delta)\operatorname{sgn}(s_\beta) \end{cases}. \tag{11}$$

where k_α and k_β are defined as (8), $\delta > 0$ is a positive constant.

Proof: The following Lyapunov function is considered:

$$V = \frac{1}{2}s^T s$$

Differentiating V with respect to time t gives:

$$\dot{V} = s^T \dot{s}$$

$$= s_\alpha \dot{s}_\alpha + s_\beta \dot{s}_\beta$$

$$= s_\alpha \dot{\bar{i}}_{as} + s_\beta \dot{\bar{i}}_{\beta s}$$

$$= s_\alpha \left(K v_{as} - K(\dot{\phi}_{as} + \eta\phi_{as} + \omega_r\phi_{\beta s}) - \frac{\eta}{\sigma}\bar{i}_{as} - \omega_r\bar{i}_{\beta s}\right)$$

$$+ s_\beta \left(K v_{\beta s} - K(\dot{\phi}_{\beta s} - \omega_r\phi_{as} + \eta\phi_{\beta s}) + \omega_r\bar{i}_{as} - \frac{\eta}{\sigma}\bar{i}_{\beta s}\right)$$

$$= s_\alpha K \left(v_{as\_n} - (\dot{\phi}_{as} + \eta\phi_{as} + \omega_r\phi_{\beta s})\right) + s_\beta K \left(v_{\beta s\_n} - (\dot{\phi}_{\beta s} - \omega_r\phi_{as} + \eta\phi_{\beta s})\right)$$

$$= s_\alpha K \left(-(k_\alpha + \delta)\operatorname{sgn}(s_\alpha) - (\dot{\phi}_{as} + \eta\phi_{as} + \omega_r\phi_{\beta s})\right)$$

$$+ s_\beta K \left(-(k_\beta + \delta)\operatorname{sgn}(s_\beta) - (\dot{\phi}_{\beta s} - \omega_r\phi_{as} + \eta\phi_{\beta s})\right)$$

$$= -K \left((k_\alpha + \delta)|s_\alpha| + (\dot{\phi}_{as} + \eta\phi_{as} + \omega_r\phi_{\beta s})s_\alpha\right)$$

$$-K \left((k_\beta + \delta)|s_\beta| + (\dot{\phi}_{\beta s} - \omega_r\phi_{as} + \eta\phi_{\beta s})s_\beta\right)$$

$$\leq -K\delta|s_\alpha| - K\delta|s_\beta|$$

$$= -K\delta\|s\|$$

that is

$$\dot{V} \le -K\delta \|s\| < 0 \quad \text{for} \quad \|s\| \ne 0$$

which means that the error system (5) can reach $s=0$ within finite time. Once on the sliding-mode manifold $s=0$, it can be seen from (6) and (7) that the estimation errors of the currents in α-β axis, $\bar{i}_{\alpha s} = \hat{i}_{\alpha s} - i_{\alpha s}$ and $\bar{i}_{\beta s} = \hat{i}_{\beta s} - i_{\beta s}$, will keep zeros. This completes the proof.

3.2   Estimation of the Rotor Fluxes

Substituting the control (9), (10) into the error observer (11) gives:

$$\begin{cases} \dot{\bar{i}}_{\alpha s} = Kv_{\alpha s\_n} - K(\dot{\hat{\phi}}_{\alpha s} + \eta\hat{\phi}_{\alpha s} + \omega_r\hat{\phi}_{\beta s}) \\ \dot{\bar{i}}_{\beta s} = Kv_{\beta s\_n} - K(\dot{\hat{\phi}}_{\beta s} - \omega_r\hat{\phi}_{\alpha s} + \eta\hat{\phi}_{\beta s}) \end{cases} \tag{12}$$

When the ideal sliding-mode $s=0$ occurs, the error observer (5) will stay on zero, that is the estimation errors of the currents in α-β axis and their derivatives will satisfy $\bar{i} = 0$, $\dot{\bar{i}} = 0$. Hence (12) can be expressed as the following form:

$$\begin{cases} v_{\alpha s\_n} = \dot{\hat{\phi}}_{\alpha s} + \eta\hat{\phi}_{\alpha s} + \omega_r\hat{\phi}_{\beta s} \\ v_{\beta s\_n} = \dot{\hat{\phi}}_{\beta s} - \omega_r\hat{\phi}_{\alpha s} + \eta\hat{\phi}_{\beta s} \end{cases} \tag{13}$$

or

$$\begin{bmatrix} \dot{\hat{\phi}}_{\alpha s} \\ \dot{\hat{\phi}}_{\beta s} \end{bmatrix} = \begin{bmatrix} -\eta & -\omega_r \\ \omega_r & -\eta \end{bmatrix} \begin{bmatrix} \hat{\phi}_{\alpha s} \\ \hat{\phi}_{\beta s} \end{bmatrix} + \begin{bmatrix} 1 & 0 \\ 0 & 1 \end{bmatrix} \begin{bmatrix} v_{\alpha s\_n} \\ v_{\beta s\_n} \end{bmatrix}. \tag{14}$$

or

$$\begin{bmatrix} \dot{\hat{\phi}}_{\alpha s} \\ \dot{\hat{\phi}}_{\beta s} \end{bmatrix} = A \begin{bmatrix} \hat{\phi}_{\alpha s} \\ \hat{\phi}_{\beta s} \end{bmatrix} + B \begin{bmatrix} v_{\alpha s\_n} \\ v_{\beta s\_n} \end{bmatrix}. \tag{15}$$

where

$$A = \begin{bmatrix} -\eta & -\omega_r \\ \omega_r & -\eta \end{bmatrix}, \quad B = \begin{bmatrix} 1 & 0 \\ 0 & 1 \end{bmatrix}. \tag{16}$$

The solution of (15) can be expressed as follows:

$$\begin{bmatrix} \hat{\phi}_{\alpha s}(t) \\ \hat{\phi}_{\beta s}(t) \end{bmatrix} = e^{At} \begin{bmatrix} \hat{\phi}_{\alpha s}(0) \\ \hat{\phi}_{\beta s}(0) \end{bmatrix} + \int_0^t e^{A(t-\tau)} B v_n(\tau) d\tau . \tag{17}$$

Since the eigenvalues of A in (are $\lambda_{1,2} = -\eta \pm j\omega$, where $\eta > 0$ is defined in (1), the solutions of $\hat{\phi}_{\alpha s}(t)$ and $\hat{\phi}_{\beta s}(t)$ (17) are stable.

After obtaining $\hat{\phi}_{\alpha s}(t)$ and $\hat{\phi}_{\beta s}(t)$, the estimate of the rotor fluxes can be obtained as follows from (2):

$$\begin{cases} \hat{\phi}_{\alpha r} = \dfrac{L_r}{L_m}(\hat{\phi}_{\alpha s} - \sigma L_s \hat{i}_{\alpha s}) \\ \hat{\phi}_{\beta r} = \dfrac{L_r}{L_m}(\hat{\phi}_{\beta s} - \sigma L_s \hat{i}_{\beta s}) \end{cases} . \tag{18}$$

and the estimate of the position of the rotor fluxes can be obtained from (18) as follows:

$$\hat{\theta}_r = \arctan(\dfrac{\hat{\phi}_{\beta r}}{\hat{\phi}_{\alpha r}}) . \tag{19}$$

Finally, the rotor flux estimation of the IMs can be summarizes as follows:

   1) design a sliding-mode observer (4) according to Theorem 1;
   2) calculate the stator fluxes using (17);
   3) calculate the rotor fluxes using (18) and (19).

4   Simulations

Some simulations are carried out to test the proposed rotor flux observer of the IMs. In the simulation, a three phase squirrel-cage IM is considered and its parameters are assumed as follows:

$$P_N = 1.5\text{kW}, \ U_N = 380\text{V}, \ R_r = 3.2\Omega, \ R_s = 6.1\Omega, \ L_r = 0.478\text{H}, \ L_s = 0.478\text{H}, \ L_m = 0.472\text{H}, \\ J = 0.033\text{kg·m}^2.$$

Considering the above parameters, the observer can be designed according to Theorem 1.

The simulation results are shown in Figs. 2-4. The actual and the estimated stator currents of the IM in the α axis are depicted in Fig. 2. The actual and the estimated stator fluxes of the IM in α axis are displayed in Fig. 3. The actual and the estimated rotor fluxes are shown in Fig. 4. The rotor flux estimation error is shown in Fig. 5. From these simulation results, it can be seen that the proposed estimation method can estimate the rotor flux of the IM quickly and actually, which validate the proposed method.

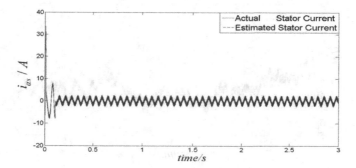

Fig. 2. Actual stator current and its estimation in α axis

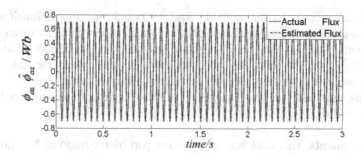

Fig. 3. Actual stator flux and its estimation in α axis

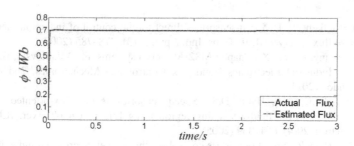

Fig. 4. Actual and estimated fluxes

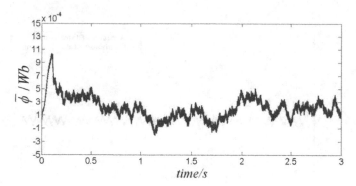

Fig. 5. Flux estimation error

5   Conclusions

This paper has proposed a sliding-mode observer based rotor flux estimation scheme for IMs. An observer is designed based on the sliding-mode technique. It can track the stator currents of an IM. The control signals of the observer can be applied to estimate the rotor flux of the IM. Since the proposed scheme does not need the stator voltage, and need only the stator currents, it has significant advantages in practical applications, especially for sensorless FOC of IMs. Its other application includes the monitoring of IMs.

Acknowledgments. This work was supported in part by the National Natural Science Foundation of China (61074015), and also in part by the Australian Research Council's Linkage Project (LP100200538) and Discovery Project (DP0986376).

References

1. Maes, J., Melkebeek, J.: Speed-sensorless direct torque control of induction motors using an adaptive flux observer. IEEE Trans. Ind. Appl. 36(3), 778–785 (2000)
2. Feng, Y., Wang, L., Yu, X.: Chapter M32 AC servo systems. In: Wilamovski, B.M., Irvin, J.D. (eds.) Industrial Electronics Handbook Control and Mechatronics, 2nd edn. CRC Press, London (2011)
3. Kwon, S., Shin, M.H., Hyun, D.S.: Speed sensorless stator flux-oriented control of induction motor in the field-weakening region using Luenberger observer. IEEE Trans. Power Electron. 20(4), 864–869 (2005)
4. Zhang, Y., Zhao, Z.: Speed sensorless control for three-level inverter-fed induction motors using an Extended Luenberger Observer. In: Proc. IEEE Veh. Power Propul. Conf., Harbin, China (2008)
5. Maes, J., Melkebeek, J.: Sensorless direct torque control of induction motors using an adaptive flux observer. IEEE Trans. Ind. 36(3), 778–785 (2000)

6. Song, J., Lee, K.-B., Song, J.-H., Choy, I., Kim, K.-B.: Sensorless vector control of induction motor using a novel reduced-order extended Luenberger observer. In: Proc. World Congress on Industrial Applications of Electrical Energy and 35th IEEE-IAS Annual Meeting, Rome, Italy, vol. 3, pp. 1828–1834 (2000)
7. Chiacchiarini, H.G., Desages, A.C.: Variable structure control with a second-order sliding condition: application to a steam generator. Automatica 131(8), 1157–1168 (1995)
8. Qi, J., Tian, Y., Gong, Y.: A sensorless initial rotor position estimation scheme and an Extended Kalman Filter observer for the direct torque controlled Permanent Magnet Synchronous Motor Drive. In: Proc. Int. Conf. Electr. Mach. Syst., Wuhan, China, pp. 3945–3950 (2008)
9. Hsin, J.S., Kuo, K.S.: Nonlinear sliding mode torque control with adaptive backstepping approach for induction motor drive. IEEE Trans. Ind. Eletron. 46(2), 380–389 (1999)
10. Lee, K.B., Blaabjerg, F.: Simple power control for sensorless induction motor drives fed by a matrix converter. IEEE Trans. Energy Conversion 23(3), 781–788 (2008)
11. Rehman, H.: Elimination of the stator resistance sensitivity and voltage sensor requirement problems for DFO control of an induction Machine. IEEE Trans. Ind. Electron. 52(1), 263–269 (2005)
12. Mitronikas, E., Safacas, A.: An improved sensorless vector-control method for an induction motor drive. IEEE Trans. Ind. Electron. 52(6), 1660–1668 (2005)
13. Levant, A.: Quasi-continuous high-order sliding-mode controllers. IEEE Trans. Autom. Control 50(11), 1812–1816 (2005)
14. Feng, Y., Yu, X., Man, Z.: Non-singular terminal sliding mode control of rigid manipulators. Automatica 38(12), 2159–2167 (2002)
15. Ohnishi, K., Suzuki, H., Miyachi, K., Terashima, M.: Decoupling control of flux and secondary current in induction motor drive with controlled voltage source and its comparison with volts/hertz control. IEEE Trans. Ind. Appl. 21(1), 241–247 (1985)

A Gasoline Engine Crankshaft Fatigue Analysis and Experiment

Jing Yang, Cheng Sun, Yi Wang, and Banglin Deng

Research Center for Advanced Powertrain Technologies,
Hunan University, Lushan SouthStreet, No.1,
Changsha, Hunan, China 410082
Yangjing10@vip.sina.com

Abstract. Analysis about a certain company's gasoline engine crankshaft system with dynamics of multi-body, analysis about the crank which work conditions are worst with the forcing displacement method for finite element analysis, based on the finite element analysis results and the load history to analysis fatigue and Take the experimental verification. The results show that the results based on the finite element analysis of fatigue analysis and the experimental results were very close, and the analysis method is more simple and high accuracy.

Keywords: Crankshaft system, Multi-body dynamics, Finite element, Fatigue analysis.

1   Introduction

Crankshaft is the main component of the Internal combustion engine, the rigidity and the strength of which has an important influence on the working reliability of internal combustion engine. On the strength and stiffness analysis, using the traditional method can only approximate the stress and deformation status, which cannot satisfy the needs of design and analysis. With the development of computer science and finite element technology rapid development, the last 30 years, the calculation of crankshaft analysis method as well as the accuracy has been greatly improved, the advanced method is multi-body dynamics combined with finite element method [1][2]. This method not only can analyze, predict, evaluate of the stress and strain distribution of these components, but also calculate accurately the dynamic stress of crankshaft.

With internal combustion engine technology developing continually, the design of internal combustion engine develop toward the direction of high efficiency, high reliability, low quality, low fuel consumption and low emissions etc. strengthen indicators continue to improve. As the crankshaft in the course of their work will bear the centrifugal force of rotating mass, the reciprocating inertial force and cyclic loads, make it under bending load. In the work process, and periodic loading acting in the crankshaft when the energizing frequency and the natural frequency of vibration of crankshaft Is multiple relationship, can make vibration increase and dynamic stress increase rapidly, resulting in fatigue failure of crankshaft. So an accurate analysis of the dynamic stress of crankshaft, to check the strength and calculation and analysis of fatigue life is very important. Considering the computational scale and accuracy of the

C.-Y. Su, S. Rakheja, H. Liu (Eds.): ICIRA 2012, Part II, LNAI 7507, pp. 540–550, 2012.
© Springer-Verlag Berlin Heidelberg 2012

results, the finite element method is adopted to establish the system of internal combustion engine crankshaft finite element model and multi body dynamics model. based on the actual conditions the purpose of this paper is calculating and analyzing the crankshaft, comprehensively analyzing of the factors which influences on the crankshaft strength and fatigue life ,comparing and analyzing the calculation results and the experimental results.

2   Finite Element Model

2.1   CAD Model Local Treatment

Before the crankshaft dynamics of multi-body calculation, mesh crankshaft parts. The crankshaft system parts including the crankshaft, flywheel, shock pulley, sprocket wheel, mesh each parts to connect parts of the grid node superposition. In order to improve the quality of the grid, make the crankshaft low stress area in the small chamfering and little round to be simplified. On the premise of the calculation precision, simplify the complex characteristics. For example, some parts of the gear tooth type to the calculation results without the influence, but the grid quality is very poor, so can consider to remove. Finally a 3 D model shown in figure 2.1.

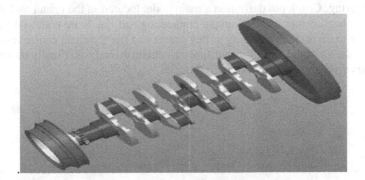

Fig. 1. Crankshaft parts assembly 3 D model after local treatment

2.2   Meshing Finite Element Grid and Model Reduction

The analysis for the concern of the crankshaft, some of the key details of crankshaft parts with hexahedron grid or two order tetrahedron grid, Tessellated tiny structures such as round place, to ensure accurate calculation results. The main journal and crank pin using hexahedral grid, refining filleted corner grid ,guarantee the accuracy of the calculation, as shown in figure 2.2.

Crank arm, flywheel and shock absorption pulley is not the major concern area ,use tetrahedron grid to accelerate the calculate speed. Whole 134952 nodes, 260018 elements.

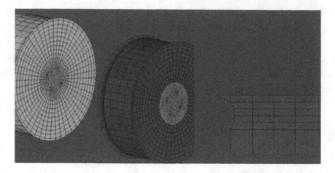

Fig. 2. The crankshaft shaft neck grid and filleted corner refining treatment

The model nodes and elements number too big, will make the computer can't operation or greatly increase the operation time if simulation directly. So it is necessary to reduce the crankshaft finite element model. Usually the model reduction can be used to characterize the dynamic characteristics of the original huge system which have smaller mass matrix and stiffness matrix in the finite element simulation[3][4][5. In this paper, the main freedom nodes of crankshaft are defined , in each one main journal, definition of uniform five main freedom nodes, each nodes with six freedom and corresponding the main journal five section and coupling with uniform distribution five rows on bearing. Crank pin definition a main node, located in the center and alignment with the big head center node of simple connecting rod, facilitate node right coupling. Definition a main node in damping pulley center and the flywheel center respectively, applied for the torsional vibration and speed fluctuation analysis. Finally the crankshaft RBE2 units distribution as shown in figure2.3.

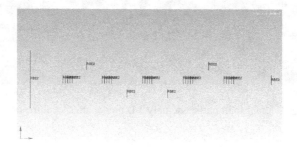

Fig. 3. The crankshaft RBE2 distribution

3   The Crankshaft Fatigue Strength Analysis

3.1   CAE Simulation

Apply AVL Excite software calculate 1000rpm-6500rpm range condition get all the conditions of the load of different the main bearing, figure 3.1-figure 3.5 shows the horizontal load and vertical load of the 1-5 main bearing in different rotating speed.

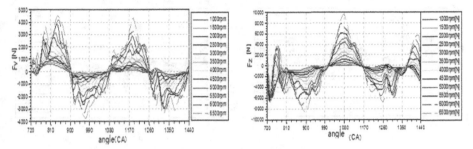

Fig. 4. The first main bearing load

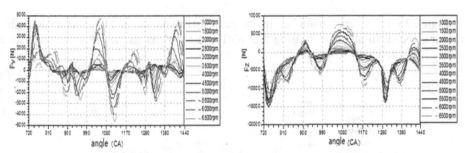

Fig. 5. The second main bearing load

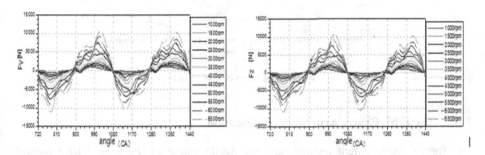

Fig. 6. The third main bearing load

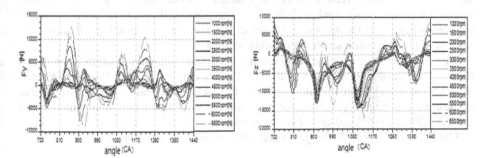

Fig. 7. The fourth main bearing load

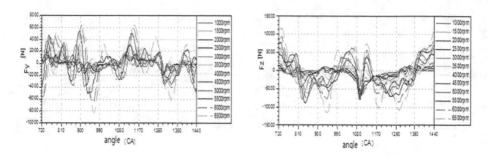

Fig. 8. The fifth main bearing load

Figure 3.6 shows each main bearing biggest instantaneous load in every crankshaft rotating speed. In all main bearing the third and fourth is the worst situation when crankshaft rotating in 6500rpm.

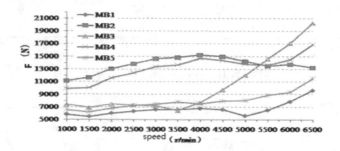

Fig. 9. The main bearing load

3.2   The Fifth Crank Arm Stress Calculation

Use forced displacement method, and the displacement of the three RBE2 control nodes of the main journal and the one RBE2 control node of the crank pin which adjacent of the fifth crank arm as the boundary conditions of the finite element analysis(step size is 10°crankshaft corner). The ABAQUS 6.10 was used for stress computation, can get its stress distribution of the every step length. Fig 3.7 shows the contour of the maximum stress distribution moment.

From the stress contour, we can learn the maximum stress area is located in below about 30° range of filleted corner of the crank pin and above about 30°range of filleted corner of the main journal. In a dangerous section, reflect the features of the structure of crank arm. The filleted corner of the main journal is 165MPa maximum stress about and 170MPa in the filleted corner of the crank pin.

The stress process of the biggest stress node should be as shown in figure 3.8.

Fig. 10. Maximum stress distribution contour

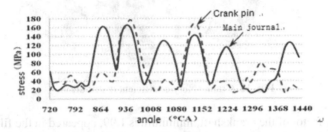

Fig. 11. The stress progress of the biggest stress nodes of the main journal and crank pin

3.3   Fatigue Analysis

Linear fatigue damage accumulation criteria: in mixed loads of different stress amplitude, the cycle load for the structural damage for :

$$\sum = \frac{n_1}{N_{f1}} + \frac{n_2}{N_{f2}} + \frac{n_3}{N_{f3}} + \cdots \tag{1}$$

Mathematical expression explanation :

$$n_1 — \Delta S_1 \text{ Load times };$$

$$n_2 — \Delta S_2 \text{ Load times };$$

$$n_3 — \Delta S_3 \text{ Load times };$$

$$N_{f1} \text{ —Life under the action of } \Delta S_1 ;$$

$$N_{f2} \text{ —Life under the action of } \Delta S_2 ;$$

$$N_{f3} \text{ —Life under the action of } \Delta S_3 。$$

For changing load according to count (rain flow count method) results, accumulated the damage of each circulation , and accumulated life.

According to the calculation of the stress distribution of the fifth crank and, using variable load linear damage cumulative principle on fatigue life calculation, fatigue calculation of used software for FEMFAT.

The calculation results of the safety factor distribution as shown in figure3.9.

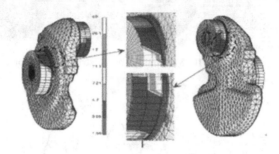

Fig. 12. Crank safety coefficient distribution

The safety factor of the crankshaft, minimum is 1.99, appeared in the filleted corner of the main journal (the main journal should be the biggest nodes). From the front stress calculation results distribution , crank pin filleted corner peak stress higher than the main journal, and the main journal safety factor is slightly less than the crank pins, this is mainly because the stress process, crank pin filleted corner peak stress times in a cycle lower than the main journal(figure3.13). Resulted in the same cycle times its cumulative damage higher than crank pin. According to experience data we think safety factor is safe when greater than 1.6, so this design is qualified.

4   Crankshaft Test

4.1   Crankshaft Fatigue Test

The general crankshaft fatigue testing machine is the excitation method loading manner. The loading method can exert a torsional load, bending load or composite loads. From the actual damage mode, most of the destruction form is bending failure.Therefore it is need to do bending fatigue test only ,for saving cost and time.This test is based on the QC/T 637-2000·Automotive engine crankshaft bending fatigue test》 .

(1)Test equipment

This test adopts DCW-400 Resonant Crankshaft Fatigue Testing Machine, as shown in Figure 4.1.   Issued by the function generator designated amplitude and frequency sine wave, drive power amplifier make vibrator which produce waveform, mechanical resonant system generates a vibration, adjust the function generator frequency to a resonance frequencies of the system, into the normal working condition.

According to the resonant frequency declines to judge the destruction of the crankshaft [6].The test according to the literature [7], as shown in the test and evaluation methods.

Fig. 13. DCW-400 Resonant Crankshaft Fatigue Testing Machine

(2) Test specification

 a) The test is used for the plane symmetric bending load and circulation base takes 1×10^7 times;

 b) The lifting of the crankshaft method determines the value of fatigue limit and the safety coefficient. Evaluate the crankshaft fatigue performance.

(3) Prepare sample•crankshaft qualified through testing and magnetic particle inspection, paying particular attention to the quality of fillet. Crankshaft input parameters, Such as table 4.1 shows:

Table 1. Crankshaft fatigue test parameter table

Parameter Name	Symbols	Unit	Value
Maximum breakout pressure	Pzmax	MPa	7.5
Cylinder diameter	D	mm	68.8
Main journal diameter	D	mm	48
Diameter of the connecting rod neck	D	mm	38
Distance from crank arm center to the main journal center	G	mm	18.88
Distance from the center of the connecting to the main journal center	L_1	mm	40.3
The main journal center distance between two	L	mm	75.4
Supporting constraint coefficients	K		0.75

(4) Name the determination of bending moment

$$M_{-1} = \pi D^2 L_1 KGP / 4L \qquad (2)$$

In formula : G—Distance from crank arm center to the main journal center, m;

  L_1—Distance from the center of the connecting to the main journal center, m;

  L—The main journal center distance between two, m;

D—Cylinder diameter, m;

K—Supporting constraint coefficients. Full support takes 0.75;

P—Maximum breakout pressure, MPa.

Take the table 4.1 related parameters generation into the formula (2), Calculated:

$$M_{-1} = 250.3 \text{N} \cdot \text{m}$$

(5) Results of fatigue test

Loading in different test under bending moment of crankshaft gets the fatigue life of the crankshaft. Test results such as 4.2 indicates:

Table 2. Data of fatigue test results

Serial number	Sample No.	Test moment N.m	Number of cycles	The results	Remarks
1	1-3	450	1×10^7	Beyond	
2	1-3	700	4.1×10^4	damage	Crank pin transition in the round
3	1-1	650	8.3×10^5	damage	Crank pin transition in the round
4	4-2	600	1.25×10^6	damage	Crank pin transition in the round
5	2-2	550	1×10^7	Beyond	
6	2-2	500	1×10^7	Beyond	
7	2-4	550	6.2×10^6	damage	Crank pin transition in the round
8	3-4	500	1×10^7	Beyond	

(6) Median fatigue limit and the safety factor

According to Table 4.2, the experimental data is shown in scatter plots 4.2:

Take the effective data scatter plot chart can be made of the crankshaft median fatigue limit and safety coefficient.

$$M_{u-1} = (\sum_{i}^{n} (Si + Si + 1)/ 2)/n \qquad (3)$$

$$= (450 + 500 \times 2 + 550 \times 2 + 600)/6 = 525 \text{N} \cdot \text{m}$$

$$n = M_{u-1} / M_{-1} = 525 / 250.3 = 2.097$$

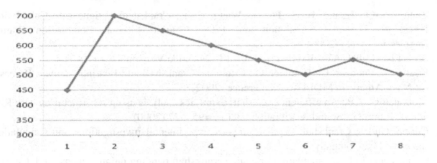

Fig. 14. Test data scatter plot chart

From that 50% lives in conditions, the safety factor of the crankshaft is for 2.097. Slightly higher than CAE calculation results, because of in the process of test without considering the surface heat treatment of the crankshaft shaft neck to the influence of the material. Position of the first part of the fatigue test of destruction and calculation of CAE minimum safety factor is not consistent, it shows that factors of the influence to fatigue are many,including the accuracy of the load on, and other factors [8]. In the test pressure due to load with only torque and no reverse bend , and did not take into account the crankshaft shaft neck surface treatment of the effects on the fatigue, this is causing a CAE analysis results and experimental results with the main factors of minor differences.

Conclusion

[1] This fatigue analysis method via calculate the crank arm which working in the worst conditions to characterize the whole crankshaft fatigue strength. In the calculation process, replace dynamic stress recovery steps after multi-body dynamics calculation to extract the displacement of the control nodes. Use forced displacement method for calculation of the crank cyclic stress process. Can reflect the torsional vibration, speed fluctuation on the effect of stress , shortened the calculation time and high precision.

[2] According to the consistency of fatigue test results and the calculation results verify the feasibility of this method in engineering.

[3] The crankshaft vibration fatigue test method and the way the actual load are inconsistency, and fatigue analysis of crankshaft without considering the neck of surface treatment will lead to the calculated results and test result differences. But do not affect the credibility of the calculation

References

1. Guo, L., Hao, Z.-Y., Liu, B., Yu, B.: Multi-body dynamics and finite element method co-simulation for crankshaft dynamical strength analysis. Journal of Zhejiang University (Engineering Science) 43(9) (2009)

2. Zhang, G.-Q., Huang, B.-C., Pu, G., Wang, C.-T.: Crankshaft Fatigue Life Calculation Based on Dynamic Simulation and FEA. Chinese Internal Combustion Engine Engineering 27(1) (2006)
3. AVL List GmbH. AVL Excite Power Unit User Guide Version 7.0.1 (2007)
4. Piraner, I., Pnueger, C., Bouthier, O.: Cummins Crankshaft and Bearing Analysis Process. In: Nonh American MDI User Conference (2002)
5. Mourelators, Z.P.: An efficient crankshaft dynamics analysis using substructuring with Ritz vetors. Journal of Sound & Vibration 238(3), 495–527 (2000)
6. Cuppo, Gudio, Crankshaft bending stresses experimental investigations and Calculation methods. Fiat Company
7. China's auto industry standard. Car engine crankshaft bending fatigue test method. China's Bureau of Machine Building Industry (2000)
8. Du, B.-P., Li, N., Zhou, H.-J.: Factors influence the effective fatigue threshold, $\Delta K_{eff,th}$. International Journal of Fatigue 9(1), 43–49 (1987)

High Precision Embedded Control of a High Acceleration Positioning System

Chao Liu, Jia Liu, Jianhua Wu, and Zhenhua Xiong

State Key Laboratory of Mechanical System and Vibration, School of Mechanical
Engineering, Shanghai Jiao Tong University, Shanghai 200240, China
{aalon,lamen,wujh,mexiong}@sjtu.edu.cn

Abstract. The research realizes a fast and high-precision positioning
control for a high acceleration X-Y platform using an embedded motion
control system. The control algorithm consists of a PD controller which
is designed by pole placement approach to implement the feedback control, a feed forward controller to improve the dynamic performance of the
servo mechanical system and a disturbance observer to suppress the external disturbances. The model of the high acceleration platform, which
is driven by permanent magnet linear synchronous motors (PMLSMs),
is first identified by a time domain relay feedback test. Then, the three
parts of the controller are designed based on the identified model. The
coefficient quantization error and the computational truncation error are
specially considered in the fix-point DSP platform, which makes the implementation feasible to run in the embedded motion system. Experimental results are presented to demonstrate the effectiveness of the proposed
control algorithm.

Keywords: Fast positioning, High acceleration, High precision, Relay
feedback, Disturbance observer, Embedded motion control.

1 Introduction

With the rapid development of semiconductor manufacturing, the advanced
packaging and electronics manufacturing equipments are required to meet the
technical demands of high acceleration, minimum positioning time, and high positioning precision. However, small positioning time requires high acceleration
in the motion system, which inevitably leads to positioning inaccuracy of the
system [2]. The constraints of high acceleration, minimum positioning time, and
high positioning precision, raise the unique requirement of high-end electronic
manufacturing equipments, such as a wire bonding machine, comparing with
other motion control systems.

In the past few years, many researchers dedicated to the servo mechanical
controller design and proposed a vast amount of algorithms. The conventional
controllers, such as a PID controller which is easily implemented in embedded
systems, have difficulties to meet the requirement of fast positioning with high
acceleration. The parameters of PID controller are commonly tuned by trial and

C.-Y. Su, S. Rakheja, H. Liu (Eds.): ICIRA 2012, Part II, LNAI 7507, pp. 551–560, 2012.

error method which mostly relies on engineering experience. This process could be time-consuming, because even if the parameters satisfy for one system, they have to be tuned again for other systems. Therefore, advanced controllers such as H_∞-based robust control [8], adaptive robust control [13], iterative learning control [1,12] are developed to further improve the servo performance. However, the applications of the advanced control algorithms are limited by its complication and the computational capacity of embedded motion control systems. An embedded system is generally resource limited, the design and implementation of embedded systems for complicated and durable industrial control have attracted a lot of attentions from both academia and industry [3,9].

With the aim of fast and high-precision positioning for a wire bonding X-Y stage, a control strategy comprises of a PD controller, a feed forward controller and a disturbance observer are implemented in an embedded motion control system. The PD controller is designed by pole placement approach to implement the feedback control. The feed forward controller is to improve the dynamics of the servo mechanical system. The disturbance observer, which applies cascade form to reduce the influence of the coefficient quantization error and the computational truncation error, suppresses the external disturbances. The model of the high acceleration X-Y positioning stage, which is driven by PMLSMs, is identified by a time-domain relay feedback technique. Experiments are conducted to show the performance improvements of the proposed controller.

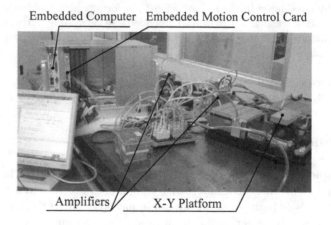

Fig. 1. The positioning control system

The remainder of this paper is organized as follows: In Section 2, the high-acceleration X-Y positioning stage and the embedded motion control system are introduced. In Section 3, the time-domain relay feedback identification and the proposed control algorithm are presented. Some implementary problems on the embedded motion control platform are also solved before the realization of the control algorithm. In Section 4, experimental results are presented to validate the effectiveness of the proposed control algorithm. Section 5 gives the conclusion.

2   The Positioning Control System

The architecture of control system is shown in Fig. 1, which consists of an X-Y positioning stage, two amplifiers, air cooling devices and an embedded motion control box. The overall hardware setup of control system is shown in Fig. 2. The embedded computer connects to the motion card via compact PCI bus. The motion control card gets the position feedback by the linear optical encoder, takes charge of both the position control loop and the driving control loop of the linear motors. In the following part, we will give the experimental results on the Y-axis.

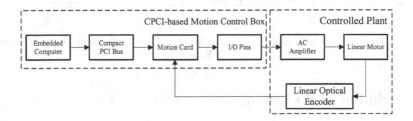

Fig. 2. The hardware setup of control system

2.1   X-Y Positioning Stage

The layout view of the PMLSMs driven X-Y positioning stage is shown in Fig. 3. The stage is designed for wire bonding application. Each axis is equipped with a non-contact linear optical encoder (Heidenhain LIF 471) with the hardware resolution of $0.4\mu m$ ($0.1\mu m$ after quadruplication) and the maximum tracking velocity of $0.5\ m/s$. An equivalent load of $2kg$ is mounted on the stage to simulate the bonding head and other components. The peak acceleration of X-axis and Y-axis are tested as $15.1g$ ($1g=9.806m/s^2$) and $14.3g$.

2.2   The Embedded Motion Control System

The embedded motion control board shown in Fig. 4 is developed by ourself, and is designed for the control of high performance electronic manufacturing machines. It is developed based on the fix-point 16-bit DSP TMS320F2812 and Cyclone II FPGA. The position loop cycle time is set to be $0.1ms$. The maximum encoder input frequency of FPGA is $4\ M$ (before quadruplication). The control algorithm described in this paper as well as the control loops is downloaded into the DSP or FPGA on the embedded card.

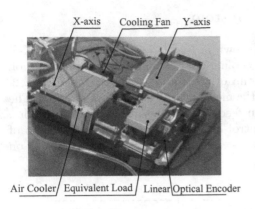

X-axis   Cooling Fan   Y-axis

Air Cooler/ Equivalent Load/ Linear\Optical Encoder

DSP Chip   DSP JTAG Interface

Compact PCI Bus\ \FPGA JTAG Interface
                        \FPGA Chip

Fig. 3. The X-Y stage

Fig. 4. The embedded motion control board

3   Modeling and Control

3.1   Modeling and Relay Feedback Identification

Taking into account the external disturbances, the dynamics of the above-mentioned servo mechanical system can be expressed as

$$m\ddot{x} = k_t u - B\dot{x} - F_d, \tag{1}$$

where m is the mass of the moving part, $\ddot{x}$ and $\dot{x}$ are the acceleration and the velocity of the moving part respectively, k_t is the motor coefficient, u is the input voltage, B is the viscous coefficients and F_d denotes the external disturbances. The model of the servo mechanical system can be written as

$$\tau\ddot{x} + \dot{x} = ku - f_d, \tag{2}$$

where $k = k_t/B$, $\tau = m/B$, $f_d = F_d/B$. The transfer functions is

$$G_n(s) = \frac{X(s)}{U(s)} = \frac{k}{(\tau s + 1)s}, \tag{3}$$

where $X(s)$ and $U(s)$ are the Laplace transformation of x and u respectively.

The model parameters in (3) are very important for the controllers tuning. Relay feedback identification technology is successfully applied to servo mechanical system by many researchers [5,10,11] by artificially adding dead time to the system with small dead time. The block diagram of relay feedback test with additional dead time is illustrated in Fig. 5. With an artificial dead time D, the relay module excites a rectangular waveform with the amplitude μ. Using the exciting signal, the servo mechanical system oscillates with the amplitudes A and the half cycle T_u.

The oscillation is characterized precisely using the time domain information, and the analytical expression in the first half cycle is

$$\dot{x}(t) = \begin{cases} k\mu(1 - e^{-t/\tau}), 0 \le t \le D \\ k\mu(1 - e^{-t/\tau}) - 2k\mu(1 - e^{-(t-D)/\tau}), D \le t \le Tu \end{cases}, \quad (4)$$

where μ is the actual force consisting of the motor generated force and disturbing forces. Given the boundary condition of the oscillation $\dot{x}(D) = A$, $\dot{x}(Tu) = 0$, the oscillation is then characterized by

$$A = k\mu(1 - e^{-D/\tau}), \quad (5)$$

$$T_u = \tau \ln(2e^{D/\tau} - 1). \quad (6)$$

Therefore, one set of relay feedback test with (μ, D) is enough to identify the two model parameters k and τ.

3.2 Design of the Control Algorithm

The proposed control framework designed in the position loop, combines a PD controller, a feed forward controller, and a disturbance observer. Consequently, the output of the proposed controllers can be expressed as

$$u = u_{pd} + u_{ff} - u_{dob}, \quad (7)$$

where u_{pd} is the output of PD controller, u_{ff} is the output of the feed forward controller and u_{dob} is the output of the disturbance observer. Fig. 6 shows the proposed control strategy of servo mechanical system.

The closed-loop transfer function of the PD controller can be expressed as

$$\frac{X(s)}{X_d(s)} = \frac{k(k_p + k_d s)}{\tau s^2 + (kk_d + 1)s + kk_p}, \quad (8)$$

where $X(s)$ and $X_d(s)$ are the Laplace transformation of the actual output x and the reference command x_d respectively, k_p is the proportional coefficient and

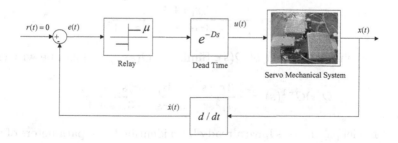

Fig. 5. Block diagram of relay-based feedback test with artificial dead time

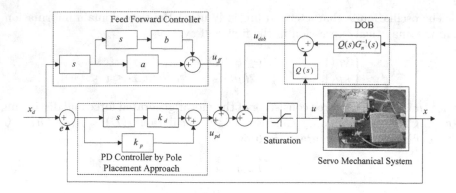

Fig. 6. The proposed control algorithm of servo mechanical system

k_d is the derivative coefficient. Take α and β as poles of the transfer function, then k_p and k_d can be written as

$$k_p = \alpha\beta\tau/k$$
$$k_d = -(1 + (\alpha + \beta)\tau)/k \qquad (9)$$

The output of feed forward controller based on the inverse model can be written as

$$u_{ff} = ax_d s + bx_d s^2, \qquad (10)$$

where x_d is the reference command, a and b are the coefficients of the feed forward controller. From the inverse of the model (3), we get

$$a = 1/k$$
$$b = \tau/k \qquad (11)$$

Disturbance observers have been successfully applied to servo systems by many researchers [4,6]. Considering the characteristics of the platform, the low-pass filter $Q(s)$ is designed in the form that the denominator of $Q(s)$ is third order, the numerator of $Q(s)$ is first order[7]. Then $Q(s)$ can be expressed as

$$Q(s) = \frac{3\tau_1 s + 1}{\tau_1^3 s^3 + 3\tau_1^2 s^2 + 3\tau_1 s + 1}, \qquad (12)$$

where τ_1 is the time constant of $Q(s)$. Similarly, $Q(s)G_n^{-1}(s)$ can be written as

$$Q(s)G_n^{-1}(s) = \frac{3\tau\tau_1 s^3 + (3\tau_1 + \tau)s^2 + s}{k(\tau_1^3 s^3 + 3\tau_1^2 s^2 + 3\tau_1 s + 1)}. \qquad (13)$$

Since the model parameters have already been identified, the parameters of three controllers can be easily calculated to improve the performance of servo mechanical system.

3.3 Implementation of the Control Algorithm

In this subsection, we will discuss the implementation of the proposed algorithm based on the fix-point 16-bit DSP device. In the embedded motion system, we use C language as the programming tool. Eq.(7) shows that the output of the proposed control algorithm can be calculated by u_{pd}, u_{ff} and u_{dob} individually. From Eqs.(9) and (11), we find that the PD controller and the feed forward controller, which is widely used in the industrial applications, can be easily implemented in the embedded motion controller. However, there are some difficulties for the implementation of DOB because of the limited resource of the fix-point 16-bit DSP device.

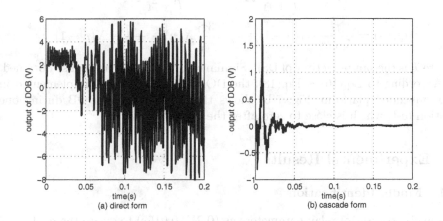

Fig. 7. The output of DOB with the direct and cascade form

In order to implement the DOB algorithm in the embedded platform, three problems should be solved, which include finite-precision effect, limited computing precision and the implementation form of DOB algorithm. Although the program running speed of DSP TMS320F2812 with fix-point variable type is much faster than float-point variable type, we still have to use the float-point variable type because data overflow could be caused by the finite-precision effect. Large amount of computation, which is more than the effective range of the variable type, can greatly affect the outcome. So the limited computing precision should be considered in the process of computation. We find that when the direct form of $Q(s)$ and $Q(s)G_n^{-1}(s)$ is used, the output of the DOB would be unstable, as shown in Fig. 7(a).

Since cascade form of the filter is insensitive to coefficient quantization compared with direct form of the filter. To avoid system instability, we adopt the cascade form of $Q(s)$ and $Q(s)G_n^{-1}(s)$ with float data format to program DOB algorithm. So, the low-pass filter $Q(s)$ can be written as

$$Q(s) = \frac{3\tau_1 s + 1}{\tau_1^3 s^3 + 3\tau_1^2 s^2 + 3\tau_1 s + 1} = \frac{Y}{Q_2} \cdot \frac{Q_2}{Q_1} \cdot \frac{Q_1}{X}, \tag{14}$$

where Y and X denotes the output and input of the $Q(s)$ respectively, Q_1 and Q_2 are the intermediate variables. Then we get

$$\frac{Y}{Q_2} = \frac{1}{\tau_1 s + 1}, \frac{Q_2}{Q_1} = \frac{1}{\tau_1 s + 1}, \frac{Q_1}{X} = \frac{3\tau_1 s + 1}{\tau_1 s + 1}. \tag{15}$$

The iterative algebraic expression above can be obtained by Euler method

$$Y(n) = \frac{\tau_1}{T + \tau_1} Y(n - 1) + \frac{T}{T + \tau_1} Q_2(n), \tag{16}$$

$$Q_2(n) = \frac{\tau_1}{T + \tau_1} Q_2(n - 1) + \frac{T}{T + \tau_1} Q_1(n), \tag{17}$$

$$Q_1(n) = \frac{\tau_1}{T + \tau_1} Q_1(n - 1) + \frac{T + 3\tau_1}{T + \tau_1} X(n) - \frac{3\tau_1}{T + \tau_1} X(n - 1), \tag{18}$$

where T is the sampling time of DSP. Similarly, $Q(s)G_n^{-1}(s)$ can be also obtained.

According to Eq.(16) $\sim$ Eq.(18), the DOB algorithm can be implemented in the embedded platform. Fig. 7(b) shows that the output of DOB during one motion test, which is close to zero after the motion is over.

4   Experimental Results

4.1   Model Identification

We utilize one set of relay parameters as ($0.2V$, $0.015s$) to excite the controlled plant. The oscillation amplitude and period are measured by averaging among ten oscillating cycles. The parameters are identified by using the Eqs. (5) and (6) in Section 3. With the oscillation characteristics $A=$ 10.54 mm/s and $T_u=$ 0.0295 s, we get the identified parameters $k=$ 61962 Vs/mm and $\tau=$ 0.435 s .

4.2   Point-to-Point Motion Experiments

A point to point motion, which is widely used in the wire bonding process, is conducted in Y-axis. The reference position profile with a travel of 0.1 inch (2.54 mm) is generated by the discrete S-curve planning. The peak planned velocity is 0.462 m/s while the peak planned acceleration is 11.8g. The planned time of the reference position profile is 11ms. The poles of α and β are set as -180, then the PD controller and feed forward controller parameters can be easily computed by the Eqs. (10) and (13).

The proposed algorithm in this paper is also implemented in the embedded system using the method given in Section 3.3. The actual displacement with the 23.5 μm of the position overshoot is displayed in Fig. 8(a). From Fig. 8(b), we find that the maximum tracking error is 37.5 μm and the positioning converging time is 22.1ms. Fig. 8(c) shows that maximum actual acceleration achieves the peak planned acceleration above-mentioned. The DAC output of the proposed

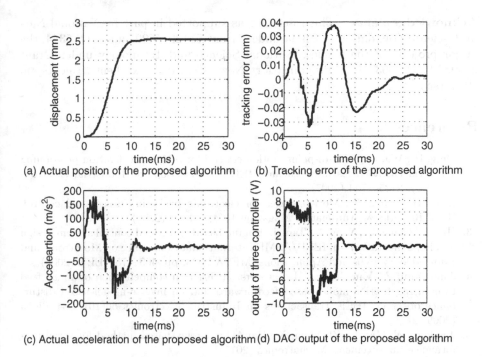

(a) Actual position of the proposed algorithm

(b) Tracking error of the proposed algorithm

(c) Actual acceleration of the proposed algorithm (d) DAC output of the proposed algorithm

Fig. 8. The performance under the proposed controller in point-to-point motion

control algorithm is given in Fig. 8(d), which shows that the maximal output is reached during the movement.

From the experimental results, we can find that the proposed algorithm has better performance in position overshoot, position tracking error and positioning time, which is desired for high-end motion control applications like electronic manufacturing machines.

5   Conclusion

A high precision controller with disturbance observer based on time-domain relay feedback approach is designed for a high acceleration X-Y positioning stage. The time-domain relay identification can be easily obtained by one set test parameter. Based on the model parameters, a control strategy comprises of a PD controller based on pole placement, a feed forward controller and a disturbance observer is developed. The parameters of the integrated algorithm are expediently tuned to improve the performance of servo mechanical system. The control algorithm is fully implemented on a self-designed embedded motion control system. Experimental results show that the proposed control scheme provides good performances in position overshoot, position tracking error and positioning time, which verify the effectiveness of the proposed control algorithm and the embedded implementation.

Acknowledgements. This research was supported in part by National Natural Science Foundation of China under Grant 51120155001 and 51175344, the major projects of the Chinese National Science and Technology under Grant 2009ZX02021-003 and Program for New Century Excellent Talents in University.

References

1. Ding, H., Wu, J.: Point-to-point motion control for a high-acceleration positioning table via cascaded learning schemes. IEEE Transactions on Industrial Electronics 54(5), 2735–2744 (2007)
2. Ding, H., Xiong, Z.: Motion stages for electronic packaging design and control. IEEE Robotics & Automation Magazine 13(4), 51–61 (2006)
3. Hu, T., Zhang, C., Yang, L., Tan, J.: Engine based embedded control system design and implementation. In: IEEE/ASME International Conference on Mechtronic and Embedded Systems and Applications, MESA 2008, pp. 469–475. IEEE (2008)
4. Jamaludin, Z., Van Brussel, H., Swevers, J.: Friction compensation of an xy feed table using friction-model-based feedforward and an inverse-model-based disturbance observer. IEEE Transactions on Industrial Electronics 56(10), 3848–3853 (2009)
5. Jianhua, W., Jia, L., Zhenhua, X., Han, D.: A relay-based method for servo performance improvement. Mechatronics (2011)
6. Kang, H., Lee, C., Chung, C., Lee, H.: Control design for self-servo track writing using a state-space disturbance observer. IEEE Transactions on Magnetics 45(11), 5094–5099 (2009)
7. Lee, H., Tomizuka, M.: Robust motion controller design for high-accuracy positioning systems. IEEE Transactions on Industrial Electronics 43(1), 48–55 (1996)
8. Liu, Z., Luo, F., Rahman, M.: Robust and precision motion control system of linear-motor direct drive for high-speed xy table positioning mechanism. IEEE Transactions on Industrial Electronics 52(5), 1357–1363 (2005)
9. Potlapally, R., Ravi, S., Raghunathan, A., Lee, R., Jha, N.: Impact of configurability and extensibility on ipsec protocol execution on embedded processors. In: 19th International Conference on VLSI Design Held Jointly with 5th International Conference on Embedded Systems and Design, p. 6. IEEE (2006)
10. Scali, C., Marchetti, G., Semino, D.: Relay with additional delay for identification and autotuning of completely unknown processes. Industrial & Engineering Chemistry Research 38(5), 1987–1997 (1999)
11. Tan, K., Lee, T., Huang, S., Jiang, X.: Friction modeling and adaptive compensation using a relay feedback approach. IEEE Transactions on Industrial Electronics 48(1), 169–176 (2001)
12. Wu, J., Ding, H.: Iterative learning variable structure controller for high-speed and high-precision point-to-point motion. Robotics and Computer-Integrated Manufacturing 24(3), 384–391 (2008)
13. Xu, L., Yao, B.: Adaptive robust precision motion control of linear motors with negligible electrical dynamics: theory and experiments. IEEE/ASME Transactions on Mechatronics 6(4), 444–452 (2001)

Rapid Control Selection through Hill-Climbing Methods

Krispin A. Davies, Alejandro Ramirez-Serrano, Graeme N. Wilson,
and Mahmoud Mustafa

Dept. of Mechanical and Manufacturing Engineering, University of Calgary, 2500 University
Drive, Calgary, Canada
{kdavies,aramirez,wilsongn,mmmustaf}@ucalgary.ca

Abstract. Consider the problem of control selection in complex dynamical and environmental scenarios where model predictive control (MPC) proves particularly effective. As the performance of MPC is highly dependent on the efficiency of its incorporated search algorithm, this work examined hill climbing as an alternative to traditional systematic or random search algorithms. The relative performance of a candidate hill climbing algorithm was compared to representative systematic and random algorithms in a set of systematic tests and in a real-world control scenario. These tests indicated that hill climbing can provide significantly improved search efficiency when the control space has a large number of dimensions or divisions along each dimension. Furthermore, this demonstrated that there was little increase in search times associated with a significant increase in the number of control configurations considered.

Keywords: Hill Climbing Search, Model Predictive Control, Random Search, Grid-Refinement Search, Mobile Robots.

1 Introduction

The past decade has witnessed a migration of autonomous systems (robots) from controlled environments, such as laboratories and factories, to the uncontrolled environments of everyday life, such as mining and other exploration areas. Diverse devices such as autonomous cars and the recently announced DARPA challenge focusing on humanoid search and rescue robots are now under development, [1,2]. These everyday scenarios present three main challenges over their controlled counterparts: i) transient vehicle models, ii) uncontrolled environments, and iii) multiple goals. The transient vehicle model refers to the vehicle dynamics and limitations (both physical limits and control bounds) which may vary in time, [3]. The second challenge, the uncontrolled environment, presents both a wide range of terrain properties (e.g., surface stiffness and frictional coefficient) and obstacles (both static and dynamic), [4]. Finally, multiple goals, potentially competing or even mutually exclusive, may exist, [5]. Traditional direct control techniques (e.g. adaptive control and optimal control) become highly complex when faced with these challenges, because they use algebraic equations to map a vehicle state, $\vec{s}$, and set of goals, $g(\vec{s})$, directly to a control configuration, $\vec{c}$, (i.e., a set of control signals completely defining

C.-Y. Su, S. Rakheja, H. Liu (Eds.): ICIRA 2012, Part II, LNAI 7507, pp. 561–570, 2012.
© Springer-Verlag Berlin Heidelberg 2012

the vehicle action), [6]. It is difficult to create equations that account for all possible combinations of input factors these challenges can produce. As an alternative, the control problem can be framed as an optimization problem within the space of all possible control configurations, $\vec{c}_i \in \vec{C}$. Within the control space, a search algorithm attempts to identify the best control configuration, $\vec{c}_{best}$, given the current goals and constraints as evaluated in a heuristic (e.g., cost) function, $h(\vec{s}, \vec{c}_i)$. Herein produces a form of model predictive control (MPC) as employed in process industries and more recently in robotics, [7].

Employing MPC creates a three part loop structure in place of a direct control law (Fig. 1) where a search algorithm suggests a control configuration, $\vec{c}_i$. The suggested control configuration is then used by a simulation algorithm to predict how the vehicle will behave (e.g., move) over a predetermined interval. The heuristic algorithm compares the predicted vehicle behavior to the defined goals in order to produce a single numerical cost, $h(\vec{s}, \vec{c}_i)$. Finally the cost, is used as feedback by the search algorithm when selecting the next control configuration, c_{i+1}.

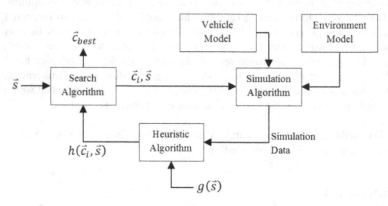

Fig. 1. Model Predictive Control Cycle

This sidesteps the need for direct control equations, and provides greater freedom. First, as the control configuration is interpreted a variety of formats can be used. For example, as a time polynomial for each control surface angle on an aerial vehicle or as a set of turning angles to be executed in sequence by an autonomous car, [3,8]. Likewise, the goals (e.g., user defined) are also interpreted granting freedom in their representation, for example: as linearly increasing time cost and as a step cost for potential collisions, [9]. Finally, the vehicle and environment models are only used in the simulation algorithm for which efficient techniques already exist, [10]. Thus, framing the control problem as MPC provides significant benefits at the expense of the time required to execute the search.

The time cost associated with simulation and heuristic evaluation is the main drawback of the MPC approach. Based on work conducted in this area, a search-simulate-evaluate loop cycle may take longer to process than an entire direct control calculation, [11]. Thus, minimizing the number of search cycles needed to select a suitable control configuration is crucial. In this case, a suitable control configuration could mean the globally optimal control configuration or simply a control configuration equal to or better than a predetermined benchmark. In an effort to reduce this search time, we propose the use of hill climbing search techniques instead of the systematic or random search algorithms employed throughout literature. It is envisioned that hill-climbing, being a subset of gradient decent, will improve performance as many of the heuristic functions produced by MPC are largely continuous, [12].

Thus, in order to determine whether the hill climbing group of search algorithms is suitable for MPC, this work compared random restart hill climbing's (RRHC) performance to a representative systematic search algorithm (progressive grid refinement search) and a representative random search algorithm (pure random search). As RRHC can be implemented readily and with computational overhead comparable to systematic and random search algorithms it was suitable for comparison, [13]. All three search algorithms are described briefly in Section 2. Initial testing of the search algorithms was conducted using a systematically defined control space heuristic, described in Section 3, to examine how performance is affected by key search parameters. As the systematic testing produced unexpectedly positive results, Section 4 applies these search algorithms to a real-world vehicle control selection problem in order to validate the systematic testing results. Finally, we present our conclusions on the potentials of both MPC in robotics and the use of hill climbing algorithms within MPC (Section 5).

2   Search Methodologies

The purpose of the search algorithm is to identify a suitable control configuration as rapidly as possible. In most scenarios, "suitable" may encompass several control configurations, all of which meet or exceed a bench mark rating. As heuristics are often evaluated on a basis of cost, in this paper it is assumed that lower heuristic costs are better. Thus, for any given control problem, there is a set of one or more control configurations which are suitable. However the number and location(s) of this/these solution(s) is/are unknown prior to conducting the search. This realization was used to select the three search algorithms: RRHC, Grid Refinement, and Random Sampling.

2.1   Hill Climbing Algorithm

Hill climbing methods were selected for their ability to rapidly identify minima within continuous spaces. As heuristic functions can be constructed to be generally continuous, though they may contain micro-discontinuities, gradient methods are suitable for solving these functions. Given the inability to analytically determine the heuristic's gradient due to the dependence on simulation results however, a numerical approach such as hill climbing is needed. Of the hill climbing methods, RRHC most closely resembled the literature methods in computational overhead making it most suitable for comparison.

Functionally, the core of RRNNHC lies in the nearest climb behavior. In this, the current control configuration's cost, $h_{current}$, is compared with the cost of those configurations closest to it within the control space. This comparison has two possible results: i) neighboring cost < current cost, or ii) neighboring cost ≥ current cost. If any of the neighboring configurations has a lower cost than the current configuration, then the current configuration is replaced by the neighboring configuration with the lowest cost. This produces the gradient descent behavior. Conversely, if the current configuration has a lower cost than all neighboring configurations, then it represents a minimum. Upon reaching a minimum, random restart is replaces the current control configuration with a randomly selected control configuration from which gradient descent can begin again.

2.2 Comparison Algorithms

The hill climbing algorithm's performance was compared with two competing algorithms (systematic searches and random based searches), each representing a method common throughout the literature. The first of these algorithms was grid refinement, which systematically searched the entire control space according to a series of progressively finer and finer grids, each with 2^i grid divisions where $i = [1, n_{div}]$, [14]. This produced rapid complete coverage of the entire control space in a coarse distribution followed by progressive increases in density, continued until the precision limit, $2^{n_{div}}$.

The second comparison algorithm was a purely random search algorithm, which repeatedly selected control configurations at random. While random searching did not always identify the global minimum within a set number of search cycles as grid refinement did, Knepper et. all demonstrated that random search patterns could perform equal to or better in terms of time performance, [9].

3   Systematic Testing

The first set of tests was conducted using a contrived heuristic function to investigate the relative performance of RRHC in response to three control space parameters. Specifically, i) the number of dimensions in the control space (dimensionality), n_{dim}, ii) the number of grid divisions along each dimension (precision), $2^{n_{div}}$, and iii) the percentage of control space sloped towards suitable control configurations (complexity).

Here, the simulation and heuristic evaluation within each search cycle was replaced by a single calculation (Eq. 1) which produced a multidimensional quadratic bowl with a superimposed wave function (Fig. 2). The bowl guaranteed that only one global minimum would exist, centered at $\vec{d}$ (randomly selected within the control space), while the cosine wave produced a set number of local minima (complexity) according to a frequency parameter, f. Furthermore, the bowl slope is controlled such that the global minimum exhibited zero cost and two locally minimal solutions will existed along each dimension with cost = 0.05.

$$h(\vec{c}) = \sum_{j=1}^{n_{dim}} \left(0.05 f^2 (d_j - c_j)^2 - \cos\left(2\pi f (d_j - c_j) \right) + 1 \right) \quad (1)$$

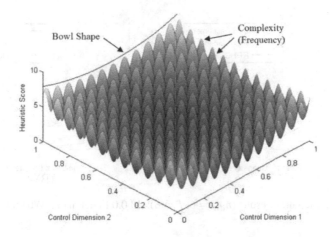

Fig. 2. Systematic Control Space Example (from Eq. 1 with $n_{dim} = 2$, $n_{div} = 2^8$, $f = 12$)

For each search algorithm, the test recorded the number of search cycles required to identify a control configuration with a cost below each benchmark. This process was repeated 100 times for each test/algorithm combination and the search cycle counts were averaged. These averaged results are presented below, normalized to the number of possible control configurations, n_{config}, per Eq. 2.

$$n_{config} = (2^{n_{div}} + 1)^{n_{dim}}$$ (2)

3.1   Dimensionality and Precision

The results of the dimensionality (Fig. 3) and precision (Fig. 4) tests indicate that RRHC has comparable performance at low dimensions/divisions. As the number of dimensions or divisions increases however, relative performance improves accordingly. This indicates that RRHC is most suitable for application on control problems with greater than 2 dimensions and 2^5 divisions where it yielded significantly improved performance over the comparison algorithms (up to 1000 faster). Also of note, the performance difference was less marked with the 0.05 benchmark than the 0.0 benchmark. This is a result of the increasing percentage of the control space with costs below the benchmark value.

3.2   Complexity

Results from the complexity test (Fig. 5) demonstrate the weakness of RRHC; specifically that the algorithm performance will decrease when used with a highly stochastic or oscillatory heuristic function, due to local minima entrapment. In comparison to the other search algorithms however, hill climbing still exhibited significantly better performance, though this improvement is inversely related to complexity.

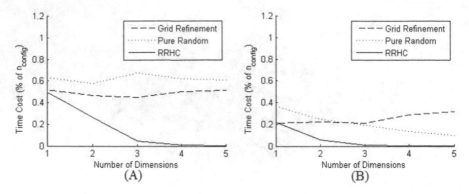

Fig. 3. Dimensionality Results ($n_{div} = 6, f = 6$): A) 0.0 Benchmark, B) 0.05 Benchmark

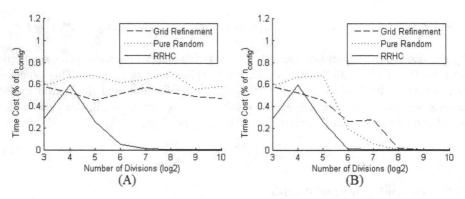

Fig. 4. Precision Results ($n_{dim} = 3, f = 6$): A) 0.0 Benchmark, B) 0.05 Benchmark

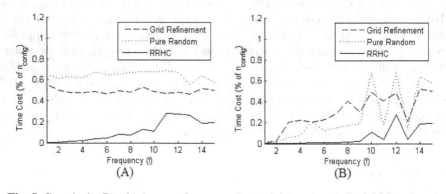

Fig. 5. Complexity Results ($n_{dim} = 3, n_{div} = 6$): A) 0.0 Benchmark, B) 0.05 Benchmark

4   Real-World Verification

While systematic testing provided insight into RRHC's performance, it produced very impressive results. To determine whether this performance increase would carry over into a real-world scenario, subsections of the experiments from Knepper et. all were recreated, [9]. In these, a differential drive robot was presented with a single path environment that it must navigate. Thus, the robot needed to select a collision free set of control outputs which would advance it along the path. The control output was a set of 4 steering rates ranging from $\pm 2.1\ rad/m$, employed in sequence for $0.3\ m$ each. This produced a 4 dimensional control space ($n_{dim} = 4$) with steering angle rates divided into either 8 divisions ($n_{div} = 3$) for coarse control or 32 divisions ($n_{div} = 5$) for fine control.

The environment (Fig. 6) contained only the path walls, generated from perlin noise to create a curving path with multiple constrictions whose curvature was bounded to the turning rate of the robot. The average length and width of the constrictions was manipulated to produce two environments i) wide paths (Fig. 6-A, $0.05\ m$ length and $0.05\ m$ width avg.) and ii) thin paths (Fig. 6-B, $0.15\ m$ length and $0.01\ m$ width avg.).

■Obstacle   □Pathway   —Sampled Route
(A)   (B)

Fig. 6. Real-World Navigation Scenario Examples. A) Wide Paths, B) Thin Paths

As the goal of the system was to produce collision free forward motion along the path, Eq. 3 was employed as the heuristic evaluation function. It was evaluated continuously along the simulation predicted line of travel, and the minimum value of the function along that line of travel was returned to the search algorithm. At each point, the function rewarded distance travelled, d_{travel}, and penalized the minimum thus far observed distance between the robot and an obstacle, $d_{obs,min}$. For mathematical reasons, $d_{obs,min}$ was limited to a minimum of 0.0001.

$$h(\vec{c}) = (0.3n_{dim} - d_{travel}) + 0.1\left(\frac{0.01}{d_{obs,min}}\right)^2 \qquad (3)$$

4.1   Performance on Wide Paths

Fig. 7 shows the cost, averaged over 100 trials, as it decreases over the first 5000 search cycles. For coarse control, RRHC reached global minimum first (468 cycles avg.), significantly faster than the comparison algorithms (3219 cycles for grid and 2735 cycles for random). Fine control showed similar relative performance with the hill climbing, grid refinement, and random algorithms taking an average $1.1e^5$, $5.5e^5$, and $5.0e^5$ cycles respectively. The average minimum cost identified by the fine control was 0.0285, slightly lower than that for coarse control at 0.0410. This demonstrates that fine control can yield better results given sufficient cycles.

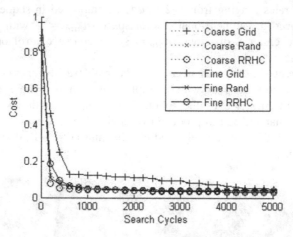

Fig. 7. Search Performance on Wide Paths

Surprisingly, fine RRHC began to surpass coarse RRHC after on a few cycles (approx. 1700 cycles). This indicates that although the fine control provides $1.1e^6$ possible control configurations (as compared to 6561 for coarse control) it can still be processed with comparable efficiency.

4.2   Performance on Thin Paths

The thin pathway performance (Fig. 8) demonstrated a significant difference between fine control (0.4527 average minimum cost) and coarse control (0.8522 average

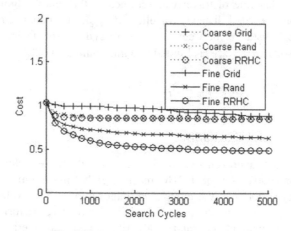

Fig. 8. Search Performance on Thin Paths

minimum cost). This disparity also caused fine RRHC to surpass coarse RRHC after only 100 cycles on average. Using fine and coarse control, RRHC required an average $4.6e^4$ and 175 cycles respectively to reach the average global minimum. Comparatively, grid refinement required an average $6.0e^5$ and 2526 cycles and pure random $4.7e^5$ and 646 cycles.

Taken together with the performance on wide paths, these results demonstrated a significant performance gain when employing RRHC, correlating with the systematic tests earlier. The performance gains within the real-world scenario (5 to 12 times faster) were not as dramatic as those from systematic testing (2 to 1000 times faster) however improvement by a factor of 5 remains a significant gain.

5   Conclusions and Future Work

The tests presented here indicate that RRHC can improve the performance of MPC. Systematic testing indicated that as the number of control dimensions and the level of control precision in each of those dimensions increases, RRHC began to significantly outperform the alternative algorithms. These performance increases carried over to a real-world test scenario, where MPC was successfully used by a simulated differential drive robot to move through a constricted path.

There remains significant investigation to be done on both MPC and the application of hill-climbing search algorithms therein. Most notably that RRHC is only one such algorithm and may not be the most suitable. In the future we intend to compare a number of hill-climbing algorithms and to conduct a wider range of real-world tests, both simulated and experimental. In the immediate future however, the application of hill climbing methods significantly improves the viability of MPC for autonomous vehicle control.

References

1. DARPA Robotics Challenge, https://www.fbo.gov/spg/ODA/DARPA/CMO/DARPA-BAA-12-39/listing.html
2. Google Official Blog, http://googleblog.blogspot.com.au/2010/10/what-were-driving-at.html#!/2010/10/what-were-driving-at.html
3. Howard, T.M., Green, C.J., Kelly, A., Ferguson, D.: State space sampling of feasible motions for high-performance mobile robot navigation in complex environments. Journal of Field Robotics, 325–345 (2008)
4. Pivtoraiko, M., Howard, T.M., Nesnas, I., Kelly, A.: Field Experiments in Rover Navigation via Model-Based Trajectory Generation and Nonholonomic Motion Planning in State Lattices. In: 9th International Symposium on Artificial Intelligence, Robotics, and Automation in Space, Pasadena, CA (2008)
5. Petti, S., Fraichard, T.: Safe motion planning in dynamic environments. In: IEEE/RSJ International Conference on Intelligent Robots and Systems, Alberta, Canada (2005)
6. Farrell, J.A., Polycarpou, M.M.: Adaptive Approximation Based Control. John Wiley & Sons Inc., New Jersey (2006)

7. Jansen, F., Ramirez-Serrano, A.: Extended MPC Strategy for Manoeuvring Unmanned Vehicles in Restricted 3D Environments. In: UVS Canada Conference, Halifax, Canada (2011)
8. Koyuncu, E., Inalhan, G.: A probabilistic B-spline motion planning algorithm for unmanned helicopters flying in dense 3D environments. In: IEEE/RSJ International Conference on Intelligent Robots and Systems, Nice, France, pp. 815–821 (2008)
9. Knepper, R.A., Mason, M.T.: Empirical Sampling of Path Sets for Local Area Motion Planning. In: 11th International Symposium on Experimental Robotics, Athens, Greece (2008)
10. Castillo-Pizarro, P., Arredondo, T.V., Torres-Torriti, M.: Introductory Survey to Open-Source Mobile Robot Simulation Software. In: 2010 Latin American Robotics Symposium and Intelligent Robotic Meeting (LARS), Sao Bernardo do Campo, Brazil, pp. 150–155 (2010)
11. Davies, K.: A Novel Control Architecture for Mapping and Motion Planning of Reconfigurable Robots in Highly Confined 3D Environments. MSc. Thesis, University of Calgary, Canada (2011)
12. Jansen, F.: Manoeuvring Unmanned Vehicles through Confined 3D Environments using Model Predictive Control. MSc. Thesis, University of Calgary, Canada (2011)
13. Smith, M., Mailler, R.: Getting What You Pay For: Is Exploration in Distributed Hill Climbing Really Worth it? In: IEEE/WIC/ACM International Conference on Web Intelligence and Intelligent Agent Technology, Toronto, Canada, pp. 319–326 (2010)
14. van den Berg, J.P., Overmars, M.H.: Roadmap-based motion planning in dynamic environments. IEEE Transactions on Robotics 21(5), 885–897 (2005)

Robust Mode-Free Sliding Mode Control of Multi-fingered Hand with Position Synchronization in the Task Space

Ming-Feng Ge[1], Zhi-Hong Guan[1,*], Tao Li[2],
Ding-Xue Zhang[3], and Rui-Quan Liao[3]

[1] Department of Control Science and Engineering
Huazhong University of Science and Technology, Wuhan, 430074, China
zhguan@mail.hust.edu.cn
[2] Electronic and Information College, Yangtze University, Jingzhou, 420400, China
[3] Petroleum and Engineering College, Yangtze University, Jingzhou, 420400, China

Abstract. In this paper, for the purpose of improving operation performance of multi-fingered hand and multiple robotic manipulators, a robust position synchronization mode-free sliding-mode control (SMC) strategy is proposed. By invoking the Lyapunov stability approach, the effectiveness of the proposed approach is testified to be robust while facing various disturbances and dynamic uncertainties. Besides, according to the practical application, the kinematic diversity is taken into consideration. We assume each individual in the multi-agent system to be with kinematic redundancy or without. Finally, we present computer simulation results to verify the effectiveness of the proposed algorithm.

Keywords: position synchronization, sliding-mode control (SMC), multi-fingered hand, dynamic uncertainty, multi-agent system, kinematic redundancy.

1 Introduction

Intelligent control of multi-fingered robot hand and multiple robotic manipulators has attracted increasing attention and has been widely studied [1]. In order to design a artificial limb which is more suitable for disabled people, coordination problem should be considered. Therefore, numerous researchers focused on the controller design of hand-object system [2],[3]. As a typical closed-chain robotic system, the coordination task in the control of hand-object system is much more important. However, since the positions and velocity of finger-tips on robotic fingers are rigidly coupled through the surface of the object, it doesn't seem to be necessary to design an algorithm to achieve coordination. Nevertheless, the research from developmental psychologists shows that the coordination task plays an important role in the stability of manipulation and grasping [4]. Unfortunately, traditional control scheme used in engineering application, either

---

* Corresponding author.

C.-Y. Su, S. Rakheja, H. Liu (Eds.): ICIRA 2012, Part II, LNAI 7507, pp. 571–580, 2012.
© Springer-Verlag Berlin Heidelberg 2012

centralized or decentralized, have not addressed coordination tasks. Therefore, it is ungent for researchers to propose an effective coordinate controller which can guarantee the stability and coordination of multi-agent systems.

In order to improve the performance of grasping and manipulation, in this paper we consider the coordination task as a position synchronization problem which has already been admitted to be effective for coordination tasks [5]. Before the proposal of synchronization methods, the coordination schemes for assembly tasks are derived by assuming there are physically connections between the individual of multi-agent systems, such as the master/slave control. Hence, recently the position synchronization theory has been widely studied [6], the physically connections are no longer indispensable. At the same time, although the algorithm is firstly derived in the purpose of solving coordination problem in assembly tasks of modern manufacturing and space applications, soon the researchers find it is also appropriate to robot manipulator tasks [7]. By such analogy, it can also be applied to multi-fingered hand systems. However, in order to mimic human, the multi-fingered hand system's inverse kinematics are ill-posed, which become a great obstacle if you want to design a high performance position synchronization controller. Besides, there still remain two main challenges: synchronization and disturbances. How to solve all these difficulties will be given by the following discussion.

To deal with the synchronization problem, a linear coupling synchronization signal will be proposed in Section 3. What's more, to improve the anti-interference abilities of the whole system, we introduced the SMC. As is mentioned above, most of the designed controllers are mode-based and lack of robustness while facing model errors and external disturbances. Meanwhile, owing to its less sensitive to the parameter variations and disturbances, the SMC is well-known as a powerful tool to deal with uncertain systems. Due to the benefit SMC is widely used in robot systems. Huang etc. proposed an SMC approach for underactuated mobile wheeled inverted pendulum systems [8]. They improved their controller and achieved greater effectiveness [9]. Whereas it is not easy to design SMC controllers for kinematic redundant manipulator systems, where the control problems have been admitted to be challenging owning to the ill-posedness of its inverse kinematics. The problem is more difficult when there exists strong coupling between the robots. What's more, SMC will cause chattering which is well-known as a crucial disadvantage to the stability of the system, which made the controller designing become extremely troublesome. In spite of this we proposed a synchronization sliding mode control which can deal with the above conditions and the detail will be discussed in Section 4.

2   Modeling of System Dynamics and Kinematics

Considering various disturbances, the dynamic model of the ith rigid-link serial robot manipulator or finger is given in the joint space as follow:

$$H_i(q_i(t))\ddot{q}_i(t) + [C_i(q_i(t), \dot{q}_i(t)) + B_i]\dot{q}_i(t) + G_i(q_i(t)) + F_i(t) = u_i(t), \qquad (1)$$

where $q_i(t) \in R^{n_i}$ denotes the joint position vector, n_i denotes the joint space dimension, $H_i(q_i(t)) \in R^{n_i \times n_i}$ is the symmetric positive definite inertia matrix, $C_i(q_i(t), \dot{q}_i(t)) \in R^{n_i \times n_i}$ represents the Coriolis and centrifugal force matrix, $G_i(q_i(t)) \in R^{n_i}$ denotes the gravity force vector, $B_i \in R^{n_i \times n_i}$ is the positive diagonal matrix that denotes viscous joint friction coefficient, $F_i(t) \in R^{n_i}$ denotes the bounded disturbance vector and $u_i(t) \in R^{n_i}$ stands for the torque input vector.

Based on the system dynamic mode, the kinematic mode of each individual can be given as follows

$$X_i = f_i(q_i), \dot{X}_i = J_i(q_i)\dot{q}_i,$$

where $X_i \in R^{m_0}$ represents the ith end-effector position, $f_i(q_i)$ is the trigonometric function of the joint position q_i, m_0 is the task space dimension of each agent, $J_i \in R^{m_0 \times n_i}$ stands for the Jacobian matrix from the joint space to the task space of the ith agent.

Remark 1. Notice that all the fingers are assumed to work in the same task space, so the task space dimension of all the agents are same. Besides, as we consider the kinematic diversity, the joint space dimension of all the individuals are different. What's more, according to the practical applications, the task space dimension m_0 is equal or lesser than the joint space dimension $n_i(m_0 \leq n_i)$, for all the agents in the whole system.

Remark 2. Notice that the Jacobian matrix J_i may be ill-posed due to the kinematic diversity. Therefore, in order to avoid the singularity position, in this paper we assume the Jacobian matrix J_i is row full rank, i.e., $rank(J_i) = m_0$. Then J_i^+ exists when the kinematic of the ith finger is redundant.

In order to make the subsequent analysis easier, some general properties of revolute joint manipulators and the Jacobian matrix from the joint space to the task space are given [10],[12].

Property 1. For any i, the following inequalities holds:

$$\begin{cases} \lambda_m I_{n_i} \leq H_i(q_i(t)) \leq \lambda_M I_{n_i} \\ \|C_i(q_i(t), \dot{q}_i(t))\| \leq k_C \|\dot{q}_i(t)\| \\ \|G_i(q_i(t))\| \leq k_G, \end{cases}$$

where I_{n_i} is the identity matrix of dimension n_i, and $\lambda_m, \lambda_M, k_C, k_G$ are positive constants.

Property 2. For any i, the matrix $\dot{H}_i(q_i(t)) - 2C_i(q_i(t), \dot{q}_i(t))$ is skew symmetric.

Property 3. For any i and all vectors $x, y \in R^{n_i}$, the following equalities holds:

$$H_i(q_i(t))x + [C_i(q_i(t), \dot{q}_i(t)) + B_i]y + G_i(q_i(t)) = Y_i(q_i(t), \dot{q}_i(t), x, y)\theta_i,$$

where $Y_i(q_i(t), \dot{q}_i(t), x, y)$ is the regressor matrix and θ_i is the constant parameter vector respected to the ith agent.

Property 4. For any i, the Jacobian matrix J_i has following properties:

$$\begin{cases} J_i(I_{n_i} - J_i^+ J_i) = 0 \\ (I_{n_i} - J_i^+ J_i)J_i^+ = 0 \\ (I_{n_i} - J_i^+ J_i)(I_{n_i} - J_i^+ J_i) = I_{n_i} - J_i^+ J_i. \end{cases}$$

3   Algorithm of Position Synchronization

Since the dynamic model and kinematic model are shown, we can define the following position error of the ith finger in the task space: $e_i = X_i - X_{di}$, where $X_{di} \in R^{m_0}$ represents the desired trajectory of the ith agent in the task space, $e_i \in R^{m_0}$ denotes the task space tracking error of the ith agent.

Therefore, assuming there are k individuals in the whole system, then the goal of task space position error synchronization is [5],[6],[7]:

$$e_1 = e_2 = e_3 = \ldots = e_k. \tag{2}$$

Obviously, if the following equation achieved, the Eq.(2) holds,

$$2e_1 - e_2 - e_k = 2e_2 - e_3 - e_1 = \ldots = 2e_k - e_{k-1} - e_1.$$

Respectively, following [7], define the synchronization error $\xi_i \in R^{m_0}$ as:

$$\begin{cases} \xi_1 = 2e_1 - e_2 - e_k \\ \xi_2 = 2e_2 - e_1 - e_3 \\ \quad \vdots \\ \xi_k = 2e_k - e_1 - e_{k-1}. \end{cases}$$

Then the integrated tracking error is defined as: $e = [e_1^T, e_2^T, \cdots, e_k^T]^T, e \in R^m, m = k \times m_0$. Respectively, the synchronization error of the whole system is $\xi = [\xi_1^T, \xi_2^T, \cdots, \xi_k^T]^T$.

Remark 3. Notice that the objective of position synchronization is to design a controller, which can guarantee that both the tracking error e and the synchronization error ξ converge to zero asymptotically.

Then define the couple matrix,

$$E_S \triangleq (I_k + \alpha L) \otimes I_{m_0}, \tag{3}$$

where L is defined as:

$$L = \begin{bmatrix} 2 & -1 & \cdots & & \cdots & -1 \\ -1 & 2 & -1 & & \cdots & 0 \\ \vdots & \ddots & \ddots & & \ddots & \vdots \\ 0 & \cdots & -1 & 2 & -1 \\ -1 & 0 & \cdots & -1 & 2 \end{bmatrix},$$

and α is a gain parameter, I_k and I_{m_0} is the identity matrix. After that we define the couple error in task space as follow: $E \triangleq E_S \cdot e$.

Lemma 1. *If $\alpha > 0$, then $E \to 0$ implies that $e \to 0, \xi \to 0$. That means, we only need to design a controller that guarantees the asymptotical convergence to zero of the couple error E then the task space position error synchronization is achieved.*

Proof. Define $m = k \times m_0$. For $x \in R^m$, decompose the vector x, then $x = [x_1^T, x_2^T, \cdots, x_k^T]^T$, where $x_i \in R^{m_0}$, for $i = 1, 2, \cdots, k$. After that, from the definition of E_S and L, we get:

$$x^T E_S x = x^T x + \alpha x^T (L \otimes I_{m_0}) x$$
$$= x^T x + \alpha \sum_{i=1}^{k} \sum_{j=1(j>i)}^{k} \|x_i - x_j\|^2. \tag{4}$$

When $E = 0$, from the definition of E, there is: $e^T E = e^T E_S e$. Then if $E = 0$, $e^T E_S e = 0$. By Eq.(4), then:

$$e^T e + \alpha \sum_{i=1}^{k} \sum_{j=1(j>i)}^{k} \|e_i - e_j\|^2 = 0.$$

Obviously, if $\alpha > 0$, $E \to 0$ implies that $e \to 0, \xi \to 0$, the proof is completed.

4   Sliding-Mode Controller Design

By the analysis of Lemma 1, we only need to design a controller that guarantees $E \to 0$. In order to make the controller design more easier, the whole system is written as:

$$H(q)\ddot{q} + [C(q, \dot{q}) + B]\dot{q} + G(q) + F(t) = u(t), \tag{5}$$

where the dimension of joint space is defined as $n = \sum_{i=1}^{k} n_i$. Besides, $q = [q_1^T, q_2^T, \cdots, q_k^T]^T, q \in R^n$, $H(q) = diag\{H_1, H_2, \cdots, H_k\}$, $H(q) \in R^{n \times n}$, $C(q, \dot{q}) = diag\{C_1, C_2, \cdots, C_k\}$, $C(q, \dot{q})\dot{q} \in R^n$, $B = diag\{B_1, B_2, \cdots, B_k\}$, $B \in R^{n \times n}$, $F(t) = (F_1^T, F_2^T, \cdots, F_k^T)^T, F(t) \in R^n$. What's more, the remaining vectors are formed as, $u(t) = (u_1^T, u_2^T, \cdots, u_k^T)^T, u(t) \in R^n$, $G(q) = (G_1^T, G_2^T, \cdots, G_k^T)^T, G(q) \in R^n$.

Meanwhile, the system kinematic is formulated as: $\dot{X} = J(q)\dot{q}$, where $J = diag\{J_1, J_2, \cdots, J_k\}, J \in R^{m \times n}$ stands for the Jacobian matrix from joint Space to task space of the whole system.

Using the property 3, with a arbitrary velocity vector $\dot{q}_r \in R^n$, the parametrization can be formulated as:

$$H(q)\ddot{q}_r + [C(q, \dot{q}) + B]\dot{q}_r + g(q) = Y(q, \dot{q}, \dot{q}_r, \ddot{q}_r)\theta. \tag{6}$$

Therefore, Substituting (6) into (5) we get the following error dynamics equation:

$$H(q)\dot{S}_r + [C(q, \dot{q}) + B]S_r + F(t) + Y(q, \dot{q}, \dot{q}_r, \ddot{q}_r)\theta = u(t), \tag{7}$$

where reference error S_r are defined as: $S_r \stackrel{\Delta}{=} \dot{q} - \dot{q}_r$.

Define the following joint reference:

$$\dot{q}_r \overset{\triangle}{=} J_S^+(E_S \dot{X}_d - \Im E) + (I_n - J^+ J)\psi + S_d - \Xi\sigma, \tag{8}$$

where $\dot{\sigma} \overset{\triangle}{=} sgn(S_q)$, $J_S \overset{\triangle}{=} E_S J$, $\Im$ and Ξ are diagonal positive definite matrices, $\psi \in R^n$ is a negative gradient for the subtask which could be optimized. The other parameters are defined as [11]:

$$\begin{cases} S \overset{\triangle}{=} J_S^+(\dot{E} + \Im E) - (I_n - J^+ J)\psi \\ S_d \overset{\triangle}{=} S(t_0)e^{-\kappa(t-t_0)} \\ S_q \overset{\triangle}{=} S - S_d. \end{cases} \tag{9}$$

Besides, $\kappa \in R^k$ is a positive definite diagonal matrix.

Then the control input is given as follow:

$$u = -K_r S_r, \tag{10}$$

where $K_r \in R^{n \times n}$ is positive definite square matrix.

Theorem 1. *For system (7) and control law (10), if the control gain α in Eq.(3) satisfies $\alpha > 0$ and K_r, the eigenvalues of Ξ are chosen to be large enough, with small initial error of e, the position error synchronization defined in Section 3 can be achieved.*

Proof. Choose the Lyapunov Function as: $V = \frac{1}{2}S_r^T H(q)S_r$. Obviously, it is positive definite. According to the property 2, the derivative of the chosen Lyapunov function can be derived as:

$$\dot{V} = -S_r^T Y(q, q, q_r, q_r)\theta - S_r^T F(t) - S_r^T(B + K_r)S_r. \tag{11}$$

Then, as the state of the system, desired trajectories and the disturbance $F(t)$ are all bounded. Using property 1, following the conclusion $\|Y(q, q, q_r, q_r)\theta\| \leq \eta(t)$ established in [11], we can conclude: $\|Y(q, q, q_r, q_r)\theta + F(t)\| \leq \eta(t) + d(t)$.

Define $\rho(t) \overset{\triangle}{=} \eta(t) + d(t)$ as the total boundary, then the following conclusion can be derived: $\dot{V} \leq -\|KS_r\|^2 + \|S_r\|\rho(t)$, where $K = (B + K_r)^T(B + K_r)$. By invoking Lyapunov stability theory, with a small initial errors ε contained in a circular neighborhood centered in zero, there exists a big enough feedback gain K_r satisfies, $K \geq \rho(t)$. Then the following conclusion can be derived: $t \to \infty$: $S_r(t) \to \varepsilon$. Since the state signals are all bounded, the following conclusion can be established: $\dot{S}_r(t) \leq \varsigma$, where ς is a bounded constant vector.

Now we should prove that the sliding mode $S_q \to 0$. Consider the Lyapunov function: $V_q = \frac{1}{2}S_q^T S_q$. According to equality (8) and (9), the following conclusion is formed: $\dot{V}_q = S_q^T \dot{S}_q \leq (\|\dot{S}_r\| - \Xi_{im})\|S_q\| = -\omega\|S_q\|$, where $\omega = \Xi_m - \varsigma_{sup}$, with Ξ_m is chosen as the minimum eigenvalue of Ξ, and the ς_{sup} is the supremum of ς. Therefore, choosing Ξ large enough, can guarantee the sliding mode approaches zero. By designing the parameters κ and Ξ, as is discussed in [11], the defined error E will exponentially converge to zero. Using Lemma 1, we can concluded that the position error synchronization is achieved through the designed controller. The proof is completed.

According to [12], we can define the subtask tracking error as: $e_N(t) = (I_n - J^+J)(\dot{q} - \psi)$. Notice that:

$$\begin{aligned}
S &= J^+E_S^{-1}(\dot{E} + \Im E) - (I_n - J^+J)\psi \\
&= J^+(\dot{e} + E_S^{-1}\Im E) - (I_n - J^+J)\psi \\
&= J^+(-\dot{X}_d + E_S^{-1}\Im E) - (I_n - J^+J)\psi + \dot{q}.
\end{aligned}$$

By using property 4, we can conclude: $e_N = (I_n - J^+J)S$. It is easy to conclude that the subtask tracking error approaches zero while S tend to zero. What's more, the subtask dose not effect the main task so it can be a extensional function of the proposed controller.

5   Simulation Study

Considering the kinematic diversity of the whole system, simulation is performed by using three 2-DOF non-linear planer robot fingers (robot 1st,3nd,4rd) and two 3-DOF non-linear planer robot fingers. The task space is assumed to be a two-dimensional space. The 2-DOF non-linear robot fingers Model follow [13],[14]. The 3-DOF planar fingers' model is derived under the same condition as the 2-DOF fingers. Assuming the mass center of each link is at the terminal, and the exact lengths of the links are all set to 1 m, the normal parameters values are given below. The 1st robot finger have two linkers, the mass and inertia of each link is: $m_{11} = 0.5, m_{12} = 1.5, I_{11} = 0.92, I_{12} = 1.13$. The 2nd robot finger's inverse kinematics are ill-posed, the mass and inertia of each link is: $m_{21} = 0.5, m_{22} = 1.5, m_{32} = 1.3, I_{21} = 0.8, I_{22} = 1.3, I_{23} = 0.4$. The 3rd: $m_{31} = 0.64, m_{32} = 0.86, I_{31} = 1.12, I_{32} = 1.04$. The 4th: $m_{41} = 0.92, m_{42} = 0.75, I_{41} = 1.14, I_{42} = 0.67$. The 5th: $m_{51} = 0.4, m_{52} = 1.5, m_{53} = 1.2, I_{51} = 0.8, I_{52} = 1.2, I_{53} = 0.4$. All the values are corresponding to international unit, that is $m \rightarrow kg, I \rightarrow kg \cdot m^2$. By considering the dynamic error and disturbance force, the following setting is implemented: $H_0 = 0.8H^*$, $C_0 = 0.8C^*$, $B_0 = 0.8B^*$, $G_0 = 0.8G^*$, $F_i(t) = 5\sin t, i = 1, 2, \ldots, 12$, where H_0, C_0, B_0, G_0 stand for the estimate value which is used in the controller designing. In correspondence, H^*, C^*, B^*, G^* denote the normal value which is calculated by the practical parameters. The normal viscous joint friction coefficients B^* is set as, $B^* = (1.1, 1.2, 1.34, 1.23, 1.52, 2.36, 3.12, 2.5, 1.2, 2.3, 1.2, 4.2)^T$.

Following [6], the desired trajectory of ith robot end-effector is assigned as: $X_{di} = X_{0i} + (X_{fi} - X_{0i})(1 - e^{-t})$. By setting, $X_0 = (1.366, 1.3660, 2.366, 3.806, 3.1248, 0.0559, 3.2412, -1.5780, 5.366, 3.806)^T$, and $X_{fi} = (0.2412, 1.832)^T, i = 1, 2, \ldots, 5$. The desired trajectory are determined.

Unlike [6], without loss of generality, the base coordination of each robot is set as, $X_{base} = (0, 0, 1, 1.44, 2, -1.41, 3, -3.41, 4, 1.44)^T$. What's more, the initial state of each robot is set as:

$X_{initial} = (0.6731, 1.6592, 0.7719, 3.2885, 2.0838, 0.1268, 1.7745, -2.1439, 6.7768,$
$2.5510)^T,$
$\dot{X}_{initial} = (-1.3281, 0.2984, -1.7438, -1.3085, -1.17, -0.256, -0.7851, -1.0891,$
$-1.0392, 2.8028)^T.$

Besides, the control gain α in Eq.(3) is designed as $0.3 \times I_5$, $\Im$ in Eq.(8) is set
as: $\Im = diag(10, 10, 20, 20, 10, 10, 10, 10, 20, 20)$, β in Eq.(8) is set as: $\Xi = I_{12}$.
The parameter $K_r = diag(30, 30, 30, 30, 30, 60, 60, 60, 60, 60, 60, 60)$.

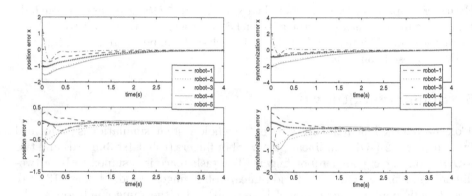

Fig. 1. The left figure shows the asymptotical convergence to zero of the finger-tip
position tracking errors. The right one shows that the synchronization tracking error
asymptotically converges to zero. Proves that the robot fingers are synchronized with
the proposed controller.

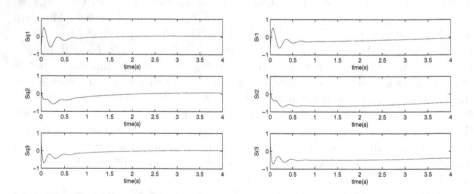

Fig. 2. The left figure shows the sliding mode s_q of robot 2nd which is assumed to be
with kinematic redundancy converge to zero. The right figure shows that the reference
error s_r of robot 2nd in the joint space is bounded in a small range.

The simulation results Fig.1 and Fig. 2 show that under various disturbances, the model-free SMC can also guarantee the asymptotical stability of task space position tracking error. Besides, it is shown that the position error of each individual is synchronized with each other. What's more, it is worth pointing out that compared with the adaptive algorithms already existed [5],[12],[15], the proposed control scheme does not need the precise dynamical model and is less sensitive to disturbances.

6   Conclusion

Normally, the design of a synchronization controller for such complicated redundant multi-fingered hand system with strong coupling is really difficult. Nevertheless, the proposed controller has great performance under various disturbances. However, the controller needs to constrain the initial position which is also its limitation. Besides, the proposed synchronization control low is more practical than the traditional coordination controllers. Finally, the numerical simulation results confirmed the effectiveness of the designed controller.

Acknowledgments. This work was supported in part by the "973" National Basic Research Program of China under Grants 2011CB013300 and 2011CB013301, and the National Natural Science Foundation of China under Grants 60834002, 60973012, 61170031 and 61170024.

References

1. Arimoto, S.: Intelligent control of multi-fingered hands. Ann. Rev. Control 28, 75–85 (2004)
2. Gueaieb, W., Al-Sharhan, S., Bolic, M.: Robust computationally efficient control of cooperative closed-chain manipulators with uncertain dynamics. Automatica 43, 842–851 (2007)
3. Zhao, Y.,Cheah, C. C.: Neural Network Control of Multifingered Robot Hands Using Visual Feedback. IEEE Trans. Neural Netw. 20, 1045–9225 (2009)
4. Sveistrup, H., Schneiberg, S., McKinley, P.A., McFadyen, B.J., Levin, M.F.: Head, arm and trunk coordination during reaching in children. Exp. Brain Res. 188, 237–247 (2008)
5. Sun, D., Mills, K.M.: Adaptive Synchronized Control for Coordination of Multi-robot Assembly Tasks. IEEE Trans. Robot. Automat. 18, 498–510 (2002)
6. Zhao, D., Li, C., Zhu, Q.: Low-pass-filter-based position synchronization sliding mode control for multiple robotic manipulator systems. Part I: J. Systems and Control Engineering 225, 1136–1148 (2011)
7. Sun, D., Shao, X.Y., Feng, G.: A Model-Free Cross-Coupled Control for Position Synchronization of Multi-Axis Motions: Theory and Experiments. IEEE Trans. Contr. Syst. Technol. 15, 306–314 (2007)
8. Huang, J., Wang, H.W., Matsuno, T., Fukuda, T., Sekiyama, K.: Robust Velocity Sliding Mode Control of Mobile Wheeled Inverted Pendulum Systems. In: 2009 IEEE International Conference on Robotics and Automation, pp. 2983–2988. IEEE Press, Kobe (2009)

9. Huang, J., Guan, Z.H., Matsuno, T., Fukuda, T., Sekiyama, K.: Sliding-Mode Velocity Control of Mobile-Wheeled Inverted-Pendulum Systems. IEEE Trans. Robot. 26, 750–758 (2010)
10. Spong, M.W., Hutchinson, S., Vidyasagar, M.: Robot modeling and control. John Wiley & Sons, Inc. (2006)
11. Parra-Vega, V., Arimoto, S., Liu, Y.H., Hirzinger, G., Akella, P.: Dynamic Sliding PID Control for Tracking of Robot Manipulators: Theory and Experiments. IEEE Trans. Robot. Automat. 19, 967–976 (2003)
12. Liu, Y.C., Chopra, N.: Controlled Synchronization of Heterogeneous Robotic Manipulators in the Task Space. IEEE Trans. Robot. 28, 268–275 (2012)
13. Yu, S.H., Yu, X.H., Shirinzadeh, B., Man, Z.H.: Continuous finite-time control for robotic manipulators with terminal sliding mode. Automatica 41, 1957–1964 (2005)
14. Feng, Y., Yu, X.H., Man, Z.H.: Non-singular terminal sliding mode control of rigid manipulators. Automatica 41, 2159–2167 (2002)
15. Damaren, C.J.: An Adaptive Controller for Two Cooperating Flexible Manipulators. J. Robotic Syst. 20(1), 15–21 (2003)

An FPGA-Based Real-Time Solution
for Networked Motion Control Systems

Maoqing Ding, Xiong Xu, Yonghua Yan, and Zhenhua Xiong

State Key Laboratory of Mechanical System and Vibration, School of Mechanical
Engineering, Shanghai Jiao Tong University, Shanghai 200240, P.R. China
{dingmaoqing,xiaoxu85,yhyan,mexiong}@sjtu.edu.cn

Abstract. In order to solve the problem of real-time communication
for multi-axis in networked motion control systems(NMCSs), a field-
programmable gate array (FPGA) based real-time solution is proposed.
In the proposed solution, a hardware data processing strategy is designed
and the data link layer of real-time communication is implemented on
FPGA. Moreover, in order to decrease the forwarding delay, the forwarding of real-time communication data is shifted down to data link
layer from application layer. Theoretical analysis and experimental results show that the FPGA-based real-time solution reduces jitter and
delay of communication. After 20000 tests, each nodes delay is 1.180 μs
in average, which achieves the same real-time performance as EtherCAT.

Keywords: networked motion control systems (NMCSs), real-time communication, data link layer, field-programmable gate array (FPGA).

1 Introduction

With the growing requirements in multi-axis coordinated motion and networked
manufacturing, embedded motion control systems with multi-node networks
have become a development trend and research focus in industrial automation
field. They are widely used in computer numerical control(CNC) systems, printing machines and robotics. However, with the development of NMCSs, a large
amount of commands and feedback information must be exchanged efficiently
and frequently among dozens or even hundreds of nodes, thus the problem of
real-time communication becomes a challenge for NMCSs [3].

Various motion control networks have been proposed by standard organiza-
tions and businesses since 1990s, such as Controller Area Network (CAN) [7]
and Servo System Control Network (SSCNET). However, their poor capability and limited transmission speed have become the bottleneck of these field
buses to provide real-time communication for NMCSs [10]. They are gradually
replaced by industrial Ethernet which has higher communication rate and better openness [6]. The existing industrial Ethernet can be classified into three
main categories [12,9]. The first category, such as Ethernet/IP [5] and FF HSE
[2], adds an industrial-automation-specific application layer on top of TCP/IP
and still adopts traditional forwarding method that the data is exchanged in

C.-Y. Su, S. Rakheja, H. Liu (Eds.): ICIRA 2012, Part II, LNAI 7507, pp. 581–591, 2012.

application layer. The data packet can not be forwarded to next node until the application layer finished receiving the packet, extracting commands from the packet, packaging and writing input data to the packet, thus forwarding delay of a node reaches dozens of microseconds. This category is therefore can only offer a real-time performance of about 100 milliseconds. The second category uses priority scheme in the Ethernet MAC layer to improve real-time performance, and they can achieve a real-time performance of about 10 milliseconds, typically. PROFINET RT [8] is an example of this category. EtherCAT is a presentative of the third category which optimizes the original MAC scheme of Ethernet. It obtains a better real-time performance by changing the data reception method used in traditional Ethernet. At the arrival of a frame, each slave extracts the output data addressed to the frame and inserts the input data for the master. Those operations are carried out "on the fly" [1]. The frame just passes through the slave and the forwarding delay of a slave is very short. With this method, EtherCAT is able to offer millisecond real-time performance, which is much better than other industrial Ethernet protocols.

However, the hardware implementation of EtherCAT which leads to the high-level performance is not available to the users since EtherCAT is not an open-source technology [4]. This means that it is difficult for technical users to do further research and development on it. Besides, end-users have to buy specific chips called EtherCAT slave controller (ESC) or get the license of its IP core from Beckhoff in practical applications, which will be expensive in the case of a large number of nodes. For example, large radio telescope uses more than one thousand nodes to adjust the attitude of the main reflector panel [11,13]. One ESC chip is about 30 dollars at present, so tens of thousands of dollars are needed to pay for the ESC chips. The cost for the specific chips or license in mass production such as robotics and printing machines is also big. At present, FPGAs are commonly used in motion control systems to create custom hardware circuit logic, so real-time solutions based on FPGA can be easily implemented by adding an Ethernet PHY module to these existing systems. The cost of an Ethernet PHY module is about 4 dollars, which is far superior to EtherCAT.

In this paper, we focus on the design and implementation of real-time communication in NMCSs. An FPGA-based real-time solution is proposed. The real-time performance of NMCSs is improved by shifting the forwarding of real-time data to data link layer from application layer, which greatly reduces the forwarding delay of slave nodes. Experimental results show that the real-time solution is as good as EtherCAT in term of real-time performance, which is one of the best industrial Ethernet protocols at present.

In detail, this paper is organized as follows: Section 2 gives a real-time analysis of the NMCSs. In section 3, we are devoted to the implementation of the proposed solution. A platform is built and experiments are conducted in section 4. Finally, the paper ends with the conclusions in section 5.

2 Real-Time Analysis

In NMCSs, real-time performance is the key element to realize complex control functions. The indicators commonly used to specify the real-time performance are forwarding delay of one node, minimum achievable cycle time and the jitter of cycle time [16,15]. In traditional forwarding methods, the data is exchanged in application layer and forwarding delay of a node reaches dozens of microseconds. In the case of a certain number of nodes and topology, longer forwarding delay means that the minimum cycle time is much greater. Furthermore, time for processing data in the application layer is uncertain, which causes the jitter of cycle time and affects real-time performance of communication systems.

In order to reduce forwarding delay and cycle time, the forwarding of real-time data is shifted down to data link layer from application layer in the proposed real-time solution. Data is extracted and inserted in the data link layer without any other operations, thus the progress of forwarding data is simplified and the real-time performance is improved.

Next, we will analyze the real-time performance of NMCSs in detail. Ring topology is used as an example, since it is widely adopted in existing NMCSs. A lumped frame technology is used to avoid collisions and conflictions in the communication progress. The lumped frame which contains command data for all slave nodes is periodically issued by the master node. At the arrival of the frame, each slave node extracts the command data from the lumped frame and inserts feedback data to the frame, and then forwards it to the next slave node. The lumped frame circulates among all the slave nodes and finally returns to the master node, which means a periodic real-time communication has been finished.

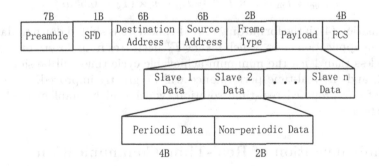

Fig. 1. Structure of a lumped frame

Fig. 1 shows the structure of the lumped frame, which is similar to standard Ethernet frame. In contrast to standard Ethernet frame, the payload of the lumped frame is separated to n fields, where n is the number of slave nodes. Each field is 6 bytes, including 4 bytes for periodic data and another 2 bytes for non-periodic data, such as alarm information.

Since we use the lumped frame technology, only one frame is required to organize the real-time data exchange in a cycle. Therefore, the cycle time T_{Cyc} can be given by the following formula:

$$T_{Cyc} = T_m + n \times T_s^{tot} + T_i, \tag{1}$$

where T_m is the total delay introduced by master node, including forwarding time of master node, PHY delay of master node (RX+TX) and propagation delay on the cables. n is the number of slave nodes. T_s^{tot} represents the total delay introduced by a slave node. T_i is the network idle time.

The total delay introduced by a slave node T_s^{tot} can be obtained as follows:

$$T_s^{tot} = T_s^f + T_p + T_c, \tag{2}$$

where T_s^f represents the forwarding delay inside the slave node. It depends on the implementation of the slave node, for example, if the forwarding of a frame is finished in application layer, the forwarding delay is up to dozens of microseconds, but it is less than $1\mu s$ if the forwarding is carried out in data link layer. T_p is PHY delay of a slave node (RX+TX). It varies between different vendors but in practice it is not above 500 ns [14]. T_c is the propagation delay on the cables. It is proportional to the length of the cable used between two nodes and typically less than 50 ns per 10 m cables [14]. Hence, T_s^{tot} can be calculated as:

$$T_s^{tot} \approx T_s^f + 0.5\mu s + 0.05\mu s = T_s^f + 0.55\mu s. \tag{3}$$

The network idle period in equation (1) is obviously set to zero when calculating the minimum achievable cycle time, so we get the following expression:

$$T_{Cyc} = T_m + n \times T_s^{tot} \approx T_m + n \times (T_s^f + 0.55\mu s). \tag{4}$$

From equation (4), if the forwarding of real-time data is shifted down to data link layer from application layer, which means T_s^f decreases from dozens of microseconds to less than 1 μs, the minimum achievable cycle time will be significantly reduced, and the real-time performance will be greatly improved. That is the reason of our proposed real-time solution, which will be implemented in the next section.

3   Implementation of Real-Time Communication

The theoretical analysis shows that real-time performance improves as a hardware data processing strategy is adopted. Its implementation on FPGA will be given in this section.

3.1   System Architecture

Fig. 2 illustrates the architecture of a networked node in NMCS, which only shows the modules used for real-time communication among nodes. Each node

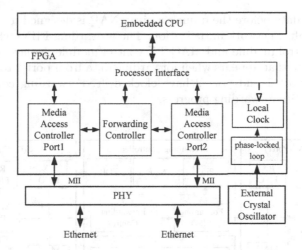

Fig. 2. System architecture of a networked node

mainly consists of an embedded CPU, an FPGA module and an Ethernet PHY module. The embedded CPU is used to realize functions of application layer, such as data processing and control tasks. Ethernet PHY module implements the physical layer of real-time communication.

The data link layer of real-time communication is implemented on FPGA and consists of a processor interface, a phase-locked loop (PLL), two media access controllers (MAC), a local clock module and a forwarding controller. A signal produced by external crystal oscillator via PLL is used as input signal of the local clock. To make sure that all the slave nodes are able to finish coordinate motions with a high precision, slave clocks are synchronized with master clock by IEEE 1588 protocol [17]. Port 1 and port 2 have the same MAC, which contains TX module (including MAC TX control and TX FIFO) and RX module (including MAC RX control and RX FIFO) and provides full transmit and receive functions [18].

3.2   Design of the Forwarding Module

As shown in Fig. 3, the key component of the forwarding module is the forwarding controller, which consists of a forwarding control module, a forwarding FIFO module, a feedback data register(FDR), a node address register(NAR) and a packet length counter(PLC). For users' convenience to process non-real-time data, the traditional forwarding method in application layer is preserved when designing the forwarding module in data link layer. The progress of forwarding a frame from port 1 to port 2 is taken as an example as the adverse progress is similar.

PLC is designed to counter the length of the frame, and it decides the field where feedback data is written in the lumped frame, which will be discussed later, therefore, complex addressing used in EtherCAT is avoid. FDR is used to store feedback data before the frame's arrival. NAR is designed to save the slave node number after network initialization. The forwarding FIFO which connects forwarding control module and MAC TX control module, is developed to avoid metastable state that appears when forwarding data from port 1 to port 2, since the clocks of port 1 and port 2 have clock drift. Forwarding control module controls the entire forwarding progress.

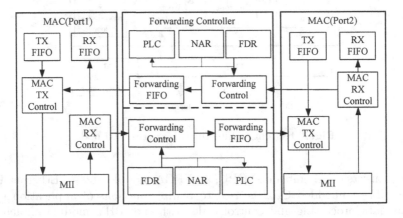

Fig. 3. Forwarding module in data link layer

The key progress of forwarding is to insert the feedback data to the correct field of the frame, which is finished by the cooperation of NAR, PLC, FDR and forwarding control module. After network initialization, the slave node number is saved in NAR and the corresponding position of the slave data in the lumped frame is calculated as:

$$L_k = 22 + 6 \times (k - 1), \tag{5}$$

where k is the slave node number and L_k denotes the corresponding position of the slave data. Besides, feedback data has been written into FDR before the frame's arrival.

When the frame reaches media independent interface (MII) of port 1, it is sent to RX FIFO of port 1 as well as the forwarding controller. The PLC starts to counter the length of the frame once the frame arrives at the forwarding control module. If the accepted length of the frame is equal to L_k, feedback data in FDR will replace the command data in the frame under the control of forwarding control module, then the new frame is written into the forwarding FIFO and transmitted to port 2. Finally, the application layer reads out the command data from RX FIFO of port 1 in event-driven manner, and finishes its control functions under synchronized clock. These operations are carried out after the forwarding progress is completed, so they do not introduce forwarding delay. The entire forwarding progress only cost less than 1 μs, which will be demonstrated in the following experiments.

4 Experimental Results

To evaluate the performance of the proposed real-time solution, we have built an experimental platform as shown in Fig. 4. There are 4 slave nodes and 1 master node in the platform, which are connected by unshielded twisted paired (UTP) in a ring topology. Each slave node mainly consists of a digital signal processor (DSP), an FPGA and an Intel LXT973. The real-time solution is implemented on an Altera Cyclone II EP2C8Q208I8N FPGA.

4.1 Forwarding Delay of a Slave Node

In this experiment, we compared the forwarding delay of a slave node between the proposed real-time solution and the traditional forwarding method. The payload of a frame were 20 bytes, 36 bytes, 64 bytes and 100 bytes, respectively. The maximum, the minimum, the average, and the jitter of the forwarding delay which were obtained from 20000 repeated tests, are outlined in Table 1. As can be seen, the forwarding delay reaches dozens of microseconds in the traditional forwarding method, but only has 0.802 μs in the real-time solution. Besides, Fig. 5(a) shows that the forwarding delay increases rapidly with the number of payloads in the traditional forwarding method, while it stays on the same value

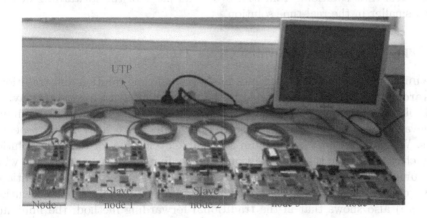

Fig. 4. Experimental set-up

Table 1. Forwarding delay in two different forwarding methods over 20000 tests

Data payload	Traditional forwarding method(μs)				Real-time solution (μs)			
(*Bytes*)	Maximum	Minimum	Average	Jitter	Maximum	Minimum	Average	Jitter
20	16.240	14.820	14.879	1.420	0.840	0.760	0.8020	0.080
36	25.600	24.220	24.276	1.380	0.840	0.760	0.8021	0.080
64	44.080	42.680	42.759	1.400	0.840	0.760	0.8021	0.080
100	65.240	63.820	63.888	1.420	0.840	0.760	0.8022	0.080

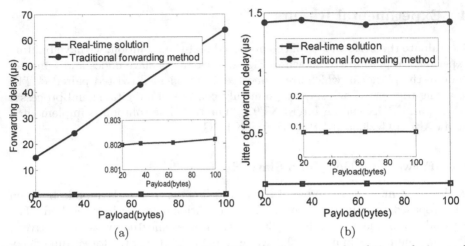

Fig. 5. A comparison of forwarding delay between the proposed real-time solution and the traditional forwarding method that forwarding is finished in application layer. (a) The average of the forwarding delay over 20000 tests; (b) The jitter of the forwarding delay over 20000 tests.

in the real-time solution. From Fig. 5(b), the jitter of the forwarding delay is much smaller in the real-time solution.

4.2   The Minimum Achievable Cycle Time

The minimum achievable cycle times for both real-time solution and traditional forwarding method were also tested in the experiment, with a constant payload of 100bytes. The number of slave nodes ranged from 1 to 4. The minimum achievable cycle time and its jitter are shown in Fig. 6 after 20000 repeated tests. We can see that the minimum achievable cycle time for real-time solution is much smaller than that for traditional forwarding method. For example, when the number of slave nodes is 4, the minimum achievable cycle time for traditional forwarding method reaches 327.2 μs, while it is only 61.9 μs in real-time solution. Fig. 6(a) also shows that in the traditional forwarding method, the minimum achievable cycle time linearly increases with the slope of 60 $\mu s/node$, but the slope is reduced to less than 2 $\mu s/node$ in real-time solution. As can be seen from Fig. 6(b), the jitter of cycle time is also much smaller in the real-time solution.

4.3   Total Delay Introduced by a Slave Node

In this experiment the total delay introduced by a slave node in real-time solution was tested. The payload of a frame respectively were 20 bytes, 36 bytes, 64 bytes and 100 bytes. The number of slave nodes ranged from 1 to 4. The minimum achievable cycle time is shown in Fig. 7(a) after 20000 repeated tests. We can see that the minimum achievable cycle time with different payloads is a set of

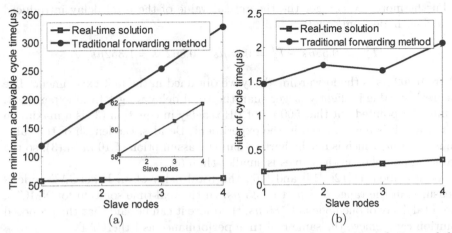

Fig. 6. A comparison of the minimum cycle time between the real-time solution and the traditional forwarding method with a constant payload of 100 bytes. (a) The minimum achievable cycle time; (b) The jitter of the cycle time over 20000 tests.

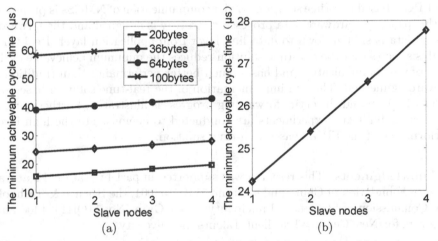

Fig. 7. The experimental results in the test of total delay introduced by a slave node. (a) The minimum achievable cycle time as a function of the number of slave nodes with different payload; (b) The minimum achievable cycle time as a function of the number of slave nodes with 36 bytes payload.

parallel lines and their slopes are the same. Therefore, the total delay introduced by a slave node is irrelevant to the payload of the frame. We select the line of 36 bytes payload to calculate the total delay of one node, as shown in Fig. 7(b). The slope of the line is 1.180, so the total delay which equals to the slope is 1.180 μs.

Furthermore, we can get the theoretical value of the total delay introduced by a slave node from equation (3):

$$T_s^{tot} = 0.55\mu s + T_s^f = 0.55\mu s + 0.802\mu s = 1.352\mu s,$$

where 0.802 μs is the forwarding delay we obtained in the first experiment. The theoretical value is slightly larger than the total delay we get from experiment. It must be pointed out that 500 ns of PHY delay in equation (3) is a maximum value, which is not achieved in the experiment. Besides, the length of the cable we use is 3 m, which is much shorter than the assumption of 10 m in (3), so the propagation delay on the cables is smaller than 50 ns.

As described in [12], [14] and [16], the total delay of an EtherCAT node is measured in the range of 1 μs to 1.35 μs. In the real-time solution for NMCSs, the total delay of one node is 1.180 μs, therefore it can be said that the proposed solution can achieve the same real-time performance as EtherCAT.

5   Conclusions

An FPGA-based real-time solution for the communication of NMCSs is proposed in this paper. A hardware data processing strategy is designed and the forwarding of data is shifted down to data link layer from application layer. Real-time analysis shows that the real-time solution reduces the minimum achievable cycle time of the communication and has a much better performance than traditional forwarding method. Then an implementation of the real-time solution based on FPGA is given and the entire forwarding progress is illustrated. Furthermore, a platform is built and experiments are conducted to demonstrate the high level performance of the FPGA-based real-time solution.

Acknowledgments. This research was supported in part by National Natural Science Foundation of China under Grant 51120155001, the Science & Technology Commission of Shanghai Municipality under Grant No. 11QH1401400 and Program for New Century Excellent Talents in University.

References

1. EtherCAT Technology Group, http://www.ethercat.org
2. Fieldbus Foundation, http://www.fieldbus.org
3. Baillieul, J., Antsaklis, P.: Control and communication challenges in networked real-time systems. Proceedings of the IEEE 95(1), 9–28 (2007)
4. Bonfe, M., Boldrin, A., Mainardi, E.: Open-source technologies for embedded control systems: from robotics to home/building automation. In: European Industrial Ethernet Award. IEEE (2011)
5. Brooks, P.: Ethernet/IP-industrial protocol. In: Proceedings of 8th IEEE International Conference on Emerging Technologies and Factory Automation, vol. 2, pp. 505–514. IEEE (2001)

6. Decotignie, J.: The many faces of industrial Ethernet. IEEE Industrial Electronics Magazine 3(1), 8–19 (2009)
7. Farsi, M., Ratcliff, K., Barbosa, M.: An overview of controller area network. Computing & Control Engineering Journal 10(3), 113–120 (1999)
8. Feld, J.: PROFINET-scalable factory communication for all applications. In: Proceedings of IEEE International Workshop on Factory Communication Systems, pp. 33–38. IEEE (2004)
9. Felser, M.: Real-time Ethernet-industry prospective. Proceedings of the IEEE 93(6), 1118–1129 (2005)
10. Flammini, A., Ferrari, P., Sisinni, E., Marioli, D., Taroni, A.: Sensor interfaces: from field-bus to Ethernet and Internet. Sensors and Actuators A: Physical 101(1), 194–202 (2002)
11. Imbriale, W.: Distortion compensation techniques for large reflector antennas. In: IEEE Proceedings of Aerospace Conference, pp. 799–804. IEEE (2001)
12. Jasperneite, J., Schumacher, M., Weber, K.: Limits of increasing the performance of industrial Ethernet protocols. In: IEEE Conference on Emerging Technologies and Factory Automation, pp. 17–24. IEEE (2007)
13. Nan, R., Ren, G., Zhu, W., Lu, Y.: Adaptive cable-mesh reflector for the FAST. Acta Astronomica Sinica 44(2), 13–18 (2003)
14. Prytz, G.: A performance analysis of EtherCAT and PROFINET IRT. In: IEEE International Conference on Emerging Technologies and Factory Automation, pp. 408–415. IEEE (2008)
15. Seno, L., Vitturi, S., Zunino, C.: Real time Ethernet networks evaluation using performance indicators. In: IEEE Conference on Emerging Technologies & Factory Automation, pp. 1–8. IEEE (2009)
16. Vitturi, S., Peretti, L., Seno, L., Zigliotto, M., Zunino, C.: Real-time Ethernet networks for motion control. Computer Standards & Interfaces 33(5), 465–476 (2011)
17. Xu, X., Sheng, X., Xiong, Z., Zhu, X.: Time-stamped cross-coupled control in networked CNC systems. In: IEEE International Conference on Robotics and Automation, pp. 4378–4383. IEEE (2011)
18. Xu, X., Xiong, Z., Wu, J., Zhu, X.: Development of a Networked Multi-agent System Based on Real-Time Ethernet. In: Jeschke, S., Liu, H., Schilberg, D. (eds.) ICIRA 2011, Part I. LNCS, vol. 7101, pp. 356–365. Springer, Heidelberg (2011)

Synchronous Control for Trajectory Tracking in Networked Multi-agent Systems

Xiong Xu, Zhenhua Xiong, Jianhua Wu, and Xiangyang Zhu

State Key Laboratory of Mechanical System and Vibration, School of Mechanical
Engineering, Shanghai Jiao Tong University, Shanghai 200240, P.R. China
{xiaoxu85,mexiong,wujh,mexyzhu}@sjtu.edu.cn

Abstract. This paper is devoted to designing a decentralized
synchronous controller for networked multi-agent systems. In the proposed controller, due to the limitations of message scheduling and network bandwidth, position synchronization error is defined as a differential
position error between current axis and its preceding one. It is proven
that the proposed controller can asymptotically stabilize both position
and synchronization errors to zero. In addition, a motion message estimator is adopted in the synchronous controller to reduce the effect
of network-induced delays. Simulations are performed on a networked
multi-axis machine tool to validate its effectiveness and demonstrate that
it can achieve good contouring performance for the multi-axis trajectory
tracking over the real-time network.

Keywords: Networked multi-agent system, multi-axis motion, position
synchronization, cross-coupled control, real-time network.

1 Introduction

Along with the continuous improvement in modern industrial and commercial
systems, there are increasing demands for applying a shared data network in control systems. For instance, in applications with a large number of sensors and
actuators, such as computer numerical control (CNC) machining centers, humanoid robots, and printing machines, real-time control networks can be used
to perform information exchanges among distributed nodes. These network systems are called networked multi-agent systems (NMASs) [7], where functional
agents such as sensors, actuators and controllers are spatially distributed and
interconnected by one communication network. Compared with traditional centralized control systems with directly wiring devices together, NMASs can reduce
the problems of wiring connection and transmit-length limitation, and decrease
installation, reconfiguration and maintenance time and costs. For a NMAS, especially in a multi-axis motion control system, synchronous errors among axes are
important aspects that significantly affect the motion accuracy [4]. To improve
the synchronization performance for centralized systems, many efforts have been
devoted to compensate different inertias and disturbances in different axes. Koren [5] proposed a cross-coupled control (CCC) for biaxial motion systems. Various improved CCC designs were later proposed to further reduce synchronous

C.-Y. Su, S. Rakheja, H. Liu (Eds.): ICIRA 2012, Part II, LNAI 7507, pp. 592–602, 2012.
© Springer-Verlag Berlin Heidelberg 2012

errors of different axes [10,3]. However, in network-based systems, besides the inertias and disturbances factors, the message scheduling and the network-induced delays also influence the synchronous performance. To the authors' knowledge, literatures focusing on NMASs study combined with the synchronous control are rarely seen. In [12], we made some attempts on this issue and have proposed a time-stamped cross-coupled controller in networked CNC systems. But this controller is based on biaxial motion systems and is still centralized. This paper furthers the research and investigates a multi-axis synchronous control over real-time networks.

The proposed controller is designed to accomplish coordination tasks in networked multi-agent systems. Based on the detailed analysis of the problems of the message scheduling in the real-time network, we choose a differential position error between current axis and its preceding one as the position synchronization error. In order to reduce the effect of network-induced delays, a motion message estimator is adopted in the synchronous controller to estimate the current position error of the preceding axis. Simulations are conducted on a networked CNC system to demonstrate the effectiveness of the proposed approach.

The remainder of this paper is organized as follows. Section 2 is devoted to the problem formulation and assumptions. In Section 3, we design a decentralized synchronous controller for networked multi-agent systems. Simulations are performed to demonstrate the effectiveness of the proposed synchronization control approach in Section 4. Conclusions and future research perspectives are given in the last section.

2 Problem Formulation and Assumptions

The main purpose of this work focuses on synchronized control of networked multi-agent systems in the manufacturing field, especially for the computer numerical control (CNC) machines. It generally consists of a set of smart networked motion control nodes, which are spatially distributed and interconnected by one real-time network. And its typical network architecture is the ring topology due to the low cabling cost, which can be shown in Fig. 1. In terms of the system architecture, the master node controls the entire digital communication and implements the key functions of a reference position generator. including code

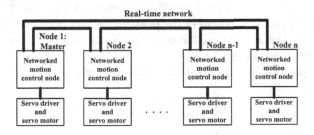

Fig. 1. Network architecture of a networked multi-agent system

interpretation, velocity planning, trajectory interpolation, etc. Meanwhile, all distributed motion control nodes can perform position-loop control and synchronous control in order to achieve the parallel computing and fast response. The detailed assumptions and notations used in the decentralized synchronous controller are described as follows:

(1) Consider that a networked multi-agent system with n agents requires motion coordination of all distributed agents. As in [9], this task requirement can be transformed to a relationship that the position errors of all agents must be regulated, namely

$$c_1 e_1 = c_2 e_2 = \cdots = c_n e_n, \tag{1}$$

where c_i denotes the coupling parameter of the ith agent and e_i is the corresponding position error. It is therefore used as the synchronization control goal in this work. Note that the relationship can be obtained for most actual applications, such as contouring error elimination problem in CNC [10] and formation control of multiple mobile robots [11].

(2) The synchronization of the networked multi-agent system can be divided into two aspects: time synchronization and position synchronization. Time synchronization is used to make all networked nodes share a common sense of a time, while the position synchronization refers to the motion synchronization by synchronizing the motion of each agent with those of others. And we focus on the decentralized motion synchronization based on the assumption that all the distributed clocks are synchronized. This can be realized by using a clock synchronization protocol, such as network time protocol or IEEE 1588 standard.

3   Control Design

In this section, a synchronous controller will be designed for networked multi-agent systems, which is then followed by the stability analysis.

3.1   Position Synchronization Errors

Consider the dynamics of a general mechanical system with n-motion axes in the matrix format [9]

$$H(x)\ddot{x} + C(x, \dot{x})\dot{x} = \tau, \tag{2}$$

where $H(x) = \{H_i(x_i)\}$ is the inertia of the system, which is positive definite, $C(x, \dot{x}) = \{C_i(x_i, \dot{x}_i)\}$ denotes the coriolis and centripetal forces, $\dot{H}(x) - 2C(x, \dot{x})$ is skew-symmetric, $x = \{x_i\}$ denotes the position coordinate, and $\tau = \{\tau_i\}$ means the input torque. Define the position error of the ith axis as $e_i = x_i^d - x_i$, where x_i^d indicates the desired position.

In [10], the position synchronization errors are defined as

$$\begin{cases} \varepsilon_1 = c_1 e_1 - c_2 e_2 \\ \varepsilon_2 = c_2 e_2 - c_3 e_3 \\ \quad \vdots \\ \varepsilon_n = c_n e_n - c_1 e_1 \end{cases}, \tag{3}$$

where ε_i denotes the position synchronization error of the ith axis. Note that the synchronization goal $c_1 e_1 = c_2 e_2 = \cdots = c_n e_n$ is achieved automatically when all position synchronization errors in (3) are zero. As in [10], a coupled position error that links e_i and ε_i together is described as

$$E_i = c_i e_i + \beta \int_0^t (\varepsilon_i - \varepsilon_{i-1}) dw, \qquad (4)$$

where β is a positive control gain, w denotes a time variable, and E_i contains the information of current axis i and two neighboring axes $i-1$ and $i+1$. From the Equation (4), $E_i \to 0$ implies $e_i \to 0$ and $\varepsilon_i \to 0$.

Then, it should be further considered when implementing the control strategy in a decentralized architecture, as shown in Fig. 1. In some real-time networks, such as the EtherCAT network with a ring topology [8], a lumped frame is periodically sent by the master node and passed through all the slave motion control nodes. The basic operating principle is that all slave nodes in the EtherCAT network can read command data (such as reference position) and write feedback data (such as position error) to the EtherCAT telegram as it passes by. It is easy for each slave node to acquire the feedback positions of its preceding nodes, but it is hard to obtain its subsequent nodes' feedback data. This problem can be settled by a high-level planner, as mentioned in [11]. However, the method would increase the network-induced delays in the networked multi-agent system because it needs more network bandwidth to transfer all slave nodes' position errors and each slave node can only receive the feedback position errors in next lumped frame.

Considering the problem of the message scheduling in the networked multi-agent system, the position synchronization error should be defined as a subset of possible pairs of preceding axes. We therefore define the position synchronization errors in this work as

$$\begin{cases} \varepsilon_1 = c_1 e_1 - c_n e_n \\ \varepsilon_2 = c_2 e_2 - c_1 e_1 \\ \quad \vdots \\ \varepsilon_n = c_n e_n - c_{n-1} e_{n-1} \end{cases} \qquad (5)$$

At the same time, the coupled position error should be rewritten as

$$E_i = c_i e_i + \beta \int_0^t \varepsilon_i dw, \qquad (6)$$

where E_i just contains the information of current axis i and its preceding axis $i-1$ when compared to [10].

In the following section, a decentralized synchronous control for position synchronization will be developed by incorporating the above cross-coupling concept into slide mode control design.

3.2   Decentralized Synchronous Control

Differentiating E_i of (6) with respect to time yields

$$\dot{E}_i = \dot{c}_i e_i + c_i \dot{e}_i + \beta \varepsilon_i. \qquad (7)$$

We then define a command vector u_i as

$$u_i = c_i \dot{x}_i^d + \dot{c}_i e_i + \beta \varepsilon_i + \Lambda E_i, \tag{8}$$

where Λ denotes a positive control gain. It also leads to the following vector combining both E_i and $\dot{E}_i$:

$$r_i = u_i - c_i \dot{x}_i = c_i \dot{e}_i + \dot{c}_i e_i + \beta \varepsilon_i + \Lambda E_i = \dot{E}_i + \Lambda E_i. \tag{9}$$

Thus, a controller is needed to restrict r_i to lie on the sliding surface such that the coupled position error E_i and its time derivative $\dot{E}_i$ tend to zero. Refer to the controller in [10], a synchronous controller is expressed by

$$\tau_i = K_i^H c_i^{-1}(\dot{u}_i - \dot{c}_i \dot{x}_i) + K_i^C c_i^{-1} u_i + K_{ri} c_i^{-1} r_i + sign(c_i^{-1} r_i) K_i^s + 2c_i^2 K_e e_i, \tag{10}$$

where K_i^H and K_i^C are positive feedforward control gains, K_{ri} and K_e are positive feedback control gains, and K_i^s is a positive parameter that satisfies the following condition:

$$K_i^s = \Delta_i^H \left\| c_i^{-1}(\dot{u}_i - \dot{c}_i \dot{x}_i) \right\| + \Delta_i^C \left\| c_i^{-1} u_i \right\|, \tag{11}$$

in which Δ_i^H and Δ_i^C are scalars. Here, we give the following assumptions: x_i^d is bounded up to its second derivative and $H_i(x_i)$ and $C_i(x_i, \dot{x}_i)$ are bounded if their arguments are bounded. Note that the control gains K_i^H and K_i^C are utilized instead of the modeling parameters $H_i(x_i)$ and $C_i(x_i, \dot{x}_i)$ so that the synchronous controller is independent of the model. In order to compensate for the nonlinear effect caused by the difference between these feedforward control gains and the real modeling parameters, a saturated control is used, which can be seen in the fourth term of the right-hand side of (10). The last term in (10) is included by reason of system stability, and is different from [10] as we adopt different definitions of position synchronization error and coupled position error.

Theorem 1: For the decentralized synchronous controller (10), the system is stable during the motion and guarantees $e_i \to 0$ and $\varepsilon_i \to 0$ as time $t \to \infty$, under the following conditions:

1) scalars Δ_i^H and Δ_i^C are large enough to satisfy $\Delta_i^H \geq \left\| K_i^H - H_i(x_i) \right\|$ and $\Delta_i^C \geq \left\| K_i^C - C_i(x_i, \dot{x}_i) \right\|$;

2) the control gain K_{ri} is properly selected to satisfy

$$\lambda_{\min}(K_{ri}) \geq \lambda_{\max}(-H_i(x_i)c_i^{-1}\dot{c}_i),$$

where $\lambda_{\min}(\cdot)$ and $\lambda_{\max}(\cdot)$ denote the minimum and maximum values of $(\cdot)$, respectively.

Proof: Define a Lyapunov function candidate as

$$V = \sum_{i=1}^{n} [\frac{1}{2} H_i(x_i)(c_i^{-1} r_i)^2 + K_e(c_i e_i)^2] + \sum_{i=1}^{n} [\frac{1}{2} K_e \Lambda \beta (\int_0^t \varepsilon_i dw)^2]. \tag{12}$$

Differentiating V with respect to time yields

$$\dot{V} = \sum_{i=1}^{n} [H_i(x_i)c_i^{-2}r_i\dot{r}_i + \tfrac{1}{2}\dot{H}_i(x_i)(c_i^{-1}r_i)^2 - H_i(x_i)c_i^{-3}\dot{c}_ir_i^2$$
$$+2K_e(c_i\dot{c}_ie_i^2 + c_i^2e_i\dot{e}_i)] + \sum_{i=1}^{n} [K_e\Lambda\beta\varepsilon_i(\int_0^t \varepsilon_i dw)] \tag{13}$$

Substituting (10) into (2) yields the closed-loop dynamics

$$H_i(x_i)c_i^{-1}\dot{r}_i + C_i(x_i,\dot{x}_i)c_i^{-1}r_i + K_{ri}c_i^{-1}r_i$$
$$+Z_i + sign(c_i^{-1}r_i)K_i^s + 2c_i^2K_ee_i = 0 \tag{14}$$

where $Z_i = (K_i^H - H_i(x_i))c_i^{-1}(\dot{u}_i - \dot{c}_i\dot{x}_i) + (K_i^C - C_i(x_i,\dot{x}_i))c_i^{-1}u_i$, which is bounded under the aforementioned assumptions. Multiplying both sides of (14) by $c_i^{-1}r_i$ yields

$$H_i(x_i)c_i^{-2}r_i\dot{r}_i + C_i(x_i,\dot{x}_i)c_i^{-2}r_i^2 + K_{ri}c_i^{-2}r_i^2$$
$$+(c_i^{-1}r_i)Z_i + \left\|c_i^{-1}r_i\right\| K_i^s + 2K_er_ic_ie_i = 0 \tag{15}$$

Substituting (15) into (13) yields

$$\dot{V} = \sum_{i=1}^{n} [-H_i(x_i)c_i^{-3}\dot{c}_ir_i^2 - K_{ri}c_i^{-2}r_i^2 + 2K_e(c_i\dot{c}_ie_i^2 + c_i^2e_i\dot{e}_i)]$$
$$- \sum_{i=1}^{n} [(c_i^{-1}r_i)Z_i + \left\|c_i^{-1}r_i\right\| K_i^s] - \sum_{i=1}^{n} 2K_er_ic_ie_i + \sum_{i=1}^{n} [K_e\Lambda\beta\varepsilon_i(\int_0^t \varepsilon_i dw)] \tag{16}$$

It should be noted that $(\tfrac{1}{2}\dot{H}_i(x_i) - C_i(x_i,\dot{x}_i))c_i^{-2}r_i^2 = 0$ because $(\tfrac{1}{2}\dot{H}(x) - C(x,\dot{x}))$ is skew symmetric. Under the conditions as in Theorem 1, namely $\Delta_i^H \geq \left\|K_i^H - H_i(x_i)\right\|$ and $\Delta_i^C \geq \left\|K_i^C - C_i(x_i,\dot{x}_i)\right\|$, it follows that

$$
\begin{aligned}
&(c_i^{-1}r_i)Z_i + \left\|c_i^{-1}r_i\right\| K_i^s \\
&\geq \left\|c_i^{-1}r_i\right\| (K_i^s - \|Z_i\|) \\
&= \left\|c_i^{-1}r_i\right\| (\Delta_i^H \left\|c_i^{-1}(\dot{u}_i - \dot{c}_i\dot{x}_i)\right\| + \Delta_i^C \left\|c_i^{-1}u_i\right\| - \|Z_i\|) \\
&\geq \left\|c_i^{-1}r_i\right\| (\left\|K_i^H - H_i(x_i)\right\| \cdot \left\|c_i^{-1}(\dot{u}_i - \dot{c}_i\dot{x}_i)\right\| \\
&\quad + \left\|K_i^C - C_i(x_i,\dot{x}_i)\right\| \cdot \left\|c_i^{-1}u_i\right\| - \|Z_i\|) \\
&\geq \left\|c_i^{-1}r_i\right\| (\left\|(K_i^H - H_i(x_i))\, c_i^{-1}(\dot{u}_i - \dot{c}_i\dot{x}_i)\right. \\
&\quad \left. +(K_i^C - C_i(x_i,\dot{x}_i))\, c_i^{-1}u_i\right\| - \|Z_i\|) \\
&= 0
\end{aligned} \tag{17}
$$

We then analyze the term $\sum_{i=1}^{n} 2K_er_ic_ie_i$ in (16). From (6)-(9), we can obtain that

$$\sum_{i=1}^{n} 2K_er_ic_ie_i = \sum_{i=1}^{n} 2K_e(\dot{c}_ie_i + c_i\dot{e}_i + \beta\varepsilon_i + \Lambda c_ie_i + \Lambda\beta\int_0^t \varepsilon_i dw)c_ie_i$$
$$= \sum_{i=1}^{n} [2K_e(c_i\dot{c}_ie_i^2 + c_i^2e_i\dot{e}_i)] + \sum_{i=1}^{n} 2K_e\Lambda c_i^2e_i^2$$
$$+ \sum_{i=1}^{n} 2K_e\beta\varepsilon_ic_ie_i + \sum_{i=1}^{n} 2K_e\Lambda\beta c_ie_i \int_0^t \varepsilon_i dw \tag{18}$$

It is noted that from (5), we have

$$
\begin{aligned}
\sum_{i=1}^{n} 2\varepsilon_i c_i e_i &= \sum_{i=1}^{n} [2(c_i e_i - c_{i-1} e_{i-1})] c_i e_i \\
&= \sum_{i=1}^{n} 2c_i^2 e_i^2 - \sum_{i=1}^{n} 2c_{i-1} c_i e_{i-1} e_i \\
&= \sum_{i=1}^{n} (c_i e_i)^2 + \sum_{i=1}^{n} (c_{i-1} e_{i-1})^2 - \sum_{i=1}^{n} 2c_{i-1} c_i e_{i-1} e_i \\
&= \sum_{i=1}^{n} (c_i e_i - c_{i-1} e_{i-1})^2 = \sum_{i=1}^{n} \varepsilon_i^2
\end{aligned}
\tag{19}
$$

Substituting (19) into (18) yields

$$
\begin{aligned}
\sum_{i=1}^{n} 2K_e r_i c_i e_i = &\sum_{i=1}^{n} [2K_e(c_i \dot{c}_i e_i^2 + c_i^2 e_i \dot{e}_i)] + \sum_{i=1}^{n} 2K_e \Lambda c_i^2 e_i^2 \\
&+ \sum_{i=1}^{n} K_e \beta \varepsilon_i^2 + \sum_{i=1}^{n} K_e \Lambda \beta \varepsilon_i \int_0^t \varepsilon_i dw
\end{aligned}
\tag{20}
$$

Therefore, we can obtain $\dot{V}$ by substituting (17) and (20) and utilizing condition 2 of Theorem 1 as follows:

$$
\begin{aligned}
\dot{V} &= \sum_{i=1}^{n} [-H_i(x_i) c_i^{-3} \dot{c}_i r_i^2 - K_{ri} c_i^{-2} r_i^2] - \sum_{i=1}^{n} 2K_e \Lambda c_i^2 e_i^2 - \sum_{i=1}^{n} K_e \beta \varepsilon_i^2 \\
&= -\sum_{i=1}^{n} [K_{ri} - (-H_i(x_i) c_i^{-1} \dot{c}_i)] c_i^{-2} r_i^2 - \sum_{i=1}^{n} 2K_e \Lambda c_i^2 e_i^2 - \sum_{i=1}^{n} K_e \beta \varepsilon_i^2 \\
&\leq -\sum_{i=1}^{n} [\lambda_{\min}(K_{ri}) - \lambda_{\max}(-H_i(x_i) c_i^{-1} \dot{c}_i)] c_i^{-2} r_i^2 - \sum_{i=1}^{n} 2K_e \Lambda c_i^2 e_i^2 - \sum_{i=1}^{n} K_e \beta \varepsilon_i^2 \\
&\leq 0
\end{aligned}
\tag{21}
$$

which indicates the system is stable. Since the Lyapunov function V is lower bounded (by zero), V tends to a constant as $t \to \infty$ and is therefore bounded for $t \in [0, \infty]$. This means that r_i, e_i and ε_i are bounded as they appear in V, and hence, $\dot{r}_i$ and $\dot{e}_i$ are bounded according to the closed-loop dynamics (14) and the expression (20). Furthermore, we can conclude that $\dot{\varepsilon}_i$ is bounded as well based on the definition (5). Therefore, r_i, e_i and ε_i are uniformly continuous, which consequently implies the uniform continuity of $\dot{V}$. From Barbalat's lemma, $r_i \to 0$, $e_i \to 0$ and $\varepsilon_i \to 0$ as time $t \to \infty$, and thus, the system is asymptotically stable.

3.3   Delay Compensation in Synchronous Control

According to the Equation (10), the synchronous controller needs the actual position error of the preceding axis to calculate the position synchronization error at the beginning of each sample period T_s. Due to the effect of network-induced delays, the sensor of the ith axis measures the position error $e_i(t)$ and sends it to the $(i+1)$th axis as the feedback signal $e_i'(t)$. These signals are related as

$$
e_i'(t) = e_i(t - TD_i),
\tag{22}
$$

where TD_i is the time delay to transmit the measured signal from the ith axis to $(i + 1)$th axis. Note that when $i = n$, $i + 1 = 1$. As aforementioned, we assume that all the distributed clocks are synchronized, and hence, the start of each period of the servo controller, including the sampling and actuation, is synchronized with a high synchronization accuracy. With adopting the real-time communication protocol, the network-induced delays are therefore constant and meet

$$TD_i = T_s \quad (i = 1, \ldots, n). \tag{23}$$

Besides, most motion measurements in real applications are smooth and predictable. We therefore adopt a motion message estimator here, which is proposed by Hsieh [2] to reduce the data-dropout effect, to estimate the current position error of the preceding axis. The estimated value of the current position error can be expressed as

$$\hat{e}_i(t) = \frac{21}{8}e_i(t - T_s) - \frac{19}{8}e_i(t - 2T_s) + \frac{7}{8}e_i(t - 3T_s) - \frac{1}{8}e_i(t - 4T_s), \tag{24}$$

where $e_i(t - T_s)$, $e_i(t - 2T_s)$, $e_i(t - 3T_s)$ and $e_i(t - 4T_s)$ mean the past four sequential position errors.

4   Simulations

Simulations will be performed to verify the motion accuracy of the proposed algorithm in a networked CNC system.

4.1   Simulation Platform

The simulation model is shown in Fig. 2, which is designed based on Matlab/Simulink and the TrueTime toolbox [1]. In the TrueTime toolbox, computer and network blocks are introduced. The computer block is based on the event-driven mechanism and executes user-defined tasks, such as sampling and actuation tasks, the control algorithm, the application layer of the communication and the network interface. For the network block, Ethernet with $100Mbps$ link speed is chosen as the transmission media of the simulation model. To simulate a real-time network with a ring topology, the lumped frame-based EtherCAT protocol was programmed into the computer block of each networked node.

The main example that we will use in the simulation is a simple three-axes milling machine for contouring applications. Each axis moves on a linear slide and is driven through a ball screw by a DC motor. The DC motor is driven by a PWM drive. The three axes operate independently, and the mathematical model of each axis between the PWM input and the position output is described as

$$P(s) = \frac{k}{s(\tau s + 1)}, \tag{25}$$

where the time constants τ (sec) for each axis are 0.055 (X $Axis$), 0.056 (Y $Axis$), and 0.040 (Z $Axis$), and the overall gains k ((mm/sec)/PWM) are 28.346 (X $Axis$), 28.956 (Y $Axis$), and 41.606 (Z $Axis$), respectively [6].

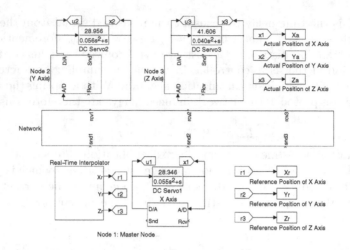

Fig. 2. Simulation model of the networked CNC system

4.2   Simulation Results

As shown in Fig. 3, simulations are conducted involving two typical motion commands to verify the performance of the proposed algorithm:

(1) linear command: a 3-D linear contour trajectory with 203.101 mm length at a speed of 1.5 m/min.

(2) circular command: a 3-D circular command is performed with 12 mm radius at a speed of 0.6 m/min.

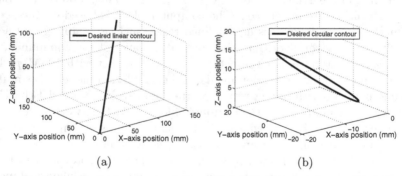

Fig. 3. Desired trajectories in simulations. (a) 3-D linear contour. (b) 3-D circular contour.

We also compare the performance among two controllers: (1) an uncoupled controller with only a standard PI position loop controller, namely, $\tau_i = K_i^P e_i + K_i^I \int_0^t e_i dw$; (2) the proposed synchronous controller for trajectory tracking in a networked multi-agent system. The control gains for the PI controller in the

3-D linear contour trajectory are $K^P = diag\{0.7817\ 0.7817\ 0.4817\}$, $K^I = diag\{0.0025\}$. And the corresponding control gains for the synchronous controller are $\beta = 0.02$, $\Lambda = 1$, $K^H = diag\{0.00194\}$, $K^C = diag\{0.03528\}$, $K_r = diag\{0.5\}$, $K^s = diag\{3\}$, $K_e = 0.7817$. For the 3-D circular contour trajectory, the control gains in the PI controller are $K^P = diag\{0.95\ 0.95\ 0.75\}$, $K^I = diag\{0.0025\}$. And the corresponding control gains for the synchronous controller are $\beta = 0.01$, $\Lambda = 1$, $K^H = diag\{0.00194\}$, $K^C = diag\{0.03528\}$, $K_r = diag\{0.5\}$, $K^s = diag\{3\}$, $K_e = 0.5$. All the control gains were obtained by the trial-and-error method.

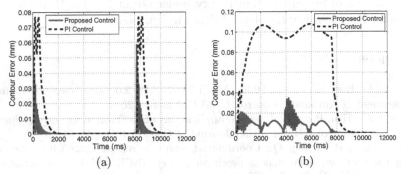

Fig. 4. Simulation results. (a) linear contouring. (b) circular contouring.

Table 1. Statistical data of linear and circular contouring

Controller	Linear Contouring		Circular Contouring	
	IAE/mm	ISE/mm^2	IAE/mm	ISE/mm^2
PI control	93.8046	4.8810	732.6286	70.3886
Synchronous control	17.3192	0.3641	74.8169	0.9306

Simulation results for the linear and circular contouring commands are shown in Fig. 4. In each plot, the horizontal axis is the simulation time and the vertical axis is the value of the contour error. Note that the contour errors are computed according to its definition. Moreover, the normalized statistical results of corresponding integrals of absolute error (IAE) and integrals of square error (ISE) are summarized in Table 1. The results indicate that compared with the standard PI control system, the proposed synchronous controller achieves better contouring accuracy over the 3-D linear and circular commands presented.

5 Conclusions and Future Work

In this paper, we propose a decentralized synchronous controller for each agent to achieve the trajectory tracking of real-time network-based systems. Simulations are conducted on a networked CNC system to demonstrate the effectiveness of the proposed synchronization control approach. It achieves improved contouring performance for the multi-axis trajectory tracking over the real-time network. Our future efforts will focus on two areas. First, experimental platform is currently built to verify the performance of our proposed algorithm in a practical networked control system. Second, the stability analysis also needs to be extended to deal with the effect of the delay compensation.

Acknowledgments. This research was supported in part by National Natural Science Foundation of China under Grant 51120155001, the Science & Technology Commission of Shanghai Municipality under Grant No. 11QH1401400 and Program for New Century Excellent Talents in University.

References

1. Cervin, A., Henriksson, D., Ohlin, M.: TRUETIME 2.0 beta-Reference Manual. Department of Automatic Control, Lund University (2009)
2. Hsieh, C.C., Hsu, P.L.: Analysis and applications of the motion message estimator for network control systems. Asian Journal of Control 10(1), 45–54 (2008)
3. Hu, C., Yao, B., Wang, Q.: Coordinated adaptive robust contouring controller design for an industrial biaxial precision gantry. IEEE/ASME Transactions on Mechatronics 15(5), 728–735 (2010)
4. Jeong, S., You, S.: Precise position synchronous control of multi-axis servo system. Mechatronics 18(3), 129–140 (2008)
5. Koren, Y.: Cross-coupled biaxial computer control for manufacturing systems. Journal of Dynamic Systems, Measurement, and Control 102, 265–272 (1980)
6. Lian, F.L., Moyne, J., Tilbury, D.: Control performance study of a networked machining cell. In: Proceedings of the American Control Conference, vol. 4, pp. 2337–2341 (2000)
7. Lian, F.L., Yook, J., Tilbury, D., Moyne, J.: Network architecture and communication modules for guaranteeing acceptable control and communication performance for networked multi-agent systems. IEEE Transactions on Industrial Informatics 2(1), 12–24 (2006)
8. Prytz, G.: A performance analysis of EtherCAT and PROFINET IRT. In: Proceedings of the IEEE International Conference on Emerging Technologies and Factory Automation, pp. 408–415. IEEE (2008)
9. Sun, D., Ge, S.: Synchronization and Control of Multiagent Systems. CRC Press (2010)
10. Sun, D., Tong, M.: A synchronization approach for the minimization of contouring errors of CNC machine tools. IEEE Transactions on Automation Science and Engineering 6(4), 720–729 (2009)
11. Sun, D., Wang, C., Shang, W., Feng, G.: A synchronization approach to trajectory tracking of multiple mobile robots while maintaining time-varying formations. IEEE Transactions on Robotics 25(5), 1074–1086 (2009)
12. Xu, X., Sheng, X., Xiong, Z., Zhu, X.: Time-stamped cross-coupled control in networked CNC systems. In: Proceedings of the IEEE International Conference on Robotics and Automation, pp. 4378–4383 (2011)

Multirobot Behavior Synchronization through Direct Neural Network Communication

David B. D'Ambrosio, Skyler Goodell, Joel Lehman,
Sebastian Risi, and Kenneth O. Stanley

Department of Electrical Engineering and Computer Science
University of Central Florida
Orlando, Florida 32816-2362, USA
{ddambro,goodsky,jlehman,srisi,kstanley}@eecs.ucf.edu
http://eplex.cs.ucf.edu/

Abstract. Many important real-world problems, such as patrol or search and rescue, could benefit from the ability to train teams of robots to coordinate. One major challenge to achieving such coordination is determining the best way for robots on such teams to communicate with each other. Typical approaches employ hand-designed communication schemes that often require significant effort to engineer. In contrast, this paper presents a new communication scheme called the *hive brain*, in which the neural network controller of each robot is directly connected to internal nodes of other robots and the weights of these connections are evolved. In this way, the robots can evolve their own internal "language" to speak directly brain-to-brain. This approach is tested in a multirobot patrol synchronization domain where it produces robot controllers that synchronize through communication alone in both simulation and real robots, and that are robust to perturbation and changes in team size.

Keywords: Evolutionary Algorithms, HyperNEAT, Multirobot Teams, Coordination, Communication, Artificial Neural Networks.

1 Introduction

As robot technology has matured and large teams of robots have become more commonplace, a research question of growing importance is how to best *coordinate* such robotic teams. While one approach is to coordinate robot teams centrally, scaling such an approach to many robots and mitigating the inherent challenges of limited bandwidth and unreliable communication in the real world may prove problematic [1]. Thus this paper instead focuses on treating robots as autonomous *communicating* agents, which notably has proven a robust and scalable strategy in nature [2, 3]. For example, insect colonies and human society itself operate by this principle.

Importantly, communication between agents enlarges the scope of their possible behaviors by enabling coordination and sharing of knowledge. In this way, teams of communicating robots may have greater potential than those without

C.-Y. Su, S. Rakheja, H. Liu (Eds.): ICIRA 2012, Part II, LNAI 7507, pp. 603–614, 2012.

communication. However, an open question in this context is how to best implement an artificial communication system that allows autonomous robotic agents to coordinate their behavior. That is, it is unclear a priori how exactly robots should pass information to each other. In nature, communication between organisms takes diverse forms. For example, ants emit and detect pheromone signals [2], bees dance and recognize visual dancing patterns [3], and humans vocalize and interpret the complex auditory signals comprising speech. Interestingly, in an artificial system it is possible to consider communication systems impossible or unlikely to be exploited by nature.

In particular, if individual robotic agents' policies are represented by artificial neural networks (ANNs), communication between agents can be implemented by connections *between* such networks. In other words, one agent's brain can directly feed into another's. By analogy, one way of understanding such a system is to imagine it as a form of telepathy; information from one agent's brain can flow into another's. The advantage of such an approach is that it bypasses the complexity of signal transduction. That is, it is unnecessary to encode a message first into an orthogonal form such as scent, movement, or sound before transmitting it, and it is symmetrically unnecessary for the recipient to decode it; a bee with such connections to other bees would not need to dance to indicate to others where to find food. While the laws of physics prevent such direct connections between the brains of biological organisms, distributed implementations of ANNs have no such limitation (though of course inter-network connections may incur some communication delay).

This insight motivates the novel approach presented in this paper, called the *hive brain*, in which agents are controlled by interconnected ANNs. This new approach for creating communicating multirobot teams is built upon the foundation of an established evolutionary algorithm called *multiagent HyperNEAT* (MAHN [4]) that is extended to represent such ANN interdependence and can scale to evolve teams with many robots. The hive brain extension allows one robot's ANN to interconnect with others' to enable communication between them. Interestingly, in this way the communication scheme itself can evolve.

This paper investigates a particular kind of collective behavior that such a hive brain can facilitate. It is inspired by an interesting physical phenomenon called *odd sympathy* [5], which is the tendency of pendulum clocks to synchronize when mounted near each other. The cause of such synchronization is that vibrations from one clock affect the other through the medium on which they are mounted. In other words, a small amount of physical *information* is transferred between the pendulums that results in a larger macrolevel effect, i.e. synchronization. An interesting analogy for robot teams would arise if communicating small amounts of information could likewise cause them to synchronize, which might have practical applications for teams that must cooperate in tasks sensitive to timing.

Thus this paper applies the hive brain approach for the first time to evolving robot teams that synchronize their movements over time. Teams that successfully synchronize are artificially evolved in a computer simulation, demonstrating that the hive brain can facilitate "odd sympathy"-like behavior in robot controllers. Furthermore, evolved teams are successfully transfered to the real world in Khepera III robots, illustrating the real-world potential of the technique. The conclusion is that the hive brain is an interesting new technique for evolving communicating teams of robots that merits further exploration.

2 Background

This section reviews past work in cooperative multiagent learning that requires communication and the NEAT and HyperNEAT methods applied in the experiments presented in this paper.

2.1 Cooperative Multiagent Learning

There are two primary traditional approaches to training multiple agents to collaborate to solve a given task. The first, multiagent reinforcement learning (MARL), encompasses several specific techniques based on off-policy and on-policy temporal difference learning [6–8]. The basic principle that unifies MARL techniques is to identify and reward promising cooperative states and actions among a team of agents [9, 10]. The other major approach, cooperative coevolutionary algorithms (CCEAs), is an established evolutionary method for training teams of agents that must work together [11, 12, 10]. The main idea is to maintain one or more populations of candidate agents, evaluate them in groups, and guide the creation of new candidate solutions based on their joint performance. However, while these approaches are effective in a number of domains [6–10], their focus is usually not on agents with explicit communication channels.

2.2 Communicating Robots

While communication among robots is not always necessary, tasks that require coordination without a central controller can benefit from robots that are able to share information about the world.

One such class of problems, which has been the subject of many studies, is known as the consensus problem [13]. In the consensus problem multiple agents must reach an *agreement* about the current state of the world, which requires shared information. Consensus schemes have been applied to various multiagent tasks, ranging from vehicle formations [14], coupled oscillators [15], and robot position synchronization [16]. While previous work on the consensus problem has focused on analytical approaches [13], if the individual robotic agents' policies are represented as ANNs, the agents should in principle be able to reach consensus through minimal communication as well.

Different ANN-based approaches to communication have been investigated in the past, in which the communication between the agents takes diverse forms. In Yong and Mikkulainen [17], each agent receives directly the position of the other agents as input. Di Palolo [18] studied agents that cooperate acoustically, while the focus of Floreano et al.'s [19] work was evolving robots that communicate by emitting light. However, unlike the approach introduced in this paper, all these approaches rely on signal transduction (i.e. a message is encoded, sent and then decoded) between a sender and a receiver.

Nevertheless, if the agents in a distributed system are controlled by neural networks, communication between agents could potentially also be implemented by direct connections between such networks. In other words, one agent's brain can directly feed into another's, which makes encoding and decoding messages unnecessary. The HyperNEAT approach should allow such controllers to be evolved because it can easily represent such ANN interdependence. The next section reviews the Neuroevolution of Augmenting Topologies (NEAT) approach, the foundation of HyperNEAT.

2.3   Neuroevolution of Augmenting Topologies

The HyperNEAT approach extended in this paper is itself an extension of the original NEAT algorithm that evolves increasing large ANNs. NEAT starts with a population of simple networks that then *increase in complexity* over generations by adding new nodes and connections through mutations. By evolving ANNs in this way, the topology of the network does not need to be known a priori; NEAT searches through increasingly complex networks to find a suitable level of complexity. Because it starts simply and gradually adds complexity, it tends to find a solution network close to the minimal necessary size. However, as explained next, it turns out that directly representing connections and nodes as explicit genes in the genome cannot scale up to large brain-like networks. For a complete overview of NEAT see Stanley and Miikkulaninen [20].

2.4   HyperNEAT

Many neuroevolution methods are *directly encoded*, which means each component of the phenotype is encoded by a single gene, making the discovery of repeating motifs expensive and improbable. Therefore, indirect encodings [21–23] have become a growing area of interest in evolutionary computation and artificial life.

One such indirect encoding designed explicitly for neural networks is the Hypercube-based NEAT (HyperNEAT) approach [24, 25], which is itself an indirect extension of the directly-encoded NEAT approach [26, 20] reviewed in the previous section. This section briefly reviews HyperNEAT; a complete introduction is in Stanley et al. [24] and Gauci and Stanley [25]. Rather than expressing connection weights as distinct and independent parameters in the genome, HyperNEAT allows them to vary across the phenotype in a regular pattern through an indirect encoding called a *compositional pattern producing network* (CPPN; [27]), which is like an ANN, but with specially-chosen activation functions.

CPPNs in HyperNEAT *encode* the connectivity patterns of ANNs as a *function of geometry*. That is, if an ANN's nodes are embedded in a geometry, i.e.

assigned coordinates within a space, then it is possible to represent its connectivity as a single evolved function of such coordinates. In effect the CPPN paints a pattern of weights across the geometry of a neural network. To understand why this approach is promising, consider that a natural organism's brain is physically embedded within a three-dimensional geometric space, and that such embedding heavily constrains and influences the brain's connectivity. Topographic maps (i.e. ordered projections of sensory or effector systems such as the retina or musculature) are realized within brains that preserve geometric relationships between high-dimensional sensor and effector fields [28, 29]. In other words, there is important information *implicit* in geometry that can only be exploited by an encoding informed by geometry.

In particular, geometric *regularities* such as symmetry or repetition are pervasive throughout the connectivity of natural brains. To similarly achieve such regularities, CPPNs exploit activation functions that induce regularities in HyperNEAT networks. The general idea is that a CPPN takes as input the geometric coordinates of two nodes embedded in the *substrate*, i.e. an ANN situated in a particular geometry, and outputs the weight of the connection between those two nodes. In this way, a Gaussian activation function by virtue of its symmetry can induce symmetric connectivity and a sine function can induce networks with repeated elements. Note that because the size of the CPPN is decoupled from the size of the substrate, HyperNEAT can compactly encode the connectivity of an arbitrarily large substrate with a single CPPN.

HyperNEAT also allows the evolution of controllers for *teams* of agents. This multiagent HyperNEAT algorithm was first introduced by D'Ambrosio and Stanley [30] and D'Ambrosio et. al [4]. It is designed to work with homogeneous and heterogeneous teams; however, in this paper the tasks only necessitates the homogeneous case. While previous experiments with multiagent HyperNEAT did not involve communication between the agents, the next section introduces such a model, which should allow the agents to synchronize their movements over time.

3   Hive Brain Approach

While HyperNEAT has been applied to multiagent problems in the past [4, 31, 30], these previous experiments did not involve communication between the agents. This paper extends HyperNEAT by allowing it to define inter-network connections that act as communication channels between agents. Such communication can be advantageous in situations where agents must cooperate closely or come to consensus, such as in this paper. Because the agents communicate through regular ANN connections, the experimenter does not need to define a specific "language" for communication, and in fact, the agents can devise one of their own that is easily integrated into their neural architecture.

For simplicity, the teams in this paper are composed of homogeneous agents, that is, agents who all have the same control policy. Thus HyperNEAT needs only to create a single ANN and communication scheme and copy this plan to all agents in the team. The substrate (i.e. the controller ANN and its geometry) for a single agent is shown in figure 1b and is made up of five layers: input, receive, hidden, transmit, and output. The input, hidden, and output layers are familiar ANN constructs, but the transmitting and receiving layers are additions that facilitate communication between agents. The transmit layer takes input from one agent's hidden layer and sends it to another agent's receiving layer, which in turn inputs into the target agent's hidden layer. In this way messages can be passed among the entire team of agents. The weights of these connections are encoded by the CPPN through the inclusion of CPPN input z_t (figure 1a) that defines the target agent of a connection. In this paper communication is limited to left and right neighbors, so z_t is defined as -1 for left neighbors, 0 for intra-agent connections, and 1 for the right neighbor, although more general communication schemes are possible.

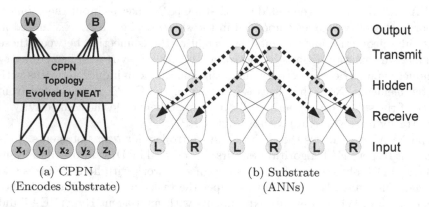

(a) CPPN	(b) Substrate
(Encodes Substrate)	(ANNs)

Fig. 1. Hive brain substrate. The CPPN (a) that encodes the connection weights in a hive substrate (b) is augmented with a z_t input that determines the target of the connection. The hive substrate (b) includes input, output, and hidden layers. However two of the hidden layers are designated as transmitting and receiving layers that are used for communication. The flow of information between agents is shown by the dashed lines. The inputs are the left and right sensors and the output is interpreted as a motor command, which are discussed in Section 4.

4   Synchronization Experiment

To demonstrate the ability to communicate, the robots are tested on their ability to synchronize their movements as they patrol a room. This domain is motivated by the natural phenomenon called odd sympathy [5], in which closely situated pendulums tend to synchronize their motions through tiny vibrations. In effect these vibrations are like simple messages; thus the hive brain communication scheme should in principle be able to produce similar results. In this domain, synchronization is defined for the robots as *moving in unison* such that their patrol trajectories begin and end at the same time. To focus on the issue of synchronization, the robots are restricted to moving left and right within a rectangular room. Thus an optimal solution would be for all robots to reverse direction at the same time before hitting a wall. Overall, the robots should oscillate back and forth between walls in synchrony, thereby covering the room reliably and systematically. The challenge is that the robots are not *started* in synchrony, so they must cooperate to achieve it, which tests the ability of the hive to produce a coordinated result. An interesting advantage of this approach is that it does not require explicit positional information to be encoded in the agents, which may not be easily obtained in the real world due to sensor ambiguity.

Each robot has left and right rangefinder sensors that return the distance of the robot to a wall, up to 30 cm, normalized between 0.0 and 1.0. The robot has a single effector that determines both the direction and speed of motion: an output between 0 and 0.5 will cause the robot to move left at a speed between 2.5 cm/sec and 5.0 cm/sec based on the value of the output. Similarly, an output between 0.5 and 1.0 will cause the robot to move right at a velocity within that same range. To determine the output for a given timestep, each network is activated four times: enough so that information about an agent's current input can travel to the output, but not enough times for information about neighbors' inputs to reach the output, effectively creating a communication delay. Importantly, the robots cannot see each other and can only see walls, so they *must* rely on communication to properly synchronize.

Training (i.e. evolution) occurs in a robot simulator (figure 2a) where teams of four agents are trained on five different initial configurations of robots between two walls between which they must patrol. These configurations are created by lining the robots up in the center of the room and then staggering their positions by different amounts. This approach forces the robots to find a general syncing policy that can work from multiple starting configurations. Teams are trained by HyperNEAT with a multiobjective reward scheme through NSGAII [32] with three objectives: (1) minimize the distance between each robot and its neighbors, (2) patrol back and forth in the room, and (3) maintain genomic diversity (calculated through NEAT speciation [20]). The distance objective is calculated by, at each time step, summing the distance from each robot to the next robot in the line and then dividing by the number of robots minus one. The average of these normalized sums over all time steps is the distance objective. The patrolling objective is simply the average number of patrol cycles performed by each robot divided by 25 (the maximum number of cycles possible in the given time).

An ideal team should quickly synchronize their behaviors so that the distances are minimized and continually patrol the room without crashing or getting stuck. Because teams start out desynchronized it is impossible to completely maximize both objectives, so a team with a normalized sum of 1.9 or greater is considered to have solved the problem in the simulator. The third objective, diversity, is only included to increase the efficiency of the optimization process, i.e. it is not the explicit goal of the experiment, so it is not included in the performance measure. The multiobjective approach was found useful in this domain because the two tasks of minimizing distance and patrolling are simple to accomplish on their own, but deceptively complex to accomplish simultaneously.

Selected teams were later transferred to actual Khepera III robots to perform the same task in the real-world (figure 2b). These robots have several IR rangefinder sensors: the rear sensor serves as the "left" sensor from simulation, and because there is no direct front sensor, the average of the two front-most sensors is used to determine the value of the "right" sensor. The robots are placed on a posterboard surface between two walls 68.5cm apart that are made of red bricks. In addition to the training size of four robots, the scalability of the solutions was also tested in the real world by testing teams of three and five robots from the *same* CPPN that was trained on only four. Furthermore, the robustness of solutions was tested by manually desynchronizing the robots once they already synchronized themselves.

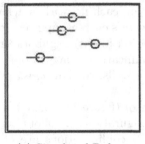

(a) Simulated Robots

(b) Actual Robots

Fig. 2. Synchronization Domain. In this domain, robots are placed inside a room such that their positions are initially staggered. The goal is for them to move such that their motions become synchronized.

4.1   Experimental Parameters

Because HyperNEAT differs from original NEAT only in its set of activation functions, it uses the same parameters [20]. The experiment was run with a modified version of the public domain SharpNEAT package [33]. The size of the population was 500 with 20% elitism. The number of generations was 300. Sexual offspring (50%) did not undergo mutation. Asexual offspring (50%) had 0.96 probability of link weight mutation, 0.03 chance of link addition, and 0.01 chance of node addition. The coefficients for determining species similarity were 1.0 for nodes and connections and 0.1 for weights. The available CPPN activation functions were sigmoid, Gaussian, absolute value, and sine, all with equal probability of being added to the CPPN. Parameter settings are based on standard Sharp-NEAT defaults and prior reported settings for NEAT [20, 34]. They were found to be robust to moderate variation through preliminary experimentation.

5   Results

From 20 simulated runs of evolution, 17 runs evolved a solution with performance above or equal to the success threshold of 1.90. On average the algorithm took 41 generations to find such a solution (stddev = 52). Of these solutions, all but two maintained a performance of 1.90 or greater when tested on untrained team sizes of three and five in simulation.

The best-performing team in each run that produced a solution was transferred to real Khepera III robots. Of the 17 runs that were successful in simulation, 15 were able to duplicate that behavior in real robots (figure 3). When robots were agitated during evaluation, i.e. removed from formation and then returned to the room out of sync, the teams could quickly resynchronize their motions. Additionally, the two teams that had the highest sum of objectives during simulation were further tested on their ability to synchronize in real robots when scaled to teams of three and five robots (on which they were not trained) and were able to successfully synchronize. Videos of the robots synchronizing can be found at http://eplex.cs.ucf.edu/demos/hive-brain-patrol.

Every working solution demonstrated a similar strategy: The team moves in the same direction towards a wall until the first agent detects the wall with its rangefinder. At that point all other agents either move towards the wall to catch up or oscillate near the wall while waiting for other agents to gather. Once enough agents gather at the wall or enough time passes all agents ultimately flip direction and run the same procedure on the opposite wall. Over several such iterations the agents lock into phase. This behavior was observed both in solutions running in the simulator and the solutions transfered to the actual Khepera III robots.

Fig. 3. Synchronization Example. The robots start out disorganized and unaligned, but using communication they are able to synchronize their movements.

Another capability that derives from this kind of team is the ability to synchronize regardless of the initial direction of each agent. With no further training the teams are able to synchronize against alternating opposite walls in real robots, creating a staggered patrolling pattern that covers more of the room at any given time (as can be seen in the videos at the above address), demonstrating that a variety of behaviors can be synchronized from this approach, and suggesting the potential for learning more complex patrol routes in the future.

6   Discussion

The results demonstrate that the hive brain approach to communication does allow agents to learn on their own to communicate effectively. Thus even with only the ability to communicate with direct neighbors the team is coming to a simple consensus about when it should leave the wall, which clearly requires communication and is the subject of many studies [35].

The hive brain approach was also often successful in real robots despite sensor and actuator noise (and manual desynchronization), implying that the policies discovered can be robust. The ability for teams to scale to new sizes, despite only being trained with four agents, also suggests that a general synchronization policy is consistently found. Perhaps most interestingly, the multiagent hive brain makes up its own communication strategy to solve the task, without any a priori programming.

These results open up a number of possible directions for future research based on the hive brain. First, a natural step would be to exploit multiagent HyperNEAT to create heterogeneous teams of communicating agents, whose communication can also thereby be heterogeneous. The robots in this paper were homogeneous and had predefined partners with which to communicate; however it would also be possible to allow HyperNEAT to decide with whom they need to talk to accomplish the task. Preliminary experiments suggest that letting every agent talk to every other agents produces too much cross-talk, resulting in poor performance. However, approaches like HyperNEAT-LEO [36] could potentially allow HyperNEAT to define appropriate patterns of communication on its own. There is also substantial room to explore how the communication connections are configured; in this paper there are explicit transmitting and receiving layers for communication, but other approaches such as directly connecting output layers to hidden layers could prove useful depending on the domain. Finally, the hive brain approach could be combined with other learning algorithms in addition to HyperNEAT.

7   Conclusion

This paper demonstrated a new multiagent communication technique called the hive brain, in which the ANNs of agents are directly connected to each other. The initial demonstration of this approach in this paper allowed simulated agents to synchronize their movements through communication and the strategies that were discovered were verified in actual Khepera III robots. This new technique opens the door to significant additional research and applications by suggesting a new way of thinking about robot communication.

Acknowledgments. This work was supported through grants from the US Army Research Office (Award No. W911NF-11-1-0489) and DARPA Computer Science Study Group Phase III (Award No. N11AP20003). This paper does not necessarily reflect the position or policy of the government, and no official endorsement should be inferred.

References

1. Busoniu, L., Babuska, R., De Schutter, B.: A comprehensive survey of multiagent reinforcement learning. IEEE Transactions on Systems, Man, and Cybernetics, Part C: Applications and Reviews 38(2), 156–172 (2008)
2. Jackson, D.E., Ratnieks, F.L.: Communication in ants. Current Biology 16(15), R570–R574 (2006)
3. Riley, J., Greggers, U., Smith, A., Reynolds, D., Menzel, R.: The flight paths of honeybees recruited by the waggle dance. Nature 435(7039), 205–207 (2005)
4. D'Ambrosio, D.B., Lehman, J., Risi, S., Stanley, K.O.: Evolving policy geometry for scalable multiagent learning. In: Proceedings of the Ninth International Conference on Autonomous Agents and Multiagent Systems (AAMAS 2010), pp. 731–738. International Foundation for Autonomous Agents and Multiagent System (2010)
5. Bennett, M., Schatz, M.F., Rockwood, H., Wiesenfeld, K.: Huygens's clocks. Proceedings of the Royal Society of London. Series A: Mathematical, Physical and Engineering Sciences 458(2019), 563–579 (2002)
6. Bowling, M., Veloso, M.: Multiagent learning using a variable learning rate. Artificial Intelligence 136(2), 215–250 (2002)
7. Hu, J., Wellman, M.P.: Multiagent reinforcement learning: theoretical framework and an algorithm. In: Proc. 15th International Conf. on Machine Learning, pp. 242–250. Morgan Kaufmann, San Francisco (1998)
8. Santana, H., Ramalho, G., Corruble, V., Ratitch, B.: Multi-agent patrolling with reinforcement learning. In: International Joint Conference on Autonomous Agents and Multiagent Systems, vol. 3, pp. 1122–1129 (2004)
9. Busoniu, L., Schutter, B.D., Babuska, R.: Learning and coordination in dynamic multiagent systems. Technical Report 05-019, Delft University of Technology (2005)
10. Panait, L., Luke, S.: Cooperative multi-agent learning: The state of the art. Autonomous Agents and Multi-Agent Systems 3(11), 383–434 (2005)
11. Ficici, S., Pollack, J.: A Game-Theoretic Approach to the Simple Coevolutionary Algorithm. In: Schoenauer, M., Deb, K., Rudolph, G., Yao, X., Lutton, E., Merelo, J.J., Schwefel, H.-P. (eds.) PPSN VI. LNCS, vol. 1917, pp. 467–476. Springer, Heidelberg (2000)
12. Panait, L., Wiegand, R., Luke, S.: Improving coevolutionary search for optimal multiagent behaviors. In: Proceedings of the Eighteenth International Joint Conference on Artificial Intelligence (IJCAI), pp. 653–658 (2003)
13. Ren, W., Beard, R., Atkins, E.: A survey of consensus problems in multi-agent coordination. In: Proceedings of the 2005 American Control Conference, vol. 3, pp. 1859–1864 (June 2005)
14. Fax, J.A., Murray, R.M.: Information flow and cooperative control of vehicle formations. IEEE Transactions on Automatic Control 49(9), 1465–1476 (2004)
15. Sepulchre, R., Leonard, N.: Collective motion and oscillator synchronization. Electrical Engineering 309, 189–205 (2004)
16. Rodriguez-Angeles, A., Nijmeijer, H.: Mutual synchronization of robots via estimated state feedback: A cooperative approach. IEEE Trans. on Control Systems Technology 12(4), 542–554 (2004)
17. Yong, C.H., Miikkulainen, R.: Coevolution of role-based cooperation in multi-agent systems. IEEE Transactions on Autonomous Mental Development 1, 170–186 (2010)

18. Di Paolo, E.A.: Behavioral coordination, structural congruence and entrainment in a simulation of acoustically coupled agents. Adaptive Behavior 8(1), 27–48 (2000)
19. Floreano, D., Mitri, S., Magnenat, S., Keller, L.: Evolutionary conditions for the emergence of communication in robots. Current Biology 17(6), 514–519 (2007)
20. Stanley, K.O., Miikkulainen, R.: Evolving neural networks through augmenting topologies. Evolutionary Computation 10, 99–127 (2002)
21. Bongard, J.C., Pfeifer, R.: Morpho-functional Machines: The New Species (Designing Embodied Intelligence). In: Evolving Complete Agents using Artificial Ontogeny, pp. 237–258. Springer (2003)
22. Hornby, G.S., Pollack, J.B.: Creating high-level components with a generative representation for body-brain evolution. Artificial Life 8(3), 223–246 (2002)
23. Stanley, K.O., Miikkulainen, R.: A taxonomy for artificial embryogeny. Artificial Life 9(2), 93–130 (2003)
24. Stanley, K.O., D'Ambrosio, D.B., Gauci, J.: A hypercube-based indirect encoding for evolving large-scale neural networks. Artificial Life 15(2) (2009)
25. Gauci, J., Stanley, K.O.: Autonomous evolution of topographic regularities in artificial neural networks. Neural Computation, 38 (2010) (to appear)
26. Stanley, K.O., Miikkulainen, R.: Competitive coevolution through evolutionary complexification. Journal of Artificial Intelligence Research 21(1), 63–100 (2004)
27. Stanley, K.O.: Compositional pattern producing networks: A novel abstraction of development. Genetic Programming and Evolvable Machines 8(2), 131–162 (2007)
28. Udin, S., Fawcett, J.: Formation of topographic maps. Annual Review of Neuroscience 11(1), 289–327 (1988)
29. Hubel, D.H., Wiesel, T.N.: Receptive fields, binocular interaction and functional architecture in the cat's visual cortex. The Journal of Physiology 160, 106–154 (1962)
30. D'Ambrosio, D.B., Stanley, K.O.: Generative encoding for multiagent learning. In: Proceedings of the Genetic and Evolutionary Computation Conference (GECCO 2008). ACM Press, New York (2008)
31. D'Ambrosio, D.B., Lehman, J., Risi, S., Stanley, K.O.: Task switching in multiagent learning through indirect encoding. In: Proceedings of the International Conference on Intelligent Robots and Systems (IROS 2011). IEEE, Piscataway (2011)
32. Deb, K., Pratap, A., Agarwal, S., Meyarivan, T.: A fast and elitist multiobjective genetic algorithm: Nsga-ii. IEEE Transactions on Evolutionary Computation 6(2), 182–197 (2002)
33. Green, C.: SharpNEAT homepage (2003-2006), http://sharpneat.sourceforge.net/
34. Stanley, K.O., Miikkulainen, R.: Competitive coevolution through evolutionary complexification 21, 63–100 (2004)
35. Ren, W., Beard, R., Atkins, E.: A survey of consensus problems in multi-agent coordination. In: Proceedings of the 2005 American Control Conference, pp. 1859–1864. IEEE (2005)
36. Verbancsics, P., Stanley, K.: Constraining connectivity to encourage modularity in HyperNEAT. In: Proceedings of the 13th Annual Conference on Genetic and Evolutionary Computation, pp. 1483–1490. ACM (2011)

Virtual Field Testing for Performance Evaluation of Cooperative Multiple Robots

Kunjin Ryu and Tomonari Furukawa

Department of Mechanical Engineering, Virginia Tech, USA
{kunjin,tomonari}@vt.edu

Abstract. This paper presents the field testing in virtual environments for performance evaluation of cooperative multi-robot systems. Once motions of robots, objects of interests are modeled, a real-like virtual environment is created. Robots are then physically linked to the virtual environment within a simulator and cooperatively operate in the environment. Unlike a real field testing, the virtual testing allows users to evaluate performance of cooperation of robots both in qualitative and quantitative ways. Additionally, due to its easiness of controlling the environmental conditions the virtual testing can be effectively utilized for testing multi robot cooperation under the same or different conditions. In this paper, a team of multiple robots are assigned to one or more missions in the virtual environment, and their cooperative performances are numerically analyzed within the simulator.

1 Introduction

Cooperative use of multiple robots has advantages over the use of a single robot in both efficiency and capability. If each robot is assigned a task which does not duplicate with those of other robots, the efficiency will be multiplied by the number of robots. If multiple robots are assigned a single task, the capability is multiplied by the number of robots. As a consequence, the last few decades have seen the increasing popularity of studying multi-robot cooperation. Contrary to single robot operation, multi-robot maneuvering is complicated, requiring additional conditions to be considered to make them work cooperatively [1].

Due to this complexity, there needs a large number of testing of not only cooperative algorithms but also hardware performance such as on-board computing and communication. One possible solution to this problem is to build a group of robots and to examine field testing within the real environment. However, several issues that make real field testing difficult exist including time for robots to be built, difficulties of repeating experiments many times, and difficulties of quantitative evaluation of performance of robots. And these issues get worse as the number of robots increases. In this respect, it is desirable that the performance of the system be tested in virtual environments before being tested in real environments.

The past efforts on the virtual testing of multi-robot systems can be divided into two areas. In the first, the primary focus has been directed to the modeling

C.-Y. Su, S. Rakheja, H. Liu (Eds.): ICIRA 2012, Part II, LNAI 7507, pp. 615–624, 2012.

of a complex system including the multi-agent system, kinematics and dynamics of each robot and its environments [2], [3], [4], [5]. Object-oriented programing and visualization belong to this area. The second area has been more focused on communication and network [6], [7]. The development of a server-client system that allows the visualization of multiple robots on multiple computers belong to this. While dramatic progress has been seen in these areas, the current systems in each area are rather evolving independently without integration. In addition, the virtual testing is mostly focused on the simulation or the qualitative analysis of the cooperative estimation and control strategy where important performance criteria such as the effect of hardware and the quantitative capability of the cooperative estimation and control strategy are completely missing.

This paper presents virtual field testing for performance evaluation of cooperative multiple autonomous robots. In order to evaluate cooperative performance of these robots as a team, virtual field testing using a simulator so-called the Platform- and Hardware-In-the-Loop Simulator (PHILS) is introduced. The cooperative performance of the team of the robots is analyzed in terms of the accuracy of the map and localization of objects of interests (OOIs), and the efficiency of the cooperative exploration by the robots. Then, the virtual field testing for quantitative analysis of cooperation of the tema of multiple robots is performed within the framework of the PHILS.

This paper is organized as follows. Section 2 deals with modeling of the OOIs, and the sensor platform for virtual environment. In section 3, the design and the development of the PHILS are presented and Section 4 describes the cooperative performance evaluation of the team of multiple robots under a simple cooperative exploration scenario. In section 6, experimental results show the qualitative and quantitative analysis of the cooperation of the team of the robots within the PHILS, and conclusions are summarized in the final section.

2   Object and Sensor Platform Model

Consider an object o of interest, the motion of which is discretely given by

$$\mathbf{x}_{k+1}^o = \mathbf{f}^o\left(\mathbf{x}_k^o, \mathbf{u}_k^o, \mathbf{w}_k^o\right), \tag{1}$$

where $\mathbf{x}_k^o \in \mathcal{X}^o$ is the state of the object at time step k, $\mathbf{u}_k^o \in \mathcal{U}^o$ is the set of control inputs of the object, and $\mathbf{w}_k^o \in \mathcal{W}^o$ is the "system noise" of the object.

In order for the formulation of the cooperative estimation and control problem, this moving object is searched and tracked by a group of sensor platforms $s = \{s_1, ..., s_{n_s}\}$. Assuming the global states of sensor platforms are assumed to be known, the motion model of sensor platform s_i is thus given by

$$\mathbf{x}_{k+1}^{s_i} = \mathbf{f}^{s_i}\left(\mathbf{x}_k^{s_i}, \mathbf{u}_k^{s_i}, \mathbf{w}_k^{s_i}\right) \tag{2}$$

where, $\mathbf{x}_k^{s_i} \in \mathcal{X}^{s_i}$ and $\mathbf{u}_i^{s_i} \in \mathcal{U}_i^s$ represent the state and control input of ith vehicle, respectively, and $\mathbf{w}_k^{s_i} \in \mathcal{W}^{s_i}$ is the "system noise" of the sensor platform. The sensor platform also carries a sensor with an "observable region" as its

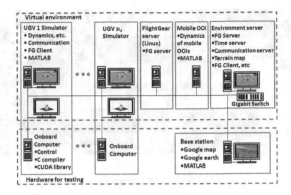

Fig. 1. Concept of the platform- and hardware-in-the-loop simulator

physical limitation to observe an object of interest. The observable region is determined not only by the properties of the sensor such as signal intensity but also the properties of the object such as the reflectivity. Defining the probability of detection (POD) $0 \leq P_D\left(\mathbf{x}_k^o | \mathbf{x}_k^{s_i}\right) \leq 1$ from these factors as a reliability measure for detecting the object o, the observable region can be expressed as $^{s_i}\mathcal{X}_O^o = \{\mathbf{x}_k^o | 0 < P_D\left(\mathbf{x}_k^o | \mathbf{x}_k^{s_i}\right) \leq 1\}$. Accordingly, the object state observed from the sensor platform, $^{s_i}\mathbf{z}_k^o \in \mathcal{X}^o$, is given by:

$$
^{s_i}\mathbf{z}_k^o = \begin{cases} ^{s_i}\mathbf{h}^o\left(\mathbf{x}_k^o, \mathbf{x}_k^{s_i}, {}^{s_i}\mathbf{v}_k^o\right) & \mathbf{x}_k^o \in {}^{s_i}\mathcal{X}_o^o \\ \emptyset & \mathbf{x}_k^o \notin {}^{s_i}\mathcal{X}_o^o \end{cases} \tag{3}
$$

where, $^{s_i}\mathbf{v}_k^o$ represents the observation noise, and ø represents an "empty element", indicating that the observation contained no information on the object or that the object is unobservable when it is not within the observable region. Note here that the terms "sensor platform" and 'robot' are used interchangeably in this paper as the configuration of sensors can be negligible.

3   Platform- and Hardware-in-the-Loop Simulator

The platform- and hardware-in-the-loop simulator (PHILS) was developed for the evaluation of cooperative performance of multiple autonomous robots and their testing in virtual environments. Figure 1 shows the schematic design of the PHILS. The PHILS consists of computers, monitors, a network switch that links the computers, and a server-client simulation software system installed on the computers. Out of the computers, three computers create an environment: one computer runs a server program so that client computers can share the same environment; another computer calculates motion of mobile objects, if there are any in the environment, using GPU since the motion of multiple objects can be parallelly calculated; the last computer with a GPU and a monitor acts as the environmental server and manages environmental parameters such as time, weather and communication speed whilst visualizing the behavior of all

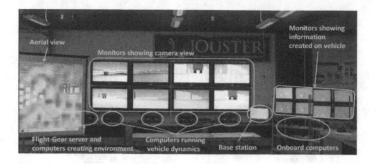

Fig. 2. Developed platform- and hardwar-in-the-loop simulator

the autonomous robots in the environment under the support of GPU. The other computers are each equipped with a GPU and connected to a monitor, run a client visualizer using the GPU and view the environment with static and mobile objects as well as autonomous robots where one computer is allocated to each autonomous robot to calculate its motion in (2) and show its view.

The cooperative performance of multiple autonomous robots can be evaluated by linking computers each to be mounted on a robot to the network switch and by testing cooperative strategies such as cooperative mapping and exploration. The PHILS provides a monitor to each on-board computer, since the performance of the on-board computers, which we check at the base station, can be monitored simultaneously. The computer to be used as the base station can also be connected and tested in the virtual environment. Unlike the conventional hardware-in-the-loop simulators or multi-robot simulators, the primary advantage of the PHILS is that it can test cooperative autonomous robots and analyze their cooperative performance as well as hardware performance in a real-time virtual environment, enabling the implementation of synchronous and asynchronous communication strategies and the control of communication delay and loss.

Figure 2 shows the PHILS developed by realizing the design. In the current setup, the PHILS has eight sets of computers meaning that it can accommodate the cooperation up to eight autonomous robots. The eight computers, as well as the other three computers that create an environment, are all those with the CPU of Dual Core 2.4GHz and the GPU of 32 stream processors. The eight monitors showing the views of autonomous robots are of 40 inch in size while the other eight monitors to connect to the on-board computers are of 19 inch in size. The network switch is of Gigabit speed so that the speed of wireless communication can be controlled with delay. The server, the client and the visualiser are all of Flight-Gear, which is an open-source simulator which was primarily designed for aerial vehicles but can now also incorporate ground vehicles. By accessing to the server, the FlightGear client can possess information on all the autonomous robots and mobile objects as well as the other environmental objects such as terrain and static objects and visualize them on the client computer. For the network communication, both the TCP/IP and the UDP are utilized.

4   Performance Evaluation within the PHILS

Environmental conditions in the PHILS can be easily controlled, which means the performance evaluation of a team of multiple robots is available under the designed conditions regardless of number of repetition. Also, true positions of objects in the environment can be easily monitored and used to numerically evaluate individual and/or cooperative performance of a team of robots. The performance of cooperative robots can be analyzed in several different ways depending on types of systems and objectives of the mission that the robots are involved. In this paper, a simple multi robot exploration scenario will be considered, where there are a number of OOIs at random positions.

The performance of a team of multiple robots can be numerically evaluated in terms of the accuracy of mapping, the efficiency of cooperative exploration, and the accuracy of OOI localization. The accuracy of mapping and OOI localization heavily relies on the solution to the problem of pose estimation and map building of each robot, and it is given by the SLAM algorithm. Let $\mathbf{Z}_k = \left\{ \mathbf{z}_k^j | \forall j \in \{1, \cdots, n_p\} \right\}$ be the current observation by the laser range finder (LRF) mounted on ith robot which is a set of points, where n_p is the number of points. Using the current and past observations, the pose of the robot and the map are computed by maximizing the joint probability shown below:

$$p(\mathbf{x}_k^{s_i}, {}^{s_i}\mathbf{M}|{}^{s_i}\mathbf{Z}_{1:k}, {}^{s_i}\mathbf{u}_{1:k}) \tag{4}$$

where, ${}^{s_i}\mathbf{M}_k$ is the map created by ith robot, ${}^{s_i}\mathbf{z}_{1:k}$ and ${}^{s_i}\mathbf{u}_{1:k}$ are observations of ith robot and control inputs for the robot up to time step k, respectively. Multi robot operation is not directly related to the problem of pose estimation and map building of each robot, however, the quality of the map of the whole environment can be associated with the cooperation of the robots. For analyzing the accuracy of the map, users of the PHILS can easily put recognizable landmarks on the virtual environment whose true locations are given only to users. While the robots cooperatively explore the environment, the combined map can be created by the maps of individual robots in the same coordinate frame. Once the team of robots is finished with building the combined map, the quality of the map can be assessed by computing position errors between true positions of landmarks and mapped positions of landmarks:

$$e = \frac{1}{n_l} \sum_{i=1}^{n_l} \left\| \mathbf{x}_k^{l_i} - \hat{\mathbf{x}}_k^{l_i} \right\|^2 \tag{5}$$

where, $\mathbf{x}_k^{l_i}$ and $\hat{\mathbf{x}}_k^{l_i}$ are true and mapped position of ith landmark, and n_l is the total number of landmarks. Similarly, the accuracy of OOI localization can be evaluated by the error between true and estimated positions of the OOIs.

In order to evaluate the efficiency of n-robot cooperation, let $t_{\beta,n}$ elapsed time for n robots to explore more than $\beta\%$ of the whole environment. $t_{\beta,n}$ may vary depending on the number of robots, thus how much the number of robots can affect the efficiency of the cooperation can be analyzed by changing the number

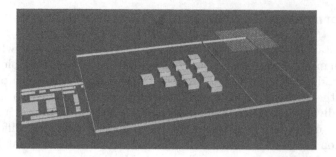

Fig. 3. Virtual environment with mobile and static OOIs

of robots and comparing elapsed times for each case. When n_1 robots and n_2 robots explore the same area separately, time difference between these two cases is given by:

$$\Delta t_{\beta,n_2,n_1} = \frac{t_{\beta,n_2} - t_{\beta,n_1}}{n_2 - n_1} \qquad (6)$$

where, n_1 and n_2 are numbers of robots to be used for autonomous exploration where $n_1 < n_2$. A negative $\Delta t_{\beta,n_2-n_1}$ means the total elapsed time for exploring $\beta\%$ of the whole space is decreased. On the other hand, if $\Delta t_{\beta,n_2-n_1}$ is nonnegative, it is not worth adding more robots.

5   Experimental Results

In this section a simplified multi robot autonomous exploration scenario was considered within a $100 \times 100m$ unknown virtual environment which had both outdoor and indoor areas (Fig. 3). There were 4 mobile OOIs and 2 static OOIs in outdoor and indoor environment, respectively, and 4 up to 8 virtual robots operated at the same time. The team of robots was required to complete the mapping task and to neutralize all the OOIs. As discussed in the previous section, cooperative performance of multiple robots was mainly evaluated based on the quality of mapping, the efficiency of the cooperative exploration, and the accuracy of OOI localization. Additionally, the robustness of the cooperative strategy applied to the team of the robots is evaluated throughout the success rate of the completion of the scenario. An OOI was regarded as being neutralized when two robots detected and successfully tracked the OOI for a few seconds keeping certain distance.

Figure 4 shows the average accumulated mapping error with respect to number of landmarks for three tests with different number of robots. Each test was conducted 50 times, and landmarks are assumed to be detected if they are within the field of view of a robot. As can be seen in the figure the average accumulated mapping error increases almost linearly, which means each mapped landmark is equally away from the true position of the corresponding landmark. The average mapping error, defined as the average accumulated error divided by the number of landmarks, is within a few centimeters regardless of the number of robots indicating that the cooperative mapping is very accurate and the accuracy is not related to the number of robots. One reason for the result is that the accuracy of the map is highly dependent on the complexity of the environment, and the virtual test environment used for performance evaluation is relatively well structured. Also, since these landmarks are not used for localization of the robot, the number of landmarks has no impact on the accuracy of the map.

Figure 5(a) shows the average percentage of the area explored out of the whole environment with respect to time when the number of robot is 4. The figure shows three different tests with different initial positions of the robots, and each test was conducted 50 times of experiments with the same initial positions of the robots. In this experiment, OOI neutralization was not included since time required to explore the environment could be significantly different depending on locations of OOIs. Although an increase of speed of each robot can accelerate exploration, it has nothing to do with efficiency of cooperative strategy. Thus, velocity of robots is set to 8 km/h for outdoor exploration and 4 km/h for indoor exploration. The result shows that the virtual environment is entirely explored ($\beta = 85$) within 19 minutes on average, and that the cooperative exploration generally works fine since the initial positions of the robots do not play significant roles during the experiment. The simplicity of the environment also helps the result be consistent. As the number of robots increases, the efficiency of exploration also improves as shown in Fig. 5(b). It can be seen that the performance of cooperative exploration gradually increases until the number of robots reaches 7, but there is no big difference between using 7 and 8 robots.

The accuracy of position estimations of the OOIs is shown in Fig. 6. Also note that each test has the same initial positions of the OOIs, and was conducted 50 times, where OOI 1 to 5 are mobile OOIs and OOI 6 and 7 are static OOIs. From this figure variance from the true position and estimated position of OOIs is small. For localization of mobile OOIs, the error rate is slightly higher than that of static OOI since the level of uncertainty is relatively large. However,

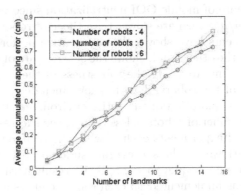

Fig. 4. Average accumulated mapping error

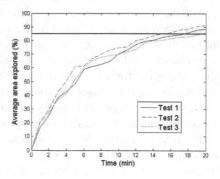

(a) Average area explored vs. time

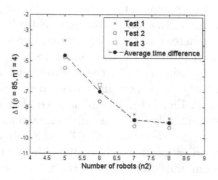

(b) time difference vs. number of robots

Fig. 5. Performance of cooperative exploration

there is no single failure of mobile OOI neutralization since velocities of mobile OOIs are set to 3 km/h, which are slower than those of robots.

Last three experiments have shown the cooperative performance of a single mission. Figure 7, on the other hand, shows the success rate of completion of two missions at the same time to verify the robustness of the cooperative strategy applied to the team of the robots. Two missions include the neutralization of all the OOIs and the exploration of the entire environment ($\beta = 85$) within 20 minutes. When the number of robots is less than 7, the success rate stays within 30% after 100 times of experiments each of which has different initial positions of robots and OOIs. However, the success rate suddenly rises when the number of robots is greater than or equal to 7. From the result it can be said that the cooperative algorithms implemented on each robot requires at least 7 robots to successfully explore the environment within 20 minutes.

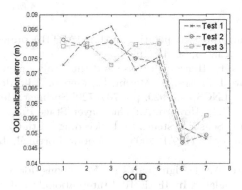

Fig. 6. OOI localization error

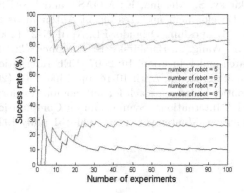

Fig. 7. Success rate of completion of two missions

6   Conclusion and Future Work

This paper has presented virtual testing for evaluation of cooperative performance of the team of robots. The PHILS that can be utilized for virtual testing was first introduced and the evaluation of cooperative performance within the PHILS was described. Virtual field testing was conducted using 4 up to 8 robots within the PHILS and the results showed that the PHILS can be effectively used for quantitative analysis of the performance of cooperative robots.

The current study is limited only to a part of cooperation between a team of robots. For the future work capabilities of autonomous robots can be evaluated in terms of different aspects of cooperation. In addition, different platforms can also be testified, and more complicated environmental parameters can be considered during virtual performance evaluation.

References

1. Alami, R., et al.: Multi-robot cooperation in the MARTHA project. IEEE Robotics and Automation Magazine 5, 36–47 (1998)
2. Jakobi, N., Husbands, P., Harvey, I.: Noise and the Reality gap: The Use of Simulation in Evolutionary Robotics. In: Morán, F., Merelo, J.J., Moreno, A., Chacon, P. (eds.) ECAL 1995. LNCS, vol. 929, pp. 704–720. Springer, Heidelberg (1995)
3. Gerkey, B., Vaughan, R.T., Howard, A.: The Player/Stage Project: Tools for Multi-Robot and Distributed Sensor Systems. In: Proceedings of the International Conference on Advanced Robotics (ICAR 2003), Coimbra, Portugal, June 30-July 3, pp. 317–323 (2003)
4. Koenig, N., Howard, A.: Design and Use Paradigms for Gazebo, An Open-source Multi-robot Simulator. In: IEEE/RSJ International Conference on Intelligent Robots and Systems, September 28-October 2, pp. 2149–2154 (2004)
5. Michel, O.: WebotsTM: Professional Mobile Robot Simulation. International Journal of Advanced Robotic Systems 1(1), 39–42 (2004)
6. Scrapper, C., Balakirsky, S., Messina, E.: MOAST and USARSim - A Combined Framework for the Development and Testing of Autonomous Systems. In: SPIE Defense and Security Symposium, Orlando, FL, April 17-21 (2006)
7. Carpin, S., Lewis, M., Wang, J., Balakirsky, S., Scrapper, C.: USARSim: A Robot Simulator for Research and Education. In: 2007 IEEE International Conference on Robotics and Automation, Roma, April 10-14, pp. 1400–1405 (2007)
8. Yamauchi, B.: A frontier-based approach for autonomous exploration. In: Proceedings of the 1997 IEEE International Symposium on Computational Intelligence in Robotics and Automation, Monterey, CA, pp. 146–151 (July 1997)

Leader-Follower Formation Control Using PID Controller

In-Sung Choi[*] and Jong-Suk Choi

Center for Bionics, Korea Institute of Science and Technology, Seoul, Korea
{cis0429,cjs}@kist.re.kr

Abstract. This paper presents a robust formation control method independent on noise of compass sensor. There are various formation control method for multi-robot system. These methods offer great way to keep the (d, φ)-formation. In real environment, however, heading angle of each robot is affected by noise of compass sensor. Because of this reason, follower can't keep exact formation. In this paper, we suggest formation control method that uses PID controller to resolve this problem. And we also prove that PID controller is effect to reduce position error.

Keywords: Formation Control, Leader-Following, Multi-agent robot, PID controller.

1 Introduction

In the last few years formation control became one challenge research topic among multi-robot research issues. This is because there are many potential advantages of such systems over a single robot, including greater flexibility, adaptability to unknown environments and robustness. Formation control is defined as the coordination of group of robots that maintain a formation within specified geometrical shapes, such as a wedge or a chain. Potential application areas of formation control include many cooperative tasks such as exploring, surveillance, search and rescue, transporting large objects and control of arrays of satellites. Several approaches have been proposed in the literature for the formation control of mobile robot[1-6]. But these approaches can be demonstrated on the assumption that all of position value are guaranteed to use for formation control. In real environment, sensor value can't satisfies this assumption. It is very important to obtain the position of the robots exactly for formation control. A state of robot is composed of x, y and θ. Of these, θ is used in prediction the movement of leader. So It is difficult to maintain the target formation effectively, if follower don't know exact value of θ. Actually value of θ measured compass sensor was inaccurate in real environment. That's why this approach in this paper is proposed. PID control is used to compensate such

---

[*] Corresponding author.

C.-Y. Su, S. Rakheja, H. Liu (Eds.): ICIRA 2012, Part II, LNAI 7507, pp. 625–634, 2012.

uncertainty of θ. By using PID control, Follower can keep the formation effectively without heading angle of each robot. This paper, first, gives the typical method of formation control[1]. Next problem occurred in real environment is verified. Finally formation control method proposed in this paper is presented.

2   Leader-Follower Formation Control

2.1   Goal of Leader-Follower Formation

In the formation, the robot can be divided into the leader and the Followers. To keep the Formation, the followers should know the position of themselves with regard to leader. There are two major methods: (d,d) control and (d,φ)-control to keep the formation in the leader-follower method. In (d,φ)-formation control, to keep the formation, the followers must maintain the relative distance and bearing angle to the leader. That is say the robots will be in formation, only if the value of (d,φ) can keep in the desired value (d^{ref},φ^{ref}). (d^{ref},φ^{ref})-formation is presented in Fig. 1.

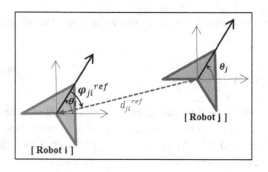

Fig. 1. (d^{ref},φ^{ref})-formation

Where d^{ref},φ^{ref} are the desired relative distance and bearing angle between two robot. With reference Fig. 1, consider the following definition.

$$d_{ji}^{ref} > 0. \tag{1}$$

$$-\frac{\pi}{2} < \varphi_{ji}^{ref} < \frac{\pi}{2}. \tag{2}$$

2.2   Typical Method of Formation Control

In order to keep the (d^{ref}, φ^{ref})-formation, follower must know the linear and angular velocities for the formation control. There are many formation control methods to obtain appropriate velocities. we choose [1] for our experiment. This formation control method is divided into step. First step is exact formation control that can keep ($d_{ji}^{ref}, \varphi_{ji}^{ref}$)-formation relative to linear velocity of leader and difference of heading angle v_j, β_{ji}. Optimal linear velocities are given by [1]

$$v_i = v_j \frac{\cos(\beta_{ji} - \varphi_{ji}^{ref})}{\cos \varphi_{ji}^{ref}}. \tag{3}$$

$$\omega_i = v_j \frac{\sin \beta_{ji}}{d_{ji}^{ref} \cos \varphi_{ji}^{ref}}. \tag{4}$$

Second step is a stabilization making the position error decrease to zero. The stabilization method in [1] is modified in a simple form in our research. The error E is decomposed with respect to E_τ and E_v.

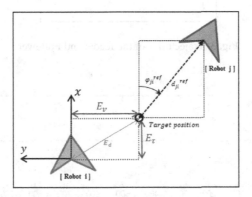

Fig. 2. Decomposition of Error

Where,

$$E_\tau = d_{ji} \cos \varphi_{ji} - d_{ji}^{ref} \cos \varphi_{ji}^{ref}. \tag{5}$$

$$E_v = d_{ji} \sin \varphi_{ji} - d_{ji}^{ref} \sin \varphi_{ji}^{ref}. \tag{6}$$

Considering above error, Eqs. (3,4) are expended as Eqs. (7,8).

$$v_i = v_j \frac{\cos(\beta_{ji} - \varphi_{ji}^{ref})}{\cos\varphi_{ji}^{ref}} + E_\tau K_v . \tag{7}$$

$$\omega_i = v_j \frac{\sin\beta_{ji}}{d_{ji}^{ref}\cos\varphi_{ji}^{ref}} + E_V K_\omega . \tag{8}$$

Where $\beta_{ji} = \theta_j - \theta_i$ and K_v, K_ω are gains of linear and angular velocities.

We simulated formation control with above method(**method 1**) as shown in Fig. 3. ($d_{ji}^{ref}, \varphi_{ji}^{ref}$) are set to (2m,-45 deg) in this Simulation.

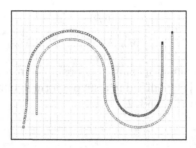

Fig. 3. Trajectories of the leader and Follower

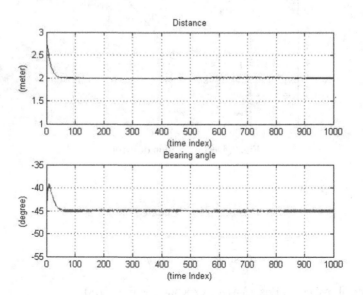

Fig. 4. (d, φ) between two robot using **method 1**

As shown in Fig. 4, the follower approaches to the leader as soon as starting. And the follower keeps the (2(m), -45(deg))-formation while following the leader. Total position error(E) obtained experiment can be presented by numerical value as following Eqs.

$$E = \frac{\sum_{k=1}^{N} E_k}{N} .$$ (9)

$$E_k = \sqrt{E_\tau^2 + E_v^2} .$$ (10)

Where N is elapsed time index. Position error(E) of Simulation result using **Method 1** is 0.021m. This Simulation experiment show that the control strategy proposed in [1] is very effective.

2.3   Problem of Inaccurate Heading Angle

Difference of heading angle(β_{ji}) is the important variable in Eqs. (7,8). Inaccurate value of the β_{ji} can bring about a bad result, because it has a bad effect. Actually, heading angle of robot($\theta_{i,j}$) has had very large noise in real environment. Robot was looking in the same direction, but β_{ji} was changing depending on location because of ground effect. $\theta_{i,j}$ is measured by compass sensor and presented as Fig. 5.

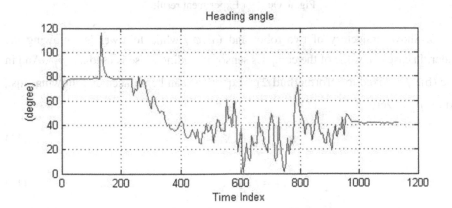

Fig. 5. Noise and ground effect

Average of above values is 47.5 degree, and standard deviation is 20.7 degree. There is problem at formation control using such value. We experimented about effect of β_{ji} in real environment.

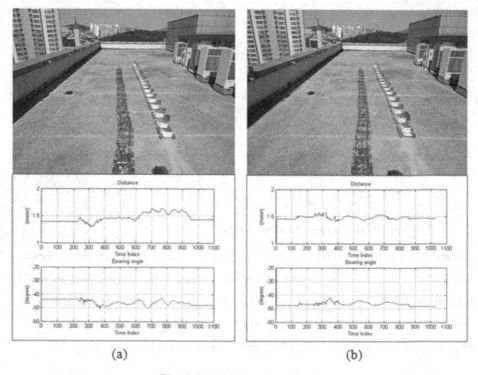

(a)   (b)

Fig. 6. Outdoor Experiment result

Fig. 6. Shows trajectory of two robot and (d, φ) while follower is following the leader. In case (a), value of the compass sensor including noise is used as β_{ji}. And in case (b), β_{ji} fixed to zero(**method 2**). Eqs. (7,8) can be reduced as following Eqs., fixing β_{ji} to zero.

$$v_i = v_j + E_\tau K_v . \tag{11}$$

$$\omega_i = E_v K_\omega . \tag{12}$$

As shown, Exact control part is removed while stabilization part is only left. Total position Errors of each case are (a) 0.096m and (b) 0.049m. method of case (b) offer much better result than case (a). In conclusion, using only stabilization part is better than adding exact control part including noise for formation control.

However, if we only use stabilization part, some problem can be occurred.

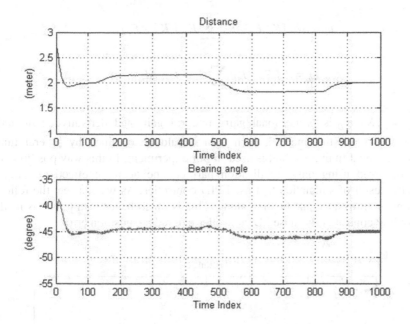

Fig. 7. (d, φ) between two robot using **method 2**

We also simulated formation control with **method 2** in same condition as Fig. 3. As we can see Fig. 7, Simulation result with **method 2** has position error in comparison with result with **method 1**(see Fig. 4). Position Error is increasing when leader begin turning the corner.

2.4   Formation Control Using PID Controller

We confirmed problems that are occurred when using exact control part including noise and only stabilization part. This paper proposes to use PID controller in order to make position error occurred in corner to zero(**method 3**). A Proportional-integral-derivative(PID) controller is generic control loop feedback mechanism widely used in industrial control systems. A PID controller calculates an error value as the difference between a measured process variable and desired setpoint. The controller attempts to minimize the error by adjusting the process control inputs. The PID controller calculation involves three separate constant parameters, and is accordingly sometimes called three-term control: the proportional, the integral and derivative values, denote P, I and D. Heuristically, these values can be interpreted in terms of time: P depends on the present error, I on the accumulation of past error, and D is a prediction of future error, based on current rate of change. Equation of formation control applied PID controller is presented as following :

$$v_i = v_j + [K_{P_\tau} E_\tau + K_{I_\tau} \sum E_\tau + K_{D_\tau} \Delta E_\tau] .\qquad(13)$$

$$\omega_i = K_{P_v} E_v + K_{I_v} \sum E_v + K_{D_v} \Delta E_v .\qquad(14)$$

Where K_P, K_I, K_D is proportional gain, integral gain and derivative gain tuning parameter. To use this method, each gain should be obtained by several tuning methods. Manual tuning method is used in out experiment. In this way position error which occurred using only stabilization part can be decrease effectively. Fig. 8. shows the result of simulation that used PID controller. As we can see, the follower maintains goal distance and bearing angle. This is much better than previous method using only P controller, because I,D controller can reduce position error.

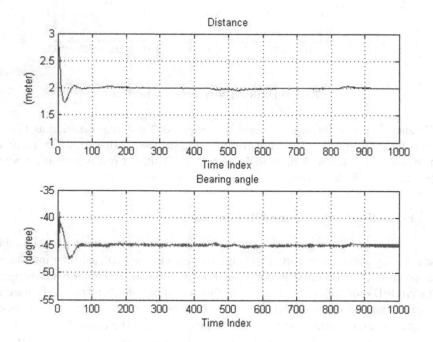

Fig. 8. (d, φ) between two robot using **method 3**

We can compare efficiency of each method through Table. 1. The position error in simulation using method 3 is small than position error using method 1 which is our target. That's why PID controller let follower moves to target position more quickly as soon as starting.

Table 1. Total Position Error in Simulation

Experiment	Error(E)
Method 1	0.021m
Method 2	0.12m
Method 3	**0.018m**

3   Experimental Results

Fig. 9 shows the result of the experiment in real environment. The leader moves along
the reverse curve with $v_j = 0.3$m/s, $\omega_j = 0.2$rad/s. The (d, φ)-formation is set to
(1.5m, -45deg). Compared with simulation result, the biggest difference is that result
using **method 1** have large amount of position error because of sensor noise.

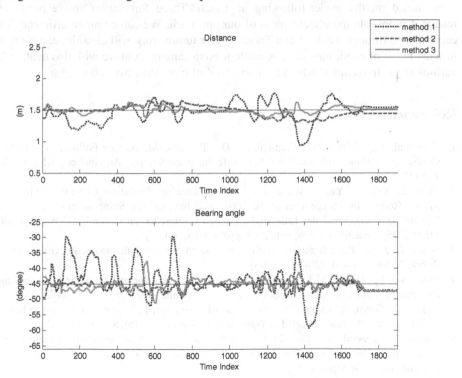

Fig. 9. Experiment result

Table 2. Total Position Error in experiment

Experiment	Error(E)
Method 1	0.165m
Method 2	0.080m
Method 3	**0.059m**

Table 2 shows the total position error in experiment.

4   Conclusions and Future Works

In this paper, we propose a new method for formation control of multiple mobile robot based on the leader-following approach. Three Simulation and experiment results demonstrate the effectiveness of our approach. We can compare efficiency of each method through Table. 1 and Table. 2. Our future work will consider experiment in wide range of conditions such as outdoor environment. And we will also deal with various Formation control which are composed of more than two robot.

References

1. Consolini, L., Morbidi, F., Prattichizzo, D., Tosques, M.: Leader-Follower Formation Control of nonholonimic mobile robots with input constraints. Automatica 44(5), 1343–1349 (2008)
2. Shao, J., Xie, G., Yu, J., Wang, L.: Leader-Following Formation Control of Multiple Mobile Robots. In: Proceedings of the 20th IEEE International Symposium on Intelligent Control, ISIC 2005 and the 13th Mediterranean Conference on Control and Automation, MED 2005, Limassol, Cyprus, vol. 2005, pp. 808–813 (2005)
3. Balch, T., Arkin, R.C.: Behavior-based formation control for multirobot team. IEEE Trans. Robot. Automat. 14(6), 926–939 (1998)
4. Fredslund, J., Mataric, M.J.: A general algorithm for robot formations using local sensing and minimal communication. IEEE Trans. Robot. Automat. 18(5), 837–846 (2002)
5. Das, A.K., Fierro, R., Kumar, V., Ostrowski, J.P., Spletzer, J., Taylor, C.J.: A vision-based formation control framework. IEEE Trans. Robot. Automat. 18(5), 813–825 (2002)
6. Ögren, P., Egerstedt, M., Hu, X.: A control Lyapunov function approach to multi-agent coordination. IEEE Trans. Robot. Automat. 18(5), 847–851 (2002)
7. PID controller – Wikipedia,
   http://en.wikipedia.org/wiki/PID_controller

Internet-Based Telerobotics of Mobile Manipulators: Application on *RobuTER/ULM*

B. Khiter[1], A. Hentout[1], E. Boutellaa[2], M.R. Benbouali[1], and B. Bouzouia[1]

[1] Division of Computer-Integrated Manufacturing and Robotics (DPR)
[2] Division of Multimedia and Systems Architecture (ASM)
Centre for Development of Advanced Technologies (CDTA)
BP 17, Baba Hassen, Algiers 16303, Algeria
{bkhiter,ahentout}@cdta.dz, hentout_abdelfetah@hotmail.com

Abstract. Few works only deal with telerobotics of mobile manipulators via the Internet. This paper consists of a contribution in this research field and describes an Internet-based multi-agent telerobotic system of such robots.

The developed system provides the operator with a human/robot interface, accessible via the Internet, for remote control of mobile manipulators. This interface displays all sensors data and video images delivered by the eye-in-hand IP camera. In addition, the interface allows the operator to perform primitive tasks, either separately by the manipulator or by the mobile base, or in cooperation by both of them.

The proposed telerobotic system is implemented on the *RobuTER/ULM* mobile manipulator. The validity of the system is demonstrated through telerobotic experiments of four primitive tasks via the Internet over a long distance.

Keywords: Mobile Manipulators, Internet-based Telerobotics, Multi-agent Architecture, *RobuTER/ULM*.

1 Introduction

Telerobotic systems are traditionally implemented by using dedicated communication channels. Moving the local/client and/or the remote sites requires the movement of all the equipments and the network reconfiguration of the communication channel connecting the two sites. Another disadvantage is that operators are, also, forced to move at the client site in order to work and to prepare tasks. Moreover, if the client machine (where the human/robot interface is implemented) breaks down, it becomes difficult (or very expensive) to continue accomplishing the task successfully.

In recent years, with the popularity of the Internet, Internet-based telerobotic systems are becoming a very interesting and promising field of researches in robotics. Telerobotics via Internet involves control of remote robots within a web browser [1]. Such a system eliminates most of the traditional problems mentioned previously. Furthermore, it allows easy and low-cost relocation of operators, and does not depend on the location of the equipment that controls the robot (located on a remote site). The development of an Internet interface, provides an opportunity for researchers to work and to cooperate together to control the robot from anywhere in the world [2].

C.-Y. Su, S. Rakheja, H. Liu (Eds.): ICIRA 2012, Part II, LNAI 7507, pp. 635–644, 2012.
© Springer-Verlag Berlin Heidelberg 2012

The literature on telerobotics over the Internet is numerous. A brief survey on the main researches is given in what follows.

In September 1994, a six-dof manipulator was put online in the *University of Western Australia* [3]. This system allowed the operators, via a web page, to control the robot located above a table with wooden blocks placed on it [4]. *Mercury Project* [5] was put online in August 1994 in the *University of Southern California*. This project consists of a *SCARA* manipulator over a semi-annular workspace containing sand and buried artifacts. The *CINEGEN* project [6] seeks to facilitate simulation aspects and offline programming of manipulators for non-specialists. The *PUMAPaint Project* [7] is an online manipulator located at *Roger Williams University*, and allowing any operator with a web browser to control a *PUMA760* manipulator in order to paint on white paper with real brushes and paint.

Other mobile base projects have been interested in Internet-based telerobotics. These systems allow the operator to control a mobile base, either in a static environment or in the exploration of dynamic ones. *KhepOnTheWeb* system [8] allows operators to control a *Khepera* mobile base in a static environment. *Carnegie Mellon University* developed *Xavier* autonomous indoor mobile base on the web [9]. This robot accepts commands to travel to different offices within a building and broadcasts camera images as it travels. Another web system is the *WebPioneer* project [10] where the operator drives a *Pioneer* mobile base in a dynamic environment.

Few researchers only have been interested in telerobotics of mobile manipulators via the Internet. In *RISCbot* project [2], the authors implemented a web-based teleoperated mobile manipulator via sensor fusion. The *RISCbot* consists of a wheelchair mobile base with an end-effector capabilities for manipulation. Carelli and colleagues [11] proposed a combination of autonomous control and teleoperation command that gave more flexibility to the entire system. Their prototype consists of a three-wheeled mobile base with a five-dof standard manipulator mounted on it.

As few works only deal with telerobotics of mobile manipulators via the Internet, this paper consists of a contribution in this field. It describes an Internet-based multi-agent telerobotic system of such robots. The paper is structured into seven sections. The first section proposed a brief state-of-the-art on Internet-based telerobotic systems. The different control modes for telerobotics are analyzed in the next section. The third section presents the hardware structure of the experimental robotic system. Section four describes the proposed Internet-based telerobotic system of mobile manipulators. The fifth section describes the human/robot interface developed for telerobotics of the *RobuTER/ULM* over the Internet. Experiments and obtained results are presented in section six. Finally, conclusions and future work are presented.

2   Control Modes for Telerobotics

Chong [12] proposed a taxonomy for telerobotic systems (*i*) *Single Operator Single Robot* (*SOSR*), (*ii*) *Single Operator Multiple Robot* (*SOMR*), (*iii*) *Multiple Operator Single Robot* (*MOSR*) and, finally, (*iv*) *Multiple Operator Multiple Robot* (*MOMR*) [13]. Fong and colleagues [14] studied *SOSR* systems, which is the case of our developed telerobotic system, where cooperation occurs between a single operator and a single robot. In this case, telerobotic control modes can be separated into four types ranging from "*no assistance provided to the operator by the robot*" to "*no assistance provided to the robot by the operator*" [15].

Direct Mode. The operator specifies all the robot motion by continuous input. He uses, thus, a suitable input device to control the movement of the robot such as a joystick, a mouse, etc. The robot does not take any initiative except to stop when it recognizes that communications breakdown [16].

Traded Mode. This mode provides alternative control of the robot. The competence of the robot includes capabilities to choose its own path, to respond intelligently to the environment, and to accomplish local goals. The operator assumes direct control in case of critical situations [15].

Shared Mode. The operator and the robot control, concurrently, different aspects of the telerobotic system. This mode relieves the operator from controlling details and lets him concentrate on the goals of telerobotics [17].

Autonomous Mode. The operator performs high-level planning and monitors the execution of the robot. He may have to interrupt the execution of the robot in dangerous situation or help it to execute tasks [17].

3   Hardware Structure of the Experimental Robotic System

The experimental robotic system, given by Fig. 1, consists of the *RobuTER/ULM* mobile manipulator. The robot is controlled by an on-board industrial PC and by four *MPC555* microcontroller cards communicating via a *CAN* bus.

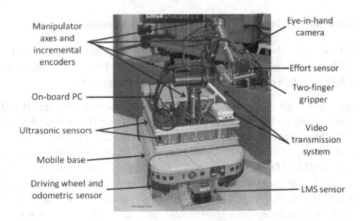

Fig. 1. Structure of the experimental robotic system (*RobuTER/ULM*)

RobuTER/ULM is composed of a six-dof ultra-light manipulator (*ULM*) with two-fingered electrical gripper, mounted upon a rectangular non-holonomic differentially-driven mobile base (*RobuTER*).

The mobile base is equipped with an odometer sensor on each driven wheel, a laser measurement system at its front and a belt of 24 ultrasonic sensors. The manipulator is equipped with an incremental position sensor for each articulation, a six-dof effort sensor and an eye-in-hand IP camera installed on the gripper. The robot has also a wireless communication system in order to communicate with an off-board PC.

4   Internet-Based Telerobotic Architecture of Mobile Manipulators

4.1   Internet Constraints

The time delay depends on the distance separating the local/client from the remote site. It depends, also, on the processing time required for coding and data transmission, the processing speed and the load of nodes, the connection bandwidth and the transmission speed, the amount of data, etc. [18]. Such delays may be constant in case of direct connection, but may be variable according to the load of the network servers and to the dynamicity of the network structure (which is the case of the Internet) [19].

It is clear that *direct control* mode needs a high-speed network to achieve online direct control of the robot. The previous constraints make direct telerobotics unsuitable for time critical, constrained and dangerous interactions (for example collision between the robot and its environment). In this case, we refer to a *shared/traded control* mode of telerobotics, with the remote robot executing a set of primitive (or more complex) tasks in a completely *autonomous mode* [20].

4.2   Internet-Based Multi-agent Telerobotic Architecture

The Internet-based telerobotic architecture of mobile manipulators is shown by Fig. 2. It consists of four local agents (*SA*, *LMRA*, *LARA* and *VSA*) and two remote agents (*RMRA* and *RARA*). The roles of each agent are given here below:

- *Supervisory Agent* (*SA*): it receives the task to be carried out and, decides on its feasibility according to the status and the availability of the required resources and sensors. If the task is accepted, *SA* distributes it on the local agents.
- *Local Mobile/Manipulator Robot Agent* (*LMRA/LARA*): it cooperates with the other local agents (*LARA/LMRA*, *VSA*) in order to build an operations plan. In addition, this agent receives information on the environment of the mobile base/manipulator and feedback (from *RMRA/RARA*) on the execution of operations. Moreover, *LMRA/LARA* sends requests to *RMRA/RARA* for execution.
- *Vision System Agent* (*VSA*): it observes the environment of the robot by the camera and, extracts useful and required information for the execution of the task from the captured images (images processing, recognition of objects, etc.).

- *Remote Mobile/Manipulator Robot Agent* (*RMRA/RARA*): it scans the sensors equipping the mobile base/manipulator and sends useful information to *LMRA/LARA*. In addition, *RMRA/RARA* controls the movement of the mobile base/manipulator in order to move to the desired situation.

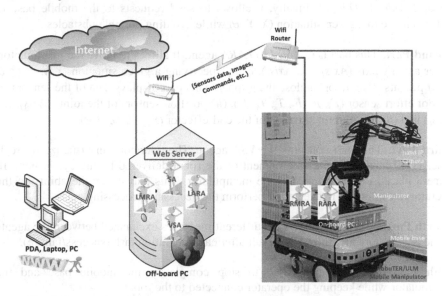

Fig. 2. Internet-based multi-agent telerobotic architecture of mobile manipulators

4.3   Implementation of the Proposed Architecture

This work was performed on a mixed environment (*i*) *Windows XP* for the off-board PC (client) and (*ii*) *Linux Redhat* for the on-board PC (robot).

The implementation of the Internet-based telerobotic architecture consists of hosting the four local agents (*SA, LMRA, LARA* and *VSA*) into a *IIS Web server* that allows to publish the control interface (the web application developed in *ASP.net*). The remote agents (*RMRA* and *RARA*) are installed on the on-board PC of the robot. The client can be any device running a web browser (PC, Laptop, PDA, Smartphone, etc.) in order to access the web page of the control application.

5   Human/Robot Interface

Following the connection of the operator to the server, an authentication page appears. The operator must enter his username and his password in order to access the control web page. Often, there are many clients making requests at the same time. Because our current system accepts one request at a time, only one client can have access to the control web page at the same time. The other clients (requests) are all ignored. Once the username and the password are verified, the control page of Fig. 3 appears. It consists mainly of six parts:

First Part. The first part concerns the *LMRA* agent. It displays all the data relative to the sensors of the mobile base (*i*) its current situation (*New_X, New_Y, New_θ*) and (*ii*) data of both right and left encoders (*E_R, E_L*). This part enables, also, activating US and LMS sensors, and computing the odometry (localization) of the mobile base (*Odo_X, Odo_Y, Odo_θ*). Finally, it allows to send requests to the mobile base in order to move to a given situation (*X, Y, θ*) while avoiding possible obstacles.

Second Part. This part is reserved to *LARA* agent. It allows to move the manipulator, either axis by axis (*Axis₁, ..., Axis₆*), or by specifying a given situation (*x, y, z, ψ, θ, φ*). It permits, also, to open/close the gripper. This part displays data of the sensors (*i*) six-dof effort sensor (*F_x, F_y, F_z, T_x, T_y, T_z*), (*ii*) position sensors of the joints (*Axis₁, ..., Axis₆*) and (*iii*) the current situation of the end-effector *(x, y, z, ψ, θ, φ)*.

Third Part. This part concerns the *VSA* agent. The operator can visualize, in real-time, video images on the environment of the robot delivered by the eye-in-hand IP camera placed on the gripper of the manipulator. This part offers the ability to the operator to capture an image and to perform the necessary processing.

Fourth Part. This area displays the different messages exchanged between the agents of the architecture and shows the result after each operation/task (success/failure).

Fifth Part. This button is used to stop completely the mobile base and the manipulator while keeping the operator connected to the robot.

Last Part. The operator can stop completely and disconnect from the robot by clicking on *Logout*.

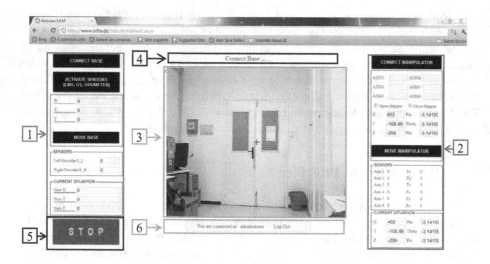

Fig. 3. Human/robot interface for Internet-based telerobotics of *RobuTER/ULM*

6   Experimental Results

In this section, we describe the manipulation progress (via the developed application) from the client connection to the complete execution of the task by the robot. Experiments have been conducted between two different locations in *Algeria* equipped with connection to the Internet and separated by more than 200km. The *RobuTER/ULM* was installed in the *CDTA Research Center* and two clients connected to the robot (*i*) the first was in *Constantine* (400km) in the east and (*ii*) the second client was in *Ain Defla* (200km) in the west.

Considering that all the tasks described in the following sub-sections are executed autonomously by the robot in the same manner and independently of the type of connection, the execution accuracy and the positioning errors are, therefore, the same. Consequently, these experiments have been performed in order to evaluate the developed telerobotic system in terms of (*i*) average connection times and (*ii*) execution times of the tasks. Both of these times are given in seconds (s).

6.1   Average Connection Times

There are many Internet nodes between the local/client site and the remote site/robot which introduce a network time delay. The average connection time is given as an indicator of such delays.

The connection to the control application (both *RMRA* and *RARA* agents) has been tested in three different cases depending on the type of connection (*i*) *direct connection* via a network cable (*ii*) the *LAN* of the *CDTA* (*iii*) the *Internet*. In all the experiments, *LMRA* agent connected first to *RMRA* agent. The average connection times are summarized in Fig. 4. As it can be seen from these results, the connection time increases as the operator moves from *direct* to *LAN* to *Internet* connection.

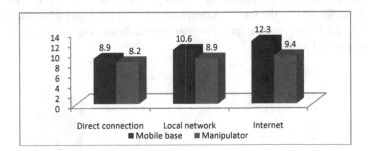

Fig. 4. Average connection times to the remote agents for the different connection types

6.2   Execution Times of the Tasks

Four basic types of tasks, illustrated in this experimental sub-section, have been performed by the mobile manipulator. The initial situation of the mobile base $Base_{Init}(x_{BInit}, y_{BInit}, \theta_{BInit})$=(0mm, 0mm, 0°). The initial configuration of the manipulator $Configuration_{Init}(Q_{1Init}, Q_{2Init}, Q_{3Init}, Q_{4Init}, Q_{5Init}, Q_{6Init})$=(0°, 0°, 0°, 0°, 0°, 0°). The initial situation of the end-effector $Effector_{Init}(x_{EInit}, y_{EInit}, z_{EInit}, \psi_{EInit}, \theta_{EInit}, \varphi_{EInit})$=(-432mm, -108.49mm, 164mm, -180°, -180°, -180°).

First Task (T1). Moving the manipulator from its initial situation to the final situation given by $Effector_{Fin}(x_{EFin}, y_{EFin}, z_{EFin}, \psi_{EFin}, \theta_{EFin}, \varphi_{EFin})$=(-330mm, -630mm, 1080mm, -135°, -88°, 5°).

The final configuration of the manipulator corresponding to this situation, computed by using the *Inverse Kinematic Model (IKM)* of the manipulator, is $Configuration_{Fin}(Q_{1Fin}, Q_{2Fin}, Q_{3Fin}, Q_{4Fin}, Q_{5Fin}, Q_{6Fin})$=(-60°, 61°, 30°, 95°, -15°, 0°).

Second Task (T2). Moving the manipulator from its initial configuration $Configuration_{Init}$ successively to three different configurations as follows:
- $Configuration_1(Q_{11}, Q_{21}, Q_{31}, Q_{41}, Q_{51}, Q_{61})$=(0°, 40°, 28°, 0°, 0°, 0°).
- $Configuration_2(Q_{12}, Q_{22}, Q_{32}, Q_{42}, Q_{52}, Q_{62})$=(20°, 32°, 28°, 0°, 0°, 0°).
- $Configuration_{Fin}(Q_{1Fin}, Q_{2Fin}, Q_{3Fin}, Q_{4Fin}, Q_{5Fin}, Q_{6Fin})$=(0°, 45°, 45°, 0°, 0°, 0°).

Third Task (T3). Moving the mobile base from its initial situation to a final situation given by $Base_{Fin}(x_{BFin}, y_{BFin}, \theta_{BFin})$=(-1920mm, 2mm, 15°) in presence of one obstacle at the position $Obstacle(x_{Ob}, y_{Ob}, z_{Ob})$=(-1000mm, 0mm, 50mm) of a size of (800x200x100)mm.

Fourth Task (T4). Moving the mobile base from its initial situation to a final situation given by $Base_{Fin}(x_{BFin}, y_{BFin}, \theta_{BFin})$=(-3440mm, 13mm, 12°). Two obstacles are present in the environment. The first one is located at the position $Obstacle_1(x_{Ob1}, y_{Ob1}, z_{Ob1})$=(-1000mm, 400mm, 50mm) of a size of (800x200x100)mm. The second obstacle is at the position $Obstacle_2(x_{Ob2}, y_{Ob2}, z_{Ob2})$=(-2000mm, -400mm, 50mm) of a size of about (600x250x100) mm.

For each primitive task considered in this sub-section (T1, T2, T3, T4), ten tests have been performed by the mobile manipulator for all the types of connection (*direct* connection, *LAN* connection and *Internet* connection). Fig. 5 gives the average execution times of all these tasks.

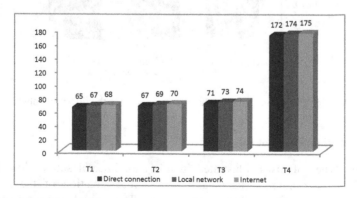

Fig. 5. Average execution times (in seconds) for the considered tasks (T1, T2, T3, T4)

7 Conclusion

The objective of this work is to develop an Internet-based telerobotic system for mobile manipulators. Such a system allows using mobile manipulators in order to accomplish complex tasks in dangerous, inaccessible and hostile environments via the Internet.

We described the control interface, available via the Internet, of the *RobuTER/ULM* mobile manipulator. Through this interface, the operator has a panel for telerobotics of the robot. The operator has all the sensors information of the *RobuTER/ULM* displayed on its web interface. He has, also, control mechanisms of the mobility, the manipulation, the sensors and the end-effector of the robot. In addition, the interface allows the operator to visualize the environment of the robot through the video images delivered by the eye-in-hand IP camera. This latter can be controlled via the web interface allowing more flexibility to view the environment.

The connection to the *RobuTER/ULM* mobile manipulator (*RMRA* and *RARA*) has been tested in three distinguished cases (*i*) *Direct connection* via a *network cable*, (*ii*) connection through the *local network of the CDTA* and, finally, (*iii*) connection via the *Internet*. It is obvious that connection over the *Internet* takes much more time compared with *direct connection* or via the *CDTA's LAN*.

While performing the tasks, we noticed a difference of less than 03 seconds (01 to 03 seconds much more) in the average total execution times of all the tasks. This augmentation is acceptable regarding all the other advantages of using the Internet.

Once the operator connected to the web control interface via a browser, he must authenticate to access the various tasks to be performed by the robot. These latter are of three categories (*i*) control of the manipulator, (*ii*) control of the mobile base and (*iii*) cooperative control of the manipulator and the mobile base.

Our system suffers by forcing operators to work sequentially and wait in a queue. Consequently, the next step is to emigrate from *Single Operator Single Robot* (*SOSR*) current system onto *Multiple Operator Single Robot* (*MOSR*) system.

References

1. Monroy, C., Kelly, R., Arteaga, M., Bugarin, E.: Remote Visual Servoing of a Robot Manipulator via Internet2. Journal of Intelligent Robotic Systems 49(1), 171–187 (2007)
2. Elkady, A., Sobh, T.: Web-Based Control of Mobile Manipulation Platforms via Sensor Fusion. In: Tzafestas, S.G. (ed.) Web-Based Control and Robotics Education, Intelligent Systems, Control and Automation: Science and Engineering, pp. 297–312. Springer Science + Business Media B.V. (2009)
3. Dalton, B., Taylor, K.: A Framework for Internet Robotics. In: The International Conference on Intelligent Robots and Systems (IROS 1998): Workshop on Web Robots, Canada (October 1998)
4. Dalton, B.: Techniques for Web Telerobotics. Ph.D. Thesis in Mechanical and Materials Engineering, University of Western Australia, Perth, Australia (2001)
5. Goldberg, K., Gentner, S., Sutter, C., Wiegley, J.: The Mercury Project: A Feasibility Study for Internet Robots. IEEE Robotics & Automation Magazine 7(1), 35–40 (2000)

6. Fluckiger, L., Baur, C., Clavel, R.: CINEGEN: a rapid prototyping tool for robot manipulators. In: Schweitzer, G., Siegwart, R., Cattin, P. (eds.) The Fourth International Conference on Motion and Vibration Control (MOVIC 1998), Zurich, Switzerland, vol. 1, pp. 129–134 (1998)

7. Stein, M.R.: The PumaPaint Project. Autonomous Robots 15(1), 255–265 (2003)

8. Simmons, R.: Xavier: An Autonomous Mobile Robot on the Web. In: The International Conference on Intelligent Robots and Systems (IROS1998): Workshop on Web Robots, Canada (October 1998)

9. Burgard, W., Cremers, A.B., Fox, D., Lakemeyer, G., Hâhnel, D., Schulz, D., Steiner, W., Thrun, S.: The interactive museum tour-guide robot. In: The 15th National Conference on Artificial Intelligence, USA (July 1998)

10. Grange, S., Fong, T., Baur, C.: Efective Vehicle Teleoperation on the World Wide Web. In: The International Conference on Robotics and Automation (ICRA 2000), USA (April 2000)

11. Carelli, R., Forte, G., Canali, L., Mut, V., Araguas, G., Destefanis, E.: Autonomous and teleoperation control of a mobile robot. Mechatronics 18(1), 187–194 (2008)

12. Chong, N., Kotoku, T., Ohba, K., Komoriya, K., Matsuhira, N., Tanie, K.: Remote coordinated controls in multiple telerobot cooperation. In: The International Conference on Robotics and Automation (ICRA 2000), San Francisco, USA (April 2000)

13. Goldberg, K., Song, D., Khor, Y., Pescovitz, D., Levandowski, A., Himmelstein, J., Shih, J., Ho, A., Paulos, E., Donath, J.: Collaborative Online Teleoperation with Spatial Dynamic Voting and a Human Tele-Actor. In: The International Conference on Robotics and Automation (ICRA 2002), Washington, USA (May 2002)

14. Fong, T., Thorpe, C., Baur, C.: Safeguarded Teleoperation Controller. In: The International Conference on Advanced Robotics (ICAR 2001), Budapest, Hungary (August 2001)

15. Ong, K.W., Seet, G., Sim, S.K.: An Implementation of Seamless Human-Robot Interaction for Telerobotics. The International Journal of Advanced Robotic Systems 5(2), 167–176 (2008)

16. Bruemmer, D.J., Dudenhoeffer, D.D., Marble, J.L.: Dynamic-Autonomy for Urban Search and Rescue. In: AAAI Mobile Robot Competition, Canada, July 28-August 1 (2002)

17. Lin, I.-.S., Wallner, F., Dillmann, R.: An Advanced Telerobotic Control System for a Mobile Robot with Multisensor Feedback. In: The Intelligent Autonomous Systems (IAS-4), Karlsruhe, Germany, March 27-30, pp. 365–372 (1995)

18. Yu, R., Huang, X.G.: Robot Remote Control Internet Architecture. In: Qi, L. (ed.) ISIA 2010. CCIS, vol. 86, pp. 514–518. Springer, Heidelberg (2011)

19. Wang, S., Xu, B., Liu, Y., Zhou, Y.: Real-time mobile robot teleoperation via Internet based on predictive control. Frontiers of Mechanical Engineering in China 2008 3(3), 299–306 (2008)

20. Tzafestas, C.S.: Web-Based Laboratory on Robotics: Remote vs. Virtual Training in Programming Manipulators. In: Tzafestas, S.G. (ed.) Web-Based Control and Robotics Education, Intelligent Systems, Control and Automation: Science and Engineering, pp. 195–225. Springer Science + Business Media B.V. (2009)

Multi-agent Control Architecture
of Mobile Manipulators: Pulling Doors Open

A. Hentout[1], A. Kimouche[2], A. Aiter[2], M.R. Benbouali[1], and B. Bouzouia[1]

[1] Computer-Integrated Manufacturing and Robotics (DPR)
Centre for Development of Advanced Technologies (CDTA)
BP 17, Baba Hassen, Algiers 16303, Algeria
[2] University of Sciences and Technology Houari Boumediene (USTHB)
BP 32, El Alia, Bab Ezzouar, Algiers 16111, Algeria
hentout_abdelfetah@hotmail.com, ahentout@cdta.dz,
alilo.ing2011@gmail.com

Abstract. This paper presents a control approach of mobile manipulators so that they can carry out the task of pulling doors open. The approach is split up into five sub-tasks (*i*) the door is located and the handle is recognized by using the sensors of the robot (*ii*) the robot moves towards the door while avoiding obstacles so that its gripper can reach the handle (*iii*) the manipulator grasps the handle of the door (*iv*) the manipulator twists the handle following a predefined trajectory and, finally, (*v*) the robot carries out a coordinated movement by requesting both of the manipulator and the mobile base to achieve the task.

The proposed approach is integrated into a multi-agent control architecture of mobile manipulators and implemented on *RobuTER/ULM*. Experimental results are presented and discussed to verify the performances of the approach.

Keywords: Mobile Manipulators, Pulling Doors Open, Multi-agent Control Architecture, *RobuTER/ULM*.

1 Introduction

Mobile manipulators have applications in several fields such as grasping and transporting objects, mining, construction, etc. Recently, the environments of such robots have migrated from industrial and factory environments to human environments [1]. Because mobile manipulators are well adapted to human tasks [2], these robots are currently present in offices, hospitals, homes for assisting disabled and/or elderly people, etc.

A mobile manipulator that evolves autonomously within human environments must be able to carry out the task of opening a door. For more than a decade, this task has served as a challenge problem for such robots. It still remains unsolved because it requires addressing of all the issues related to (*i*) the accurate identification of the position and the size of the door and its handle, (*ii*) the computation of the right approach to grasp and to manipulate the handle, (*iii*) the computation of a coordinated movement between the mobile base and the manipulator that allows opening the door and, finally, (*iv*) the navigation through the opened door. In addition, this task is

C.-Y. Su, S. Rakheja, H. Liu (Eds.): ICIRA 2012, Part II, LNAI 7507, pp. 645–655, 2012.

difficult because of the high variability in the conditions under which the doors may be opened (*i*) doors vary in their sizes and types, (*ii*) some doors are opened by pulling and others by pushing, (*iii*) some doors are opened to the left and others to the right and, finally (*iv*) environment around the door may contain obstacles which limit how wide the door can be opened and the space where the robot can move [3].

Several approaches were proposed in the literature. Klingbeil et al. [4] used a vision-based learning algorithm that can locate the handle of the door and decide the direction in which it should be turned. Once this step accomplished, a pre-planned trajectory is executed for twisting the handle. Niemeyer et al. [5] presented a method which is based on an online estimation of the kinematics of the door. During the movement, the actual velocity of the system is observed and the robot pushes into the direction of the least resistance in order to open the door. In [6], a door opening system was presented that was able to open a series of doors by pushing them. Reactive controllers were used to coordinate the motion of the manipulator and the mobile base with the door. Ott and colleagues [7] used a Cartesian impedance controller to make a mobile manipulator able to push to open doors. In this work, the authors assume the direction of twisting the handle of the door. Jain and Kemp presented in [8] a door opening approach using equilibrium point control. The robot could detect, navigate towards and push open doors. Rhee et al. considered in [9] this task with a compliance controlled mobile manipulator. The size of the door and its direction of opening are fixed before carrying out the task. The robot grasps the handle of the door by its multi-fingered hand by using map matching, vision and tactile sensing. Finally, the robot plans a door opening trajectory and pulls door open.

As it can be noticed, most of the works presented above deal with the problem of pushing doors open and few researchers attempted to pull doors open. For this reason, this paper tries to propose a simple approach for the problem of pulling doors open by a mobile manipulator. This task is considered as a benchmark for the multi-agent control architecture of mobile manipulators proposed previously in [10]. Our approach implies a knowledge of the size of the door and the direction of its opening (left or right). It needs, moreover, pre-planned trajectories for the mobile base and the manipulator in order to accomplish the task.

The paper is structured into six sections. The first section presented a brief state-of-the-art on the task of opening doors by mobile manipulators. The different parameters of the task, in a cluttered environment, are presented in the next section. The third section presents the structure of the experimental robotic system. Section four describes the proposed approach for dealing with the task of opening a door by pulling on it. Experiments and obtained results are presented and discussed in section five. Finally, conclusions and future work are presented.

2   Parameters of the Task

Fig. 1 gives a simple representation of the task of opening doors by mobile manipulators in presence of obstacles. The different parameters are given as follows:

- $R_A(O_A, x_A, y_A, z_A)$: it represents the absolute reference frame.
- $R_B(O_B, x_B, y_B, z_B)$: this frame is attached to the mobile base.
- $R_M(O_M, x_M, y_M, z_M)$: this frame is fixed to the basis of the manipulator.

- $R_E(O_E, x_E, y_E, z_E)$: it is attached to the end-effector.
- $Base_{Init}(x_{BInit}, y_{BInit}, \theta_{BInit})$: it is the initial situation of the mobile base given in R_A.
- $Base_{Fin}(x_{BFin}, y_{BFin}, \theta_{BFin})$: $Base_{Fin}$ is the final situation of the mobile base in R_A. It is computed so that the handle of the door belongs to the new workspace of the robot.
- $Handle_{Init}(x_{PInit}, y_{PInit}, z_{PInit})$: it is the position of the handle of the door given in R_A.
- $Handle_{Fin}(x_{PFin}, y_{PFin}, z_{PFin})$: it is the new position of the handle of the door given in the new R_M when the mobile base arrives to $Base_{Fin}$.
- $Config_{Init}(Q_{1Init} ..., Q_{dofInit})$: it represents the initial configuration of the manipulator where dof is the number of degrees of freedom.
- $Config_{Fin}(Q_{1Fin} ..., Q_{dofFin})$: it corresponds to $Handle_{Fin}$. $Config_{Fin}$ is computed by using the *Inverse Kinematic Model (IKM)* of the manipulator.
- $Effector_{Init}(x_{EInit}, y_{EInit}, z_{EInit}, \theta_{EInit}, \psi_{EInit}, \varphi_{EInit})$: it represents the initial situation of the end-effector given in R_A.
- $Effector_{Fin}(x_{EFin}, y_{EFin}, z_{EFin}, \theta_{EFin}, \psi_{EFin}, \varphi_{EFin})$: it represents the final situation of the end-effector given in R_A.
- $Obstacle_i(x_{Obi}, y_{Obi}, z_{Obi})$: it is the position of the obstacle i ($i=0...n$) given in R_A where n is the number of obstacles present in the environment.
- $^M T_E$: this matrix defines R_E in R_M and corresponds to the *Direct Kinematic Model (DKM)* of the manipulator.
- $^A T_E$: this matrix defines R_E in R_A.
- $^A T_B$: it defines R_B in R_A.
- $^B T_M$: it is the matrix defining R_M in R_B.

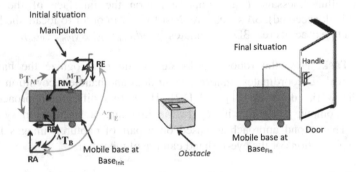

Fig. 1. Parameters of the task of opening a door

3 Proposed Approach

3.1 Multi-agent Control Architecture

A multi-agent architecture has been proposed in [10] for remote control (telerobotics) of mobile manipulators. It consists of four local agents and two remote agents. The roles of each agent are given here below:

- *Supervisory Agent (SA)*: this first agent receives the task to be carried out and, decides on its feasibility according to the status and the availability of the required resources and sensors. If the task is accepted, *SA* distributes it on the local agents.
- *Local Mobile/Manipulator Robot Agent (LMRA/LARA)*: *LMRA/LARA* cooperates with the other local agents (*LARA/LMRA, VSA*) in order to build an operations plan. In addition, this agent receives information on the environment of the mobile base/manipulator and feedback (from *RMRA/RARA*) on the execution of operations. Also, *LMRA/LARA* sends requests to *RMRA/RARA* for execution.
- *Vision System Agent (VSA)*: it observes the environment of the robot by the camera and, extracts useful and required information for the execution of the task from the captured images (images processing, recognition of objects, etc.).
- *Remote Mobile/Manipulator Robot Agent (RMRA/RARA)*: it scans the sensors equipping the mobile base/manipulator and sends useful information to *LMRA/LARA*. In addition, *RMRA/RARA* controls the movement of the mobile base/manipulator in order to move to the desired situation.

3.2   Proposed Approach

The proposed approach can be split up into five consecutive sub-tasks. Each one can be considered as a distinguished whole problem. Only the last four phases are described in this paper. The other phases have been the objects of other works.

When the operator introduces the task to be carried out, *SA* receives that task and tests whether the robot is able to perform it. If the robot cannot execute the task, *SA* displays a failure message (Task impossible) on the interface of the operator. Otherwise (Task accepted), *SA* sends a request to *VSA* in order to locate the handle of the door and to extract its real 3D coordinates $Handle_{Init}(x_{PInit}, y_{PInit}, z_{PInit})$.

First Sub-Task. How the robot can locate the door, recognize the handle and compute its real 3D coordinates $Handle_{Init}$? Our door and handle recognition system is built on the works done in [11] and [12]. Here, two different approaches were proposed to compute $Handle_{Init}$ in R_A. In the first one, a laser-vision system was developed. The second approach is based on a pair of captured images from two different configurations of the eye-in-hand camera of the robot.

Second Sub-Task. How to control the manipulator to reach the handle of the door and to adjust the gripper on the exact position of the handle? As shown by Fig. 2, two possible cases can be distinguished when *LARA* receives $Handle_{Init}$ from *VSA*:

- *$Handle_{Init}$ is within the current workspace of the robot ($Handle_{Init} \equiv Handle_{Fin}$)*: LARA uses the *IKM* of the manipulator to compute $Config_{Fin}(Q_{1Fin}, ..., Q_{dofFin})$ and sends it to *RARA*. After that, the manipulator opens its gripper and moves to reach the computed configuration $Config_{Fin}$ as shown by (1). When the robot reaches the handle, it adjusts the position of the gripper relatively to the handle and, finally, closes its gripper to grasp the handle. If the manipulator succeeds these operations, *LARA* sends another request to *RARA* to twist the handle.

$$Effector_{Fin} \equiv Handle_{Fin} \qquad (1)$$

- *Handle$_{Init}$ is outside the current workspace of the robot (Handle$_{Init}$≠Handle$_{Fin}$)*: The mobile base moves towards the door and stops at a certain distance from it (more details are given below). The process continues as in the preceding case.

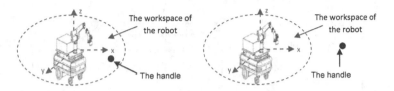

Fig. 2. Possible configurations of a handle

Third Sub-Task. At the end of the second sub-task, another problem must be solved: How the mobile base will move in order to approach the door? If *Handle$_{Init}$* is outside the current workspace of the manipulator (Fig. 3), *LARA* will send *Handle$_{Init}$* to *LMRA*. After that, this latter agent computes *Base$_{Fin}$* by using (2). *LMRA* sends this information to *RMRA* to move to *Base$_{Fin}$*. For this aim, the neural-based navigation approach developed in [13] is used in order to navigate and to avoid obstacles on the trajectory of the mobile base while moving to *Base$_{Fin}$*.

$$Base_{Fin} = \begin{cases} x_{BFin} = x_{PInit} + \alpha \\ y_{BFin} = y_{PInit} + \beta \end{cases} \quad (\alpha, \beta \in R) \tag{2}$$

Fourth Sub-Task. Once the previous sub-tasks are accomplished, a pre-planned trajectory is executed by the manipulator (fourth, fifth and sixth axes) for twisting the handle of the door. If the robot cannot twist the handle in the first direction (according to the information delivered by the six-dof effort sensor), it will try to twist the handle is the other direction. If it does not work again, the door is considered as closed and *LARA* sends an error message (Door closed) to *SA*.

Fifth Sub-Task. The last sub-task consists of moving backwards the robot while holding the handle of the door until it is fully open. This sub-task requires cooperation between the mobile base and the manipulator. Three different ways exist for pulling door open:

- The mobile base is stopped at a certain distance in front of the door and the manipulator performs it alone. In this case, *SA* sends a request to *LARA* to track a predefined operational trajectory for the manipulator in order to complete the task.
- The manipulator grasps the handle of the door and remains fixed in this configuration whereas the mobile base moves backwards until the door is fully opened. For this second manner, *SA* sends a request to *LMRA* to track a pre-planned trajectory in form of an arc.
- Both of the mobile base and the manipulator realize, simultaneously, a combined movement. Here, *SA* sends a request to both *LMRA* and *LARA* to achieve the task.

The protocol diagram of Fig. 3 shows the execution progress of the task rather than the agents that work together in order to achieve it.

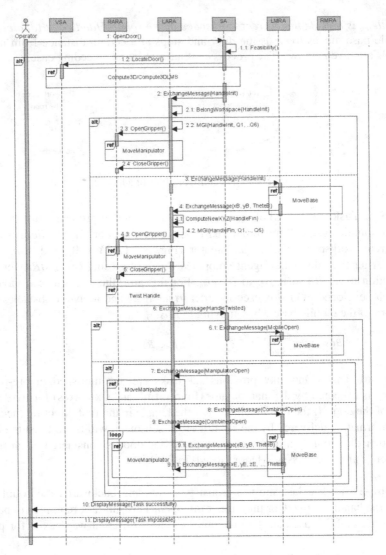

Fig. 3. Protocol diagram of the execution of the task of opening doors

4   Experimental Results

4.1   Structure of the Experimental Robotic System

RobuTER/ULM, given by Fig. 4, consists of a six-dof ultra-light manipulator (*ULM*) with two-fingered electrical gripper, carried on a rectangular non-holonomic differentially-driven mobile base (*RobuTER*). The robot is equipped with an odometer sensor on each driven wheel, a laser measurement system at the front of the mobile base, a belt of 24 ultrasonic sensors, an incremental position sensor for each

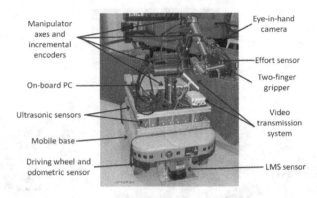

Fig. 4. Structure of the *RobuTER/ULM* mobile manipulator

articulation of the manipulator, a six-dof effort sensor integrated on the gripper and an eye-in-hand camera.

4.2   Obtained Results

The approach described above has been implemented on *RobuTER/ULM*. The manipulator is supposed to be fixed rigidly on the mobile base which is assumed, in its turn, moving on the plan. Also, no sliding is considered between the wheels of the mobile base and the ground. In addition, the obstacles are considered only on the ground and they do not interfere (no collision) with the manipulator while moving to the desired configuration. Finally, the environment around the door is considered free of obstacles and the mobile base can move freely in front of the door.

Table 1. Initial and final conditions of the task of opening doors

$Base_{Init}(x_{BInit}, y_{BInit}, \theta_{BInit})$	(0mm, 0mm, 0°)
$Config_{Init}(Q_{1Init}, Q_{2Init}, Q_{3Init}, Q_{4Init}, Q_{5Init}, Q_{6Init})$	(0°, 0°, 0°, 0°, 0°, 0°)
$Effector_{Init}(x_{EInit}, y_{EInit}, z_{EInit}, \psi_{EInit}, \theta_{EInit}, \varphi_{EInit})$	(-432mm, -108.49mm, 164mm, -180°, -180°, -180°)
$Handle_{Init}(x_{pInit}, y_{pInit}, z_{pInit})$	(-4800mm, 190mm, 1050mm)
$Obstacle_1(x_{Ob1}, y_{Ob1}, z_{Ob1})$	(-1800mm, 50mm, 150mm)
$Base_{Fin}(x_{BFin}, y_{BFin}, \theta_{BFin})$ (α=650, β=-10)	(-4150mm, 200mm, 0°)
$Handle_{Fin}(x_{PFin}, y_{PFin}, z_{PFin})$	(-650mm, -10mm, 410mm)
$Config_{Fin}(Q_{1Fin}, Q_{2Fin}, Q_{3Fin}, Q_{4Fin}, Q_{5Fin}, Q_{6Fin})$	(0°, 15°, 105°, 0°, 0°, 0°)

The door is about 500mm width and must be open to the right by a combined movement of the mobile base and the manipulator for an angle of 60°. The obtained results are shown by the following snapshots of Fig. 5:

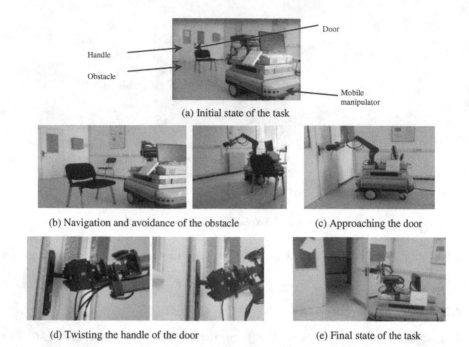

(a) Initial state of the task

(b) Navigation and avoidance of the obstacle   (c) Approaching the door

(d) Twisting the handle of the door   (e) Final state of the task

Fig. 5. Opening the door by a combined movement of the mobile base and the manipulator

Fig. 6a shows the real trajectory of the mobile base while moving towards $Base_{Fin}$ and avoiding the obstacle present in the environment. The real operational trajectory of the end-effector and that of the mobile base while pulling the door open are shown, respectively, by Fig. 6b and Fig. 6c.

4.3   Discussions of Obtained Results

25 tests have been carried out for the task of pulling doors open by the *RobuTER/ULM* mobile manipulator. An initial success rate of about 25% has been obtained. This very low rate is due to the sliding of the gripper from the handle of the door which is a very disadvantageous problem when performing the task. This problem is caused mainly by the form and the nature of the gripper which is not suitable for such tasks. Furthermore, this problem becomes more serious with the rotation of the gripper and the twisting of the handle.

To solve this problem, the gripper was covered with rubber to create more friction between it and the handle. This last operation has doubled the success rate of the task. Thus, 13 tests have succeeded and 12 tests failed, i.e., a success rate of about 52%.

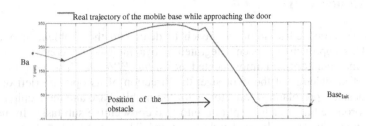

(a)   Real trajectory of the mobile base while approaching the door and avoiding the obstacle

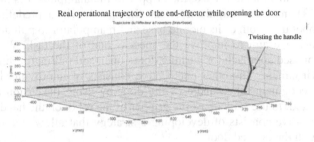

(b) Operational trajectory of the end-effector

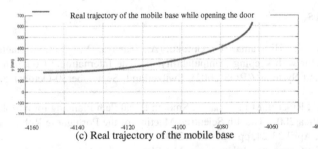

(c) Real trajectory of the mobile base

Fig. 6. Combined movement of the robot while pulling door open

4.4   Manual vs. Autonomous Control

The average execution times of the task for both manual and autonomous control modes are summarized and distributed as shown in Table 2. A great difficulty has been noticed while opening the door manually and most of the tests have failed.

Table 2. Average execution time for both manual and autonomous modes

	Time of the task of opening a door (seconds)					Success rate (%)
	Total time	Navigation of the mobile base (a distance of 4m without obstacles)	Movement of the manipulator	Twisting the handle	Open the door	
Autonomous	42	20	05	05	12	52%
Manual	87	20	25	12	30	08%

5   Conclusion

This paper proposed a simple approach to deal with the problem of pulling doors open. This approach has been integrated into a multi-agent control architecture of mobile manipulators and implemented on *RobuTER/ULM*. The proposed approach implies a knowledge of the door size, the direction of its opening (left or right) and needs, besides, pre-planned trajectories for the mobile base and the manipulator.

The proposed approach is split up into five consecutive sub-tasks. In the first one, the handle of the door is located and recognized. The second sub-task moves the robot in front of the door while avoiding obstacles so that handle belongs to the new workspace of the manipulator. Next, the gripper of the manipulator is inserted into the door handle. Then, the manipulator twists the handle via a predefined trajectory. Finally, the robot uses both of its mobile base and manipulator to pull door open.

In the future, we aim to improve the success rate of the task. We aim, also, to extend the proposed approach for pushing doors open and pulling/pushing doors close in indoor environment. The other perspective consists of improving the sub-task of locating and recognizing the handle of the door by using the vision and the laser-vision system and, to use it to adjust the gripper of the robot on the handle of the door. The last perspective consists of developing a strategy that allows the mobile base to navigate through the opened door.

References

1. Nagatani, K., Hirayama, T., Gofuku, A., Tanaka, Y.: Motion planning for mobile manipulator with keeping manipulability. In: The International Conference on Intelligent Robots and Systems (IROS 2002), Switzerland, September30-October 5, pp. 1663–1668 (2002)
2. Alfaro, C., Ribeiro, M.I., Lima, P.: Smooth Local Path Planning for a Mobile Manipulator. In: Robotica 2004, The 4th Scientific Meeting of the Portuguese Robotics Festival, Porto, Protugal, April 23-24, pp. 127–134 (2004)
3. Chitta, S., Cohen, B., Likhachevy, M.: Planning for Autonomous Door Opening with a Mobile Manipulator. In: The International Conference on Robotics and Automation (ICRA 2010), Anchorage, USA, May 3-7, pp. 1799–1806 (2010)
4. Klingbeil, E., Saxena, A., Ng, A.Y.: Learning to open new doors. In: The International Conference on Intelligent Robots and Systems (IROS 2010), Taipei, Taiwan, October 18-22, pp. 2751–2757 (2010)
5. Niemeyer, G., Slotine, J.J.E.: A simple strategy for opening an unknown door. In: The International Conference of Robotics and Automation (ICRA 1997), USA, pp. 1448–1453 (April 1997)
6. Meeussen, W., Wise, M., Glaser, S., Chitta, S., McGann, C., Mihelich, P., Marder-Eppstein, E., Muja, M., Eruhimov, V., Foote, T., Hsu, J., Rusu, R.B., Marthi, B., Bradski, G., Konolige, K., Gerkey, B., Berger, E.: Autonomous Door Opening and Plugging In using a Personal Robot. In: The International Conference on Robotics and Automation (ICRA 2010), USA, May 3-7, pp. 729–736 (2010)
7. Ott, C., Baeuml, B., Borst, C., Hirzinger, G.: Autonomous Opening of a Door with a Mobile Manipulator: A Case Study. In: The 6th IFAC Symposium on Intelligent Autonomous Vehicles (IAV), Toulouse, France, September 3-5, pp. 349–354 (2007)

8. Jain, A., Kemp, C.C.: Behavior-Based Door Opening with Equilibrium Point Control. In: The RSS Workshop on Mobile Manipulation in Human Environments, USA, June 28 (2009)
9. Rhee, C., Chung, W., Kim, M., Shim, Y., Lee, H.: Door opening control using the multi-fingered robotic hand for the indoor service. In: The International Conference on Robotics and Automation (ICRA 2004), USA, April 26-May 01, pp. 4011–4016 (2004)
10. Hentout, A., Bouzouia, B., Toukal, Z.: Multi-agent Architecture Model for Driving Mobile Manipulator Robots. The International Journal of Advanced Robotic Systems 5(3), 257–269 (2008)
11. Hentout, A., Bouzouia, B., Akli, I., Bouskia, M.A., Ouzzane, E.A., Benbouali, M.R.: Multi-Agent Control Architecture of Mobile Manipulators: Extraction of 3D Coordinates of Object Using an Eye-in-Hand Camera. In: The International Conference on Signals, Circuits and Systems (SCS 2009), Tunisia, November 06-08 (2009)
12. Hentout, A., Bouzouia, B., Akil, I., Toumi, R.: Mobile Manipulation: A Case Study. In: Robot Manipulators: New Achievements. Edited by Aleksandar Lazinica and Hiroyuki Kawai, pp. 145–167, 718 pages (April 2010) ISBN 978-953-307-090-2
13. Azouaoui, O., Kadri, M., Ouadah, N.: Implementation of a neural-based navigation approach on indoor and outdoor mobile robots. In: The 5th International Conference on Soft Computing as Transdisciplinary Science and Technology (CSTST 2008), France, October 27-31, pp. 71–77 (2008)

Planar Surface Area Transformation and Calculation Using Camera and Orientation Sensor

Miti Ruchanurucks[1,*], Surangrak Sutiworwan[1], and Pongthorn Apiroop[2]

[1] Faculty of Engineering, Kasetsart University, Bangkok, Thailand
[2] Huawei Technologies Co., Ltd, Bangkok, Thailand
fengmtr@ku.ac.th, rhoii@hotmail.com,
pongthorn.apiroop@huawei.com

Abstract. This research presents a planar area calculation method, focusing on image warping to top view. An orientation sensor attached to a camera is used to acquire the camera's orientation in real time. In practice, alignment between camera and sensor is imperfect. Therefore, calibration between camera and sensor is addressed using Iterative Least Square method. Then, extrinsic parameters derived from the calibrated sensor and pre-computed intrinsic parameters will be used to generate homography matrix. Homography matrix and a separately required translation matrix will be used to generate a top view image. In the top view image, we can directly count the number of target pixel. Finally, the number of pixel is converted to area size in real-world unit.

Keywords: Area calculation, orientation sensor, multi-sensor calibration, homography, image warping, iterative least square.

1 Introduction

Presently, in agricultural field, it is highly beneficial to correctly predict yield of crops such as maize, wheat, rice and so on. Ground survey is one method to approximate such number. However, it uses a lot of man-power, time, and expense. On the other hands, remote sensing using satellite image is sensitive to weather. Also a scheme to perform image classification of satellite data is inadequate [1]. Therefore, automatic ground survey system is proposed for crop calculation to reduce time and cost.

A good practical example of automatic ground survey system is China's Crop Watch program. [2], [3] applies their algorithm with using Vehicle & GIS & GPS & Video System (VGGVS) for navigation, data collection, and computation. On the top of a vehicle, a camera and an orientation sensor are attached together in order to control the estimation precision. The camera receives an angle from the sensor to adjust a motor to be perpendicular with ground plane all the time. Therefore, the motor adjusting is necessary for the algorithm.

In our work, the motor adjusting is removed by applying image warping instead. Homography information based on the orientation sensor generates top view image

---

* Corresponding author.

C.-Y. Su, S. Rakheja, H. Liu (Eds.): ICIRA 2012, Part II, LNAI 7507, pp. 656–665, 2012.
© Springer-Verlag Berlin Heidelberg 2012

similar to [4]. Then, counting the number of pixel followed by calculating the actual area size in the real world can be performed in the real time.

Our assumption is the system would be installed on a vehicle. We also assume that height between the camera and the planar field is known. All calibrations explained in this paper would be done offline.

For programming, a camera model in OpenCV (Open Source Computer Vision library) is used as it has many good features, such as the precise calibration results, efficient computing, a fast computing speed, etc. as discussed in [5],[6]. Homography is applied for the warping that transforms a perspective view to a top view image. For each frame of image, the homography matrix can be derived from camera's intrinsic and extrinsic parameters. Camera calibration technique with checker board method is used to identify intrinsic parameters as in [7], whereas extrinsic parameters are derived in real time using information from an orientation sensor.

Furthermore, we address a problem of translational parameters in homography matrix. We found out that two (out of three) translation parameters make the output image's size changes dramatically if Roll angle changes. So instead of doing translation directly in the homography matrix, a separate translation matrix would be applied after the image was warped to top view.

Moreover, as alignment between camera and sensor is not perfect, we need to find rotational relationship between them. Ideally, the camera coordinate must be parallel with the sensor coordinate. Thus, calibration between camera and sensor is required for more accurate area calculation. Iterative Least Square (ILS) method [8] is proposed to solve this problem.

Finally, our final contribution is finding a relationship between the top view pixel size and the actual area size.

2   Study Area and Experimental Setup

Our experiments consist of three phases. Pre-processing step consists of camera calibration, sensor calibration and calibration between camera and sensor. Processing step consists of warping to top view using orientation sensor in real time. Post-processing step consists of comparing the warped image with the ground truth and mapping factor from pixel to actual area size. These steps require parameters as will be shown below.

As mentioned earlier, we assume that the height between the camera and the planar area is known. Orientation of the camera around present axis is defined using Roll, Pitch, Yaw angles, as shown in Fig. 1. We found that change in roll and yaw angle does not affect mapping factor from pixel to actual area size. So, only change in pitch angle is study extensively in this work.

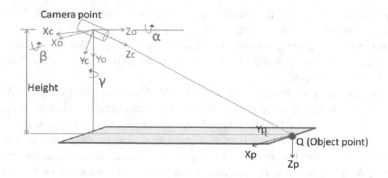

Fig. 1. Angle between object and camera coordinates: Roll (α), Pitch (β) and Yaw (γ) around world axis are the rotation around the Zo-Xo-Yo axis respectively. We illustrate it as Zo-Xo-Yo just to be compatible with the notion of 'angle between object and camera'. For other parts in this paper, the angle will be defined as Roll Yaw Pitch around present axis (Zc-Yc-Xc, respectively).

Images are captured in arbitrary perspective views. Distortion parameters are used to undistort the input image. Viewpoint is changed to top view using homography, which consists of intrinsic and extrinsic parameters. Whereas extrinsic parameters will be derived in real time, intrinsic parameters are shown in Table 1.

Table 1. Experimental parameter

Parameters	Values
Intrinsic parameters	$f_x =1038.71, f_y =1037.18$ $c_x = 471.87, c_y =361.42$
Distortion parameters	$k_1=-0.243, k_2=0.14, k_3=0$ $p_1=-0.0031\ p_2= -0.004836$

3   Method

Our area calculation scheme relies a lot on warping based on homography matrix. So instead of starting from calibration, this chapter explains about homography, rotational parameters from sensor, warping, quality enhancement by calibration between camera and orientation sensor, and area mapping, respectively.

3.1   Homography

Homography matrix (H) is a transformation matrix from a perspective view to a top view which consists of intrinsic matrix (M) and extrinsic matrix ($[R|T]$). It relates points in real-world coordinate (Q) to points in camera coordinate (q). Intrinsic parameters, namely focal length (f_x, f_y) and principal point (c_x, c_y) are generated by camera calibration. Extrinsic parameters, namely rotation (R) and translation (T), in general, can be derived by the calibration as well. We will explain the basic of calibration first, and will show how to further calculate extrinsic matrix for moving camera later.

According to a pinhole camera model, the camera performs a perspective projection of a 3D point onto an image point located on a retinal plane. Using homogenous coordinates, the projective relation between a 3D point and its image can be expressed as (1) and (2)

$$sq = M[R \mid T]Q \cdot \qquad (1)$$

$$s\begin{bmatrix} x \\ y \\ 1 \end{bmatrix} = \begin{bmatrix} f_x & 0 & c_x \\ 0 & f_y & c_y \\ 0 & 0 & 1 \end{bmatrix} \begin{bmatrix} r_{11} & r_{12} & r_{13} & t_1 \\ r_{21} & r_{22} & r_{23} & t_2 \\ r_{31} & r_{32} & r_{33} & t_3 \end{bmatrix} \begin{bmatrix} X \\ Y \\ Z \\ 1 \end{bmatrix} \cdot \qquad (2)$$

Where, s is an arbitrary scale factor for the pinhole camera model [9]. In other words, the quantities in projective geometry are determined up to a constant factor [10].

When the structure under observation is a plane, a simpler formulation of $[R\mid T]$ becomes available. Since the world coordinate system can be set anywhere, it can be conveniently positioned on the plane, such that latter has zero Z coordinate. From (2), it can be rewritten as (3) and (4), which is homography.

$$s\begin{bmatrix} x \\ y \\ 1 \end{bmatrix} = \begin{bmatrix} f_x & 0 & c_x \\ 0 & f_y & c_y \\ 0 & 0 & 1 \end{bmatrix} \begin{bmatrix} r_{11} & r_{12} & t_1 \\ r_{21} & r_{22} & t_2 \\ r_{31} & r_{32} & t_3 \end{bmatrix} \begin{bmatrix} X \\ Y \\ 1 \end{bmatrix} \cdot \qquad (3)$$

$$sq = H\tilde{Q} \cdot \qquad (4)$$

3.2   Rotational Parameters from Orientation Sensor

The extrinsic parameters based on (3) are the projection matrix. In this work, it is derived in real time using an orientation sensor. 9DOF Razor IMU [11] incorporates four sensors which can become an Attitude and Heading Reference System that compose of:

LY530AL (single-axis gyro) and LPR530AL (dual-axis gyro) measure the angular velocity.

ADXL345 (triple-axis accelerometer) measures the acceleration.

HMC5843 (triple-axis magnetometer) is tilt compensated in Yaw axis.

The 9DOF board is programmed with DCM algorithm on the 8MHz Arduino bootloader by Arduino IDE. The outputs of all sensors are processed by an on-board ATmega328 to Roll, Pitch, Yaw angles. The three parameters are output through a serial interface with baud rate of 57600 bps.

3.3   Warping

Warping from perspective view to top view is done by inverting homography matrix and set $s = 1$, in (4). This can be written as (5).

$$\tilde{Q} = H^{-1}q \; .\tag{5}$$

(5) can generate real time top view image using rotational parameters (α, β, γ) from the orientation sensor. For translation parameters (t_1, t_2, t_3), they are set to $(0, 0, f_x /2)$. Setting t_3, zoom, to $f_x /2$ makes the top view image covers as many pixels in its original image as possible. This is preferable as we are going to apply the top view image for area calculation.

For t_1 and t_2, shift, normally it is used to shift the warped image to be viewable. However, doing so introduces output image's size changes dramatically when roll angle changes. One example is in Fig. 2. The reason can be analyzed by replacing (5) with (6).

(a)   (b)

Fig. 2. Warping to top view using (t_1, t_2, t_3) equal to $(c_x, c_y, f_x /2)$, from (a) input perspective image, resulting in (b) output unorganized top view image

$$\tilde{Q} = \begin{bmatrix} r_{11} & r_{12} & t_1 \\ r_{21} & r_{22} & t_2 \\ r_{31} & r_{32} & t_3 \end{bmatrix}^{-1} \begin{bmatrix} f_x & 0 & c_x \\ 0 & f_y & c_y \\ 0 & 0 & 1 \end{bmatrix}^{-1} q \; .\tag{6}$$

Then, look at the first term on the right side of the equation. It defines (inverse) rotational and translational relationship between perspective view and top view when intrinsic parameters are neglected. By inputting roll and pitch angles, we found that (6) will be different between one with t_1 or t_2 and one with t_3, as shown in (7), (8), and (9), respectively.

$$
\begin{bmatrix} r_{11} & r_{12} & t_1 \\ r_{21} & r_{22} & 0 \\ r_{31} & r_{32} & 0 \end{bmatrix}^{-1} = \begin{bmatrix} 0 & \dfrac{1}{\sin(\alpha)} & \dfrac{-1}{\tan(\alpha)\tan(\beta)} \\ 0 & 0 & \dfrac{1}{\sin(\beta)} \\ \dfrac{1}{t_1} & \dfrac{-1}{t_1\tan(\alpha)} & \dfrac{1}{t_1\sin(\alpha)\tan(\beta)} \end{bmatrix} \cdot
\tag{7}
$$

$$
\begin{bmatrix} r_{11} & r_{12} & 0 \\ r_{21} & r_{22} & t_2 \\ r_{31} & r_{32} & 0 \end{bmatrix}^{-1} = \begin{bmatrix} \dfrac{1}{\cos(\alpha)} & 0 & \dfrac{\tan(\alpha)}{\tan(\beta)} \\ 0 & 0 & \dfrac{1}{\sin(\beta)} \\ \dfrac{-\tan(\alpha)}{t_2} & \dfrac{1}{t_2} & \dfrac{-1}{t_2\cos(\alpha)\tan(\beta)} \end{bmatrix} \cdot
\tag{8}
$$

$$
\begin{bmatrix} r_{11} & r_{12} & 0 \\ r_{21} & r_{22} & 0 \\ r_{31} & r_{32} & t_3 \end{bmatrix}^{-1} = \begin{bmatrix} \cos(\alpha) & \sin(\alpha) & 0 \\ -\sin(\alpha) & \cos(\alpha) & 0 \\ \dfrac{\cos(\beta)}{\sin(\alpha)\tan(\beta)} & \dfrac{\cos(\beta)}{-\cos(\alpha)\tan(\beta)} & \dfrac{1}{t_3} \\ t_3 & t_3 & t_3 \end{bmatrix} \cdot
\tag{9}
$$

To understand the effect of (7)-(9), let's focus on 2-by-2 left upper members of each matrix. We can compare them to 2D image's affine transformation. For (7)-(8), they introduces unorganized output image when Roll (α) changes, as mentioned. For (9) they are similar to rotational plus shear and scaling, which is what we need to do warping, as expected. This is the reason why we need to do translation in row and column of each image separately, as shown in (10).

$$
\tilde{Q} = SH^{-1}q \; .
\tag{10}
$$

Where, $S = \begin{bmatrix} 1 & 0 & c_x \\ 0 & 1 & c_y \\ 0 & 0 & 1 \end{bmatrix}$ performs shifting as required, resulting in an appropriate top view image as will be shown in Fig. 3.

3.4   Calibration between Camera and Sensor

To compensate for imperfect alignment, from (1), rotation matrix (R) acquired from the sensor must be transferred to that of the camera using a correction matrix (R_{offset}). In our calibration, the world coordinate (Q) and the imager coordinate (q) are known. The intrinsic (M) and translation vector (T) are pre-defined. In (11), we need to find R_{offset} for correcting R_{sensor} to R_{camera}. Iterative Least Square (ILS) technique [8] is applied to find R_{offset} as follow.

$$R_{camera} = R_{offset}R_{sensor} \quad . \tag{11}$$

(11) can be represented as (12) which consists of 9 unknown parameters. We rearrange (12) as (13).

$$\begin{bmatrix} b_{11} & b_{12} & b_{13} \\ b_{21} & b_{22} & b_{23} \\ b_{31} & b_{32} & b_{33} \end{bmatrix} = \begin{bmatrix} r_{11} & r_{12} & r_{13} \\ r_{21} & r_{22} & r_{23} \\ r_{31} & r_{32} & r_{33} \end{bmatrix} \begin{bmatrix} a_{11} & a_{12} & a_{13} \\ a_{21} & a_{22} & a_{23} \\ a_{31} & a_{32} & a_{33} \end{bmatrix} \quad . \tag{12}$$

$$\begin{bmatrix} b_{11} \\ b_{12} \\ b_{13} \\ b_{21} \\ b_{22} \\ b_{23} \\ b_{31} \\ b_{32} \\ b_{33} \end{bmatrix} = \begin{bmatrix} a_{11} & a_{21} & a_{31} & 0 & 0 & 0 & 0 & 0 & 0 \\ a_{12} & a_{22} & a_{32} & 0 & 0 & 0 & 0 & 0 & 0 \\ a_{13} & a_{23} & a_{33} & 0 & 0 & 0 & 0 & 0 & 0 \\ 0 & 0 & 0 & a_{11} & a_{21} & a_{31} & 0 & 0 & 0 \\ 0 & 0 & 0 & a_{12} & a_{22} & a_{32} & 0 & 0 & 0 \\ 0 & 0 & 0 & a_{13} & a_{23} & a_{33} & 0 & 0 & 0 \\ 0 & 0 & 0 & 0 & 0 & 0 & a_{11} & a_{21} & a_{31} \\ 0 & 0 & 0 & 0 & 0 & 0 & a_{12} & a_{22} & a_{32} \\ 0 & 0 & 0 & 0 & 0 & 0 & a_{13} & a_{23} & a_{33} \end{bmatrix} \begin{bmatrix} r_{11} \\ r_{12} \\ r_{13} \\ r_{21} \\ r_{22} \\ r_{23} \\ r_{31} \\ r_{32} \\ r_{33} \end{bmatrix} \quad . \tag{13}$$

Alternatively (13) can be written as (14), where i is the ith sample in the data collection process.

$$[M_i]_{9 \times 1} = [N_i]_{9 \times 9}[O]_{9 \times 1} \quad . \tag{14}$$

To estimate 9 parameters in O, it can be determined in a least-squares sense.

$$[O]_{9 \times 1} = ([N_i^T]_{9 \times 9}[N_i]_{9 \times 9})^{-1}([N_i^T]_{9 \times 9}[M_i]_{9 \times 1}) \quad . \tag{15}$$

The large number of sample significantly increases the system accuracy. Thus, to update (15) after every control point is collected, Iterative Least Squares method [8] is applied as in (16)

$$[O]_{9 \times 1} = (\sum_i [N_i^T]_{9 \times 9}[N_i]_{9 \times 9})^{-1} \sum_i ([N_i^T]_{9 \times 9}[M_i]_{9 \times 1}) \quad . \tag{16}$$

After O is calculated, it means the imperfect alignment can be corrected by getting O rearranged in the form of R_{offset} before multiply R_{offset} back into (10). And then, apply it in homography matrix.

3.5   Area Mapping

Finally, the number of target pixels must be mapped to area size in real world unit by a pre-calibrated equation. Such equation is derived by (17). The calibration requires a known planar area (K) and its corresponding number of pixels (k). By rule of three, unknown planar area (A) can be estimated from its corresponding number of pixels (a).

$$\frac{A(cm^2)}{K(cm^2)} = \frac{a(pixel)}{k(pixel)} . \tag{17}$$

The number of pixels of the known area varies according to pitch angle (β). Hence (17) can be replaced by (18). Where, gradient (m) and intercept (c) of linear equation can be known from the pre-calibrated equation.

$$A(cm^2) = \frac{a(pixel) * K(cm^2)}{m\beta + c(pixel)} . \tag{18}$$

The next chapter explains such mapping in more detail based on an experimental result.

4   Experiment

In the experimental setup, the pitch angle was manually varied from 20 degree to 80 degree. In case of pitch angle are 0-20 and 80-90 degree, the top view cannot be generated by the orientation information effectively due to a limitation of sensor. The experiment parameters are stated in Table1.

Fig. 3 (a) and (b) shows the perspective view, top view warped image, and the number of red pixels at 20 and 70 degree pitch angle, respectively.

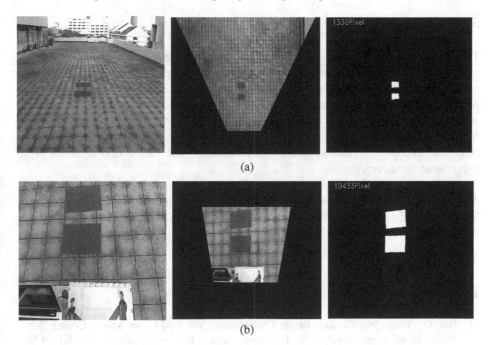

Fig. 3. Perspective view input, top view output, and the number of target pixels with (a) pitch angle of 20° and (b) pitch angle of 70°

After comparing the warped image with the ground truth, we could get the mapping factor from pixel to the real world unit. From many captured data, linear equation for area size approximation is illustrated in Fig. 4. We found that the size of the field linearly depends on the pitch angle. After sensor alignment compensation, the line fitting is more linear which R-square increases from 0.9885 to 0.9978. For accuracy, it is improved from 94.01% to 97.86% without and with sensor alignment compensation, respectively.

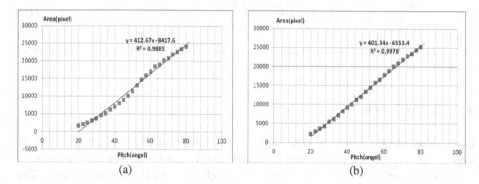

(a)   (b)

Fig. 4. Relation between pitch angle and pixel numbers of the same object, (a) without sensor alignment compensation and (b) with sensor alignment compensation

5   Conclusion

This paper addresses three issues of image transformation and warping and area calculation. First, warping an image to its top view can be made effectively by performing shifting separately from homography matrix. Second, to use a camera with an orientation sensor attached effectively, a method to calibrate orientation between them is proposed using Iterative Least Square. Finally, a closed-form formula to approximate an area size in real world from its number of pixels is proposed. The overall method of area transformation and calculation achieves high approximation accuracy.

Acknowledgments. This research is financially supported by Thailand Advanced Institute of Science and Technology (TAIST), National Science and Technology Development Agency (NSTDA), Tokyo Institute of Technology, and Kasetsart University (KU).

References

1. Dai, D., Yang, W.: Satellite Image Classification via Two-Layer Sparse Coding With Biased Image Representation. IEEE Geoscience and Remote Sensing Letters 8(1), 173–176 (2011)

2. Suxia, W.: A Statistic Method of Crop Acreage Based on Image Recognition. In: International Conference on Intelligent Systems Design and Applications, October 16-18, vol. 2, pp. 418–422 (2006)
3. Tian, Y., Wu, B., Xu, W., Huang, J., Xu, W.: An Effective Field Method of Crop Proportion Survey in China Based on GVG Integrated System. In: IEEE International Geoscience and Remote Sensing Symposium, September 20-24, vol. 6, pp. 4028–4030 (2004)
4. Luo, L.B., Koh, I.S., Park, S.Y., Ahn, R.S., Chong, J.W.: A Software-Hardware Cooperative Implementation of Bird's-Eye View System for Camera-on-Vehicle. In: IEEE International Conference on Network Infrastructure and Digital Content, November 6-8, pp. 963–967 (2009)
5. Wang, Y.M., Li, Y., Zheng, J.B.: A Camera Calibration Technique Based on OpenCV. In: International Conference on Information Sciences and Interaction Sciences, June 23-25, pp. 403–406 (2010)
6. Xin, Y., Ruishuang, Z., Li, S.: A Calibration Method Based on OpenCV. In: International Workshop on Intelligent Systems and Applications, May 28-29, pp. 1–4 (2011)
7. OpenCV 2.0 documentation, Machine Learning Library,
   http://opencv.willowgarage.com/documentation/
   camera_calibration_and_3d_reconstruction.html
8. Ziraknejad, N., Tafazoli, S., Lawrence, P.D.: Autonomous Stereo Camera Parameter Estimation for Outdoor Visual Servoing. In: IEEE Workshop on Machine Learning for Signal Processing, August 27-29, pp. 157–162 (2007)
9. Zhang, Z.: Flexible Camera Calibration by Viewing a Plane from Unknown Orientations. In: IEEE International Conference on Computer Vision, vol. 1, pp. 666–673 (1999)
10. Faugeras, O.: Three-Dimensional Computer Vision. A Geometric Viewpoint. The MIT Press (1993)
11. 9 Degrees of Freedom - Razor IMU - AHRS compatible,
    http://www.sparkfun.com/products/9623

Multi-modal People Tracking for an Awareness Behavior of an Interactive Tour-Guide Robot

Peter Poschmann*, Sven Hellbach, and Hans-Joachim Böhme

Artificial Intelligence Group, UAS Dresden, Germany
{poschmann,hellbach,boehme}@htw-dresden.de
http://www.htw-dresden.de/

Abstract. We propose a system for enhancing a human-robot interaction system. The goal is to embrace surrounding persons into a conversation with the robot by means of establishing or keeping eye contact. For this, a simple and hence computationally efficient people tracking algorithm has been developed, which in itself is an enhancement of existing approaches. As the foundation of our approach we use a vanilla Kalman filter that explicitly models the velocity in the state space, while the observations are transformed into a unified global coordinate system. We evaluate different integration strategies for multiple sensor cues. Furthermore, we extend an algorithm for group detection to be able to recognize individuals.

Keywords: people tracking, sensor fusion, Kalman filter, multi-modality, human-robot interaction.

1 Introduction

Our goal is to develop an interactive musem tour-guide robot. While interacting with the visitors, the robot should show an observable awareness behavior, like moving the head to its interaction partners. Coming from the fact that eyes play a central role in human-human communication, Ito et al. [8] and Yoshikawa et al. [18] investigated the influence of establishing eye-contact between robot and human user. They argue that eye-contact is not only simple "looking at each others eyes", but is itself a procedure to confirm the partner's intention. To do so, the robot first has to perceive the persons within its vicinity. Mostly, the robot is interacting with groups of persons. It is not necessary to sense all of them all of the time, because the robot can only look at one person at a time. Right now the verbal interaction is controlled by a human in a Wizard of Oz scenario, as we are still evaluating our dialog model. The head of the robot is not controlled by the human, so he can concentrate on the dialog. Therefore we need the people tracking and autonomous awareness behavior to give persons the impression that the robot is listening and encourage them to speak to it in a natural way.

---

* This work was supported in part by ESF grant number 100071902.

C.-Y. Su, S. Rakheja, H. Liu (Eds.): ICIRA 2012, Part II, LNAI 7507, pp. 666–675, 2012.

Our robot (figure 1) is a SCITOS G5 platform equipped with two laser range finders 40 cm above the ground, an omnidirectional camera above the head, a depth camera on top, a ring of sonar sensors and a head with two eyes that has no further sensor capabilities, but is used for interaction purposes. Except for the sonar, all of the mentioned sensors are used for detecting and tracking persons.

We need to be able to robustly track groups of persons in a cluttered environment and it has to be simple and computationally efficient, as other processes are running (localization, navigation, etc.). In the past decade, a variety of approaches have been proposed for the detection and tracking of people. The detection of persons in laser scans can be done via learned features [1], predefined patterns (e.g. spatially related local scan minima) [3] or clustering algorithms [14,10]. While feature based techniques (trained or predefined) show decreasing robustness in case of highly variable appearances of people due to occlusions, clothing, or scene content, clustering does not require special assumptions of people's appearance and is computationally efficient. Histograms of oriented gradients (HOG) [6] are very successful at detecting pedestrians in still images and extensions even make use of the data of depth cameras [12], but suffer from a high computational complexity. The Viola-Jones-Detector [11,9] is an efficient alternative for detecting persons within images.

Fig. 1. Our robot

For robust tracking in real-world environments, the fusion of multiple sensors in a probabilistic framework is often utilized to compensate for errors of single sensors [14,2]. In case of non-linear transition and measurement models, extended or unscented Kalman filters as well as particle filters can be used for probabilistic tracking. The vanilla Kalman filter could only be used if the models were linear. When new observations arrive, they have to be assigned to existing tracks. There are many probabilistic approaches to solve this data association problem, like multi-hypotheses tracking [15] and joint-probabilistic data association [7,16], but they are quite complex and computationally expensive. A very simple, yet sufficient, solution is the nearest neighbor technique with a one-to-one association [2].

This paper is structured as follows. Section 2 describes our approach, section 3 shows and discusses experimental results and section 4 concludes the paper.

2   Approach

In order to look at people, the robot has to know the position of the head of each person. The measurements of all sensors will be transformed into a global coordinate system. Laser and sonar sensors can only see the legs of the persons and have no possibility to sense the height of the head, while cameras can only give rough estimations of the distance to the detected head based on assumptions of the size of that head. Therefore the information of different sensor cues should be fused and uncertainties should be modeled to account for uncertain information (like the distance from the camera cues).

We use a tracking-by-detection approach, where a sensor cue detects persons at certain times and passes those detections to the tracker, which updates tracks to combine them with previous detections. In fact, each object is tracked independently of others using a Kalman filter. To keep the sensor cues consistent and make integration of new cues easy, their detections will be converted into normal distributions describing the estimated position of the detected person's head in three-dimensional Euclidean space before passing them to the tracker.

2.1   Detection

Laser Scan Clustering. To detect most of the persons even in cluttered scenes with many people partially occluding each other, we do not use features or patterns for detection inside the laser scans. Instead, our approach, that is inspired by [10], uses cluster algorithms to estimate the positions of the persons. The laser scan gets preprocessed to distinguish between static and dynamic objects. We use the estimated pose of the robot and an occupancy grid map of the environment that is dilated to compensate for uncertain localization. The endpoints of the laser measurements will be extracted and the points that end in an occupied cell will be removed. Hence, the only remaining observations are the ones that can not be explained by the environment model. To prevent outlier measurements, the points get clustered using single-linkage-clustering with a small distance (5 cm) and all clusters with less than three points will be removed.

Starting with each point being its own cluster, single-linkage-clustering will combine the two clusters closest to each other as long as their distance is below a threshold that defines the minimum distance between two clusters. With a distance bigger than a typical step width of a human (e.g. 50 cm) in the mounting height of the laser range finder, the points can be clustered into groups of persons. If there is enough space between them, each group will only contain one person, but if they are close to each other, there may be more than one per group.

Similar to [10] we estimate the legs of the persons, but unlike them, we use complete-linkage-clustering. Like single-linkage-clustering, it will start with each point being its own cluster, where two clusters will be combined to a bigger cluster, but it uses the maximum distance (between the farthest points) instead. A threshold of 25 cm should be more than the diameter of a single leg, but less than two legs, so in most cases there will be one cluster per leg. Wide skirts, coats or bags might lead to a slight over-estimation of the number of legs. Then, the legs will be assigned to each other in a pairwise manner using a nearest neighbor algorithm with a maximum distance between the centers of the legs of 60 cm. The average of the assigned legs (and single legs, if there are remaining ones) will be the centers of the persons.

The covariance matrix of the resulting observation will be chosen depending on the number of detected persons inside a group. If there are more than two legs inside a group, then legs of two different persons might be assigned incorrectly

Fig. 2. Clustering approach to people detection in laser range scans. Black dots indicate points that were removed because they represent the background or are outliers. *Left:* Outlier and background points are removed, the remaining laser points are clustered into separate groups of people. The colors represent different group clusters. *Center:* Each group is clustered to roughly identify legs of people. The colors represent different leg clusters. *Right:* The big circles correspond to persons that result from the pairwise assignments of the legs and the remaining ones.

and therefore the positions of the persons could be wrong. Because of that, the algorithm chooses a covariance matrix with higher uncertainty. If there are just two legs in a group (or only one), then the uncertainty will be lower, as there is only one possible assignment.

That clustering approach is simple and delivers reliable results on groups of people even with partial occlusions, where approaches using explicit detections might fail. The clusters and resulting person detections are shown in figure 2.

Face and Upper Body Detection. The images of the omnidirectional (color values) and depth camera (intensity values) are used to detect faces as well as upper bodies using OpenCV's Viola-Jones-Detector [11,9], which is known to be very efficient. Although they operate on the same sensor, the two detectors result in two different cues per camera.

To reduce processing time, the search windows for the omnidirectional camera will be limited to regions where tracks of persons already exist [5]. Therefore, only parts of the image have to be analyzed, but the detection is dependent on the observations of other sensor cues, which might lead to a delayed or prevented track initialization if other cues do not detect the person.

Using the known field of view of the camera, the resolution of the image, the width of the detection window and the estimated width of that window in real space, the distance to the detected face or upper body can be estimated. Because this estimation is pretty rough, the uncertainty in the camera's direction is chosen to be higher than the lateral uncertainty. For the depth images there is no need to estimate the distance based on that calculation, as the depth is given. It will be averaged using 25 measurements around the center of the head.

2.2 Tracking

Because sensor measurements are uncertain and prone to error, probabilistic approaches are most often used in mobile robotics for state estimation [17].

Instead of including the positions of all persons into one joint state space, we do track them independently of each other, so the state space has a low dimensionality and the problem remains computationally efficient. To be able to look at people, we have to know the position of the heads, so the important part of the state of a person is the three-dimensional position of the head in Euclidean space, represented in Cartesian coordinates. A constant velocity model will help predicting new positions and therefore make the assignment of observations to tracks less error-prone. But instead of modeling the velocity as a three-dimensional vector, we assume the velocity parallel to the z-axis to be zero [2], because persons rarely change their height (at least in our scenario). The length of the resulting two-dimensional velocity vector encodes the walking speed in meters per second. The state vector $x_t = (p_x, p_y, p_z, v_x, v_y)^T$ consists of position of the head p and the velocity v. We assume the state to be normally distributed, and make use of the Kalman filter for estimation. Unlike [2], our motion and measurement models are linear, and therefore we can use the vanilla Kalman filter instead of the extended or unscented one. Linearization, if necessary, lies within the responsibility of the sensor cues. The following noisy linear equations express the motion (eq. 1) and measurement model (eq. 2), where ε_t and δ_t are zero-mean Gaussian distributions.

$$x_t = A_t x_{t-1} + \varepsilon_t, \qquad A_t = \begin{pmatrix} 1 & 0 & 0 & \Delta t & 0 \\ 0 & 1 & 0 & 0 & \Delta t \\ 0 & 0 & 1 & 0 & 0 \\ 0 & 0 & 0 & 1 & 0 \\ 0 & 0 & 0 & 0 & 1 \end{pmatrix} \qquad (1)$$

$$z_t = C_t x_t + \delta_t, \qquad C_t = \begin{pmatrix} 1 & 0 & 0 & 0 & 0 \\ 0 & 1 & 0 & 0 & 0 \\ 0 & 0 & 1 & 0 & 0 \end{pmatrix} \qquad (2)$$

The time Δt since the last update will be used to predict the position using the velocity and the observation z_t will consist of the observed head position, which is equivalent to the first three dimensions of the state.

The assignments of new observations to the correct tracks was kept computationally efficient. A gating step removes assignments that are highly unlikely and a nearest neighbor approach assigns observations to tracks, so each track is updated by at most one observation and each observation will update at most one track. The gating and assignment is based on the Mahalanobis distance between the track and observation distributions. Measurements that are not associated with any track will be used to initialize new tracks.

Our approach benefits from the availability of different, at least partially complementary sensor cues. But in order to obtain a confident and robust tracking result, some specific aspects have to be considered. As there may be false detections, it is useful to assign to each track a likelihood for being a human at all [13,14]. An estimation in Bayesian manner is not possible, because there are only observations that state the presence of humans and the update rates of the sensors influence the resulting probability. Different to [13,14], we want that

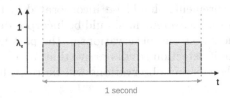

Fig. 3. Contribution to the likelihood of being a human of an example sensor cue. The contribution per update depends on the confidence value λ_c of the cue and the update rate of the sensor. The contributions of the last second of all cues will be summed up and capped at one, so the resulting value lies between zero and one.

likelihood to be stable if the person is constantly measured by one or more sensors. That way we avoid problems with the likelihood approaching zero even if the track is consistently confirmed. If the likelihood reaches zero, the track is deleted. We simply add a likelihood fraction of each sensor cue update within the last second and cap values above one. Figure 3 (left) shows the likelihood that is contributed by an example sensor cue. The amount per update depends on the chosen confidence value λ_c and the update rate of the sensor, the colored area represents the likelihood fraction. That area will be equal to the confidence value if the sensor cue does confirm the presence of a person with each update within the last second. To ensure that at least two sensor cues must confirm the presence of a person, the threshold for the likelihood for being a human must simply be higher than the confidence value of each cue. Equation 3 shows the computation of the likelihood l_h of a track for being a human. C is the set of sensor cues, U_c is the set of updates of sensor cue c of the last second, I_u equals one if the track was confirmed within that update and zero otherwise, f_c is the update rate of the sensor cue in seconds and λ_c is the confidence value of the cue.

$$l_h = \min(1, \sum_{c \in C} \sum_{u \in U_c} I_u f_c \lambda_c)) \qquad (3)$$

Because of missing detections and sensor data arriving asynchronously, the likelihood is not as stable as one would hope and it may drop below the threshold, even if the person is reasonably detectable. Therefore a second threshold is introduced that must be undercut by the likelihood for the person to not be regarded as a human anymore. This leads to a hysteresis behavior. To prevent non-human objects to be regarded as a person, the second threshold should be above the confidence of sensor cues that state the existence of some object, but not the kind of object, like the laser cue. At the same time, detection cues of camera images are not as likely to return detections of objects that are not recognizable as persons, so their confidence may be higher than the second threshold.

Because the detections inside the camera images take considerably longer than others (like detections in laser scans), the order the results arrive in might not be the order the sensor measurements were taken in. We want to ensure two things: The measurements should be incorporated in the right order and the latest arriving sensor measurement should be incorporated, no matter what. Therefore we save the states and observations of the past few seconds and roll back the current state if detection results arrive that are older than the current state. In this case, the existing observations will be re-evaluated based on the new past state.

2.3   Behavior

To give surrounding persons the impression that the robot is aware of them, it turns its head, so it appears as it would look at them. To give the people a stronger feeling of being looked at [18], the robot changes the person he looks at from time to time (every ten seconds if there are other persons). The choice of the person to look at is random, but not each person has the same probability of being chosen. The probability is computed from the distance to the robot, the necessary head movement and the time since the person was looked at before. Therefore, the robot prefers nearby persons, little head movement, and persons it has not looked at for a while or at all.

3   Results

For the evaluation of our people tracking approach, we used log data from our robot. The logs consist of sensor measurements and show some persons that stand close to the robot and look at it for most of the time. The location on the ground plane of each person was labeled manually for every five seconds, so an evaluation is possible for these times only. The height of a person was not included in the ground truth data, because the estimation based solely on the camera images would be quite uncertain.

The tracking was evaluated by simulating the robot using the sensor data of the log files and comparing the tracked persons to the labeled persons whenever this information is available (every five seconds). Persons whose distance to the robot was more than three meters were ignored because the robot was interacting with people right next to the robot and a robust tracking was not possible in that distance, because of the low camera resolution and laser range. We tried to stay close to the CLEAR MOT metrics [4] with the difference that we did not evaluate every frame and were not able to detect mismatches with our labeled data, as we did not add IDs to persons. CLEAR MOT measures the error in estimated position for matched tracks and persons (multiple object tracking precision MOTP) and the misses, false positives and mismatches compared to the overall number of objects (multiple object tracking accuracy MOTA).

The output of the people tracker was compared against the labeled ground truth data by assigning them to each other in a one-to-one manner based on the Euclidean distance using a global nearest neighbor algorithm with a correspondence threshold of 50 cm.

We recorded and labeled two different kinds of logs, one with persons only slightly moving (except for approaching and leaving the robot) and one with

Table 1. Results of the experiments. Test A was done using our approach, test B using the likelihood computation of [14], test C using leg patterns for laser based people detection [3] and D with using leg patterns with additional background subtraction.

Log	Test	Miss rate	False positive rate	MOTA	MOTP
	A	39.35 %	0 %	60.98 %	6.44 cm
first	B	47.1 %	0 %	52.9 %	5.48 cm
	C	43.23 %	6.45 %	50.32 %	6.27 cm
	D	49.03 %	0 %	50.91 %	5.73 cm
	A	46.64 %	0.45 %	52.91 %	9.06 cm
second	B	49.78 %	0 %	50.22 %	9.03 cm
	C	55.95 %	1.01 %	43.4 %	8.94 cm
	D	48.32 %	0.11 %	51.57 %	10.68 cm

more people, which were moving from time to time, even outside of the viewing area of the robot (far away or occluded). The logs together had a length of around ten minutes. Test A in table 1 shows the average results after repeating each experiment three times. The high amount of misses is explained by the necessity of detections within the camera images (as otherwise the likelihood for being human will drop below the threshold, when only the laser cue is confirming a track). Those detections are not available when persons are occluded within the images, do not look to the camera, are seen from the side or are moving fast (due to motion blur).

Because there were no bags, coats or skirts on any of the persons, there were hardly any false positive detections of the laser cues. Therefore the results might have been better if the confidence of that cue was chosen higher than the lower likelihood threshold. But just because the sensor logs are quite ideal in that regard, that does not mean that it is always like that and therefore we chose the parameters to cope with cases of false detections in the laser cues.

To evaluate our improvements, we compared them to other approaches. We begin with the computation of the likelihood for a track of being a human, where our computation differs from the one of [14]. The parameters were chosen to kind of copy the behavior of our system - in both cases it should need around one second for a track to become a confirmed person if it is detected by a laser and one camera detection cue and it should need the same time to become non-human when the camera detection stays away and only the laser cue confirms the track. We also included the second threshold, because otherwise our solution of the asynchronicity issue would interfere with the likelihood computation. Test B in table 1 shows the results. While the MOTA is worse than with our approach, the precision is higher. This can be explained by the fact that the persons, that count as misses in test B but were detected in test A, are not confirmed that much by different sensor cues (compared to the persons that were detected in both cases) and that the uncertainty of the position estimation was higher because of the lower number of observations.

With our computation, a steady detection will lead to an increasing likelihood until the maximum confidence of the sensor cue is reached, then it will stay at that value until the person is not detected anymore or other cues start to deliver detections. With the other computation method, the likelihood will increase or decrease most of the time and it will decrease whenever only a single cue confirms the track until the track disappears (likelihood reached zero) and in the next time frame the track re-appears because of the detection. This unstable behavior influences the results of the first sensor log more than of the second one.

We compared our clustering approach to people detection in laser scans to the leg patterns of [3], the results can be seen in table 1, test C. The Hokuyo laser range finder, that is mounted at the back of the robot, does not deliver smooth, consistent measurements, but misses some of them if they are few meters away or have a certain color and structure. Therefore in the first log the leg pattern approach spots patterns in the background, detects two persons where there is only one and misses one person completely, that is subsequently missed in the omni-image, because of the missing track and the restriction of the search window for detections. The cluttered environment of the second sensor log is especially bad for that approach, as there are many false positive detections that enlarge the search windows of the face and upper body detections and make those detections need more time. Additionally there are missed detections inside the laser scans, just like with the first log file.

To make the comparison with our approach more fair, we made a second try with background subtraction, see table 1, test D. The problems with false positives in the background are gone, but the others that arise from the unsteady measurements of the back laser range finder still remain, just like problems with persons occluding each other. Additionally there were some measurements of a person's leg in the first log that were removed, because the person stood near a table, and therefore the leg pattern was destroyed, leading to a higher miss rate.

Even though some of the results show a better MOTP than our approach, the difference is at most 1 cm, which is not that much. Furthermore, the MOTA is quite a bit worse in that cases, as both values depend on the chosen assignment threshold.

4   Conclusion

We have introduced a people tracking approach that enables our robot to look at people during an interaction situation. It can cope with groups of people in a cluttered environment and is computationally efficient.

Our approach for people detection within the laser scan detects persons even if they are occluded by others or have a high variety of appearances, though it assumes that most of the non-human objects were removed by the background subtraction. Problems may arise with persons wearing coats or bags, but that is quite uncommon in our scenario, as most of the visitors leave their wardrobes at the cloakroom. The introduced likelihood computation leads to stable likelihoods, is a filtering mechanism for false positives and a way to remove tracks that are not confirmed anymore. Our approach is simple and efficient, yet works very well.

References

1. Arras, K.O., Martínez Mozos, Ó., Burgard, W.: Using boosted features for the detection of people in 2d range data. In: Proc. of ICRA, pp. 3402–3407 (2007)
2. Bellotto, N., Hu, H.: Vision and laser data fusion for tracking people with a mobile robot. In: Proc. of ROBIO, Kunming, China, pp. 7–12 (December 2006)
3. Bellotto, N., Hu, H.: Multisensor-based human detection and tracking for mobile service robots. IEEE Trans. Syst., Man, Cybern. B 39(1), 167–181 (2009)
4. Bernardin, K., Stiefelhagen, R.: Evaluating multiple object tracking performance: the clear mot metrics. Journal on Image and Video Processing 2008, 1 (2008)
5. Blanco, J., Burgard, W., Sanz, R., Fernandez, J.: Fast face detection for mobile robots by integrating laser range data with vision. In: Proc. of ICAR (2003)
6. Dalal, N., Triggs, B.: Histograms of oriented gradients for human detection. In: Proc. of CVPR, vol. 1, pp. 886–893 (2005)
7. Fortmann, T.E., Bar-Shalom, Y., Scheffe, M.: Sonar tracking of multiple targets using joint probabilistic data association. IEEE J. Oceanic Eng. 8(3), 173–184 (1983)
8. Ito, A., Hayakawa, S., Terada, T.: Why robots need body for mind communication - an attempt of eye-contact between human and robot. In: Proc. of ROMAN Workshop, pp. 473–478 (2004)
9. Kruppa, H., Castrillón Santana, M., Schiele, B.: Fast and robust face finding via local context. In: Proc. of VS-PETS, pp. 157–164 (2003)
10. Lau, B., Arras, K.O., Burgard, W.: Multi-model hypothesis group tracking and group size estimation. International Journal of Social Robotics 2(1), 19–30 (2010)
11. Lienhart, R., Maydt, J.: An extended set of haar-like features for rapid object detection. In: Proc. of ICIP, vol. 1, pp. 900–903 (2002)
12. Luber, M., Spinello, L., Arras, K.O.: People tracking in rgb-d data with on-line boosted target models. In: Proc. of IROS (2011)
13. Martin, C., Schaffernicht, E., Scheidig, A., Groß, H.M.: Sensor fusion using a probabilistic aggregation scheme for people detection and tracking. In: Proc. of ECMR, pp. 176–181 (2005)
14. Müller, S., Schaffernicht, E., Scheidig, A., Böhme, H.J., Groß, H.M.: Are you still following me? In: Proc. of ECMR, pp. 211–216 (2007)
15. Reid, D.B.: An algorithm for tracking multiple targets. IEEE Trans. Automat. Contr. 24(6), 843–854 (1979)
16. Schulz, D., Burgard, W., Fox, D., Cremers, A.B.: People tracking with a mobile robot using sample-based joint probabilistic data association filters. Int. J. Robot. Res. 22(2), 99–116 (2003)
17. Thrun, S., Burgard, W., Fox, D.: Probabilistic Robotics. The MIT Press (2005)
18. Yoshikawa, Y., Shinozawa, K., Ishiguro, H., Hagita, N., Miyamoto, T.: Responsive robot gaze to interaction partner. In: Proc. of RSS (2006)

A Robotic Pan and Tilt 3-D Target Tracking System by Data Fusion of Vision, Encoder, Accelerometer, and Gyroscope Measurements

Tae-Il Kim[1], Wook Bahn[1], Chang-Hun Lee[1], Tae-Jae Lee[1], Byung-Moon Jang[1],
Sang-Hoon Lee[2], Min-Wug Moon[2], and Dong-Il "Dan" Cho[1,*]

[1] Department of Electrical Engineering and Computer Science/ASRI/ISRC,
Seoul National University, Seoul, Korea
{ehoiz,wook03,chlee84,ltj88,jbm4693,dicho}@snu.ac.kr
[2] RS Automation, Gyeonggi-do, Korea
{shlee,mwmoon}@rsautomation.co.kr

Abstract. This paper presents a vision-tracking system for mobile robots, which travel in a 3-dimentional environment. The developed system controls pan and tilt actuators attached to a camera so that a target is always directly in the line of sight of the camera. This is achieved by using data from robot wheel encoders, a 3-axis accelerometer, a 3-axis gyroscope, pan and tilt motor encoders, and camera. The developed system is a multi-rate sampled data system, where the sampling rate of the camera is different with that of the other sensors. For the accurate estimation of the robot velocity, the developed system detects the slip of robot wheels, by comparing the data from the encoders and the accelerometer. The developed system estimates the target position by using an extended Kalman filter. The experiments are performed to show the tracking performance of the developed system in several motion scenarios, including climbing slopes and slip cases.

Keywords: Vision tracking system, Sensor data fusion, Kalman filter, Slip detection.

1 Introduction

Continuous monitoring of a target is one of the most important issues in the human robot interaction (HRI) research area. Several studies in the visual servoing area have proposed methods to control the motion of a camera which senses the object of interest [1-5]. The feedback information for the camera-motion-control is extracted from the data of the camera, by using the computer vision processes. However, the vision data have some weaknesses, such as the time delay of the data due to the relatively heavy computational load of the computer vision processing and the noise of the data due to the motion of the camera. To overcome these problems of the vision data, several approaches are proposed, which integrate the vision data and the robot motion data [6-13]. The robot motion data are measured by the physical sensors such

---

* Corresponding author.

C.-Y. Su, S. Rakheja, H. Liu (Eds.): ICIRA 2012, Part II, LNAI 7507, pp. 676–685, 2012.
© Springer-Verlag Berlin Heidelberg 2012

as inertial sensors. Recently, some studies present effective data fusion methods for the control of camera motion, which improve vision-tracking performance while a robot moves around [11-13]. The systems presented by Hwang et al. [11], Park et al. [12], and Kim et al. [13] use the data from a camera, inertial sensors and encoders to control the motion of camera. Hwang et al. [11] and Park et al. [12] proposed vision-tracking systems for mobile robots using two Kalman filters and a slip detector. These systems show high tracking performance even when the robot wheels slip. Since these systems are designed for use in flat surfaces, the systems may not provide satisfactory performances when the robots climb slopes. Kim et al. [13] proposed a vision system for mobile robots for tracking moving targets using stereo vision and motion information. This system is designed for use in a 3-dimentional environment, and estimates the target position with respect to the robot. However, this system requires a relatively high computational load in stereo vision processing.

This paper presents a vision-tracking system for mobile robots, which travel in a 3-dimensional environment. The developed system controls pan and tilt motors attached to a camera so that a target is in the line of sight of the camera. The developed system calculates the actuation angles of the pan and tilt motors, by estimating the 3-dimensional coordinates of the target with respect to the robot. In the estimation process, the developed system uses the data from robot wheel encoders, a 3-axis accelerometer, a 3-axis gyroscope, pan and tilt motor encoders, and camera. The developed system is a multi-rate sampled data system that the sampling rate of the camera is different with that of the other sensors of the developed system. For the effective estimation, Kalman filters are applied to the developed system. The developed system detects the situation that robot wheels slip, and changes the measurement model of robot velocity estimator. As a result, the developed system can continue the vision-tracking while intermittent slip occurs.

2   System Configuration

The purpose of the presented system is the vision-tracking of a target while the mobile robot, on which the developed system is installed, moves on a 3-dimentional terrain. The developed system actuates pan and tilt motors attached to a camera so that a target is in the line of sight of the camera. The main structure of the developed system is shown in Fig. 1.

The image processor uses the face detection algorithm, developed by Postech and Electronics and Telecommunication Research Institute (ETRI), to extract the position and the size information of the target [14]. The developed system calculates the position of center point of the detected target, to compute the error to the set point (0, 0). The frame transformation calculator generates the vision data, by combining the output data of the image processor and the pan and tilt angle data. The controller receives the vision data and the robot motion data, to estimate the position of target. The structure of the controller is explained in detail in Section 3.

The kinematic modeling of the developed system is shown in Fig. 2. The designed model is similar with the model presented by Kim et al. [13]. The motion of the robot is represented as the change in the target position vector with respect to the robot frame. The hardware of the developed system is shown in Fig. 3.

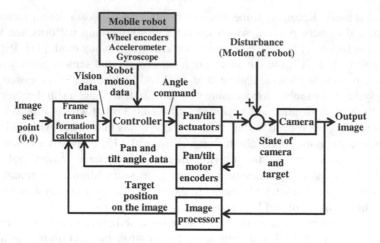

Fig. 1. The structure of the developed vision-tracking system

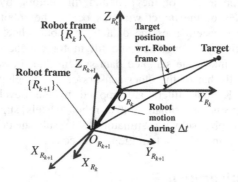

Fig. 2. The kinematic modeling of the developed system

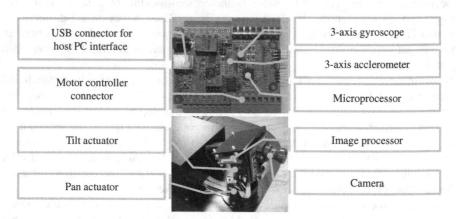

Fig. 3. The hardware of the developed system

3   Sensor Data Fusion Method

The detailed structure of the controller is shown in Fig. 4. The designed controller includes the robot velocity estimator, the target position estimator and the actuation angle calculator. The controller receives the robot wheel encoder data, the accelerometer data, the gyroscope data, and the vision data as input. The controller outputs the angle command for the pan and tilt actuators.

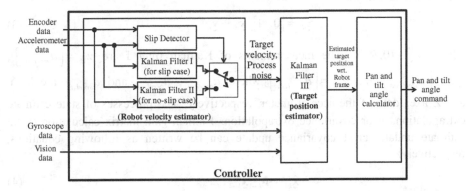

Fig. 4. The structure of the controller

3.1   Robot Velocity Estimation

The robot velocity estimator is composed of a slip detector and two Kalman filters. The Kalman filter I and the Kalman filter II are designed for slip case and no-slip case, respectively. The robot wheel encoder data and the accelerometer data are the input of the robot velocity estimator. The robot velocity data and the process noise data for Kalman filter III are the output of the robot velocity estimator.

The wheel encoders provide fairly accurate displacement data when the robot wheels do not slip. However, the encoder data are not reliable, when the wheels slip, or when the robot is kidnapped. The slip detector finds out the slip case, by comparing the data from the encoders and the accelerometer. The following statement shows the condition of the slip cases.

$$\sum_{i=k-l+1}^{k} \left(\left| v_{enc,k} - v_{accel,xk} \right| + \left| v_{accel,yk} \right| + \left| v_{accel,zk} \right| \right) > threshold \qquad (1)$$

where $v_{enc,k}$ is the X-axis velocity of the target, which is calculated by using encoder data, and $v_{accel,xk}$, $v_{accel,yk}$ and $v_{accel,zk}$ are the X-axis, Y-axis and Z-axis velocities of the target, respectively, which are calculated by using accelerometer data. When the slip case is detected, the proposed system does not use encoder data in the estimation of the robot velocity by selecting Kalman filter I as the velocity estimator. It is supposed that the state of each axis is uncorrelated. The states of Kalman filter I are

$\underset{\sim}{x}_{1k} = \begin{bmatrix} v_{xk} & a_{xk} \end{bmatrix}^T$, $\underset{\sim}{x}_{2k} = \begin{bmatrix} v_{yk} & a_{yk} \end{bmatrix}^T$ and $\underset{\sim}{x}_{3k} = \begin{bmatrix} v_{zk} & a_{zk} \end{bmatrix}^T$. The system model of Kalman filter I can be written as follows:

$$\underset{\sim}{x}_{ik} = \begin{bmatrix} 1 & \Delta t \\ 0 & 1 \end{bmatrix} \underset{\sim}{x}_{i(k-1)} + \underset{\sim}{w}_{i(k-1)} . \tag{2}$$

where $i = 1, 2, 3$ and $\underset{\sim}{w}_{ik} \sim (0, Q_{ik})$. The measurement model of Kalman filter I is represented as follows:

$$\underset{\sim}{z}_{ik} = \begin{bmatrix} 0 & 1 \end{bmatrix} \cdot \underset{\sim}{x}_{ik} + \underset{\sim}{v}_{ik} \tag{3}$$

where $\underset{\sim}{v}_{ik} \sim (0, R_{ik})$. The measurements of Kalman filter I are $\underset{\sim}{z}_{1k} = \begin{bmatrix} a_{accel,xk} \end{bmatrix}$, $\underset{\sim}{z}_{2k} = \begin{bmatrix} a_{accel,yk} \end{bmatrix}$ and $\underset{\sim}{z}_{3k} = \begin{bmatrix} a_{accel,zk} \end{bmatrix}$ where $a_{accel,xk}$, $a_{accel,yk}$ and $a_{accel,zk}$ are X, Y and Z axes data of the accelerometer, respectively. The processes of state estimate extrapolation, error covariance extrapolation, Kalman gain matrix calculation, state estimate update, error covariance update can be written as following equations, respectively:

$$\hat{\underset{\sim}{x}}_k^- = \Phi_{k-1} \hat{\underset{\sim}{x}}_{k-1}^+ , \tag{4}$$

$$P_k^- = \Phi_{k-1} P_{k-1}^+ \Phi_{k-1}^T + Q_{k-1} , \tag{5}$$

$$K_{ik} = P_{ik}^- H_{ik}^T (H_{ik} P_{ik}^- H_k^T + R_{ik})^{-1} , \tag{6}$$

$$\hat{\underset{\sim}{x}}_k^+ = \hat{\underset{\sim}{x}}_k^- + K_k (\underset{\sim}{z}_k - H_k \hat{\underset{\sim}{x}}_k^-) , \tag{7}$$

and

$$P_k^+ = (I - K_k H_k) P_k^- . \tag{8}$$

For the no-slip case, it is supposed that the translational motion of the robot can be expressed by using only X-axis data with respect to the robot frame, i.e. v_{yk}, v_{zk}, a_{yk}, and a_{zk} are zero. The states of Kalman filter II is $\underset{\sim}{x}_{1k} = \begin{bmatrix} v_{xk} & a_{xk} \end{bmatrix}^T$ The system model of Kalman filter II is same with that of Kalman filter I, except the process noise $\underset{\sim}{w}_{1k} \sim (0, Q'_{1k})$. The measurement model of Kalman filter II is represented as follows:

$$\underset{\sim}{z}_{1k} = \begin{bmatrix} 1 & 0 \\ 0 & 1 \end{bmatrix} \cdot \underset{\sim}{x}_{1k} + \underset{\sim}{v}_{1k} . \tag{9}$$

where $\underset{\sim}{v}_{1k} \sim (0, R'_{1k})$. The measurements of Kalman filter II is

$$\underset{\sim}{z}_{1k} = \begin{bmatrix} v_{enc,k} & a_{accel,xk} \end{bmatrix}^T . \tag{10}$$

where $v_{enc,xk}$ is the velocity of robot measured by the encoders. The other processes of Kalman filter II are same with that of Kalman filter I.

3.2   Target Position Estimation

The target position estimator is composed of a Kalman filter III, which is an extended Kalman filter. The states of Kalman filter III is $\underset{\sim}{\mathbf{x}}_k = \begin{bmatrix} x_k & y_k & z_k \end{bmatrix}^T$, where x_k, y_k and z_k are X, Y and Z axis coordinates of the target position, respectively, with respect to the robot frame. The input of Kalman filter III is $\underset{\sim}{\mathbf{u}}_k = \begin{bmatrix} v_{xk} & v_{yk} & v_{zk} \end{bmatrix}^T$. The state transition model of Kalman filter III is incremental ZXY Euler angle rotation matrix using gyroscope data $[\omega_{xk} \quad \omega_{yk} \quad \omega_{zk}]^T$ and sampling time Δt. The system model of Kalman filter III can be written as follows:

$$\underset{\sim}{\mathbf{x}}_k = f_{k-1}(\underset{\sim}{\mathbf{x}}_{k-1}, \underset{\sim}{\mathbf{u}}_{k-1}, \underset{\sim}{\mathbf{w}}_{k-1}) = F_{k-1} \cdot \underset{\sim}{\mathbf{x}}_{k-1} - \Delta t \cdot \underset{\sim}{\mathbf{u}}_{k-1} + \underset{\sim}{\mathbf{w}}_{k-1} \tag{11}$$

where

$$[\Delta\theta_{1k} \quad \Delta\theta_{2k} \quad \Delta\theta_{3k}]^T = [\omega_{zk} \cdot \Delta t \quad \omega_{xk} \cdot \Delta t \quad \omega_{yk} \cdot \Delta t]^T , \tag{12}$$

$$c_{ik} = \cos \Delta\theta_{ik} , \tag{13}$$

$$s_{ik} = \sin \Delta\theta_{ik} , \tag{14}$$

$$F_k = \begin{bmatrix} c_{1k}c_{3k} - s_{1k}s_{2k}s_{3k} & -s_{1k}c_{2k} & c_{1k}s_{3k} + s_{1k}s_{2k}c_{3k} \\ c_{1k}s_{3k} + s_{1k}s_{2k}c_{3k} & c_{1k}c_{2k} & s_{1k}s_{3k} - c_{1k}s_{2k}c_{3k} \\ -c_{2k}s_{3k} & s_{2k} & c_{2k}c_{3k} \end{bmatrix} , \tag{15}$$

and $\underset{\sim}{\mathbf{w}}_k \sim (0, Q_k)$. The measurement model of Kalman filter III is

$$\underset{\sim}{\mathbf{z}}_k = h_k(\underset{\sim}{\mathbf{x}}_k, \underset{\sim}{\mathbf{v}}_k) = H \cdot \begin{bmatrix} x_k & y_k & z_k \end{bmatrix}^T + \underset{\sim}{\mathbf{v}}_k , \tag{16}$$

where

$$H_k = \begin{bmatrix} 1 & 0 & 0 \\ 0 & 1 & 0 \\ 0 & 0 & 1 \end{bmatrix}. \tag{17}$$

and $\underset{\sim}{\mathbf{v}}_k \sim (0, R_k)$. The measurement of Kalman filter III is the vision data, which are the coordinate of the target with regard to the robot frame. The processes of state estimate extrapolation, error covariance extrapolation, Kalman gain matrix calculation, state estimate update, error covariance update can be written as following equations, respectively:

$$\hat{\mathbf{x}}_k^- = f_{k-1}(\hat{\mathbf{x}}_{k-1}^+, \mathbf{u}_{k-1}, 0) \ , \tag{18}$$

$$P_k^- = F_{k-1} P_{k-1}^+ F_{k-1}^T + Q_{k-1} \ , \tag{19}$$

$$K_{ik} = P_{ik}^- H_{ik}^T (H_{ik} P_{ik}^- H_k^T + R_{ik})^{-1} \ , \tag{20}$$

$$\hat{\mathbf{x}}_k^+ = \hat{\mathbf{x}}_k^- + K_k(\mathbf{z}_k - h_k(\hat{\mathbf{x}}_k^-, 0)) \ , \tag{21}$$

and

$$P_k^+ = (I - K_k H_k) P_k^- \ , \tag{22}$$

where

$$\hat{\mathbf{x}}_k^- = \begin{bmatrix} \hat{x}_k^- & \hat{y}_k^- & \hat{z}_k^- \end{bmatrix}^T \ . \tag{23}$$

The sampling rate of the vision data is 27 Hz, and therefore, the sampling rate of the other sensors are synchronized at 108 Hz, which is an integer multiple of the vision rate. If the vision data are not ready after the Kalman gain matrix calculation, the developed system repeats the state estimate extrapolation with the updated data from the gyroscope and the velocity estimator. When the vision data are not ready, the following are used:

$$\hat{\mathbf{x}}_{k-1}^+ = \hat{\mathbf{x}}_{k-1}^- \tag{24}$$

and

$$P_{k-1}^+ = P_{k-1}^- \ . \tag{25}$$

3.3   Actuation Angle Calculation

The actuation angle calculator transforms the target position vector with respect to the robot frame to the position vector with respect to the actuator frame, of which the camera is located on the origin. The pan angle α and the tilt angle β are calculated as follows:

$$\alpha = \tan^{-1}\left(\frac{^A y_T}{^A x_T}\right) \ , \tag{26}$$

and

$$\beta = -\tan^{-1}\left(\frac{^A z_T}{\sqrt{\left(^A x_T\right)^2 + \left(^A y_T\right)^2}}\right) \tag{27}$$

where $^A P_T = \begin{bmatrix} ^A x_T & ^A y_T & ^A z_T \end{bmatrix}^T$ is the target position with respect to the actuator frame.

4 Experimental Results

To show the performance of the developed system, two kinds of experiments are performed. In the experiment 1, the robot moves on the trajectory, which includes 10 ° slopes. The trajectory of the robot in experiment 1 is shown in Fig. 3. In translation sections, the motion commands are given to the robot to move forward at 0.5 m/sec. In rotation sections, the motion commands are given to the robot to rotate at 50 °/sec. In the experiment 2, the motion command is given to the robot to move forward for 1 m. The robot is forced to stay at the initial position while the wheels slip. When the robot wheels stop, the robot is released, and the motion command is given to the robot to move forward for 1.5 m. The trajectory of the robot in experiment 2 is shown in Fig. 4. The vision error and its root mean square (RMS) are measured in each experiment with following equations:

$$(\text{Vision error})=\sqrt{\varepsilon_{i,x}^{2}+\varepsilon_{i,y}^{2}} \tag{28}$$

and

$$(\text{RMS of vision error})=\sqrt{\sum_{i=1}^{N}\frac{(\varepsilon_{i,x}^{2}+\varepsilon_{i,y}^{2})}{N}} \tag{29}$$

where $\varepsilon_{i,x}$ and $\varepsilon_{i,y}$ are vision errors of X and Y axes in i-th image, respectively. The size of the images is VGA (640 by 480 pixels).

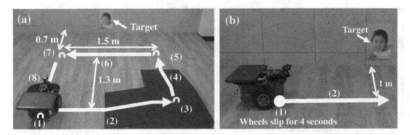

Fig. 5. The trajectory of the robot in the experiments. (a) Experiment 1. (b) Experiment 2.

Experiment 1 is performed with two systems, the developed system and the vision-tracking system which has the 2-dimentional model. The RMS vision error of the former is 8.92 pixels, and that of the latter is 27.50 pixels. The vision errors of the systems in experiment 2 are shown in Fig. 5. It is shown that the developed system has improved performance in section (2) ~ (4), especially, in Fig. 7-(a), compared with Fig. 7-(b). In section (2) ~ (4), the robot has pitch motions and displacement in Z-axis, which the 2-dimentional model cannot cover. However, the developed system compensates for the disturbances made by the slopes, to perform vision-tracking successfully.

Experiment 2 is performed with two systems, the developed system and the vision-tracking system which does not have slip detection function. The RMS vision error of the former is 8.48 pixels, and that of the latter is 96.26 pixels. The vision errors of the systems in experiment 2 are shown in Fig. 8. It is shown that the developed system has improved performance in section (2), especially, in Fig. 8-(a), compared with Fig. 8-(b). Since the robot stays at one place in section (1), the measurement update of the position estimator enables the system to find the direction of the target, even if the system cannot detect the slip case. However, the error of estimated target position increases rapidly in the system without slip detector. In section (2), since the robot has motion, the error of estimated target position in the system without slip detector diminishes the performance of the system. On the other hand, the developed system can perform successful vision-tracking, even if the slip case occurs, since the accumulated error does not increase fast in the developed system.

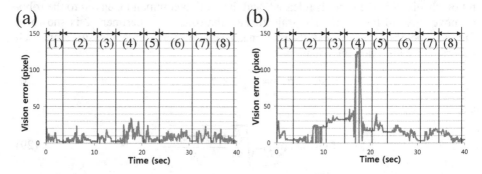

Fig. 6. Results of the experiment 1. (a) The developed system. (b) The vision-tracking system which has the 2-dimentional model

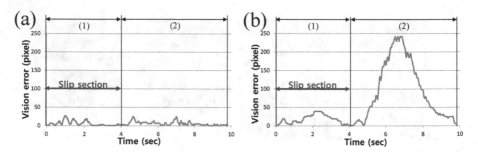

Fig. 7. Results of the experiment 2. (a) The developed system. (b) The vision-tracking system which does not have slip detection function.

5   Conclusion

In this paper, the vision-tracking system for mobile robots which travel in a 3-dimentional environment is presented. The developed system controls pan and tilt motors attached to a camera so that a target is in sight of the camera. The developed system calculates the actuation angles of the pan and tilt motors by estimating the 3-dimentional coordinates of the target with respect to the robot. For the effective estimation, Kalman filters are applied to the developed system. In the estimation process, the developed system uses the data from robot wheel encoders, a 3-axis accelerometer, a 3-axis gyroscope, pan and tilt motor encoders, and camera. The developed system is a multi-rate sampled data system that the sampling rate of the camera is different with that of the other sensors of the developed system. Since the sampling rate of camera is relatively low, the developed system uses the data from the other sensors between the samples of the camera, to estimate the target position with respect to the robot. The developed system detects the situation that robot wheels slip, and changes the measurement model of robot velocity estimator. As a result, the developed system can continue the vision-tracking while the slip cases occur temporarily. The experimental results show that the developed system achieves improved tracking performance in the various scenarios.

Acknowledgment. This work was supported by the R&D program of MKE (10040157, Development of Rotational Transducer SoC and Module with 21bit Resolution for Robot Actuators) and the R&D program of SBMA (S2043246, Development of SLAM Module, using Vision and Motion Information).

References

1. Espiau, B., Chaumette, F., Rives, P.: A New Approach to Visual Servoing in Robotics. IEEE Transactions on Robotics and Automation 8(3), 313–326 (1992)
2. Hutchinson, S., Hager, G.D., Corke, P.I.: A tutorial on visual servo control. IEEE Transactions on Robotics and Automation 12(5), 615–670 (1996)
3. Corke, P.I., Hutchinson, S.: A New Partitioned Approach to Image Based Visual Servo Control. IEEE Transactions on Robotics and Automation 17(4), 507–515 (2001)
4. Hamel, T., Mahony, R.: Visual Servoing of an Under-Actuated Dynamic Rigid-Body System: An Image-Based Approach. IEEE Transactions on Robotics and Automation 18(2), 507–515 (2002)
5. Chena, J., Dawsonb, D.M., Dixonc, W.E., Chitrakaran, V.K.: Navigation Function-Based Visual Servo Control. Automatica 43(7), 1165–1177 (2007)
6. Algrain, M.C., Quinn, J.: Accelerometer Based Line-of-Sight Stabilization Approach for Pointing and Tracking Systems. In: Second IEEE Conference on Control Applications, vol. 1, pp. 159–163 (1993)
7. Panerai, F., Metta, G., Sandini, G.: Visuo-Inertial Stabilization in Space-Variant Binocular Systems. Robotics and Autonomous Systems 30(1-2), 195–214 (2000)
8. Xie, S., Luo, J., Gong, Z., Ding, W., Zou, H., Fu, X.: Biomimetic Control of Pan-Tilt-Zoom Camera for Visual Tracking Based-on an Autonomous Helicopter. In: IEEE/RSJ International Conference on Intelligent Robots and Systems, pp. 2138–2143 (2007)
9. Lenz, A., Balakrishnan, T., Pipe, A.G., Melhuish, C.: An Adaptive Gaze Stabilization Controller Inspired by the Vestibulo-Ocular Reflex. Bioinspiration & Biomimetics 3, 1–11 (2008)
10. Hwangbo, M., Kim, J., Kanade, T.: Inertial-Aided KLT Feature Tracking for a Moving Camera. In: Intelligent Robots and Systems, pp. 1909–1916 (2009)
11. Hwang, W., Park, J., Kwon, H., Anjum, M., Kim, J., Lee, C., Kim, K., Cho, D.D.: Vision Tracking System for Mobile Robots Using Two Kalman Filters and a Slip Detector. In: International Conference on Control, Automation and Systems, pp. 2041–2046 (2010)
12. Park, J., Hwang, W., Kwon, H., Kim, K., Cho, D.D.: A Novel Line of Sight Control System for a Robot Vision Tracking System, Using Vision Feedback and Motion-Disturbance Feedforward Compensation. Robotica (accepted)
13. Kim, T., Bahn, W., Lee, C., Lee, T., Shaikh, M.M., Kim, K.: Vision System for Mobile Robots for Tracking Moving Targets, Based on Robot Motion and Stereo Vision Information. In: 2011 IEEE/SICE International Symposium on System Integration, pp. 634–639 (2011)
14. Jun, B., Kim, D.: Robust Real-Time Face Detection Using Face Certainty Map. In: Lee, S.-W., Li, S.Z. (eds.) ICB 2007. LNCS, vol. 4642, pp. 29–38. Springer, Heidelberg (2007)

A DSmT-Based Approach for Data Association in the Context of Multiple Target Tracking

Mohamed Airouche[1, 2], Layachi Bentabet[2], and Mimoun Zelmat[1]

[1] Applied Automation Laboratory, FHC, Boumerdes University, Boumerdes, Algeria
[2] Computer Sciences Department, Bishop's University, Sherbrooke, Canada
airouche_m@umbb.dz, lbentabe@ubishops.ca,
zelmat_mimoun@yahoo.com

Abstract. This paper presents a multiple target tracking method that uses the Dezert-Smarandache Theory (DSmT) for data association. A detailed framework is developed to show how the DSmT can be used to associate measurements with the corresponding correct targets. We will discuss the choices of the tracking hypotheses in the DSmT and we will demonstrate the effectiveness of the developed approach on simulated and real tracking scenarios that uses color and infrared cues.

Keywords: DSmT, Multiple Target Tracking, Data association.

1 Introduction

The purpose of Multi-target tracking (MTT) systems is to provide a unified and comprehensive picture of the environment using data reported by one or more sensors. The goal of an MTT system is to form and maintain tracks on targets of interest from scans of measurement provided by the sensors. The MTT problem is made more difficult by manoeuvring targets and by the presence of clutter [1]. The detection and tracking of multiple targets is a problem that arises in a wide variety of context. Examples include radar based tracking of aircraft, video-based tracking of people for surveillance or security purposes, mobile robotics, and many more.

Data association is of crucial importance for multiple target because of the necessity to relate each measurement to correct object [1,2]. Simpler techniques such as Nearest-Neighbour approaches are commonly used in MTT systems, but their performance degrades in clutter. The more complex Multiple Hypotheses Tracker (MHT) [3] provides improved performance, but it's difficult to implement and in clutter environments a large number of hypotheses may have to be maintained, which require extensive computational resource. The Joint Probabilistic Data Association (JPDA) approach, which is an extension of the Probabilistic Data Association (PDA) algorithm, has been widely applied to perform data association in MTT systems. The JPDA can be implemented successfully even in the presence of heavy clutter [4][5].

Evidential data fusion processes such as Dempster-Shafer Theory (DST) [6] and the recent Dezert-Smarandache Theory (DSmT) [7] have also been applied to achieve multiple target tracking. The classical Dempster-Shafer Theory (DST) represents the uncertainty and imprecision in the measurements via confidence values that are

C.-Y. Su, S. Rakheja, H. Liu (Eds.): ICIRA 2012, Part II, LNAI 7507, pp. 686–695, 2012.

committed to single or a union hypotheses. DST does not require the knowledge of prior probabilities. Dempster's rule combines the issued measurements and provides a reliable assessment of the uncertainty, especially in case of low conflicts between the measurements. When the conflict increases the Dempster's rule of combination leads to false conclusions or cannot provide a reliable result at all. While DST considers the tracking hypotheses as a set of exclusive elements, DSmT relaxes this condition and allows for overlapping and intersecting hypotheses. This allows for quantifying the conflict that might arise between the different sources throughout the assignment of non-null confidence values to the intersection of distinct hypotheses. Recently, many DSmT−based approaches for multiple target tracking were proposed in the literature. In [8], a particle filter using a DSmT step is proposed to achieve multiple targets tracking in cluttered scenes with location and colour cues. In [9], the DSmT is used to track pedestrians using a combination of infrared, color and location cues. In [8] and [9], the notion of plausibility was used to calculate and update the particle weights. In [10], fuzzy memberships are used to generate DSmT's mass functions and produce a Belief matrix, which in turn is used to undergo on-road vehicle tracking. The authors presented a comparison of their experimental results with those obtained using the JPDA. In [11], the concept of generalized data (kinematics and attribute) association is used to improve track maintenance performance in complicated situations (closely spaced targets). A combination of the Global Nearest Neighbour-like approach and the Munkres algorithm is proposed to resolve the generalized association matrix. The DSm hybrid rule of combination is used to deal with particular integrity constraints associated with some elements of the free Dedekind's distributive lattice.

In the DSmT based tracking techniques proposed in the literature, the DSmT framework was used to achieve data fusion between multiple measurements associated with the same individual target. In this paper, we assume that the measurement-target association is unknown, and we apply the DSmT to estimate the best association scheme. We will focus on the calculation steps of the association probabilities using the DSmT. The paper is organized as follows: Section 2 presents the tracking model. The principles of data association using DSmT is presented in section 3. The experimental results are given in section 4.

2   Background

In the following, let's assume that the number of targets, τ, and the number of measurements, d, are known up to time $t - 1$. Each target is associated with a track $\{\theta_j\}_{j=1}^{\tau}$. The objective is to combine the d measurements to determine the best track for each candidate at time t. The measurements are considered to originate from targets, if detected, or from clutter. The clutter is a special model for so-called false alarms, whose statistical proprieties are different from the targets. We describe the motion of the jth target by the following nonlinear discrete time equation:

$$x_{t,j} = f_t(x_{t-1,j}) + w_{t,j}, \tag{1}$$

Where $X_{t,j} = (x_{1,j}, x_{2,j}, \cdots, x_{t,j})$ is a first order Markov process that describes the state vector of the jth target. At time t, the received measurements are given by

$z_t = \{z_l\}_{l=1}^d$. The measurement vector up to time t is given by $Z_t = (z_1, z_2, \cdots, z_t)$. In (1), f_t is a transition function of states and w_t is a random vector describing noise and uncertainties in the state transition model.

3   Dezert-Smarandache Theory (DSmT) and Data Association

3.1   Basics of DSmT

DSm Theory of plausible and paradoxical reasoning is a generalization of the classical DST [7], which allows formal combining of rational, uncertain and paradoxical sources. In DST [6], there is a fixed set of mutually exclusive and exhaustive elements, called the frame of discernment, which is symbolized by $\Theta = \{\theta_1, \theta_2, \cdots, \theta_N\}$. The frame of discernment Θ defines the hypotheses for which the information sources can provide confidence. While DST considers Θ as a set of exclusive elements, DSmT relaxes this condition and allows for overlapping and intersecting hypotheses. This allows for quantifying the conflict that might arise between the different sources due to occlusion and clutter. This is done throughout the assignment of non-null confidence values to the intersection of distinct hypotheses. In DSmT, a hyper-power set D^Θ is defined as the set of all composite hypotheses obtained from the frame Θ with $\cup$ and $\cap$ operators. D^Θ constitutes the free DSm model $\mathcal{M}^f(\Theta)$, which allows to work with vague concepts when there is no constraint on the elements of the frame Θ. For a given fusion problem, some exclusivity constraints and possibly non-existential constraints have to be taken into account on the element of D^Θ. This allows to construct a hybrid DSm model $\mathcal{M}(\Theta)$. Each hybrid fusion problem is then characterized by a proper hybrid DSm model. Shafer's model, denoted $\mathcal{M}^0(\Theta)$, corresponds to a very specific hybrid DSm model where all the elements of Θ are truly exclusive.

A map $m(\cdot)$ is defined from D^Θ to $[0,1]$ to assign to each hypothesis A in D^Θ a mass function $m(A)$ that satisfies the following conditions [7]:

$$\begin{cases} 0 \leq m(A) \leq 1 \\ m(\emptyset) = 0, \\ \sum_{A \in D^\Theta} m(A) = 1 \end{cases} \tag{2}$$

If $m(A) > 0$, then A is called a *focal element*.

Two functions are usually evaluated to characterize the uncertainty about a hypothesis A. The belief function, Bel, measures the minimum uncertainty value of A; whereas, the plausibility function, Pl, reflects the maximum uncertainty value. Belief and plausibility functions are defined from D^Θ to $[0,1]$ as follows [7]:

$$\begin{cases} Bel(A) = \sum_{\substack{B \in D^\Theta \\ B \subseteq A}} m(B) \\ Pl(A) = \sum_{\substack{B \in D^\Theta \\ B \cap A \neq \emptyset}} m(B) \end{cases} \tag{3}$$

DSmT uses the classical DSm Conjunctive (DSmC) rule to combine the mass functions from the sensors when assuming a free DSm model $\mathcal{M}^f(\Theta)$ according the following equation [7]:

$$m(A) = \sum_{\substack{B_1, B_2, \cdots, B_d \in D^\Theta \\ B_1 \cap B_2 \cap \cdots \cap B_d = A}} \prod_{l=1}^{d} m_l(B_l). \tag{4}$$

The hybrid DSm (DSmH) rule of combination is a generalization of the DSmC combination rule which allows to work on any hybrid model. The DSmH combination rule for d independent sources is defined for all $A \in D^\Theta$ as follows [7]:

$$m(A) = \phi(A) \cdot [S_1(A) + S_2(A) + S_3(A)], \tag{5}$$

where:

$$S_1(A) = \sum_{\substack{B_1, B_2, \cdots, B_d \in D^\Theta \\ B_1 \cap B_2 \cap \cdots \cap B_d = A}} \prod_{l=1}^{d} m_l(B_l);$$

$$S_2(A) = \sum_{\substack{B_1, B_2, \cdots, B_d \in D^\Theta \\ B_1 \cup B_2 \cup \cdots \cup B_d = A \\ B_1 \cap B_2 \cap \cdots \cap B_d \in \emptyset}} \prod_{l=1}^{d} m_l(B_l);$$

$$S_3(A) = \sum_{\substack{B_1, B_2, \cdots, B_d \in \emptyset \\ [U=A] \vee [(U \in \emptyset) \wedge (A=I_T)]}} \prod_{l=1}^{d} m_l(B_l).$$

Note that the function $\phi(A)$ is *the characteristic non-emptiness function* of a set A i.e. $\phi(A) = 1$ if $A \notin \emptyset$, and $\phi(A) = 0$ otherwise. The empty set $\emptyset$ is the set of all elements of D^Θ, which have been forced to be empty through the constraints of the model, and the classical/universal empty set. $S_1(A)$ is the DSmC combination rule for d independent sources based on $\mathcal{M}^f(\Theta)$ given in equation (4). $S_2(A)$ is the mass of all relatively and absolutely empty sets that is transferred to the total or relative ignorance associated with non existential constraints. $S_3(A)$ transfers the sum of relatively empty sets directly into the canonical disjunctive form of non-empty sets. $U = B_1 \cup B_2 \cup \cdots \cup B_d$ and I_T is the total ignorance. The DSmH rule is mathematically well defined and works with any model independently of the value of the degree of conflict.

3.2   DSmT-Based Data Association

Even though DSmT was originally developed to carry out data fusion from multiple sensors, it can also achieve data association when applied in the context of multiple target tracking. Unlike probabilistic data association techniques such as the JPDA, which associates measurements with individual tracks only, the DSmT allows the association of measurements with the union and intersection of tracks to tackle the uncertainties and conflicts that might arise during the tracking. For this purpose, The DSmT defines a hyper-power set D^Θ which contains all the association hypotheses for which measurements can provide confidence values. These hypotheses are:

1) The empty set: $\emptyset$;
2) Individual tracks: $\{\theta_j\}_{j=0}^{\tau}$;

3) Unions of tracks: $\theta_r \cup \cdots \cup \theta_s$;

4) Intersections of tracks: $\theta_r \cap \cdots \cap \theta_s$;

5) Tracks combined using $\cup$ and $\cap$ operators.

The confidence value is expressed in terms of mass functions $\{m_l(\cdot)\}_{l=1}^d$ that are committed to each association hypothesis. Given this framework, $m_l(\theta_j)$, expresses the confidence level with which measurement z_l is associated with track θ_j, for $j = 1, \cdots, \tau$, and the false alarm hypothesis θ_0. A mass $m_l(\theta_r \cup \cdots \cup \theta_s)$ models the ignorance in assigning measuremement z_l to any of the hypotheses included in $\theta_r \cup \cdots \cup \theta_s$. This situation occurs when some targets share a similar profile, and therefore they are difficult to separate. A mass $m_l(\theta_r \cap \cdots \cap \theta_s)$ quantifies the conflict that might arise between tracks $\theta_r, \cdots, \theta_s$ regarding the origin of measurement z_l. The conflict can result from clutter or targets' occlusion. If some exclusivity or non-existential constraints have to be taken into account, the empty set $\emptyset$ should be updated to contain the excluded hypotheses.

The pairings' confidences $\{m_l(\cdot)\}_{l=1}^d$ for each individual measurement are then combined into a single map function $m(\cdot)$ which quantifies the overall confidence level with which all the measurements can be jointly associated with every hypothesis in D^Θ. $m(\cdot)$ can be derived according to the DSmC combination rule in (4) if an $\mathcal{M}^f(\Theta)$ is considered, or according to DSmH combination rule in (5), in case of an $\mathcal{M}(\Theta)$ hybrid model. Other combination rules such as the Proportional Redistributions Rules (PCR), Dempster's rule or the Uniform Redistribution Rule can be considered as well [7]. Some rules can be better justified than others depending on their ability or not to preserve associativity and commutativity properties of the combination. However, they are all based in the calculation of the conjunctive rule and the redistribution of the conflict if there are some constraints. A general combination rule of d independent measurements can then be written as follows

$$m(A) = \phi(A) \cdot [m^c(A) + m^r(A)] \tag{6}$$

for all $A \in D^\Theta$. As in equation (5), $\phi(A)$ is the characteristic non-emptiness function of A. $m^c(A)$ is the DSmC combination rule based on $\mathcal{M}^f(\Theta)$ given in equation (4). $m^r(A)$ is the portion of partial or total conflict that is redistributed on A.

For the purpose of tracking, only individual targets modeled by individual hypotheses in D^Θ are considered for decision making. This is carried out by transferring the confidence values of combined hypotheses towards single hypotheses using the belief function or the plausibility function as follows [7]:

$$Bel(\theta_j) = \sum_{\substack{A \in D^\Theta \\ A \subseteq \theta_j}} m(A), Pl(\theta_j) = \sum_{\substack{A \in D^\Theta \\ A \cap \theta_j \notin \emptyset}} m(A) \tag{7}$$

$Bel(\theta_j)$ and $Pl(\theta_j)$ quantify the detection belief and the detection plausibility of target θ_j by d independent measurements. The belief function sums over all hypotheses A contained in θ_j; whereas, the plausibility function sums over all hypotheses A containing θ_j.

To illustrate the data association process using DSmT, let's consider the tracking case of two targets using two measurements. This tracking problem is characterized by the following frame of discernment:

$$\Theta = \{\theta_0, \theta_1, \theta_2\}$$

Where θ_1 and θ_2 refer to individual targets and θ_0 refer to the false alarm hypothesis. Measurements can originate from the targets and the false alarm. Furthermore, we assume that individual measurements cannot be associated with composite hypotheses built with the union and/or intersection operators. Consequently, all the measurements share the same set of focal elements which we define as follows:

$$G_l = \Theta = \{\theta_0, \theta_1, \theta_2\}, \quad l = 1,2 \tag{8}$$

As an exclusivity constraint, we assume that two measurements cannot originate from the same target. It follows then a hybrid model $\mathcal{M}(\Theta)$ where $\phi(\theta_j) = 0$ for $j = 1,2$. It is important to note that this assumption is not mandatory. It however makes the tracking scenario similar to the one used in the JPDA [4][5]. The confidence values assigned to the hypotheses in G_l are then combined using the rule in (6). The resulting set of focal elements is denoted by $G \subset D^\Theta$ and it is given by:

$$G = \{\theta_0, \theta_0 \cap \theta_1, \theta_0 \cap \theta_2, \theta_1 \cap \theta_2\}, \tag{9}$$

If $A \in G$, then $m(A) > 0$. In fact, G is a unified frame that contains all the possible association hypotheses for $\tau = d = 2$ and the given exclusivity constraint. Table 1 illustrates how G is constructed from G_1 and G_2.

Table 1. DSmT association hypotheses for 2 targets and 2 measurements

$G_2 \backslash G_1$	θ_1	θ_2	θ_0
θ_1	$\emptyset$	$\theta_1 \cap \theta_2$	$\theta_1 \cap \theta_0$
θ_2	$\theta_1 \cap \theta_2$	$\emptyset$	$\theta_2 \cap \theta_0$
θ_0	$\theta_1 \cap \theta_0$	$\theta_2 \cap \theta_0$	θ_0

Hypothesis $\theta_1 \cap \theta_2$ results from the association of measurement 1 with target 1 and measurement 2 with target 2 or from the association of measurement 1 with target 2 and measurement 2 with target 1. Hypothesis $\theta_j \cap \theta_0$, for $j = 1,2$, results from the association of measurement 1 with target 1 or target 2 and measurement 2 with the false alarm or vice versa. Hypothesis θ_0 results from the association of both measures with the false alarm. Simple hypotheses θ_1 and θ_2 are excluded due to the fact that only one measurement can originate from a target. The total conflict resulting from such a constraint is given by:

$$K = m_1(\theta_1) \cdot m_2(\theta_1) + m_1(\theta_2) \cdot m_2(\theta_2), \tag{10}$$

The conflict can be redistributed proportionally on the focal elements $A \in G$ using Dempster's rule as follows:

$$m^r(A) = \frac{K}{1-K} \cdot m^c(A), \tag{11}$$

Therefore:

$$m(A) = m^c(A) + \frac{K}{1-K} \cdot m^c(A) = \frac{1}{1-K} \cdot m^c(A), \tag{12}$$

which satisfies (2). Using (12) and the DSmC rule in (6), we obtain the confidence value of each association hypothesis in G:

$$m(\theta_0) = m_1(\theta_0) \cdot m_2(\theta_0)/(1-K)$$
$$m(\theta_1 \cap \theta_2) = [m_1(\theta_1) \cdot m_2(\theta_2) + m_1(\theta_2) \cdot m_2(\theta_1)]/(1-K)$$
$$m(\theta_1 \cap \theta_0) = [m_1(\theta_1) \cdot m_2(\theta_0) + m_1(\theta_0) \cdot m_2(\theta_1)]/(1-K)$$
$$m(\theta_2 \cap \theta_0) = [m_1(\theta_2) \cdot m_2(\theta_0) + m_1(\theta_0) \cdot m_2(\theta_2)]/(1-K)$$

Finally, the plausibility of detecting each target is calculated by summing over the hypotheses using (7):

$$\text{Pl}(\theta_1) = m(\theta_1 \cap \theta_2) + m(\theta_1 \cap \theta_0) \text{ and } \text{Pl}(\theta_2) = m(\theta_1 \cap \theta_2) + m(\theta_2 \cap \theta_0)$$

4   Experimental Results

4.1   Multiple Target Tracking Simulation

In this section, the DSmT data association technique developed in this paper is applied to track two simulated targets using two measurements ($\tau = 2$ and $d = 2$). Unlike the example described in section 3.2, the DSmT is implemented using a full set of hypotheses that includes also the individual hypotheses (i.e. $\phi(\theta_j) = 1$ for $j = 1,2$). This aims to show the contribution of the mass functions of individual hypotheses in the decision process. We recall that a mass function assigned to an individual hypothesis results from the association of two measurements to the same target, which is explicitly excluded in the JPDA framework.

The position $(x_{t,j}, y_{t,j})$ of the jth target and its velocity $(u_{t,j}, v_{t,j})$ in Cartesian coordinates are used to describe the target's state $X_{t,j} = (x_{t,j}, y_{t,j}, u_{t,j}, v_{t,j})^T$ at time t. The following discrete time system is used for the state transition:

$$X_{t,j} = F \cdot X_{t-1,j} + W_{t,j}, \quad j = 1,2 \tag{13}$$

In equation (13), F is a square matrix defining the deterministic component of the target's motion model, and $W_{t,j}$ is its random component. We set $F = \begin{pmatrix} I_{2\times2} & \Delta t \cdot I_{2\times2} \\ 0_{2\times2} & I_{2\times2} \end{pmatrix}$ and $W_{t,j}$ is assumed to follow a Gaussian distribution $\mathcal{N}(0, \text{diag}(\sigma_{xx}^2, \sigma_{yy}^2, \sigma_{uu}^2, \sigma_{vv}^2))$. The two-by-two null matrix and unity matrix are denoted $0_{2\times2}$ and $I_{2\times2}$ respectively. Tentative measurements are simulated from true position and velocity as follows:

$$Z_{t,j} = \left(\sqrt{x_{t,j}^2 + y_{t,j}^2}, \arctan\left(\frac{y_{t,j}}{x_{t,j}}\right), u_{t,j}, v_{t,j} \right)^T + \mathcal{E}, \tag{14}$$

Where $\mathcal{E}$ is an additive noise that is assumed to follow a Gaussian distribution $\mathcal{N}(0, \text{diag}(\sigma_{rr}^2, \sigma_{\theta\theta}^2, \sigma_{uu}^2, \sigma_{vv}^2))$.

In the following experiments, we set $\sigma_{xx} = \sigma_{yy} = 1.5m$, $\sigma_{rr} = 0.1m$, $\sigma_{\theta\theta} = 0.05rad$, $\sigma_{uu} = \sigma_{vv} = 0.75\,m/s$, and a time step $\Delta t = 0.1s$. The initial state vectors are $X_{0,1} = (200,110,-20,20)^T$, $X_{0,2} = (110,110,20,20)^T$. At each time step two measurements are generated using equation (14). To evaluate the performances of our method, a root mean square error (RMSE) is calculated over Ns=100 tracking simulations and 40 time samples.

Figure 1 presents the tracking result in the xy plane.

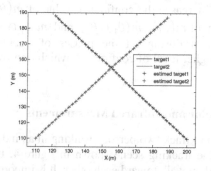
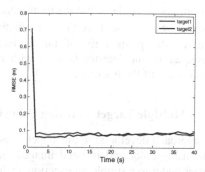

Fig. 1. Tracking in the xy plane using DSmT

Fig. 2. RMSE of tracking during the occlusion

From figure 1, we notice that our method is able to track the two targets before, during and after the occlusion. The RMSE of the position, shown in figure 2, demonstrated the robust behavior of the DSmT.

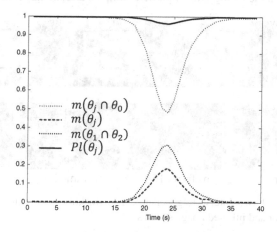

Fig. 3. Plausibility of detection of target $j = 1, 2$

Figure 3 shows the DSmT's mass functions and the plausibility of detecting each target. From the results, we see that the mass function of $\theta_1 \cap \theta_2$ characterizes the occlusion between the two targets. This mass function is low before and after the occlusion and is high in between.

The mass function of hypotheses $\theta_j \cap \theta_0$ characterizes the ability to detect the target by only one measurement. The other measurement is supposed to originate from the clutter. However during the occlusion phase, the first measurement results from the occluding target while the second one results from the occluded target. Consequently, the mass function of $\theta_j \cap \theta_0$ decreases as illustrated in figure 3. The mass function $m(\theta_j)$ represents the confidence level of having both measurements originate from the same target. $m(\theta_j)$ is low before and after the occlusion where only one measurement originates from each target. However, during the occlusion, both targets share the same position which increases the confidence value of $m(\theta_j)$. Figure 3 shows also that the combination of $m(\theta_j)$, $m(\theta_1 \cap \theta_2)$ and $m(\theta_j \cap \theta_0)$ increases the plausibility of target detection during all the phases of tracking. Consequently, the decision is made with a higher level of confidence, which improves the accuracy of the tracking.

4.2   Multiple Target Tracking Using Color and Infrared Measurements

The approach developed in this paper is used to track two persons walking in an indoor scene using color and infrared images. In the tracking scene shown in figure 4, two persons undergo a simple intersection while they walk toward each other. It is important to note that both thermal and Color frames were synchronized and corrected for minor misalignments before the tracking. The tracking was carried out using the particle filtering algorithm described in [8]. Unlike [8], the data association is not done manually; but using the approach described in section 3. At each time step, two measurements were generated from the scene. Each measurement is composed of a color and an infrared component. These components are evaluated as the bhattacharya distances between the histograms of particle samples and the target models [9].

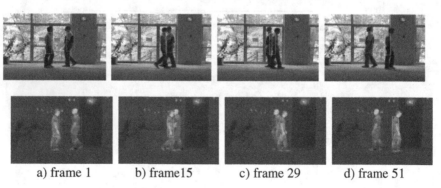

a) frame 1   b) frame15   c) frame 29   d) frame 51

Fig. 4. Tracking of two intersecting persons. The tracking results are shown with colored rectangles on color and infrared image streams.

As shown in figure 4, the tracking is accurate before, during and after the occlusion. During the occlusion phase, the tracking is particularly challenging due to the closeness of the targets, which perturbs the color cue and might lead to a false identification. The color measurement loses gradually its ability to separate the targets as they converge to the intersection point. During the occlusion, all the color measurements are associated with the occluding target. However, the infrared cue remains stable given the similarity of the thermal profile of the targets. Consequently, the thermal profile of the occluding target keeps the particles of the occluded target in a correct position. Once, the hidden target appears again, the mass functions associating the measurements with the occluded target increase again, and as a result the particles are attracted to the right target.

5 Conclusion

In this paper, we presented a new method for data association in the context of multiple targets tracking using multiple sensors. The presented approach is based on the Dezert-Smarandache Theory (DSmT). In this work we show that the DSmT can be employed to carry out data association. The experiments of tracking two targets using two measurements given in this paper demonstrated that the developed approach provides accurate tracking. Future work will focus on tests with increased number of targets and measurements.

References

1. Bar-Shalom, Y.: Multitarget-Multisensor Tracking: Advanced Applications. Artech House (1990)
2. Bar-Shalom, Y., Dale Blair, W.: Multitarget-Multisensor Tracking: Application and Advances, vol. III. Artech House, Massachusetts (2000)
3. Blackman, S.S.: Multiple hypotheses tracking for multiple target tracking. IEEE A&E Systems Magazine 19(1), 5–15 (2004)
4. Frank, O., Nieto, J., Guivant, J., Scheding, S.: Multiple target tracking using sequential Monte Carlo Methods and statistical data association. In: Proceedings of the IEEE International Conference on Intelligence Robotics and Systems, vol. 3, pp. 2718–2723 (2003)
5. Vermaak, J., Godsill, S., Pérez, P.: Monte Carlo Filtering for Multi-Target Tracking and data association. IEEE Trans. Aerosp. Electron. Syst. 41(1), 309–332 (2005)
6. Shafer, G.: A Mathematical Theory of Evidence. Princeton University Press, Princeton (1976)
7. Smarandache, F., Dezert, J.: Advances and applications of DSmT for information Fusion. Collected works, vol. 3. Am. Res. Press, ARP (2009)
8. Sun, Y., Bentabet, L.: A particle filtering and DSmT Based Approach for conflict resolving in case of Target Tracking with multiple cues. J. Math. Imag. Vis. 36(2), 159–167 (2010)
9. Airouche, M., Bentabet, L., Zelmat, M., Gao, G.: Pedestrian tracking using color, thermal and location cue measurements: a DSmT-based framework. Machine Vision and Applications (2011), doi: 10.1007/s00138-011-0342-z
10. Dang, H., Han, C.: Multi-target data association approach for vehicle tracking in road situation. In: Proceedings of IEEE on Intelligent Transportation Systems, vol. 1, pp. 379–383 (2003)
11. Dezert, J., Tchamova, A., Smarandache, F., Konstantinova, P.: Target Type Tracking with different fusion rules: A Comparative Analysis. In: Application and Advances of DSmT for Information Fusion, vol. 2, ch. 13. American Research Press (2006)

Planning Sensor Feedback for Assembly Skills by Using Sensor State Space Graphs

U. Thomas[1] and F. M. Wahl[2]

[1] Institute of Robotics and Mechatronics, DLR,
Muenchner Strasse 20, 82234 Wessling, Germany
http://www.robotics.dlr.de/Ulrike.Thomas
[2] Institute for Robotics and Process Control,
Technical University of Braunschweig, Germany
http://www.rob.cs.tu-bs.de

Abstract. In this paper, it is shown how robust execution of assembly skills can be planned by using sensor state space graphs. The here proposed method is evaluated by some assembly skills in which force feedback is applied. Assembly skills are implemented by manipulation primitive nets which constitute an interface between planning and execution of robotic systems. The sensor state space graph is introduced, which is an extension of the contact formation graph in a more general way, when various sensors might be used simultaneously for assembly execution. It is shown, how contact formation graphs can be generated by simulation of rigid body motions. The known contact formation graphs are enhanced by the definition of contact types between higher order surfaces. Additionally, a more general view is given by introducing sensor state space graphs. It is shown how contact formation graphs can be mapped to manipulation primitive nets, which allow the robust execution of assembly skills, despite the appearance of uncertainties. The approach is demonstrated successfully on some assembly tasks. Here the task of plugging a power socket on a top hat rail is illustrated due to its complex sequence. The shown assembly task is characterized by small fitting tolerances, where the application of force feedback is indispensable.

Keywords: Assembly skills, sensor state space graphs, contact formation graphs, manipulation primitive nets.

1   Introduction

Skill based robot programming has become very popular in last decades in particular for assembly tasks. Sensors are highly needed in order to guide the robot during the assembly process due to the appearance of uncertainties. Thus, the usage of various sensors in assembly skills increases continuously. Most of the implementation process for assembly skills is done by time consuming and expensive manual work. One aim is to let skills be reused by different robots in different environments and another aim is to let the implementation process be done automatically. In this paper, a generic framework is suggested in order to automize these time consuming programming tasks. Fig 1 illustrates the various levels of abstraction for robot programming. On the top level an

C.-Y. Su, S. Rakheja, H. Liu (Eds.): ICIRA 2012, Part II, LNAI 7507, pp. 696–707, 2012.

assembly process consisting for example of a sequence of tasks. Each task is implemented as a state chart of skills. The instantiation of the skills can be taken out of a predefined skill library or can be generated automatically. Each skill is implemented as a net of manipulation primitives. This instantiation is shown in the second middle level. The execution of elemental motions (manipulation primitives) is illustrated in the lowest level of abstractions. In the terminology of manipulation primitive nets, a single manipulation primitive belongs to the lowest level, a net of the manipulation primitives constitutes an assembly skill and refers to the middle level of abstraction. Based on this, each assembly skill can be coded as net of manipulation primitives. For more information on this topic refer to [4,13,7]. The specification of manipulation primitive follow Mason's compliance-frame concept as well as De Schutters and Van Brussel's task-frame formalism [8,11]. Meanwhile Smits et al. [12] suggest the iTaSC formalism in order to specify robot motions, in which relative transformations between feature frames of objects need to be controlled to let the robot successfully execute e.g. assembly operations. In order to estimate the possible feedback and to guide the robot through several states during assembly the contact formation graph has been introduced by Ji and Xiao [6]. The contact formation graph is widely used for planning the execution of complex robot tasks see Meeussen et al. [9] or for recognizing contacts during the learning of assembly skills compare to Hertkorn et al. [5]. Therewith the contact states during the execution of an assembly process can be estimated, but each elementary motion has to be instantiated off-line by advanced robot programmers familiar with the task-frame formalism. Considering the iTaSC approach, which is based on Ambler and Poppelstones' symbolic special relations [1]. A single instantiation may establish the relation between two feature frames, which can be monitored by a camera system.

As the numbers of sensors in the assembly process is increased, contact formation graphs need to be extended to the more general sensor state space graph which is able to represent relations between two objects according to different sensors. For force feedback controlled robots the contact formation graph is sufficient to own all possible contact states. For other sensors like camera systems, the contact formation graphs need to be enhanced to sensor state space graphs. Here a theoretical introduction into the sensor state space graphs is given. The contact formation graph can be considered as an instance of the sensor state space graph. With contact formation graphs planning for force feedback controlled robots becomes possible and with sensor state space graphs the planning for other sensors can be achieved. In the next section the sensor state space graph is defined. As an example the generation of contact formation graphs is shown. The section next after defines assembly skills as manipulation primitive nets. Section number four illustrates how the contact formation graph can be mapped to manipulation primitive net in order to be executed by force controlled robots.

2   The Sensor State Space Graph

The sensor state space graph constitutes an extension of the former known contact formation graph. A contact formation graph is here considered as a sensor state space graph in which only force feedback is used. A state between two rigid objects can be described by the relative transformation between two object features. Hence we need a clear definition of features. An object may have various features. A feature can either be a vertex, an edge, a circular arc, a face, a cylindrical face or a spherical face in cases where sensor states are estimated by force feedback. For vision feedback a feature can also be a circle, a shaft, or even an edge. In particular it can be everything which is measurable by any sensor. Hence a node in the sensor state space graph is a measurable constraint between two or even more features. The edges between the nodes in the sensor state space graph represent a possible elemental motion to switch between these two sensor states.

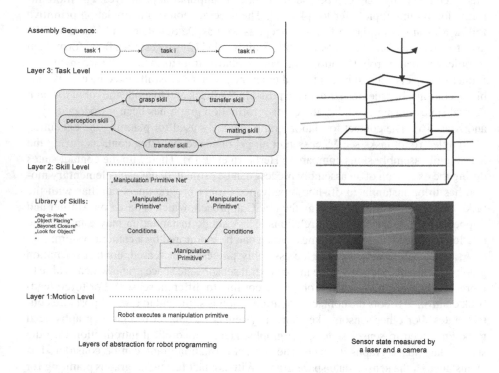

Layers of abstraction for robot programming   Sensor state measured by a laser and a camera

Fig. 1. On the left side the abstraction layers for robot programming are shown. The entire assembly sequence is instantiated by a sequence of skills. Each skill can be coded as a net of manipulation primitives, which are mapped to a robot controller for execution. Each manipulation primitive changes the contact states in cases where force feedback is applied. Manipulation primitive nets can be coded by hand, but in this paper an algorithm is shown to automize this process. On the right side it is shown how the rotational degree of freedom for the upper object can be measured by a laser and a camera. The state with front faces parallel is represented by a node in the sensor state space graph can can be detected by a camera system.

2.1 Generating Features from Object Models

In order to obtain possible sensor states, features need to be extracted automatically from model data. The relation between features corresponds to a measurable state in the sensor state space graph. Objects are often represented by triangle meshes. Thus,

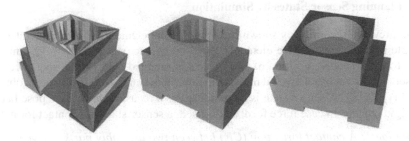

Fig. 2. Left: Original data (triangle mesh); middle: segmentation into planes, and right: segmentation into cylindrical and spherical surfaces

it is necessary to extract features from this model information. For general planning purposes as many features as possible need to be extract. Taking as an example force feedback, the following features (topological elements) need to be segmented from triangles meshes, because the relations between theses features can be recognized by using force feedback:

$$te_i \in TE := \{vertex(V), edge(E), circular\ arc(A), face(F), \qquad (1)$$
$$cylindrical\ surface(C), spherical\ surface(S)\}$$

The idea is to fit planes, cylinders and spheres in the triangle mesh and then define contact states between theses elemental features. Therefore, an algorithm according to [2] is implemented which works on closed loop meshes, represented as a queue of neighboring edges. Here the algorithm is implemented as a greedy approach, meaning that as many neighboring triangles are taken to enlarge a given primitive shape as the least square error is less than a predefined threshold. For example, for fitting a face primitive consisting of $3d$ points $\{\mathbf{p}_1, \ldots, \mathbf{p}_n\}$ with center point $\mathbf{c}$ into the mesh the covariance matrix $\mathbf{M}_{cov}$ is estimated according to

$$\mathbf{M}_{cov} = \sum_i a(\mathbf{p_i})(\mathbf{p_i} - \mathbf{c})(\mathbf{p_i} - \mathbf{c})^T \qquad (2)$$

where $a(\mathbf{p}_i)$ can be considered as a weight for the influence of $\mathbf{p}_i$. The new fitting plane segment $seg = seg_k \cup seg_l$ passes through $\mathbf{c}$ and its normal vector $\mathbf{n}$ is the eigenvector, corresponding to the minimum eigenvalue of $\mathbf{M}_{cov}$. When estimated the fitting plane given by parameters $(\mathbf{n}, d)$ the least square error L^2 is consequently obtained by:

$$L^2 = \sum_i a(\mathbf{p_i}) \cdot (\mathbf{n} \cdot \mathbf{p}_i - d)^2 \quad \forall \mathbf{p}_i \in seg_k \cup seg_l \qquad (3)$$

If the least square error is less than a certain threshold the two segments $seg := seg_k \cup seg_l$ are merged into a new segment. For fitting other shape primitives into the triangulated objects the procedure is equivalent. Therewith after this segmentation procedure an object is attached with many features called topological elements. Fig. 2 illustrates the results of the segmentation algorithm for the power socket.

In cases where lasers and cameras are used, symbolic spatial relations like the ones suggested in [1] can be used.

2.2 Planning Sensor States by Simulation

In the previous section, it is shown how topological elements can be generated from triangle meshes. Given these elements, possible contact states need to be simulated. Therefore, the relative position of two objects is sampled by a Halton sequence. From this sequence a set of relative 6d transformations between two rigid objects is obtained: $X = \{x_1, \ldots, x_n\}$. A sensor state is then defined as a measurable relative pose between two rigid objects. In case force feedback is used, a sensor state is a contact formation:

Definition 1: A contact formation (CF) between two assembly parts is given by a set of main contacts: $CF := \{MC_1, \ldots, MC_n\}$. Additionally, we write CF^X, where X represents the set of relative object poses between A and B, which ensure the contact state.

with a main contact defined as:

Definition 1: A main contact (MC) between two topological elements is given by a tuple $(te_i, te_j) \in TE_A \times TE_B$, where the sets TE_A are all topological elements of assembly part A and TE_B respectively of part B.

In a more general form a sensor state is:

Definition 2: A sensor state (ST) between two assembly parts is given by a set of measurable pose constraints $PC : ST := \{PC_1, \ldots, PC_n\}$. Additionally, we write ST^X, where X represents the set of relative object poses between two objects.

Thus, the sensor states are obtained from simulation of possible relative object transformations and considerations of their relative feature pose. For example considering two edges, each of it belongs to another part. During simulation all the samples for the rigid body motion can be collected, which ensure a relative motion, where these edges are kept in parallel.

A vision sensor could be used to monitor this constraint during assembly. Hence this extracted sensor state may help to guide the assembly process. Thus the sensor state space graph is a more general way to describe assembly process states and can be exhaustively used to plane sensor feedback for assembly skills. At first the nodes are generated by simulation and then the edges are inserted into the sensor state space graph as described in the following section.

2.3 Generating Sensor State Transitions

For the extraction of nodes all sensor states, which may occur, or which are useful to be considered need to be generated. Further on it is important to ensure correct transitions between these sensor states. Again, considering force feedback only the neighborhood of two nodes in the sensor state space graph according to Xiao [14] can easily be defined:

Definition 3: Two contact formations $CF_i^{X_i}$ and $CF_j^{X_j}$ are neighbors, if either $CF_i^{X_i} \subset CF_j^{X_j}$ or $CF_j^{X_j} \subset CF_i^{X_i}$ applies. The relation is given, if all reducible main contacts $MC \in CF_i^{X_i}$ are within $CF_j^{X_j}$.

For a more general view, the neighborhood of sensor states can be defined as follows:

Definition 4: Two sensor states $ST_i^{X_i}$ and $ST_j^{X_j}$ are neighbors, if either $ST_i^{X_i} \subset ST_j^{X_j}$ or $ST_j^{X_j} \subset ST_i^{X_i}$ applies. The relation is given, if all relations between features are within their neighboring state.

This implies that sensor state spaces are neighbors if the features expressing the rigid body transformation between objects are neighbors, too. This means that during transitions the dofs are reduced step by step. Consequently, a sensor state space graph consists of a set of nodes, the sensor states. In cases where only force feedback is used a sensor state is a contact formation, $\mathscr{CF} := \{CF_1^{X_1}, \ldots, CF_n^{X_n}\}$, enriched with a set of edges called transitions $\mathscr{T}$.

2.4   The Algorithm for Generating Enhanced Contact Formation Graphs

Here an contact formation graph is considered as an instance of the sensor state space graph. In order to simulate contact states, relative object poses are sampled. Then the nodes are extracted and in a next step the possible transitions are predicted and inserted into the graph. This computation is shown for the contact formation graphs $G := (\mathscr{CF}, \mathscr{T})$, but can also be applied for sensor state space graphs.

3   Definition of Skills by Manipulation Primitive Nets

In this section a brief introduction into manipulation primitive nets is given, because the sensor state space graph is mapped to manipulation primitives which build the interface to the control system. For a more detailed description please refer to Finkemeyer et al. [3], Kroeger et al. [7] or an earlier description of nets of skill primitives to Thomas et al. [13].

Definition 5: A manipulation primitive is a hybrid robot motion parametrized by the four elements
$MP := \langle HM, \lambda, \tau, \sigma \rangle$, *where each element is:*

- *HM it is the hybrid robot motion specified with respect to a given task frame:* **TF**
- *λ it is a stop condition, which maps the measured and filtered sensor values in a given time window to a boolean expression.*
- *τ is a set of tool commands, which can be executed simultaneously to the hybrid robot motion.*
- *σ provides the current sensor values as return values, when the hybrid motion is finished, which means that λ could be evaluated to true.*

The hybrid motion is defined wrt. a given task frame. The task frame is a reference system in which the hybrid motion is specified. In most cases, the task frame is set to the contact point. Additionally, for each dof the appropriate controller needs to be selected. This can either be a position, force or velocity controller or a controller, which automatically switches between free space and contact as implemented by Reisinger [10].

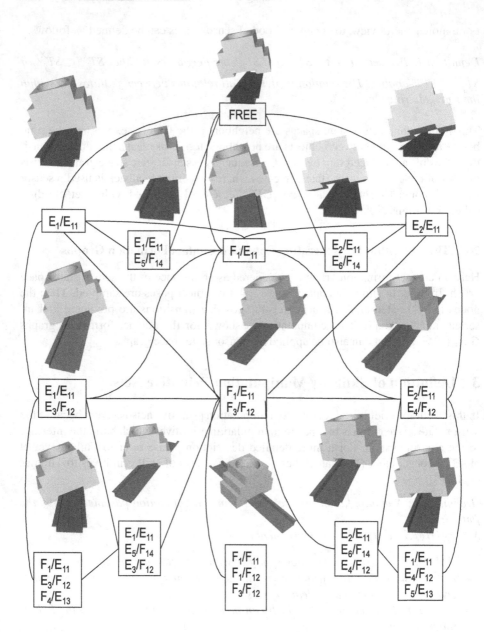

Fig. 3. A generated contact formation graph for the power socket to be assembled on top of the hat rail

For each dof at least one controller is selected. For example, in a second controller hierarchy a position controller might be selected additionally to a force controller. Each manipulation primitive owns a stop condition λ and can return required sensor values σ. Furthermore a tool command τ can be invoked. Moreover, for the execution of complex assembly tasks manipulation primitive nets are needed, which are defined as follows:

Algorithm 1. Generate Contact-Formation-Graph

Require: active part $A := \{TE_A\}$, passive part $B := \{TE_B\}$ consisting of their topological elements.

Ensure: $G = (\mathscr{CF}, \mathscr{T})$

1: $\mathscr{CF} \leftarrow \emptyset, \mathscr{T} \leftarrow \emptyset, X := \{x_1, \ldots, x_m\}$ samples
2: **for** each $x_i \in X$ **do**
3:     $\mathscr{CF} \leftarrow \mathscr{CF} \cup \text{CONTACTFORMATION}(TE_A, TE_B, x_i)$
4: **for** each $CF_i^{X_i} \in \mathscr{CF}$ **do**
5:     **for** each $CF_j^{X_j} \in \mathscr{CF}$ **do**
6:         **if** $(i \neq j) \wedge (CF_i = CF_j)$ **then)**
7:             $\mathscr{CF} \leftarrow \mathscr{CF} \setminus CF_j^{X_j}$
8:             $X_i \leftarrow X_i \cup X_j$
9: **for** each $CF_i \in \mathscr{CF}$ **do**
10:     **for** each $CF_j \in \mathscr{CF}$ **do**
11:         **if** $i \neq j \wedge (CF_i \subset CF_j \vee CF_j \subset CF_i)$ **then**
12:             $\mathscr{T} \leftarrow \mathscr{T} \cup (CF_i, CF_j)$ ▷ add transition
    return $(\mathscr{CF}, \mathscr{T})$
13: **function** CONTACTFORMATION(TE_A, TE_B, x_i)
14:     $CF_k^X \leftarrow \emptyset$ with $X \leftarrow \{x_i\}$
15:     **for** each $te_{i,A} \in TE_A$ **do**
16:         **for** each $te_{j,B} \in TE_B$ **do**
17:             **if** $(te_{i,A}, te_{j,B}, x_i) \in MC$ and is contact **then**
18:                 $CF_k \leftarrow CF_k \cup$ contact type of $(te_{i,A}, te_{j,B})$
19:         **for** each $MC_i \in CF_k$ **do**
20:             **for** each $MC_j \in CF_k$ **do**
21:                 **if** $(i \neq j) \vee (MC_i \in MC_j)$ **then**
22:                     $CF_k \leftarrow CF_k \setminus MC_i$ ▷ reduce contacts
        return CF_k^X

Definition 6: A manipulation primitive net $MPN := \langle \Sigma, \Pi, \Xi, \Omega, \Psi \rangle$ is defined by the items:

- *Σ is the set of manipulation primitives $\Sigma = \{MP^*\}$,*
- *Π is a set of defined start MPs $\Pi \subseteq \Sigma$,*
- *Ξ is a set of defined stop MPs $\Xi \subseteq \Sigma$,*
- *Ω is a set of transitions. A transition is given by $\omega_{ij} := (\sigma_i, \sigma_j)$, which fulfills $\forall \omega_{ij} \in \Omega \; \exists \; \sigma_i, \sigma_j \in \Sigma$. Hence a transition represents the edge and it is a connection between the previous manipulation primitive $\sigma_i \in \Sigma$ and its succeeding manipulation primitive $\sigma_j \in \Sigma$*
- *Ψ is a set of global net variables, which can be changed by traversing an edge. To each global variable a $\psi := \langle value, type \rangle \in \Psi$ belongs a basic data type $type \in \{int, double, float\}$ and its value.*

Each node in the net represents a single manipulation primitive net, where the arcs represent possible transitions from one manipulation primitive to the next. Each arc obtains an equation, which triggers the arc if the equation given over measured sensor values is fulfilled.

Based on the computed contact formation graph and additional absolute values regarding the expected contact forces, manipulation primitive nets can be generated.

4   Planning Force Feedback for Assembly Skills by Mapping Contact Formation Graphs to Executable Nets

To generate manipulation primitive nets, rules have to be applied in order to transform nodes and edges of an enhanced contact formation graph into respective manipulation primitives and transitions. In addition to these rules, a look-up table is used for the selection of appropriate controller values. Each edge in the contact formation graph represents a change of the contact state, which could be carried out by one manipulation primitive. But, the following example should be considered: Given the contact state called *free* and the succeeding contact states in Fig. 3; only one manipulation primitive lets the contact situation switch from *free* into all succeeding contact states. Thus, only one manipulation primitive is necessary. Each contact formation CF is annotated by a set of configurations X. Therewith, the algorithm searches for a transformation from free space into all other succeeding contact states, which can be reached according to the inertial object pose. In the given example, a single translational transformation is necessary. The free space node has five succeeding contact states, thus five transitions are needed to decide, in which situation the assembly task is after the execution of the first manipulation primitive. Hence iteratively the manipulation primitives need to be filled with the following parameters: A) The task frame, B) parameters for the hybrid robot motion and C) stop condition and equations for the transitions.

4.1   Computation of the Task Frame

As mentioned above the task frame should be placed in the contact point. For each contact formation CF all main contact types are known: $\{MC_1,\ldots,MC_n\}$. Hence the task frame can be placed inside the convex hull of all contact points:

$$CH\{\cup_{\forall p_i \in TE_A}\{p_i|\forall p_j \in TE_B : p_i = p_j\}\} \tag{4}$$

with $TE_A = \cup_{\forall MC_i \in CF}\{te_A|te_A \in MC_i\}$ and $TE_B = \cup_{\forall MC_i \in CF}\{te_B|te_B \in MC_i\}$. Therewith, the position of the task frame is assigned. For the orientation, we determine the longest contact region, which serves as the x-axis. For the z-axis the normal vector of the contact region is applied. By supplement to the right hand rule, the y-axis is given, hence we obtain a specification for the task frame.

4.2   Parametrizing the Hybrid Robot Motion

For the automatical parametrization of the hybrid motion, the contact formation graph needs to be enhanced by directions. A contact formation CF^X is annotated by a set of relative object poses X between part A and part B, hence the $CF_j^{X_j}$ is successor of $CF_i^{X_i}$ if

$$\min\{\cup_{\forall x_l \in CF_i^{X_i}}||x_l - x_{goal}||\} > \min\{\cup_{\forall x_k \in CF_j^{X_j}}||x_k - x_{goal}||\} \tag{5}$$

holds. This means a configuration exists in the successor, which is closer to the given goal position. Now, a constraint is introduced in order to reduce the further search problem: Each manipulation primitive should only reduce one degree of freedom at a time. Hence a transformation $^{xi}T_{xj}$ with a single movement in one direction is searched. Given this parameter and assuming contact the switching controller is selected. The controller set values are taken from the look-up-table.

4.3   Setting Up the Stop Condition and Transitions

Setting up the stop condition can be arranged quite easily, because we apply the constraint again; that one dof (degree of freedom) is reduced by one manipulation primitive. The stop condition values need to be set up and are caused by the direction the motion is specified. Additionally a time out is set and bounds are specified for the other axes to ensure an appropriate motion. For conditions annotated at the transitions the inequations need to be determined. Hence, we assume a motion according to the hybrid motion and the given task frame. Thereafter, we divide the possible contact surfaces into regions according to the topological elements of the active object. Therewith we obtain equations for reaction forces and torques. The conjunctions of all outgoing transition cover the entire possible contact space, such that no deadlock arises.

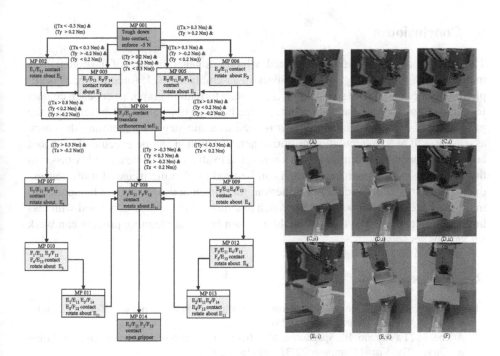

Fig. 4. Generated manipulation primitive net (left) for the shown robot task (right)

5 Experiments

The experiments have been carried out with various robot tasks started in different poses. A success rate close to a 100 % could be reached. Here the assembly task "plugging a power socket on a top hat rail" is depicted in Fig. 4 on the right side. The situations, in which the colored manipulation primitives in Fig. 4 (left side) are executed, are illustrated on the right side. First of all, with a translational movement, the socket comes in contact with the top hat rail, and in our example an edge/edge contact is established (MP 001). With the evaluation of the condition $(T_x < -0.3\,Nm) \wedge (Ty > 0.2\,Nm)$ the contact E_1/E_{11} is recognized (image B in Fig. 4). Now, with the next manipulation primitive (MP 002), the robot rotates the socket about edge E_1 until a surface/edge contact F_1/E_{11} is established (C, i and C, ii in Fig. 4). With a translational orthogonal movement to edge E_{11}, the next contact state $E_1/E_{11}, E_3/F_{12}$ is ensured and recognized by evaluating the equation $((Ty > 0.3\,Nm) \wedge (Tz > -0.2\,Nm))$ (Fig. 4 right (D, i) and (D, ii)). Subsequently, a rotation about the edge E_3 is executed, such that further rotation about E_{11} is necessary in order to assemble the socket on the top hat rail successfully (images (E, i) and (E, ii)). The longest edge of the hat rail is now collinear with the edge E_{11}. Finally, the power socket is rotated about this edge as long as the measured torque is less than a determined threshold of $2,5\,Nm$. When the stop condition is evaluated to be true, the socket is fixed on the top hat rail (Fig. 4 right, image (F)).

6 Conclusion

The sensor state space graph is suggested, which is a generalization of the contact formation graph, for planning sensor feedback in assembly skills. If force feedback is applied only, the sensor state space graph is a contact formation graph, where each contact formation represents a measurable contact state between objects. In the current state the generation of contact formation graphs is used as a sub-step for generating the entire assembly skill as a manipulation primitive net, which then can be executed by a robot controller supporting primitives. This approach is evaluated by some assembly tasks. In the future the sensor state space graph can be used to plan the usage of more sensors during assembly skill execution. Further on, the shown approach should be applied to more examples. Overall with this approach assembly skills can be generated with less human interaction. In the future it will be shown how this planning process can work for various sensors.

References

1. Ambler, A.P., Popplestone, R.J.: Inferring the position of bodies from specified spatial relationships. Artificial Intelligence 6 (1975)
2. Attene, M., Falcidieno, B., Spagnuolo, M.: Hierarchical mesh segmentation based on fitting primitives. The Visual Computer 22(3), 181–193 (2006)
3. Finkemeyer, B., Kroeger, T., Wahl, F.M.: Executing Assembly Tasks Specified by Manipulation Primitive Nets. Advanced Robotics 19, 591–611 (2005)
4. Hasegawa, T., Suehiro, T., Takase, K.: A Model-Based Manipulation System with Skill-Based Execution. IEEE Transactions on Robotics and Automation 8(5), 535–544 (1992)

5. Hertkorn, K., Roa, M.A., Preusche, C., Borst, C., Hirzinger, G.: Identification of contact formations: Resolving ambiguous force torque information. In: International Conference on Robotics and Automation (2012)

6. Ji, X., Xiao, J.: Planning Motions Compliant to Complex Contact States. The International Journal of Robotics Research 20(6), 446–465 (2001)

7. Kroeger, T., Finkemeyer, B., Wahl, F.M.: A Task Frame Formalism for Practical Implementations. In: IEEE International Conference on Robotics and Automation, pp. 5218–5223 (2004)

8. Mason, M.T.: Compliance and force control for computer controlled manipulators. IEEE Transactions on Systems, Man, and Cybernetics 11, 418–432 (1981)

9. Meeussen, W., Schutter, J.D., Bruyninckx, H., Xiao, J., Stafetti, E.: Integration of Planning and Execution in Force Controlled Compliante Motion. In: IEEE/RSJ International Conference on Intelligent Robotic Systems, pp. 2550–2555 (2005)

10. Reisinger, T.: Force Control of Parallel Robots based on skill primitives. Ph.D. thesis, Technical University of Braunschweig (2007) (in German)

11. Schutter, J.D., Brussel, H.V.: Compliant Robot Motion II. A Control Approach Based on External Control Loops. The International Journal of Robotics Research 7(4), 18–33 (1988)

12. Smits, R., Laet, T.D., Claes, K., Bruyninckx, H., Schutter, J.D.: iTASC: a tool for multi-sensor integration in robot manipulation. In: Multisensor Fusion and Integration for Intelligent Systems, pp. 445–452 (2008)

13. Thomas, U., Finkemeyer, B., Kroeger, T., Wahl, F.M.: Error-tolerant execution of complex robot tasks based on skill primitives. In: IEEE International Conference on Robotics and Automation, pp. 3069–3075 (2003)

14. Xiao, J., Zhang, L.: Computing Rotational Distances between Contacting Polytops. In: IEEE International Conference on Robotics and Automation, pp. 791–797 (1996)

Author Index